BUSINESS MATHEMATICS AND STATISTICS

CLASS 12

Special Features

- Learning Objectives, Illustrations & Practical Problems
- Theoretical Questions : Long, Short & Objective Type Questions
- Numerical Questions
- Latest Model Paper & Board Examination Paper

Book Code : 6338
ISBN : 978-93-82883-06-7
Price : ₹ 385.00

BUSINESS MATHEMATICS AND STATISTICS

CLASS 12

Strictly according to latest
Syllabus and Question Pattern prescribed by the
Jharkhand Academic Council, Ranchi
for Class XII

Dr. S. K. Singh
M. Com., Ph. D.
Recipient of
Rashtriya Gaurav Award &
included in Asian Admirable Achiever
Asia/Pacific Who's who

Dr. Awadhesh Kumar Singh
M. Sc. (Maths.), Ph. D.

Sudha Singh

Special Features

- Learning Objectives, Illustrations & Practical Problems
- Theoretical Questions : Long, Short & Objective Type Questions
- Numerical Questions
- Latest Model Paper & Board Examination Paper

Revised Edition

SBPD PUBLICATIONS

If you have any doubts or corrections regarding textbook, please scan the QR Code and contact us through WhatsApp

Scan the given QR Code

MAKING EDUCATION AFFORDABLE DIGITALLY

SAVE MONEY AND PLANET, BUY eBook

उपरोक्त QR Code Scan करके हमारी वेबसाइट www.sbpdpublications.com पर जाएँ।

(A) यदि आप नए User हैं तो Register करें।

(B) यदि आप पहले से रजिस्टर हैं तो Login करें।

eBook के Menu Option या Search Button पर अपनी eBook को Search करें।

eBook खरीदने के लिए Add to Cart या Buy Now पर क्लिक करें और Checkout करें।

अब आप Go to Library या Manage My Library Click करें। अब आप अपनी eBook Library में पढ़ सकते हैं।

Our Books are also available at :

amazon Flipkart

www.sbpdpublications.com

Revised Edition

Book Code : 6338

ISBN : 978-93-82883-06-7

Price : ₹ 385.00

SBPD Publications

3/20B, Agra-Mathura Bye Pass Road, Near Tulsi Cinema, Agra-282 002

Phones : (0562) 4304545; Mobile : 09412258082-85; 7055711052, 8218493141;

sbpd.publications@gmail.com; website : www.sbpdpublications.com

Preface

We feel privileged to present our readers a thoroughly revised edition of our book **'Business Mathematics and Statistics'**. The book has been written in teach and test pattern primarily for the students appearing for Business Mathematics and Statistics paper at 10 + 2 level/I. Com. second year of Jharkhand Academic Council, Ranchi.

Special Features of the Book :

- Each chapter in the book contains Learning Objectives, Illustrations and Numerical Problems.
- At the end of each chapter practice questions are provided for the students.
- The book is based on Latest Syllabus and Question Pattern.
- Including Previous Years and Latest Board Examination Question Paper.
- Latest Model Paper is also provided at end of the book.

We sincerely express our thanks to Dr. Amrit Kumar, New Saket Nagar, Hinoo, Ranchi, who not only removed the rough edges of this book but also helped in revising and presenting of this book in simplified manner.

We hope that this book will meet the expectations of the students. We shall be thankful to them it they let us know what needs to be done to raise their level of satisfaction.

—Publisher

Syllabus

Jharkhand Academic Council (JAC), Ranchi

BUSINESS MATHEMATICS AND STATISTICS

For I. Com. Second Year + 2 (Class XII)

A. BUSINESS MATHEMATICS

Unit 1 : Progressions

(a) Elementary Idea of A.P., G.P. and H.P.

(b) Properties of A.P., G.P. and H.P.

Unit 2 : Permutation and Combination

(a) Elementary Idea of Permutation.

(b) To find the Number of Permutations of n Different Things taken r at the time.

(c) Elementary Idea of Combination.

(d) To find the Number of Combinations of n Different Things taken r at the time.

Unit 3 : Determinants

(a) Introduction, Expansion and Properties of Determinants.

(b) Uses of Determinants.

Unit 4 : Matrices

(a) Definition and Kinds of Matrices.

(b) Laws of Matrix Algebra.

(c) Laws of Matrix Multiplication and Division.

Unit 5 : Sets

(a) Definition, Notation and Kinds of Sets.

(b) Set Relations, Proper Sub-set.

(c) Venn Diagrams and Power Set.

Unit 6 : Differentiation

(a) Introduction, Increment, Differential Co-efficients.

(b) General Rule of Differentiation.

Unit 7 : Integration

(a) Introduction, Constant of Integration, Indefinite Integrals.

(b) Basic Rules of Integration.

B. STATISTICS

Unit 1 : Measures of Central Tendency : Mean, Median, Mode

Unit 2 : Geometric Mean and Harmonic Mean

Unit 3 : Time Series :

(i) Trend or Secular Trend.
(ii) Seasonal Variation.
(iii) Cyclical Variation.
(iv) Irregular Movements.
(v) Analysis of Time Series.
(vi) Mathematical Models for Time Series.
(vii) Measurement of Secular Trend :
  (a) Freehand Curve Method.
  (b) Method of Averages : Selected Point Method; Semi-average Method; Moving Average Method.
  (c) Method of Least Squares : Arithmetic Straight Line; Logarithmic Straight Line; Parabolic Curve.
(viii) Seasonal Variation; Measurement of Cyclical Variation.

Unit 4 : Theory of Probability

Basic Concepts : Random Experiment; Sample Space; Discrete Events; Complementary Event, Exhaustive Event; Equal Likely Events.

Meaning and Definition of Probability; Probability Theorems; Bayes' Theorem; Permutation and Combination in the Theory of Probability; Bernaulli Trials.

Unit 5 : Interpolation and Extrapolation

Meaning; Importance; Assumption, Methods of Interpolation—Graphical; Algebraic; Binomial Expansion; Parabolic; Newton's Method of Finite; Newton's Forwards and Backward; Lagrange's; Newton-Gauss Forward; Backward; Sterling's and Newton's Divided Difference Methods.

Contents

(A) BUSINESS MATHEMATICS

Unit 1 : Progressions :

- Elementry Idea of A.P., G.P. and H.P.
- Properties of A.P., G.P. and H.P.

Unit 2 : Permutation and Combination

Unit 3 : Determinants

Unit 4 : Matrices

Unit 5 : Sets

Unit 6 : Differentiation

Unit 7 : Integration

1

ARITHMETIC PROGRESSION (A.P.)

LEARNING OBJECTIVES

After studying this chapter, you will be able to know :

- **1.1 Sequence**
- **1.2 Series**
- **1.3 Progression :**
  - **1.3.1 Arithmetic Progression**
  - **1.3.2 To find the *n*th term of an A.P., where *n* is any Positive Integers**
  - **1.3.3 To find the sum of *n*th terms of an A.P.**
  - **1.3.4 Arithmetic Means**

SOLVED EXAMPLES AND PRACTICAL PROBLEMS : AT A GLANCE

No. of Examples		*No. of Problems*
	To find the *n*th term of an A.P. where *n* is any Positive Integers	
1 to 5	Type I : Based on Sequence	Exercise 1(A) 1 to 4
6A to 17	Type II : Based on $t_n = a + (n - 1)d$	5 to 17A
18 to 19	Type III : Based on Three, Four or Five Numbers	18 to 25
	Miscellaneous Problems	26 to 28
1 to 19	To find the sum of first *n*th terms of an A.P.	Exercise 1 (B) 1 to 22
1 to 9	To insert *n* Arithmetic Means between Two given Quantities	Exercise 1 (C) 1 to 11
	Arithmetic Mean	Exercise 1 (D) 1 to 7
	Objective Questions	Exercise 1 (E) 27 + 8 + 2
47	**Total**	**68 + 37**

(1.1) SEQUENCE

A succession of numbers written according to some definite rule is called a sequence.

The first, second, third terms of a sequence are denoted by t_1, t_2, t_3 respectively.

Some Examples of Sequences

(i) 2, 4, 6, 8, ...

Here each term of the sequences can be obtained by adding 2 to the preceding term. This is the definite rule of this sequence.

(ii) 3, 6, 12, 24, ...

Here each term can be obtained by multiplying the preceding term by 2. This is the definite rule of this sequence.

KINDS OF SEQUENCE

Sequence

Finite Sequence | Infinite Sequence

(i) Finite Sequence : A sequence is said to be a finite sequence if it has finite number of terms.

Example : 1, 3, 5, 7.

(ii) Infinite Sequence : A sequence is said to be an infinite sequence if it has infinite number of terms.

Example : 1, 3, 5, 7, ...

(1.2) SERIES

If the terms of a sequence are connected with *plus* (+) or *minus* (–), then the numbers are called a series.

Example : 2, 4, 6, 8, ...is a sequence.

So 2 + 4 + 6 + 8 + ... is a series.

TYPE OF SERIES

Series

Finite Series | Infinite Series

(i) Finite Series : A series having finite number of terms is called a finite series.

Example : 1 + 3 + 5 + 7 is a finite series.

(ii) Infinite Series : A series having infinite number of terms is called an infinite series.

Example : 1 + 3 + 5 + 7 + ... is a infinite series.

(1.3) PROGRESSION

Meaning : If the terms of a sequence or a series are written under specific conditions, then the sequence or the series is called a progression.

TYPES OF PROGRESSION

Progression

Arithmetic Progression (A.P.) | Geometric Progression (G.P.) | Harmonic Progression (H.P.)

1.3.1 Arithmetic Progression

If the difference between any two consecutive terms of a progression, are same, then the progression is known as A. P. (Arithmetic progression). The difference between any term and the term preceding it is constant throughout, this constant is called the *common difference* (c.d.) of the A.P. Common difference is generally denoted by '*d*'.

Example : 1, 4, 7, 10, ... are in A.P.

because
$$t_2 - t_1 = 4 - 1 = 3$$
$$t_3 - t_2 = 7 - 4 = 3$$
$$t_4 - t_3 = 10 - 7 = 3$$

....

....

$$\because t_2 - t_1 = t_3 - t_2 = t_4 - t_3 = \ldots\ldots$$

So the sequence is in A.P. and its common difference is 3.

Thus if three numbers a, b, c are in A.P.

then $b - a = c - b$

or $\boxed{2b = a + c \Rightarrow b = \frac{a+b}{2}}$

1.3.2 To find the *n*th term of an A. P. where *n* is any positive integers

Solution :

Let first term of the A.P. $= a$

and c.d. $= d$

then First term $t_1 = a = a + (1-1)d$

Second term $t_2 = a + d = a + (2-1)d$

Third term $t_3 = a + 2d = a + (3-1)d$

Fourth term $t_4 = a + 3d = a + (4-1)d$

....

....

*n*th term $t_n = a + (n-1)d$

Thus for an A.p. $\boxed{t_n = a + (n-1)d}$

Formula 1

SOLVED EXAMPLES

Problems Based on Sequence

✎ Type I

Example 1

If *n*th term of a sequence is $\frac{n^2}{n+1}$, then find the sequence.

Solution :

Let *n*th term of the sequence is t_n

then $t_n = \frac{n^2}{n+1}$

So $t_1 = \frac{1^2}{1+1} = \frac{1}{2}$; (Putting $n = 1$)

$t_2 = \frac{2^2}{2+1} = \frac{4}{3}$; (Putting $n = 2$)

$t_3 = \frac{3^2}{3+1} = \frac{9}{4}$; (Putting $n = 3$)

$t_4 = \frac{4^2}{4+1} = \frac{16}{5}$; (Putting $n = 4$)

....

....

Hence the sequence is $\frac{1}{2}, \frac{4}{3}, \frac{9}{4}, \frac{16}{5}$, ...

Example 2

If *n*th term of a sequence is $(2n^2 + 1)$ then find the sequence. Is this sequence in A. P. ?

Solution :

Let nth term of the sequence is t_n

then $t_n = 2n^2 + 1$

So
$t_1 = 2 \times 1^2 + 1 = 3;$ (Putting $n = 1$)
$t_2 = 2 \times 2^2 + 1 = 9;$ (Putting $n = 2$)
$t_3 = 2 \times 3^2 + 1 = 19;$ (Putting $n = 3$)
$t_4 = 2 \times 4^2 + 1 = 33;$ (Putting $n = 4$)

So the sequence is, 3, 9, 19, 33, ...

Now $t_2 - t_1 = 9 - 3 = 6$

$t_3 - t_2 = 19 - 9 = 10$

$\because \quad t_2 - t_1 \neq t_3 - t_2$

So the sequence is not in A. P.

Example 3

Find the first five terms of the sequence for which $t_1 = 1, t_2 = 2$ and $t_{n+2} = t_n + t_{n+1}$.

Solution :

By the question,

$$t_{n+2} = t_n + t_{n+1} \quad ...(i)$$

Putting $n = 1$ in (i), $t_3 = t_1 + t_2 = 1 + 2 = 2$

Putting $n = 2$ in (i), $t_4 = t_2 + t_3 = 2 + 3 = 5$

Putting $n = 3$ in (i), $t_5 = t_3 + t_4 = 3 + 5 = 8$

So the first five terms of the sequence are 1, 2, 3, 5 and 8.

Example 4

Find the first four terms of the sequence for which

$t_1 = 2, t_{n+1} = \dfrac{t_n}{t_n + 1}$.

Solution :

By the question

$$t_{n+1} = \frac{t_n}{t_n+1} \quad ...(i)$$

Putting $n = 1$ in eq. (i), $t_2 = \dfrac{t_1}{t_1+1} = \dfrac{2}{2+1} = \dfrac{2}{3}$

Putting $n = 2$ in eq. (i), $t_3 = \dfrac{t_2}{t_2+1} = \dfrac{\frac{2}{3}}{\frac{2}{3}+1}$

$$= \frac{\frac{2}{3}}{\frac{2+3}{3}} = \frac{2}{3} \times \frac{3}{5} = \frac{2}{5}$$

Putting $n = 3$ in eq. (i), $t_4 = \dfrac{t_3}{t_3+1} = \dfrac{\frac{2}{5}}{\frac{2}{5}+1} = \dfrac{\frac{2}{5}}{\frac{2+5}{5}}$

$$= \frac{\frac{2}{5}}{\frac{7}{5}} = \frac{2}{5} \times \frac{5}{7} = \frac{2}{7}$$

So the first four terms of the sequence are : 2, $\frac{2}{3}$, $\frac{2}{5}$, $\frac{2}{7}$.

Example 5

Find the first five terms of the sequence for which $t_1 = 3, t_{n+1} = \dfrac{1+t_n}{1+2t_n}$.

Solution :

By the question

$$t_{n+1} = \frac{1+t_n}{1+2t_n} \quad ...(i)$$

Putting $n = 1$ in eq. (i),

$$t_2 = \frac{1+t_1}{1+2t_1} = \frac{1+3}{1-2\times 3} = \frac{4}{7}$$

Putting $n = 2$ in eq. (i),

$$t_3 = \frac{1+t_2}{1+2t_2} = \frac{-+\frac{4}{7}}{1-2\times\frac{4}{7}} = \frac{\frac{7+4}{7}}{\frac{7+8}{7}} = \frac{\frac{11}{7}}{\frac{15}{7}} = \frac{11}{15}$$

Putting $n = 3$ in eq. (i),

$$t_4 = \frac{1+t_3}{1+2t_3} = \frac{1+\frac{11}{15}}{1+2\times\frac{11}{15}} = \frac{\frac{15+11}{15}}{\frac{15+22}{15}} = \frac{\frac{26}{15}}{\frac{37}{15}} = \frac{26}{37}$$

Putting $n = 4$ in eq. (i),

$$t_5 = \frac{1+t_4}{1+2t_4} = \frac{1+\frac{26}{37}}{1+2\times\frac{26}{37}} = \frac{\frac{37+26}{37}}{\frac{37+52}{37}} = \frac{\frac{63}{37}}{\frac{89}{37}} = \frac{63}{89}$$

So the first five terms of the sequence are 3, $\frac{4}{7}$, $\frac{11}{15}$, $\frac{26}{37}$ and $\frac{63}{89}$.

✎ Type II

Problems based on $t_n = a + (n - 1)d$

Example 6(A)

Find the 10th term of the A. P. 3, 8, 13, 18, ...

Solution :

The given sequence is in A.P.

Its first term $a = 3$

c.d., $d = 8 - 3 = 5;$

$t_{10} = ?$

$\because \quad t_n = a + (n-1)d$

$\therefore \quad t_{10} = a + (10-1)d$

$= 3 + 9 \times 5 = 48$

$\therefore \quad t_{10} = 48$ **Ans.**

Example 6(B)

Find the 12th term of the A. P. 7, 10, 13, 16, ... (*JAC, 2024*)

Solution :

Given $a = 7, n = 12, d = 10 - 7 = 3$

c.d., $d = 10 - 7 = 3$

$n = 12$

$t_n = a + (n-1)d$

$t_{12} = 7 + (12-1)3$

$= 7 + 33 = $ **40** **Ans.**

Example 7

How many terms are there in A. P. 20, 25, 35, ..., 100 ?

Solution :

By the question, first term

$a = 20$

c.d., $d = 25 - 20 = 5$

$t_n = 100$, then $n = ?$

$\because$ $t_n = a + (n-1)d$

$\therefore$ $100 = 20 + (n-1) \times 5$

$\Rightarrow$ $100 - 20 = (n-1) \times 5$

$\Rightarrow$ $80 = (n-1)5$

$\Rightarrow$ $n - 1 = \dfrac{80}{5} = 16$

$\Rightarrow$ $n = 16 + 1$

$\therefore$ $n = 17$ **Ans.**

So there are 17 terms in the given A.P.

Example 8

If 8th and 25th terms of an A.P. are 15 and 49 respectively, then find its first term and common difference.

Solution :

For this A.P.

let first term $= a$

and c.d. $= d$

By the question $t_8 = 15$

or $a + (8-1)d = 15$

or $a + 7d = 15$ ...(i)

Again $t_{25} = 49$

or $a + (25-1)d = 49$

or $a + 24d = 49$ ...(ii)

Subtracting (i) from (ii),

$a + 24d = 49$

$a + 7d = 15$

$-\quad -\quad -$

$17d = 34$

$\therefore$ $d = 2$

Putting d = 2 in eq. (i)

from (i), $a + 7 \times 2 = 15$

$\therefore$ $a + 14 = 15$

So first term $a = 1$

and c.d. $= 2$ **Ans.**

Example 9

Find the A. P. whose 7th and 13th terms are 34 and 64 respectively.

Solution :

For the A. P. let first term $= a$

and c.d. $= d$

By the question $t_7 = 34$

$\Rightarrow$ $a + (7-1)d = 34$

$\Rightarrow$ $a + 6d = 34$ ...(i)

Again $t_{13} = 64$

$\Rightarrow$ $a + (13-1)d = 64$

$\Rightarrow$ $a + 12d = 64$ ...(ii)

Subtracting (i) from (ii),

$a + 12d = 64$

$a + 6d = 34$

$-\quad -\quad -$

$6d = 30$

$\therefore$ $d = 5$

Putting $d = 5$ in eq. (i),

$a + 6 \times 5 = 34$

or $a + 30 = 34$

$\therefore$ $a = 4$

So for this A.P. First term $= 4$

c.d. $= 5$

So the A. P. is 4, 9, 14, 19...............

Example 10

If the third term of an A.P. is 18 and seventh term is 30, find the 17th term. *(JAC, 2019, 26)*

Solution :

Let First term $= a$,

Common difference $= d$

Given : T_3 or $a + 2d = 18$ ...(i)

T_7 or $a + 6d = 30$ ...(ii)

From eq. (i) and (ii) $a + 2d = 18$

$a + 6d = 30$

$-\quad -$

$-4d = -12$

$\therefore$ $d = \dfrac{-12}{-4} = 3$

Putting the value of d in equ. (i),

$a + 2d = 18$

$\Rightarrow$ $a + 2 \times 3 = 18$

$\Rightarrow$ $a = 18 - 6$

$\therefore$ $a = 12$

17th term $T_{17} = a + 16d$

$= 12 + 16 \times 3$

$= 12 + 48$

$= 60$ **Ans.**

Example 11

How many terms are identical in the two arithmetic progressions 2, 4, 6, 8, ... upto 100 terms and 3, 6, 9, ... upto 80 terms.

Solution :

The first A .P. is 2, 4, 6, 8, 10, 12, 14, 16, 18, ... to 100 terms.

Here First term $= 2$, $n = 100$ and c.d. $= 2$

Last term of A.P. $t_{100} = a + (100-1)d$

$= 2 + 99 \times 2 = 200$

The second A.P. is 3, 6, 9, 12, 15, 18, ... to 80 terms,

Here first term, $a = 3$, $n = 80$ and c.d. $= 3$

Last term of this A. P.

$t_{80} = 3 + (80-1)\,3 = 3 + 79 \times 3 = 240$

Common terms of both the A. Ps 6, 12, 18,.....which are in A.P.

First term $= 6$

and c.d. = 6

Let last term of this A.P. = t_n

$\therefore \quad t_n \le 200$

or $\quad 6 + (n-1)\,6 \le 200$

or $\quad 6n \le 200$

or $\quad n \le \dfrac{100}{3}$

or $\quad n \le 33\dfrac{1}{3}$

$\therefore \quad n = 33$

So 33 terms of both the A.P.s are common. **Ans.**

Example 12

A person was appointed in the scale of ₹ 5,000-500-10,000. Find in how many years he will reach the maximum of the scale ?

Solution :

Initial scale of the person = ₹ 5,000

Since his scale increases by ₹ 500 per year,

So after one year scale = 5,000 + 500 = ₹ 5,500

So after two years scale = 5,500 + 500 = ₹ 6,000

5,000 ↓ 5,500 ↓ 6,000 ↓ 6,500 ↓

Since 5,000, 5,500, 6,000, ... are in A. P.

First term $\quad a = 5{,}000$

$d = 500$

Let $\quad t_n = 10{,}000$

or $\quad a + (n-1)d = 10{,}000$

or $\quad 5{,}000 + (n-1)\,500 = 10{,}000$

or $\quad (n-1)\,500 = 5{,}000$

or $\quad n - 1 = 10$

or $\quad n = 11$

So after 11 years he will reach maximum of the scale. **Ans.**

Example 13

Is 105 a term of the arithmetic sequence 4, 9, 14, 19, ... ?

Solution :

The given sequence is 4, 9, 14, 19,...which are in A. P.

Its first term $a = 4$

c.d. = 5

for this A. P.,

Let $\quad t_n = 105$

$\therefore \quad a + (n-1)d = 105$

or $\quad 4 + (n-1)\,5 = 105$

or $\quad (n-1)\,5 = 101$

or $\quad n - 1 = \dfrac{101}{5}$

or $\quad n = \dfrac{101}{5} + 1 = \dfrac{106}{5} = 21\dfrac{1}{5}$,

which is a fraction.

So 105 is not any term of this A.P. **Ans.**

Example 14

Find the first negative term of the sequence 999, 995, 991, 987, ...

Solution :

The given A. P. is 999, 995, 991, 987,...

its first term $\quad a = 999$

$d = -4$

Let t_n is the first negative term of the A. P.

$\therefore \quad t_n < 0$

or $\quad a + (n-1)d < 0$

or $\quad 999 + (n-1)(-4) < 0$

or $\quad 999 - 4n + 4 < 0$

or $\quad 1\,003 - 4n < 0$

or $\quad 1{,}003 < 4n$

or $\quad 4n > 1{,}003$

or $\quad n > \dfrac{1{,}003}{4}$

or $\quad n > 250\dfrac{3}{4}$

$\therefore \quad n = 251$

$\therefore \quad t_n = a + (n-1)d$

$t_{251} = 999 + (251-1)(-4)$

$= 999 - 1{,}000 = -1$

So the first negative term of the A.P. is – 1. **Ans.**

Example 15

How many terms are there in the A. P. 7, 13, 19, ..., 205 ?

Solution :

Series 7, 13, 19 is in A.P.,

where $a = 7 \qquad n = ?$

$d = 13 - 7 = 6 \qquad T_n = 205$

Now, $\quad T_n = a + (n-1)d$

or $\quad 205 = 7 + (n-1)6$

or $\quad 205 = 7 + 6n - 6$

or $\quad 205 = 6n + 1$

or $\quad 6n = 205 - 1$

or $\quad n = \dfrac{204}{6}$

= 34th term **Ans.**

Example 16

The first three terms of an A. P. are 20, 16 and 12. Which term is – 96 ?

Solution :

20, 16 and 12 is in A.P.

So $\quad a = 20 \qquad T_n = -96$

$d = 16 - 20 = -4 \qquad n = ?$

Now $\quad T_n = a + (n-1)d$

or $\quad -96 = 20 + (n-1) - 4$

or $\quad -96 = 20 - 4n + 4$

or $\quad -96 = 24 - 4n$

or $\quad 4n = 96 + 24$

or $$n = \frac{120}{4}$$

$\therefore$ $$n = 30\text{th term}$$ **Ans.**

Example 17

Find the number of integers between 100 and 1000 that are

(i) divisible by 7, (ii) not divisible by 7.

Solution :

(i) Integers between 100 and 1,000 that are divisible by 7

105, 112, 119,....,994

which are in A.P.

Its first term $a = 105$

and $d = 7$ then $n = ?$

Let last term $t_n = 994$

or $a + (n-1)d = 994$

or $105 + (n-1)7 = 994$

or $(n-1)7 = 889$

or $n - 1 = 127$

$\therefore$ $n = 128$ **Ans.**

(ii) Number of integers between 100 and 1,000 = 901 in which number of integers divisible by 7 = 128

So number of such integers not divisible by 7 = 901 – 128 = 773 **Ans.**

✎ Type III

Problems based on three, four or five numbers in A.P. when their sum is given

Working Rule :

(i) If three numbers are in A.P. and their sum is given, then the numbers are $\alpha - \beta, \alpha, \alpha + \beta$.

(ii) If four numbers are in A. P. and their sum is given, then the numbers are $\alpha - 3\beta, \alpha - \beta, \alpha + \beta, \alpha + 3\beta$.

(iii) If five numbers are in A. P. and their sum is given, then the numbers are $\alpha - 2\beta, \alpha - \beta, \alpha, \alpha + \beta, \alpha + 2\beta$.

Example 18

Divide 15 into three parts which are in A. P. and the sum of their squares is 83.

Solution :

Let three numbers in A. P. are $\alpha - \beta, \alpha, \alpha + \beta$.

By the question,

$$\alpha - \beta + \alpha + \alpha + \beta = 15$$

or $3\alpha = 15$

or $\alpha = 15$

Again by the question,

$$(\alpha - \beta)^2 + \alpha^2 + (\alpha + \beta)^2 = 83$$

or $\alpha^2 + \beta^2 - 2\alpha\beta + \alpha^2 + \alpha^2 + \beta^2 + 2\alpha\beta = 83$

or $3\alpha^2 + 2\beta^2 = 83$

or $3(5)^2 + 2\beta^2 = 83$

or $75 + 2\beta^2 = 83$

or $2\beta^2 = 83 - 75 = 8$

or $\beta^2 = 4$

$\beta = \pm 2$

When $\alpha = 5$ and $\beta = 2$

then First Number $= \alpha - \beta = 5 - 2 = 2$

Second Number $= \alpha = 5$

Third Number $= \alpha + \beta = 5 + 2 = 7$

Then the three numbers are 3, 5, 7. **Ans.**

Again when $\alpha = 5$ and $\beta = -2$, then

First Number $= \alpha - \beta = 5 - (-2) = 7$

Second Number $= \alpha = 5$

Third Number $= \alpha + \beta = 5 + (-2) = 3$

then the three numbers are 7, 5, 3. **Ans.**

Example 19

The sum of four integers in A. P. is 24 and their product is 945. Find the numbers.

Solution :

Let four numbers in A. P. are $\alpha - 3\beta, \alpha - \beta, \alpha + \beta, \alpha + 3\beta$.

By the question,

$$\alpha - 3\beta + \alpha - \beta + \alpha + \beta + \alpha + 3\beta = 24$$

or $4\alpha = 24$

or $\alpha = 6$

Again by the question,

$$(\alpha - 3\beta)(\alpha - \beta)(\alpha + \beta)(\alpha + 3\beta) = 945$$

or $\{(\alpha - 3\beta)(\alpha + 3\beta)\}\{(\alpha - \beta)(\alpha + \beta)\} = 945$

or $(\alpha^2 - 9\beta^2)(\alpha^2 - \beta^2) = 945$

or $(36 - 9\beta^2)(36 - \beta^2) = 945$

or $9(4 - \beta^2)(36 - \beta^2) = 945$

or $(4 - \beta^2)(36 - \beta^2) = 105$

or $144 - 4\beta^2 - 36\beta^2 + \beta^4 = 105$

or $\beta^4 - 40\beta^2 + 144 - 105 = 0$

or $\beta^4 - 40\beta^2 + 39 = 0$

or $\beta^4 - \beta^2 - 39\beta^2 + 39 = 0$

or $\beta^2(\beta^2 - 1) - 39(\beta^2 - 1) = 0$

or $(\beta^2 - 1)(\beta^2 - 39) = 0$

So either $\beta^2 - 39 = 0$

$\Rightarrow \beta = \pm\sqrt{39}$ Impossible

as the four numbers are integers

So $\beta^2 - 1 = 0$

$\Rightarrow$ $\beta^2 = 1 \Rightarrow \beta = \pm 1$

When $\alpha = 6$ and $\beta = 1$, then

$\alpha - 3\beta = 6 - 3 \times 1 = 3$

$\alpha - \beta = 6 - 1 = 5$

$\alpha + \beta = 6 + 1 = 7$

$\alpha + 3\beta = 6 + 3 \times 1 = 9$

then the required numbers are 3, 5, 7, 9. **Ans.**

Again when $\alpha = 6$ and $\beta = -1$,

then
$$\alpha - 3\beta = 6 - 3 \times (-1) = 9$$
$$\alpha - \beta = 6 - (-1) = 7$$
$$\alpha + \beta = 6 + (-1) = 5$$
$$\alpha + 3\beta = 6 + 3 \times (-1) = 3$$

then the required numbers are 9, 7, 5, 3. **Ans.**

Working Rules of A.P. : If $a_1, a_2, a_3, \ldots\ldots\ldots a_n$ are in A. P.

then (1) $a_1 + k, a_2 + k, a_3 + k, \ldots\ldots\ldots, a_n + k$ will be in A. P.

(2) $a_1 - k, a_2 - k, a_3 - k, \ldots\ldots\ldots, a_n - k$ will be in A. P.

(3) $ka_1, ka_2, ka_3, \ldots\ldots\ldots, ka_n$ will be in A. P.

(4) $\frac{a_1}{k}, \frac{a_2}{k}, \frac{a_3}{k}, \ldots\ldots, \frac{a_n}{k}, k \neq 0$ will be in A. P.

Exercise 1(A)

✎ Type I

Problems Based on Sequence

1. Write the sequence whose nth term is $\frac{n}{n+1}$.
2. If nth terms of a sequence is $2na + b$, where a, b are constants, is this sequence an A.P. ?
3. Show that $(a-b)^2, (a^2+b^2), (a+b)^2$ are in A.P.
4. The nth term of a sequence is $3n - 2$. Is the sequence an A.P. ? If so, find its 10th term.

✎ Type II

Problems Based on $t_n = a + (n-1)d$

5. Find the 10th term of the sequence 10, 5, 0, – 5, – 10, ...
6. Find the 10th term of the sequence 3, 5, 7, 9, ...
7. How many terms are there in A.P. 1, 3, 5, 7, ..., 99 ? *(JAC, 2022)*
8. Which term of the A.P. 1, 3, 5, 7, 9, ... is 65 ?
9. Find the A.P. whose 7th and 12th terms are 34 and 64 respectively. Also find its 10th term.
10. How many terms are indentical in the two A.P. if each of the A.P. 3, 5, 7, and 4, 7, 10, ... is continued to 100 terms?
11. Is 254 a term of the A.P. 4, 9, 14, 19, ... ?
12. If $(x + 2)$, $3x$ and $(4x + 1)$ are in A.P. then find x.
13. Which term of the A.P. 3, 7, 11, ... will be 59 ? *(JAC, 2025)*
14. If 24th term of an A.P. is twice the 10th term, prove that 72th term is twice the 34th term.
15. If 3rd term of an A.P. is four times the first term and 6th term is 17, find the A.P.
16. Find the value of k, if 5, k, 11 are in A.P.
17. In a certain A.P. 11th and 16th terms are 44 and 19 respectively, then find the A.P. Also find its 20th term.

17A. If 40th and 80th terms of an A.P. are 119 and 239, find the A.P. *(JAC, 2025)*

✎ Type III

Problems Based on Three, Four or Five Numbers in A.P When There sum in Given

18. If the sum of three numbers in A.P. is 12 and sum of their cubes is 408, find the numbers.
19. If the sum of three consecutive terms of an A.P. is 51 and the product of two extremes is 273, find the numbers.
20. Divide 24 into four parts which are in A.P. such that the sum of their squares is 164.
21. The sum of three no. in A.P. is – 24 and their product is 288. Find the numbers.
22. The sum of three no. in A.P. is 15 and the product of 1st and the last is 21. Find the numbers.
23. Divide 20 into 4 parts which are in A.P. and such that the product of first and fourth is to product of the second and third in the ratio 2 : 3.
24. The sum of digits of a three digit number is 12 and the digits are in A.P. If the digits are reversed, then the number is diminished by 396. Find the number.
25. The three nos. are in the ratio of 3 : 7 : 9. If 5 subtracted from the second, the resulting number form an A.P. Find the original numbers.

Miscellaneous Problems

26. Which term of the sequence 72, 70, 68, 66, ... is 40 ?
27. Is 184 a term of the sequence 3, 7, 11, ... ?
28. How many numbers of two digits are divisible by 7 ?

Answers

1. $\frac{1}{2}, \frac{2}{3}, \frac{3}{4}, \ldots$	2. Yes	4. 28
5. – 35	6. 21	7. 50
8. 33	9. – 2, 4, 10, 16, ... $t_{10} = 52$	
10. 33	11. Yes, 51st term	12. $x = 3$
13. 15th	15. 2, 5, 8, 11, 14, ...	16. $k = 8$
17. A.P. : 94, 89, 84, ...$t_{20} = -1$	17A. 2, 5, 8, 11, ...	
18. 1, 4, 7, or 7, 4, 1	19. 13, 17, 21 or 21, 17, 13	
20. 3, 5, 7, 9 or 9, 7, 5, 3	21. – 18, – 8, 2 or 2, – 8, –18	
22. 3, 5, 7 or 7, 5, 3	23. 2, 4, 6, 8	24. 642
25. 15, 35, 45	26. 17th term	
27. Not a term	28. 13	

1.3.3 To find the sum of nth terms of an A.P.

For the A.P.

Let first term = a

c.d. = d

Sum of first n terms
$$= S_n$$

Now S_n and nth term
$$= t_n \; a + (a + d) + (a + 2d) + \ldots + (t_n - 2d) + (t_n - d) + t_n \quad \ldots(i)$$

Again S_n and nth term
$$= t_n + (t_n - d) + (t_n - 2d) + \ldots + (a + 2d) + (a + d) + a \quad \ldots(ii)$$

Adding the corresponding terms of eq. (i) and (ii),
$$2S_n = (a + t_n) + (a + t_n) + (a + t_n) + \ldots + (a + t_n) + (a + t_n) + (a + t_n)$$
$$= (a + t_n) + (a + t_n) + (a + t_n) + \ldots \text{ to } n \text{ terms}$$
$$= n\,(a + t_n)$$

$$\therefore \quad \boxed{S_n = \frac{n}{2}(a + t_n)} \quad \textbf{Formula 1} \ldots(iii)$$

$$= \frac{n}{2}[a + a + (n-1)d] \quad [\because t_n = a + (n-1)d]$$

$$= \frac{n}{2}[2a + (n-1)d]$$

$$\therefore \quad \boxed{S_n = \frac{n}{2}[2a + (n-1)d]} \qquad \textbf{Formula 2}$$

Note : An important formula when S_n is given, then find t_n.

$$\boxed{t_n = S_n - S_{n-1}} \qquad \textbf{Formula 3}$$

SOLVED EXAMPLES

Example 1

Find the sum of first n odd natural numbers.

Or

Prove that $1 + 3 + 5 + 7 + ...$ to n terms $= n^2$.

Solution :

The given series is in A.P.

Its first term $a = 1$

c.d. $d = 2$

and number of terms $= n$

$$\because \quad S_n = \frac{n}{2}[2a + (n-1)d]$$

$$S_n = \frac{n}{2}[2 \times 1 + (n-1).2]$$

$$= \frac{n}{2}[2 + 2n - 2]$$

$$= \frac{n}{2}.2n = n^2 \qquad \textbf{Proved}$$

Example 2

Find the sum of the following series upto 9th term :

$$2\sqrt{3} + \frac{9}{\sqrt{3}} + \frac{12}{\sqrt{3}} + ...$$

Solution :

The series is in A.P., where

$$a = 2\sqrt{3}$$

$$d = \frac{9}{\sqrt{3}} - 2\sqrt{3}$$

$$= \frac{9-6}{\sqrt{3}} = \frac{3}{\sqrt{3}} = \sqrt{3}$$

$$n = 9$$

Now $S_n = \frac{n}{2}[2a + (n-1)d]$

$$= \frac{9}{2}\left[2(2\sqrt{3}) + (9-1)\sqrt{3}\right]$$

$$= \frac{9}{2}\left[4\sqrt{3} + 8\sqrt{3}\right] = \frac{9}{2}\left[12\sqrt{3}\right]$$

$$= 9(6\sqrt{3})$$

$$= 54\sqrt{3} \qquad \textbf{Ans.}$$

Example 3

If the sum of n terms of a series be $2n^2 + 7n$, then find the first five terms of the progression.

Solution :

Here $S_n = 2n^2 + 7n$

$\therefore \quad S_{n-1} = 2(n-1)^2 + 7(n-1)$

$\because \quad t_n = S_n - S_{n-1}$

$$= (2n^2 + 7n) - \{2(n-1)^2 + 7(n-1)\}$$

$$= (2n^2 + 7n) - 2(n-1)^2 - 7(n-1)$$

$$= 2n^2 + 7n - 2(n^2 - 2n + 1) - 7n + 7$$

$$= 2n^2 + 7n - 2n^2 + 4n - 2 - 7n + 7$$

$$t_n = 4n + 5$$

$\therefore \quad t_1 = 4 \times 1 + 5 = 9$

$t_2 = 4 \times 2 + 5 = 13$

$t_3 = 4 \times 3 + 5 = 17$

$t_4 = 4 \times 4 + 5 = 21$

$t_5 = 4 \times 5 + 5 = 25$

So the first five terms of the progression are 9, 13, 17, 21, 25. **Ans.**

Example 4

Find the sum of the series upto 8th term

$$3\frac{1}{3} + 4 + 4\frac{2}{3} + 6 + ...$$

Solution :

Given $a = \frac{10}{3}$

$$d = \frac{14}{3} - \frac{10}{3} = \frac{4}{3}, n = 8$$

$$S_n = \frac{n}{2}[2a + (n-1)d]$$

$$S_8 = \frac{8}{2}\left[2 \times \frac{10}{3} + (8-1)\frac{4}{3}\right]$$

$$= 4\left[\frac{20}{3} + \frac{28}{3}\right]$$

$$= 4 \times \frac{48}{3}$$

$$= 4 \times 16$$

$$= 64 \qquad \textbf{Ans.}$$

Example 5

Find the value of x in the following series :

$1 + 6 + 11 + ... + x = 148$

Solution :

The given series is in A.P. in which

$a = 1, d = 6 - 1 = 5,$

$S_n = 148$

Then, $S_n = \frac{n}{2}\left[2a + (n-1)d\right]$

$\Rightarrow \quad 148 = \frac{n}{2}\left[2 \times 1 + (n-1)5\right]$

$\Rightarrow \quad 148 \times 2 = n[2 + 5n - 5]$

$\Rightarrow \quad 296 = n[5n - 3]$

$\Rightarrow \quad 296 = 5n^2 - 3n$

$\Rightarrow \quad 5n^2 - 3n - 296 = 0$

$\Rightarrow \quad 5n^2 - 40n + 37n - 296 = 0$

$\Rightarrow \quad 5n(n-8) + 37(n-8) = 0$

$\Rightarrow \quad (5n+37)(n-8) = 0$

$\therefore \quad n = \frac{-37}{5}$

and $\quad n = 8$

$n = 8 \quad \left[\because n \neq \frac{-37}{5}\right]$

Now 8th term $\quad T_n = a + (n-1)d$

$T_8 = 1 + (8-1)5$

$= 1 + 35 = 36$

$\therefore \quad x = 36$ **Ans.**

Example 6

Prove that : $1 + 2 + 3 + \ldots\ldots$ to n terms $= \frac{n(n+1)}{2}$.

Solution :

For the given A. P. first term $a = 1$

Common difference $d = 1$

Number of terms $= n$

$\because \quad S_n = \frac{n}{2}\left[2a + (n-1)d\right]$

$= \frac{n}{2}\left[2\times1 + (n-1).1\right]$

$= \frac{n}{2}\left[2 + n - 1\right] = \frac{n}{2}(n+1)$

$S_n = \frac{n(n+1)}{2}$ **Proved.**

Example 7

Find the sum of the series $1 - 3 + 5 - 7 + 9 - 11 + \ldots$ to n terms.

Solution :

Case (i) : If n is an even positive integer, then let $n = 2m$, where m is any positive integer.

$\therefore 1 - 3 + 5 - 7 + 9 - 11 + \ldots$ to n terms

$= 1 - 3 + 5 - 7 + 9 - 11 + \ldots\ldots$ to $2m$ terms

$= (1-3) + (5-7) + (9-11) + \ldots$ to m terms

$= (-2) + (-2) + (-2) + \ldots$ to m terms

$= 2m = -n \quad [\because n = 2m]$

Case (ii) : If n is an odd positive integer, then let $n = 2m + 1$, where m is any positive integer.

$\therefore 1 - 3 + 5 - 7 + 9 - 11 + \ldots$ to n terms

$= 1 - 3 + 5 - 7 + 9 - 11 \ldots$ to $(2m+1)$ terms

$= 1 - [3 - 5 + 7 - 9 + 11 + \ldots$ to $2m$ terms$]$

$= 1 - [(3-5) + (7-9) + \ldots$ to m terms$]$

$= 1 - [(-2) + (-2) + \ldots$ to m terms$]$

$= 1 - [-2m] = 2m + 1 = n$ **Ans.**

Example 8

A person was appointed at a salary of ₹ 700 p.m. The condition of appointment was that he would receive ₹ 740 p.m. in the second year, ₹ 780 p.m. in the third year and so on. Find the total salary he would expect to have received by the end of 10 years.

Solution :

Total income in first year,

$a = 700 \times 12 =$ ₹ 8,400

Common difference,

$d = 40 \times 12 = 480$

Number of years, $n = 10$

So total salary at the end of 10 years

$= \frac{n}{2}[2a + (n-1)d]$

$= \frac{10}{2}[2 \times 8{,}400 + (10-1).480]$

$= 5[16{,}800 + 4{,}320]$

$= 5 \times 21{,}120$

$=$ ₹ 1,05,600 **Ans.**

Example 9

The sum of how many terms of the series $5 + 7 + 9 + \ldots\ldots\ldots$ will be 572 ? (*JAC*, 2018)

Solution :

Here $\quad a = 5, d = 7 - 5 = 2,$

$S_n = 572, n = ?$

We know that, $\quad S_n = \frac{n}{2}[2a + (n-1)d]$

$572 = \frac{n}{2}[2(5) + (n-1)2]$

or $\quad 1144 = n[10 + 2n - 2]$

or $\quad 1144 = n(8 + 2n)$

or $\quad 1144 = 8n + 2n^2$

or $\quad 2n^2 - 8n - 572 = 0$

or $\quad n^2 - 4n - 572 = 0$

or $\quad n^2 + 26n - 22n - 572 = 0$

or $\quad n(n+26) - 22(n+26) = 0$

or $\quad (n+26)(n-22) = 0$

or $\quad n = 22 \quad [\because n \neq 26]$

$\therefore \quad n = 22$

Example 9 (A)

How many terms of the series $54 + 51 + 48 + 45 + \ldots\ldots$ must be taken to make 513 ? Explain the double answer.

Solution :

For the given A.P.

Let sum to n terms $= 513$

Here $\quad a = 54, d = -3$

$\because \quad S_n = \frac{n}{2}\left[2a + (n-1)d\right]$

$513 = \frac{n}{2}[2 \times 54 + (n-1)(-3)]$

or $\quad 513 = \frac{n}{2}[108 - 3n + 3]$

$$\text{or} \quad 513 = \frac{n}{2}(111-3n)$$
$$\text{or} \quad 1026 = n(111-3n)$$
$$\text{or} \quad 1026 = 111n - 3n^2$$
$$\text{or} \quad 3n^2 - 111n + 1026 = 0$$
$$\text{or} \quad n^2 - 37n + 342 = 0$$
$$\text{or} \quad n^2 - 18n - 19n + 342 = 0$$
$$\text{or} \quad n(n-18) - 19(n-18) = 0$$
$$\text{or} \quad (n-18)(n-19) = 0$$
$$\therefore \quad n = \mathbf{18, 19}$$

Explanation of double answer :

$$S_{18} = \frac{18}{2}[2\times 54 + (18-1)(-3)]$$
$$= 9(108-51) = 9\times 57 = 513$$
$$\text{and} \quad t_{19} = a + (19-1)d$$
$$= 54 + 18\times(-3)$$
$$= 54 - 54 = 0$$

$t_{19} = 0$, so the sum of the 18 terms and sum of the first 19 terms are equal.

Example 10

Find the maximum sum of the A.P. 40, 38, 36, 34, ...

Solution :

The sum will be maximum when we take only positive terms.

Let t_n is the first negative term.

$$a = 40, d = -2$$
$$\therefore \quad t_n < 0$$
$$\text{or} \quad a + (n-1)d < 0$$
$$\text{or} \quad 40 + (n-1).(-2) < 0$$
$$\text{or} \quad 40 - 2n + 2 < 0$$
$$\text{or} \quad 42 < 2n$$
$$\text{or} \quad 2n > 42$$
$$n > 21$$

So the first negative term = 22th term

So for maximum sum we should add only 21 terms.

$$\text{So required max. sum} = \frac{21}{2}[2\times 40 + (21-1)(-2)]$$
$$= \frac{21}{2}\times 40$$
$$= 21\times 20$$
$$= 420$$

Ans.

Example 11

25 trees are planted in a straight line of a well at equal intervals of 5 metre. To water them the gardener must bring water for each tree separately from a well 10 metre from the first tree in a line with the trees. How far he will have to cover in order to water all the trees beginning with the first if he start from the well.

Solution :

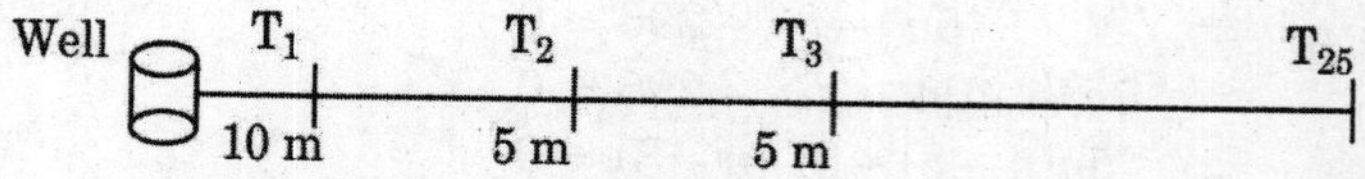

Let the well is 'W' and T_1, T_2, T_3 ,......, T_{25} are positions of the given trees and the distance in two is 5 metre. The distance of T_1 from the well is 10 m and $T_1 - T_2 = T_2 - T_3 = \ldots\ldots = T_{24} - T_{25} = 5$ m.

So distance covered to water the first tree = 10 m, distance covered to water the 2nd tree = 10 + 15 = 25 m, distance covered to water the 3rd tree = 15 + 20 = 35 m, distance covered to water the 4th tree = 20 + 25 = 45 m and so on.

So total distance covered to water all the trees

$$= 10 + 25 + 35 + 45 + \ldots \text{ to 25 terms}$$
$$= 10 + [25 + 35 + 45 + \ldots \text{ to 24 terms}]$$
$$= 10 + \frac{24}{2}[2\times 25 + (24-1).10]$$
$$= 10 + 12[50 + 230] = 10 + 12\times 280$$
$$= 10 + 3{,}360$$
$$= 3{,}370 \text{ m}$$

Ans.

Example 12

Find the sum upto 100 terms of following series :
0.70 + 0.71 + 0.72 + 0.73 + ...

Solution :

Series is in A.P.

$$\text{So} \quad a = 0.70$$
$$d = 0.71 - 0.70 = 0.01$$
$$n = 100$$

$$\text{By formula } S_n = \frac{n}{2}\left[2a + (n-1)d\right]$$
$$\therefore \quad S_{100} = \frac{100}{2}\left[2\times 0.70 + (100-1)\times 0.01\right]$$
$$= 50[1.4 + (99\times 0.01)]$$
$$= 50[1.4 + 0.99]$$
$$= 50\times 2.39$$
$$= 119.5$$

Ans.

Example 13

Prove that the sum of the later half of the first $2n$ terms of a series in A.P. is equal to one-third of the sum of the first $3n$ terms.

Solution :

For the A.P.,

Let first term = a

and c.d. = d

The sum of later half of the first $2n$ terms

$$= S_{2n} - S_n$$
$$= \frac{2n}{2}[2a + (2n-1)d] - \frac{n}{2}[2a + (n-1)d]$$

$= \frac{n}{2}[4a + 2(2n-1)d - 2a - (n-1)d]$

$= \frac{n}{2}[4a + (4n-2)d - 2a - (n-1)d]$

$= \frac{n}{2}[2a + (4n - 2 - n + 1)d]$

$= \frac{n}{2}[2a + (3n-1)d]$

$= \frac{1}{3}\cdot\frac{3n}{2}[2a + (3n-1)d]$

$= \frac{1}{3}S_{3n} = \frac{1}{3}$ (the sum of first 3n terms)

Proved

Example 14

Find the sum upto 12th term

$\sqrt{5} + \sqrt{5}(1-\sqrt{5}) + \sqrt{5}(1-2\sqrt{5}) + \ldots\ldots$

Solution :

Given $a = \sqrt{5}$

$d = \sqrt{5}(1-\sqrt{5}) - \sqrt{5}$

$= \sqrt{5} - 5 - \sqrt{5}$

$= -5$

$n = 12$

$S_{12} = \frac{12}{2}[2a + (n-1)d]$

$= 6[2 \times \sqrt{5} + (12-1)(-5)]$

$= 6(2\sqrt{5} - \sqrt{5})$ **Ans.**

Example 15

12th term of an A.P. is 12 more than sixth term and their sum is 38. Find the series.

Solution :

Given $T_{12} = 12 + T_6$

$a + (12-1)d = 12 + a + (6-1)d$

$a + 11d = 12 + a + 5d$

$11d - 5d = 12$

$6d = 12$

$d = \frac{12}{6} = 2$

and $T_{12} + T_6 = 38$

$a + 11d + a + 5d = 38$

$2a + 16d = 38$

$2a + (16 \times 2) = 38$

$2a = 38 - 32$

$2a = 6$

$a = 3$

Series

$a = 3$

$a + d = 3 + 2 = 5$

$a + 2d = 3 + (2 \times 2) = 7$

So, $= 3, 5, 7$ **Ans.**

Example 16

Find the sum of the series : 72 + 68 + 66 + ... + 40.

Solution :

Let the number of terms in A.P. be n

According to question,

first term $(a) = 72$

Common difference $(d) = -4$

and Last term $(t_n) = 40$

$\because$ $t_n = a + (n-1)d$

$\therefore$ $40 = 72 + (n-1)(-4)$

or $40 = 72 - 4n + 4$

or $40 = 76 - 4n$

or $4n = 36$

$\therefore$ $n = 9$

$\because$ $S_n = \frac{n}{2}[2a + (n-1)d]$

$\therefore$ $S_9 = \frac{9}{2}[2\times72 + (9-1)(-4)]$

$= \frac{9}{2}[144 - 32]$

$= \frac{9}{2}[112]$

Hence Required sum = 504 **Ans.**

Example 17

The sum of all natural numbers between 100 and 1,000; which are multiple of 5 is : (*JAC*, 2016)

(a) 98,450 (b) 96,450

(c) 97,450 (d) 95,450

Solution :

The following are the numbers of the multiple of 5 in between 100 and 1,000.

105, 110, 115, ..., 995, this $a = 105$, $d = 110 - 105 = 5$ and $t_n = 995$

$\because$ $t_n = a + (n-1)d$

$\therefore$ $995 = 105 + (n-1) \times 5$

$\therefore$ $(n-1)5 = 995 - 105$

$\Rightarrow$ $n - 1 = \frac{890}{5}$

$\Rightarrow$ $n - 1 = 178$

$\Rightarrow$ $n = 178 + 1$

$\therefore$ $n = 179$

then Sum of 179 digits

$(S_{179}) = \frac{n}{2}[a + t_n]$

$= \frac{179}{2}[105 + 995]$

$= \frac{179}{2} \times 1,100$

$= 179 \times 550$

$= 98,450$

Hence the option (a) is right.

Example 18

The sum of how many terms of the series : (*JAC*, 2018)

$5 + 7 + 9 + ...$ will be 572 ?

Solution :

For the given A.P.

Let sum of n terms $= 572$

Here $a = 5, d = 7 - 5 = 2$

$\therefore \quad S_n = \frac{n}{2}[2a + (n-1)d]$

$572 = \frac{n}{2}[2 \times 5 + (n-1)2]$

or $572 = \frac{n}{2}[10 + 2n - 2]$

or $572 = \frac{n}{2}[8 + 2n]$

or $572 = \frac{n}{2}2[4 + n]$

or $572 = n[4 + n]$

or $572 = 4n + n^2$

or $n^2 + 4n - 572 = 0$

or $n^2 + 26n - 22n - 572 = 0$

or $n(n + 26) - 22(n + 26) = 0$

or $(n + 26)(n - 22) = 0$

or $n - 22 = 0, n + 26 = 0$

$n = 22, n = -26$ (– ve)

Hence the sum of 22 terms of the sence will be 572.

Example 19

Find the sum of all three-digit numbers divisible by ? (*JAC*, 2018)

Solution :

Three-digit numbers, divisible by 9

108, 117, 126 999

which are in A.P.

I[st] term, $a = 108, \quad d = 117 - 108 = 9$

$t_n = 999$

or $a + (n-1)d = 999$

$\Rightarrow 108 + (n-1)9 = 999$

$\Rightarrow 108 + 9n - 9 = 999$

$\Rightarrow 99 + 9n = 999$

$\Rightarrow 9n = 999 - 99$

$\Rightarrow 9n = 900$

$\therefore \quad n = \frac{900}{9} = 100$

$S_n = \frac{n}{2}(a + l)$

$S_{100} = \frac{100}{2}(108 + 999)$

$= 50(1107) = 55350$

Exercise 1(B)

Based on the Formula $S_n = \frac{n}{2}[2a + (n-1)d]$

1. Find the sum of the following series :

   (i) $\frac{3}{\sqrt{5}} + \frac{4}{\sqrt{5}} + \sqrt{5} + ...$ upto 19 terms

   (ii) $\frac{n-1}{n} + \frac{n-2}{n} + \frac{n-3}{n} + \frac{n-4}{n} + ...$ upto n terms

   (iii) $1 + 5 + 3 + 9 + 5 + 13 + 7 + 17 + ...$upto 30 terms

   (iv) $2 + 3\frac{1}{3} + 4\frac{2}{3} + ...$ upto 60 terms

   (v) $\sqrt{3} + \sqrt{3}(1 - \sqrt{3}) + \sqrt{3}(1 - 2\sqrt{3}) + ...$ upto 21 terms

   (vi) $2 + 3 + 5 + 6 + 8 + 9 + ... + (3n - 1) + (3n)$

2. Find the sum of the series $1 - 2 + 3 - 4 + 5 - 6 + ...$upto n terms.
3. Find the least value of n such that $2 + 5 + 8 + 11 + ...$upto n terms ≥ 200.
4. Find the sum of all integers of 3 digits which are divisible by 7.
5. How many terms of the series $20 + 19\frac{1}{3} + 18\frac{2}{3} + ...$ must be taken to make 300. Explain the double answer.
6. The third and seventh term of an A.P. are 18 and 30 respectively, find the sum of their 17 terms. (*J.A.C.*, 2016)
7. The sum of n terms of an A.P. is 136 and common difference is 4. If the last term is 31, then find the number of terms.
8. Find the maximum sum of the A.P. 30, 27, 24, 21, 18, ...
9. How many integers between 10 and 100 are divisible by 3 ? Solve by a formula.
10. Find the sum of all integers between 100 and 400 which are divisible by 7.
11. There are 30 trees at equal distance of 5 metre in a line with a well, the distance of the well from the nearest tree being 10 metre. A gardener waters all the trees separately starting from the well and he returns to the well after watering each tree to get water for the next. Find the total distance the gardener will cover in order to water all the trees.
12. Find the sum of all natural numbers between 500 and 1000 which are divisible by 13.
13. Find the sum of the numbers lying between 1 and 100 which are divisible by 2 or 5.
14. Find the sum of all odd numbers of 4 digits which are divisible by 9.
15. For any series $5 + 7 + 9 + ...$ the sum of how many terms will be 480 ?
16. A man saves ₹ 20 in the first month, ₹ 30 in the 2nd month, ₹ 40 in the third month and so on upto five years. Find the total amount saved in five years.
17. Find the sum of the series $1\frac{1}{7}, 1, \frac{6}{7}, \frac{5}{7}$, ... upto 16th term.
18. How many terms of the progression 15, 12, 9........ should be taken so that their sum is 36 ?
19. For A.P. 3, 5, 7, 9........ the sum of how many terms will be 120.

20. The sum of how many terms of the progression 25, 22, 19, 16...... will be 116 ? Also find the last term.
21. How many terms of the series 2 + 4 + 6 + ... amount to 42 ?
22. Find the three numbers in an A.P. such that their sum is 15 and their product is 105. (*JAC*, 2025)

Answers

1. (i) $\frac{228}{\sqrt{5}}$ (ii) $\frac{1}{2}(n-1)$ (iii) 720
(iv) 2480 (v) $21(\sqrt{3}-30)$ (vi) $n(2+3n)$
2. $-\frac{n}{2}$, if n is even and $\frac{n+1}{2}$, if n is odd
3. 12
4. 70,336
5. n = 25 or 36
6. 612
7. 8
8. 165
9. n = 30
10. S_{43} = 10,836
11. 4,795 m
12. 28,405
13. 3,050
14. n = 500, S_n = 27,54,000
15. 20
16. ₹ 18,900
17. $\frac{8}{7}$
18. n = 8 or n = 3
19. n = 10
20. n = 8
21. n = 6
22. 3, 5, 7 or 7, 5, 3

1.3.4 Arithmetic Means

Definition : If three numbers be in A.P. then the middle one is called the Arithmetic Mean (A.M.) of the other two.

Example : Thus if a, x, b are in A.P. the x is said to be the A.M. of a and b.

Since a, x, b are in A.P.

$$\therefore \quad x - a = b - x$$

$$\Rightarrow \quad 2x = a + b$$

$$\Rightarrow \quad x = \frac{a+b}{2}$$

To insert n Arithmetic Means between Two given Quantities

Let $A_1, A_2, A_3, \ldots, A_n$ are n A.M.s between two given quantities a and b.

So $a, A_1, A_2, A_3, \ldots, A_n, b$ are in A.P.

Let its c.d. = d

Number of terms in this A.P. = $n + 2$

$$\therefore \quad b = (n+2)\text{th term} = a + (n+2-1)d$$

$$\Rightarrow \quad b - a = (n+1)d$$

$$\Rightarrow \quad d = \frac{b-a}{n+1}$$

$$\therefore \quad A_1 = a + d = a + \frac{b-a}{n+1} = \frac{an+b}{n+1}$$

$$A_2 = a + 2d = a + 2\left(\frac{b-a}{n+1}\right) = \frac{a(n-1)+2b}{n+1}$$

$$A_3 = a + 3d = a + 3 \times \left(\frac{b-a}{n+1}\right) = \frac{a(n-2)+3b}{n+1}$$

....

$$A_n = a + nd = a + n \times \left(\frac{b-a}{n+1}\right) = \frac{a+nb}{n+1}$$

So n A.M.s between two numbers a and b

$$\frac{an+b}{n+1}, \frac{a(n-1)+2b}{n+1}, \frac{a(n-1)+3b}{n+1} \ldots\ldots\ldots \frac{an+b}{n+1}$$

SOLVED EXAMPLES

Example 1

Find the arithmetic mean between 4 and 10.

Solution :

We know that single A.M. between

$$a \text{ and } b = \frac{a+b}{2}$$

So $$\text{A.M. of 4 and 10} = \frac{4+10}{2} = 7$$

Example 2

If n arithmetic mean (A.M.s) are inserted between 20 and 80 such that first mean : last mean = 1 : 3. Find n.

Solution :

Let n A.M.s between 20 and 80 are $A_1, A_2, A_3, \ldots, A_n$.

So 20, $A_1, A_2, A_3, \ldots, A_n$, 80 are in A.P. in which number of terms = $n + 2$

its c.d. $$d = \frac{80-20}{n+1} = \frac{60}{n+1}$$

Now $$A_1 = a + d = 20 + \frac{60}{n+1} = \frac{20n+80}{n+1} \quad \ldots(i)$$

and $$A_n = a + nd = 20 + n \times \frac{60}{n+1} = \frac{80n+20}{n+1} \quad \ldots(ii)$$

By the question, $$\frac{A_1}{A_n} = \frac{1}{3}$$

$$\therefore \quad \frac{20n-80}{80n-20} = \frac{1}{3}$$

or $$\frac{n+4}{4n+1} = \frac{1}{3}$$

$$\Rightarrow \quad 3n + 12 = 4n + 1$$

$$\Rightarrow \quad n = 11$$

Example 3

Insert 4 arithmetic mean between 4 and 19.

Solution :

Let four A.M.s between 4 and 19 are A_1, A_2, A_3, A_4.

So 4, A_1, A_2, A_3, A_4, 19 are in A.P.

Here $a = 4$

$n = 6$

Let its c.d. $= d$

$t_6 = 19$

$4 + (6-1)d = 19$

$\Rightarrow 5d = 15$

$\therefore d = 3$

$\therefore A_1 = (4 + d) = 7$

$A_2 = (4 + 2d) = 10$

$A_3 = (4 + 3d) = 13$

$A_4 = (4 + 4d) = 16$

So four A.M.s are 7, 10, 13, 16. **Ans.**

Example 4

A man saves ₹ 50 in the first month, ₹ 60 in the second month, ₹ 70 in the third month and so on up to 4 years. Find the total amount saved in 4 years. (*JAC*, 2023)

Solution :

Saving in first month = ₹ 50

Saving in second month = ₹ 60

Given $d = 60 - 50 = 10$

$a = 50$

$n = 4 \times 12$

$= 48$

$S_n = \frac{n}{2}[2a + (n^{-1})d]$

$= \frac{48}{2}[2 \times 50 + (48 - 1)\ 10]$

$= 24\ [100 + 470]$

$= 24 \times 570$

= ₹ 13,680

So, Total savings in four years

= 13,680

Example 5

Which term of the A.P. 1, 3, 5, 7, 9 .... is 65 ? [*Mock Test Paper (JAC)*]

(i) 23 (ii) 33 (iii) 43 (iv) 40

Solution :

This $a = 1$, $d = 3 - 1 = 2$ and $T_n = 65$

$\because T_n = a + (n-1)\,d$

$\Rightarrow 65 = 1 + (n-1)\,2$

$\Rightarrow 65 = 1 + 2n - 2$

$\Rightarrow 65 = 2n - 1$

$\Rightarrow 2n = 66$

$\Rightarrow n = 33$

then (ii) objective truth.

Example 6

Find the 10th term of the sequence 10, 5, 0, – 5, – 10, ... [*Mock Test Paper (JAC)*]

(i) – 47 (ii) – 35

(iii) – 37 (iv) – 29

Solution :

This $a = 10$, $d = 5 - 10 = -5$ and $n = 10$

$\because T_n = a + (n-1)\,d$

$= 10 + (10 - 1) \times (-5)$

$= 10 + 9 \times (-5)$

$= 10 - 45 = -35$

Hence the option (ii) is correct.

Example 7

What is the value of common difference of the A.P. 10, 22, 34, 46, ... ? [*Mock Test Paper (JAC)*]

(i) 6 (ii) 12 (iii) 18 (iv) 10

Solution :

General Difference, d = Second digit – First digit

$\therefore d = 22 - 10 = 12$

Hence the option (ii) is correct.

Example 8

Divide 24 into four parts which are in A.P. such that the sum of their squares is 164. (*JAC*, 2017)

Solution :

Assume four parts of 24 is $a - 3d, a - d, a + d$ and $a + 3d$. Hence according to the question,

$a - 3d + a - d + a + d + a + 3d = 24$

$\Rightarrow 4a = 24$

$\Rightarrow a = 6$

again $(a - 3d)^2 + (a - d)^2 + (a + d)^2 + (a + 3d)^2 = 164$

$\Rightarrow a^2 + 9d^2 - 6ad + a^2 + d^2 - 2ad + a^2 + d^2 + 2ad + a^2 + 9d^2 + 6ad = 164$

$\Rightarrow 4a^2 + 20d^2 = 164$

$\Rightarrow 4 \times 6^2 + 20d^2 = 164$

$\Rightarrow 144 + 20d^2 = 164$

$\Rightarrow d^2 = 1$

$\Rightarrow d = \pm 1$

When $a = 6$ and $d = 1$, then

$a - 3d = 3$

$a - d = 5$

$a + d = 7$

$a + 3d = 9$

When $a = 6$ and $d = -1$, then

$a - 3d = 9$

$a - d = 7$

$a + d = 5$

$a + 3d = 3$

Hence, four parts of 24 are 3, 5, 7 and 9.

Example 9

The monthly salary of a person in first year is ₹ 300 per month. He gets an increment of ₹ 20 per year. What were his total earning during 10 years of services ? (*JAC*, 2017)

Solution :

Given, $a = 300 \times 12 =$ ₹ 3,600 per year

$n = 10, d = 20, S_{10} = ?$

$S_n = \frac{n}{2}[2a + (n-1)d]$

$S_{10} = \frac{10}{2}[2 \times 3{,}600 + (10 - 1) \times 20]$

$= 5\,(7{,}200 + 180)$
$= 5 \times 7{,}380$
$= ₹\,36{,}900$ **Ans.**

Exercise 1(C)

1. A man saved ₹ 50 in first month, ₹ 80 in second month, ₹ 110 in the third month and so on. How much he save in 5 years ?
2. A man saves ₹ 32 during the first year, ₹ 36 during the second year and in this way he increases his savings ₹ 4 per year. Find in that time his savings will be ₹ 200 ?
3. A man arrange to pay off a debt of ₹ 4,860 by 10 instalments which are in A.P. If he increases his instalment by ₹ 24 annually, find the value of his first instalment.
4. A person buys National Savings Certificate of value exceeding of the last year purchase by ₹ 100. After 12 years he finds that the total value of certificate purchased by him is ₹ 7,200. Find the value of the certificate purchased by him (i) In the first year and (ii) In the eighth year.
5. Gul repays a loan of ₹ 3,250 by paying ₹ 20 in the first month and then increase the payment of ₹ 15 every month. How long will it take to clear her loan ?
6. 'A' arrange to pay off a debt of ₹ 4,800 in 24 monthly instalments which form an A.P. After 20 instalment, A becomes insolvent and his creditors finds that ₹ 1,200 still remains unpaid. Find the value of first four instalments.
7. Raju agrees to pay off a debt of ₹ 3,600 in 40 annual instalments which form an A.P. When 30 of the instalment are paid, he dies leaving one-third of the debt unpaid. Find the value of first four instalments.
8. The cost of drilling a tubewell is ₹ 2.50 per foot for the first 100 feet and an additional ₹ 0.25 for every subsequent foot. Find the cost of the last foot and the total cost of 220 feet deep tubewell.
9. A man saved ₹ 16,500 in ten years. In each year after the first he saved ₹ 100 more than he did in the preceding year. How much did he saved in the first year ?
10. Shri Ram paid ₹ 200 for a machine. At the end of 7th year it was valued at ₹ 95. Assuming the yearly depreciation is a constant amount, find the annual depreciation.
11. A person was appointed at a salary of ₹ 700 per month. The condition of appointment was that he would receive ₹ 740 per month in the second year, ₹ 780 per month in the third year and so on the salary will increase. Find the total salary he would expect to have received by the end of 10 years. *(JAC, 2026)*

Answers

1. ₹ 56,100 2. $n = 5$ year 3. ₹ 378
4. ₹ 50 and ₹ 750 5. $n = 20$ months
6. ₹ 85, 95, 105, 115 7. ₹ 51
8. $l =$ ₹ 32.50, S = 250 + 2,115 = ₹ 2,365
9. $a =$ ₹ 1200 10. ₹ 15 11. ₹ 8,400

Exercise 1(D)

Arithmetic Mean

1. Find the A.M. between the following numbers :
   (i) 3, 9 (ii) – 3, 5 (iii) 7, 11
2. Insert 8 arithmetic means between 2 and 11.
3. Insert 12 arithmetic means between $-3\frac{1}{2}$ and $-42\frac{1}{2}$.
4. Insert 8 A.M.s between 5 and 32.
5. Between 1 and 31 n A.M.s inserted such that the ratio of the 7th and $(n-1)$th means is 5 : 9, find n.
6. If x, y, z are in A.P. and A_1 is the arithmetic mean of x, y and A_2 is the arithmetic mean of y, z, then prove that the arithmetic mean of A_1 and A_2 is y.

[**Hint :** x, y, z are in A.P.

$\therefore$ $x + z = 2y$ ...(i)

$A_1 = \frac{x+y}{2}$ ...(ii)

and $A_2 = \frac{y+z}{2}$ ....(iii)

Now $A_1 + A_2 = \frac{x+y+y+z}{2}$

$= \frac{x+z+2y}{2} = \frac{2y+2y}{2} = 2y$

$\therefore$ $y = \frac{A_1 + A_2}{2}$

$\therefore$ So arithmetic mean of A_1 and A_2 is y.]

7. If n A.M.s are inserted between two numbers, prove that the sum of the means equidistant from the beginning and the end is constant.

[**Hint :** Let n A.M.s between a and b are $A_1, A_2, A_3, \ldots\ldots, A_n$.
So $a, A_1, A_2, A_3 \ldots\ldots\ldots A_n, b$ are in A.P.
Let its c.d. $= d$
Then rth mean from the beginning $= a + rd$
If we start from the end then c.d. $= -d$
So rth mean from the end $= b + r(-d) = b - rd$
Now rth mean from the beginning + rth mean from the end $= a + rd + b - rd$
$= a + b$]

Answers

1. (i) 6 (ii) 1 (iii) 9, 2. 3, 4, 5, 6, 7, 8, 9, 10
3. $-6\frac{1}{2}, -9\frac{1}{2}, -12\frac{1}{2}, \ldots\ldots, -39\frac{1}{2}$
4. 8, 11, 14, 17, 20, 23, 26, 29. 5. 14

Exercise 1(E)

Objective Type Questions

❑ Multiple Choice Questions

1. Which is the 27th term of the sequence 5, 14, 23, ... ?
   (a) 239 (b) 100 (c) 101 (d) 900
2. In an A.P. if $t_n = 3n + 5$, then the common difference will be :
   (a) 1 (b) 2 (c) 3 (d) 4
3. In an A.P. if 6th and 12th terms are 13 and 25, then its 20th term will be :
   (a) 41 (b) 39 (c) 43 (d) 37
4. Which term will be 27 the sequence 5, 7, 9, 11, ... : *(JAC, 2022)*
   (a) 13th (b) 12th (c) 11th (d) 10th

5. If pth term is q and qth term is p of an A.P., then its rth term is :
(a) $p+q+r$ (b) $p-q-r$ (c) $p+q-r$ (d) $p-q+r$
6. 10th term of the A.P. 2, 5, 8, 11 .... : *(JAC, 2015, 19)*
(a) 47 (b) 33 (c) 37 (d) 28
7. If 9 times of the 9th term of an A.P. is equal to 13 times to 13th term, then the 22nd term of the A.P. is :
(a) 0 (b) 22 (c) 220 (d) 198
8. If the sum of n terms of an A.P. is given by $S_n = 3n + 2n^2$, then the common difference of the A.P. is :
(a) 3 (b) 2 (c) 6 (d) 4
9. If in an A.P. third term is 18 and 7th term is 30, then the 17th term is :
(a) 60 (b) 12 (c) 24 (d) 16
10. In an A.P. first term is 1 and last term is 11. If the sum of n terms is 36, the value of n will be :
(a) 10 (b) 7 (c) 6 (d) 5
11. The 7th and 13th terms of an A.P. are 34 and 64 respectively. The second term of the series is :
(a) 9 (b) 10 (c) 15 (d) 23
12. If 6th and 12th terms of an A.P. are 13 and 25 respectively, then its 20th term is :
(a) 4 (b) 39 (c) 43 (d) 37
13. The 10th term of sequence 10, 5, 0, – 5, – 10, ... is : *(JAC, 2015, 20)*
(a) 30 (b) 35 (c) – 35 (d) 25
14. How many terms are there in A.P. 1, 3, 5, 7, ..., 99 ? *(JAC, 2015)*
(a) 40 (b) 30 (c) 50 (d) 45
15. The 15th term of the A.P. 7, 14, 21, ... is. *(JAC, 2017, 22)*
(a) 98 (b) 91 (c) 105 (d) 84
16. If 70, k, 100 are in AP the value of k is : *(JAC, 2018, 20, 22, 24)*
(a) 80 (b) 85 (c) 90 (d) 95
17. 16th term of A. P. 2 + 5 + 8 + 11 + ... will be :
(a) 21 (b) 20 (c) 47 (d) 45
18. 20th term of A.P. 1, 5, 9, 13, ... is :
(a) 76 (b) 77 (c) 75 (d) 101
19. The sum of A.P. 2, 4, 6, 8.......upto 25th term will be :
(a) 650 (b) 600 (c) 350 (d) 675
20. The sum of A.P. 1, – 3, – 7........ upto 20th term will be :
(a) 740 (b) – 740 (c) – 700 (d) – 760
21. The sum of odd numbers from 1 to 100 is :
(a) 2500 (b) 250 (c) 500 (d) 5,000
22. If a person saves ₹ 10 in first month, ₹ 20 in second month, ₹ 30 in third month and so on. The total saving of the person in 6 years will be :
(a) ₹ 26,000 (b) ₹ 26,280
(c) ₹ 25,560 (d) ₹ 26,300
23. The 12th term of A.P. 7, 10, 13, 16,......... is : *(JAC, 2023)*
(a) 19 (b) 22 (c) 25 (d) 40
24. The value of k in A.P. 3, k, 17 is : *(JAC, 2023)*
(a) 10 (b) 20 (c) 30 (d) 40
25. The nth term of A.P. is : *(JAC, 2024)*
(a) $T_2 - T_1$ (b) $a+(n-1)d$
(c) ar^{n-1} (d) $\dfrac{1}{a+(n-1)d}$
26. 10th term of A.P. 2, 5, 8, ... is : *(JAC, 2025)*
(a) 29 (b) 32 (c) 35 (d) 26
27. How many terms are there in the A.P. 7, 13, 19, ..., 205 ? *(JAC, 2026)*
(a) 30 (b) 35 (c) 34 (d) 31

Answers

1. (a)	2. (c)	3. (a)	4. (d)	5. (c)	6. (d)	7. (a)
8. (a)	9. (a)	10. (c)	11. (a)	12. (a)	13. (c)	14. (c)
15. (c)	16. (b)	17. (c)	18. (b)	19. (a)	20. (b)	21. (a)
22. (b)	23. (d)	24. (a)	25. (b)	26. (a)	27. (c)	

❑ Fill in the blanks

1. If the sum of n terms of an A.P. is $5n^2 + 2n$, then the second term = ...
2. If the sum of three consecutive terms of an A.P. is 24 and sum of their squares is 200, then the numbers are ....
3. The sum of four consecutive numbers of an A.P. is 40 and product of the two extremes is 91, then the numbers are.................
4. If $\dfrac{1}{b+c}, \dfrac{1}{c+a}, \dfrac{1}{a+b}$ are in A.P., then a^2, b^2, c^2, are in ....
5. $\dfrac{a^{n+1}+b^{n+1}}{a^n+b^n}$ will be arithmetic mean of a and b if n = ...
6. The sum of the first n terms of the A.P. a, $a+d$, $a+2d$, ... is given by $S_n = \dfrac{n}{2}[......+(n-1)d]$.
7. The sum of an infinite A.P. is 50. If the first term is 10, then the common ratio is ....
8. Which term of the A.P. 1, $\sqrt{3}$, 3, ... will be 81.

Answers

1. 17	2. 6, 8, 10	3. 7, 9, 11, 13	4. A.P.
5. 0	6. 2a	7. 4/5	8. 9th

❑ Write True or False

1. In usual notation for an A.P. $S_n = \dfrac{n}{a}(a+1)$.
2. The number of terms in A.P. 4, 7, 10, ..., 148 is $n = 49$.

Answers

1. True 2. True

❖❖

2

GEOMETRIC PROGRESSION (G.P.)

LEARNING OBJECTIVES

After studying this chapter, you will be able to know :

- **2.1 Definition**
- **2.2 To find the *n*th term of a G.P., where *n*th is any Positive Integer**
- **2.3 Properties of G.P.**
- **2.4 To find the sum of *n* terms of a G.P.**
- **2.5 Geometric Mean, G.M.**
- **2.6 Mixed Problems on A.M. and G.M.**
- **2.7 Objective Questions on G.P.**

SOLVED EXAMPLES AND PRACTICAL PROBLEMS : AT A GLANCE

No. of Examples		*No. of Problems*
	To Find the *n*th term of a G.P. where *n* is any Positive Integer	
1 to 4	Type I	Exercise 2(A) 1 to 14
5 to 10	Type II	15 to 23
1 to 12	Find the sum of *n* terms of G.P.	Exercise 2(B) 1 to 20
1 to 2	Geometric Mean	Exercise 2(C) 1 to 4
3 to 7	Mixed Problems on A.M. and G.M.	5 to 7
1 to 5	Objective Questions on G.P.	Exercise 2(D) 22 + 1 + 4
34	**Total**	**50 + 27**

(2.1) DEFINITION

The sequence or series in which the ratio of two consecutive terms are same, is called G. P.

In this the ratio of any term and the preceding term is constant throughout, this constant is known as the common ratio (C.R or r) of the G.P.

As, 1, 4, 16, 64, ...

Here $\qquad \dfrac{t_2}{t_1} = \dfrac{4}{1} = 4$

$$\frac{t_3}{t_2} = \frac{16}{4} = 4$$

$$\frac{t_4}{t_3} = \frac{64}{16} = 4$$

$$\frac{t_2}{t_1} = \frac{t_3}{t_2} = \frac{t_4}{t_3}$$

So the sequence is in G.P.

and $\quad$ its common ratio = 4

(2.2) TO FIND THE *n*th TERM OF A G. P. WHERE *n*th IS ANY POSITIVE INTEGER

For the G. P. Let first term = a

and Common ratio = r

then

$$t_1 = a = ar^0 = ar^{1-1}$$
$$t_2 = ar = ar^{2-1}$$
$$t_3 = ar^2 = ar^{3-1}$$
$$t_4 = ar^3 = ar^{4-1}$$

....

....

$$t_n = ar^{n-1}$$

$\therefore$ nth term of G.P. = $t_n = ar^{n-1}$

Formula 1

(2.3) PROPERTIES OF GEOMETRIC PROGRESSION

(i) If each term of a G.P. be multiplied by a non zero number, then the sequence obtained is also a G.P.

Example : a, ar, ar^2, ar^3 are in G.P.

Let b is any non zero number.

The sequence obtained by multiplying each term by 'b' is

ab, abr, abr^2, abr^3,..............

Here this new sequence is also in G.P. whose common ratio is r and first term is ab.

(ii) If each term of a G.P. be divided by a non zero number, then the sequence obtained is also a G.P.

Example : a, ar, ar^2, ar^3, ... are in G.P.

Let 'b' is any non zero number the sequence obtained by dividing each term by 'b' is $\frac{a}{b}, \frac{ar}{b}, \frac{ar^2}{b}, \frac{ar^3}{b}$, G.P...

Here this new sequence is also in G.P. whoswe common ratio = r and first term = a/b.

(iii) The reciprocals of the term of a G.P. are also in G.P.

Example : a, ar, ar^2, ar^3, ... are in G.P.

The sequence obtained by reciprocals of the corresponding terms of the given G.P. are :

$\frac{1}{a}, \frac{1}{ar}, \frac{1}{ar^2}, \frac{1}{ar^3}$, ... G. P.

Clearly this sequence is a G.P. whose common ratio $= \frac{1}{r}$ and first term $= \frac{1}{a}$.

SOLVED EXAMPLES

✎ Type I

Example 1

How many terms are there in G. P. 0.03, 0.06, 0.12, ..., 3.84.

Solution :

Let number of terms in G.P. = n

Now $a = 0.03,\ r = 2,\ t_n = 3.84,\ n = ?$

$$t_n = ar^{n-1} = 3.84$$
$$\Rightarrow (0.03)2^{n-1} = 3.84$$
$$\Rightarrow 2^{n-1} = \frac{3.84}{0.03}$$
$$\Rightarrow 2^{n-1} = 128 = 2^7$$
$$\Rightarrow n-1 = 7$$
$$\therefore n = 8$$

Ans.

Example 2(A)

Find the 8th term of the progression 1, $\sqrt{3}$, 3 ....

Solution :

The given progression $1, \sqrt{3}, 3$,............ is in G.P.

Its first term (a) = 1 and c.r. = $\sqrt{3}$

$\because$ nth term of G.P. = ar^{n-1}

$\therefore$ 8th term of given G.P. (t_8) = $1 \times (\sqrt{3})^{8-1}$

$= 1 \times (\sqrt{3})^7 = 27\sqrt{3}$

Ans.

Example 2(B)

Find the 5th term of the following series

3 + 6 + 12 + ...

Solution :

Given $a = 3$, $r = \frac{T_2}{T_1} = \frac{6}{3} = 2$, $n = 5$

$$\text{5th Term} = ar^{5-1}$$
$$= 3 \times 2^{5-1}$$
$$= 3 \times 2^4$$
$$= 3 \times 16$$
$$= 48$$

Ans.

Example 2(C)

Which term of the G.P. 2, 8, 32, ... is 32768 ?

Solution :

Given $a = 2$

$$r = \frac{8}{2} = 4$$
$$T_n = ar^{n-1}$$
$$32768 = 2 \times 4^{n-1}$$
$$\frac{32768}{2} = 4^{n-1}$$
$$16384 = 4^{n-1}$$
$$(4)^7 = 4^{n-1}$$
$$7 = n-1$$
$$n = 7+1$$
$$n = 8^{th} \text{ term}$$

Ans.

Example 3

Find the G.P. where 7th term is 320 and 10th term is 2,560.

Solution :

Let first term = a, Common ratio = r,

$$7\text{th Term} = ar^{7-1} = ar^6 = 320 \quad ...(1)$$
$$10\text{th Term} = ar^{10-1} = ar^9 = 2560 \quad ...(ii)$$

$$\frac{ar^9}{ar^6} = \frac{2,560}{320} \text{ [or Dividing]}$$
$$r^3 = 8$$
$$r^3 = 2^3$$
$$\therefore \quad r = 2$$

After putting the value of r in Equ. (i)

$$ar^6 = 320$$
$$a \times 2^6 = 320$$
$$a \times 64 = 320$$
$$a = \frac{320}{64} = 5$$

Hence G.P is 5, 10, 20, 40, 80......... **Ans.**

Example 4

The population of a city in Jan. 2000 was 20,000. It increased at the rate of 2% per annum. Find the population of the city in Jan. 2010.

Solution :

Population in Jan. 2000 = 20,000

Rate of increasing = 2% per annum

$$\text{So Population in Jan. 2001} = 20,000\left(1+\frac{2}{100}\right)$$
$$= 20,000\,(1.02)$$

Similarly Population in Jan. 2002

$$= 20,000\,(1.02)^2$$

Here $a = 20,000, r = 1.02$

then Population in Jan. 2010

$$t_{11} = ar^{11-1} = ar^{10}$$
$$= 20,000\,(1.02)^{10} \text{ **Ans.**}$$

✎ Type II

Working Rules

1. If three numbers are in G.P. and their product is given, then take the three numbers as $\frac{a}{r}, a, ar$. If the product of the three numbers is not given, then take the numbers as a, ar, ar^2.

2. If four numbers are in G.P. and their product is given, then take the four numbers as $\frac{a}{r^3}, \frac{a}{r}$ ar, ar^3. If the product of the four numbers is not given, then take the four numbers as a, ar^2, ar^3, ar^4.

3. If the five numbers are in G.P. and their product is given, then take the five numbers as $\frac{a}{r^2}, \frac{a}{r}, a, ar, ar^2$. If the product of five numbers is not given, then take the numbers as $a, ar^2, ar^3, ar^4, ar^5$.

Example 5

Mr. Amrit borrows a certain amount without interest from Angel and pays it in 10 instalments, each instalment being twice the preceding one. If the first instalment is ₹ 60, find the last instalment.

Solution :

Mr. Amrit pays ₹ 60 in first instalment.

Hence $a = 60$ (First instalment)

Second instalment = ₹ 120

Third instalment = ₹ 180

$$\text{So} \quad r = \frac{120}{60} = 2$$
$$\because \quad T_n = ar^{n-1}$$
$$\therefore \quad T_{10} = 60 \times 2^{10-1}$$
$$= 60 \times 2^9$$
$$= 60 \times 512$$
$$= ₹\,30,720$$ **Ans.**

Example 6

If the product of three numbers in G.P. be 216 and their sum is 19, Then find the numbers.

Solution :

Let three numbers in G.P. are $\frac{a}{r}$, a and ar.

By the question, $\frac{a}{r}.a.ar = 216$

or $a^3 = 6^3$

$\Rightarrow$ $a = 6$

Again $\frac{a}{r} + a + ar = 19$

or $\frac{6}{r} + 6 + 6r = 19$

or $6 + 6r + 6r^2 = 19r$

or $6r^2 + 6r + 6 - 19r = 0$

or $6r^2 - 13r + 6 = 0$

or $6r^2 - 9r - 4r + 6 = 0$

or $3r(2r-3) - 2(2r-3) = 0$

or $(2r-3)(3r-2) = 0$

$$r = \frac{3}{2}, \frac{2}{3}$$

When $r = \frac{3}{2}$, then the numbers are 4, 6, 9.

and when $r = \frac{2}{3}$, then the numbers are 9, 6, 4.

So the required numbers = 4, 6, 9 **Ans.**

Example 7

The sum of three numbers in G. P. is 21 and the sum of their squares is 189, find the numbers.

Solution :

Let the three numbers in G.P. are a, ar and ar^2.

By the question, $a + ar + ar^2 = 21$

or $a(1 + r + r^2) = 21$ ....(i)

and $a^2 + a^2r^2 + a^2r^4 = 189$

or $a^2(1 + r^2 + r^4) = 189$ ....(ii)

Dividing (ii) by the square of eq. (i),

$$\frac{a^2(1 + r^2 + r^4)}{a^2(1 + r + r^2)^2} = \frac{189}{441} = \frac{3}{7}$$

or $\frac{1 + 2r^2 + r^4 - r^2}{(1 + r + r^2)^2} = \frac{3}{7}$

or $\frac{(1 + r^2)^2 - r^2}{(1 + r + r^2)^2} = \frac{3}{7}$

or $\frac{(1 + r^2 + r)(1 + r^2 - r)}{(1 + r + r^2)^2} = \frac{3}{7}$

or $\frac{1 + r^2 - r}{1 + r + r^2} = \frac{3}{7}$

or $7 + 7r^2 - 7r = 3 + 3r + 3r^2$

or $4r^2 - 10r + 4 = 0$

or $2r^2 - 5r + 2 = 0$

or $2r^2 - 4r - r + 2 = 0$

or $2r(r - 2) - 1(r - 2) = 0$

or $(r - 2)(2r - 1) = 0$

$\therefore$ $r = 2, \frac{1}{2}$

When $r = 2$, then from eq. (i),

$$a = \frac{21}{1 + 2 + 2^2} = \frac{21}{7} = 3$$

When $r = \frac{1}{2}$, then

$$a = \frac{21}{1 + \frac{1}{2} + \left(\frac{1}{2}\right)^2} = \frac{21}{1 + \frac{1}{2} + \frac{1}{4}} = \frac{21}{7} \times 4 = 12$$

When $a = 3$ and $r = 2$ then the numbers are 3, 6, 12.

When $a = 12$, $r = \frac{1}{2}$, then the numbers are 12, 6, 3.

So the required numbers are 3, 6, 12. **Ans.**

Example 8

Find three numbers in G. P. whose sum is 52 and the sum of whose product in pair is 624.

Solution :

Let the required number be a, ar, ar^2.

Then $(a + ar + ar^2) = 52$

$\Rightarrow$ $a(1 + r + r^2) = 52$ ....(i)

and $a.ar + a.ar^2 + a.ar^3 = 624$

or $a^2r(1 + r + r^2) = 624$ ....(ii)

On dividing (ii), by (i), we get

$ar = 12 \Rightarrow a = \frac{12}{r}$

Putting $a = \frac{12}{r}$ in (i), we get

$\frac{12}{r}(1 + r + r^2) = 52$

$\Rightarrow$ $3(1 + r + r^2) = 13r$

$\Rightarrow$ $3r^2 - 10r + 3 = 0$

$\Rightarrow$ $(3r - 1)(r - 3) = 0$

$\Rightarrow$ $r = \frac{1}{3}, r = 3$

$\therefore$ $a = 36$

or $a = 4$

Hence the required numbers are (36, 12, 4) or (4, 12, 36). **Ans.**

Example 9

Find the 4th term from end of the G. P. 3, 6, 12, 24 ....., 3, 072.

Solution :

If we start from end, then common ratio = 1/2

$\therefore$ 4th term from end$(T_4) = T_n\left[\frac{1}{2}\right]^{4-1}$

$= 3{,}072\left[\frac{1}{2}\right]^3$

$= \frac{3{,}027 \times 1}{8} = 384$ **Ans.**

Example 10

Find the 10th term of the progression 1, $\sqrt{3}$, 3.

Solution :

1, $\sqrt{3}$, 3 is in G. P.

So $a = 1, r = \sqrt{3}$

$T_{10} = ar^{n-1}$

$= 1 \times (\sqrt{3})^{10-1} = 1 \times (\sqrt{3})^9$

$= 81\sqrt{3}$ **Ans.**

Exercise 2(A)

✎ Type I

1. Which term of G. P. 1, $\sqrt{3}$, 3, ... will be 81 ?
2. Write down the 9th term of G. P. $\sqrt{3}, \frac{1}{\sqrt{3}}, \frac{1}{3\sqrt{3}}$, ...
3. How many terms are there in the G. P. 5, 20, 80, ..., 5,120 ?
4. Which term of G. P. 1, $\frac{1}{2}, \frac{1}{4}, \frac{1}{8}$, ... will be $\frac{1}{512}$?

5. Find the seventh term of the G. P. $2^2, 2^3, 2^4$, ...
6. If the fifth term of a G. P. is 81 and second term is 24, find the G. P. (*JAC*, 2020)
7. The first terms of a G. P. is 5 and the common ratio is – 2. What is the 6th term ?
8. If 5th and 8th terms of a G. P. be 48 and 384 respectively. Find the G. P.
9. Fourth term of a G. P. is 40 and the tenth term is 2,560. Find the seventh term.
10. The 4th and 8th terms of a G. P. are 24 and 384 respectively, find the Ist term and the common ratio.
11. The second term of a G. P. is 27 and 7th term is 1/9. Find the first term and the common ratio. (*JAC*, 2026)
12. The 7th term of a G. P. is 8 times of the 4th term then find the series if its 5th term is 48.
13. Find the value of k if 3, k, 48 are in G. P.
14. Quantities $x, 8, y$ $(x \neq y)$ are in G. P. and $x, y, -8$ in A. P. Find the value of x and y. (*JAC*, 2024)

✎ Type II

15. Three numbers whose sum is 15 are in A. P. If 1, 4, 19 be added to them respectively the resulting numbers are in G. P. Find the numbers.
16. The product of three terms in G. P. is 216 and their sum is 21. Find the terms.
17. If the continued product of three numbers in G. P. is 216 and the sum of their products in pair is 156. Find the numbers.
18. If the sum of three numbers in G.P. is 28 and their product is 512, find the G.P.
19. If for a G. P. $S_2 = 8$ and $S_4 = 80$, find its first term and the common ratio.
20. The ratio of the fourth and 12th term of a G. P. with positive common ratio is 1 : 256. If the difference of two terms be 61.2, find the sum of 8 terms of the series.
21. The sum of three consecutive numbers in G. P. is 35 and their product is 1,000. Find the numbers. (*JAC*, 2024)
22. For what value of x the numbers $x-2, x, x+3$ are in G. P.
23. If the 4th term of a G. P. be 8 and 9th term be 256, find the nth term. Also determine which term of the progression is 64.

Answers

1. 9th term	2. $\frac{\sqrt{3}}{3^8}$	3. 6	4. 10th item
5. 256	6. 16, 24, 36, ...		7. – 160
8. 3, 6, 12, 24	9. 320	10. $a = 3, r = 2$	
11. $a = 81, r = 1/3$		12. 3, 6, 12, ...	
13. ± 12		14. 16 and 4	
15. 2, 5, 8 or 26, 5, – 16		16. 3, 6, 12 or 12, 6, 3	
17. 2, 6, 18		18. 4, 8, 16 or 16, 8, 4	
19. $a = 2, r = 3$		20. $r = 2, a = 0.03, S_8 = 7.65$	
21. 5, 10, 20		22. 6	
23. $r = 2, a = 1, n = 7$			

(2.4) TO FIND THE SUM OF n TERMS OF A G. P.

For the G.P. let

first term $= a$

and c.r. $= r$

and S_n denotes the sum of first n terms of G.P.

$$S_n = a + ar + ar^2 + ar^3 + \ldots\ldots + ar^{n-2} + ar^{n-1} \quad \ldots(i)$$

Now multiplying both sides by r,

$$rS_n = ar + ar^2 + ar^3 + \ldots\ldots + ar^{n-1} + ar^n \quad \ldots(ii)$$

Subtracting eq. (ii) from (i),

$$S_n - rS_n = a - ar^n$$

or $$S_n(1-r) = a(1-r^n)$$

$$S_n = \frac{a(1-r^n)}{1-r}, \text{ when } r < 1$$

Formula 1

Multiplying the numerator and denominator by (–1),

$$S_n = \frac{a(1-r^n)}{1-r}, \text{ when } r > 1$$

Formula 3

To find the sum of infinite terms of a G. P. when the value of the common ratio is less than one

For the G.P. let

first term $= a$ and c.r. $= r$

(where $|r| < 1$)

Let S_n denotes the sum of first n terms,

then $$S_n = a + ar + ar^2 + ar^3 + \ldots\ldots\ldots + ar^{n-2} + ar^{n-1} \quad \ldots(i)$$

$\therefore$ $$rS_n = ar + ar^2 + ar^3 + \ldots\ldots\ldots + ar^{n-1} + ar^n \quad \ldots(ii)$$

Subtracting (ii) from (i),

$$S_n(1-r) = a - ar^n$$

or $$S_n = \frac{a - ar^n}{1-r}$$

or $$S_n = \frac{a}{1-r} - \frac{ar^n}{1-r} \quad \ldots(iii)$$

$\because$ $|r| < 1$ *i.e.*, $-1 < r < 1$.

$\therefore$ $n \to \infty$

$r^n \to 0$

$\therefore$ $$\frac{ar^n}{1-r} \to 0$$

So from (iii), $$S_n = \frac{a}{1-r}$$

SOLVED EXAMPLES

Example 1

Find the sum of 8 terms of the following G. P. :

$$\frac{1}{2} + 1 + 2 + \ldots\ldots\ldots$$

Solution :

The given series is $\frac{1}{2} + 1 + 2 + \ldots\ldots\ldots$

Here first term $(a) = \frac{1}{2}$

and c.r. $(r) = 2$

$n = 8$

$$S_8 = \frac{a(r^8 - 1)}{r - 1} = \frac{\frac{1}{2}(2^8 - 1)}{2 - 1}$$

$$= \frac{1}{2}(256 - 1)$$

$$= \frac{255}{2}$$

$$= 127\frac{1}{2}$$ **Ans.**

Example 2

Find the sum of the following series :

$2 + 6 + 18 + ... + 4374.$

Solution :

The given series is in G.P.

Here First term $(a) = 2$

c.r. $(r) = 3\ (r > 1)$

Let $t_n = 4{,}374$

$\because$ $t_n = ar^{n-1}$

$4{,}374 = 2.(3)^{n-1}$

or $2{,}187 = 3^{n-1}$

or $3^7 = 3^{n-1}$

or $n - 1 = 7$

or $n = 8$

$\therefore$ $S_n = \frac{a(r^n - 1)}{r - 1}$

$$= \frac{2(3^8 - 1)}{3 - 1} = \frac{2(3^8 - 1)}{2}$$

$= 3^8 - 1 = 6{,}561 - 1$

$= 6{,}560.$ **Ans.**

Example 3

How many terms of the series $2 + 6 + 18 + ...$must be taken to make the sum equal to 728.

Solution :

$a = 2, r = 3, Sn = 728, n = ?$

$$S_n = \frac{a(r^n - 1)}{r - 1}, r > 1$$

$$728 = \frac{2(3^n - 1)}{3 - 1}$$

$$728 = \frac{2(3^n - 1)}{2}$$

$3^n = 729$

$3^n = 3^6$

$n = 6$ **Ans.**

Example 4

Find the least value of n for which

$1 + 3 + 3^2 + ... + 3^{n-1} > 1000.$

Solution :

Given that

$1 + 3 + 3^2 + ... + 3^{n-1} > 1000$

or $1\left(\frac{3^n - 1}{3 - 1}\right) > 1000 \left[\because S_n = \frac{a(r^n - 1)}{(r - 1)}\right]$

or $\frac{3^n - 1}{2} > 1000$

or $3^n - 1 > 2000$

or $3^n > 2001$

Now $3^1 = 3, 3^2 = 9, 3^3 = 27, 3^4 = 81, 3^5 = 243, 3^6 = 729, 3^7 = 2187$

Clearly $2187 > 2001$

$\therefore$ So the least value of n for which

$3^n > 2000 = 7$ **Ans.**

Example 5

Find $1 + \frac{1}{2} + \frac{1}{4} + \frac{1}{8} + ...$ to ∞. *(JAC, 2022)*

Solution :

Here first term, $a = 1$

c.r., $r = \frac{1}{2} (r < 1)$

Now $S_\infty = \frac{a}{1 - r} = \frac{1}{1 - \frac{1}{2}} = 2$ **Ans.**

Example 6

Find $1 + \frac{x}{1 + x} + \frac{x^2}{(1 + x)^2} + ...\ \infty$, if $x > 0$.

Solution :

Here $a = 1, r = \frac{x}{1 + x}, r = \frac{x}{1 + x} < 1 \quad (\because x > 0)$

Now $S_\infty = \frac{a}{1 - r} = \frac{1}{1 - \frac{x}{1 + x}} = 1 + x$ **Ans.**

Example 7

Express 0.4.23 as a rational number (or quotient of two integers).

Solution :

$0.4.23 = 0.423232323$ .... ∞

$= 0.4 + 0.023 + 0.00023 + ...\infty$

$$= \frac{4}{10} + \frac{23}{1000} + \frac{23}{100000} + ...\ \infty$$

$$= \frac{4}{10} + \frac{23}{1000}\left[1 + \frac{1}{100} + \frac{1}{10000} + ...\ \infty\right]$$

$$= \frac{4}{10} + \frac{23}{1000}\left(\frac{1}{1 - \frac{1}{100}}\right)\left[\because S_\infty = \frac{a}{1 - r}\right]$$

$$= \frac{4}{10} + \frac{23}{1000} \times \frac{100}{99}$$

$$= \frac{4}{10} + \frac{23}{990} = \frac{396 + 23}{990} = \frac{419}{990}$$ **Ans.**

Example 8

Fifth term of G.P. is 81 where as its second term is 24. Find the series and its sum of first four terms.

Solution :

Let first term = a

Common Ratio = r

Given $T_5 = 81$

$$ar^{5-1} = 81$$

$$ar^4 = 81 \quad ...(i)$$

$$T_2 = 24$$

$$ar^{2-1} = 24$$

$$ar = 24 \quad ...(ii)$$

From Equ. (i) & (ii)

$$\frac{ar^4}{ar} = \frac{81}{24} = \frac{27}{8}$$

$$r^3 = \left[\frac{3}{2}\right]^3$$

and from Equ. (ii)

$$ar = 24$$

$$a \times \frac{3}{2} = 24$$

$$a = 24 \times \frac{3}{2} = 16$$

Series = 16, 24, 36 ....

Again

$$S_4 = \frac{a(r^4 - 1)}{r - 1}$$

$$S_4 = \frac{16\left\{\left(\frac{3}{2}\right)^4 - 1\right\}}{\frac{3}{2} - 1}$$

$$S_4 = \frac{16\left[\frac{81}{16} - 1\right]}{\frac{3-2}{2}}$$

$$S_4 = \frac{16 \times 2}{1}\left[\frac{81 - 16}{16}\right]$$

$$S_4 = 2 \times 65$$

$$S_4 = 130$$ **Ans.**

Example 9

Find the sum to n terms of the following series : (*JAC*, 2019)

8 + 88 + 888 + ...

Solution :

$$S_n = 8 + 88 + 888 + \text{.........} \ n \text{ term}$$

$$= 8\,[1 + 11 + 111 + \text{.........} \ n \text{ term}]$$

$$= \frac{8}{9}\,[9 + 99 + 999 + \text{.........} \ n \text{ term}]$$

$$= \frac{8}{9}\,[(10-1) + (100-1) + (1000-1) + \text{....} \ n \text{ term}]$$

$$= \frac{8}{9}\,[(10 + 100 + 1000 + \text{.......} \ n \text{ term}) - (1 + 1 + 1 + \text{.........} \ n \text{ term})]$$

$$= \frac{8}{9}\left[10.\left(\frac{1 - 10^n}{1 - 10}\right) - n\right] = \frac{8}{9}\left[10.\left(\frac{10^n - 1}{10 - 1}\right) - n\right]$$

$$= \frac{8}{81}(10^{n+1} - 10 - 9n)$$ **Ans.**

Example 10

Sum up the series : (*JAC*, 2016)

$$\frac{3}{4} - \frac{5}{4^2} + \frac{3}{4^3} - \frac{5}{4^4} + \frac{3}{4^5} - \frac{5}{4^6} + \text{.........} \infty$$

Solution :

$$\frac{3}{4} - \frac{5}{4^2} + \frac{3}{4^3} - \frac{5}{4^4} + \frac{3}{4^5} - \frac{5}{4^6} + \text{.........} \infty$$

$$= 3\left[\frac{1}{4} + \frac{1}{4^3} + \frac{1}{4^5} + \text{....} \infty\right] - 5\left[\frac{1}{4^2} + \frac{1}{4^4} + \frac{1}{4^6} + \text{....} \infty\right]$$

$$= 3 \times \frac{\frac{1}{4}}{1 - \frac{1}{4^2}} - 5 \times \frac{\frac{1}{4^2}}{1 - \frac{1}{4^2}} \qquad \left[\because S_\infty = \frac{a}{1 - r}\right]$$

$$= 3 \times \frac{\frac{1}{4}}{\frac{15}{16}} - 5\,\frac{\frac{1}{16}}{\frac{15}{16}}$$

$$= 3\left[\frac{4}{15}\right] - 5\left[\frac{1}{15}\right]$$

$$= \frac{4}{5} - \frac{1}{3}$$

$$= \frac{12 - 5}{15} = \frac{7}{15}$$ **Ans.**

Example 11

The sum of infinite term of a G. P. is 32 and the sum of first two terms is 24. Find the progression.

Solution :

$$S_\infty = \frac{a}{1 - r}$$

Given $$\frac{a}{1 - r} = 32$$

and $$a + ar = 24$$

or $$a\,(1 + r) = 24$$

$$\therefore \quad (1 + r)(1 - r) = \frac{24}{32} = \frac{3}{4}$$

$$1 - r^2 = \frac{3}{4}$$

$$\Rightarrow \qquad r^2 = \frac{1}{4}$$

$$\therefore \qquad r = \frac{1}{2}$$

$$a = 16$$

$\therefore$ G.P. = 16, 4, 4,.......... **Ans.**

Example 12

A boy agrees to work at the rate of the one-rupee the first day, two rupess the second day, four rupees the third day, eight rupees the forth day and so on. How much would he get at the end of 120 days ?

Solution :

Total amount he got at the end of 120 days

$$= 1 + 2 + 4 + 8 + \text{.........} \; 120 \text{ days}$$

$$= \frac{1\,(1 - 2^{120})}{1 - 2} = \frac{2^{120} - 1}{2 - 1}$$

$$= ₹(2^{120} - 1)$$

Exercise 2(B)

1. Find the sum of the series $1 + \frac{1}{3} + \frac{1}{9} + \frac{1}{27} + \ldots$to n terms.
2. Find the sum of the series 1 + 2 + 4 + 8 + ... upto 12 terms.
3. Find the sum of the series $1 - \frac{1}{2} + \frac{1}{4} - \frac{1}{8} + \ldots$ to n terms.
4. Find the sum of the series 4 + 44 + 444 + ... to n terms.
5. Find the sum of the series 0.5 + 0.55 + 0.555 + ... to n terms.
6. Find the sum of 8 terms of the G. P. 3, 6, 12, 24, ...
7. How many terms of the series $1 + 2 + 2^2 + \ldots$ must be taken to make 511.
8. If a be the first term, b the nth term and p the product of n terms of G. P., show that $p^2 = (ab)^n$.
9. The sum of n terms of a series is $a.2^n - b$, find its nth term. Are the terms of this series in G. P. ?
10. Find the nth term and the sum to n terms of the series : $1 + (1 + 2) + (1 + 2 + 2^2) + \ldots$
11. Find the sum of the series :
$$1 + 3x + 9x^2 + 27x^3 + \ldots \text{ to } \infty.$$
12. Find the sum of the series :
$$\frac{1}{5} + \frac{1}{7} + \frac{1}{5^2} + \frac{1}{7^2} + \ldots \text{ to } \infty$$
13. Find the sum of the geometric sequence $1 + \frac{1}{2} + \frac{1}{4} + \frac{1}{8} +$ ...... to 12th terms.
14. First term and the sum of an infinite G. P. are 2 and 3 respectively. Find the common ratio and sum upto n terms.
15. Find the sum upto infinite :
$$\frac{2}{5} + \frac{3}{5^2} + \frac{2}{5^3} + \frac{3}{5^4} + \frac{2}{5^5} + \frac{3}{5^6} + \ldots$$
16. Express 0.5.4 as a rational number.
17. The sum of an infinite G. P. whose common ratio is numerically less than 1 is 32 and sum of the first two is 24, the find the G.P.
18. The sum of infinite number of terms of a decreasing G. P. is 4 and sum of the squares of its terms to infintiy is $\frac{16}{3}$, find the G. P.
19. The first term of an infinite Geometric progression is 1 and the sum of the terms is 13, find the common ratio.
20. Find the sum to n terms : 5 + 55 + 555 + ...

Answers

1. $\left[\frac{3}{2}\left(1 - \frac{1}{3^n}\right)\right]$ 2. 4,095 3. $\frac{2}{3}\,[1 - (-1)^n/2^n]$

4. $\left[\frac{4}{81}(10^{n+1} - 9n - 10)\right]$ 5. $\left[\frac{5}{9}\left(n - \frac{10^n - 1}{9 \times 10^n}\right)\right]$

6. 765, 7. 9, 9. a^{2n-1}; yes

10. $2^n - 1$; $2^{n+1} - 2 - n$ 11. $\left[\frac{1}{1 - 3x}\right]$ 12. $\left[\frac{5}{12}\right]$

13. $\left[\frac{4{,}095}{2{,}048}\right]$ 14. $\left[\frac{1}{3}\left[\frac{1}{2}\left(3 - \frac{1}{3^{n-1}}\right)\right]\right]$

15. $\left[S_\infty = \frac{13}{24}\right]$ 16. $\left[\frac{6}{11}\right]$

17. 16, 8, 4, 2, ... or 48, – 24, 12, – 6 18. $\left[2, 1, \frac{1}{2}, \frac{1}{4} \ldots\right]$

19. $\left[\frac{12}{13}\right]$ 20. $\left[\frac{5}{81}(10^{n+1} - 9n - 10)\right]$

(2.5) GEOMETRIC MEAN, G. M.

When three numbers a, b, c are in G. P., then b is called G. M. of a and c.

Geometric Mean is generally denoted by G.

To find One Geometric Mean between any Two Numbers

Let G is the Geometric Mean of two numbers a and b. So a, G, b are in G.P.

$$\therefore \qquad \frac{G}{a} = \frac{b}{G}$$

$$\Rightarrow \qquad G^2 = a.\,b$$

$$\therefore \qquad G = \sqrt{ab}$$

So G.M. of a and b $= \sqrt{ab}$

To Insert n Geometric Means between Two Given Quantities

Let $G_1, G_2, G_3, \ldots, G_n$, n are geometric means between two given quantities a and b, then $a, G_1, G_2, G_3, \ldots, G_n, b$ are in G.P.

$$b = (n+2)\text{th term of the G.P.}$$
$$= ar^{n+2-1} = ar^{n+1}$$
$$\therefore \quad r^{n+1} = \frac{b}{a}$$
$$\Rightarrow \quad r = \left(\frac{b}{a}\right)^{\frac{1}{n+1}}$$

So
$$G_1 = ar = a\left(\frac{b}{a}\right)^{\frac{1}{n+1}}$$
$$G_2 = ar^2 = a\left(\frac{b}{a}\right)^{\frac{2}{n+1}}$$
$$G_3 = ar^3 = a\left(\frac{b}{a}\right)^{\frac{3}{n+1}}$$
....
$$G_n = ar^n = \left(\frac{b}{a}\right)^{\frac{n}{n+1}}$$

So the required G.M.s are $a\left(\frac{b}{a}\right)^{\frac{1}{n+1}}$, $a\left(\frac{b}{a}\right)^{\frac{2}{n+1}}$, $a\left(\frac{b}{a}\right)^{\frac{3}{n+1}}$, ..., $a\left(\frac{b}{a}\right)^{\frac{n}{n+1}}$.

SOLVED EXAMPLES

Example 1

Insert 4 G. M. s between 5 and 160.

Solution :

Let for G.M.s between 5 and 160 are G_1, G_2, G_3, G_4, then 5 G_1, G_2, G_3, G_4, 160 are in G. P.

$$t_6 = 160$$
$$5.r^5 = 160$$
$$r^5 = 32 = 2^5$$
$$r = 2 \text{ (where } c.r. = r)$$
$$\therefore \quad G_1 = 5r = 5 \times 2 = 10$$
$$G_2 = 5r^2 = 5 \times 4 = 20$$
$$G_3 = 5r^3 = 5 \times 8 = 40$$
and
$$G_4 = 5r^4 = 5 \times 16 = 80$$

Thus 4 G.M.s between 5 and 160 are 10, 20, 40, 80.

Example 2

Find the value of n, when $\dfrac{a^{n+1} + b^{n+1}}{a^n + b^n}$ is the G. M. of any two numbers a and b.

Solution :

$$\text{G. M. of } a \text{ and } b = \sqrt{ab} = a^{1/2}b^{1/2}$$

By the question,

$$\text{G. M. of } a \text{ and } b = \frac{a^{n+1} + b^{n+1}}{a^n + b^n}$$
$$\therefore \quad \frac{a^{n+1} + b^{n+1}}{a^n + b^n} = a^{1/2}b^{1/2}$$
or $$a^{n+1} + b^{n+1} = a^{1/2}b^{1/2}(a^n + b^n)$$
or $$a^{n+1} + b^{n+1} = a^{n+1/2}b^{1/2} + a^{1/2} + b^{n+1/2}$$
or $$a^{n+1} - a^{n+1/2}b^{1/2} = a^{1/2}b^{n+1/2} - b^{n+1}$$
or $$a^{n+1/2}(a^{1/2} - b^{1/2}) = b^{n+1/2}(a^{1/2} - b^{1/2})$$
or $$a^{n+1/2} = b^{n+1/2} \qquad [\because a \neq b]$$
or $$\left(\frac{a}{b}\right)^{n+1/2} = 1 = \left(\frac{a}{b}\right)^0$$
$$\therefore \quad n + \frac{1}{2} = 0$$
$$\therefore \quad n = -\frac{1}{2}$$
Ans.

(2.6) MIXED PROBLEMS ON A.M. AND G.M.

Example 3

If a be one A. M. and G_1 and G_2 be two geometric means between b and c, prove that

$$G_1^3 + G_2^3 = 2abc$$

Solution :

$$\text{A. M. of } b \text{ and } c = \frac{b+c}{2}$$
$$\Rightarrow \quad 2a = b + c \qquad \ldots(1)$$

$\because$ G_1 and G_2, are two G.M.s between b and c.

$\therefore$ b, G_1, G_2, c are in G. P.

Let c.r. in r of G. P.

$$\therefore \quad G_1 = br,\ G_2 = br^2 \text{ and } c = br^3 \qquad \ldots(2)$$

Now $$(G_1)^3 + (G_2)^3 = (br)^3 + (br^2)^3 = b^3r^3(1 + r^3)$$
$$= b^3.\frac{c}{b}\left(1 + \frac{c}{b}\right)$$
$$\left[\because \text{ from eq. (2), } r^3 = \frac{c}{b}\right]$$
$$= b^2c\frac{(b+c)}{b}$$
$$= bc(b+c)$$
$$= bc.\,2a$$
$$= 2abc \quad [\because \text{ from eq. (1), } b + c = 2a]$$
$$G_1^3 + G_2^3 = 2abc$$
Proved

Example 4

If a, b and c be in G. P. and x, y be the A. M. between a, b and b, c respectively, show that :

$$\frac{a}{x} + \frac{c}{y} = 2$$

Solution :

By the question, a, b, c are in G.P.

$$\therefore \quad b^2 = ac \qquad \ldots(1)$$

Again x is the A.M. of a and b

$$x = \frac{a+b}{2} \quad ...(2)$$

$$y = \frac{b+c}{2} \quad ...(3)$$

$$\therefore \quad \text{L. H. S.} = \frac{a}{x} + \frac{c}{y}$$

$$= \frac{2a}{a+b} + \frac{2c}{b+c}$$

$$= 2\left\{\frac{ab+ac+ac+bc}{ab+ac+b^2+bc}\right\}$$

$$= \frac{2(ab+2ac+bc)}{(ab+ac+ac+bc)}$$

[$\because b^2 = ac$, from eq. (1)]

$$= \frac{2(ab+2ac+bc)}{(ab+2ac+bc)}$$

$$= 2 \qquad \textbf{Proved}$$

Example 5

If the A. M. between two numbers be twice their G. M., show that the ratio of the numbers is $2+\sqrt{3} : 2-\sqrt{3}$.

Solution :

Let the two numbers are a and b, their A.M. = A and G.M. = G

Then $\quad A = \dfrac{a+b}{2}$ and $G = \sqrt{ab} \quad ...(1)$

By the question,

$$\frac{a+b}{2} = 2\sqrt{ab}$$

or $$\frac{a+b}{2\sqrt{ab}} = \frac{2}{1}$$

$$\Rightarrow \frac{a+b+2\sqrt{ab}}{a+b-2\sqrt{ab}} = \frac{2+1}{2-1}$$

[By Componendo and Dividendo]

$$\Rightarrow \frac{(\sqrt{a}+\sqrt{b})^2}{(\sqrt{a}-\sqrt{b})^2} = \frac{3}{1}$$

$$\Rightarrow \frac{\sqrt{a}+\sqrt{b}}{\sqrt{a}-\sqrt{b}} = \frac{\sqrt{3}}{1}$$

$$\Rightarrow \frac{2\sqrt{a}}{2\sqrt{b}} = \frac{\sqrt{3}+1}{\sqrt{3}-1}$$

[By Componendo and Dividendo]

$$\Rightarrow \frac{\sqrt{a}}{\sqrt{b}} = \frac{\sqrt{3}+1}{\sqrt{3}-1}$$

$$\Rightarrow \frac{a}{b} = \left(\frac{\sqrt{3}+1}{\sqrt{3}-1}\right)^2 = \frac{3+1+2\sqrt{3}}{3+1-2\sqrt{3}}$$

$$= \frac{4+2\sqrt{3}}{4-2\sqrt{3}}$$

$$\therefore \quad \frac{a}{b} = \frac{2+\sqrt{3}}{2-\sqrt{3}}$$

or $\quad a : b = 2+\sqrt{3} : 2-\sqrt{3}$ **Proved**

Example 6

If one G. M., G. and two A. Ms. p and q be inserted between two given quantities, prove that

$$G^2 = (2p-q)(2q-p)$$

Solution :

G.M. of a and b = G

$\therefore$ a, G, b are in G. P.

$$G^2 = ab \quad ...(1)$$

Again a, p, q, b are in A.P.

So $\quad p - a = q - p$

$\quad = b - q$

Now $\quad p - a = q - p$

$\Rightarrow \quad 2q - q = a \quad ...(2)$

Again $\quad q - p = b - q$

or $\quad q + q - p = b$

or $\quad 2p - p = b \quad ...(3)$

From eq. (1) $\quad G^2 = ab$

$\quad = (2p-q)(2q-p)$ **Proved**

Example 7

The first, second and seventh terms of an A.P. are in G.P. and the common difference is 2, then 2nd term of the A.P. is :

(a) $\frac{5}{2}$ (b) 2 (c) $\frac{3}{2}$ (d) $\frac{1}{2}$

Solution :

a and d $\quad$ first term = a

Second term = $a + b$

or $\quad$ Seventh term = $a + 6d$

By the question $\quad (a+d)^2 = a \times (a+6d)$

$$a^2 + d^2 + 2ad = a^2 + 6ad$$

$$d^2 = 4ad$$

$$d = 4a$$

$$d = 2$$

$$a = \frac{2}{4} = \frac{1}{2}$$

second term = $a + d$

$$= \frac{1}{2} + 2 = \frac{5}{2} \qquad \textbf{Ans. (a)}$$

Exercise 2(C)

Geometric Mean (G.M.)

1. Insert 6 G. Ms between $\frac{8}{27}$ and $-5\frac{1}{16}$.
2. Insert 6 G. Ms between $\frac{1}{27}$ and 81.
3. Insert 6 G. Ms between 27 and $\frac{1}{81}$.
4. If a is the G. M. of a 2 and $\frac{1}{4}$, then find a.

Problems Based on A. M. and G.M.

5. Find the G. M. between 8 and 32.
6. Insert 3 G. P. between 486 and 6.
7. Insert 5 G. M. between 3 and 192 *i. e.* insert 5 numbers of terms between 3 and 192 such that the whole series formed shall be in G. P.

Answers

1. $\left[\frac{-4}{9}, \frac{2}{3}, -1, \frac{3}{2}, \frac{-9}{4}, \frac{27}{8}\right]$ 2. $\left[\frac{1}{9}, \frac{1}{3}, 1, 3, 9, 27\right]$

3. $\left[9, 3, 1, \frac{1}{3}, \frac{1}{9}, \frac{1}{27}\right]$ 4. $\left[\frac{1}{\sqrt{2}}\right]$

5. 16 6. 162, 54, 18 7. 6, 12, 24, 48, 96

(2.7) OBJECTIVE QUESTIONS ON G. P.

SOLVED EXAMPLES

Example 1

If $a, a+1, a+3$, are in G. P. then the value of a is :

(a) 2 (b) 1 (c) 4 (d) None of these

Solution :

$\because a, a+1, a+3$ are in G. P.

$$\therefore \quad \frac{a+1}{a} = \frac{a+3}{a+1}$$

$$\Rightarrow \quad a^2 + 2a + 1 = a^2 + 3a$$

$$\Rightarrow \quad 2a + 1 = 3a$$

$$\therefore \quad a = 1$$

Ans. (b)

Example 2

The fifth term of the sequence 4, 12, 36, ...is :

(a) 332 (b) 348 (c) 324 (d) None of these

Solution :

Given G. P. = 4, 12, 36,..........

Here $a = 4$

$$r = \frac{12}{4} = 3$$

$$\therefore \quad t_5 = ar^{5-1} = ar^4$$

$$= 4.(3)^4 = 324$$

Ans. (c)

Example 3

If the third term of a G. P. is 8, then the product of its first five terms is :

(a) 8 (b) 8^2 (c) 8^5 (d) None of these

Solution :

Here $t_3 = 8$

$$ar^2 = 8 \quad ...(1)$$

$\therefore$ Product of the first five terms

$$= a.\, ar.\, ar^2.ar^3.\, ar^4$$

$$= a^5.r^{1+2+3+4}$$

$$= a^5 r^{10} = (ar^2)^5 = 8^5$$

Ans. (c)

Example 4

If the first term of G. P. is 'a' and the common ratio is r, then the sum of infinity will be term $\frac{a}{1-r}$ when :

(a) $r \geq 1$ (b) $r \leq 1$

(c) $-1 \leq r \leq 1$ (d) $-1 < r < 1$

Solution :

$$\therefore \quad S_n = \frac{a(1-r^n)}{1-r} \quad ...(i)$$

If $-1 < r < 1$, then $\lim_{n\to\infty} r^n = 0$

$$\therefore \text{ From eq. (1),} \quad S_\infty = \frac{a(1-0)}{1-r} = \frac{a}{1-r}$$

So the condition (d) is true. **Ans. (d)**

Example 5

If $S = 1 + a + a^2 + a^3 + a^4 + \dots$ infinite term, then a :

(a) $\frac{S}{S-1}$ (b) $\frac{S}{1-S}$ (c) $\frac{S-1}{S}$ (d) $\frac{1-S}{S}$

Solution :

$$\therefore \quad S = 1 + a + a^2 + a^3 + a^4 + \dots \text{ to } \infty \text{ terms}$$

$$\Rightarrow \quad S = \frac{1}{1-a}$$

$$\Rightarrow \quad 1 = S - aS$$

$$\Rightarrow \quad aS = S - 1$$

$$\Rightarrow \quad a = \frac{S-1}{S}$$

Ans. (c)

Exercise 2(D)

Objective Type Questions

❑ Multiple Choice Questions

1. Find $\frac{1}{2} + \frac{3}{4} + \frac{7}{8} + \frac{15}{16}, \dots n$

(a) $2^n - 1$ (b) $2^n - n - 1$

(c) $1 - 2^{-n}$ (d) $2^{-n} + n - 1$

[**Hint :** Sum of the given series

$$= \left(1-\frac{1}{2}\right) + \left(1-\frac{1}{4}\right) + \left(1-\frac{1}{8}\right) + \left(1-\frac{1}{16}\right) + \dots n \text{ terms}$$

$$= n - \left(\frac{1}{2} + \frac{1}{4} + \frac{1}{8} + \dots n \text{ terms}\right)]$$

2. Find : $9^{1/3+1/9+1/27}+ \ldots$ to ∞ terms :
(a) 2 (b) 3
(c) 4 (d) None of these

3. If nth term of a G.P. is 3^n, then its sum to n terms :
(a) $\frac{5}{2}(2^n - 1)$ (b) $\frac{3}{2}(3^n - 1)$
(c) $\frac{2}{3}(3^n - 1)$ (d) None of these

4. If a, b, c, d are in G.P., then $(a-b)^2, (b-c)^2, (c-d)^2$ are :
(a) In A.P. (b) In G.P.
(c) In H.P. (d) None of these

5. If the first and 8th terms of a G.P. is x^{-4} and x^{52} and the second term is x^t, then t :
(a) 4 (b) – 12
(c) $\frac{3}{2}$ (d) 7

6. Geometric mean of a and b is : (JAC, 2015)
(a) $\frac{a+b}{2}$ (b) ab^2
(c) $\sqrt{ab}$ (d) None of these

7. The term of a G.P. is 4. The product of its first 5 terms is :
(a) 4^3 (b) 4^4
(c) 4^5 (d) None of these

8. In a G.P. if the $(m+n)^{th}$ term is p and $(m-n)^{th}$ term is q, then its mth term is :
(a) 0 (b) pq (c) $\sqrt{pq}$ (d) $\frac{p+q}{2}$

9. The 3rd term in a G.P. is 4. The product of first 5 terms is :
(a) 256 (b) 2,048
(c) 512 (d) 1,024

10. If the pth, qth and rth terms of a G.P. are a gain in G.P. the $p.q.r.$ are in :
(a) A.P. (b) G.P.
(c) Both in A.P. and G.P. (d) None of these

11. The sum of infinite terms of the G.P. $1+\frac{1}{2}+\frac{1}{2^2}+ \ldots$ is :
(a) 4 (b) $\frac{5}{2}$ (c) $\frac{3}{2}$ (d) 2

12. Five numbers are in geometric progression such that their product is 1,024, then the third number will be :
(a) 1 (b) 4 (c) 6 (d) 12

13. The sum of first five terms of the series 2,8,32....... is : (JAC, 2018)
(a) 682 (b) 748 (c) 996 (d) 1024

14. The 8th term of a G.P. $1-\frac{2}{3}+\frac{4}{9}-\frac{8}{27}+ \ldots$ will be :
(a) $\frac{-128}{2187}$ (b) $\frac{-64}{729}$ (c) $\frac{2187}{-128}$ (d) $\frac{120}{2100}$

15. The sum of G. P. 2.5 + 5 + 10 + 20 + ... upto 10 terms will be :
(a) 2500 (b) 2557.5 (c) 5115 (d) 255.7

16. Find the geometric mean between 2 and 32 :
(a) 16 (b) 64 (c) 8 (d) 128

17. The first, second and seventh terms of an A.P. are in G.P. and the common difference is 2. The 2nd term of the A.P. is : (JAC, 2016)
(a) 5/2 (b) 2 (c) 3/2 (d) 1/2

18. The value of m in G.P. 4, m, 64 is : (JAC, 2023)
(a) 8 (b) 16 (c) 4 (d) 2

19. If 4, k, 64 are in G. P. then k is : (JAC, 2025)
(a) 8 (b) 16 (c) 64 (d) 4

20. Geometric mean of 4 and 9 is : (JAC, 2026)
(a) 6 (b) 7 (c) 6.5 (d) 12

21. The nth term of a G.P. is : (JAC, 2026)
(a) $a+(n-1)d$ (b) ar^{n-1}
(c) ar (d) $\frac{a}{r}$

22. The first term of a G.P. is 5 and the common ratio is – 2. What is the 6th term ? (JAC, 2026)
(a) – 100 (b) 100 (c) – 160 (d) 160

Answers

1. (d) 2. (a) 3. (b) 4. (b) 5. (a) 6. (c) 7. (c) 8. (c) 9. (d) 10. (a) 11. (d) 12. (b) 13. (b) 14. (a) 15. (b) 16. (c) 17. (a) 18. (b). 19. (b) 20. (a) 21. (b) 22. (c)

❑ Fill in the blank

1. The geometric mean of 3 and 75 is............

Answer

1. 15

❑ Write True or False

1. If the sum of the first 6 terms of a G.P. is 9 times the sum of first three terms, then common ratio connot be equal to 1.
2. If the common ratio of G.P. from the beginning is r, then common ratio of this progression from end (*i.e.*, writing the terms by reverting their order) will be $1/r$.
3. The quartiles whose reciprocals are in A.P. are called G.P.
4. Geometric mean is the nth root of the sum of n terms.

Answers

1. True 2. True 3. False 4. True

3

HARMONIC PROGRESSION (H.P.)

LEARNING OBJECTIVES

After studying this chapter, you will be able to know :

- **3.1 Definition**
- **3.2 Properties of H.P.**
- **3.3 To find the *n*th term of a Harmonic Progression**
- **3.4 Harmonic Mean**
- **3.5 Summation of Some Special Series**

SOLVED EXAMPLES AND PRACTICAL PROBLEMS : AT A GLANCE

No. of Examples		*No. of Problems*
1 to 10	To find the *n*th term of a Harmonic Progression	Exercise 3(A) : 1 to 14
1 to 8	Harmonic Mean	Exercise 3(B) : 1 to 8
1 to 8	Summation of Some Special Series	Exercise 3(C) : 1 to 11
	Mixed Objective Questions on A.P., G.P., H.P. and A.M., G.M., H.M.	Exercise 3(D) : 13 + 5 + 6
26	**Total**	**33 + 24**

(3.1) DEFINITION

If the reciprocals of each term of a progression are in A. P., then the sequence is said to be in H.P.

Note : No Term of H.P. can be zero.

Example : $a, b, c,$ .... will be in H.P if $\frac{1}{a}, \frac{1}{b}, \frac{1}{c},$ .... are in A. P.

Thus, nth term of H.P.

$$= \frac{1}{n\text{th term of the corresponding A.P.}}$$

(3.2) PROPERTIES OF H.P.

(i) a_1, a_2, a_3 ,.................., a_n are in H.P. if and only if $\frac{1}{a_1}, \frac{1}{a_2}, \frac{1}{a_3},$ ...., $\frac{1}{a^n}$ are in A. P.

(ii) If a be the first term, b be the last term and n be the number of terms of the H.P., the cd of A. P. corresponding to the given H. P.= $\frac{a-b}{ab\,(n-1)}$.

(iii) nth term of H. P.

$$= \frac{1}{n\text{th term of the corresponding A.P.}}$$

(3.3) TO FIND THE *n*th TERM OF A HARMONIC PROGRESSION

For the H.P.

let the First term = a

Second term = b

and nth term = x

So for the corresponding A.P.

and common difference = 4

First term $= \frac{1}{a}$

Second term $= \frac{1}{b}$

and nth term $= \frac{1}{x}$

its c.d. = (2nd term – 1st term)

$$= \left(\frac{1}{b}\right) - \left(\frac{1}{a}\right)$$

$$= \frac{a-b}{ab}$$

$= d$ (say)

nth term $= a + (n-1)d$

$$t_n = \frac{1}{a} + (n-1)\frac{a-b}{ab}$$

$$\frac{1}{x} = \frac{b+(n-1)(a-b)}{ab}$$

$$\therefore \quad x = \frac{ab}{b+(n-1)(a-b)}$$

If a, b, c are in H.P., then find the value of b.

$\because a, b, c$ are in H. P.

$\therefore \frac{1}{a}, \frac{1}{b}, \frac{1}{c}$ are in A. P.

$$\therefore \quad \frac{1}{b} - \frac{1}{a} = \frac{1}{c} + \frac{1}{b}$$

$$\Rightarrow \quad \frac{1}{b} + \frac{1}{b} = \frac{1}{c} + \frac{1}{a}$$

$$\Rightarrow \quad \frac{2}{b} = \frac{a+c}{ac}$$

$$\Rightarrow \quad b(a+c) = 2ac$$

$$\therefore \quad b = \frac{2ac}{a+c}$$

Thus if $a, b\ c$ are in H. P.,

then $b = \frac{2ac}{a+c}$.

SOLVED EXAMPLES

Example 1

If $\frac{1}{8}, x, \frac{3}{2}$ are in H. P., then find the value of x.

Solution :

$\because \frac{1}{8}, x, \frac{3}{2}$ are in H.P.

$$\therefore \quad x = \frac{2 \times \frac{1}{8} \times \frac{3}{2}}{\frac{1}{8} + \frac{3}{2}} = \frac{\frac{3}{8}}{\frac{13}{8}} = \mathbf{\frac{3}{13}}$$ **Ans.**

Example 2

Write down the seventh term of $\frac{1}{5}, \frac{1}{9}, \frac{1}{13}, \ldots\ldots$

Solution :

Reciprocals of the given terms are 5, 9, 13, ... which are in H. P

Its first term = 5

and common difference = 4

$\because \quad t_n = a + (n-1)d$

$\therefore \quad t_7 = 5 + (7-1)4$

$= 29$

So t_7 of the corresponding H.P. $= \mathbf{\frac{1}{29}}$ **Ans.**

Example 3

If pth term of an H. P. be qr and qth term be rp, prove that its rth term is pq.

Solution :

For the H.P. $\quad t_p = qr, t_q = rp$

So for the corresponding

A.P. $= t_p = \frac{1}{qr}, t_q = \frac{1}{rp}$

Let its first term $= a$ and c.d. $= d$

$\because \quad t_p = a + (p-1)d$

$\therefore \quad \frac{1}{qr} = a + (p-1)d$ ...(i)

Again $\quad t_q = a + (q-1)d$

$\frac{1}{rp} = a + (q-1)d$ ...(ii)

Subtracting (i) form (ii),

$$\frac{1}{pr} - \frac{1}{qr} = (q-p)d$$

or $\quad \frac{q-p}{pqr} = (q-p)d$

$\therefore \quad d = \frac{1}{pqr}$ $(\because p \neq q)$ ...(iii)

From equ. (i), $\frac{1}{qr} = a + (p-1).\frac{1}{pqr}$

$$\Rightarrow \quad \frac{1}{qr} = a\frac{1}{qr} - \frac{1}{pqr}$$

$\Rightarrow \quad a = \frac{1}{pqr}$ ...(iv)

$$\therefore \quad t_r = a + (r-1)d = \frac{1}{pqr} + (r-1)\frac{1}{pqr}$$

$$= \frac{1+r-1}{pqr} = \frac{1}{pq}$$

So for the corresponding

H.P. $t_r = pq$ **Proved**

Example 4

Find the 14th term of the series $\frac{6}{5}, 1, \frac{6}{7}, \ldots\ldots\ldots\ldots$

Solution :

Let x is the 14th term of the H.P.

Then $\frac{5}{6}, 1, \frac{7}{6}$ is in A.P. and 14th term is $\frac{1}{v}$.

Then $1-\frac{5}{6}=\frac{7}{6}-1=\frac{1}{6}=d$

So 14th term $=\frac{1}{v}$

$$=\frac{5}{6}+(14-1)\times\frac{1}{6}$$

$[\because T_n = a+(n-1)d]$

$$=\frac{5}{6}+\frac{13}{6}=\frac{18}{6}=3$$

Hence 14th term is $\frac{1}{3}$. **Ans.**

Example 5

Find the H. P. whose fifth and eighth terms are $-\frac{7}{26}$ and $-\frac{1}{8}$.

Solution :

Let the three terms in H.P. are $\frac{1}{a}, \frac{1}{a+b}, \frac{1}{a+2d}$.

So The Fifth term $=\frac{7}{-26}=\frac{1}{a+4d}$

and Eight term $=\frac{1}{-8}=\frac{1}{a+7d}$

when substracted $3d=-8+\frac{26}{7}$

$$=\frac{-56+26}{7}=\frac{-30}{7}$$

$\therefore$ $d=-\frac{10}{7}$

Now $a+4d=-\frac{26}{7}$

$$a=-4d-\frac{26}{7}$$

$$=\frac{4\times 10}{7}-\frac{26}{7}$$

$$=\frac{40-26}{7}$$

$$=\frac{14}{7}=2$$

Hence $\frac{1}{2}, \frac{1}{2-\frac{10}{7}}, \frac{1}{2-\frac{20}{7}}, \ldots\ldots$ *i.e.*, $\frac{1}{2}, \frac{7}{4}, -\frac{7}{6}, \ldots\ldots$

Ans.

Example 6

If a, b, c are in H. P., then prove that $\frac{a}{b+c}, \frac{b}{c+a}, \frac{c}{a+b}$ are in H. P.

Solution :

$\because a, b, c$ are in H. P.

$\therefore \frac{1}{a}, \frac{1}{b}, \frac{1}{c}$ are in A. P.

Multiplying each term by $(a+b+c)$

$\frac{a+b+c}{a}, \frac{a+b+c}{b}, \frac{a+b+c}{c}$ are in A. P.

$\Rightarrow \left(1+\frac{b+c}{a}\right), \left(1-\frac{c+a}{b}\right), \left(1+\frac{a+b}{c}\right)$ are in A. P.

Subtracting 1 from each term,

$\frac{b+c}{a}, \frac{c+a}{b}, \frac{a+b}{c}$ are in A. P.

$\therefore \frac{a}{b+c}, \frac{b}{c+a}, \frac{c}{a+b}$ are in H. P. **Proved**

Example 7

Find the sum of the Harmonic Progression.

$$\frac{1}{4}, \frac{1}{7}, \frac{1}{10}, \frac{1}{13}.$$

Solution :

$$S_4=\frac{1}{4}+\frac{1}{7}+\frac{1}{10}+\frac{1}{13}$$

$$=\frac{910+520+364+280}{4\times 7\times 10\times 13}$$

$$=\frac{2074}{3640}=\frac{1037}{1820}$$ **Ans.**

Example 8

The sum of first three terms of a H.P. is $\frac{33}{40}$ and first term is $\frac{1}{2}$. Find the Progression.

Solution :

Given first term in H.P. is $\frac{1}{2}$

or in A.P. is $\frac{2}{1}=2$

Now let the A.P. is $a, a+d, a+2d$ .....

and H.P. is $\frac{1}{a}, \frac{1}{a+d}, \frac{1}{a+2d}$ .....

Given,

$$S_3=\frac{1}{a}+\frac{1}{a+d}+\frac{1}{a+2d}=\frac{33}{40}$$

$$=\frac{1}{2}+\frac{1}{2+d}+\frac{1}{2+2d}=\frac{33}{40}$$

$$=\frac{1}{2+d}+\frac{1}{2+2d}=\frac{33}{40}-\frac{1}{2}$$

$$\Rightarrow \quad \frac{4+3d}{(2+d)(2+2d)} = \frac{13}{40}$$

$$\Rightarrow \quad 40(4+3d) = 13(2+d)(2+2d)$$

$$\Rightarrow \quad 160 + 120d = 13(4 + 4d + 2d + 2d^2)$$

$$\Rightarrow \quad 160 + 120d = 52 + 52d + 26d + 26d^2)$$

$$\Rightarrow \quad 26d^2 - 120d + 78d + 52 - 160 = 0$$

$$\Rightarrow \quad 26d^2 - 42d - 108 = 0$$

$$\Rightarrow \quad 13d^2 - 21d - 54 = 0$$

$$\Rightarrow \quad 13d^2 - 39d + 18d - 54 = 0$$

$$\Rightarrow \quad 13d(d-3) + 18(d-3) = 0$$

$$(d-3)(13d+18) = 0$$

$$\Rightarrow \quad d - 3 = 0$$

$$\Rightarrow \quad d = 3$$

$$\Rightarrow \quad 13d + 18 = 0$$

$$13d = -18$$

$$d = \frac{-18}{13}$$

Taking $d = 3$

$$\text{H.P.} = \frac{1}{2}, \frac{1}{2+3}, \frac{1}{2+6}$$

$$= \frac{1}{2}, \frac{1}{5}, \frac{1}{8} \text{ ....}$$

Taking $d = \frac{-18}{13}$

$$\text{H.P.} = \frac{1}{2}, \frac{1}{2-\frac{18}{13}}, \frac{1}{2-\frac{36}{13}}$$

$$= \frac{1}{2}, \frac{13}{8}, \frac{-13}{10} \text{ ....} \quad \textbf{Ans.}$$

Example 9

The sum of three numbers in H. P. is 37 and the sum of their reciprocals is $\frac{1}{4}$, find the numbers.

Solution :

Let three mumbers in H.P. are $\frac{1}{\alpha-\beta}, \frac{1}{\alpha}, \frac{1}{\alpha+\beta}$.

By the question,

$$\alpha - \beta + \alpha + \alpha + \beta = \frac{1}{4}$$

$$\Rightarrow \quad 3\alpha = \frac{1}{4}$$

$$\therefore \quad \alpha = \frac{1}{12}$$

Now $\frac{1}{\alpha-\beta} + \frac{1}{\alpha} + \frac{1}{\alpha+\beta} = 37$

$$\Rightarrow \quad \frac{1}{\alpha-\beta} + 12 + \frac{1}{\alpha+\beta} = 37$$

$$\Rightarrow \quad \frac{\alpha+\beta+\alpha-\beta}{(\alpha-\beta)(\alpha+\beta)} = 25$$

$$\Rightarrow \quad \frac{2\alpha}{\alpha^2-\beta^2} = 25$$

$$\Rightarrow \quad \frac{2.\frac{1}{12}}{\frac{1}{144}-\beta^2} = 25$$

$$\Rightarrow \quad \frac{1}{6} \times \frac{144}{1-144\beta^2} = 25$$

$$\Rightarrow \quad \frac{24}{1-144\beta^2} = 25$$

$$\Rightarrow \quad 25 - 25 \times 144\beta^2 = 24$$

$$\Rightarrow \quad 1 = 25 \times 144\beta^2$$

$$\Rightarrow \quad \beta^2 = \left(\frac{1}{5 \times 12}\right)^2$$

$$\therefore \quad \beta = \pm \frac{1}{60}$$

When $\alpha = \frac{1}{12}, \beta = \frac{1}{60}$

Then
$$\frac{1}{\alpha-\beta} = \frac{1}{\frac{1}{12}-\frac{1}{60}}$$

$$= \frac{60}{5-1} = 15$$

$$\frac{1}{\alpha} = 12$$

and
$$\frac{1}{\alpha+\beta} = \frac{1}{\frac{1}{12}+\frac{1}{60}}$$

$$= \frac{60}{5+1} = 10$$

Similarly, when $\alpha = \frac{1}{12}, \beta = \frac{1}{60}$

Then
$$\frac{1}{\alpha-\beta} = \frac{1}{\frac{1}{12}+\frac{1}{60}}$$

$$= \frac{60}{5+1} = \frac{60}{6} = 10$$

$$\frac{1}{\alpha} = \frac{1}{\frac{1}{12}} = 12$$

$$\frac{1}{\alpha+\beta} = \frac{1}{\frac{1}{12}-\frac{1}{60}}$$

$$= \frac{60}{5-1} = \frac{60}{4} = 15$$

So the required three numbers are 15, 12, 10. **Ans.**

Example 10

If a, b, c be in H. P., prove that

$$\frac{1}{b-a}+\frac{1}{b-c}=\frac{1}{a}+\frac{1}{c}$$

Solution :

$\because$ a, b, c are in H. P.

$$\therefore \quad b=\frac{2ac}{a+c}$$

Now L.H.S. $=\dfrac{1}{b-a}+\dfrac{1}{b-c}$

$$=\frac{1}{\frac{2ac}{a+c}-\frac{a}{1}}+\frac{1}{\frac{2ac}{a+c}-\frac{c}{1}}$$

$$=\frac{a+c}{2ac-a^2-ac}+\frac{a+c}{2ac-ac-c^2}$$

$$=(a+c)\left[\frac{1}{ac-a^2}+\frac{1}{ac-c^2}\right]$$

$$=(a+c)\left[\frac{1}{a(c-a)}-\frac{1}{c(c-a)}\right]$$

$$=(a+c)\left[\frac{c-a}{ac(c-a)}\right]=\frac{a+c}{ac}$$

$$=\frac{1}{c}+\frac{1}{a}$$

Proved

Exercise 3(A)

1. Find the sequence whose nth term is $\dfrac{1}{3n-2}$. Is this sequence an H. P. ?
2. Find the 4th term of the sequence $2, 2\frac{1}{2}, 3\frac{1}{3}, \ldots\ldots\ldots\ldots$
3. Which term is $\left(-\frac{1}{26}\right)$ of progression $\frac{1}{10}, \frac{1}{8}, \frac{1}{6}, \frac{1}{4}, \ldots\ldots\ldots\ldots$?
4. Find the 7th term of the series $\frac{1}{3}+\frac{8}{23}+\frac{4}{11}+\ldots\ldots\ldots\ldots$
5. Find the 4th term of an H. P., whose 7th term is $\frac{1}{20}$ and 13th term is $\frac{1}{38}$.
6. Find first three terms of a H.P., whose 4th and 8th terms are 3/5 and 1/3 respectively.
7. Find the nth term of the series $\frac{5}{2}+\frac{20}{13}+\frac{10}{9}+\frac{20}{23}+\ldots$
8. Find the 4th term of the series $4, 5, 6\frac{2}{3}$.
9. Find the H. P. whose 6th term is 1 and 10th term is 5. Find 15th term of the series also.
10. The arithmetic mean of two numbers exceeds the geometric mean by $\frac{3}{2}$ and geometric mean exceeds the harmonic mean by $\frac{6}{5}$. Find the numbers.
11. If a, b, c are in H. P., then prove that $\frac{a}{b+c-a}, \frac{b}{c+a-b}, \frac{c}{a+b-c}$ are in H. P.
12. If a^2, b^2, c^2 are in A. P. Then prove that $b+c, c+a, a+b$ are in H. P.
13. Find the sum of five terms of the given harmonic series $\frac{1}{2}, \frac{1}{4}, \frac{1}{6}, \ldots$ (*JAC, 2026*)
14. Find the H.P. whose 7th term and 12th term are $\frac{1}{10}$ and $\frac{1}{25}$ respectively. (*JAC, 2026*)

Answers

1. $1, \frac{1}{4}, \frac{1}{7}, \frac{1}{10}, \ldots\ldots\ldots$, Yes
2. 5
3. 19th term
4. $\frac{4}{9}$
5. $\frac{1}{11}$
6. $\frac{3}{2}, 1, \frac{3}{4}$
7. $\frac{20}{5n+3}$
8. 10
9. $\frac{1}{2}, \frac{5}{9}, \frac{5}{8}, \frac{5}{7}, \frac{5}{6}, \frac{1}{1}$ and 15th term $=-\frac{5}{4}$
10. 3 and 12

(3.4) HARMONIC MEAN

Definition : If three numbers a, b, c be in H. P., then b is called H. M. of a and c.

Harmonic Mean is generally denoted by H.

To Insert One Harmonic Mean between any Two Numbers

Let the two numbers are a and b and H is the single H.M. between them, so a, H, b are in H.P.

$\therefore$ $\frac{1}{a}, \frac{1}{H}, \frac{1}{b}$ are in A.P.

$$\therefore \quad \frac{1}{H}-\frac{1}{a}=\frac{1}{b}-\frac{1}{H}$$

$$\Rightarrow \quad \frac{1}{H}+\frac{1}{H}=\frac{1}{b}+\frac{1}{a}$$

$$\Rightarrow \quad \frac{2}{H}=\frac{a+b}{ab}$$

$$\Rightarrow \quad H(a+b)=2ab$$

$$\therefore \quad H=\frac{2ab}{a+b}$$

Thus H. M.of a and b $=\dfrac{2ab}{a+b}$

To Insert n Harmonic Means between Two Given Quantities

Let the two given quantities are a and b and H_1, H_2, H_3 ,................, H_n are H.M.s between them a, H_1, H_2, H_3, ..., H_n, b are in H.P.

$\therefore$ $\frac{1}{a}, \frac{1}{H_1}, \frac{1}{H_2}, \ldots\ldots\ldots\ldots, \frac{1}{H_n}, \frac{1}{b}$ are in A. P.

Number of terms in it $= n+2$

first term $= \frac{1}{a}$

and last term $= (n+2)$th term$= \frac{1}{b}$

Let the common difference $= d$

then $t_{n+2} = \frac{1}{b}$

$$\frac{1}{a} + (n+2-1)d = \frac{1}{b}$$

$$\therefore \quad (n+1)d = \frac{1}{b} - \frac{1}{a}$$

$$\therefore \quad d = \frac{a-b}{ab(n+1)}$$

$$\therefore \quad \frac{1}{H_1} = \frac{1}{a} + d$$

$$= \frac{1}{a} + \frac{a-b}{ab(n+1)}$$

$$= \frac{a+nb}{ab(n+1)}$$

$$\therefore \quad H_1 = \frac{ab(n+1)}{a+nb}$$

Again $\frac{1}{H_2} = \frac{1}{a} + 2d$

$$= \frac{1}{a} + \frac{2(a-b)}{ab(n+1)}$$

$$= \frac{2a+(n-1)b}{ab(n+1)}$$

$$\therefore \quad H_2 = \frac{ab\,(n+1)}{2a+(n-1)b}$$

Again $\frac{1}{H_3} = \frac{1}{a} + 3d$

$$= \frac{1}{a} + \frac{3(a-b)}{ab(n+1)}$$

$$= \frac{3a+(n-2)b}{ab(n+1)}$$

$$\therefore \quad H_3 = \frac{ab\,(n+1)}{3a+(n-2)b}$$

....

....

$$\frac{1}{H_n} = \frac{1}{a} + nd$$

$$= \frac{1}{a} + \frac{n(a-b)}{ab(n+1)}$$

$$= \frac{na+b}{ab(n+1)}$$

$$\therefore \quad H_n = \frac{ab(n+1)}{na+b}$$

So n H. M.s between a and b are

$$\frac{ab(n+1)}{a+nb}, \frac{ab(n+1)}{2a+(n-1)b}, \frac{ab(n+1)}{3a+(n-2)b}, \ldots\ldots\ldots\ldots, \frac{ab(n+1)}{na+b}$$

Relation between A. M., G.M. and H.M. of Two Unequal, Real and Positive Numbers

To prove that (i) A.M., G.M., H.M., are in G.P.,

i.e., $(G.M.)^2 = A.M. \times H.M.$

and (ii) A.M., G.M., H.M., are in descending order of magnitude

i.e., A.M. > G.M. > H.M.

Proof :

Let the two unequal 'positive' real numbers are a and b.

Their sign A.M. = A, G.M. = G and H.M. = H

$$\therefore \quad A = \frac{a+b}{2}; \; G = \sqrt{ab}; \; H = \frac{2ab}{a+b}$$

$$\because \quad A \times H = \frac{a+b}{2} \times \frac{2ab}{a+b}$$

$$= ab = G^2$$

$$\therefore \quad G^2 = A \times H \qquad \ldots(i)$$

So A, G and H are in G.P.

Again $\because \quad A - G = \frac{a+b}{2} - \sqrt{ab}$

$$= \frac{a+b-2\sqrt{ab}}{2}$$

$$= \frac{\left(\sqrt{a}-\sqrt{b}\right)^2}{2} > 0 \qquad \ldots(ii)$$

$\because$ A > G [$\because a \neq b$] ...(iii)

$\therefore$ $A \times H = G^2$ [From eq. (i)]

or $A \times H = G \times G$

$\because$ A > G

$\therefore$ H > G

or A > G > H

or A.M. > G.M. > H.M.

SOLVED EXAMPLES

Example 1

Insert six H. M.s between 3 and $\frac{6}{23}$.

Solution :

Let six H.M.s between 3 and $\frac{6}{23}$ are $H_1, H_2, H_3, H_4, H_5, H_6$.

So $3, H_1, H_2, H_3, H_4, H_5, H_6, \frac{6}{23}$ are in A. P.

$\therefore \frac{1}{3}, \frac{1}{H_1}, \frac{1}{H_2}, \ldots\ldots\ldots\ldots, \frac{1}{H_6}, \frac{6}{23}$ are in A.P.

$\therefore \quad t_8 = \frac{23}{6}$

or $\quad \frac{1}{3} + (8-1)d = \frac{23}{6}$

or $\quad 7d = \frac{23}{6} - \frac{1}{3} = \frac{23-2}{6} = \frac{21}{6} = \frac{7}{2}$

$\therefore \quad d = \frac{1}{2}$

$\therefore \quad \frac{1}{H_1} = \frac{1}{3} + d = \frac{1}{3} + \frac{1}{2} = \frac{5}{6}$

$\frac{1}{H_2} = \frac{1}{3} + 2d + \frac{1}{3} + 1 = \frac{4}{3}$

$\frac{1}{H_3} = \frac{1}{3} + 3d = \frac{1}{3} + \frac{3}{2} = \frac{11}{6}$

$\frac{1}{H_4} = \frac{1}{3} + 4d = \frac{1}{3} + 2 = \frac{7}{3}$

$\frac{1}{H_5} = \frac{1}{3} + 5d = \frac{1}{3} + \frac{5}{2} = \frac{17}{6}$

$\frac{1}{H_6} = \frac{1}{3} + 6d = \frac{1}{3} + 3 = \frac{10}{3}$

$\therefore \quad H_1 = \frac{6}{5}; H_2 = \frac{3}{4}; H_3 = \frac{6}{11};$

$H_4 = \frac{3}{7}; H_5 = \frac{6}{17}; H_6 = \frac{3}{10}.$ **Ans.**

Example 2

Find 'One Harmonic Mean' between 1 and 9.

Solution :

Let single H.M. between 1 and 9 = H

$\because \quad H = \frac{2ab}{a+b} = \frac{2 \times 1 \times 9}{1+9}$

$= \frac{18}{10} = \mathbf{1.80}$ **Ans.**

Example 3

Find n such that $\frac{a^{n+1} + b^{n+1}}{a^n + b^n}$ may be the single harmonic mean between a and b.

Solution :

$\because \quad$ H.M. of a and $b = \frac{2ab}{a+b}$

By the question,

H.M. of a and $b = \frac{a^{n+1} + b^{n+1}}{a^n + b^n}$

$\therefore \quad \frac{a^{n+1} + b^{n+1}}{a^n + b^n} = \frac{2ab}{a+b}$

$\Rightarrow a^{n+2} + ab^{n+1} + a^{n+1}b + b^{n+2} = 2a^{n+1}b + 2ab^{n+1}$

$\Rightarrow \quad a^{n+2} + b^{n+2} = a^{n+1}b + ab^{n+1}$

$\Rightarrow \quad a^{n+2} - a^{n+1}b = ab^{n+1} - b^{n+2}$

$\Rightarrow \quad a^{n+1}(a-b) = b^{n+1}(a-b)$

$\Rightarrow \quad a^{n+1} = b^{n+1} \quad [\because a \neq b]$

$\Rightarrow \quad \frac{a^{n+1}}{b^{n+1}} = 1$

$\Rightarrow \quad \left(\frac{a}{b}\right)^{n+1} = \left(\frac{a}{b}\right)^0$

$\Rightarrow \quad n + 1 = 0$

$\therefore \quad n = -1$ **Ans.**

Examples based on A.M., G.M. and H.M.

Example 4

If A be the A.M. and H be the H.M. between two quantities a and b, prove that :

$$\frac{a-A}{a-H} \cdot \frac{b-A}{b-H} = \frac{A}{H}$$

Solution :

By the question,

$$A = \frac{a+b}{2} \quad \text{...(i)}$$

and $$H = \frac{2ab}{a+b} \quad \text{...(ii)}$$

Now L.H.S. $= \frac{a-A}{a-H} \cdot \frac{b-A}{b-H}$

$$= \frac{a - \frac{a+b}{2}}{a - \frac{2ab}{a+b}} \cdot \frac{b - \frac{a+b}{2}}{b - \frac{2ab}{a+b}}$$

$$= \frac{(a-b)}{2} \cdot \frac{(a+b)}{a^2 - ab} \times \frac{(b-a)}{2} \cdot \frac{(a+b)}{b^2 - ab}$$

$$= \frac{(a-b)(a+b)}{2a(a-b)} \times \frac{(b-a)(a+b)}{2b(b-a)}$$

$$= \frac{(a+b)^2}{4ab}$$

and $$\frac{A}{H} = \frac{a+b}{2} \times \frac{a+b}{2ab}$$

$$= \frac{(a+b)^2}{4ab}$$

$$\therefore \frac{a-A}{a-H} \cdot \frac{b-A}{b-H} = \frac{A}{H}$$

L.H.S. = R.H.S. **Proved**

Example 5

If 9 arithmetic means and 9 harmonic means be inserted between 2 and 3, prove that $A + \frac{6}{H} = 5$, where A is any arithmetic mean and H the corresponding harmonic mean.

Solution:

Let 9 A.M.s between 2 and 3 are $A_1, A_2, A_3, \ldots\ldots, A_9$.

$\therefore$ 2, $A_1, A_2, \ldots\ldots\ldots\ldots A_9$, 3 are in A.P.

For this A.P let c.d = d

$$d = \frac{3-2}{9+1} = \frac{1}{10} \quad \left[\because d = \frac{b-a}{n+1}\right]$$

$\therefore$ nth arithmetic mean A_n

$$= 2 + nd = 2 + \frac{n}{10}$$

$$= \frac{20+n}{10} = A \text{ (say)}$$

Again let 9 H.M.s between 2 and 3 are $H_1, H_2, H_3, \ldots\ldots\ldots\ldots, H_9$.

$\therefore$ 2, $H_1, H_2, H_3, \ldots\ldots\ldots\ldots, H_9$, 3 are in H.P.

$\therefore$ $\frac{1}{2}, \frac{1}{H_1}, \frac{1}{H_2}, \frac{1}{H_3}, \ldots\ldots\ldots\ldots, \frac{1}{H_9}, \frac{1}{3}$ are in A. P.

For this A.P. let c.d. = d_1

$$d_1 = \frac{\frac{1}{3} - \frac{1}{2}}{9+1} = \frac{\frac{2-3}{6}}{10} = \frac{-1}{60}$$

For this A.P.,

$$\frac{1}{H_n} = \frac{1}{2} + nd_1 = \frac{1}{2} + n\left(-\frac{1}{60}\right)$$

$$= \frac{30-n}{60}$$

$$\therefore \quad H_n = \frac{60}{30-n} = H \text{ (say)}$$

Now

$$\text{L.H.S.} = A + \frac{6}{H}$$

$$= \frac{20+n}{10} + \frac{6(30-n)}{60}$$

$$= \frac{20+n}{10} + \frac{30-n}{10}$$

$$= \frac{20+n+30-n}{10}$$

$$= \frac{50}{10} = 5$$

Proved

Example 6

The A.M. between two numbers exceeds their G.M. by 2 and G.M. exceeds the H.M. by $1\frac{3}{5}$. Find the numbers.

Solution :

Lew the two numbers are a and b.

According to question,

$$\text{A.M.} = \text{G.M.} + 2$$

or $A = G + 2$ ...(i)

and $\text{G.M.} = \text{H.M.} + 1\frac{3}{5}$

or $G = H + \frac{8}{5}$

or $H = G - \frac{8}{5}$ ...(ii)

$\because$ $G^2 = AH$

$\therefore$ $G^2 = (G+2)\left(G - \frac{8}{5}\right)$

$$= G^2 - \frac{8G}{5} + 2G - \frac{16}{5}$$

or $2G - \frac{8G}{5} = \frac{16}{5}$

or $\frac{2G}{5} = \frac{16}{5}$

or $G = \frac{16}{5} \times \frac{5}{2} = 8$

and $\sqrt{ab} = G = 8$ ...(iii)

$\therefore$ $ab = 64$ ...(iv)

From eqns. (i) and (iii),

$A = 8 + 2 = 10$ ...(v)

$\Rightarrow$ $\frac{a+b}{2} = 10$

$\Rightarrow$ $a + b = 10 \times 2 = 20$ ...(vi)

From Eqns. (iv) and (vi),

$a = 16$

$b = 4$

or $a = 4$

$b = 16$

Ans.

Example 7

If A and G are A.M. and G.M. of two positive unequal real numbers respectively then prove that A > G.

Solution :

$\because$ $A = \frac{a+b}{2}$

$G = \sqrt{ab}$

$$A - G = \frac{a+b}{2} - \sqrt{ab}$$

$$= \frac{a+b-2\sqrt{ab}}{2}$$

$$= \frac{\left(\sqrt{a}-\sqrt{b}\right)^2}{2} > 0$$

$\because$ $A - G > 0$

$\therefore$ $A > G$ $[\because a \neq b]$

Proved

Example 8

If the numbers a, b, c are in A.P. and the numbers b, c, d are in H.P., then prove that :

$$ad = bc.$$

Solution :

Here a, b, c are in A.P.

$\therefore$ $b = \frac{a+c}{2}$ ...(1)

and b, c, d are in H.P.

$$\therefore \quad c = \frac{2bd}{b+d} \quad ...(2)$$

From Equation 2,

$$c(b+d) = 2bd$$

or $\quad bc + cd = 2bd$

or $\quad bc + cd = (a+c)d \quad (\because 2b = a+c)$

or $\quad bc + cd = ad + cd$

or $\quad bc = ad$ **Proved**

Exercise 3(B)

1. Insert 4 H.M.s between 1 and $\frac{1}{11}$.
2. Insert 4 H.M.s between 1 and 16.
3. Insert 4 H.M.s between 1 and $\frac{1}{16}$.
4. n harmonic means have been inserted between 1 and 4 such that first mean : last mean = 1 : 3, find n.
5. Insert three H.M. between $\frac{4}{9}$ and $-2\frac{2}{5}$.
6. The harmonic mean of two numbers is 4, their A.M., A and G.M., G satisfy the relation $2A + G^2 = 27$. Find the numbers.
7. If a, b, c are in H. P., prove that :
(i) $a^2 + c^2 > 2b^2$ (ii) $a^5 + c^5 > 2b^5$
8. The H.M. and A.M. of two numbers are 3 and 4 respectively. Find the numbers.

Answers

1. $\left[\frac{1}{3}, \frac{1}{5}, \frac{1}{7}, \frac{1}{9}\right]$ 2. $\left[\frac{16}{13}, \frac{16}{10}, \frac{16}{7}, \frac{16}{4}\right]$ 3. $\left[\frac{1}{4}, \frac{1}{7}, \frac{1}{10}, \frac{1}{13}\right]$

4. 11 5. $\left[\frac{12}{19}, \frac{12}{11}, 4\right]$, 6. 6, 3,

7. (i) $a^2 + c^2 > 2b^2$, (ii) $a^5 + c^5 > 2b^5$ 8. 6 or 2

(3.5) SUMMATION OF SOME SPECIAL SERIES

We have learnt to find the sum of a series whose terms are in A.P. or in G.P. Now we will find the sum of some series whose terms are related to A.P. or G.P.

Σ Notation : 'Σ' is letter of Greek alphabets and it is called 'sigma'. Sigma means the sum of similar terms. The sum of any series is calculated by using Σ sign befor its general term.

For Example :

$$\sum_{1}^{25} n = 1 + 2 + 3 + ... + 25$$

Similarly $$\sum_{1}^{30} n^3 = 1^3 + 2^3 + 3^3 + ... + 30^3$$

and $$\sum_{1}^{n} n^2 = 1^2 + 2^2 + 3^2 + ... + n^2$$

Clearly $\sum_{r=1}^{r=n} r$ and $\sum_{n=1}^{n=n} n$ are of the same meaning.

In start, Σn is simply written in place of $\sum_{1}^{n}$.

So
$$\Sigma n = 1 + 2 + 3 + ... + n$$
$$\Sigma n^2 = 1^2 + 2^2 + 3^2 + ... + n^2$$
$$\Sigma n^3 = 1^3 + 2^3 + 3^3 + ... + n^3$$

To Find the Sum of the Squares of the First n Natural Numbers

Let the required sum be S.

Then $\quad S = 1^2 + 2^2 + 3^2 + ... + n^2 = ?$

Now we take an identity which is true for each value of r.

$$r^3 - (r-1)^3 = 3r^2 - 3r + 1 \quad ...(i)$$

Now putting $r = 1, 2, 3, ..., (n-1), n$ in eq. (i),

If $r = 1$, then $\quad 1^3 - 0^3 = 3.1^2 - 3.1 + 1$

If $r = 2$, then $\quad 2^3 - 1^3 = 3.2^2 - 3.2 + 1$

If $r = 3$, then $\quad 3^3 - 2^3 = 3.3^2 - 3.3 + 1$

....

....

$r = (n-1)$, then

$$(n-1)^3 - (n-2)^3 = 3(n-1)^2 - 3(n-1) + 1$$

$r = n$, then $\quad n^3 - (n-1)^3 = 3n^2 - 3.n + 1$

Adding both sides

$$n^3 = 3(1^2 + 2^2 + ... + n^2) - 3(1 + 2 + ... + n) + (1 + 1 + ... + n)$$

or $$n^3 = 3S - 3.\frac{n(n+1)}{2} + n$$

or $$3S = n^3 - n + \frac{3n(n+1)}{2}$$

$$= n(n-1)(n+1) + \frac{3n(n+1)}{2}$$

$$= n(n+1)\left(n - 1 + \frac{3}{2}\right)$$

$$= \frac{n(n+1)(2n+1)}{2}$$

$$\therefore \quad S = \frac{n(n+1)(2n+1)}{6}$$

Independent Proof

Let $\quad S = 1^2 + 2^2 + 3^2 + ... + n^2$

Now we take an identity which is true for each value of r.

$$(2r+1)^3 - (2r-1)^3 = 24r^2 + 2 \quad ...(i)$$

Now putting $\quad r = 1, 2, 3, ..., (n-1), n$ in eq. (i),

$$3^3 - 1^3 = 24.1^2 + 2$$
$$5^3 - 3^3 = 24.2^2 + 2$$
$$7^3 - 5^3 = 24.3^2 + 2$$

....

....

$$(2n-1)^3 - (2n-3)^3 = 24.(n-1)^2 + 2$$
$$(2n+1)^2 - (2n-1)^3 = 24.n^2 + 2$$

Adding them

$$(2n+1)^3 - 1^3 = 24(1^2 + 2^2 + \dots + n^2) + 2n$$
$$= 24S + 2n$$
$$\therefore \quad 24S = (2n+1)^3 - 1 - 2n$$
$$= (2n+1)^3 - (2n+1)$$
$$= (2n+1)\{(2n+1)^2 - 1\}$$
$$= (2n+1)\{4n^2 + 4n\}$$
$$= 4n(n+1)(2n+1)$$
$$\therefore \quad S = \frac{4n(n+1)(2n+1)}{24}$$
$$= \frac{n(n+1)(2n+1)}{6}$$
$$\therefore \quad \Sigma n^2 = 1^2 + 2^2 + 3^2 + \dots + n^2$$
$$= \frac{n(n+1)(2n+1)}{6}$$

To Find the Sum of the Cubes of the First *n* Natural Numbers

Let $S = 1^3 + 2^3 + 3^3 + \dots + n^3$

To find the value of S we take an identity

$$r^4 - (r-1)^4 = 4r^3 - 6r^2 + 4r - 1 \quad \dots(i)$$

which is true for all values of r.

$r = 1$, then $1^4 - 0^4 = 4.1^3 - 6.1^2 + 4.1 - 1$

$r = 2$, then $2^4 - 1^4 = 4.2^3 - 6.2^2 + 4.2 - 1$

$r = 3$, then $3^4 - 2^4 = 4.3^3 - 6.3^2 + 4.3 - 1$

....

....

$r = (n-1)$, then

$(n-1)^4 - (n-2)^4 = 4.(n-1)^3 - 6(n-1)^2 + 4(n-1) - 1$

$r = n$, then $n^4 - (n-1)^4 = 4n^3 - 6.n^2 + 4.n - 1$

Adding them

$$n^4 = 4(1^3 + 2^3 + 3^3 + \dots + n^3) - 6(1^2 + 2^2 + 3^2 + \dots + n^2) + 4(1 + 2 + 3 + \dots + n) - n$$
$$= 4S - \frac{6n(n+1)(2n+1)}{6} + \frac{4n(n+1)}{2} - n$$

or

$$4S = n^4 + n(n+1)(2n+1) - 2n(n+1) + n$$
$$= n[n^3 + (n+1)(2n+1) - 2(n+1) + 1]$$
$$= n[n^3 + 2n^2 + 3n + 1 - 2n - 2 + 1]$$
$$= n(n^3 + 2n^2 + n)$$
$$= n^2(n^2 + 2n + 1)$$
$$= n^2(n+1)^2$$
$$\therefore \quad S = \frac{n^2(n+1)^2}{4} = \left[\frac{n(n+1)}{2}\right]^2$$
$$= \left[\sum n\right]^2$$
$$\therefore \quad \Sigma n^3 = \left[\sum n\right]^2$$

Independent Proof

We take an identity

$$(r+1)^2 - (r-1)^2 = 4r$$

Which is true for all real values of r.

Multiplying both sides by r^2,

$$r^2(r+1)^2 - r^2(r-1)^2 = 4r^3 \quad \dots(i)$$

In eq. (i) if

$r = 1$, then $1^2.2^2 - 1^1.0^2 = 4.1^3$

$r = 2$, then $2^2.3^2 - 1^2.2^2 = 4.2^3$

$r = 3$, then $3^2.4^2 - 2^2.3^2 = 4.3^3$

....

....

$r = (n-1)$ them, $(n-1)^2.n^2 - (n-2)^2.(n-1)^2 = 4(n-1)^3$

$r = n$ them, $n^2(n+1)^2 - n^2(n-1)^2 = 4n^3$

Adding them $n^2(n+1)^2 = 4(1^3 + 2^3 + 3^3 + \dots + n^3)$

or $S = 1^3 + 2^3 + 3^3 + \dots + n^3$

$$= \frac{1}{4}n^2(n+1)^2$$
$$= \left[\frac{n(n+1)}{2}\right]^2$$

Similarly $S = \Sigma n^2 = 1^3 + 2^3 + 3^3 + \dots + n^3$

$$= \left[\frac{n(n+1)}{2}\right]^2$$
$$= (1 + 2 + 3 + \dots + n)^2$$
$$= (\Sigma n)^2$$

SOVLED EXAMPLES

Example 1

Find the sum of n terms of the series $1^2 + 3^2 + 5^2 + 7^2 + \dots\dots\dots\dots$.

Solution :

The given terms of the series are not in A.P. but 1, 3, 5, 7, ... are in A. P.

Its nth term $= 1 + (n-1).2$

$= 2n - 1$

$\therefore$ nth term of the given series

$$t_n = (2n-1)^2$$
$$= 4n^2 - 4n + 1$$

So, sum of n terms of the given series

$$S_n = \Sigma t_n = \Sigma(4n^2 - 4n + 1)$$
$$= \Sigma 4n^2 - \Sigma 4n + \Sigma 1$$
$$= 4\Sigma n^2 - 4\Sigma n + n$$
$$= \frac{4n(n+1)(2n+1)}{6} - \frac{4n(n+1)}{2} + n$$

$$= n\left[\frac{2}{3}(n+1)(2n+1) - 2(n+1) + 1\right]$$

$$= n\left[\frac{2(2n^2+3n+1) - 6(n+1) + 3}{3}\right]$$

$$= \frac{n(4n^2-1)}{3}$$ **Ans.**

Example 2

Find the sum to n terms of the series :

1.2.3 + 2.3.4. + 3.4.5. + ...

Solution :

$$t_n = \{1+(n-1).1\}\{2+(n-1).1\}\{3+(n-1).1\}$$
$$= n(n+1)(n+2)$$
$$= n(n^2+3n+2)$$
$$= n^3 + 3n^2 + 2n$$

$$\therefore \quad S_n = \sum_{n=1}^{n} t_n = \Sigma n^3 + 3\Sigma n^2 + 2\Sigma n$$

$$= \left\{\frac{n(n+1)}{2}\right\}^2 + \frac{3n(n+1)(2n+1)}{6} + \frac{2n(n+1)}{2}$$

$$= \frac{n(n+1)}{2}\left[\frac{n(n+1)}{2} + 2n + 1 + 2\right]$$

$$= \frac{n(n+1)}{2}\left(\frac{n^2+n+4n+2+4}{2}\right)$$

$$= \frac{1}{4}.n(n+1)(n^2+5n+6)$$

$$= \frac{1}{4}.n(n+1)(n+2)(n+3)$$ **Ans.**

Example 3

Find the sum of the series to 16 terms :

$$\frac{1^3}{1} + \frac{1^3+2^3}{1+3} + \frac{1^3+2^3+3^3}{1+3+5} + \ldots\ldots\ldots\ldots$$

Solution :

$$t_n = \frac{1^3+2^3+3^3+\ldots+n^3}{1+3+5+\ldots \text{ nth terms}}$$

$$= \frac{\left\{\frac{n(n+1)}{2}\right\}^2}{n/2\{2.1+(n-1)2\}} = \frac{\left\{\frac{n(n+1)}{2}\right\}^2}{n^2}$$

$$= \frac{(n+1)^2}{4} = \frac{n^2+2n+1}{4}$$

So sum of nth terms

$$S_n = \sum_{n=1}^{n} t_n$$

$$= \frac{1}{4}\sum_{n=1}^{n}(n^2+2n+1)$$

$$= \frac{1}{4}\left\{\sum_{n=1}^{n} n^2 + 2\sum_{n=1}^{n} n + \sum 1\right\}$$

$$= \frac{1}{4}\left\{\frac{n(n+1)(2n+1)}{6} + \frac{2n(n+1)}{2} + n\right\}$$

$\therefore$ So sum of 16 terms

$$S_{16} = \frac{1}{4}\left\{\frac{16(16+1)(16\times 2+1)}{6} + 16.(16+1) + 16\right\}$$

$$= \frac{1}{4}\left[\frac{16\times 17\times 33}{6} + 16\times 17 + 16\right]$$

$$= \frac{1}{4}\times 16\left[\frac{17\times 33}{6} + 17 + 1\right]$$

$$= 4\left[\frac{561}{6} + 18\right]$$

$$= 4\times\left[\frac{561+108}{6}\right]$$

$$= 4\times\frac{669}{6} = 446$$ **Ans.**

Arithmetico-Geometric Progression

A series is said to be an arithmetico-geometric series if its each term is the product of the corresponding terms of an A.P. and a G.P.

To obtain the sum of an arithmetico-geometric series.

Working Rules :

(i) Let the sum of the series = S

(ii) Multiply S by the common ratio of the geometric series.

(iii) Subtract this new series from S.

(iv) Then simplify them and obtains.

Example : If the arithmetic series 1 + 3 + 5 + 7+ .... be multiplied by the corresponding terms of the geometric series $1 + x + x^2 + x^3 + \ldots\ldots$ in order, then we obtain the following arithmetico-geometric series :

$$1 + 3x + 5x^2 + 7x^3 + \ldots\ldots\ldots\ldots$$

Example 4

Find the sum to n terms of the series :

$1 + 2x + 3x^2 + 4x^3 + \ldots\ldots\ldots\ldots\ldots\ldots\ldots\ldots$

Solution :

Let
$$S = 1 + 2x + 3x^2 + 4x^3 + \ldots + nx^{n-1}$$
$$xS = x + 2x^2 + 3x^3 + \ldots + (n-1)x^{n-1} + nx^n$$
$$- \quad - \quad - \quad - \quad - \quad -$$

Subtracting

$$(1-x)\,S = 1 + x + x^2 + x^3 + \ldots + x^{n-1} - nx^n$$

$$(1-x)\,S = \frac{(1-x^n)}{1-x} - nx^n$$

$$\therefore \quad S = \frac{(1-x^n)}{(1-x)^2} - \frac{nx^n}{1-x}$$ **Ans.**

Example 5

Find the sum of the series $1 + 2^2x + 3^2x^2 + 4^2x^3 + \ldots$ to ∞, where $-1 < x < 1$.

Solution :

$$\text{Let} \quad S = 1 + 2^2x + 3^2x^2 + 4^2x^3 + \ldots \infty \text{ terms} \quad \ldots(i)$$

$$\therefore \quad x.S = x + 2^2x^2 + 3^2x^3 + \ldots \infty \text{ terms} \quad \ldots(ii)$$

Subtracting

$$S - xS = 1 + 3x + 5x^2 + 7x^3 + \ldots \text{ to } \infty \text{ terms}$$

$$(1-x)S = 1 + 3x + 5x^2 + 7x^3 + \ldots \text{ to } \infty \text{ terms} \quad \ldots(iii)$$

Again multiplying both sides by x,

$$x(1-x)S = x + 3x^2 + 5x^2 + 7x^3 + \ldots \text{ to } \infty \text{ terms} \quad \ldots(iv)$$

Subtracting (iv) from (iii),

$$(1-x)S = 1 + 3x + 5x^2 + 7x^3 + \ldots \text{ to } \infty \text{ terms} \quad \ldots(v)$$

$$x(1-x)S = x + 3x^2 + 5x^3 + \ldots \text{ to } \infty \text{ terms} \quad \ldots(vi)$$

Subtracting

$$(1-x)(1-x)S = 1 + 2x + 2x^2 + 2x^3 + \ldots \text{ to } \infty \text{ terms}$$

$$(1-x)(1-x)S = 1 + (2x + 2x^2 + 2x^3 + \ldots \text{ to } \infty \text{ terms})$$

$$= 1 + \frac{2x}{1-x} = \frac{1-x+2x}{1-x}$$

$$= \frac{1+x}{1-x}$$

$$\therefore \quad S = \frac{1+x}{(1-x)^3} \qquad \textbf{Ans.}$$

Mixed Problems on A.P., G.P. and H.P.

Example 6

If $a^x = b^y = c^z$ and a, b, c are in G. P., show that x, y, z are in H.P.

Solution :

$$a^x = b^y = c^z = k \text{ (say)}$$

$$\therefore \quad a = (k)^{1/x}$$

$$b = (k)^{1/y}$$

$$c = (k)^{1/z}$$

Now ∵ a, b, c are in G.P.

$$\therefore \quad b/a = c/b$$

$$\Rightarrow \quad \frac{k^{1/y}}{k^{1/x}} = \frac{k^{1/z}}{k^{1/y}}$$

$$\Rightarrow \quad (k)^{1/y - 1/x} = (k)^{1/z - 1/y}$$

$$\Rightarrow \quad \frac{1}{y} - \frac{1}{x} = \frac{1}{z} - \frac{1}{y}$$

$\therefore \frac{1}{x}, \frac{1}{y}, \frac{1}{z}$ are in A.P.

$\Rightarrow x, y, z$ are in H.P.

Example 7

If three positive numbers a, b, c are in A.P., G.P. and H.P. as well, then find their values.

Solution :

∵ a, b, c are in A.P., G.P. and H.P.

$$\therefore \quad b = \frac{a+c}{2} \quad \ldots(i)$$

$$b^2 = ac \quad \ldots(ii)$$

$$\text{and} \quad b = \frac{2ac}{a+c} \quad \ldots(iii)$$

From eq. (i) and (ii),

$$\left(\frac{a+c}{2}\right)^2 = ac$$

$$\Rightarrow \quad (a+c)^2 = 4ac$$

$$\Rightarrow \quad (a+c)^2 - 4ac = 0$$

$$\Rightarrow \quad (a-c)^2 = 0$$

$$\therefore \quad a = c$$

Putting $c = a$ in eqs. (i), $b = \frac{a+a}{2} = a$

$$\therefore \quad a = b = c$$

So the three numbers are equal.

Example 8

If $\frac{x+y}{2}, y, \frac{y+z}{2}$ be in H.P., prove that x, y, z are in G.P.

Solution :

∵ $\frac{x+y}{2}, y, \frac{y+z}{2}$ are in H.P.

$$\therefore \quad y = \frac{2\left(\frac{x+y}{2}\right)\left(\frac{y+z}{2}\right)}{\frac{x+y}{2} + \frac{y+z}{2}}$$

$$= \frac{(x+y)(y+z)}{x+2y+z}$$

$$\Rightarrow \quad xy + 2y^2 + yz = xy + y^2 + xy + yz$$

$$\Rightarrow \quad y^2 = xz$$

∴ x, y, z are in G.P. **Proved**

Exercise 3(C)

Find the sum of the following series :

1. $1^3 + 3^3 + 5^3 + \ldots$ to n terms.
2. $1.3 + 3.5 + 5.7 + \ldots$ to n terms.
3. $1^2 + 4^2 + 7^2 + 10^2 + \ldots$ to n terms.
4. $1^2 + (1^2 + 2^2) + (1^2 + 2^2 + 3^2) + \ldots$ to 10 terms.

[Hint : $t_n = 1^2 + 2^2 + 3^2 + \ldots + n^2 = \Sigma n^2$

$$= \frac{n(n+1)(2n+1)}{6}$$

$$= \frac{1}{6} n(2n^2 + 3n + 1)$$

$\therefore \quad S_n = \frac{1}{6}[2\Sigma n^3 + 3\Sigma n^2 + \Sigma n]$

$$= \frac{1}{6}\left[2\left(\frac{n(n+1)}{2}\right)^2 + \frac{3n(n+1)(2n+1)}{6} + \frac{n(n+1)}{2}\right]$$

Putting $n = 10$,

$$S_{10} = \frac{1}{6}\left[2\left\{\frac{10(10+1)}{2}\right\}^2 + \frac{3\times 10\times 11\times 21}{6} + \frac{10\times 11}{2}\right]$$

5. 1.2.3 + 2.3.5. + 3.4.7 + ... to n terms.

6. $1 + \frac{1}{1+2} + \frac{1}{1+2+3} + \ldots$ to n terms.

[**Hint:** $t_n = \frac{1}{1+2+3+\ldots n} = \frac{1}{\frac{n(n+1)}{2}} = \frac{2.1}{n(n+1)}$

$= 2\left[\frac{1}{n} - \frac{1}{n+1}\right]$

putting $n = 1, 2, 3, \ldots, n$ and then add them.]

7. Find the sum of the series, if the numbers of terms is infinite :

$\frac{1}{2.4} + \frac{1}{4.6} + \frac{1}{6.8} + \frac{1}{8.10} + \ldots$

[**Hint:** $\therefore\ t_n = \frac{1}{2n(2n+2)}$

$= \frac{1}{4n(n+1)}$

$= \frac{1}{4}\left[\frac{1}{n} - \frac{1}{n+1}\right]$

$n = 1, 2, 3, 4, \ldots$ and then add them then put $\lim_{n\to\infty}$]

8. If $\frac{a-x}{px} = \frac{a-y}{qy} = \frac{a-z}{rz}$ and p, q, r be in A.P., show that x, y, z are in H.P.

9. If a, b, c, d, be in G.P. and $a^x = b^y = c^z = d^w$, prove that x, y, z, w are in H.P.

10. Show that if three quantities be in any two of the three progressions, A.P., G.P. and H.P., they will be also in the third progression.

11. If $(y - x), 2(y - a), (y - z)$ are in H.P., prove that $x - a, y - a, z - a$ are in G.P.

Answers

1. $n^2(2n^2 - 1)$
2. $\left[\frac{1}{3}n(4n^2 + 6n - 1)\right]$
3. $\left[\frac{1}{2}n(6n^2 - 3n - 1)\right]$
4. 1,210
5. $\left[\frac{1}{2}n(n+1)^2(n+2)\right]$
6. $\left[\frac{2n}{n+1}\right]$
7. $\left[\frac{1}{4}\right]$

Exercise 3(D)

Objective Type Questions

❒ Multiple Choice Questions

Select the correct answer :

1. If a, b, c are in A.P. and a^2, b^2, c^2 are in H.P. and $2b^2 \neq -ac$, then :
(a) $a = b = c$ (b) $a + b = c$
(c) $b + c = a$ (d) $a + a = b$

2. If $\frac{a}{b} = \frac{c}{d}$ and a, b, c are in A.P., then b, c, d are in :
(a) A.P. (b) G.P. (c) H.P. (d) None of these

3. If the numbers a, b, c are in A.P. and b, c, d in H.P., then :
(a) $ad = bc$ (b) $ab = cd$
(c) $ac = bd$ (d) None of these

4. If a, b, c are in H.P., then :
(a) $\frac{a}{c} = \frac{a+b}{b-c}$ (b) $\frac{a}{c} = \frac{a-b}{b-c}$
(c) $\frac{a}{c} = \frac{a-b}{c-b}$ (d) $\frac{a}{c} = \frac{a-b}{c+b}$

5. If the A.M., G.M. and H.M. of the two real positive quantities are A, G and H, then :
(a) $AH = G^2$ (b) $AH = G$
(c) $A \geq G < H$ (d) $(AH)^2 = G^2$

6. Four harmonic means are inserted between 1 and $\frac{1}{16}$. The first harmonic mean from the beginning is :
(a) $\frac{1}{7}$ (b) $\frac{1}{4}$ (c) $\frac{1}{13}$ (d) $\frac{1}{10}$

7. The arithmetic mean between two numbers is A, geometric mean is G, harmonic mean is H, then A, G, H are in :
(a) A.P. (b) G.P. (c) H.P. (d) None of these

8. What is the harmonic mean between $\frac{8}{3}$ and 4 ?
(a) $\frac{35}{24}$ (b) $\frac{24}{35}$ (c) $\frac{3}{2}$ (d) $\frac{5}{7}$

9. If $\frac{1}{4}, x, \frac{4}{3}$ are in H.P., then the value of x is :
(a) $\frac{8}{19}$ (b) $\frac{19}{8}$ (c) $\frac{8}{18}$ (d) $\frac{19}{18}$

10. Which term of H.P. $1, \frac{1}{5}, \frac{1}{9}, \ldots$ is $\frac{1}{25}$? (JAC, 2023)
(a) 6 (b) 7 (c) 8 (d) 9

11. In H.P. $\frac{1}{10}, \frac{1}{8}, \frac{1}{6}$ the fifth term is (JAC, 2024)
(a) $\frac{1}{2}$ (b) 0 (c) -2 (d) 12

12. 6th term of H.P. $\frac{1}{5}, \frac{1}{7}, \frac{1}{9}, \ldots$ is : (JAC, 2025)
(a) $\frac{1}{18}$ (b) $\frac{1}{12}$ (c) $\frac{1}{15}$ (d) $\frac{1}{17}$

13. Harmonic mean of a and b is : (JAC, 2026)

(a) $\frac{2ab}{a+b}$ (b) $\sqrt{ab}$ (c) $\frac{a+b}{2}$ (d) $\frac{a+b}{2ab}$

Answers

1. (a)	2. (c)	3. (a)	4. (b)	5. (a)	6. (b)	7. (b)
8. (b)	9. (a)	10. (b)	11. (a)	12. (c)	13. (a).	

❐ Fill in the blanks

1. The G.M. of any two unequal positive quantities is .... their A.M.
2. G.M. of two numbers is the .... of their product.
3. If a be the A.M. between b and c and b the G.M. between c and a, then c is the .... between a and b.
4. A harmonic mean between 2 and 8 is ....
5. If $a^x = b^y = c^z$ and a, b, c are in G.P., then x, y, z will be in ...., P.

Answers

1. Less than 2. Square root 3. A.M. 4. 3.2
5. Harmonic or Σ(H)

❐ Write True or False

1. Series a, ar, ar^2, ..., is in H.P.
2. There is no suitable formula for determining the sum of n terms of a H.P.
3. If x_1, x_2, x_3, x_4 are in H.P. then $x_1x_2 + x_2x_3 + x_3x_4 = 4x_1x_4$.
4. If $\frac{1}{x}$, $\frac{1}{x+1}$ and $\frac{1}{7}$ are in H.P., then the value of x will be 4.
5. The harmonic mean between $\frac{3}{8}$ and 4 is $\frac{24}{35}$.
6. If a, b, c are in H.P. then $a - \frac{b}{2}, \frac{b}{2}, c - \frac{b}{2}$ are in H.P. Is it true ?

Answers

1. False 2. True 3. False 4. True
5. True 6. False.

❖❖

4

PROPERTIES OF A.P., G.P. AND H.P.

LEARNING OBJECTIVES

After studying this chapter, you will be able to know :

- **4.1 Properties of A.P.**
- **4.2 Properties of G.P.**
- **4.3 Properties of H.P.**
- **4.4 Relation between A.M., G.M. and H.M.**

SOLVED EXAMPLES AND PRACTICAL PROBLEMS : AT A GLANCE

No. of Examples		*No. of Problems*
		Exercise 4
1 to 5	Find the *n*th term of A.P.	1 to 12
6 to 8	Geometric Progression	
9 to 12	Harmonic Progression	1 to 3
12	**Total**	**12 + 3**

(4.1) PROPERTIES OF A.P.

We know that the sequence, in which every term is obtained by adding a fixed number to just previous term, is called and A.P. Fixed number is called the common difference, denoted by '*d*'.

If a be the first term then A.P. in general form is

$$a, a + d, a + 2d, a + 3d, \ldots\ldots$$

Properties of A.P. are following :

(1) The series obtained by adding or subtracting a fixed number to every term of an A.P. is also an A.P. and whose common difference remains the same. ***e.g.***

A.P. is 2, 4, 6, 8..........., common difference = + 2

by adding 5 to each term, we get

New series 7, 9, 11, 13.....

which is also an A.P., whose common difference is also + 2.

(2) The series, obtained by multiplying a fixed number K to every term of an A.P., is also an A.P. and whose common difference is equal to the K times of the common difference of former series. ***e.g.***

A.P. is 2, 4, 6, 8,...........common difference = + 2

by multiplying 3 to each term, we get

6, 12, 18, 24,.....

which is also an A.P. and common difference

$= 6 = 3 \times 2$

(3) If we divide every term of the series 9, 15, 21, 27,.....by 3, then new series is

3, 5, 7, 9,.......

which is also an A.P.

$$\text{Com. diff.} = 2 = \frac{6}{3}$$

$$= \frac{\text{Common difference of former series}}{3}$$

(4) The series obtained by adding corresponding terms of two A.P.'s is also an A.P. e.g.

First A.P. is 2, 3, 4, 5, ... $d_1 = 1$

Second A.P. is 5, 7, 9, 11, ... $d_2 = 2$

then by adding the corresponding terms

New series is 7, 10, 13, 16, ... also an A.P.

Common difference $= 3 = 1 + 2 = d_1 + d_2$

(5) Similarly, the series obtained by subtracting corresponding terms of two A.P.s is also an A.P. whose common difference $= d_1 - d_2$

(6) The series obtained by multiplying or dividing the corresponding terms is not an A.P.

Points to Remember

1. Three numbers in A.P. are $a-d, a, a+d$.
2. Four numbers in A.P. are $a-3d, a-d, a+d, a+3d$.
3. Five numbers in A.P. are $a-2d, a-d, a, a+d, a+2d$.
4. In an A.P. of even terms.
   No. of terms = $2n$ and in this A.P. there are two middle terms nth and $(n+1)$th.
5. In an A.P. of odd terms
   No. of terms = $2n+1$
   and in this A.P. there are only one middle term $(n+1)$th term.
6. The sum of terms equidistant from the beginning and from the end is constant and equal to the sum of first and last terms.
7. The sum of n arithmetic means between two quantities a, b in n times of their arithmetic mean.
8. If the sum of n terms S_n of an A.P. is given then by applying the formula $T_n = S_n - S_{(n-1)}$ We get the nth term T_n of this A.P.

SOLVED EXAMPLES

Example 1

Find the sum of seventh terms from the beginning and from the end of an A.P. whose first term is 2 and last term is 98.

Solution :

∵ Sum of terms equidistant from the beginning and from the end = first term + last term

∴ 7th term from the beginning + 7th term from the last = 2 + 98 = 100

Example 2

The sum of five terms of an A.P. is 30, find the middle term of the series.

Solution :

Let the five terms be

$a-2d, a-d, a, a+d, a+2d$

Given $(a-2d)+(a-d)+a+(a+d)+(a+2d) = 30$

or $5a = 30$

or $a = 6$

∴ Middle term = 6

Example 3

The sum of n terms of an A.P. is n^2+n, then find the nth term of this series.

Solution :

Given $S_n = n^2 + n$ ...(i)

Put $(n-1)$ in place of n,

$S_{(n-1)} = (n-1)^2 + n - 1$

nth term $= n^2 - 2n + 1 + n - 1$

$= n^2 - n$

∵ Formula : $T_n = S_n - S_{(n-1)}$

$T_n = (n^2+n) - (n^2-n)$

$= n^2 + n - n^2 + n = 2n$

Example 4

Find the sum of 11 arithmetic means between 1 and 25.

Solution :

∵ No. of arithmetic means $n = 11$

∴ Sum of 11 arithmetic means = 11 × (Arithmetic mean of 1 and 25)

$= 11 \times \left(\frac{1+25}{2}\right)$

$= 11 \times 13 = 143$

Example 5

If a, b, c are in A.P., then prove that :

(i) $\frac{1}{bc}, \frac{1}{ca}, \frac{1}{ab}$ are in A.P.

(ii) $\frac{ab+ac}{bc}, \frac{bc+ab}{ca}, \frac{ca+cb}{ab}$ are in A.P.

(iii) $a^2(b+c), b^2(c+a), c^2(a+b)$ are in A.P.

Solution :

(i) Let $\frac{1}{bc}, \frac{1}{ca}, \frac{1}{ab}$ are in A.P.

Multiplying every term by abc,

$\frac{abc}{bc}, \frac{abc}{ca}, \frac{abc}{ab}$ are in A.P.

⇒ a, b, c are in A.P. **Proved**

(ii) Let $\frac{ab+ac}{bc}, \frac{bc+ab}{ca}, \frac{ca+cb}{ab}$ are in A.P.

Adding 1 to each term,

$\frac{ab+ac}{bc}+1, \frac{bc+ab}{ca}+1, \frac{ca+cb}{ab}+1$ are in A.P.

$\frac{ab+ac+bc}{bc}, \frac{bc+ab+ca}{ca}, \frac{ca+cb+ab}{ab}$ are in A.P.

Divide each term by $(ab+bc+ca)$,

$\frac{1}{bc}, \frac{1}{ca}, \frac{1}{ab}$ are in A.P.

Multiplying every term by abc,

a, b, c are in A.P. **Proved**

(iii) Let $a^2(b+c), b^2(c+a), c^2(a+b)$ are in A.P.

Adding abc to each term,

$a^2(b+c)+abc, b^2(c+a)+abc, c^2(a+b)+abc$ are in A.P.

⇒ $a(ab+ac+bc), b(bc+ba+ac), c(ca+cb+ab)$ are in A.P.

Divide by $(ab+ac+bc)$,

a, b, c are in A.P. **Proved**

(4.2) PROPERTIES OF G.P.

We know that the sequence, in which every term is obtained by multiplying a fixed number to just previous term is called a G.P. The fixed number is called the common ratio denoted by 'r'. If a be the first term then G.P. in its general form is a, ar, ar^2, ar^3, ...

Properties of G.P. are following :

1. The new series obtained by multiplying or dividing every term to a fixed number, is also a G.P. and common ratio of the new series remains the same.

e.g., G.P. is 4, 12, 38, 108, ...; $r = 3$
Each term is multiplied by 2,
New series 8, 24, 72, 216, ...
which is also a G.P., $r_1 = 3$
If each term is divided by 4,
New series 1, 3, 9, 27,......., $r_2 = 3$
which is also a G.P.

2. The series, obtained by multiplying corresponding terms of two G.P. is also a G.P. whose common ratio is the product of common ratios of two series, e.g.

First G.P. is 1, 2, 4, 8 ....., $r_1 = 2$
Second G.P. is 3, 9, 27, 81, ..., $r_2 = 3$
New series 3, 18, 108, 648, ... is also a G.P.
whose common ratio = $6 = r_1 \times r_2$

3. Similarly, the series, obtained by dividing the corresponding terms of two G.P. is also a G.P. whose common ratio is $\frac{r_1}{r_2}$.

4. The series, obtained by the reciprocals of terms of a G.P., is also a G.P. whose common ratio is the reciprocal of common ratio of former G.P.

5. If a series is an A.P. as well as a G.P. then all the terms of this series are same, e.g., 3, 3, 3, 3, 3, ...

It is an A.P. whose common difference = 0
and it is a G.P. whose common ratio = 1

6. If common ratio $r = 1$ of a G.P. then sum of n terms = na, where a is the first term.

Points to Remember

1. Three numbers in G.P. are $\frac{a}{r}$, a, ar.
2. Four numbers in G.P. are $\frac{a}{r^3}, \frac{a}{r}, ar, ar^3$.
3. Five numbers in G.P. are $\frac{a}{r^2}, \frac{a}{r}, a, ar, ar^2$.
4. The product of terms equidistant from the beginning and from the last is constant and is equal to the product of first and last terms.
5. Product of n Geometric means between two numbers a, b is equal to the nth power of the Geometric mean of a, b.
6. Geometric mean of two negative numbers is also negative.
   e.g., if a and b are two negative numbers then
   $$G = -\sqrt{ab}$$
   i.e., Geometric mean of -9 and -16
   $$= \sqrt{-9\times(-)16}$$
   $$= -\sqrt{144} = -12$$
7. If a and b are two real, positive numbers then their A.M. is greater than their G.M.

Example 6

The sum of three consecutive numbers in G.P. is 38 and their product is 1,728. Find the numbers.

Solution :

Let three numbers be $\frac{a}{r}, a, ar$.

Given $\frac{a}{r} + a + ar = 38$ ...(i)

and $\frac{a}{r} \times a \times ar = 1728$

$\Rightarrow a^3 = 12^3$

$\Rightarrow a = 12$

Putting this value of a in equation (i),

$$\frac{12}{r} + 12 + 12r = 38$$

or $\frac{12}{r} + 12r = 26$

or $12 + 12r^2 = 26r$

or $12r^2 - 26r + 12 = 0$

or $6r^2 - 13r + 6 = 0$

or $6r^2 - 9r - 4r + 6 = 0$

or $3r(2r-3) - 2(2r-3) = 0$

or $(3r-2)(2r-3) = 0$

or $3r - 2 = 0$

or $2r - 3 = 0$

$\therefore r = \frac{2}{3}$ or $r = \frac{3}{2}$

When $a = 12$, and $r = \frac{2}{3}$

Numbers $\frac{12}{2/3}, 12, 12 \times \frac{2}{3}$

$\Rightarrow$ 18, 12, 8

When $a = 12$, and $r = \frac{2}{3}$

Numbers $\frac{12}{3/2}, 12, 12 \times \frac{3}{2}$

$\Rightarrow$ 8, 12, 18

Example 7

Find the product of three geometric means between 2 and 32.

Solution :

Product of 3 G.M.s $= \left(\sqrt{2\times 32}\right)^3 = (8)^3 = 512$

Example 8

If A be the arithmetic mean and p, q be two geometric means between two numbers, then prove that

$$\frac{p^2}{q}+\frac{q^2}{p} = 2A.$$

Solution :

Let a and b be two numbers.

$$\therefore \quad A = \frac{a+b}{2} \Rightarrow a + b = 2A \quad ...(i)$$

and a, p, q, b are in G.P.

$$\therefore \quad p^2 = aq \text{ and } q^2 = pb$$

$$\Rightarrow \quad \frac{p^2}{q} = a \text{ and } \frac{q^2}{p} = b$$

On adding, $\frac{p^2}{q}+\frac{q^2}{p} = a + b = 2A$ [using (i)]

(4.3) PROPERTIES OF H.P.

The series is called Harmonic series if the reciprocal of terms make an A.P. *e.g.*

$\frac{1}{2}, \frac{1}{5}, \frac{1}{8}, \frac{1}{11}$, ... are in H.P.

$g\frac{1}{b}, \frac{1}{a+2b}, \frac{1}{a+4b}$,....... are in H.P.

In other words, Harmonic series is that series in which three consecutive terms are such that

$$\frac{\text{First term}}{\text{Third term}} = \frac{\text{First term} - \text{Second term}}{\text{Second term} - \text{Third term}}$$

(4.4) RELATION BETWEEN ARITHMETIC MEAN (A.M.), GEOMETRIC MEAN (G.M.) AND HARMONIC MEAN (H.M.)

If a and b are two real and positive numbers or quantities or (AM). (HM) = $(GM)^2$, then :

(i) $AH = G^2$ *i.e.,* A, G, H are in G.P.

(ii) A > G > H *i.e.,* A, G, H are in descending order.

(iii) AM ≥ GM ≥ HM, Sign of equality holds, *i.e.,* AM = GM = HM when two quantities are equal.

Proof (i) : a and b are two numbers then

$$\text{Arithmetic Mean } A = \frac{a+b}{2}$$

$$\text{Geometric Mean } G = \sqrt{ab}$$

$$\text{Harmonic Mean } H = \frac{2ab}{a+b}$$

$$\therefore \quad AH = \frac{a+b}{2} \times \frac{2ab}{a+b}$$

$$= ab = G^2$$

$$\therefore \quad AH = G^2$$

$\therefore$ A, G, H are in G.P.

Proof (ii) : $A - G = \frac{a+b}{2} - \sqrt{ab}$

$$= \frac{a+b-2\sqrt{ab}}{2}$$

$$= \frac{(\sqrt{a}-\sqrt{b})^2}{2} = \text{Positive number}$$

$$\therefore \quad \boxed{A > G}$$

$$\text{and } G - H = \sqrt{ab} - \frac{2ab}{a+b}$$

$$= \frac{\sqrt{ab}(a+b)-2ab}{a+b}$$

$$= \frac{\sqrt{ab}\left[a+b-2\sqrt{ab}\right]}{a+b}$$

$$= \frac{\sqrt{ab}\left(\sqrt{a}-\sqrt{b}\right)^2}{a+b} = \text{Positive number}$$

$$\boxed{G > H}$$

On combining these two relations

A > G > H

Proved

Three numbers a, b, c will be in A.P., G.P. and H.P. if

$$\frac{a-b}{b-c} = \frac{a}{a} = \frac{a}{b} = \frac{a}{c} \text{ respectively}$$

(i) $\because \quad \frac{a-b}{b-c} = \frac{a}{a} = 1$

$\Rightarrow \quad a - b = b - c$

$\Rightarrow \quad a + b = 2b$

$\Rightarrow \quad b = \frac{a+c}{2}$

$\therefore$ a, b, c are in A.P.

(ii) $\because \quad \frac{a-b}{b-c} = \frac{a}{b}$

$\Rightarrow \quad ab - b^2 = ab - ac$

$\Rightarrow \quad b^2 = ac$

$\therefore$ a, b, c are in G.P.

(iii) $\because \quad \frac{a-b}{b-c} = \frac{a}{c}$

$\Rightarrow \quad ac - bc = ab - ac$

$\Rightarrow \quad 2ac = bc + ab$

$\Rightarrow \quad 2ac = b(c + a)$

$\Rightarrow \quad b = \frac{2ac}{a+c}$

$\therefore$ a, b, c are in H.P.

Example 9

A.M. and G.M. between two real and positive numbers are 9 and 6 respectively, then find the harmonic mean between them.

Solution :

Given $A = 9, G = 6$

$\because$ $G^2 = AH$ [from formula]

$\therefore$ $H = \dfrac{G^2}{A} = \dfrac{(6)^2}{9}$

$= \dfrac{6\times 6}{9} = 4$

Example 10

If a, b, c are in A.P., b, c, d are in G.P. and c, d, e are in H.P., then prove that a, c, e are in G.P.

Solution :

$\because$ a, b, c are in A.P.

$\therefore$ $b = \dfrac{a+c}{2}$ ...(i)

$\because$ b, c, d are in G.P. $c^2 = bd$ ...(ii)

$\because$ c, d, e are in H.P. $d = \dfrac{2ce}{c+e}$ ...(iii)

Putting the value of b and d in equation (2),

$c^2 = \left(\dfrac{a+c}{2}\right)\left(\dfrac{2ce}{c+e}\right)$

$\Rightarrow$ $c = \dfrac{e(a+c)}{c+e}$

$\Rightarrow$ $c(c+e) = e(a+c)$

$\Rightarrow$ $c^2 + ce = ae + ce$

$\Rightarrow$ $c^2 = ae$

i.e., a, c, e are in G.P.

Example 11

If a, b, c are in A.P. and a, mb, c in G.P., then prove that a, m^2b, c will be in H.P.

Solution :

$\because$ a, b, c are in A.P. $b = \dfrac{a+c}{2}$ ...(i)

$\because$ a, mb, c are in G.P.

$\therefore$ $m^2b^2 = ac$ ...(ii)

Dividing eq. (2) by eq. (1),

$\dfrac{m^2b^2}{b} = \dfrac{ac}{\frac{a+c}{2}}$

$\Rightarrow$ $m^2b = \dfrac{2ac}{a+c}$

a, m^2b, c are in H.P.

Example 12

If a, b, c, d are in H.P., prove that

$ab + bc + cd = 3ad$

Solution :

$\because$ a, b, c are H.P.

$\therefore$ $b = \dfrac{2ac}{a+c}$

$\Rightarrow$ $a + c = \dfrac{2ac}{b}$ ...(i)

$\because$ b, c, d are in H.P.

$\therefore$ $c = \dfrac{2bd}{b+d}$

$\Rightarrow$ $b + d = \dfrac{2bd}{c}$ ...(ii)

Multiplying eq. (i) and eq. (ii),

$(a+c)(b+d) = \dfrac{2ac}{b}\times\dfrac{2bd}{c}$

$\Rightarrow$ $ab + ad + bc + cd = 4ad$

$\Rightarrow$ $ab + bc + cd = 4ad - ad$

$\therefore$ $ab + bc + cd = 3ad$ **Proved**

Exercise 4

1. The sum of n terms of an A.P. is $3n^2 + 2n$, then find its pth term.
2. Find the sum of n arithmetic means between x and $3x$.
3. The sum of four terms of an A.P. 4 and the sum of product of first and last term and product of middle terms is -38, then find the numbers.
4. The sides of a right angled triangle are in A.P., prove that they are in the ratio of 3 : 4 : 5.
5. If a,b,c are in A.P. prove that $a\left(\dfrac{1}{b}+\dfrac{1}{c}\right), b\left(\dfrac{1}{c}+\dfrac{1}{a}\right), c\left(\dfrac{1}{a}+\dfrac{1}{b}\right)$ are also in A.P.
6. If $\dfrac{1}{3}, a, b, c, d, e, f, g, 432$ are in G.P., then find the product of c and e.
7. If arithmetic mean and geometric mean between two numbers are 20 and 16 respectively, then find the numbers.
8. Three numbers, whose sum is 15, are in A.P. If 1, 4, 9 be added to them respectively, they are in G.P., find the numbers.
9. If G be the G.M. between two given numbers and A_1, A_2 be the two A.M.s between them, prove that :
   $G^2 = (2A_1 - A_2)(2A_2 - A_1)$
10. If $(a + b)$, $2b$, $(b + c)$ are in H.P. then prove that a, b, c are in G.P.
11. Find two positive numbers whose difference is 12 and whose A.M. exceeds the G.M. by 2.
12. Find the sum of series :
    $\dfrac{3}{4} - \dfrac{5}{4^2} + \dfrac{3}{4^3} - \dfrac{5}{4^4} + \dfrac{3}{4^5} - \dfrac{5}{4^6} + \ldots\ldots$ upto infinite terms.

Answers

1. $6p - 1$ 2. $2nx$ 3. $-5, -1, 3, 7$ 6. 144
7. 8, 32 8. 26, 5, -16 or 2, 5, 8
11. 16 and 4 12. $\dfrac{7}{15}$

❑ Short Answer Type Questions

1. State any three properties of a A.P.
2. State any three properties of a G.P.
3. Explain the relationship among Arithmetic mean, Geometric mean and Harmonic mean of two quantities.

5

PERMUTATION AND COMBINATION

LEARNING OBJECTIVES

After studying this chapter, you will be able to know :

- **5.1 Permutation**
- **5.2 Fundamental Principle of Counting**
  - **To find the number of permutation of *n* different things taken *r* at a time.**
  - **To find the number of permutations of *n* different things taken *r* at a time when each thing can be repeated *r* times.**
- **5.3 Circular Permutation**
- **5.4 Combination**
  - **Definition**
  - **To find the number of combinations of *n* different things taken *r* at a time.**
  - **Properties of ^nC_r.**

SOLVED EXAMPLES AND PRACTICAL PROBLEMS : AT A GLANCE

No. of Examples		*No. of Problems*
	Permutation	
1 to 6	Type I : Short Answer Type Questions	Exercise 5 (A) 1 to 19
7 to 10	Type II : Long Answer Type Questions	Exercise 5(A) 1 to 21
11 to 12	Type III : Long Answer Type Questions	
13 to 14	Type IV : Long Answer Type Questions	
15 to 25	Type V : Long Answer Type Questions	
26 to 28	Circular Permutation	Exercise 5(B) 1 to 10
	Combination	
1A to 7(C)	Short Answer Type Questions	Exercise 5(C) 1 to 18
8 to 23	Long Answer Type Questions	Exercise 5(C) 1 to 16
	Objective Type Questions	Exercise 5(D) 24 + 2 + 5
51	**Total**	**84 + 31**

(5.1) PERMUTATION

Definition : Each of the different arrangements which can be made by taking some or all of a number of given things or object at a time is called permutation.

Example : (1) Consider two letters A and B. Supposing we are asked to select two things out of the two letters. This can be done in only one way by selecting both A and B and putting it together AB.

If we are asked to arrange there two letters by taking both at a time, this we can do it by two ways by writing (i) AB or (ii) BA. Thus, in this case of arrangement the order of appearance of A and B is important.

(2) If we are given three things, say a, b and c and asked to select two things at a time, this we can do it by arranging them in the following way :

ab, ba, ac, ea, bc, cb

Thus, we have two types of classification of things (i) selection and (ii) arrangement selection of things is called combination and the arrangements of things is called permutation. In the above example, *ab, ba, ac, ca, bc, cb* each is called permutation. Here the number of permutation is 6.

(3) The permutations of the three things, namely a, b and c taken all at a time are :

abc, bca, cab, bac, acb, cba

Here also, the number of permutations is 6.

However, permutations of the three things a, b and c taken one at a time will be 3 only.

(4) Similarly, the permutations of four things. A, B, C and D taken two at a time will be as follows :

AB, AC, AD, BC, BD, CD, BA, CA, DA, CB, DB, DC

In this case the number of permutations is 12.

Notation for Permutation

The number of permutations of n different objects taking r at a time is denoted by the symbol ^nP_r.

where,

$$^nP_r = \frac{\text{Product of first } n \text{ natural numbers}}{\text{Product of first } (n-1) \text{ natural numbers}}$$

Some Symbols

Factorial *n* : The product of first n natural numbers is denoted by $|\underline{n}$ or by $n!$ and read as 'factorial n'.

Thus $\quad |\underline{n} = 1.\ 2.\ 3.4.\ \ldots\ldots\ldots\ (n-1)\ n$

$\qquad\quad = n\ (n-1)\ (n-2)\ \ldots\ldots\ 4.3.2.1.$

Example $\quad |\underline{4} = 1.2.3.4.5.$

$\qquad\quad = 120 = 5.4.3.2.1.$

$\qquad |\underline{4} = 1.2.3.4 = 24 = 4.3.2.1.$

Some results related to factorial *n* :

(1) $\quad |\underline{n} = 1.2.3\ \ldots\ldots\ (n-1)\ n$

$\qquad = \{1.2.3.\ \ldots\ldots\ (n-1)\}n$

Home $\quad |\underline{n} = n\ |\underline{n-1}$

Similarly $\quad |\underline{(n-1)} = (n-1)\ |\underline{n-2}$

Thus $\quad |\underline{n} = n\ |\underline{n-1}$

$\qquad = n\ (n-1)\ |\underline{n-2}$

$\qquad = n\ (n-1)\ (n-2)\ |\underline{n-3}$ etc.

(2) If n and r are positive integers, then

$$\frac{n!}{r!} = \frac{1.2.3.\ldots\ldots n}{1.2.3.\ldots\ldots r}$$

$$= \frac{1.2.3.\ \ldots\ldots\ (r-1)\ r\ \ (r+1)\ (r+2)\ \ldots\ldots\ (n-1)\ n}{1.2.3.\ (r-1)\ r}$$

$= (r+1)\ (r-2)\ \ldots\ldots\ (n-1)\ n$

$= n\ (n-1)\ (n-2)\ \ldots\ldots\ (r+1)$

$$\frac{|\underline{n}}{|\underline{n-1}} = \frac{1.2.3.\ \ldots\ldots\ (n-r)\ (n-r+1)\ \ (n-r+2)\ \ldots\ldots\ (n-1)\ n}{1.2.3\ (n-r)}$$

$= (n-r+1)\ (n-r+2)\ \ldots\ldots\ (n-1)\ n$

$= n\ (n-1)\ (n-2)\ \ldots\ldots\ (n-r+2)\ (n-r+1)$

$= n\ (n-1)\ (n-2)\ \ldots\ldots\ r$

> **Remarks** : Factorial n! is defined for positive integers only. Factorials of proper functions or negative integers are not defined. Zero factorial is assumed to be = 1

(5.2) FUNDAMENTAL PRINCIPLE OF COUNTING

(1) **Multiplication Rule :** If a work can be done independently in m different ways and another work can be done independently in n different ways, then number of ways of doing the work together $m \times n$ ways

Generalisation of Principle : If a work can be done independently in p different ways, the second work after this can be done independently in q different ways. The third work after the second can be done independently in r different ways. The fourth work after the third can be done independently in s different ways........etc.

Then number of ways to do all the work together =

$p \times q \times r \times s \times \ldots\ldots$

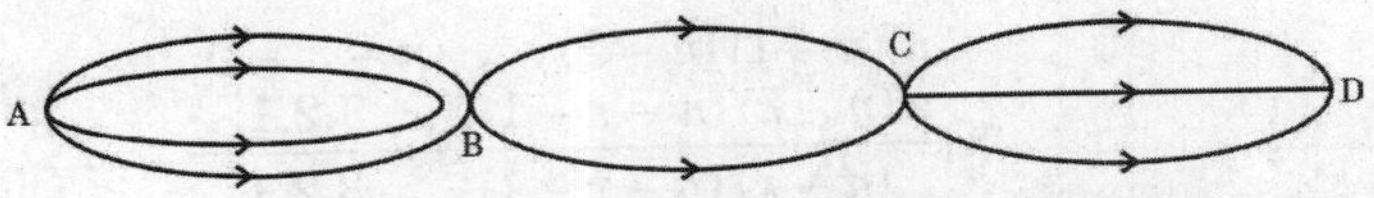

There are four trains between A and B, there are two trains between B and C. If there is a train in each route, then number of ways to reach A to C = 4 × 2 = 8. Similarly if there are three trains between C and D, then total number of ways to reach A to D = 4 × 2 × 3 = 24.

(2) **Addition Rule :** If a work A can be done in m ways and another work B can be done in n ways and C is a work which is done only when either A or B is done, then number of ways of doing the work C is $(m+n)$ ways.

To Find the Number of Permutation of *n* Different things taken *r* at a Time

Or

To establish the formula

$$^np_r = \frac{|\underline{n}}{|\underline{(n-r)}} \text{ or } ^nP_r = \frac{n!}{(n-r)!}$$

Proof : $\quad ^np_r$ = Number of permutations of r different things out of n different things.

= Number of ways of filling up r vacant places with n different ways.

Let the n different things be a_1, a_2, a_3 .... a_n

1st	2nd	3rd	..... (r – 1)th	rth
↓	↓	↓		↓
n ways	$(n-1)$ ways	$(n-2)$ ways		$(n-r+1)$ ways

First place can be filled up by any one of n things a_1, a_2. a_3 ,.........., a_n in n ways.

Number of things left after filling up the first place $= (n-1)$

Second place can be filled up by any one of the remaining $(n-1)$ things in $(n-1)$ ways.

Number of things left after fling up the first and second place $= (n-2)$

Third place can be filled by any one of the remaining $(n-2)$ things in $(n-2)$ ways.

Thus number of ways of filling up first place $= n$

Number of ways of filling up second place $= (n-1)$

Number of ways of filling up third place $= (n-2)$

Number of ways of filling up fourth place $= (n-3)$

....

....

Number of ways of filling up rth place $= n-(r-1)$
$= n-r+1$

By the multiplication rule of counting first, second, third, fourth,....,rth places can be together filled up
$= n(n-1)(n-2)$ .... $(n-r+1)$ ways

Hence $^np_r = n(n-1)(n-2)$ .... $(n-r+1)$

$$= \frac{n(n-1)(n-2)\ldots\ldots(n-r+1) \times (n-r)(n-r-1)\ldots\ldots 3.2.1.}{(n-r)(n-r-1)\ldots\ldots 3.2.1.}$$

Then $^np_r = \dfrac{\underline{|n}}{\underline{|(n-r)}}$ or $\dfrac{n!}{(n-r)!}$

Number of permutations of n different things taken all at a time = $\underline{|n}$

Proof :

1st	2nd	3rd	.....	nth
↓	↓	↓		↓
n ways	$(n-1)$ ways	$(n-2)$ ways		$(n-r+1)$ ways = 1 way

As above

Number of ways of filling up first place $= n$

Number of ways of filling up second place $= n-1$

Number of ways of filling up third place $= n-2$

....

....

Number of ways of filling up nth place $= n-(n-1)$
$= 1$

By multiplication rule, number of ways of filling up first, second, third,....., nth place together.

$$^np_r = n(n-1)(n-2) \ldots\ldots 3.2.1 = \underline{|n}$$

Thus $^np_r = \underline{|n}$

Meaning of $\underline{|0}$

We know that

$$^np_r = \frac{\underline{|n}}{\underline{|(n-r)}}$$

Putting $r = n$

$$^np_r = \frac{\underline{|n}}{\underline{|n-n}} = \frac{\underline{|n}}{\underline{|0}} \quad \ldots(i)$$

But we know that

$$^np_r = \underline{|n} \quad \ldots(ii)$$

From (i) and (ii),

$$\frac{\underline{|n}}{\underline{|0}} = \underline{|n}$$

or $\underline{|0}\,.\,\underline{|n} = \underline{|n}$

or $\underline{|0} = \dfrac{\underline{|n}}{\underline{|n}}$

$\therefore$ $\underline{|0} = 1$

*** If r is a positive integer, then**

$$\frac{1}{\underline{|-r}} = 0$$

Proof : $\because\ ^np_r = \dfrac{\underline{|n}}{\underline{|n-r}}$ ...(i)

$^np_r = n(n-1)(n-2)$ .... $(n-r+1)$ ...(ii)

From (i) and (ii),

$$\frac{\underline{|n}}{\underline{|n-r}} = n(n-1)(n-2) \ldots\ldots\ldots (n-r+1) \ldots\text{(iii)}$$

Putting $n = 0$ in (iii),

$$\frac{\underline{|0}}{\underline{|0-r}} = 0$$

or $\dfrac{\underline{|1}}{\underline{|-r}} = 0$ **Proved**

*** To Find the Permutation of n things taking all at a time when things are not all Different**

Let total number of things $= n$

p things are identical and of one type, q things are identical and are of second type, r things are identical and are of third type and rest are all different.

Let the required number of permutations $= x$

Since p different things can be arranged among themselves in $\underline{|p}$ ways. Therefore, if we replace p identical things by p different things which are also different from the rest things, then number of permutation will become $x\,\underline{|p}$. Again if we replace q identical things by q different things, then number of permutations will become $x\underline{|p}\underline{|q}$. Again if we replace r identical things by r different things which are different from rest, then number of permutations will become $x \times \lfloor p \times \lfloor q \times \lfloor r$.

Now all the n things are different and therefore number of permutations should be $\lfloor n$.

Thus $\quad x \times \lfloor p \times \lfloor q \times \lfloor r = \lfloor n$

$$\therefore \quad x = \frac{\lfloor n}{\lfloor p \lfloor q \lfloor r}$$

Example : How many words can be formed with all the letters of the word 'Vice-chancellor'.

Solution : Here total number of letters = 14

In which 'c' occurs three times, 'l' occurs two times, and 'c' occurs two times, other letters are different to each other. So number of ways to arrange these letters among themselves $d = \dfrac{\lfloor 14}{\lfloor 3 \lfloor 2 \lfloor 2}$

To Find the Number of Permutations of *n* Different things taken *r* at a time when each thing can be repeated *r* times

1st Place	2nd	......	rth
↓	↓		↓
n ways	n ways		n ways

Number of permutations of n different things taken r at a time when repetition is allowed = Number of ways in which r blank places can be filled up by n different things when repetition is allowed.

Now first place can be filled up by any one of the n different things.

$\therefore$ Number of ways in which first place can be filled up = n

Number of ways in which second place can be filled up = n

....

....

Number of ways in which rth place can be filled up = n

Now by multiplication rule of fundamental principle of counting number of ways in which first, second, third,....., rth places can be together filled up

$= n \times n \times n$ .... r times

$= n^r$

Theorem : Prove that

$${}^np_r = r.{}^{n-1}p_{r-1} + {}^{n-1}p_r$$

Proof : $\quad {}^np_r = \dfrac{\lfloor n}{\lfloor n-1}$ ...(i)

Now

$$r.{}^{n-1}p_{r-1} + {}^{n-1}p_r = \frac{r\lfloor n-1}{\lfloor n-r} + \frac{\lfloor n-r}{\lfloor n-r-1}$$

$$= \frac{r\lfloor n-1}{\lfloor n-r} + (n-r)\frac{\lfloor n-1}{\lfloor n-r}$$

$$= \frac{\lfloor n-r[r+n-r]}{\lfloor n-r}$$

$$= \frac{n\lfloor n-1}{\lfloor n-r}$$

$$= \frac{\lfloor n}{\lfloor n-r} = {}^np_r \quad \text{...(ii)}$$

From (i) and (ii), ${}^np_r = r.{}^{n-1}p_{r-1} + {}^{n-1}p_r$

Important Formulae to find out the Number of Permutations : At a Glance

1. Number of Permutations of n different things taken r at a time : ${}^np_r = \dfrac{\lfloor n}{\lfloor (n-r)}$ or $\dfrac{n!}{(n-r)!}$ *(JAC, 2023)*
2. Number of permutations of n distinguishable things taken all at a time :
   (a) ${}^nP_n = \lfloor n$ or $n!$ (without replacement)
   (b) ${}^nP_n = n^n$ (with replacement)
   Here, ${}^nP_n = \dfrac{n!}{(n-n)!} = \dfrac{n!}{0!} = n!$ $(\because 0! = 1)$
3. Number of permutations of n things taken all at a time when p of them are alike and of one kind, q of them are alike and of second kind and r things are alike and third kind and so on, then total number of permutations $= \dfrac{n!}{p!q!r!.....}$ or $\dfrac{\lfloor n}{\lfloor p \lfloor q \lfloor r....}$
4. Number of permutation of n distinguishable things taken r at a time when a particular thing is selected each time :
   ${}^np_r = r \times {}^{n-1}P_{r-1} = {}^{n-1}P_{r-1} + {}^{n-1}P_{r-1} +$ ...., r times.
5. Total number of permutations of a dissimilar things taken r at a time with repetition = n^r
6. **Circular Permutation** : To find the number of circular permutation of n different things taken r at a time.

   Case 1 : The number of permutation of n distinct objects to a circle if their anticlockwise and clockwise orders are distinct = $\lfloor n-1$ or $(n-1)!$ and the total number when taken r at time will be $\dfrac{{}^nP_r}{r}$.

   Case 2 : If no distinction is made between anticlockwise and clockwise order : Total number of circular permutations of n things taken all at a time is $\dfrac{(n-1)!}{2}$ or $\dfrac{1}{2}\lfloor n-1$ and the total number when taken r at n time will be $\dfrac{{}^nP_r}{2r}$.

SOLVED EXAMPLES

✎ Type I

❐ Short Answer Type Questions

Example 1

The value of $^7p_4$ is : *(JAC, 2022)*

Solution :

$$^7p_4 = \frac{7!}{(7-4)!} = \frac{7!}{3!}$$

$$= \frac{7\times6\times5\times4\times3!}{3!}$$

$$= 7\times6\times5\times4$$

$$= 840$$ **Ans.**

Example 2

If $^np_5 = 20 \times {}^np_3$, then find the value of n.

Solution :

$$^np_5 = 20 \times {}^np_3$$

or $$\frac{\underline{|n}}{\underline{|n-5}} = 20 \times \frac{\underline{|n}}{\underline{|n-3}}$$

or $$\frac{\underline{|n}}{\underline{|n-5}} = \frac{20 \times \underline{|n}}{(n-3)(n-4)\underline{|n-5}}$$

or $(n-3)(n-4) = 20$

or $(n-3)(n-4) = 5\times4$

or $n-3 = 5$

$\therefore$ $n = 8$ **Ans.**

Example 3

If $^np_4 = 360$, then find the value of n.

Solution :

$\because$ $^np_4 = 360$

$\therefore$ $$\frac{\underline{|n}}{\underline{|n-4}} = 360$$

or $n(n-1)(n-2)(n-3) = 360 = 6\times5\times4\times3$

$\therefore$ $n = 6$ **Ans.**

Example 4

Find the value of r, if $^6p_r = 30$.

Solution :

$\because$ $^6p_r = 30$

$\therefore$ $6\times5\times$ .... r factors $= 6\times5$

$\therefore$ $r = 2$ **Ans.**

Example 5

If $^{22}p_{r+1} : {}^{20}p_{r+2} = 11 : 52$, then find the value of r.

Solution : $$\frac{^{22}p_{r+1}}{^{20}p_{r+2}} = \frac{11}{52}$$

$$\frac{\dfrac{\underline{|22}}{\underline{|21-r}}}{\dfrac{\underline{|20}}{\underline{|18-r}}} = \frac{11}{52}$$

or $$\frac{22\times21\times\underline{|20}}{\underline{|20}} \times \frac{\underline{|18-r}}{(21-r)(20-r)(19-r)\underline{|18-r}} = \frac{11}{52}$$

or $$\frac{22\times21}{(21-r)(20-r)(19-r)} = \frac{11}{52}$$

or $(21-r)(20-r)(19-r) = 2\times21\times52$

$= 12\times13\times14$

$21-r = 14$

$\therefore$ $r = 7$ **Ans.**

Example 6

If $^9P_r = 3024$, find the value of r. *(JAC, 2018)*

Solution :

$$^9P_r = 3024$$

$\Rightarrow$ $$\frac{\underline{|9}}{\underline{|9-r}} = 3024$$

$\Rightarrow$ $$\frac{9\times8\times7\times6\times\underline{|5}}{\underline{|9-r}} = 3024$$

$\Rightarrow$ $$\frac{9\times8\times7\times6\times\underline{|5}}{3024} = \underline{|9-r}$$

$\Rightarrow$ $\underline{|5} = \underline{|9-r}$

$\Rightarrow$ $\underline{|9-4} = \underline{|9-r}$

$r = 4$

✎ Type II

❐ Long Answer Type Questions

Example 7

How many numbers between 400 and 1000 can be made with the digits 2, 3, 4, 5, 6 and 0 ?

Solution :

Here nothing has been given about repetition of digits, therefore we will assume that repetition of digits is not allowed.

Any number between 400 and 1000 will be three digits

4 or 5 or 6		
↓ 3 types		↓ $^5p_2$

Since the number should be greater than 400, therefore hundred place can be filled up by any one of the three digits, 4, 5 and 6 in 3 ways.

Remaining two places can be filled up be remaining five digits in $^5p_2$ ways.

$\because$ Required number $= 3 \times {}^5p_2$

$$= 3 \times \frac{\underline{|5}}{\underline{|5-2}} = 3 \times \frac{\underline{|5}}{\underline{|3}}$$

$= 3\times5\times4 = 60$ **Ans.**

Example 8

How many even numbers of four digits can be formed with the digits 0, 1, 2, 3, 4, 5 and 6, no digit being used more than once ?

Solution :

Each even number must have 0, 2, 4 or 6 in its units place. Here total number of digits = 7

			0 or 2 or 4 or 6

When 0 occurs at units place, there is no restriction on other places and when 2 or 4 or 6 occurs at units place, there is restriction on thousand places as 0 can not be put at thousand place.

Case I. When 0 occurs at unit place :

			0
${}^6p_3$ ways			1 way

Units place can be filled up with 0 in 1 way and remaining three places can be filled up by remaining 6 digits in ${}^6p_3$.

∴ Number of numbers formed in this case

$$= 1 \times {}^6p_3$$

$$= \frac{|\underline{6}}{|\underline{(6-3)}} = \frac{|\underline{6}}{|\underline{3}}$$

$$= \frac{6 \times 5 \times 4|\underline{3}}{|\underline{3}}$$

$$= 6 \times 5 \times 4 = 120$$

Case II. When 0 does not occur at unit place :

Any one of remaining six digits except zero			2 or 4 or 6
↓ 5 ways	${}^5p_2$ ways		↓ 3 way

Unit place an be filled up by any one of the three digits 2, 4 and 6 in 3 ways.

Thousands place can be filled up by any one of the remaining six digits except zero in 5 ways.

Remaining two places can be filled by any remaining five digits in ${}^5p_2$ ways.

∴Number of numbers formed in this case

$$= 3 \times 5 \times {}^5p_2$$

$$= 15 \times \frac{|\underline{5}}{|\underline{3}} = 300$$

∴ Required number = 120 + 300 = 420 **Ans.**

Example 9

Find the sum of all four digits numbers that can be formed with the digits 3, 2, 3, 4.

Solution :

To find the sum of all the numbers formed with 3, 2, 3, 4, it is neceseary to know in how many numbers each of 2, 3, 4 will be in the units place.

The number of numbers having 2 in the unitsplace

$$= \frac{|\underline{3}}{|\underline{2}} = 3$$

Since tens place, hundreds place and thousands place are to be filled up by 3, 3, 4.

The number of numbers having 3 in the units place

$$= |\underline{3} = 6$$

Since other three places are to be filled up by 3, 2, 4.

Similarly, the number of numbers having 4 in the units place

$$= \frac{|\underline{3}}{|\underline{2}} = 3$$

∴ The sum of the digits in the units place of all the numbers $= 3 \times 2 + 6 \times 3 + 3 \times 4$

$$= 6 + 18 + 12 = 36$$

Similarly the sum of the digits of all numbers in each of the other places = 36

∴The required sum

$$= 36 \times 1{,}000 + 36 \times 100 + 36 + 10 + 36 \times 1$$

$$= 36{,}000 + 3{,}600 + 360 + 36$$

$$= 36\,(1{,}000 + 100 + 10 + 1)$$

$$= 36 \times 1{,}111$$

$$= 39{,}996$$ **Ans.**

Example 10

Find the sum of all the 4 digits numbers that can be formed with the digits 1, 2, 3 and 4.

Solution :

Total number of digits = 4

Number of 4 digits are to be formed

∴ Number of numbers formed = ${}^4p_4 = 24$

Sum of the numbers formed.

When 2 occurs at units place

Number of numbers formed = ${}^3p_3 \times 1 = 6$

			2
${}^3p_3 = |\underline{3}$ ways			1 ways

Similarly 1, 2, 3 and 4 also occur $1 \times |\underline{3} = 6$ times at unit place, so the sum of numbers at unit place

$$= 6\,(1 + 2 + 3 + 4)$$

$$= 60$$

Similarly sum of digits at tens, hundreds and thousands places will be 60 each.

So sum of numbers formed.

$$= 60 \times 1 + 60 \times 10 + 60 \times 100 + 60 \times 1{,}000$$

$$= 60 + 600 + 6{,}000 + 60{,}000$$

$$= 66{,}660$$ **Ans.**

✎ Type III

Example 11

In how many ways 3 prizes can be given away to 7 boys when each boy is eligible for any of the prizes.

Solution :

Each of the three prizes can be given away to any one of the 7 days.

So, number of ways of distribute the first prize = 7

Similarly, number of ways to distribute the second prize = 7

Number of ways to distribute the third prize = 7

So required ways to distribute the three prizes among 7 days = $7 \times 7 \times 7 = 343$ **Ans.**

Example 12

A gentleman has 6 friends of invite. In how many ways can he send invitation cards to them, if he has three servants to carry the cards.

Solution :

Invitation cards may be sent to each of the 6 friends by any one of the three servants.

So number of ways to invite the first friend = 3

Similarly, number of ways to invite the second friend = 3

Other remaining friends also can be invite by 3 ways each.

So required number of ways to sent the invitation cards

$$= 3 \times 3 \times 3 \times 3 \times 3 \times 3$$
$$= (3)^6 = 729$$ **Ans.**

✎ Type IV

Example 13

There are two books each of three volumes and two books each of two volumes. In how many ways can be ten books be arranged on a long table so that the volumes of the same book are not separated.

Solution :

According to question, there are four types of books.

Number of volumes of first book = 3

Number of volumes of second book = 3

Number of volumes of third book = 2

Number of volumes of fourth book = 2

If we assume one book for all the volumes of same book, then number of books = 4

Number of ways to arrange these four books on a long table = ${}^4p_4 = \underline{|4}$

Again number of ways to arrange all the three volumes of first book among themselves = $\underline{|3}$

Similarly three volumes of the second book can be arranged among themselves by $\underline{|3}$ ways.

Number of ways to arrange the two volumes of the third book = $\underline{|2}$

Thus required number of ways to arrange these ten books on a long table

$$= \underline{|4}\ \underline{|3}\ \underline{|3}\ \underline{|2}\ \underline{|2}$$
$$= 24 \times 6 \times 6 \times 2 \times 2$$
$$= 3,456$$ **Ans.**

Example 14

In how many ways can 8 Indians, 4 Americans and Englishmen be seated in a row so that all persons of the same nationality sit together.

Solution :

Assuming all persons of the same nationality as one person we have only three persons.

These three persons can be seated in a row in $\underline{|3}$ ways.

But 8 Indians can be arranged among themselves in $\underline{|8}$ ways; 4 Americans can be arranged among themselves in $\underline{|4}$ ways and 4 Englishmen can be arranged among themselves in $\underline{|4}$ ways.

$\therefore$ Required number = $\underline{|3}\ \underline{|8}\ \underline{|4}\ \underline{|4}$ **Ans.**

✎ Type V

Example 15

In how many ways 4 boys and 4 girls can be seated in a row so that boys and girls are alternate.

Solution :

Case I. When a boy sits at the first place. Possible arrangement will be of the form

B	G	B	G	B	G	B	G

Now there are four places namely. 1st, 3rd, 5th and 7th for four boys, therefore four boys can be seated in $\underline{|4}$ ways. Again there are four places namely 2nd, 4th, 6th and 8th for four girls.

$\therefore$ four Girls can be seated in $\underline{|4}$ ways in the case $= \underline{|4}\,.\underline{|4}$

Case II. When a girl sits at the first place. Possible arrangement will be of the form

G	B	G	B	G	B	G	B

$\therefore$ Number of arrangement in this case

$$= \underline{|4}\,.\underline{|4}$$

$\therefore$ Required number $= \underline{|4}\,.\underline{|4} + \underline{|4}\,.\underline{|4}$

$$= 2(\underline{|4}\,.\underline{|4})$$
$$= 2,112$$ **Ans.**

Example 16

In how many ways can 7 I. A. and 5 I. Sc. students be seated in a row so that no two of the I. Sc. students may sit together ?

Solution :

Here, there is no restriction on I.A. students, therefore, first we must fix the position of 7 I.A. students.

I. A.	I. A.	I. A.	I. A.	I. A.	I. A.	I. A.

×	I.A.	×	I.A.	×	I.A.	×	I.A.	×	I.A.	×	I.A.	×	I.A.	×

Now 7 I.A. students can be seated in a row in $\underline{|7}$ ways.

Now if I. Sc. students sit at the place (Including the two ends) indicated by 'x', then no two of the five I.Sc. students will come together.

Now there are 8 places for 5 I.Sc. students.

The five I.Sc. students can be seated in ${}^8p_5$ ways.

∴ Required number of ways in which 7 I.A. students and 5 I.Sc. students can sit

$$= {}^8p_5 \times \underline{|7} = \frac{\underline{|8}}{\underline{|3}} \times \underline{|7} \quad \textbf{Ans.}$$

Example 17(A)

There are 5 boys and 3 girls. In how many ways can they be seated in a row so that three girls do not sit together.

Solution :

Total number of persons = 5 + 3 = 8

When there is no restriction, they can be seated in a row in $\underline{|8}$ ways.

But when all the three girls sit together regarding the three girls as one person, we have only 5 + 1 = 6 persons.

These 6 persons can be arranged in a row in $\underline{|6}$ ways.

But the three girls can be arranged among themselves in $\underline{|6}$ ways.

∴ Number of ways when three girls are together = $\underline{|6}\,\underline{|3}$ ways.

∴ Required number of ways in which all the three girls do not sit together

$$= \underline{|8} - \underline{|6}\,\underline{|3}$$
$$= \underline{|6}\,(8-7-6)$$
$$= 50 \times \underline{|6} = 36{,}000 \quad \textbf{Ans.}$$

Example 17(B)

In how many ways 5 boys and 4 girls can be seated in a row so that no two girls are together ? (*JAC*, 2024)

Solution :

5 boys can be seated in a row in $5\,P_5 = 5! = 120$ ways

In each of these arrangement 6 places are seated, shown by the letter G as given below

G	B	G	B	G	B	G	B	G	B	G

Since no two girls are to sit together, so we may arrange 4 girls in 6 places. Thus 4 girls can be seated in $6P_4$ ways.

So total arrangements $= 120 \times 6\,P_4$

$$= 120 \times 6 \times 5 \times 4 \times 3$$
$$= 43{,}200 \quad \textbf{Ans.}$$

Example 18

In how many ways can 10 different questions in an examination paper be arranged so that (i) best and worst always come together, (ii) they never come together ?

Solution :

The number of permutations of 10 papers when there is no restriction = $\underline{|10}$

(i) When the best and the worst papers come together, regarding the two or one paper.

Then number of papers = 9

Number of ways to arrange these 9 papers = $\underline{|9}$

But the two papers can be arranged among themselves in $\underline{|2}$ ways.

So number of permutation when the best and worst papers always come together

$$= \underline{|2}\,\underline{|9} = 2\underline{|9} \quad \textbf{Ans.}$$

(ii) So required number of arrangement when the best and the worst papers do not come together

$$= \underline{|10} - 2\,\underline{|9}$$
$$= 36{,}28{,}800 - 7{,}25{,}760$$
$$= 29{,}03{,}040 \quad \textbf{Ans.}$$

Example 19

In a town the car plate number contain only three or four digits, not containing the digit 0. What is the maximum number of cars that can be numbered ?

Solution :

Any number not containing the digit 0 can be made by the digits 1, 2, 3, 4, 5, 6, 7, 8, 9.

Case I. When the number plate is made of three non zero digits, then maximum number of number plates

$$= 9 \times 9 \times 9 = 9^3$$

As repetition of digits are allowed in number plate

↓	↓	↓
9	9	9

Case II. When the number plate is made of four non zero digits.

↓	↓	↓	↓
9	9	9	9

Then maximum number of number plates

$$= 9 \times 9 \times 9 \times 9 = 9^4$$

So Maximum number of cars

$$= 9^3 + 9^4 \quad \textbf{Ans.}$$

Example 20

In how many ways can a 10 questions multiple choice examination be answered if there are four choice, a, b, c and d to each question ? If no two consecutive questions are answered alike, how many ways are there?

Solution :

In the first part there is no restriction.

So number of ways to answer the first question = 4

Because there are four choice a, b, c and d for the first question.

Similarly number of ways to answer the second question = 4 and other remaining questions can also be answered in 4 ways each.

So number of ways to answer the ten questions

$= 4 \times 4 \times 4 \times 4 \times$ .... 10 times

$= 4^{10}$ **Ans.**

In the second part of the question there is a restriction that no two questions are answered the same so number of ways to answer the first question = 4

Since no two questions are answered the same. It means that the answer of the first question can not be the answer of the second question.

So answer of ways to answer the second question = 3

Similarly other remaining questions can also be answered in 3 ways each. So number of ways to answer the ten questions

$= 4 \times 3 \times 3 \times 3 \times 3 \times 3 \times 3 \times 3 \times 3 \times 3$

$= 4 \times 3^9$ **Ans.**

Permutation (Arrangements) of the Letters in a Word

While making various arrangements of the letters in a word, it is not necessary that word has a significant meaning. That is a 'word' in this sense (ordered arrangment or permutation) does not need to be meaningful word.

Restricted or Conditional Permutation : Sometimes arrangements are made with some conditions, for example, to place a particular letter at a particular place. In such a case, permutation is obtained by keeping in view the conditions and placing the remaining letters or things on remaining blank places.

Example 21

How many words can be formed with the letters of the word "LAHORE" ? How many words of them begin with L ?

Solution :

(i) Total number letters in the word "LAHORE" = 6

Here, all letters are different.

Hence, the number of arrangements of them 6 letters = $^6P_6$.

$= 6! = 6 \times 5 \times 4 \times 3 \times 2 \times 1 = 720$

(ii) Put L in the first place and arrange the rest. Now there are 5 (6 – 1) letters, all q them being different. Hence, Number of permutations which begin with L = $^5P_5$

$= 5! = 5 \times 4 \times 3 \times 2 \times 1 = 120$

Example 22

How many permutations can be formed from the letters of the word "MANGO"—(i) taking all the letters at a time, (ii) taking 3 letters at a time, (iii) talking all the letters at a time when 'M' may appear always in the beginning, (iv) taking all the letters provided 'M' may appear always in the beginning and 'O' always in the end.

Solution :

The number of letters in the word "MANGO" = 5

All letters are different.

(i) Taking all the letters, 5 different letters can be arranged in 5!.

$\therefore\ ^5P_5 = 5! = 5 \times 4 \times 3 \times 2 \times 1 = 120$ ways.

(ii) Taking 3 letters at a time,

No. of permutations = $^5P_3$

$$^5P_3 = \frac{5!}{3!} = \frac{5 \times 4 \times 3 \times 2 \times 1}{3 \times 2 \times 1} = 20$$

(iii) Taking all the letters at a time when 'M' may appear always in the beginning.

Now there are 5 – 1 = 4 letters.

Hence, $^4P_4 = 4! = 4 \times 3 \times 2 \times 1 = 24$

(iv) When 'M' always appear in the beginning and 'O' in the end

5 – 2 = 3 letters

Hence, $^3P_3 = 3! = 3 \times 2 \times 1 = 6$

Example 23

In how many ways can the letters of the word "Director" be arranged so that the three vowels are never together ? *(JAC, 2016, 19)*

Solution :

Number of letters in the word Director = 8

> *** Formula :** Number of permutation of n things when p things are similar and are of one type. q of them are similar and are of second type others are different = $\dfrac{\lfloor n}{\lfloor p \lfloor q}$

In which r occurs 2 times other letters are different to each other.

So number of ways to arrange these letters = $\dfrac{\lfloor 8}{\lfloor 2}$

= 20, 160

There are three vowels *i.e.*,o and five consonants in the word 'Director'.

When three vowels are together, assuming the 3 vowels as one letter.

Then number of letters = 5 + 1 = 6 in which r occurs 2 times.

So number of ways to arrange these 6 letters = $\dfrac{\lfloor 6}{\lfloor 2}$

= 360

Again number of ways to arrange the 3 vowels among themselves = $\lfloor 3$ = 6

So number of arrangements that all the three vowels are together

$= \dfrac{\lfloor 6}{\lfloor 2} \times \lfloor 3 = 360 \times 6$

= 2,160

So required number of arrangements that all the vowels are never together

= 20,160 – 2,160

= 18,000 **Ans.**

Example 24

In how many ways the letters of the word INTERMEDIATE can be arranged so that the vowels always occupy even places ?

Solution :

Number of letters in the word INTERMEDIATE = 12

In which 'I' occurs two times, 'E' occurs three times, T occurs two times, other letters are different to each other.

The word INTERMEDIATE contains six vowels I, E, E, I, A, E and six consonants N, T, R, M, D, T.

If we want to put in the vowels at even places, then there are six places for the vowels.

So number of ways to put the given six vowels at six even places $= \frac{\lfloor 6}{\lfloor 2 . \lfloor 3} = 60$

Again Number of ways to arrange the given six consonants among themselves

$$= \frac{\lfloor 6}{\lfloor 2} = 360$$

Thus number of ways to arrange the letters of the word INTERMEDIATE. So that the vowels always occurs at even places = 60 × 360 = 21,600 **Ans.**

Example 25

How many words can be formed with the letters of the word "Pataliputra" without changing the relative order of the vowels and consonants ? *(J.A.C., 2016)*

Solution :

Number of letters in the word 'Pataliputra' = 11

In which fire vowels and six consonants. The letter 'a' occurs three times, 't' occurs two times and 'p' occurs two times. Other letters are different to each other.

Since the relative order of the vowels and consonants cannot change so the vowels can put in only at the place of vowels and consonants can be put in the place of consonants. So number of ways to arrange the given five vowels among themselves.

$$= \frac{\lfloor 5}{\lfloor 3} = 20$$

Similarly number of ways to arrange the given six consonants among themselves

$$= \frac{\lfloor 6}{\lfloor 2 \lfloor 2} = 180$$

So Required number of words = 20 × 180 = 3,600 **Ans.**

Exercise 5 (A)

❑ Short Answer Type Questions

1. Find the values of: (i) ${}^6p_2$, (ii) ${}^{20}p_6$, (iii) ${}^{13}p_3$, (iv) ${}^{11}p_4$, (v) ${}^{10}p_2$ *(JAC, 2023, 24)*
2. (a) If ${}^{2n}p_3 = 100 \times {}^np_2$ find the value of n.
   (b) If ${}^np_4 = 12 \times {}^np_2$, find n. *(JAC, 2020, 23)*
3. If ${}^np_5 : {}^np_3 = 2 : 1$, find n.
4. If ${}^np_4 : {}^{n+1}p_4 = 3 : 4$, find n.
5. If ${}^{10}p_{n-1} : {}^{11}p_{n-2} = 30 : 11$, find n.
6. If ${}^{20}p_r = 6{,}840$, find r.
7. If ${}^{m+n}p_2 = 90$ and ${}^{m-n}p_2 = 30$, find m and n. *(JAC, 2020)*

[Hint : ${}^{m+n}p_2 = 90$

or $\frac{\lfloor m+n}{\lfloor m+n-2} = 90$

or $(m+n)(m+n-1) = 10 \times 9$

$\therefore$ $m+n = 10$ ...(i)

and ${}^{m-n}p_2 = 30$

or $\frac{\lfloor m-n}{\lfloor m-n-2} = 30$

or $(m-n)(m-n-1) = 6 \times 5$

$\therefore$ $m-n = 6$ ...(ii)

8. If ${}^{12}p_r = 11{,}880$, find r.
9. In how many ways 4 books can be selected out of 6 books ? Find also the permutation of the books selected.
10. (i) In how many ways can 10 seats in a bus be occupied by 4 passengers.
    (ii) In how many ways 6 prices can be distributed to 3 persons when each person is eligible for any of the prizes ?
11. (i) How many words can be formed with the letters of the word SUNDAY taken two at a time ?
    (ii) How many different words of 3 letters can be formed out of the letters of the word 'PRODUCT' ?
12. How many numbers between 100 and 1,000 can be made with the digits 1, 2, 3, 4, 5, 6, 7, 8, 9 ?
13. If ${}^np_3 = 60$, find n.
14. How many different words can be formed out of the letters of the following words ?
    (a) STATISTICS (b) ACCOUNTANCY
15. How many words can be formed by taking all the letters of the word 'MATHEMATICS' ?
16. How many words can be formed by taking all the letters from the following words ?
    (i) INDIA, (ii) BHARAT, (iii) BANKER, (iv) COMMITTEE
17. Find the number of arrangment that can be made out of the letters of the word BANANA. *(JAC, 2023)*
18. In how many ways 5 bulbs of different colours can be arranged in one live ?
19. In how many ways can the letters of the word 'DIRECTOR' be arranged ? *(JAC, 2025)*

Answers

1. (i) 30, (ii) 27907200, (iii) 1716, (iv) 7920, (v) 90 2. (a) $n = 13$, 2. (b) $n = 6$, 3. $n = 5$ 4. $n = 15$ 5. $n = 7$ 6. $r = 3$ 7. $m = 8, n = 2$ 8. $r = 4$ 9. 15, 360 10. (i) 5,040, (ii) 360 11. (i) 30, (ii) 210 12. 504 13. $n = 5$ 14. (a) 50,400; (b) 16,63,200 15. 49,89,600 16. (i) 60 (ii) 360, (iii) 720, (iv) 45360 17. 60 18. 120. 19. 10080 ways

❑ Long Answer Type Questions

1. In how many ways can three prizes be given away to 5 students when each student is eligible for any of the prizes?
2. In how many ways n things be given to p persons, when each person can get any number of things $(n > p)$?
3. How many numbers of 5 digits can be formed with the digits 0, 1, 2, 3, 4 ?
4. How many numbers between 100 and 1,000 can be formed with the digits 1, 2, 3, 4, 5, 6, 7. No digit being repeated.
5. How many numbers lying between 100 and 1,000 can be formed with the digits 2, 3, 4, 0, 8, 9, no digit being repeated?

6. Three are m men and n monkeys ($m < n$) If a man have any number of monkeys, in how many ways may every monkey have a master ?

[**Hint :** The way to give a master to first monkey = m

The way to give a master to second monkey = m

The way to give a master to third monkey = m

In this way the way of give the master to all n monkeys = $m \times m \times m \times$ ..... n times $= m^n$]

7. In how many ways 5 delegates can be put in 6 hotels of a city if there is no restriction ?

8. In how many ways 6 rings of different types can be had in 4 fingers ?

[**Hint :** No. of Fingers = 6

No. of different type rings = 6

Because any ring can wear in any finger from four fingers.

The way of wearing second ring = 4

This way the way of wearing all rings will be different = 4

So the total way of wearing all 6 rings in 4 fingers = $4 \times 4 \times 4 \times 4 \times 4 \times 4 = 4^6$]

9. How many different words can be formed with the letters of the word 'MATHEMATICS' ? In how many of them the vowels are together and consonants are together ?

10. In how many ways can the letters of the word 'BANARAS' be arranged so that the letters n and s are never together ?

11. 3 women and 5 men are to sit in a row for a dinner. Find in how many ways they can be arranged so that no two women sit next to each other ?

12. In a dinner party there are 10 Indians, 5 Americans and 5 Englishmen. In how many ways can they be arranged in a row so that all persons of the same nationality sit together ?

13. In a class of students there are 4 girls and 6 boys. In how many ways can they be seated in a row so that all the four girls are not together ?

14. In how many ways can the letters of the word 'VIOLENT' be arranged so that vowels occupy only the odd places ?

15. How many words can be formed by using the letters of the word 'BHARAT' ? How many of these words will not contain B and H together. How many of these start with B and end with T ?

16. Find the numbers of the words formed by the letters of the word 'DELHI' : Which (i) begin with D. (ii) End with I. (iii) The letter L being always in the middle. (iv) Begin with D and end with I.

17. (a) In how many different ways can the letters of the word 'SALOON' be arranged, if the consonants and vowels must occupy alternate places ?

(b) How many arrangements can be made of the letters of the word 'DRAUGHT' ? How many arrangements can be made where in the two vowels are not separated ?

18. How many different can be made of by hoisting 6 differently coloured flags one above the other when other number of them may be hoisted at once ?

19. How many words can be formed with the letters of the word "HAZIPUR" ? How many words of them begen with H ?

20. In how many ways 7 men and 7 women can stand in a straight line so that no two women stand togather.

21. In how many ways 3 boys and 5 girls can be arranged in a row so that :

(i) No two boys are together.

(ii) All the girls are together.

Answers

1. 5^3 2. p^n 3. 96 4. 210

5. 100 6. m^n, 7. 6^5 8. 4^6

9. $\left[\frac{\underline{|11}}{\underline{|2}\,\underline{|2}\,\underline{|2}}, \frac{\underline{|2}\,\underline{|7}\,\underline{|4}}{\underline{|2}\,\underline{|2}\,\underline{|2}}\right]$ 10. 600 11. $\underline{|5} \cdot {}^6p_3$

12. $\underline{|3}\,\underline{|10}\,\underline{|5}\,\underline{|5}$ 13. $\underline{|10}\;\underline{|7}\;\underline{|4}$

14. 576 15. 360, 240, 12

16. (i) 24, (ii) 24, (iii) 24, (iv) 6 17. (a) 36, (b) 5,040 ; 1,440

18. ${}^6p_1 + {}^6p_2 + {}^6p_3 + {}^6p_4 + {}^6p_5 + {}^6p_6 = 1{,}956$

19. (i) 5040, (ii) 720 20. $\underline{|7}\;\underline{|8}$

21. (i) 14400, (ii) 2880

5.3 CIRCULAR PERMUTATION

Definition : If all the given things are placed round the circumference of a circle, then each arrangement is called a circular permutation.

There is no end point in a circular permutation whereas there are two end points of a linear permutation.

Principle of Circular Permutation

If we take four letters A, B, C, D together, then they can form the following linear and cyclic permutation :

Linear—

A B C D   D A B C   C D B A   B C D A

Cyclic—

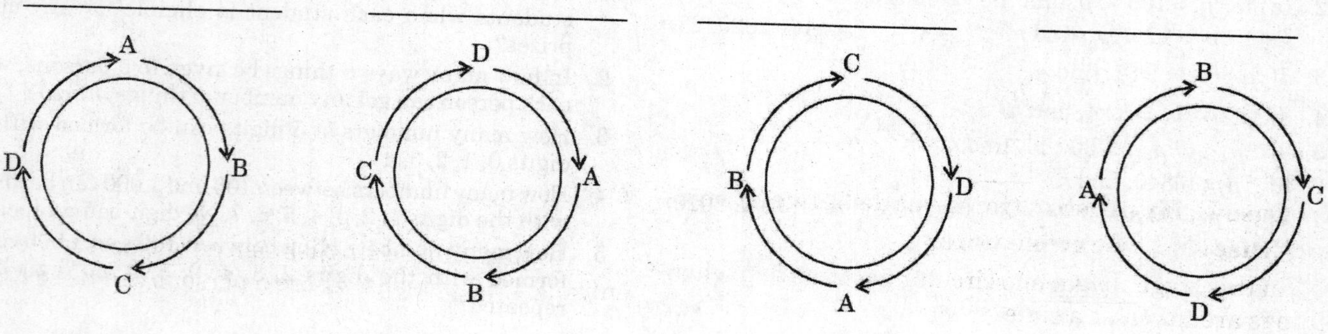

If we see the linear permutation of A, B, C, D, then we get four different arrrangements for the same relative order of the given letters. But if we arrange them in cyclic order, then all the arrangements are same which are show in the above figure. Thus we get only one circular permutation for the different linear permutation when some or all things are taken at a time. There are two types of circular permutation.

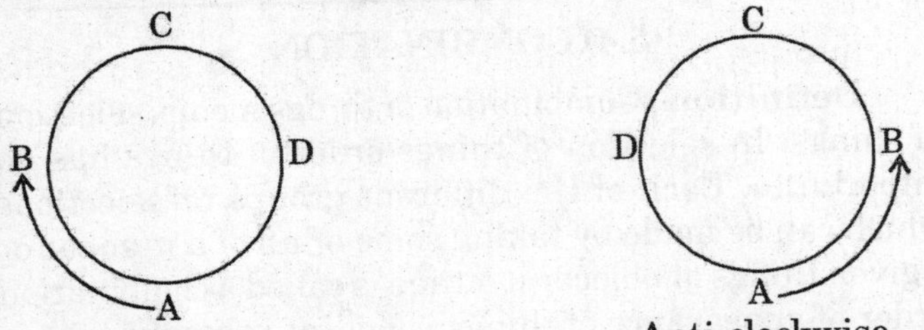

Clockwise Anti-clockwise

(1) In circular permutation, if anticlockwise and clockwise order arrangements are *distinct*, then permutations are different and in this case the number of permutations is $\lfloor n-1$ or $(n-1)!$.

(2) If in a circular permutations, the anti-clockwise and clockwise order of arrangements are *not distinct* them they are considered as the same permutations. This can be seen in the case of arrangements of beads or flowers around a circle. In this case, then number of permutations of n things, is $\frac{1}{2}(n-1)!$ or $\frac{\lfloor n-1}{2}$

To Find the Number of Circular Permutation of n different things taken r at a time

Let the number of circular permutation of n different things taken r at a time $= x$

Case I. When distinction is made between the anti-clockwise and clockwise order :

In this stage we get 'r' linear permutation for a circular permutation when r things are taken at a time.

So for x circular permutation number of linear permutations $= x.r$

But we know that number of linear permutation of n different things taken r at a time ^np_r.

So $\quad xr = {}^np_r$

$\therefore \quad x = \frac{{}^np_r}{r}$

If all the things are taken at a time, then $r = n$

So $\quad x = \frac{{}^np_r}{n}$

$\Rightarrow \quad x = \frac{\lfloor n}{\lfloor n} = \frac{n\lfloor n-1}{\lfloor n}$

$\therefore \quad x = \lfloor n-1$

Case II. If no distinction is made between anti-clockwise and clockwise order :

In this stage we get one circular permutation when r things are taken at a time.

So for x circular permutation number of linear permutation $= 2xr$

So $\quad 2xr = {}^np_r$

$\therefore \quad x = \frac{{}^np_r}{2r}$

If all the n things are taken at a time, then $r = n$

So $\quad x = \frac{{}^np_n}{2n} = \frac{\lfloor n}{2n} = \frac{1}{2}\frac{n\lfloor n-1}{n}$

$= \frac{1}{2}\lfloor n-1$

Example 26

In how many ways can 5 Indians and 5 Englishmen be seated along a circle so that they are alternate ?

Solution :

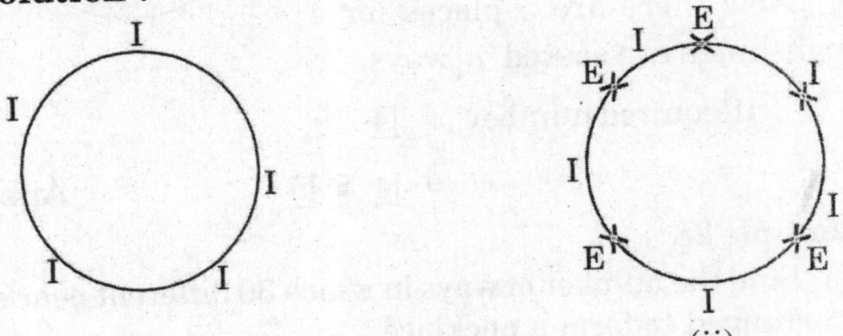

(i) (ii)

5 Indians an be seated along a circle in $\lfloor 4$ ways.

If the Englishmen sit at the places indicated by cross 'x', then Indians and Englishmen will be alternate.

Now there are 5 places for 5 Englishmen.

$\therefore$ 5 Englishmen can be seated in $\lfloor 5$ ways.

$\therefore$ Required number $= \lfloor 4.\lfloor 5$ **Ans.**

Example 27

In how many ways 5 Indians and 4 Englishmen can be seated at a round table if

(i) there is no restriction ?

(ii) all the four englishmen sit together ?

(iii) all the four Englishmen do not sit together ?

(iv) no two Englishmen sit together ?

Solution :

(i) Total number of persons = 5 + 4 = 9

These 9 persons can be seated at the round table in $\lfloor 8$ ways.

$\therefore$ Required number $= \lfloor 8$

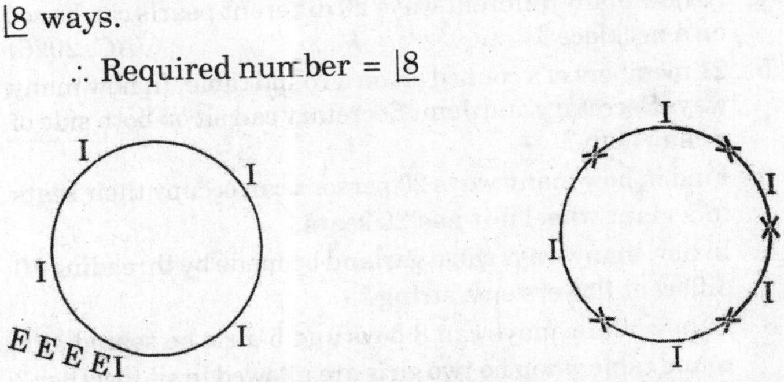

(ii) Regarding 4 Englishmen as one person we have only 5 + 1 = 6 persons. These 6 persons can be seated at the round table in $|\underline{5}$ ways but 4 Englishmen can be arranged among themselves in $|\underline{4}$ ways.

$\therefore$ Required number = $|\underline{5}.|\underline{4}$

(iii) Total number of arrangement when there is no restriction = $|\underline{8}$,

Number of arrangement when all four Englishmen do not sit together = $|\underline{8} - (|\underline{5} \times |\underline{4})$

(iv) Since there is no restriction on Indians therefore, first of all we arrange the 5 Indians.

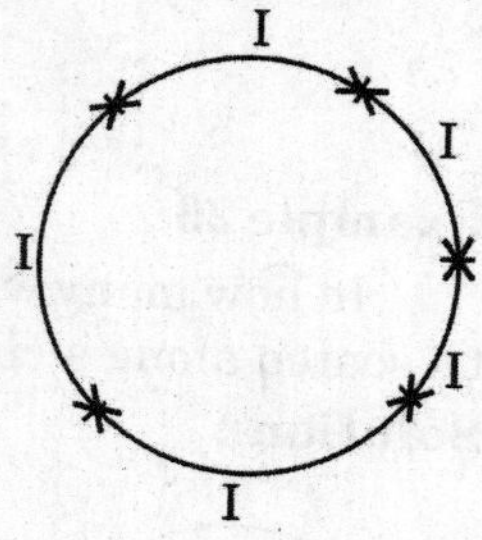

Now 5 Indians can be seated around a table in $|\underline{4}$ ways. If the Englishmen sit at the place indicated by '×', then no two Englishmen will $|\underline{5-1}$ sit together.

Now there are 5 places for 4 Englishmen can seated ${}^5p_4$ ways.

$\therefore$ Required number = $|\underline{4} \cdot {}^5p_4$

= $|\underline{4} \times |\underline{5}$ **Ans.**

Example 28

Find the number of ways in which 30 different pearls be arranged to form a necklace.

Solution :

Number of different pearls = 30

In a necklace the clockwise and anti-clockwise direction are same, so number of ways to arrange the 30 pearls

$$a = \frac{|\underline{30-1}}{2} = \frac{|\underline{29}}{2}$$ **Ans.**

Exercise 5 (B)

Problems based on Cyclic Permutation

1. In how many ways can 5 men sit around a table ?
2. In how many ways can 7 Englishmen and 6 Indians sit down around a table so that no two Indians are together ?
3. 4 Gentlemen and 4 Ladies are invited to a certain party. Find the number of ways of seating them around a table so that only ladies are seated on the two sides of each gentlemen ? *(JAC, 2016)*
4. In how many different ways 20 different pearls can be set on a necklace ? *(JAC, 2026)*
5. 21 members of a council sit on a round table. In how many ways Secretary and Joint Secretary can sit on both side of a chairman ?
6. Find in how many ways 20 persons can occupy their seats in a giant wheel if it has 20 seats.
7. In how many ways can a garland be made by threading 10 different flowers on a string ?
8. In how many mays can 8 boys and 5 girls be seated at a round table when no two girls are allowed to sit together ?
9. In how many ways can 7 men and 7 women be seated at a round table that no two ladies sit together ?
10. In how many ways can 8 persons be seated at a round table ?

Answers

1. 24	2. $|\underline{6}$; ${}^7p_6$	3. 144	4. ½, $|\underline{19}$
5. 18 ! × 1 × 2!	6. $|\underline{19}$	7. 9! × ½ = 181440	
8. 7! 5! or 5040 × 120		9. 6! 7! = 3628800	
10. 5040			

(5.4) COMBINATION

Definition : Combination of things means selection of things. In selection of things order of things has no importance. Each of the different groups or selections which can be made by taking some or all of a number or a given things or objects at a time is called a combination order of appearance of things is not into account.

Example 1. Following groups can be made with three different objects *a, b, c* taking two at a time.

ab, bc, ac

Hence *ab* and *ba* are the same group. Here it is also clear that for each combination (selection or group) of two things, number of permutations (arrangements) is $|\underline{2}$. For example, for combination *ab* there are two permutations *ab* and *ba*.

Example 2. Following four groups can be made with 4 different things *a, b, c, d* taking three at a time *abc, abd, acd, bcd*. Now for each combination (group) of three things, number of permutations is $|\underline{3}$ = 6. For example for the group *abc*, there are 6 permutations (arrangements) *abc, acb, bac, bca, cab, cba*.

To find the number of Combinations of *n* different things taken *r* at a time

or $${}^nC_r = \frac{|\underline{n}}{|\underline{r}\,|\underline{n-r}}$$

or $${}^nC_r = \frac{|\underline{n!}}{|\underline{r!}\,|\underline{(n-r)!}}$$

or $${}^nC_r = \frac{{}^nP_r}{r!}$$

Here

${}^nC_r$ = Number of Combinaitons with *r* things at a time

n = Number of all items

${}^np_r$ = Number of Combinations with *r* things at a time

r = Items taken together

$|\underline{or!}$ = Factorial

$|\underline{r}$ or $r!$ = Factorial *r* or number of permutations with a combination.

Proof : Number of combinations of *n* different things taken *r* at a time is ${}^nC_r$. Now each combination consists of *r* different things and these *r* things can be arranged among themselves in $|\underline{r}$ ways.

Thus for one combination of r different things.

Number of arrangements = $\underline{|r}$

For ^nC_r Combinations number of arrangemnets = $\underline{|r}\ ^nC_r$

But number of permutation of n different of n things taken r at a time = ^nP_r

$$\therefore \quad x.\ \underline{|r} = {}^nP_r$$

$$\text{or} \quad x.\ \underline{|r} = \frac{\underline{|n}}{\underline{|n-r}}$$

$$\text{or} \quad x = \frac{\underline{|n}}{\underline{|r}\,\underline{|n-r}}$$

$$\text{or} \quad {}^nC_r = \frac{\underline{|n}}{\underline{|r}\,\underline{|n-r}} = \frac{{}^nP_r}{\underline{|r}}$$

Some Important Results :

(i) $^nC_n = 1$

Proof : $\because$ $^nC_r = \dfrac{\underline{|n}}{\underline{|n}\,\underline{|n-r}}$

Putting $r = n$,

$$^nC_n = \frac{\underline{|n}}{\underline{|n}\,\underline{|n-n}}$$

$$= \frac{\underline{|1}}{\underline{|0}} = \frac{1}{1} = 1$$

(ii) $^nC_0 = 1$

Proof : $\because$ $^nC_r = \dfrac{\underline{|n}}{\underline{|r}\,\underline{|n-r}}$

Putting $r = 0$,

$$^nC_0 = \frac{\underline{|n}}{\underline{|0}\,\underline{|n-0}}$$

$$= \frac{\underline{|n}}{1.\underline{|n}} = 1$$

Properties of ^nC_r

1. To prove that :

$$^nC_r = {}^nC_{n-r}$$

Proof : $^nC_r = \dfrac{\underline{|n}}{\underline{|r}\,\underline{|n-r}} = \dfrac{\underline{|n}}{\underline{|n-r}\,\underline{|n-(n-r)}}$

$$= {}^nC_{n-r}$$

2. To prove that :

$$^nC_x = {}^nC_y \Rightarrow x = y \text{ or } x + y = n$$

Proof : $^nC_x = {}^nC_y$

So by the definition of Combination

$$x = y$$

$$^nC_r = {}^nC_{n-r}$$

$$\therefore \quad {}^nC_x = {}^nC_{n-x}$$

$$y = n - x \Rightarrow x + y = n$$

Hence $\quad {}^nC_x = {}^nC_y \Rightarrow x = y \text{ or } x + y = n$

3. To prove that :

$$^nC_r + {}^nC_{r-1} = {}^{n+1}C_r$$

Proof : $^nC_r + {}^nC_{r-1}$

$$= \frac{\underline{|n}}{\underline{|r}\,\underline{|n-r}} + \frac{\underline{|n}}{\underline{|r-1}\,\underline{|n-r+1}}$$

$$= \underline{|n}\left\{\frac{1}{r\,\underline{|r-1}\,\underline{|n-r}} + \frac{1}{\underline{|r-1}\,(n-r+1)\,\underline{|n-r}}\right\}$$

$$= \underline{|n}\left\{\frac{n-r+1+r}{r\,\underline{|r-1}\,(n-r+1)\,\underline{|n-r}}\right\}$$

$$= \frac{(n+1)\,\underline{|n}}{r\,\underline{|r-1}\,(n-r+1)\,\underline{|n-r}}$$

$$= \frac{\underline{|n+1}}{r.\underline{|n+1-r}} = {}^{n+1}C_r \qquad \textbf{Proved}$$

4. Prove that :

$$r.\ {}^nC_r = n.\ {}^{n-1}C_{r-1}$$

Proof :

$$r.\ {}^nC_r = r.\ \frac{\underline{|n}}{\underline{|r}.\,\underline{|n-r}}$$

$$= \frac{\underline{|n}}{\underline{|r-1}\,\underline{|n-r}}$$

$$= \frac{\underline{|n-1}}{n\underline{|r-1}\,\underline{|(n-1)-(r-1)}}$$

$$= n.\ {}^{n-1}C_{r-1}$$

5. To prove that :

$$\frac{1}{r+1}.\ {}^nC_r = \frac{1}{n+1}\ {}^{n+1}C_{r+1}$$

Proof :

$$\frac{1}{r+1}.\ {}^nC_r = \frac{1}{r+1}\ \frac{\underline{|n}}{\underline{|r}\,\underline{|n-r}}$$

$$= \frac{\underline{|n}}{\underline{|r+1}\,\underline{|n-r}}$$

$$= \frac{1}{n+1}\ \frac{\underline{|n+1}}{\underline{|r+1}\,\underline{|n-r}}$$

$$= \frac{1}{n+1}\ \frac{\underline{|n+1}}{\underline{|n+1}\,\underline{|(n+1)-(r+1)}}$$

$$= \frac{1}{n+1}.\ {}^{n+1}C_{r+1} \qquad \textbf{Proved}$$

SOLVED EXAMPLES

❑ Short Answer Type Questions

Example 1(A)

Find the values of the following :

(i) $^5C_3$ (ii) $^{11}C_4$ (iii) $^9C_6$ (iv) $^{20}C_{15}$

Solution :

$$^nC_r = \frac{\underline{|n}}{\underline{|r}\,\underline{|(n-r)}}$$

(i) $$^5C_3 = \frac{\underline{|5}}{\underline{|3}\,\underline{|(5-3)}} = \frac{\underline{|5}}{\underline{|3}\,\underline{|2}}$$
$$= \frac{5\times4\times3\times2\times1}{3\times2\times1\times2\times1} = 10$$

(ii) $$^{11}C_4 = \frac{11!}{4!\,(11-4)!} = \frac{11!}{4!\,7!}$$
$$= \frac{11\times10\times9\times8}{4\times3\times2\times1} = 330$$

(iii) $$^9C_6 = \frac{9!}{6!\,(9-6)!} = \frac{9!}{6!\,3!}$$
$$= \frac{9\times8\times7}{3\times2\times1} = 84$$

(iv) $$^{20}C_{15} = \frac{\underline{|20}}{\underline{|15}\,\underline{|(20-15)}}$$
$$= \frac{20\times19\times18\times17\times16\times\underline{|15}}{\underline{|15}\,\underline{|5}}$$
$$= \frac{20\times19\times18\times17\times16}{5\times4\times3\times2\times1}$$
$$= 19\times18\times17\times16 = 15504$$

Example 1(B)

If $^nC_3 = 120$ then find n. (*JAC, 2024*)

Solution :

$$^nC_3 = 120$$
$$\frac{n!}{3!(n-3)!} = 120$$
$$\frac{n(n-1)(n-2)(n-3)!}{3!(n-3)!} = 120$$
$$n(n-1)(n-2) = 120\times3!$$
$$n(n-1)(n-2) = 120\times3\times2\times1$$
$$n(n-1)(n-2) = 720$$
$$n(n-1)(n-2) = 10\times9\times8$$
$$n = 10$$ **Ans.**

Example 2(A)

If $^{2n}C_3 : {^nC_2} = 44 : 3$, find the value of n.

Solution :

$\because$ $$^{2n}C_3 : {^nC_2} = 44 : 3$$

$\therefore$ $$\frac{\underline{|2n}}{\underline{|3}\,\underline{|2n+3}} \div \frac{\underline{|n}}{\underline{|2}\,\underline{|n-2}} = \frac{44}{3}$$

or $$\frac{2n\,(2n-1)\,(2n-2)}{\underline{|3}} \div \frac{n\,(n-1)}{\underline{|2}} = \frac{44}{3}$$

or $$\frac{2n\,(2n-1)\,(2n-2)}{3n\,(n-1)} = \frac{44}{3}$$

or $$\frac{4\,(2n-1)}{3} = \frac{44}{3}$$

or $$2n-1 = 11$$

or $$2n = 12$$

$\therefore$ $$n = 6$$

Example 2(B)

If $^nC_5 = {^nC_7}$, find n.

Solution :

First Method : $^nC_5 = {^nC_7}$

or $$\frac{\underline{|n}}{\underline{|5}\,\underline{|n-5}} = \frac{\underline{|n}}{\underline{|7}\,\underline{|n-7}}$$

or $$\frac{1}{\underline{|5}\,(n-5)\,(n-6)\,\underline{|n-7}} = \frac{1}{7.\,6.\,\underline{|5}.\,\underline{|n-7}}$$

or $$\frac{1}{(n-5)\,(n-6)} = \frac{1}{7.\,6}$$

or $$(n-5)\,(n-6) = 7.\,6$$

$\therefore$ $$n-5 = 7$$
$$n = 12$$ **Ans.**

Second Method : $^nC_5 = {^nC_7}$

$\because$ $5 \neq 7$

$\therefore$ $5+7 = n$

$\therefore$ $n = 12$

Formula :	
If	$^nC_x = {^nC_y}$
then either	$x = y$
or	$x + y = n$

Example 3

If $^{2n}C_3 : {^nC_3} :: 11 : 1$, find n.

Solution :

$$^{2n}C_3 : {^nC_3} :: 11 : 1$$

or $$\frac{^{2n}C_3}{^nC_3} = \frac{11}{1}$$

or $$\frac{\underline{|2n}}{\underline{|3}\,\underline{|2n-3}} \times \frac{\underline{|3}\,\underline{|n-3}}{\underline{|n}} = 11$$

or $$\frac{2n\,(2n-1)\,(2n-2)\,\underline{|2n-3}\times\underline{|3}\,\underline{|n-3}}{\underline{|(2n-3}\,\underline{|3}n\,(n-1)\,(n-2)\,\underline{|n-3}} = 11$$

or $$\frac{2n\,(2n-1)\,(2n-2)}{n\,(n-1)\,(n-2)} = 11$$

or $$\frac{4\,(2n-1)}{n-2} = 11$$

or $$11n - 22 = 8n - 4$$

or $$11n - 8n = 22 - 4$$

or $$3n = 18$$

$\therefore$ $$n = 6$$ **Ans.**

Example 4

If $^nC_{10} = {^nC_{12}}$, find $^nC_5$.

Solution :

$$^nC_{10} = {^nC_{12}}$$

$\because$ $10 \neq 12$

$\therefore$ $10 + 12 = n$

$\therefore$ $n = 22$

$$^nC_5 = {^{22}C_5} = \frac{\underline{|22}}{\underline{|5}\,\underline{|17}}$$

$$= \frac{22\times21\times20\times19\times18\,\underline{|17}}{5\times4\times3\times2\times1\times\underline{|17}}$$

$$= 26{,}334$$ **Ans.**

Example 5(A)

Find the value of r if ${}^n p_r = 720$ and ${}^nC_r = 120$.

Solution :

$${}^nC_r = \frac{{}^n p_r}{\lfloor r}$$

or $$120 = \frac{720}{\lfloor r}$$

or $$\lfloor r = 6 = (3 \times 2 \times 1)$$

or $$\lfloor r = \lfloor 3$$

$\therefore$ $$r = 3$$ **Ans.**

Example 5(B)

Find the value of n and r if ${}^nC_r = 56$ and ${}^nP_r = 336$.

Solution :

$${}^nC_r = 56, \quad {}^nP_r = 336$$

We know that $${}^nC_r = \frac{{}^nP_r}{\lfloor r}$$

$$56 = \frac{336}{\lfloor r}$$

or $$\lfloor r = \frac{336}{56} = 6 = 3 \times 2 \times 1 = \lfloor 3$$

$\therefore$ $$r = 3$$

$\therefore$ $${}^nP_r = 336$$

Putting the value of r

$${}^nP_3 = 336$$

$$n(n-1)(n-2) = 336$$

$$n(n-1)(n-2) = 8 \times 7 \times 6$$

$\therefore$ $$n = 8$$

$\therefore$ $$n = 8, r = 3$$

Example 6

Find n if ${}^nC_6 : {}^{n-3}C_3 = 33 : 4$.

Solution :

$\because$ $${}^nC_6 : {}^{n-3}C_3 = 33 : 4$$

or $$\frac{\lfloor n}{\lfloor 6 \lfloor n-6} \times \frac{\lfloor 3 \lfloor n-3-3}{\lfloor n-3} = \frac{33}{4}$$

or $$\frac{\lfloor n}{\lfloor n-3} \frac{\lfloor 3}{\lfloor 6} = \frac{33}{4}$$

or $$\frac{n(n-1)(n-2)}{6 \times 5 \times 4} = \frac{33}{4}$$

$$n(n-1)(n-2) = 6 \times 5 \times 33$$

or $$= 2 \times 3 \times 5 \times 11 \times 3$$

$$= 11 \times 10 \times 9$$

$\therefore$ $$n = 11$$ **Ans.**

Example 7 (A)

If ${}^{15}C_{3r} = {}^{15}C_{r+3}$, then find r.

Solution :

$\because$ $${}^{15}C_{3r} = {}^{15}C_{r+3}$$

$\therefore$ $$3r = r + 3$$

or $$2r = 3$$

$\therefore$ $$r = \frac{3}{2} \text{ Impossible}$$

$\therefore$ $$3r + r + 3 = 15$$

$\Rightarrow$ $$4r = 12 \text{ or } r = 3$$ **Ans.**

Example 7 (B)

If ${}^{20}C_{r-1} = {}^{20}C_{r+1}$, find the value of r.

Solution :

$\because$ $${}^{20}C_{r-1} = {}^{20}C_{r+1}$$

$$(r-1) + (r+1) = 20$$

$$2r = 20$$

$\therefore$ $$r = 10$$

Example 7 (C)

If ${}^{10}C_r = {}^{10}C_{r+2}$, find ${}^5C_r$.

Solution :

$${}^{10}C_r = {}^{10}C_{r+2}$$

$$r + r + 2 = 10$$

$$2r + 2 = 10$$

or $$2r = 10 - 2 = 8$$

$\therefore$ $$r = 4$$

Put the value of r in

$${}^5C_r = {}^5C_4$$

$\Rightarrow$ $$\frac{5!}{(5-4)!\,4!} = \frac{5!}{1!\,4!} = 5$$ **Ans.**

Theorem 2 : *The number of combinations of n different things taking r at a time (without replacement)*

(i) **When particular element is always included in the combination :**

The number of combinations = ${}^{n-p}C_{r-p}$

(ii) **When particular element always excluded that is not included at all from the combination :**

The number of combination = ${}^{n-p}C_r$

❐ Long Answer Type Questions

Example 8

In how many ways can 11 players can be selected from 15 players if (i) one particular players is always to be included in the team and (ii) one particular players is always to be excluded from the team.

Solution :

Total Players (n) = 15

Number of players to be selected (r) = 1

(i) One particular player is always included *i.e.*, only 10 players (11 – 1) have to be selected out 14 (*i.e.*, 15 – 1).

So the total ways are :

$${}^{n-P}C_{r-P} = {}^{15-1}C_{11-1} = {}^{14}C_{10}$$

$$= \frac{\lfloor 14}{\lfloor 10 \lfloor (14-10)} = \frac{\lfloor 14}{\lfloor 10 \lfloor 4}$$

$$= \frac{14\times13\times12\times11\times\lfloor 10}{\lfloor 10\times\lfloor 4}$$

$$= \frac{14\times13\times12\times11}{4\times3\times2\times1} = 1001 \quad ...(i)$$

(ii) One particular player is always to be excluded. It means out of 14 players, 11 players have to be selected. Therefore,

$$^{n-P}C_r = {}^{15-1}C_{11} = {}^{14}C_{11}$$

$$^{14}C_{11} = \frac{\lfloor 14}{\lfloor 11\,\lfloor(14-11)} = \frac{\lfloor 14}{\lfloor 11\,\lfloor 3}$$

$$= \frac{14\times13\times12\times\lfloor 11}{\lfloor 11\times3\times2\times1}$$

$$= \frac{14\times13\times12}{3\times2\times1} = 364 \quad ...(ii)$$

Theorem 3 : *Division in Groups*

The number of combinations of taking some or all things at a time from n distinguishable things is :

$${}^nC_1 + {}^nC_2 + {}^nC_3 + ... {}^nC_n = 2^n - 1$$

Example 9

A person has 7 friends. In how many ways can be invite one or more of them on dinner ?

Solution :

Required ways $= 2_n - 1 = 2^7 - 1 = 128 - 1 = 127$

Alternatively, ${}^7C_1 + {}^7C_2 + {}^7C_3 + {}^7C_4 + {}^7C_5 + {}^7C_6 + {}^7C_7$
$= 7 + 21 + 35 + 35 + 21 + 7 + 1$
$= 127$

Example 10

In how many ways Ankit can invite at least one friend at dinner out of 4 friends ?

Solution :

(i) Ways of inviting 1 friend out of $4 = {}^4C_1 = 4$
(ii) Ways of inviting 2 friends out of $4 = {}^4C_2 = 6$
(iii) Ways of inviting 3 friends out of $4 = {}^4C_3 = 4$
(iv) Ways of inviting 4 friends out of $4 = {}^4C_4 = 1$

Hence, the required number of ways
$= {}^4C_1 + {}^4C_2 + {}^4C_3 + {}^4C_4$
$= 4 + 6 + 4 + 1 = 15$

Alternatively,
Required number of ways $= 2_n - 1 = 2^4 - 1$
$= 2 \times 2 \times 2 \times 2 - 1 = 15$

Remember : Important Formulae Relating to Combination

Theorem 1 : The number of combinations of n different things taken r at a time is given by ${}^nC_r$.

(A) ${}^nC_r = \frac{\lfloor n}{\lfloor r\,\lfloor(n-r)}$ or (B) ${}^nC_r = \frac{n!}{r!\,\lfloor(n-r)!}$

(*JAC*, 2023)

or (C) $= \frac{{}^nP_r}{r!}$

Some Results based on theorem A

(i) On taking $r = n$, ${}^nC_n = \frac{n!}{n!\,(n-n)!} = \frac{n!}{n!\,0!}$

$\therefore$ ${}^nC_n = 1$

(ii) On taking $r = 0$, ${}^nC_0 = \frac{n!}{0!\,n!}$ $\therefore$ ${}^nC_0 = 1$

(iii) On taking $n - r$ in placed of r,

$${}^nC_{n-r} = \frac{n!}{n-r!\,\{n-(n-r)\}!}$$

$$= \frac{n!}{r!\,(n-r)!} \qquad \therefore {}^nC_r = {}^nC_{n-r}$$

(iv) If ${}^nC_x = {}^nC_y$ and $x \neq y$, them $x + y = n$
(v) ${}^nC_r = {}^nC_{r-1}$
(vi) ${}^nC_r + {}^nC_{r-1} = {}^{n+1}C_{r-1}$
(vii) $r.{}^nC_r = n.\,{}^{n-1}C_{r-1}$
(viii) $\frac{1}{r+1}\,.\,{}^nC_r = \frac{1}{n+1} = {}^{n+1}C_{r+1}$

Theorem 2 : The number of combinations of taking some or all things at a time from n distinguishable things $= 2^n - 1$

Theorem 3 : The number of combinations of n different things taking r at a time (without replacement) when :

(i) Specified P things are always included $= {}^{n-P}C_{r-p}$
(ii) Specified P things are always excluded or never included $= {}^{n-P}C_r$

Example 11

There are 50 students in a class of a College. In how many ways can they select 3 representatives for the College union ?

Solution :

Required Ways $= {}^{50}C_3 = \frac{\lfloor 50}{\lfloor 3\,\lfloor 47}$ $\left[\because {}^nC_r = \frac{\lfloor n}{\lfloor n-r}\right]$

$= \frac{50 \times 49 \times 48}{3 \times 2} = 19{,}600$ **Ans.**

Example 12

On a new year day every student of a class sends a card to every other student. The post-man delivers 600 cards. How many students are there in the class ?

Solution :

Let n be the number of students. Now number of ways in which two students can be selected out of n students is ${}^nC_2$.

$\therefore$ Number of pairs of students $= {}^nC_2$ .But for each pair of students, number of cards sent is 2 (since if there are two students A and B, A will send a card to B and B will send to A).

For ${}^nC_2$ pairs, numbers of cards sent $= 2.\,{}^nC_2$

According to the question,

$$2.\,{}^nC_2 = 600$$

$$\Rightarrow \quad \frac{\underline{|n}}{\underline{|2}\,\underline{|n-1}} = 600$$

$$\Rightarrow \quad n(n-1) = 600$$

$$\Rightarrow \quad n(n-1) = 25 \times 24$$

$$\therefore \quad n = 25$$

$\therefore$ Number of students = 25 **Ans.**

Example 13

Out of 6 gentlemen and 4 ladies a committee of 5 is to be formed. In how many ways can this be done so as to include atleast one lady in each committee. (*JAC*, 2016)

Solution :

First Method :

We have to form a committee of 5 persons including atleast one lady.

Number of gentlemen = 6

Number of ladies = 4

So total number of persons = 10

Number of ways to choose 5 persons out of 10 = ${}^{10}C_5$

If we want to choose those 5 persons in which no lady. Then number of ways to select them = ${}^6C_5$

So Required Permutation = ${}^{10}C_5 - {}^6C_5$

$$= \frac{\underline{|10}}{\underline{|5}\,\underline{|5}} - \frac{\underline{|6}}{\underline{|5}\,\underline{|1}}$$

$$= \frac{10 \times 9 \times 8 \times 7 \times 6}{5 \times 4 \times 3 \times 2 \times 1} - 6$$

$$= 252 - 6 = 246$$ **Ans.**

Second Method :

Number of gentlemen = 6

Number of ladies = 4

We have to form a committee of 5 persons including atleast one lady. This committee can be formed by the following ways :

Number of Ladies	*Number of Gentlemen*	*Number of Committee*
1	4	${}^4C_1 . {}^6C_4$
2	3	${}^4C_2 . {}^6C_3$
3	2	${}^4C_3 . {}^6C_2$
4	1	${}^4C_4 . {}^6C_1$

$\therefore$ Required Ways = ${}^4C_1.{}^6C_4 + {}^4C_2.{}^6C_3 + {}^4C_3.{}^6C_2 + {}^4C_4.{}^6C_1$

$$= 4 \times 15 + 6 \times 20 + 4 \times 15 + 1 \times 6$$

$$= 60 + 120 + 60 + 6 = 246$$ **Ans.**

Example 14

There are ten points in a plane of these ten points four points are in a straight line and with the exception of these four points, no other three points are in the same straight line. Find the number of triangles formed.

Solution :

First Method :

Number of points = 10. In which 4 points are collinear and in other 6 points no three points are collinear. We know that a triangle can be formed after selection of three non collinear points. Number of ways to choose three points out of 10 = ${}^{10}C_3$.

Number of ways to choose three points out of 4 Collinear points = ${}^4C_3$

But we cannot form a triangle in this selection.

So Required number of triangles = ${}^{10}C_3 - {}^4C_3$

$$= \frac{\underline{|10}}{\underline{|3}\,\underline{|7}} - \frac{\underline{|4}}{\underline{|3}\,\underline{|1}}$$

$$= \frac{10 \times 9 \times 8}{6} - 4$$

$$= 120 - 4 = 116$$ **Ans.**

Second Method :

Number of given points = 10

In which number of collinear points = 4

We can form a triangle after selection of 3 non-collinear points which can be chosen by the following ways :

Number of points selected out of collinear points	*Number of points selected out of remaining 6 points*	*Number of triangles forced*
0	3	${}^4C_0 \times {}^6C_3 = 20$
1	2	${}^4C_1 \times {}^6C_2 = 60$
2	1	${}^4C_2 \times {}^6C_1 = 36$
3	0	0
	Total	116

Hence, Required ways = 20 + 60 + 36 + 0

= 116 **Ans.**

Example 15

A boat has a crew of 10 men of which 3 can row only on one side and 2 only on the other. In how many ways the crew can be arranged ?

Solution :

For manning the crew, 5 men will sit on each side. Since 3 men can row only on one side and 2 only on the other side, therefore any 2 out of the remaining 5 men are selected for sitting on the side of 3 and the remaining 3 men for sitting on the side of 2.

$\therefore$ The number of selections for manning the crew on both sides

$$= {}^5C_2 \times {}^3C_3 = 10$$

Corresponding to each selection, the crew of 5 men on both sides can be arranged in $\underline{|5} \times \underline{|5}$ ways.

$\therefore$ The required number of arrangements

$$= 10 \times \underline{|5} \times \underline{|5}$$

= 1,44,000 **Ans.**

Example 16

In how many ways can a team of 11 be chosen from 14 football players, if two of them can only be goal keepers.

Solution :

Total number of football players = 14

Number of players to be chosen = 11

Which number of goal keepers = 2

Thus number of players except goal keepers

$= 14 - 2 = 12$

We have to choose 10 players out of these 12.

Number of ways to choose them $= {}^{12}C_{10}$

$$= \frac{\lfloor 12}{\lfloor 10 \lfloor 2}$$

$$= \frac{12 \times 11}{2} = 66$$

Again number of ways to choose one goal keeper out of 2

$= {}^{2}C_{1} = 2$

So required number of Selection $= 66 \times 2$

$= 132$ **Ans.**

Example 17

There are 10 Professors and 20 Students out of whom a committee of 2 Professors and 3 Students to be formed. Find how many ways these committees can be formed, if

(i) A particular professor is included ?

(ii) A particular professor is excluded ?

Solution :

Number of Professors = 10

Number of Students = 20

We have to form a committee of 2 professors and 3 students.

(i) Since a particular professor included so we have to choose only one professor out of remaining 3, number of ways to choose them $= {}^{9}C_{1}$

Now number of ways to choose three students out of 20 $= {}^{20}C_{3}$

So total number of ways to form the Committee in this case $= {}^{9}C_{1} \times {}^{20}C_{3}$

(ii) If a particular professor is excluded, then we have to choose any two professors out of 9.

Number of ways to choose them $= {}^{9}C_{2}$

Again Number of ways to choose three students out of 20 $= {}^{20}C_{3}$

The number of ways to form the committee $= {}^{9}C_{2} \times {}^{20}C_{3}$

Ans.

***Use the following results whichever is required**

(i) Number of ways of selecting r different things out of n different things

$= {}^{n}C_{r}$

(ii) Number of ways of selecting r things out of n identical things

$= 1$ for $r = 0, 1, 2, 3, \ldots, n$

(iii) Number of ways of selecting zero or more things out of n identical things

$= 1 + 1 + 1 + \ldots + (n+1)$ terms $= n + 1$

(iv) Number of ways of selecting one or more things out of n identical things

$= n$

(v) Number of ways of selecting zero or more out of n different things

$= {}^{n}C_{0} + {}^{n}C_{1} + {}^{n}C_{2} + \ldots + {}^{n}C_{n} = 2^{n}$

(iv) Number of ways of selecting one or more out of n different things

$= {}^{n}C_{1} + {}^{n}C_{2} + \ldots + {}^{n}C_{n} = 2^{n} - 1$

Example 18

From 5 Apples, 4 Oranges and 3 Mangoes, how many selections of fruit can be made ?

Solution :

Number of apples = 5

Zero or more apples can be select out of 5 identical apples in $5 + 1 = 6$ ways

Number of oranges = 4

Zero or more oranges can be selected out of 4 identical oranges in $4 + 1 = 5$ ways

Number of mangoes = 3

Zero of more mangoes can be selected out of 3 identical mangoes in $3 + 1 = 4$ ways.

∴ Total number of selection, when all the three types of fruits are selected $= 6 \times 5 \times 4$

But in one of these selections number of each type of fruit is zero. Hence this selection must be excluded.

So required number of selections $= 6 \times 5 \times 4 - 1$

$= 120 - 1$

$= 119$ **Ans.**

Example 19

Gives 5 different green dyes, 4 different blue and 3 different red dyes. How many combinations of dyes can be chosen taking atleast one green and one blue dyes ?

Solution :

One or more green dyes can be selected out of 5 different green dyes in

$${}^{5}C_{1} + {}^{5}C_{2} + {}^{5}C_{3} + {}^{5}C_{4} + {}^{5}C_{5}$$

$= 2^{5} - 1 = 31$ ways

One or more blue dyes can be selected out of 4 different blue dyes in

$${}^{4}C_{1} + {}^{4}C_{2} + {}^{4}C_{3} + {}^{4}C_{4}$$

$= 2^{4} - 1 = 15$ ways

Zero or more red ways can be selected out of 3 different red dyes in

$${}^{3}C_{0} + {}^{3}C_{1} + {}^{3}C_{2} + {}^{3}C_{3}$$

$= 2^{3} = 8$ ways

∴ Required mumber of selections

$= 31 \times 15 \times 8 = 3{,}720$ **Ans.**

Example 20

In how many ways 12 different things can be equally distributed among 4 persons ? If they are divided in four groups instead to giving to 4 persons, what will be the number of ways ?

Solution :

We have to distribute 12 different things among 4 persons. So each person will get 3 things. Number of ways to choose 3 things out of 12 for the first person = ${}^{12}C_3$

Number of ways to choose 3 things out of remaining 9 things for the second person = ${}^{9}C_3$

Again number of ways to choose 3 things out of remaining 6 things for the third person = ${}^{6}C_3$

Again number of ways to choose 3 things out of 3 remaining things for the fourth person = ${}^{3}C_3$

So required selections = ${}^{12}C_3 \times {}^{9}C_3 \times {}^{6}C_3 \times {}^{3}C_3$ **Ans.**

Second Part

Here the 12 different things are divided in four groups,

Then required number of ways to distribute them

$$= \frac{{}^{12}C_3 \times {}^{9}C_3 \times {}^{6}C_3 \times {}^{3}C_3}{\underline{|4}}$$

$$= \frac{\underline{|12}}{\underline{|3}\,\underline{|9}} \times \frac{\underline{|9}}{\underline{|3}\,\underline{|6}} \times \frac{\underline{|6}}{\underline{|3}\,\underline{|3}} \times \frac{\underline{|3}}{\underline{|3}\,\underline{|0}}$$

$$= \frac{\underline{|12}}{\underline{|4}\,(\underline{|3})^4}$$

Example 21

What is the value of 4 ! ? [*Mock Test Paper* (*JAC*)]

(a) 6 × 5 × 4 × 3 × 2 × 1 (b) 4 × 3 × 2 × 1

(c) 4 + 3 + 2 + 1 (d) none of these

Solution :

$$4\,! = 4 \times 3 \times 2 \times 1$$

Hence, the option (b) is right.

Example 22

How many different signals can be made by hoisting 6 differently coloured flags one above the other when any number of them may be hoisted at once ?

[*Mock Test Paper* (*JAC*)]

Solution :

Total number of signals

$= {}^6p_1 + {}^6p_2 + {}^6p_3 + {}^6p_4 + {}^6p_5 + {}^6p_6$

$= \frac{\underline{|6}}{\underline{|6-1}} + \frac{\underline{|6}}{\underline{|6-2}} + \frac{\underline{|6}}{\underline{|6-3}} + \frac{\underline{|6}}{\underline{|6-4}} + \frac{\underline{|6}}{\underline{|6-5}} + \frac{\underline{|6}}{\underline{|6-6}}$

$= \frac{\underline{|6}}{\underline{|5}} + \frac{\underline{|6}}{\underline{|4}} + \frac{\underline{|6}}{\underline{|3}} + \frac{\underline{|6}}{\underline{|2}} + \frac{\underline{|6}}{\underline{|1}} + \frac{\underline{|6}}{\underline{|0}}$

$= 6 + 6 \times 5 + 6 \times 5 \times 4 + 6 \times 5 \times 4 \times 3 + 6 \times 5 \times 4 \times 3 \times 2 + 6 \times 5 \times 4 \times 3 \times 2 \times 1$

$= 6 + 30 + 120 + 360 + 720 + 720$

$= 1956$ ways

Example 23

In how many wags can a team of 11 be chosen from 15 cricketers if two of them can only be wicketkeepers ?

(*JAC*, 2018)

Solution :

Total number of cricketers = 15

Number of players to be chosen = 11

Which number of wicketkeepers = 2

Thus number of cricketer execpt wicketkeepers

= 15 – 2 = 13

We have to choose 10 cricketers out of these 13

Number of was to choose them = ${}^{13}C_{10}$

$$= \frac{\underline{|13}}{\underline{|10}\,\underline{|13-10}}$$

$$= \frac{\underline{|13}}{\underline{|10}\,\underline{|3}}$$

$$= \frac{13 \times 12 \times 11}{3 \times 2}$$

$$= 13 \times 12 \times 11$$

$$= 286$$

Again number of ways to choose one wicketkeeper out of 2 = ${}^2C_1 = 2$

So, required number of selection

= 286 × 2 = 572

Exercise 5 (C)

❑ Short Answer Type Questions

1. Find the values of :
   (i) ${}^{12}C_4$ (ii) ${}^{10}C_3$ (iii) ${}^{8}C_8$ (iv) ${}^{20}C_{17}$
2. Find the value of '*r*' if ${}^{18}C_r = {}^{18}C_{r+2}$
3. Find the value of '*n*' if ${}^nC_2 = 10$
4. Find the value or '*r*' if ${}^{15}C_{r+3} = {}^{15}C_{2r-3}$
5. If ${}^{20}C_{r-1} = {}^{20}C_{r+1}$, find the value of *r*.
6. If ${}^{18}C_{r-1} = {}^{18}C_{r+2}$, find the value of ${}^rC_5$.
7. Find the value of *n* if ${}^{2n}C_3 : {}^nC_2 = 44 : 3$. (*JAC*, 2025)
8. If ${}^{18}C_r = {}^{18}C_{r+2}$, find ${}^rC_6$. (*JAC*, 2016)
9. If ${}^nC_{12} = {}^nC_8$, find ${}^nC_{17}$ and ${}^{22}C_n$.
10. If ${}^nC_{r-1} = 36$, ${}^nC_r = 84$ and ${}^nC_{r+1} = 126$, find *n* and *r*.
11. If ${}^np_r = 2{,}520$ and ${}^nC_r = 21$, find *r*.
12. A delegation of 6 members is to be sent abroad out of 12 members. In how many ways can selection be made so that :
    (i) a particular member is included ?
    (ii) a particular member is excluded ?
13. A committee consisting of 2 men and 2 women is to be chosen from 5 men and 6 women. In how many ways can this be done ?
14. There are 10 points in a plain of which 4 are collinear. How many different straight lines can be drawn by joining them ?
15. In how many ways 12 different books can be distributed equally in 4 persons ?
16. How many numbers can be formed by using 3 digits at a time out of 1, 3, 5, 7, 8 and 9. no digit being repeated ?

17. A bag contains 5 black, 3 white and 3 red balls. In how many ways can 3 black balls be drawn ?
18. If ${}^nP_r = 336$ and ${}^nC_r = 56$, them find r.

Answers

1. (i) 495, (ii) 210, (iii) 1, (iv) 1140 2. 8
3. 5 4. 6 or 5 5. 10 6. 56
7. 34 8. 28 9. 1, 140, 231
10. $n = 9, r = 3$ 11. 5 12. (i) 462, (ii) 462
13. 150 14. 40 15. $\frac{\lfloor 12}{(\lfloor 3)^4}$ 16. 120
17. 10 18. $r = 3$

❑ Long Answer Type Questions

1. Find the total number of selection of atleast one red ball from 4 red and 3 green balls, if the balls of the same colour are different.
2. In an election for 3 seats there are 6 candidates. A voter cannot vote for more than 3 candidates. In how many ways can he vote ?
3. From 7 gentlemen and 5 ladies a boat party is to be formed. In how many ways can this be done so as to include atleast one day ?
4. There are n stations on a railway line. The number of kinds of tickets printed (no return ticket) is 105. Find the number of stations.

[**Hint :** Let the number of stations $= n$

$\therefore$ No. of Tickets $= 1 \times {}^nC_2 = {}^nC_2$

From the question, ${}^nC_2 = 150$

$\because \; {}^nC_r = {}^nC_{n-r}$
$\therefore \; {}^{20}C_{13} = {}^{20}C_{20-13}$
and ${}^{20}C_{14} = {}^{20}C_{20-14}$

or $\frac{\lfloor n}{\lfloor 2 \lfloor n-2} = 105$

or $\frac{n(n-1)\lfloor n-2}{\lfloor n-2} = 210$

or $n(n-1) = 15 \times 14$

$\therefore$ $n = 15$

5. To fill 12 vacancies there are 25 candidates of which 5 are from scheduled castes. If 3 of the vacancies are reserved for scheduled caste candidates while the rest are open to all, find the number of ways in which the selections can be made.
6. At an election three wards of a town are convassed by 4, 5 and 8 men respectively. If there are 20 volunteers, in how many ways can they be allotted to different wards ?
7. A man has 7 friends and he wants to invite 3 of them at a party. Find how many parties to each of 3 different friends he can give and how many times any particular friend will attend the parties ?
8. Out of 7 men and 4 ladies a committee of 5 is to be formed. In how many ways can this be done so as to include atleast 3 ladies ?
9. A candidate is required to answer 6 out of 10 questions which are divided into groups, each containing five questions and he is not permitted to attempt more than 4 from any group. In how many ways can he make up his choice ?
10. From 8 gentlemen and 4 ladies a committee of 5 is to be formed. In how many ways can this be done so as to include atleast one lady ?
11. From 7 gentlemen and 4 ladies a committee of 5 is to be formed. In how many ways can this be done so as to include atleast one lady ? (*JAC*, 2024)
12. From 6 boys and 7 girls a committee of 5 is to be formed so as to include atleast one girl. Find the number of ways in which this can be done. (*JAC*, 2017)
13. In a group of 15 boys there are 6 hockey players. In how many ways can 12 boys be selected so as to include atleast 4 hockey players ?
14. In how many can a first eleven be selected from 20 players if—(i) 8 particular players are always to be included in the team, (ii) 8 particular players are to be excluded from the team, (iii) one particular players is not to be taken in the team.
15. In an examination, a candidate has to pass in each of the 6 subjects. In how many ways can be fail.
16. If ${}^nP_r = 6720$ and ${}^nC_r = 56$ then find the values of 'n' and 'r'.

Answers

1. 120 2. 41 3. 771 4. 15
5. ${}^5C_3 \times {}^{20}C_9 \times {}^5C_4 \times {}^{20}C_8 \times {}^5C_5 \times {}^{20}C_7$
6. ${}^{20}C_4 \times {}^{16}C_5 \times {}^{11}C_8$ 7. 35, 15 8. 91
9. 200 10. 736 11. 441
12. ${}^7C_1 \times {}^6C_4 + {}^7C_2 \times {}^6C_3 + {}^7C_3 \times {}^6C_2 + {}^7C_4 \times {}^6C_1 + {}^7C_5 \times {}^6C_0$
13. 435 14. (i) 220, (ii) 12, (iii) 75582 15. 63
16. $n = 8, r = 5$

Exercise 5 (D)

Objective Type Questions

❑ Multiple Choice Questions

1. If ${}^{15}P_r = 2{,}730$ then the value of r will be :
(a) 3 (b) 4 (c) 5 (d) 6
2. If ${}^nC_{12} = {}^nC_8$ then n is equal to :
(a) 20 (b) 12 (c) 6 (d) 30
3. The number of ways in which 6 prizes can be given to 3 persons, if a person may get any number of prizes is :
(a) 3^6 (b) 6^3 (c) ${}^6P_3$ (d) ${}^6C_3$
4. How many different words of 2 letters can be formed out of the letters of the word CAT ?
(a) 8 (b) 6 (c) 3 (d) 2
5. The total number of answering 5 objectives type questions each question having 4 choices is :
(a) 256 (b) 512 (c) 1,024 (d) 4,096
6. ${}^nP_r$ is equal to : (*JAC*, 2024)
(a) $\frac{n}{n(n-r)!}$ (b) $\frac{n!}{r-n!}$
(c) $\frac{n!}{n-r!}$ (d) None of these

7. If $^nP_4 = 360$ then the value of n will be : *(JAC, 2020, 22)*
(a) – 5 (b) – 6
(c) 6 (d) None of these

8. If $^nP_3 = 60$ then the value of n is : *(JAC, 2018)*
(a) 3 (b) 5 (c) 9 (d) 20

9. The value of $^{10}C_6$ is : *(JAC, 2018, 20, 24)*
(a) 210 (b) 100 (c) 60 (d) 1024

10. The value of $^7P_4$ is : *(JAC, 2019)*
(a) $7 \times 6 \times 5 \times 4$ (b) $4 \times 3 \times 2 \times 1$
(c) 7×4 (d) $\underline{|7} \times \underline{|4}$

11. Value of $^{60}C_{60}$ is : *(JAC, 2019, 26)*
(a) 1 (b) 0 (c) 60 (d) – 1

12. In how many ways 5 persons can sit around the circular table ? *(JAC, 2022, 23)*
(a) 4 (b) 8 (c) 12 (d) 24

13. In how many ways Mayank can invite at least one friend at dinner out of 4 friends ?
(a) 5 (b) 10 (c) 15 (d) 16

14. In how many ways a party of 4 men and 4 women be seated at a circular table, so that the two women are not adjacent ?
(a) 164 (b) 174 (c) 144 (d) 154

15. The number of circular permutations of n things taken r at a time is :
(a) $^nP_{r \times r}$ (b) $^nC_r \times r!$ (c) $\frac{^nC_r}{r!}$ (d) $\frac{^nP_r}{r}$

16. $7! - 5!$ is equal to : *(JAC, 2022)*
(a) 5,040 (b) 4,920 (c) 5,703 (d) 5,000

17. If $^nC_{10} = {^nC_4}$ then n is : *(JAC, 2022)*
(a) 14 (b) 10 (c) 4 (d) 40

18. The number of ways to arrange the letter of the word BIPIN is : *(JAC, 2022)*
(a) 120 (b) 60
(c) 130 (d) None of these

19. The value of 5! is equal to : *(JAC, 2022)*
(a) 4! (b) $3 \times 2 \times 1$
(c) $\frac{1}{5!}$ (d) $5 \times 3 \times 3 \times 2 \times 1$

20. The value of $^{10}C_3$ is : *(JAC, 2023)*
(a) 120 (b) 60 (c) 30 (d) 180

21. The value of $^{12}C_2$ is : *(JAC, 2025)*
(a) 60 (b) 30 (c) 50 (d) 66

22. If $^{15}C_{3r} = {^{15}C_{r+3}}$ then r is : *(JAC, 2025)*
(a) 6 (b) 9 (c) 3 (d) 4

23. If $^nC_{18} = {^nC_6}$ then n is equal to : *(JAC, 2026)*
(a) 20 (b) 12 (c) 24 (d) 6

24. 0 ! is equal to : *(JAC, 2026)*
(a) 1 (b) ∞ (c) 0 (d) 5

Answers

1. (a) 2. (a) 3. (a) 4. (b) 5. (c) 6. (c) 7. (c)
8. (b) 9. (a) 10. (a) 11. (a) 12. (d) 13. (c) 14. (c)
15. (d) 16. (b) 17. (a) 18. (b) 19. (d) 20. (a) 21. (d)
22. (c) 23. (c) 24. (a)

❐ Fill in the Blanks

1. In an exam, a candidate has to pass in each of the five subjects. The number of ways he can fails ....
[Hints : $^5C_1 + {^5C_2} + {^5C_3} + {^5C_4} + {^5C_5} = 2^5 - 1 = 31$]
2. The number of permutations of the letters of MATHEMATICS is ....

Answers

1. 31 2. $\frac{1!}{2!\,2!\,2!}$

❐ Write True or False

1. $^5C_5 = 5$.
2. $^{10}C_3 = 840$.
3. $^8P_3 = 100$.
4. 3 letters can be posted in 5 letter boxes in 3^5 ways. **[Note :** Correct 5^3 ways.]
5. $^5C_3 = 10$

Answers

1. True 2. False 3. False 4. False
5. True.

❖❖

6

DETERMINANTS

LEARNING OBJECTIVES

After studying this chapter, you will be able to know :

- **6.1 Definition of Determinants**
- **6.2 Rows and Columns of Determinants**
- **6.3 Rules for Expanding a Determinant**
  - **6.3.1 Sign of a Determinant**
  - **6.3.2 Minors and Co-factors of Determinant**
  - **6.3.3 Expansion of Second Order Determinants**
  - **6.3.4 Expansion of Third Order Determinants**
- **6.4 Properties of Determinants**
- **6.5 Cramer's Rule**
- **6.6 Applications of Determinants**

SOLVED EXAMPLES AND PRACTICAL PROBLEMS : AT A GLANCE

No. of Examples		*No. of Problems*
1 to 5	Minors and Cofactors	Exercise 6(A) 1 to 7
6A to 24	Determinants	Exercise 6(B) 1 to 23
1 to 8	Cramer's Rule	Exercise 6(C) 1 to 11
	Short Answer Type Questions	Exercise 6(D) 1 to 8
	Long Answer Type Questions	Exercise 6(E) 1 to 4
	Objective Type Questions	Exercise 6(F) 15 + 6 + 6
32	**Total**	**53 + 27**

(6.1) DEFINITION OF DETERMINANTS

Determinant can be defined as *"a numerical value obtained from a square matrix of the coefficients of certain unknown variables enclosed by two bars by the process of diagonal expansion to tell upon a given algebraic system."*

In other words an arrangement of $n \times n$ quantities in a square array between two parallel lines is called a determinant of order n. A determinant denoted by Δ or by a capital letter.

In symbols, it may be expressed as

$$\Delta \text{ or } A = \begin{vmatrix} a_{11} & a_{12} \ldots & \alpha_{1n} \\ a_{21} & a_{22} \ldots & \alpha_{2n} \\ a_{n_1} & a_{n_2} \ldots & \alpha_{nn} \end{vmatrix}$$

Terms related to Determinants :

1. **Elements or Constituents :** The n^2 quantities (or objects), a_{ij}, $i = 1, 2, 3, \ldots\ldots\ldots, n$, $j = 1, 2, 3, \ldots\ldots n$ are called the elements or constituents of determinants.
2. **Suffix :** In elements a_{ij} first suffix i stamps for row and second suffix j stands for column.
3. **Row Elements :** Horizontal elements (a_{11}, a_{12} , ………, a_{nn}) are called row elements.
4. **Column Elements :** Vertical elements form a column and so vertical elements are called column elements.
5. **Order of Determinants :** When the number of rows and number of columns are written with multiplication sign, then it is called order of determinant.

Important Points

1. The diagonal begins with left upper most ($a_{11}, a_{22}, \ldots\ldots\ldots, a_{nn}$) end is called ***Principal* Diagonal** and its elements are called diagonal elements.
2. Horizontal elements form 'rows' and vertical elements form 'columns'.
3. Order of Determinants = Number of rows × Number of columns.
4. The number of rows and columns in a determinant are equal.
5. So, the shape of the determinant is square type.

We take two linear equations

$$a_1x + b_1y = 0 \quad \ldots\text{(i)}$$

and

$$a_2x + b_2y = 0 \quad \ldots\text{(ii)}$$

We want to eliminate x and y

From (i), $\frac{x}{y} = \frac{-b_1}{a_1}$ ...(iii)

From (ii), $\frac{x}{y} = \frac{-b_2}{a_2}$ ...(iv)

From (iii) and (iv),

$$\frac{-b_1}{a_1} = \frac{-b_2}{a_2}$$

$$\Rightarrow \quad a_1b_2 = a_2b_1$$

$$\Rightarrow \quad a_1b_2 - a_2b_1 = 0$$

We can write $a_1b_2 - a_2b_1$ as $\begin{vmatrix} a_1 & b_1 \\ a_2 & b_2 \end{vmatrix}$

This form is called determinant, expansion of the determinant

$$\begin{vmatrix} a_1 & b_1 \\ a_2 & b_2 \end{vmatrix} = a_1b_2 - a_2b_1$$

This is a determinant of second order and a_1b_2 and a_2b_1 are its elements.

Now we take three linear eqns. in x, y and z.

$$a_1x + b_1y + c_1z = 0 \quad \ldots\text{(i)}$$
$$a_2x + b_2y + c_2z = 0 \quad \ldots\text{(ii)}$$
$$a_3x + b_3y + c_3z = 0 \quad \ldots\text{(iii)}$$

We want to eliminate x, y, z from the above three eqns.

From (i) and (ii) (by cross multiplication),

$$\frac{x}{b_1c_2 - b_2c_1} = \frac{y}{a_2c_1 - a_1c_2} = \frac{z}{a_1b_2 - a_2b_1}$$
$$= k \text{ (say), where } k \neq 0$$

$$\Rightarrow \quad x = k(b_1c_2 - b_2c_1)$$
$$y = k(a_2c_1 - a_1c_2)$$
$$z = k(a_1b_2 - a_2b_1)$$

Putting the above value of x, y, z in (iii), we get

$$ka_3(b_1c_2 - b_2c_1) + kb_3(a_2c_1 - a_1c_2) + kc_3(a_1b_2 - a_2b_1) = 0$$

$$\because \quad k \neq 0$$

$$\therefore \quad a_3(b_1c_2 - b_2c_1) + b_3(a_2c_1 - a_1c_2) + c_3(a_1b_2 - a_2b_1) = 0$$

$$\Rightarrow a_3b_1c_2 - a_3b_2c_1 + a_2b_3c_1 - a_1b_3c_2 + a_1b_2c_3 - a_2b_1c_3 = 0$$

$$\Rightarrow a_1(b_2c_3 - b_3c_2) + a_2(b_1c_3 - b_3c_1) + a_3(b_1c_2 - b_2c_1) = 0$$

The determinant form of the above relation is :

$$\begin{vmatrix} a_1 & b_1 & c_1 \\ a_2 & b_2 & c_2 \\ a_3 & b_3 & c_3 \end{vmatrix}$$

This is called a determinant of third order in which three rows and three columns. The expansion of the determinant :

$$\begin{vmatrix} a_1 & b_1 & c_1 \\ a_2 & b_2 & c_2 \\ a_3 & b_3 & c_3 \end{vmatrix} = a_1\begin{vmatrix} b_2 & c_2 \\ b_3 & c_3 \end{vmatrix} - a_2\begin{vmatrix} a_1 & c_1 \\ b_3 & c_3 \end{vmatrix} + a_3\begin{vmatrix} b_1 & c_1 \\ b_2 & c_2 \end{vmatrix}$$

$$= a_1(b_2c_3 - b_3c_2) - a_2(b_1c_3 - b_3c_1) + a_3(b_1c_2 - b_2c_1)$$

Expansion or Value of a Determinant of 1st Order

The value of a determinant of a (1 × 1) matrix $|a|$ is defined as $|a| = a$.

Expansion or Value of a Determinant of 2nd Order

We define $\begin{vmatrix} a_1 & b_1 \\ a_2 & b_2 \end{vmatrix} = a_1b_2 - a_2b_1$

Expansion or Value of a Determinant of 3rd Order

For finding the value of a determinant of 3rd order or more, we need the definition of minor and factor.

Value of Determinant : The value of a determinant is the sum products of elements of a row (or a column) with their corresponding co-factors.

We expand a determinant by any arbitrary choosen row or column.

(6.2) ROWS AND COLUMNS OF DETERMINANTS

In a determinant the horizontal lines from left to right are called first, second, third, ... rows respectively which are represented by $R_1, R_2, R_3, \ldots$ In a determinant from upper to lower vertical lines are called first, second, third, ... columns which are represented by $C_1, C_2, C_3, \ldots$ respectively.

Value of determinant of first order (or order 1)

The value of a determinant of (1 × 1) matrix $|a|$ is defined as $|a| = a$.

Therefore, $|a_{21}| = a_{21}$, $|20| = 20$, $|-15| = -15$

Value of Determinant of Second order (or Order 2)

Let $A = \begin{vmatrix} a_1 & b_1 \\ a_2 & b_2 \end{vmatrix}$ be a matrix of order 2 × 2

then the determinant of A is defined as

$$\begin{vmatrix} a_1 & b_1 \\ a_2 & b_2 \end{vmatrix} = a_1 b_2 - a_2 b_1$$

Value of Determinant of Third Order (or Order 3)

Determinant of order three can be determined by expressing in terms of second order determinants. This is known as an expansion of a determinant along a row (or a column). For expansion or finding the value of determinant of third order we will need the definitions of Minor and Co-factor (defined later on).

Value of determinant

The value of a determinant is the sum of the products of elements of a row (or a column) with their respective co-factors.

We may expand a determinant by any arbitrary chosen row or column.

(6.3) RULES FOR EXPANDING A DETERMINANT

To find the value of a determinant we expand them by the elements of any row or by the elements of any column. This representation is called expansion of a determinant. In the expansion of a determinant we multiply the elements of any row or column by their respective co-factors.

6.3.1 Sign of a Determinant

If we expand a determinant by any row or column using minors, we keep in view the following symbols (+) and (–) *i.e.*, in alternative order for a determinant of order three :

$$\begin{vmatrix} + & - & + \\ - & + & - \\ + & - & + \end{vmatrix}$$

6.3.2 Minors and Co-factors of a Determinant

Minor : Minor of an element a_{ij} of a determinant is the determinant obtained by deleting its *i*th row and *j*th column in which element a_{ij} lies. Minor of an element a_{ij} is devoted by M_{ij}.

Co-factors : Co-factor of an element a_{ij} is devoted by A_{ij}.

It is defined by A_{ij} = (–1) $i + j$, M_{ij}, where, M_{ij} is minor of a_{ij}.

If the element of a_{ij} is expressed by cofactor c_{ij}, then

$$C_{ij} = (-1)^{i+j}.\ M_{ij}$$

i.e., Co-factor = $(-1)^{i+j}$ × Minor

Where, C_{ij} = the co-factor of the element in the *i*th row and *j*th column of the determinant.

$(-1)^{i+j}$ = the factors determining the algebraic sign depending upon the number of rows (*i*) and the number of columns (*j*) in which the element occurs in the element.

M_{ij} = the minor of the element in the *i*th row and *j*th column of the determinant.

Thus, $C_{11} = (-1)^{1+1}.\ M_{11}$; $C_{12} = (-1)^{1+2}.\ M_{12}$ and $C_{13} = (-1)^{1+3}.M_{13}$.

Rule of Sign

The co-factor of an element a_{ij} is obtained by multiplying minor of that element by $(-1)^{i+j}$.

Here, (1) $(-1)^{i+j}$ will be +1 if $i + j$ is even number, *e.g.* 4, 6, 8 etc., and

(2) $(-1)^{i+j}$ will be – 1 if $i + j$ is odd, e.g. 5, 7, 9 etc.

In other words, (i) If the sum of *i* and *j* in a determinant is even, the sign of minor and co-factor is the same, *i.e.*, $C_{ij} = M_{ij}$, If $i + j$ = Even number.

(ii) If the sum of *i* and *j* in a determinant is odd, then the sign of co-factor will be reverse of that of the minor, *i.e.*, $C_{ij} = -M_{ij}$, if $i + j$ = Odd number.

$$\text{Let } A = \begin{vmatrix} a_{11} & a_{12} & a_{13} \\ a_{21} & a_{22} & a_{23} \\ a_{31} & a_{32} & a_{33} \end{vmatrix}$$

Example : For the matrix A written above

$$A_{11} = (-1)^{1+1} \begin{vmatrix} a_{22} & a_{23} \\ a_{32} & a_{33} \end{vmatrix} = a_{22}\, a_{33} - a_{23}\, a_{32}$$

$$A_{32} = (-1)^{3+2} \begin{vmatrix} a_{11} & a_{13} \\ a_{21} & a_{23} \end{vmatrix} = -(a_{11}\, a_{23} - a_{13}\, a_{21})$$

and so on.

Example 1

Find minors and co-factors of all the elements of the determinant $\begin{vmatrix} 1 & -2 \\ 4 & 3 \end{vmatrix}$.

Solution :

Minor of the element a_{ij} is M_{ij}.

Here a = 11. So M_{11} = Minor of a_{11} = 3

$Minor_{12}$ = Minor of the element a_{12} = 4

$Minor_{21}$ = Minor of the element a_{21} = – 2

$Minor_{22}$ = Minor of the element a_{22} = 1

Now, Co-factor of a_{ij} is A_{ij}. So,

$A_{11} = (-1)^{1+1}$ $M_{11} = (-1)^2 (3) = 3$

$A_{12} = (-1)^{1+2}$ $M_{12} = (-1)^3 (4) = -4$

$A_{21} = (-1)^{2+1}$ $M_{21} = (-1)^3 (-2) = 2$

$A_{22} = (-1)^{2+2}$ $M_{22} = (-1)^4 (1) = 1$

Example 2

Find minors and co-factors of the elements a_{11} and a_{21} in the determinant $\Delta = \begin{vmatrix} a_{11} & a_{12} & a_{13} \\ a_{21} & a_{22} & a_{23} \\ a_{31} & a_{32} & a_{33} \end{vmatrix}$.

Solution :

$$\text{Minor of } a_{11} = M_{11} = \begin{vmatrix} a_{22} & a_{23} \\ a_{32} & a_{33} \end{vmatrix} = a_{22}\, a_{33} - a_{23}\, a_{32}$$

$$\text{Co-factor of } a_{11} = A_{11} = (-1)^{1+1}\ M_{11} = a_{22}\, a_{33} - a_{23}\, a_{32}$$

Minor of $a_{21} = M_{11} = \begin{vmatrix} a_{12} & a_{13} \\ a_{32} & a_{33} \end{vmatrix} = a_{12}\,a_{33} - a_{13}\,a_{32}$

Co-factor of $a_{21} = A_{21} = (-1)^{2+1}$

$M_{21} = (-1)(a_{12}\,a_{33} - a_{13}a_{32})$

$= -a_{12}\,a_{33} + a_{13}\,a_{32}$

Example 3

Find the minors and co-factors of the first row of determinant $\begin{vmatrix} 3 & -3 & -4 \\ 1 & 2 & -2 \\ -1 & 2 & 1 \end{vmatrix}$.

Solution :

Elements of $R_1 = 3, -3$ and -4

Minor of 3 = $\begin{vmatrix} 2 & -2 \\ 2 & 1 \end{vmatrix}$

Minor of – 3 = $\begin{vmatrix} 1 & -2 \\ -1 & 1 \end{vmatrix}$

Minor of – 4 = $\begin{vmatrix} 1 & 2 \\ -1 & 2 \end{vmatrix}$

and co-factor of

$3 = A_{11} = (-1)^{1+1}, M_{11}$

[Formula $(-1)^{i+j} M_{ij}$]

$= (-1)^2 \begin{vmatrix} 2 & -2 \\ 2 & 1 \end{vmatrix} = (2+4) = 6$

Co-factor of – 3 = $A_{12} = (-1)^{1+2} \begin{vmatrix} 1 & -2 \\ -1 & 1 \end{vmatrix} = -(1-2) = 1$

Co-factor of 4 = $A_{13} = (-1)^{1+3} \begin{vmatrix} 1 & 2 \\ -1 & 2 \end{vmatrix} = (2+2) = 4$

Value of Determinant

Example 4

Find the value of the determinant given below using the Minor and Co-factor expansion method :

$$|A| = \begin{vmatrix} 2 & 3 \\ 1 & 5 \end{vmatrix}$$

Solution :

Determination of the value of |A| by the Minor expansion method :

Given $|A| \begin{vmatrix} 2 & 3 \\ 1 & 5 \end{vmatrix}$

Expanding the minors along the R_1, and chaining the products, we have,

$|A| = a_{11}\,M_{11} - a_{12}\,M_{12}$

Given $a_{11} = 2, a_{12} = 3, M_{11} = 5$ and $M_{12} = 1$

$|A| = (2 \times 5) - (3 \times 1) = 10 - 3 = 7$

Determination of the value |A| by co-factor expansion method :

$|A| = a_{11}.\,C_{11} + a_{12}.C_{12}$

where, $a_{11} = 2, a_{12} = 3$

$C_{11} = (-1)^{1+1}.\,M_{11} = 1(5) = 5$

$C_{12} = (-1)^{1+2}.\,M_{12} = -1\,(1) = -1$

we have, $|A| = a_{11}\,C_{11} + a_{12}\,C_{12}$

Thus, $|A| = (2 \times 5) + (3 \times -1) = 10 - 3 = 7$

Hence, the numerical value of the determinant

A = 7.

Example 5

Find the value of the determinant |A| from the following using the Minor and Co-factor expansion method :

$$|A| = \begin{vmatrix} 2 & -5 & 3 \\ 3 & -1 & 2 \\ 1 & -2 & 1 \end{vmatrix}$$

Solution :

Determination of the value of determinant A, by the Minor expansion method :

Given $|A| = \begin{vmatrix} 2 & -5 & 3 \\ 3 & -1 & 2 \\ 1 & -2 & 1 \end{vmatrix}$

Here, $a_{11} = 2, a_{12} = -5, a_{13} = 3$

$M_{11} = \begin{vmatrix} -1 & 2 \\ -2 & 1 \end{vmatrix}, M_{12} = \begin{vmatrix} 3 & 2 \\ 1 & 1 \end{vmatrix}$

and $M_3 = \begin{vmatrix} 3 & -1 \\ 1 & -2 \end{vmatrix}$

Expanding the Minors along the R_1 and chaining the products, we have,

$|A| = a_{11}\,M_{11} - a_{12}\,M_{12} + a_{13}\,M_{13}$

Substituting the respective values in the above, we have,

$|A| = 2\begin{vmatrix} -1 & 2 \\ -2 & 1 \end{vmatrix} - (-5)\begin{vmatrix} 3 & 2 \\ 1 & 1 \end{vmatrix} + 3\begin{vmatrix} 3 & -1 \\ 1 & -2 \end{vmatrix}$

$= 2\,[(-1 \times 1) - (2 \times -2)] + 5\,[(3 \times 1) - (2 \times 1)] + 3\,[(3 \times -2) - (-1 \times 1)]$

$= 2 \times 3 + 5 \times 1 + 3 \times -5$

$= 6 + 5 - 15 = -4$

Determination of the value of determinant by co-factor expansion method :

The co-factor of the det. A along its Row – 1 are :

$C_{11} = (-1)^{1+1}.M_{11} = 1\begin{vmatrix} -1 & 2 \\ -2 & 1 \end{vmatrix}$

$= 1\,[(-1 \times 1) - (2 \times -2)] = 3$

$C_{12} = (-1)^{1+2}.M_{12} = -1\begin{vmatrix} 3 & 2 \\ 1 & 1 \end{vmatrix}$

$= -1[(3 \times 1) - (2 \times 1)] = -1$

$C_{13} = (-1)^{1+3}.\,M_{13} = 1\begin{vmatrix} 3 & -1 \\ 1 & -2 \end{vmatrix}$

$= 1\,[(3 \times -2) - (-1 \times 1)] = -5$

The determinant is given by

$|A| = a_{11}.c_{11} + a_{12}.c_{12} + a_{13}.c_{13}$

Substituting the respective values in the above, we get, $|A| = (2 \times 3) + -5 \times (-1) + 3 \times (-5)$

$= 6 + 5 - 15 = -4$

Hence, the numerical value of the given 3 × 3 determinant A both the above ways = – 4.

Exercise 6 (A)

1. Find the minor of element 6 in the determinant :

$$\Delta = \begin{vmatrix} 1 & 2 & 3 \\ 4 & 5 & 6 \\ 7 & 8 & 9 \end{vmatrix}$$

2. Find the co-factors of 10, 11, 12, in the determinants :

$$\begin{vmatrix} 10 & 13 & 16 \\ 11 & 14 & 17 \\ 12 & 15 & 18 \end{vmatrix}$$

3. Find the minor and co-factors of determinant : $\begin{vmatrix} 2 & -4 \\ 0 & 3 \end{vmatrix}$

4. Find minor and co-factors of the elements 2, 6 in the determinant :

$$\begin{vmatrix} 2 & -3 & 5 \\ 6 & 0 & 4 \\ 1 & 5 & 7 \end{vmatrix}$$

5. Find the minors and co-factors of the first row of the determinant :

$$\begin{vmatrix} 1 & 2 & 3 \\ 3 & 4 & 5 \\ 5 & 6 & 7 \end{vmatrix}$$

6. Find the value of determinant $|A|$ from the following using Minor and Co-factor expansion method :

$$|A| = \begin{vmatrix} 7 & 17 \\ 9 & 22 \end{vmatrix}$$

7. Find the value of the determinant $|B|$ from the following using Minor and Co-factor expansion method along column 3 :

$$|B| = \begin{vmatrix} 1 & 3 & 1 \\ 2 & 5 & 4 \\ 6 & 1 & 5 \end{vmatrix}$$

Answers

1. – 6 2. – 3, 6, – 3
3. Minors : 3, 0, – 4, 2; Co-factors : 3, 0, 4, 2
4. Minors : $\begin{vmatrix} 0 & 4 \\ 5 & -7 \end{vmatrix}, \begin{vmatrix} -3 & 5 \\ 5 & -7 \end{vmatrix}$; Co-factors : – 20, – 4
5. Minors : $\begin{vmatrix} 4 & 5 \\ 6 & 7 \end{vmatrix}, \begin{vmatrix} 3 & 5 \\ 5 & 7 \end{vmatrix}, \begin{vmatrix} 3 & 4 \\ 5 & 6 \end{vmatrix}$; Co-factors : – 2, 4, – 2
6. 1 7. 35

6.3.3 Expansion of Second Order Determinants

The value of order two is the difference of the products of the principal diagonal elements and the product of second diagonal elements :

$$\begin{vmatrix} a_1 & b_1 \\ a_2 & b_2 \end{vmatrix} = \begin{vmatrix} a_1 & \\ & b_2 \end{vmatrix} - \begin{vmatrix} & b_1 \\ a_2 & \end{vmatrix}$$

$$= a_1b_2 - a_2b_1 \text{ or } b_1a_2 \begin{vmatrix} a_1 & b_1 \\ a_2 & b_2 \end{vmatrix}$$

Here every term on RHS has two elements.

Example :

$$\begin{vmatrix} 3 & -2 \\ -1 & 4 \end{vmatrix} = \begin{vmatrix} 3 & \\ & 4 \end{vmatrix} - \begin{vmatrix} & -2 \\ -1 & \end{vmatrix}$$

$$= (3 \times 4) - [(-2) \times (-1)]$$

$$= 12 - 2 = 10$$

6.3.4 Expansion of Third Order Determinants

First Method (Expansion by Row) :

$$\text{Let } \Delta = \begin{vmatrix} a_1 & b_1 & c_1 \\ a_2 & b_2 & c_2 \\ a_3 & b_3 & c_3 \end{vmatrix}$$

$$= a_1\begin{vmatrix} b_2 & c_2 \\ b_3 & c_3 \end{vmatrix} - b_1\begin{vmatrix} a_2 & c_2 \\ a_3 & c_3 \end{vmatrix} + c_1\begin{vmatrix} a_2 & b_2 \\ a_3 & b_3 \end{vmatrix}$$

$$= a_1(b_2c_3 - b_3c_2) - b_1(a_2c_3 - a_3c_2) + c_1(a_2b_3 - a_3b_2)$$

First method has been given before.

Second Method (Sarrus Expansion Method) : The numerical value of a determinant of the order three can be determined by Sarrus Expansion method. The following process should be followed to obtain the numerical value of a determinant by this method :

1. At first we write all the three columns. After this again write the first and second column as given below :

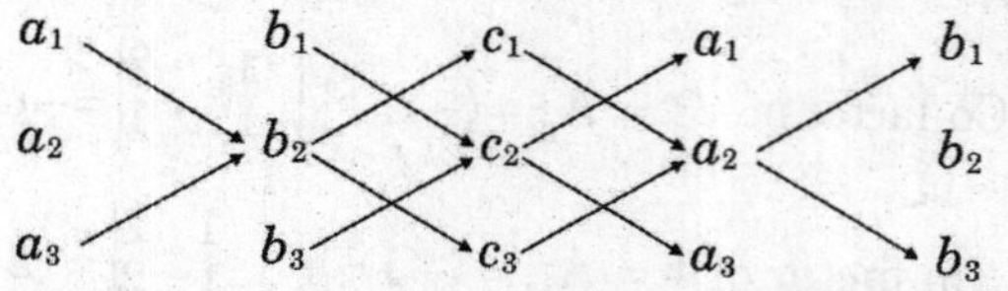

2. Now from upper left to right multiply a_1 by the numbers according to leading diagonal.

3. Similarly multiply b_1 by the numbers as above and then multiply c_1 by the numbers as above.

4. Adding them, we get

$$a_1b_2c_3 + b_1c_2a_3 + c_1a_2b_3 \quad \text{...(i)}$$

5. Again from lower left to right multiply a_3 by the numbers according to leading diagonal. Similarly multiply b_3 and c_3 by the numbers according to leading diagonals and adding them

$$a_3b_2c_1 + b_3c_2a_1 + c_2a_2b_1 \quad \text{...(ii)}$$

6. Now subtracting (ii) from (i), we get the expansion of the determinant.

That is

$$\Delta = a_1b_2c_3 + b_1c_2a_3 + c_1a_2b_3 - a_3b_2c_1 - b_3c_2a_1 - c_3a_2b_1$$
$$= a_1(b_2c_3 - b_3c_2) + b_1(c_2a_3 - c_3a_2) + c_1(a_2b_3 - a_3b_2)$$

6.3.5 Features of Determinant

1. The number of rows and columns in a determinant is equal, *i.e.*,

Number of Rows = Number of Columns
= Order of Determinant

2. Each element occurs only once in the products in the expansion of a determinant.

3. The number of terms in the expansion of 2 × 2 determinants is $\lfloor 2$ or 2! = 2

4. Out of there $n!$ or $\lfloor n$ terms (or products) half are with *plus sign* and half are with *minus sign*.

5. In determinant every element is written in + and – in alternative order.

6. The value of any element in the determinant is equal to the product of its place value and written number, therefore,

Value of element $a_{ij} = (-1)^{i+j} \times a_{ij}$

(6.4) PROPERTIES OF DETERMINANTS

Property I : The value of a determinant does not change when rows are changed into corresponding columns.

Proof :

Let $\Delta = \begin{vmatrix} a_1 & b_1 & c_1 \\ a_2 & b_2 & c_2 \\ a_3 & b_3 & c_3 \end{vmatrix}$ and $\Delta' = \begin{vmatrix} a_1 & a_2 & a_3 \\ b_1 & b_2 & b_3 \\ c_1 & c_2 & c_3 \end{vmatrix}$

Then we have to prove that

$\Delta' = \Delta$

$$\Delta = \begin{vmatrix} a_1 & b_1 & c_1 \\ a_2 & b_2 & c_2 \\ a_3 & b_3 & c_3 \end{vmatrix}$$

$$= a_1(b_2c_3 - b_3c_2) - b_1(a_2c_3 - a_3c_2) + c_1(a_2b_3 - a_3b_2) \quad \text{...(i)}$$

$$\text{Now } \Delta' = \begin{vmatrix} a_1 & a_2 & a_3 \\ b_1 & b_2 & b_3 \\ c_1 & c_2 & c_3 \end{vmatrix}$$

$$= a_1(b_2c_3 - b_3c_2) - a_2(b_1c_3 - b_3c_1) + a_3(b_1c_2 - b_2c_1)$$

$$= a_1(b_2c_3 - b_3c_2) - a_2b_1c_3 + a_2b_3c_1 + a_3b_1c_2 - a_3b_2c_1$$

$$= a_1(b_2c_3 - b_3c_2) - b_1(a_2c_3 - a_3c_2) + c_1(a_2b_3 - a_3b_2) \quad \text{...(ii)}$$

From (i) and (ii),

$\Delta' = \Delta$

Example :

$$\Delta = \begin{vmatrix} 1 & 2 & 3 \\ 2 & 3 & 4 \\ 0 & 1 & 5 \end{vmatrix} = 1(15-4) - 2(10-0) + 3(2-0)$$

$$= -3$$

$$\text{and } \Delta' = \begin{vmatrix} 1 & 2 & 0 \\ 2 & 3 & 1 \\ 3 & 4 & 5 \end{vmatrix} = 1(15-4) - 2(10-3) + 0(8-9)$$

$$= -3$$

So $\Delta' = \Delta$

Property II : If any two rows or columns of a determinant are inter-changed, the sign of the determinant is changed, but its value remains the same.

Proof :

Let $\Delta = \begin{vmatrix} a_1 & b_1 & c_1 \\ a_2 & b_2 & c_2 \\ a_3 & b_3 & c_3 \end{vmatrix}$ and $\Delta' = \begin{vmatrix} a_3 & b_3 & c_3 \\ a_2 & b_2 & c_2 \\ a_1 & b_1 & c_1 \end{vmatrix}$

Then we have to prove that

$\Delta' = -\Delta$

Expanding the determinant along row

$$\Delta = a_1(b_2c_3 - b_3c_2) - b_1(a_2c_3 - a_3c_2) + c_1(a_2b_3 - a_3b_2) \quad \text{...(i)}$$

$$\text{Now } \Delta' = \begin{vmatrix} a_3 & b_3 & c_3 \\ a_2 & b_2 & c_2 \\ a_1 & b_1 & c_1 \end{vmatrix} \; [R_1 \to R_3]$$

$$\Delta' = a_3(b_2c_1 - b_1c_2) - b_3(a_2c_1 - a_1c_2) + c_3(a_2b_1 - a_1b_2)$$

$$= a_3b_2c_1 - a_3b_1c_2 - b_3a_2c_1 + a_1b_3c_2 + c_3a_2b_1 - a_1b_2c_3$$

$$= a_1(b_2c_3 - b_3c_2) + b_1(a_2c_3 - a_3c_2) - c_1(a_2b_3 - a_3b_2) \quad \text{...(ii)}$$

From (i) and (ii),

$\Delta' = \Delta$

Example :

$$\Delta = \begin{vmatrix} 1 & 2 & 3 \\ 2 & 3 & 4 \\ 0 & 1 & 5 \end{vmatrix} = 1(15-4) - 2(10-0) + 3(2-0)$$

$$= -3$$

$$\text{and } \Delta' = \begin{vmatrix} 2 & 3 & 4 \\ 1 & 2 & 3 \\ 0 & 1 & 5 \end{vmatrix} \; [R_1 \leftrightarrow R_2]$$

$$= 2(10-3) - 3(5-0) + 4(1-0) = 3$$

so $\Delta' = -\Delta$

Property III : The value of a determinant is zero, if any two rows or columns are identical.

Proof : Let $\Delta = \begin{vmatrix} a_1 & b_1 & c_1 \\ a_2 & b_2 & c_2 \\ a_1 & b_1 & c_1 \end{vmatrix}$ then we have to prove that $\Delta = 0$

$$\text{then } \Delta = \begin{vmatrix} a_1 & b_1 & c_1 \\ a_2 & b_2 & c_2 \\ a_1 & b_1 & c_1 \end{vmatrix}$$

$$= -\begin{vmatrix} a_1 & b_1 & c_1 \\ a_2 & b_2 & c_2 \\ a_1 & b_1 & c_1 \end{vmatrix}$$

$$= -\Delta \; [R_1 \leftrightarrow R_3]$$

Thus $\Delta = -\Delta \Rightarrow 2\Delta = 0 \Rightarrow \Delta = 0$

Example :

$$\Delta = \begin{vmatrix} 1 & 2 & 3 \\ 2 & 3 & 4 \\ 1 & 2 & 3 \end{vmatrix}$$

$$= 1(9-8) - 2(6-4) + 3(4-3)$$
$$= 1 - 4 + 3 = 0$$

Property IV : If each constituent in any row or in any column is multiplied by the same factor then the determinant is multiplied by that factor.

In other words, if a factor is common in any row or column, then that common factor can be taken out as a product to the determinant.

Thus $\begin{vmatrix} ma_1 & mb_1 & mc_1 \\ a_2 & b_2 & c_2 \\ a_3 & b_3 & c_3 \end{vmatrix} = m\begin{vmatrix} a_1 & b_1 & c_1 \\ a_2 & b_2 & c_2 \\ a_3 & b_3 & c_3 \end{vmatrix}$

Proof : Let $\Delta = \begin{vmatrix} a_1 & b_1 & c_1 \\ a_2 & b_2 & c_2 \\ a_3 & b_3 & c_3 \end{vmatrix}$

then $\Delta = a_1(b_2c_3 - b_3c_2) - b_1(a_2c_3 - a_3c_2) + c_1(a_2b_3 - a_3b_2)$

Let $\Delta' = \begin{vmatrix} ma_1 & mb_1 & mc_1 \\ a_2 & b_2 & c_2 \\ a_3 & b_3 & c_3 \end{vmatrix}$

then $\Delta' = ma_1(b_2c_3 - b_3c_2) - mb_1(a_2c_3 - a_3c_2) + mc_1(a_2b_3 - a_3b_2)$

$= m[a_1(b_2c_3 - b_3c_2) - b_1(a_2c_3 - a_3c_2) + c_1(a_2b_3 - a_3b_2)]$

$= m\Delta$

Example :

$$\begin{vmatrix} 32 & 24 & 16 \\ 8 & 3 & 5 \\ 4 & 5 & 3 \end{vmatrix} = 8\begin{vmatrix} 4 & 3 & 2 \\ 8 & 3 & 5 \\ 4 & 5 & 3 \end{vmatrix}$$

[taking common 8 from first row]

$$= 8 \times 4\begin{vmatrix} 1 & 3 & 2 \\ 2 & 3 & 5 \\ 1 & 5 & 5 \end{vmatrix}$$

[taking common 4 from first column]

Property V : If each element of any row or column of a determinant is the sum of two quantities then determinant can be expressed as the sum of two determinants.

Example :

$$\Delta = \begin{vmatrix} a_1+\alpha_1 & b_1 & c_1 \\ a_2+\alpha_2 & b_2 & c_2 \\ a_3+\alpha_3 & b_3 & c_3 \end{vmatrix} = \begin{vmatrix} a_1 & b_1 & c_1 \\ a_2 & b_2 & c_2 \\ a_3 & b_3 & c_3 \end{vmatrix} + \begin{vmatrix} \alpha_1 & b_1 & c_1 \\ \alpha_2 & b_2 & c_2 \\ \alpha_3 & b_3 & c_3 \end{vmatrix}$$

Proof :

$$\Delta = \begin{vmatrix} a_1+\alpha_1 & b_1 & c_1 \\ a_2+\alpha_2 & b_2 & c_2 \\ a_3+\alpha_3 & b_3 & c_3 \end{vmatrix}$$

$$= (a_1+\alpha_1)\begin{vmatrix} b_2 & c_2 \\ b_3 & c_3 \end{vmatrix} - (a_2+\alpha_2)\begin{vmatrix} b_1 & c_1 \\ b_3 & c_3 \end{vmatrix} + (a_3+\alpha_3)\begin{vmatrix} b_1 & c_1 \\ b_2 & c_2 \end{vmatrix}$$

$$= a_1\begin{vmatrix} b_2 & c_2 \\ b_3 & c_3 \end{vmatrix} - a_2\begin{vmatrix} b_1 & c_1 \\ b_3 & c_3 \end{vmatrix} + a_3\begin{vmatrix} b_1 & c_1 \\ b_2 & c_2 \end{vmatrix} + \alpha_1\begin{vmatrix} b_2 & c_2 \\ b_3 & c_3 \end{vmatrix} - \alpha_2\begin{vmatrix} b_1 & c_1 \\ b_3 & c_3 \end{vmatrix} + \alpha_3\begin{vmatrix} b_1 & c_1 \\ b_2 & c_2 \end{vmatrix}$$

$$= \begin{vmatrix} a_1 & b_1 & c_1 \\ a_2 & b_2 & c_2 \\ a_3 & b_3 & c_3 \end{vmatrix} + \begin{vmatrix} \alpha_1 & b_1 & c_1 \\ \alpha_2 & b_2 & c_2 \\ \alpha_3 & b_3 & c_3 \end{vmatrix}$$

Notes : $\begin{vmatrix} a_1+b_1 & c_1+d_1 & e_1 \\ a_2+b_2 & c_2+d_2 & e_2 \\ a_3+b_3 & c_3+d_3 & e_3 \end{vmatrix} = \begin{vmatrix} a_1 & c_1 & e_1 \\ a_2 & c_2 & e_2 \\ a_3 & c_3 & e_3 \end{vmatrix} + \begin{vmatrix} a_1 & d_1 & e_1 \\ a_2 & d_2 & e_2 \\ a_3 & d_3 & e_3 \end{vmatrix} + \begin{vmatrix} b_1 & c_1 & e_1 \\ b_2 & c_2 & e_2 \\ b_3 & c_3 & e_3 \end{vmatrix} + \begin{vmatrix} b_1 & d_1 & e_1 \\ b_2 & d_2 & e_2 \\ b_3 & d_3 & e_3 \end{vmatrix}$

Property VI : The value of a determinant does not change when any row or column is multiplied by a number or expression and is then added to or subtracted from any other row or column.

Example :

Let $\Delta = \begin{vmatrix} 1 & 2 & 3 \\ 2 & 3 & 4 \\ 2 & 0 & 5 \end{vmatrix} = -7,$

$\Delta' = \begin{vmatrix} 5 & 2 & 13 \\ 2 & 3 & 4 \\ 2 & 0 & 5 \end{vmatrix}, R_1 \to R_1 + 2R_3$

$= 5(15-0) - 2(10-8) + 13(0-6)$

$= 75 - 4 - 78 = -7$

$\Delta'' = \frac{1}{3} R_1 \to 3R_1 + 2R_3 \begin{vmatrix} 7 & 6 & 19 \\ 2 & 3 & 4 \\ 2 & 0 & 5 \end{vmatrix}$

[Δ'' has been made by Δ]

$= \frac{1}{3}[7(15-0) - 6(10-8) + 19(0-6)]$

$= \frac{1}{3}(-21) = -7$

In Δ'' R_1 has been changed and R_1 has been multiplied by 3. So $\frac{1}{3}$ has been written out side the determinant.

Proof : We have to prove that

$$\begin{vmatrix} a_1 & b_1 & c_1 \\ a_2 & b_2 & c_2 \\ a_3 & b_3 & c_3 \end{vmatrix} = \begin{vmatrix} a_1+mb_1 & b_1 & c_1 \\ a_2+mb_2 & b_2 & c_2 \\ a_3+mb_3 & b_3 & c_3 \end{vmatrix}$$

Let $\Delta = \begin{vmatrix} a_1+mb_1 & b_1 & c_1 \\ a_2+mb_2 & b_2 & c_2 \\ a_3+mb_3 & b_3 & c_3 \end{vmatrix}$

Then $\Delta = \begin{vmatrix} a_1 & b_1 & c_1 \\ a_2 & b_2 & c_2 \\ a_3 & b_3 & c_3 \end{vmatrix} + \begin{vmatrix} mb_1 & b_1 & c_1 \\ mb_2 & b_2 & c_2 \\ mb_3 & b_3 & c_3 \end{vmatrix}$

$= \begin{vmatrix} a_1 & b_1 & c_1 \\ a_2 & b_2 & c_2 \\ a_3 & b_3 & c_3 \end{vmatrix} + m\begin{vmatrix} b_1 & b_1 & c_1 \\ b_2 & b_2 & c_2 \\ b_3 & b_3 & c_3 \end{vmatrix}$

$= \begin{vmatrix} a_1 & b_1 & c_1 \\ a_2 & b_2 & c_2 \\ a_3 & b_3 & c_3 \end{vmatrix} \quad \left[\because \begin{vmatrix} b_1 & b_1 & c_1 \\ b_2 & b_2 & c_2 \\ b_3 & b_3 & c_3 \end{vmatrix} = 0 \right]$

SOLVED EXAMPLES

Example 6. (A)

Find the value of $\begin{vmatrix} 9 & 3 \\ 12 & 4 \end{vmatrix}$. (*JAC*, 2015, 18, 19)

Solution :

Given determinant $= \begin{vmatrix} 9 & 3 \\ 12 & 4 \end{vmatrix} = 9 \times 4 - 3 \times 12$

$= 36 - 36$

$= 0$ **Ans.**

Example 6. (B)

Find the value of determinant $\begin{vmatrix} 3 & -4 \\ 5 & 9 \end{vmatrix}$.

Solution :

Let $\Delta = \begin{vmatrix} 3 & -4 \\ 5 & 9 \end{vmatrix}$

$= 3 \times 9 - 5 \times (-4)$

$= 27 + 20$

$= 47$ **Ans.**

Example 6. (C)

The value of $\begin{vmatrix} 2 & 4 \\ -1 & 3 \end{vmatrix}$ is (*JAC*, 2022)

Solution :

$= 2 \times 3 - (-1 \times 4)$

$= 6 - (-4)$

$= 6 + 4$

$= 10$ **Ans.**

Example 7. (A)

If $\begin{vmatrix} x & 5 \\ x & x \end{vmatrix} = 24$, then find the value of x. (*JAC*, 2015, 23)

Solution :

Here $\begin{vmatrix} x & 5 \\ x & x \end{vmatrix} = 24$

or $x^2 - 5x = 24$

or $x^2 - 5x - 24 = 0$

or $x^2 - 8x + 3x - 24 = 0$

or $x(x-8) + 3(x-8) = 0$

or $(x-8)(x+3) = 0$

$\therefore$ $x = 8$ or $x = -3$ **Ans.**

Example 7. (B)

If $\begin{vmatrix} 3 & -2 \\ -4 & x \end{vmatrix} = 15$, then find the value of x

Solution :

Here $\begin{vmatrix} 3 & -2 \\ -4 & x \end{vmatrix} = 15$

or $3 \times x - (-4)(-2) = 15$

or $3x - 8 = 15$

or $3x = 15 + 8$

or $3x = 23$

$\therefore$ $x = \frac{23}{3}$ **Ans.**

Example 7. (C)

Find the values of x and y when

$\begin{bmatrix} 1 & -2 \\ y & x \end{bmatrix} = 0$ and $\begin{bmatrix} 7 & 6 \\ y & x \end{bmatrix} = 40$. (*JAC*, 2024)

Solution :

Given $\begin{bmatrix} 1 & -2 \\ y & x \end{bmatrix} = 0$ and $\begin{bmatrix} 7 & 6 \\ y & x \end{bmatrix} = 40$.

$x(1) + 2(y) = 0$ and $7(x) - 6(y) = 40$

$x + 2y = 0$ ....(i)

$7x - 6y = 40$ ...(ii)

From Equ. (i) & (ii)

$x + 2y = 0$

$7x - 6y = 40$

$7x + 14y = 0$

$7x - 6y = 40$

$- \quad + \quad -$

$20y = -40$

$y = \frac{-40}{20}$

$y = -2$

Now,

$$x + 2y = 0$$
$$x + 2(-2) = 0$$
$$x = 4$$

Hence

$$x = 4, y = -2$$ **Ans.**

Example 8.

Evaluate : $\begin{vmatrix} 1 & 2 & 4 \\ 1 & 3 & 9 \\ 1 & 4 & 16 \end{vmatrix}$ (*JAC*, 2016)

Solution :

Let $a = 2, b = 3, c = 3$

Now $\Delta = \begin{vmatrix} 1 & a & a^2 \\ 1 & b & b^2 \\ 1 & c & c^2 \end{vmatrix}$, where $\begin{matrix} a = 2 \\ b = 3 \\ c = 4 \end{matrix}$

$$= (a-b)(b-c)(c-a)$$
$$= (2-3)(3-4)(4-2) = 2$$ **Ans.**

Example 9.

Prove that $\begin{vmatrix} 1 & a & a^2 \\ 1 & b & b^2 \\ 1 & c & c^2 \end{vmatrix} = (a-b)(b-c)(c-a).$

Solution :

Let $\Delta = \begin{vmatrix} 1 & a & a^2 \\ 1 & b & b^2 \\ 1 & c & c^2 \end{vmatrix}$

Now $\Delta = \begin{vmatrix} 0 & a-b & a^2-b^2 \\ 0 & b-c & b^2-c^2 \\ 1 & c & c^2 \end{vmatrix}$

$[R_1 \to R_1 - R_2, R_2 \to R_2 - R_3]$

$$= (a-b)(b-c)\begin{vmatrix} 0 & 1 & a+b \\ 0 & 1 & b+c \\ 1 & c & c^2 \end{vmatrix}$$

$$= (a-b)(b-c).1\begin{vmatrix} 1 & a+b \\ 1 & b+c \end{vmatrix}$$

$$= (a-b)(b-c)(b+c-a-b)$$
$$= (a-b)(b-c)(c-a)$$ **Ans.**

Example 10.

Prove that $\begin{vmatrix} 23 & 12 & 11 \\ 36 & 10 & 26 \\ 63 & 26 & 37 \end{vmatrix} = 0.$

Solution :

$$\Delta = 23\begin{vmatrix} 10 & 26 \\ 26 & 37 \end{vmatrix} - 12\begin{vmatrix} 36 & 26 \\ 63 & 37 \end{vmatrix} + 11\begin{vmatrix} 36 & 10 \\ 63 & 26 \end{vmatrix}$$

$$= 23[(10 \times 37 - 26 \times 26)] - 12[(36 \times 37 - 26 \times 63)] + 11[(36 \times 26 - 10 \times 63)]$$
$$= 23(370-676) - 12(1{,}332-1{,}638) + 11(936-630)$$
$$= -23 \times 306 - 12 \times (-306) + 11 \times 306$$
$$= (-23 + 12 + 11) \times 306$$
$$= 0 \times 306 = 0$$ **Proved**

Example 11.

Find the value of determinant :

$$\begin{vmatrix} 265 & 240 & 219 \\ 240 & 225 & 198 \\ 219 & 198 & 181 \end{vmatrix}.$$

Solution :

$$\Delta = \begin{vmatrix} 265 & 240 & 219 \\ 240 & 225 & 198 \\ 219 & 198 & 181 \end{vmatrix}$$

By $C_1 - C_2 \to C_1$ and $C_2 - C_3 \to C_2$,

$$\Delta = \begin{vmatrix} 25 & 21 & 219 \\ 15 & 27 & 198 \\ 21 & 17 & 181 \end{vmatrix}$$

By $C_1 - C_2 \to C_1$ and $C_3 - 8C_1 \to C_3$,

$$\Delta = \begin{vmatrix} 4 & 21 & 19 \\ -12 & 27 & 78 \\ 4 & 17 & 13 \end{vmatrix}$$

By $R_1 - R_3 \to R_1$ and $R_2 + 3R_3 \to R_2$,

$$\Delta = \begin{vmatrix} 0 & 4 & 6 \\ 0 & 78 & 117 \\ 4 & 17 & 13 \end{vmatrix}$$

$$= \begin{vmatrix} 0 & 2 \times 2 & 2 \times 3 \\ 0 & 39 \times 2 & 39 \times 3 \\ 4 & 17 & 13 \end{vmatrix}$$

$$= 2 \times 39\begin{vmatrix} 0 & 2 & 3 \\ 0 & 2 & 3 \\ 4 & 17 & 13 \end{vmatrix}$$

$$= 2 \times 39 \times 4(6-6) = 0$$ **Ans.**

Example 12.

Evaluate : $\Delta = \begin{vmatrix} b+c & a+b & a \\ c+a & b+c & b \\ a+b & c+a & c \end{vmatrix}.$

Solution :

$$\Delta = \begin{vmatrix} a+b+c & a+b & a \\ a+b+c & b+c & b \\ a+b+c & c+a & c \end{vmatrix} \quad [C_1 \to C_1 + C_3]$$

$$= (a+b+c)\begin{vmatrix} 1 & a+b & a \\ 1 & b+c & b \\ 1 & c+a & c \end{vmatrix}$$

$$= (a+b+c)\begin{vmatrix} 1 & a+b & a \\ 0 & c-a & b-a \\ 0 & c-b & c-a \end{vmatrix}$$

$[R_2 \to R_2 - R_1 ; R_3 \to R_3 - R_1]$

$= (a + b + c) [(c - a)^2 - (c - b) (b - a)]$

$= (a + b + c) [c^2 + a^2 - 2ca - (cb - ca - b^2 + ba)]$

$= (a + b + c) [a^2 + b^2 + c^2 - bc - ca - ab]$

$= a^3 + b^3 + c^3 - 3abc$ **Ans.**

Example 13.

Evaluate : $\Delta = \begin{vmatrix} 1+a_1 & a_2 & a_3 \\ a_1 & 1+a_2 & a_3 \\ a_1 & a_2 & 1+a_3 \end{vmatrix}$

Solution :

$$\Delta = \begin{vmatrix} 1+a_1+a_2+a_3 & a_2 & a_3 \\ 1+a_1+a_2+a_3 & 1+a_2 & a_3 \\ 1+a_1+a_2+a_3 & a_2 & 1+a_3 \end{vmatrix}$$

$[C_1 \to C_1 + C_2 + C_3]$

$$= (1+a_1+a_2+a_3)\begin{vmatrix} 1 & a_2 & a_3 \\ 1 & 1+a_2 & a_3 \\ 1 & a_2 & 1+a_3 \end{vmatrix}$$

$$= (1+a_1+a_2+a_3)\begin{vmatrix} 0 & -1 & 0 \\ 0 & 1 & -1 \\ 1 & a_2 & 1+a_3 \end{vmatrix} \quad [R_1 \to R_1 - R_2; R_2 \to R_2 - R_3]$$

$$= (a+a_1+a_2+a_3)\begin{vmatrix} -1 & 0 \\ 1 & -1 \end{vmatrix}$$

$= (1+a_1+a_2+a_3)(1-0)$

$= 1+a_1+a_2+a_3$ **Ans.**

Example 14.

Prove that $\begin{vmatrix} a-b-c & 2a & 2a \\ 2b & b-c-a & 2b \\ 2c & 2c & c-a-b \end{vmatrix} = (a+b+c)^3$

Solution :

$$\Delta = \begin{vmatrix} a+b+c & a+b+c & a+b+c \\ 2b & b-c-a & 2b \\ 2c & 2c & c-a-b \end{vmatrix}$$

$[R_1 \to R_1 + R_2 + R_3]$

$$= (a+b+c)\begin{vmatrix} 1 & 1 & 1 \\ 2b & b-c-a & 2b \\ 2c & 2c & c-a-b \end{vmatrix}$$

$$= (a+b+c)\begin{vmatrix} 1 & 0 & 0 \\ 2b & -b-c-a & 0 \\ 2c & 0 & -c-a-b \end{vmatrix}$$

$[C_1 \to C_2 - C_1; C_3 \to C_3 - C_1]$

$$= (a+b+c)\begin{vmatrix} -b-c-a & 0 \\ 0 & -c-a-b \end{vmatrix}$$

$= (a + b + c) [-(b + c + a) \times -(c + a + b)]$

$= (a + b + c) (a - b + c)^2 = (a + b + c)^3$ **Proved**

Example 15.

Prove that $\begin{vmatrix} a+b+2c & a & b \\ c & b+c+2a & b \\ c & a & c+a+2b \end{vmatrix} = 2(a + b + c)^3.$

Solution :

$$\Delta = \begin{vmatrix} 2(a+b+c) & a & b \\ 2(a+b+c) & b+c+2a & b \\ 2(a+b+c) & a & c+a+2b \end{vmatrix}$$

$[C_1 \to C_2 + C_2 + C_3]$

$$= 2(a+b+c)\begin{vmatrix} 1 & a & b \\ 1 & b+c+2a & b \\ 1 & a & c+a+2b \end{vmatrix}$$

$$= 2(a+b+c)\begin{vmatrix} 0 & -(b+c+a) & 0 \\ 0 & (b+c+a) & -(a+b+c) \\ 1 & a & c+a+2b \end{vmatrix}$$

$[R_1 \to R_1 - R_2; R_2 \to R_2 - R_3]$

$$= 2(a+b+c)(a+b+c)^2\begin{vmatrix} 0 & -1 & 0 \\ 0 & 1 & -1 \\ 1 & a & c+a+2b \end{vmatrix}$$

$= 2 (a + b + c)^3 \, 1 \, [\{(-1)(-1) - 1.0\}]$

$= 2 (a + b + c)^3$ **Proved**

Example 16.

Evaluate :

$\begin{vmatrix} b+c & a & c \\ b & c+a & b \\ c & c & a+b \end{vmatrix}$. (*JAC*, 2017)

Solution :

$$\Delta = \begin{vmatrix} 0 & -2c & -2b \\ b & c+a & b \\ c & c & a+b \end{vmatrix} \quad [R_1 \to R_1 - R_2 - R_3]$$

$$= \frac{1}{bc}\begin{vmatrix} 0 & -2c & -2b \\ bc & c(c+a) & bc \\ bc & bc & a(a+b) \end{vmatrix}$$

$[R_2 \to c.R_2,\ R_3 \to bR_3]$

$$= \frac{1}{bc}\begin{vmatrix} 0 & -2c & -2b \\ 0 & c(c+a-b) & b(c-a-b) \\ bc & bc & a(a+b) \end{vmatrix}$$

$[\text{by } R_2 \to R_2 - R_3]$

$$= \frac{1}{bc}.bc\begin{vmatrix} -2c & -2b \\ c(c+a-b) & b(c-a-b) \end{vmatrix}$$

$= -2bc\,(c-a-b) + 2bc\,(c+a-b)$

$= 2bc\,(-c+a+b+c+a-b)$

$= 2bc\,(2a) = 4abc$ **Ans.**

Example 17.

Find the value of $\begin{vmatrix} b^2+c^2 & ab & ac \\ ab & c^2+a^2 & bc \\ ca & cb & a^2+b^2 \end{vmatrix}$.

Solution :

Multiplying C_1 by a, C_2 by b and C_3 by c respectively, we get

$$\Delta = \frac{1}{abc}\begin{vmatrix} a(b^2+c^2) & ab^2 & ac^2 \\ a^2b & b(c^2+a^2) & bc^2 \\ ca^2 & cb^2 & c(a^2+b^2) \end{vmatrix}$$

$$= \frac{1}{abc} \times abc\begin{vmatrix} b^2+c^2 & b^2 & c^2 \\ a^2 & c^2+a^2 & c^2 \\ a^2 & b^2 & a^2+b^2 \end{vmatrix}$$

Using $C_1 \to C_1 - (C_2 + C_3)$

$$\Delta = \begin{vmatrix} 0 & b^2 & c^2 \\ -2c^2 & c^2+a^2 & c^2 \\ -2b^2 & b^2 & a^2+b^2 \end{vmatrix}$$

$$= -2\begin{vmatrix} 0 & b^2 & c^2 \\ c^2 & c^2+a^2 & c^2 \\ b^2 & b^2 & a^2+b^2 \end{vmatrix}$$

Again using $C_2 \to C_2 - C_1$ and $C_3 \to C_3 - C_1$

$$\Delta = -2\begin{vmatrix} 0 & b^2 & c^2 \\ c^2 & a^2 & 0 \\ b^2 & 0 & a^2 \end{vmatrix}$$

$$= -2\left[0.\begin{vmatrix} a^2 & 0 \\ 0 & a^2 \end{vmatrix} - b^2\begin{vmatrix} c^2 & 0 \\ b^2 & a^2 \end{vmatrix} + c^2\begin{vmatrix} c^2 & a^2 \\ b^2 & 0 \end{vmatrix}\right]$$

$= -2[0 - b^2(a^2c^2) + c^2(-a^2b^2)]$

$= -2(-2a^2b^2c^2)$

$= 4a^2b^2c^2 = (2abc)^2$ **Ans.**

Example 18.

If $a+b+c=0$, then find $\begin{vmatrix} a-x & c & b \\ c & b-x & a \\ b & a & c-x \end{vmatrix} = 0.$

Solution :

By given determinants

$$\begin{vmatrix} a+b+c-x & c & b \\ a+b+c-x & b-x & a \\ a+b+c-x & a & c-x \end{vmatrix} = 0$$

$[\text{Using } C_1 \to C_1 + C_2 + C_3]$

or $(a+b+c-x)\begin{vmatrix} 1 & c & b \\ 1 & b-x & a \\ 1 & a & c-x \end{vmatrix} = 0$

or $(-x)\begin{vmatrix} 1 & c & b \\ 0 & b-c-x & a-b \\ 0 & a-c & c-b-x \end{vmatrix} = 0$

$[\text{Using } R_2 \to R_2 - R_1,\ R_3 \to R_3 - R_1]$

$[\because a+b+c=0]$

or $x\,[(b-c-x)(c-b-x) - (a-c)(a-b)] = 0$

or $x\,(x^2 - b^2 - c^2 + 2bc - a^2 + ab + ca - bc) = 0$

or $x(x^2 - a^2 - b^2 - c^2 + ab + bc + ca) = 0$

$\therefore$ $x = 0$

or $x^2 = a^2 + b^2 + c^2 - (ab + bc + ca)$

$= (a^2+b^2+c^2) - \frac{1}{2}[(a+b+c)^2 - (a^2+b^2+c^2)]$

$= \frac{3}{2}(a^2+b^2+c^2)$ $[\because a+b+c=0]$

$x = 0$ or $x = \pm\sqrt{\left\{\frac{3}{2}(a^2+b^2+c^2)\right\}}$

Example 19.

Solve : $\begin{vmatrix} a & a & x \\ a & a & a \\ b & x & b \end{vmatrix} = 0.$

Solution :

By the given determinant $\begin{vmatrix} 0 & a & x \\ 0 & a & a \\ b-x & x & b \end{vmatrix} = 0$

$[\text{Using } C_1 \to C_1 - C_2]$

$\Rightarrow$ $(b-x)\begin{vmatrix} a & x \\ a & a \end{vmatrix} = 0$

$\Rightarrow \quad (b-x)(a^2-ax) = 0$

$\therefore \quad b-x = 0$ and $a^2-ax=0$

$\Rightarrow \quad x = b$ and $ax = a^2$

$\therefore \quad x = b$ and $x = a$ **Ans.**

Example 20.

Solve : $\begin{vmatrix} x+a & b & c \\ a & x+b & c \\ a & b & x+c \end{vmatrix} = 0.$

Solution :

$$\begin{vmatrix} x+a+b+c & b & c \\ x+a+b+c & x+b & c \\ x+a+b+c & b & x+c \end{vmatrix} = 0$$

[Using $C_1 \to C_1 + C_2 + C_3$]

$$\text{or} \quad (x+a+b+c)\begin{vmatrix} 1 & b & c \\ 1 & x+b & c \\ 1 & b & x+c \end{vmatrix} = 0$$

$$\text{or} \quad (x+a+b+c)\begin{vmatrix} 0 & -x & 0 \\ 0 & x & -x \\ 1 & b & x+c \end{vmatrix} = 0$$

[Using $R_1 \to R_1 - R_2, R_2 \to R_2 - R_3$]

$$\text{or} \quad (x+a+b+c)\,1\begin{vmatrix} -x & 0 \\ x & -x \end{vmatrix} = 0$$

or $\quad (x+a+b+c)(x^2) = 0$

$\therefore \quad x^2 = 0$

or $\quad x+a+b+c = 0$

$\Rightarrow \quad x = 0$

$\Rightarrow \quad x = -(a+b+c)$

Ans.

Example 21.

Show without expanding: $\begin{vmatrix} a & bc & abc \\ b & ca & abc \\ c & ab & abc \end{vmatrix} = \begin{vmatrix} a & a^2 & a^3 \\ b & b^2 & b^3 \\ c & c^2 & c^3 \end{vmatrix}.$

Solution :

$$\text{L.H.S.} = \frac{1}{a^2b^2c^2}\begin{vmatrix} a^3 & a^2bc & a^3bc \\ b^3 & ab^2c & ab^3c \\ c^3 & abc^2 & abc^3 \end{vmatrix}$$

[Using $R_1 \to a^2R_1, R_2 \to b^2R_2, R_3 \to c^2R_3$]

$$= \frac{(abc)(abc)}{a^2b^2c^2}\begin{vmatrix} a^3 & a & a^2 \\ b^3 & b & b^2 \\ c^3 & c & c^2 \end{vmatrix}$$

$$= -\begin{vmatrix} a & a^3 & a^2 \\ b & b^3 & b^2 \\ c & c^3 & c^2 \end{vmatrix}$$

[Using $C_1 \leftrightarrow C_2$] Inter-change C_1 and C_2

$$= \begin{vmatrix} a & a^2 & a^3 \\ b & b^2 & b^3 \\ c & c^2 & c^3 \end{vmatrix} = \text{R.H.S.} \quad [\text{Using } C_2 \leftrightarrow C_3]$$

Proved

Example 22.

Show without expanding :

$$\begin{vmatrix} b+c & c+a & a+b \\ q+r & r+p & p+q \\ y+z & z+x & x+y \end{vmatrix} = 2\begin{vmatrix} a & b & c \\ p & q & r \\ x & y & z \end{vmatrix}.$$

Solution :

$$\text{L.H.S.} = \Delta = \begin{vmatrix} b-c & c+a & a+b \\ q-r & r+p & p+q \\ y\,z & z+x & x+y \end{vmatrix}$$

[Using $C_1 + (C_2 - C_3)$]

$$= \begin{vmatrix} 2c & c+a & a+b \\ 2r & r+p & p+q \\ 2z & z+x & x+y \end{vmatrix}$$

$$= \begin{vmatrix} c & c+a & a+b \\ 2r & r+p & p+q \\ z & z+x & x+y \end{vmatrix} \quad [\text{Using } C_2 - C_1]$$

$$= 2\begin{vmatrix} c & c & a+b \\ r & p & p+q \\ z & z & x+y \end{vmatrix} \quad [\text{Using } C_3 - C_2]$$

$$= 2\begin{vmatrix} c & a & b \\ r & p & q \\ z & z & y \end{vmatrix}$$

$$= 2(-1)^2\begin{vmatrix} a & b & c \\ p & q & r \\ x & y & z \end{vmatrix} = 2\begin{vmatrix} a & b & c \\ p & q & r \\ x & y & z \end{vmatrix}$$

Using $C_1 \leftrightarrow C_2$, then $C_2 \leftrightarrow C_3$ = R.H.S. **Proved**

Example 23.

Show that $\begin{vmatrix} 0 & p-q & p-r \\ q-p & 0 & q-r \\ r-p & r-q & 0 \end{vmatrix} = 0.$

Solution :

$$\text{L.H.S.} = \begin{vmatrix} 0 & p-q & p-r \\ q-p & 0 & q-r \\ r-p & r-q & 0 \end{vmatrix}$$

$$= \begin{vmatrix} q-p & r-q & p-r \\ q-p & r-q & q-r \\ q-p & r-q & 0 \end{vmatrix}$$

Using $C_1 \to C_1 - C_2$ and $C_2 \to C_2 - C_3$

$$= (q-p)(r-q) \begin{vmatrix} 1 & 1 & p-r \\ 1 & 1 & q-r \\ 1 & 1 & 0 \end{vmatrix}$$

$= 0$ **Proved**

Example 24.

Find the value of $A = \begin{vmatrix} 2 & 2 & 3 \\ 3 & 4 & 5 \\ 6 & 7 & 8 \end{vmatrix}$ (*JAC*, 2018, 26)

Solution :

$$A = \begin{vmatrix} 2 & 2 & 3 \\ 3 & 4 & 5 \\ 6 & 7 & 9 \end{vmatrix}$$

$$= 2\begin{vmatrix} 4 & 5 \\ 7 & 9 \end{vmatrix} - 2\begin{vmatrix} 3 & 5 \\ 6 & 9 \end{vmatrix} + 3\begin{vmatrix} 3 & 4 \\ 6 & 7 \end{vmatrix}$$

$= 2(36-35) - 2(27-30) + 3(21-24)$

$= 2(1) - 2(-3) + 3(-3)$

$= 2 + 6 - 9$

$= 8 - 9$

$= -1$ **Proved**

Exercise 6 (B)

1. (a) Evaluate :

(i) $\begin{vmatrix} 7 & 15 \\ 8 & 20 \end{vmatrix}$ (ii) $\begin{vmatrix} 6 & -3 \\ 7 & 2 \end{vmatrix}$

(b) (i) Find the value of x, when

$\begin{vmatrix} x & 1 \\ x & x \end{vmatrix} = 20$ (*JAC*, 2020)

(ii) Find the value of x if $\begin{vmatrix} 4x & 16 \\ x & x \end{vmatrix} = -15$

2. Find x and y when $\begin{vmatrix} -6 & 5 \\ x & y \end{vmatrix} = -9$, $\begin{vmatrix} 7 & 4 \\ y & x \end{vmatrix} = 37$. (*JAC*, 2025)

3. Find the value of :

$$\begin{vmatrix} 4 & 9 & 7 \\ 3 & 5 & 7 \\ 5 & 4 & 5 \end{vmatrix}$$

4. Find the value of :

$$\begin{vmatrix} 1 & 2 & 4 \\ 1 & 3 & 6 \\ 1 & 4 & 7 \end{vmatrix}$$

5. Find the value of : (*JAC*, 2024)

$$\begin{vmatrix} a & h & g \\ h & b & f \\ g & f & c \end{vmatrix}$$

6. Find the value of :

$$\begin{vmatrix} 1 & a^2 & a^3 \\ 1 & b^2 & b^3 \\ 1 & c^2 & c^3 \end{vmatrix}$$

7. Find the value of : (*JAC*, 2016)

$$\begin{vmatrix} 1 & 1 & 1 \\ a & b & c \\ a^2 & b^2 & c^2 \end{vmatrix}$$

8. Find the value of : (*JAC*, 2015)

$$\begin{vmatrix} 1 & a & a^2-bc \\ 1 & b & b^2-ca \\ 1 & c & c^2-ab \end{vmatrix}$$

9. Find the value of : (*JAC*, 2015)

$$\begin{vmatrix} 1 & bc & bc(b+c) \\ 1 & ca & ca(c+a) \\ 1 & ab & ab(a+b) \end{vmatrix}$$

10. Evaluate : (*JAC*, 2026)

$$\begin{vmatrix} 1 & a & b+c \\ 1 & b & c+a \\ 1 & c & a+b \end{vmatrix}$$

11. Prove that :

$$\begin{vmatrix} 1 & a & bc \\ 1 & b & ca \\ 1 & c & ab \end{vmatrix} = (a-b)(b-c)(c-a)$$

12. Prove that :

$$\begin{vmatrix} a & a+b & a+2b \\ a+2b & a & a+b \\ a+b & a+2b & a \end{vmatrix} = 9b^2(a+b)$$

13. Prove that :

$$\begin{vmatrix} x+a & x+b & x+c \\ y+a & y+b & y+c \\ z+a & z+b & z+c \end{vmatrix} = 0$$

14. Prove that :

$$\begin{vmatrix} a+b & b+c & c+a \\ b+c & c+a & a+b \\ c+a & a+b & b+c \end{vmatrix} = -2(a^3+b^3+c^3-3abc)$$

15. If a, b, c are in A.P., show that :

$$\begin{vmatrix} x+1 & x+2 & x+a \\ x+2 & x+3 & x+b \\ x+3 & x+4 & x+c \end{vmatrix} = 0$$

[**Hint :** a, b, c are in A.P

$\therefore a-b = b-c = K$

$$\Delta = \begin{vmatrix} -1 & -1 & a-b \\ -1 & -1 & b-c \\ x+3 & x+4 & x+c \end{vmatrix}$$ [Using $R_1 \to R_1 - R_2$, $R_2 \to R_2 - R_3$]

$$= \begin{vmatrix} -1 & -1 & K \\ -1 & -1 & K \\ x+3 & x+4 & x+c \end{vmatrix} = 0 \; [\because R_1 = R_2]$$ **Proved**

16. Solve : (*JAC*, 2023)

$$\begin{vmatrix} x & 2 & 3 \\ 4 & x & 1 \\ x & 2 & 5 \end{vmatrix} = 0$$

17. Solve :

$$\begin{vmatrix} 3+x & 5 & 2 \\ 1 & 7+x & 6 \\ 2 & 5 & 3+x \end{vmatrix} = 0$$

18. Show without expanding at any stage that :

$$\begin{vmatrix} 0 & c & b \\ -c & 0 & a \\ -b & -a & 0 \end{vmatrix} = 0$$

[Hint: $\Delta = \begin{vmatrix} 0 & c & b \\ -c & 0 & a \\ -b & -a & 0 \end{vmatrix}$

$= \begin{vmatrix} 0 & -c & -b \\ c & 0 & -a \\ b & a & 0 \end{vmatrix}$ Using Row ↔ Column

$= \begin{vmatrix} 0 & c & b \\ -c & 0 & a \\ -b & -a & 0 \end{vmatrix}$ $\begin{bmatrix} \text{Using } -1.R_1 \to R_1 \\ -1.R_2 \to R_2 \\ -1.R_3 \to R_3 \end{bmatrix}$

$= -\Delta$

or $\Delta = -\Delta$

or $\Delta + \Delta = 0$

or $2\Delta = 0$

∴ $\Delta = 0$

or $\begin{vmatrix} 0 & c & b \\ -c & 0 & a \\ -b & -a & 0 \end{vmatrix} = 0$]

19. Show without expanding at any stage that :

$$\begin{vmatrix} (a-1)^2 & a^2+1 & a \\ (b-1)^2 & b^2+1 & b \\ (c-1)^2 & c^2+1 & c \end{vmatrix} = 0$$

20. Show without expanding at any stage that : (*JAC*, 2015)

$$\begin{vmatrix} 1 & a & bc \\ 1 & b & ca \\ 1 & c & ab \end{vmatrix} = \begin{vmatrix} 1 & a & a^2 \\ 1 & b & b^2 \\ 1 & c & c^2 \end{vmatrix}$$

21. Evaluate :

$$\begin{vmatrix} 5 & 10 & 8 \\ 4 & 3 & 2 \\ 7 & 9 & 8 \end{vmatrix}$$

22. Prove that :

$$\begin{vmatrix} 0 & ab^2 & ac^2 \\ a^2b & 0 & bc^2 \\ a^2c & b^2c & 0 \end{vmatrix} = 2a^3b^3c^3$$

23. Solve the equation :

$$\begin{vmatrix} 15-x & 1 & 10 \\ 11-3x & 1 & 16 \\ 7-x & 1 & 13 \end{vmatrix} = 0$$

Answers

1. (a) (i) 20, (ii) 33, (b) $x = (5, -4)$, $\left[x = \dfrac{5}{2}, \dfrac{3}{2}\right]$

2. $x = \dfrac{129}{31}, y = -\dfrac{62}{31}$ 3. 77 4. – 1

5. $abc + 2fgh - af^2 - bg^2 - ch^2$

6. $(a-b)(b-c)(c-a)(ab+bc+ca)$

7. $(b-c)(c-a)(a-b)$

8. 0 9. 0 16. $\pm 2\sqrt{2}$

17. 0, – 1, – 12, 21. – 30, 23. $x = 6$

(6.5) CRAMER'S RULE

Use of Determinants in Solving Linear Equation (Cramer's Rule)

System of Linear Equations of Two Variables

Let the system of eqs. are

$$a_1x + b_1y + c_1 = 0 \quad \text{...(i)}$$
$$a^2x + b_2y + c_2 = 0 \quad \text{...(ii)}$$

where $\begin{vmatrix} a_1 & b_1 \\ a_2 & b_2 \end{vmatrix} \neq 0$

By cross multiplication,

$$\frac{x}{b_1c_2 - b_2c_1} = \frac{-y}{a_1c_2 - a_2c_1} = \frac{1}{a_1b_2 - a_2b_1}$$

or
$$\frac{x}{\begin{vmatrix} b_1 & c_1 \\ b_2 & c_2 \end{vmatrix}} = \frac{-y}{\begin{vmatrix} a_1 & c_1 \\ a_2 & c_2 \end{vmatrix}} = \frac{1}{\begin{vmatrix} a_1 & b_1 \\ a_2 & b_2 \end{vmatrix}}$$

We can find the value of x and y from the above relation.

System of Linear Equations in Three Variables

Let the system of equations in three variable x, y and z are

$$a_1x + b_1y + c_1z = d_1 \quad \text{...(i)}$$
$$a_2x + b_2y + c_2z = d_2 \quad \text{...(ii)}$$
$$a_3x + b_3y + c_3z = d_3 \quad \text{...(iii)}$$

Let $\Delta = \begin{vmatrix} a_1 & b_1 & c_1 \\ a_2 & b_2 & c_2 \\ a_3 & b_3 & c_3 \end{vmatrix}$, $\Delta_1 = \begin{vmatrix} d_1 & b_1 & c_1 \\ d_2 & b_2 & c_2 \\ d_3 & b_3 & c_3 \end{vmatrix}$

$\Delta_2 = \begin{vmatrix} a_1 & d_1 & c_1 \\ a_2 & d_2 & c_2 \\ a_3 & d_3 & c_3 \end{vmatrix}$, $\Delta_3 = \begin{vmatrix} a_1 & b_1 & d_1 \\ a_2 & b_2 & d_2 \\ a_3 & b_3 & d_3 \end{vmatrix}$

Let $\Delta \neq 0$

Now $\Delta_1 = \begin{vmatrix} d_1 & b_1 & c_1 \\ d_2 & b_2 & c_2 \\ d_3 & b_3 & c_3 \end{vmatrix}$

$$= \begin{vmatrix} a_1x+b_1y+c_1z & b_1 & c_1 \\ a_2x+b_2y+c_2z & b_2 & c_2 \\ a_3x+b_3y+c_3z & b_3 & c_3 \end{vmatrix}$$

$$= \begin{vmatrix} a_1x & b_1 & c_1 \\ a_2x & b_2 & c_2 \\ a_3x & b_3 & c_3 \end{vmatrix}$$

$$= x\begin{vmatrix} a_1 & b_1 & c_1 \\ a_2 & b_2 & c_2 \\ a_3 & b_3 & c_3 \end{vmatrix} = x\Delta$$

By $(C_1 \rightarrow C_1 - yC_2 - zC_3)$

$\therefore$ $x = \dfrac{\Delta_1}{\Delta}$, where $\Delta \neq 0$

$\Delta_2 = y\Delta$

$\therefore$ $y = \dfrac{\Delta_2}{\Delta}$ or $z = \dfrac{\Delta_3}{\Delta}$

$$x = \frac{\Delta_1}{\Delta}, y = \frac{\Delta_2}{\Delta}, z = \frac{\Delta_3}{\Delta}$$

$$\Rightarrow \quad \frac{x}{\Delta_1} = \frac{y}{\Delta_2} = \frac{z}{\Delta_3} = \frac{1}{\Delta} \quad ...(1)$$

To find the values of x, y, z from eqn. (1) is called Cramer's Rule.

Nature of Solution

By Cramer's Rule, $x = \dfrac{\Delta_1}{\Delta}, y = \dfrac{\Delta_2}{\Delta}, z = \dfrac{\Delta_3}{\Delta}$

(i) If $\Delta \neq 0$, then we can find unique solution of x, y, z. In this case the system of equations are said to be consistent.

(ii) If $\Delta = 0$, then there are two cases :

(a) $\Delta = 0$ and at least one of Δ_1, Δ_2 and Δ_3 are non zero.

(b) $\Delta = 0$ and $\Delta_1 = \Delta_2 = \Delta_3 = 0$

Case (a) :

If $\Delta = 0$ and at least one of Δ_1, Δ_2 and Δ_3 are non zero, then the value of x or y or z will be ∞ and this value can not satisfy the system of equation.

Thus in this case the system of equations will be inconsistent. *i.e.*, we can not find the value of x, y and z in this case.

Case (b) :

If $\Delta = 0$ and $\Delta_1 = \Delta_2 = \Delta_3 = 0$, then the value of x, y and z are $\dfrac{0}{0}$ which is indeterminate form.

So in this case we get infinite number of solution for x, y and z.

Condition for Consistency

When there are three equations in two variables :

Let the system of equations are :

$$a_1x + b_1y + c_1 = 0 \quad ...(i)$$
$$a_2x + b_2y + c_2 = 0 \quad ...(ii)$$
and $$a_3x + b_3y + c_3 = 0 \quad ...(iii)$$

The system of equations will be consistent if the value of x and y obtained by any two satisfies the third equation.

Solving (i) and (ii) by Cramer's Rule,

$$\frac{x}{\begin{vmatrix} b_1 & c_1 \\ b_2 & c_2 \end{vmatrix}} = \frac{-y}{\begin{vmatrix} a_1 & c_1 \\ a_2 & c_2 \end{vmatrix}} = \frac{1}{\begin{vmatrix} a_1 & b_1 \\ a_2 & b_2 \end{vmatrix}}$$

where $\begin{vmatrix} a_1 & b_1 \\ a_2 & b_2 \end{vmatrix} \neq 0$

Putting the value of x and y in (iii),

$$a_3\begin{vmatrix} b_1 & c_1 \\ b_2 & c_2 \end{vmatrix} - b_3\begin{vmatrix} a_1 & c_1 \\ a_2 & c_2 \end{vmatrix} + c_3\begin{vmatrix} a_1 & b_1 \\ a_2 & b_2 \end{vmatrix} = 0$$

thus $$\begin{vmatrix} a_1 & b_1 & c_1 \\ a_2 & b_2 & c_2 \\ a_3 & b_3 & c_3 \end{vmatrix} = 0$$

or $$\Delta = 0$$

This is the required condition for consistency.

SOLVED EXAMPLES

Example 1.

Solve the following system of equations by Cramer's Rule :

$$x + y = 4$$
$$2x - 3y = 9$$

Solution :

Here $\Delta = \begin{vmatrix} 1 & 1 \\ 2 & -3 \end{vmatrix} = -3 - 2 = -5 \neq 0$

$\Delta_1 = \begin{vmatrix} 4 & 1 \\ 9 & -3 \end{vmatrix} = -21$, $\Delta_2 = \begin{vmatrix} 1 & 4 \\ 2 & 9 \end{vmatrix} = 1$

By Cramer's Rule,

$$\frac{x}{\Delta_1} = \frac{y}{\Delta_2} = \frac{1}{\Delta}$$

$$\therefore \quad \frac{x}{-21} = \frac{y}{1} = \frac{1}{-5}$$

$$\therefore \quad x = \frac{21}{5}, y = -\frac{1}{5}$$ **Ans.**

Example 2.

Solve the following equations by Cramer's Rule :

$$2x - y + 3z = 9$$
$$x + y + z = 6$$
$$x - y + z = 2$$

Solution :

Here, $\Delta = \begin{vmatrix} 2 & -1 & 3 \\ 1 & 1 & 1 \\ 1 & -1 & 1 \end{vmatrix}$

$= 2(1+1) + 1(1-1) + 3(-1-1)$

$= 4 - 6 = -2$

$\Delta_1 = \begin{vmatrix} 9 & -1 & 3 \\ 6 & 1 & 1 \\ 2 & -1 & 1 \end{vmatrix}$

$= 9(1+1) + 1(6-2) + 3(-6-2)$

$= 18 + 4 - 24 = -2$

$\Delta_2 = \begin{vmatrix} 2 & 9 & 3 \\ 1 & 6 & 1 \\ 1 & 2 & 1 \end{vmatrix}$

$= 2(6-2) - 9(1-1) + 3(2-6)$

$= 8 - 12 = -4$

$\Delta_3 = \begin{vmatrix} 2 & -1 & 9 \\ 1 & 1 & 6 \\ 1 & -1 & 2 \end{vmatrix}$

$= 2(2+6) + 1(2-6) + 9(-1-1)$

$= 16 - 4 - 18 = -6$

By Cramer's Rule,

$$\frac{x}{\Delta_1} = \frac{y}{\Delta_2} = \frac{z}{\Delta_3}$$

$\Rightarrow \quad \frac{x}{-2} = \frac{y}{-4} = \frac{z}{-6} = \frac{1}{-2}$

$\therefore \quad x = 1, y = 2, z = 3$ **Ans.**

Example 3.

Determine whether the following system of equations has no solution, unique solution or infinite number of solutions :

$$2x + 3y = 6$$
$$4x + 6y = 10$$

Solution :

$\Delta = \begin{vmatrix} 2 & 3 \\ 4 & 6 \end{vmatrix} = 0;$

$\Delta_1 = \begin{vmatrix} 6 & 3 \\ 10 & 6 \end{vmatrix} = 6 \neq 0$

Thus the system of equations is inconsistent, so it has no solution.

Example 4.

Determine whether the following system of equations has no solution, unique solution or infinite number of solutions :

$$x + y = 2$$
$$2x + 2y = 4$$

Solution :

$\Delta = \begin{vmatrix} 1 & 1 \\ 2 & 2 \end{vmatrix} = 0$

$\Delta_1 = \begin{vmatrix} 2 & 1 \\ 4 & 2 \end{vmatrix} = 0$

$\Delta_2 = \begin{vmatrix} 1 & 2 \\ 2 & 4 \end{vmatrix} = 0$

$\because \quad \Delta = 0$ and $\Delta_1 = \Delta_2 = 0$

Thus the system of equations is inconsistent and it has infinite solution.

Example 5.

Show that the following system of equations is consistent :

$$x + y - z = 1$$
$$2x + 3y + z = 4$$
$$4x + 3y + z = 16$$

Solution :

$\Delta = \begin{vmatrix} 1 & 1 & -1 \\ 2 & 3 & 1 \\ 4 & 3 & 1 \end{vmatrix}$

$= \begin{vmatrix} 0 & 0 & -1 \\ 3 & 4 & 1 \\ 5 & 4 & 1 \end{vmatrix}$

$(C_1 \to C_1 + C_3, C_2 \to C_2 + C_3)$

$= -1(12 - 20) = 8 \neq 0$

Thus the system of equations is consistent and it has unique solution.

Example 6(A)

Find the value of x when : *(JAC, 2019)*

$\begin{vmatrix} x & 5 \\ x & x \end{vmatrix} = 24$

(a) $x = 8$ or $x = -3$ (b) $x = 5$ or $x = 4$

(c) $x = 6$ or $x = 7$ (d) $x = 9$ or $x = 0$

Solution :

$\begin{vmatrix} x & 5 \\ x & x \end{vmatrix} = 24$

$\therefore \quad x^2 - 5x = 24$

$\Rightarrow \quad x^2 - 5x - 24 = 0$

$\Rightarrow \quad x^2 - 8x + 3x - 24 = 0$

$$\Rightarrow \quad x(x-8)+3(x-8) = 0$$
$$\Rightarrow \quad (x-8)(x+3) = 0$$
$$\therefore \quad x = 8 \text{ or } -3$$

Hence, option (a) is right.

Example 6(B)

If $\begin{vmatrix} 5 & 10 \\ 2 & x \end{vmatrix} = 0$ then the value of x is : *(JAC, 2024)*

(a) 8 (b) 4 (c) 2 (d) 1

Solution :

$$\begin{vmatrix} 5 & 10 \\ 2 & x \end{vmatrix} = 0$$
$$\Rightarrow \quad 5x-(10\times 2) = 0$$
$$\Rightarrow \quad 5x-20 = 0$$
$$\Rightarrow \quad 5x = 20$$
$$\Rightarrow \quad x = \frac{20}{5} = 4$$

Hence, option (b) is right

Example 7.

Find the value of : $\begin{vmatrix} 1 & 2 & 4 \\ 1 & 3 & 6 \\ 1 & 4 & 7 \end{vmatrix}$

(a) – 1 (b) 5 (c) 9 (d) 7

Solution :

$$\begin{vmatrix} 1 & 2 & 4 \\ 1 & 3 & 6 \\ 1 & 4 & 7 \end{vmatrix}$$
$$= 1(3\times 7-4\times 6)-2(1\times 7-6\times 1)+4(1\times 4-1\times 3)$$
$$= (21-24)-2(7-6)+4(4-3)$$
$$= -3-2+4 = -5+4 = -1$$

Hence the option (a) is correct.

Example 8.

Prove that :

$$\begin{vmatrix} 1 & a & bc \\ 1 & b & ca \\ 1 & c & ab \end{vmatrix} = (a-b)(b-c)(c-a).$$

Solution :

$$\text{L.H.S.} = \begin{vmatrix} 1 & a & bc \\ 1 & b & ca \\ 1 & c & ab \end{vmatrix}$$

When $R_1 \to R_1 - R_2$, $R_2 \to R_2 - R_3$,

$$= \begin{vmatrix} 0 & a-b & bc-ca \\ 0 & b-c & ca-ab \\ 1 & c & ab \end{vmatrix}$$
$$= (a-b)(b-c)\begin{vmatrix} 0 & 1 & -c \\ 0 & 1 & -a \\ 1 & c & ab \end{vmatrix}$$
$$= (a-b)(b-c)\begin{vmatrix} 1 & -c \\ 1 & -a \end{vmatrix}$$
$$= (a-b)(b-c)(-a+c)$$
$$= (a-b)(b-c)(c-a)$$
$$= \text{R.H.S.}$$

Exercise 6 (C)

Solve the following equations by Cramer's Rule :

1. $x+2y = 5$, $3x-y = 1$
2. (a) $x-2y = 0$, $7x+6y = 40$
2. (b) $5x-2y = 3$, $x+7y = 45$
3. $5x-6y+9 = 0$, $7x+4y = 37$
4. $2x+3y-3z = 0$, $5x-2y+2z = 19$, $x+7y-5z = 5$
5. $3x+2y-2z = 1$, $-x+y-4z = 13$, $2x-3y+4z = 8$
6. $2x+y+6z = 46$, $5x-6y+4z = 15$, $7x+4y-3z = 19$
7. $x+y+z = 6$, $2x+y-3z = -5$, $3x-2y+z = 2$

Determine whether the following system of equations has no solution, unique solution or infinite number of solutions :

8. $5x-3y = 3$, $x+y = 7$
9. $x+2y = 5$, $3x+6y = 15$
10. $2x+3y+z = 5$, $3x+y+5z = 7$, $x+4y-2z = 3$
11. $x+y-z = -2$, $6x+4y+6z = 26$, $2x+7y+4z = 31$

Answers

1. $x=1, y=2$
2. (a) $x=4, y=2$, (b) $x=3, y=6$
3. $x=3, y=4$
4. $x=3, y=6, z=8$
5. $x=\frac{41}{17}, y=\frac{-158}{17}, z=\frac{-105}{17}$
6. $x=3, y=4, z=6$,
7. $x=1, y=2, z=3$,
8. Unique Solution
9. Infinite Solution
10. No Solution
11. Unique Solution

(6.6) APPLICATIONS OF DETERMINANTS

Determinant is the important introduction in the study of mathematics. It is very useful in all branches of Science and Engineering. In 1893, Leibnitz discovered the typical methods of expression by the study of getting expression from elimination of unknown terms in linear equations of 1st power, which is used in many branches of Science and Engineering.

Important Points

1. **Determinant :** If the elimination of x and y from the system of equations $a_1x+b_1y=0$ and $a_2x+b_2y=0$ gets $\frac{a_1}{b_1}=-\frac{y}{x}=\frac{a_2}{b_2}$ or $a_1b_2-a_2b_1=0$. Term $a_1b_2-a_2b_1$ is called a determinant. Its denoted by $\begin{vmatrix} a_1 & b_1 \\ a_2 & b_2 \end{vmatrix}$. Here a_1b_2 is called leading diagonal or principal diagonal. Terms a_1, a_2, b_1 and b_2 are the entries of a determinant. Rows and columns denoted from horizontal entries and perpendicular entries.

∴ Given 2 columns and 2 rows.

∴ It is called a determinant of the second order,

$\begin{vmatrix} a_1 & b_1 & c_1 \\ a_2 & b_2 & c_2 \\ a_3 & b_3 & c_3 \end{vmatrix}$ is called a determinant of 3×3 order because it contains 3 rows and 3 columns.

2. **Determinant's Expansion or Evaluating a Determinant** : To evaluate a determinant we expand it in terms of the elements of any row or any column. To expand a determinant means to find its value.
In the expansion of a determinant each element of a row or a column is multiplied with a determinant of order one less then the order of the original determinant which is obtained by eleminating the row and column passing through this element and putting the proper sign before each element.

3. **Minor** : By the minor of an element of a determinant we mean the subsquare-determinant of the given determinant along which this particular element (a_{ij}) does not exist. It is obtained by deleting the row and the column on which the particular element (a_{ij}) lies. It is represented by M_{ij}, which denotes the minor of an element in which ith row and jth column of the determinant.

4. **Co-factor** : By the co-factor of an element of a determinant we mean the product of $(-1)^{i+j}$ and the minor of the concerned element (M_{ij}). Symbolically it is given by
C_{ij} or $A_{ij} = (-1)^{i+j}.\ M_{ij}$

5. **Properties of Determinants :**

(i) If rows be changed into columns and columns into rows of a determinant, then the value of a determinant unchanged.

(ii) If any two parallel adjacent rows or adjacent columns of a determinant particularly interchanged then the value of a determinant does not change but sign changed.

(iii) If all elements in any row or any column of a determinant are zeros, then the determinant is equal to zero.

(iv) If all the elements of any row or any column be multiplied by any number then the value of a determinant also be multiplied by that number.

(v) If each element of any row or column is written as the sum of two terms, then the determinant can be written as the sum of two terms.

(vi) Any row or column of any determinant is multiplied by any number and the resulting product is added or subtracted in other row or column, then the value of a determinant does not change.

(vii) If any two rows or two columns of a determinant are identical, then the value of a determinant is zero.

Exercise 6 (D)

❐ Short Answer Type Questions

1. What is meant by determinants?
2. Explain determinant's expansion.
3. State the properties of expanding determinants.
4. State any two characteristics of determinants.
5. State the uses of determinants.
6. Describe any one property of determinants.
7. What is meant by minor determinant?
8. Explain co-factor.

Exercise 6 (E)

❐ Long Answer Type Questions

1. Give the definition of determinant and write its mai properties.
2. Give the definition of determinant and explain its rule
3. What do you understand by determinants of third orde Explain its co-factor.
4. Explain 'Laplace's Expansion' under determinants wi examples.

Exercise 6 (F)

Objective Type Questions

❐ Multiple Choice Questions

1. The value of $\begin{vmatrix} 10 & 7 \\ 8 & 5 \end{vmatrix}$ is :
(a) 15 (b) 5
(c) – 6 (d) None of these

2. If $\begin{vmatrix} x & 8 \\ 3 & 3 \end{vmatrix} = 0$, then the value of x is : (*JAC*, 202
(a) 7 (b) 3
(c) 8 (d) None of these

3. One method of expanding determinant of order 3 is :
(a) Sarrus Method (b) Bayes Method
(c) Pascal Rule (d) None of these

4. The value of determinant $\begin{vmatrix} x^2 & x \\ 5x & 5 \end{vmatrix}$ is : (*JAC*, 2018, 23, 2
(a) 0 (b) 1 (c) 5 (d) 25

5. The value of x in the determinant $\begin{vmatrix} 3 & x \\ 2 & 4 \end{vmatrix} = 0$ is :
(a) 2 (b) 4 (c) 6 (d) 8

6. The value of determinant $\begin{vmatrix} 2 & -3 \\ 4 & 9 \end{vmatrix}$ is :
(a) 18 (b) 30 (c) 20 (d) 6

7. The number of elements in 2 order determinant will b
(a) 1 (b) 2 (c) 3 (d) 4

8. If 3 is the number of elements in a determinant, th the number of rows will be :
(a) 4 (b) 3 (c) 2 (d) 1

9. The value of determinant $\begin{vmatrix} 0 & -5 \\ -3 & 0 \end{vmatrix}$ will be :

(a) 0 (b) 2 (c) 15 (d) – 15

10. The value of $\begin{vmatrix} 0 & 0 & 0 \\ 1 & 0 & 3 \\ 2 & 6 & 5 \end{vmatrix}$ is : *(JAC, 2022)*

(a) 10 (b) 0 (c) 3 (d) 8

11. If two rows of a determinant are equal then the value of determinant is : *(JAC, 2022, 26)*

(a) – 1 (b) 1 (c) 0 (d) 2

12. The value of determinant $\begin{vmatrix} 3 & 9 \\ 2 & 12 \end{vmatrix}$ is : *(JAC, 2023)*

(a) 12 (b) 16 (c) 18 (d) 20

13. The value of $\begin{vmatrix} 9 & 3 \\ 12 & 4 \end{vmatrix}$ is : *(JAC, 2019)*

(a) 0 (b) 4 (c) 6 (d) 12

14. The values of x when $\begin{vmatrix} x & 8 \\ 2 & x \end{vmatrix} = 0$ are : *(JAC, 2025)*

(a) ± 4 (b) ± 2 (c) ± 3 (d) ± 5

15. If $\begin{bmatrix} 2 & x \\ 5 & 0 \end{bmatrix} = \begin{bmatrix} 2 & 1 \\ 5 & 0 \end{bmatrix}$ then the value of x is : *(JAC, 2026)*

(a) 2 (b) 5 (c) 1 (d) 0

Answers

1. (c) 2. (c) 3. (a) 4. (a) 5. (c) 6. (b) 7. (d)
8. (b) 9. (d) 10. (b) 11. (c) 12. (c) 13. (a) 14. (d)
15. (c).

❒ Fill in the Blanks

1. Determinant is a .... matrix.
2. A determinant of order two contains .... elements.
3. The value of $\begin{vmatrix} 7 & 17 \\ 9 & 22 \end{vmatrix}$ = ...
4. If the two columns of determinant are identical then its value is :
5. Cramer's rule can be applied only when if ......
6. In the expansion of a determinant, the small determinant multiplied with an element is called ....

Answers

1. Square, 2. 4 3. 1
4. zero 5. $\Delta \neq 0$ 6. minor

❒ Write True or False

1. The number of rows and columns in a determinant is necessarily equal.
2. Co-factor is minor with corresponding sign.
3. Expansion of a determinant means its evaluation.
4. If two rows or columns of a determinant are identical, the value of determinant is 1.
5. The value of $\begin{vmatrix} 2 & 3 \\ 1 & 4 \end{vmatrix} = -2$.
6. The value of $\begin{vmatrix} 1 & -1 \\ -1 & 1 \end{vmatrix} = 4$.

Answers

1. True 2. True 3. True 4. False
5. False 6. False.

❖❖

7

MATRICES

LEARNING OBJECTIVES

After studying this chapter, you will be able to know :

- **7.1 Definition of a Matrix**
- **7.2 Elements of a Matrix**
- **7.3 Types of Matrices**
- **7.4 Laws of a Matrices Algebra**
  - **7.4.1 Addition of Matrices**
  - **7.4.2 Subtraction of Matrices**
  - **7.4.3 Multiplication of Matrices**

SOLVED EXAMPLES AND PRACTICAL PROBLEMS : AT A GLANCE

No. of Examples		*No. of Problems*
1 to 6	Short Answer Type Questions	Exercise 7(A) 1 to 13
7 to 28	Long Answer Type Questions	Exercise 7(B) 1 to 23
	Objective Type Questions	Exercise 7(C) 28 + 5 + 5
28	**Total**	**36 + 38**

(7.1) DEFINITION OF A MATRIX

Matrix is a rectangular array of real or complex numbers in rows and columns. Such an array is enclosed by [ ] or ( ).

A matrix is denoted by the capital letters A, B, C etc.

Example : $A = \begin{pmatrix} 1 & 4 & 5 \\ 6 & 3 & -7 \end{pmatrix}$ or $\begin{bmatrix} 1 & 4 & 5 \\ 6 & 3 & -7 \end{bmatrix}$

Here A is a 2×3 matrix because A has two rows and three columns.

(7.2) ELEMENTS OF A MATRIX

The numbers occurring in the rectangular array are called the elements of a matrix. Elements of a matrix are denoted by small letters. If A is a matrix of the type $m \times n$, then the element of the *i*th row and *j*th column is usually denoted by a_{ij}. The matrix A is some-times also written as (a_{ij}) or $[a_{ij}]$.

Example : Let $A = \begin{bmatrix} 4 & 3 & 5 \\ -4 & 0 & 3 \end{bmatrix}$

Here 4, 3, 5, – 4, 0, 3 are called elements of the matrix.

Here the element of first row and second column is 3. So $a_{12} = 3$.

(7.3) TYPES OF MATRICES

1. Rectangular Matrix : If the number of rows and columns in a matrix is not equal *i.e.*, $m \neq n$, then the matrix is said to be a rectangular matrix.

Example : $A = \begin{bmatrix} 1 & 5 & 7 & 4 \\ 3 & 6 & 9 & 8 \end{bmatrix}$

this is a rectangular matrix of the order 2×4.

2. Square Matrix : A matrix having equal number of rows and columns is called a square matrix.

Example : $A = \begin{bmatrix} 1 & 2 & 3 \\ 2 & 3 & 4 \\ 2 & 0 & 5 \end{bmatrix}$ is a square matrix of order 3×3.

3. Horizontal Matrix : The matrix in which number of columns is greater than number of rows. *i.e.*, A, $m \times n$ matrix is called a horizontal matrix if $m < n$.

Example : $A = \begin{bmatrix} 1 & 0 & 2 \\ 3 & 4 & 5 \end{bmatrix}$ is a horizontal matrix.

4. Vertical Matrix : The matrix in which number of rows is greater than number of columns, *i.e.*, A, $m \times n$ matrix is called a vertical matrix if $m > n$.

Example : $B = \begin{bmatrix} 1 & 0 \\ 2 & 7 \\ 4 & 8 \end{bmatrix}$ is a vertical matrix.

5. Row Matrix : A matrix having only one row is called a row matrix or a row vector, *i.e.*, A matrix of the type $1 \times n$ is called a row matrix.

Example : A = [5, 7, 8] is a row matrix.

6. Column Matrix : A matrix having only one column is called a column matrix or a column vector, *i.e.*, A matrix of the type $n \times 1$ is called a column matrix.

Example : $A = \begin{bmatrix} 5 \\ 7 \\ 3 \end{bmatrix}$ is a column matrix.

7. Zero Matrix or Null Matrix : A matrix whose each element is zero, is called a zero matrix or null matrix.

Example : $B = \begin{bmatrix} 0 & 0 & 0 \\ 0 & 0 & 0 \\ 0 & 0 & 0 \end{bmatrix}$ is a null matrix.

Diagonal of a Matrix : Let A is a square matrix of order n.

$$\text{Let } A = \begin{bmatrix} a_{11} & a_{12} & a_{13} & \ldots & a_{1n} \\ a_{21} & a_{22} & a_{23} & \ldots & a_{2n} \\ a_{31} & a_{32} & a_{33} & \ldots & a_{3n} \\ \ldots & \ldots & \ldots & \ldots & \ldots \\ \ldots & \ldots & \ldots & \ldots & \ldots \\ a_{n1} & a_{n2} & a_{n3} & \ldots & a_{nn} \end{bmatrix}$$

Here the elements $a_{11}, a_{22}, a_{33}, \ldots, a_{nn}$ are called the diagonal elements and the line along which these elements lie, is called principal diagonal of the matrix.

Example : $A = \begin{bmatrix} 1 & 5 & 9 \\ 2 & 7 & 3 \\ 3 & 8 & 5 \end{bmatrix}$

Here 1, 7, 5 are diagonal elements of matrix A.

8. Diagonal Matrix : A square matrix having all elements not occurring along the *principal diagonal* elements equal to zero is called a diagonal matrix. Thus the square matrix (a_{ij}) is called the diagonal matrix if $a_{ij} = 0$ for $i \neq j$.

Example :

$A = \begin{bmatrix} 7 & 0 \\ 0 & 3 \end{bmatrix}_{2\times2}$ $B = \begin{bmatrix} 5 & 0 & 0 \\ 0 & 3 & 0 \\ 0 & 0 & 3 \end{bmatrix}_{3\times3}$

$C = \begin{bmatrix} 8 & 0 & 0 & 0 \\ 0 & 7 & 0 & 0 \\ 0 & 0 & 6 & 0 \\ 0 & 0 & 0 & 5 \end{bmatrix}_{4\times4}$

Here A, B and C are diagonal matrix.

Principal Diagonal Element : An element both the subscripts (i and j) of which are euqal is called a principal element. The line along which the principal diagonal elements are pretioned is called the principal or leading diagonal.

9. Scalar Matrix : A square matrix is said to be a scalar matrix if all elements along the principal diagonal are equal and all elements not occurring the principal diagonal are zero.

Example : $A = \begin{bmatrix} 5 & 0 & 0 \\ 0 & 5 & 0 \\ 0 & 0 & 5 \end{bmatrix}$, here A is a scalar matrix.

10. Unit Matrix or Identity Matrix : A square matrix is said to be a unit matrix if all the elements along the principal diagonal are unity and all elements not occurring along the principal diagonal are zero.

In other words, "A scalar matrix is said to be a unit matrix if all the elements along the principal diagonal are unity (1)."

Example : $A = \begin{bmatrix} 1 & 0 & 0 \\ 0 & 1 & 0 \\ 0 & 0 & 1 \end{bmatrix}$ is a unit matrix of order 3.

A unit matrix of order n is denoted by I_n.

Thus in the example given above $A = I_3$.

11. Triangular Matrix : There are two types of triangular matrix :

(a) Lower Triangular Matrix : A square matrix (a_{ij}) is called a lower triangular matrix if $a_{ij} = 0$ for $i<j$.

Example : $A = \begin{bmatrix} 5 & 0 & 0 \\ 8 & 7 & 0 \\ -9 & 0 & 6 \end{bmatrix}$, $B = \begin{bmatrix} 2 & 0 & 0 \\ 5 & 3 & 0 \\ 0 & 2 & 1 \end{bmatrix}$

Here A and B are lower triangular matrices.

(b) Upper Triangular Matrix : A square matrix (a_{ij}) is said to be an upper triangular matrix if $a_{ij} = 0$ for $i > j$.

Example : $A = \begin{bmatrix} 5 & 8 & 7 \\ 0 & 9 & 4 \\ 0 & 0 & 6 \end{bmatrix}$, $B = \begin{bmatrix} 6 & 5 & 9 \\ 0 & 3 & 0 \\ 0 & 0 & 6 \end{bmatrix}$

Here A and B are upper triangular matrices.

12. Sub-Matrix : A matrix obtained by omitting some rows or some columns from the given matrix A'is called a sub-matrix of the matrix A.

Example : Let $A = \begin{bmatrix} 2 & 3 & 4 & 5 \\ 7 & 0 & 8 & 9 \\ 6 & 5 & 7 & 3 \end{bmatrix}$, $B = \begin{bmatrix} 2 & 4 & 5 \\ 6 & 7 & 3 \end{bmatrix}$

Here B has been obtained by omitting 2nd row and 2nd column of A. Hence B is a sub-matrix of A. Each matrix is a sub-matrix of itself.

13. Equal Matrix : Two matrix A and B are said to be equal if :

(i) Number of rows in A = Number of rows in B.

(ii) Number of columns in A = Number of columns in B.

(iii) Corresponding elements of A and B are equal, in other words, if $A = (a_{ij})_{m \times n}$ and $B = (b_{ij})_{m \times n}$,

then A = B if $a_{ij} = b_{ij}$, where $i = 1, 2, 3, \ldots m, j = 1, 2, 3 \ldots n$

Example : $A = \begin{bmatrix} 5 & 7 & 8 \\ 9 & 6 & 4 \end{bmatrix}$, $B = \begin{bmatrix} 5 & 7 & 8 \\ 9 & 6 & 4 \end{bmatrix}$

then A = B because number of rows and columns are euqal and corresponding elements of A and B are same.

Equal Matrix is also known as *comparable matrix.*

14. Symmetric Matrix : A square matrix A is called symmetric matrix if it is equal to its transpose A. A square matrix is called negative symmetric matrix if transpose is equal to –A, where –A is obtained from A by changing the sign of all elements of A. The matrix –A is known as the negative matrix of A.

Example : $A = \begin{bmatrix} 1 & 2 & 3 \\ 2 & 5 & 4 \\ 3 & 4 & 7 \end{bmatrix}$, $A^T = \begin{bmatrix} 1 & 2 & 3 \\ 2 & 5 & 4 \\ 3 & 4 & 7 \end{bmatrix}$

$$A = A^T$$

In symbols, $A = [a_{ij}]_{n \times n}$ is said to be symmetric if $a_{ij} = a_{ji}$.

15. Skew-Symmetric Matrix : A square matrix A $= [a_{ij}]_{n \times n}$ is said to be skew-symmetric if $a_{ji} = a_{ij}$

Example : $A = \begin{bmatrix} 0 & -4 \\ 4 & 0 \end{bmatrix}$, $B = \begin{bmatrix} 0 & 3 & 4 \\ -3 & 0 & 10 \\ -4 & -10 & 0 \end{bmatrix}$

In other words a square matrix is called skew-symmetric if A′ = A.

(7.4) LAWS OF A MATRICES ALGEBRA

7.4.1. Addition of Matrices

If A and B are two matrices of the same type *i.e.,* number of rows in A = number of rows in B and number of columns in A = number of columns in B, then matrices A and B are of the same type. The elements of A + B will be obtained by the sum of the corresponding elements of A and B.

Thus if $A = (a_{ij})_{m \times n}$ and $B = (b_{ij})_{m \times n}$

then $A + B = (a_{ij} + b_{ij})_{m \times n}$

Example (i) :

Find the value of A + B, if :

$$A = \begin{bmatrix} 5 & 1 \\ 1 & 2 \end{bmatrix}, B = \begin{bmatrix} 3 & 0 \\ -5 & 7 \end{bmatrix}$$

Solution :

$$A + B = \begin{bmatrix} 5 & 1 \\ 1 & 2 \end{bmatrix} + \begin{bmatrix} 3 & 0 \\ -5 & 7 \end{bmatrix}$$

$$= \begin{bmatrix} 5+3 & 1+0 \\ 1+(-5) & 2+7 \end{bmatrix} = \begin{bmatrix} 8 & 1 \\ -4 & 9 \end{bmatrix}$$

Example (ii) :

$A = \begin{bmatrix} 5 & 4 & 6 \\ 9 & 8 & 7 \end{bmatrix}$, $B = \begin{bmatrix} 6 & 4 & -7 \\ 9 & -3 & 2 \end{bmatrix}$, then find the value of A + B.

Solution :

$$A + B = \begin{bmatrix} 5+6 & 4+4 & 6-7 \\ 9+9 & 8-3 & 7+2 \end{bmatrix} = \begin{bmatrix} 11 & 8 & -1 \\ 18 & 5 & 9 \end{bmatrix}$$

Example (iii) :

Find the value of A + B + C, if :

$$A = \begin{bmatrix} 4 & 5 & 7 \\ 3 & 8 & 2 \end{bmatrix}, B = \begin{bmatrix} 6 & 4 & -2 \\ 5 & 3 & -6 \end{bmatrix}, C = \begin{bmatrix} 3 & -2 & 1 \\ 4 & 3 & -2 \end{bmatrix}$$

Solution :

$$A + B + C = \begin{bmatrix} 4 & 5 & 7 \\ 3 & 8 & 2 \end{bmatrix} + \begin{bmatrix} 6 & 4 & -2 \\ 5 & 3 & -6 \end{bmatrix} + \begin{bmatrix} 3 & -2 & 1 \\ 4 & 3 & -2 \end{bmatrix}$$

$$= \begin{bmatrix} 4+6+3 & 5+4+(-2) & 7+(-2)+1 \\ 3+5-4 & 8+3+3 & 2+(-6)+(-2) \end{bmatrix}$$

$$= \begin{bmatrix} 13 & 7 & 6 \\ 12 & 14 & -6 \end{bmatrix}$$

Properties of Matrix Addition

(i) Commutative Law : If A and B are two matrices of the same type, then A + B = B + A.

Proof : Let $A = (a_{ij})_{m \times n}$, $B = (b_{ij})_{m \times n}$, then

$$A + B = (a_{ij})_{m \times n} + (b_{ij})_{m \times n}$$

($\because a_{ij}$ and b_{ij} are numbers by addition of matrices)

$$= (a_{ij} + b_{ij})_{m \times n}$$
$$= (b_{ij} + a_{ij})_{m \times n}$$
$$= (b_{ij})_{m \times n} + (a_{ij})_{m \times n}$$
$$= B + A$$

(ii) Associative Law : If A, B and C are three matrices of the same type, then

$$A + (B + C) = (A + B) + C$$

Proof : Let $A = (a_{ij})_{m \times n}$

$B = (b_{ij})_{m \times n}$

and $C = (c_{ij})_{m \times n}$

now $A + (B + C) = (a_{ij}) + \{(b_{ij}) + (c_{ij})\}$

$= (a_{ij}) + (b_{ij} + c_{ij})$

($\because a_{ij}, b_{ij}$ and c_{ij} are numbers)

$= \{(a_{ij} + b_{ij}) + (c_{ij})\}$

$= \{(a_{ij}) + (b_{ij}) + (c_{ij})\}$

$= (A + B) + C$

Other Laws of Matrix Addition

(i) A + 0 = 0 + A = A, where 0 is a zero matix.

(ii) A + (– A) = (– A) + A = 0

(iii) A + B = A + C ⇒ B = C

B + A = B + C ⇒ A = C

7.4.2. Subtraction of Matrices

If A and B are two matrices of the same type, then A – B will be a matrix of the same type that of A or B.

(A – B) can be obtain by the subtraction of corresponding elements of A and B. Hence to obtain (A – B) the following two conditions are necessary :

(i) Number of rows in A = Number of rows in B.

(ii) Number of columns in A = Number of columns in B.

Example (i) :

Subtract matrix B form matrix A, where :

$$A = \begin{bmatrix} 8 & 18 \\ 28 & 38 \end{bmatrix},\ B = \begin{bmatrix} 6 & 16 \\ 20 & 50 \end{bmatrix}$$

Solution :

$$A - B = \begin{bmatrix} 8-6 & 18-16 \\ 28-20 & 38-50 \end{bmatrix} = \begin{bmatrix} 2 & 2 \\ 8 & -12 \end{bmatrix}$$

Example : (ii)

If $A = \begin{bmatrix} 4 & 6 & 10 \\ 8 & 10 & 18 \end{bmatrix}$ and $B = \begin{bmatrix} 16 & 4 & 14 \\ 24 & 6 & 18 \end{bmatrix}$, then find the value of A – B.

Solution :

$$A - B = \begin{bmatrix} 4 & 6 & 10 \\ 8 & 10 & 18 \end{bmatrix} - \begin{bmatrix} 16 & 4 & 14 \\ 24 & 6 & 18 \end{bmatrix}$$

$$= \begin{bmatrix} 4-16 & 6-4 & 10-14 \\ 8-24 & 10-6 & 18-18 \end{bmatrix}$$

$$= \begin{bmatrix} -12 & 2 & -4 \\ -16 & 4 & 0 \end{bmatrix}$$

Example (iii) :

$A = \begin{bmatrix} a_1 & b_1 & c_1 \\ a_2 & b_2 & c_2 \end{bmatrix}$ and $B = \begin{bmatrix} d_1 & e_1 & f_1 \\ d_2 & e_2 & f_2 \end{bmatrix}$, find (A – B)

Solution :

$$A - B = \begin{bmatrix} a_1 - d_1 & b_1 - e_1 & c_1 - f_1 \\ a_2 - d_2 & b_2 - c_2 & c_2 - f_2 \end{bmatrix}$$

7.4.3. Multiplication of Matrices

If A and B are two matrices such that number of columns in A = number of rows in B, then AB will be defined. AB will be a matrix in which :

(i) Number of rows in AB = Number of rows in A.

(ii) Number of columns in AB= Number of columns in B.

(iii) Element of *i*th row and *j*th column of AB = the sum of the product of element in *i*th row of A and corresponding *j*th column of B thus if $A = (a_{ij})_{m \times n}$, $B = (b_{jk})_{n \times p}$, **then** $AB = (C_{ik})_{m \times p}$, where $C_{ik} = \sum_{j=1}^{n} a_{ij}\, b_{ik}$.

If A = $m \times n$ matrix

B = $n \times p$ matrix

then AB = $m \times p$ matrix

Example (i) :

$A = [2\ \ 3\ \ 4]$, $B = \begin{bmatrix} 5 & 2 \\ 6 & 8 \\ 7 & 1 \end{bmatrix}$, then find the value of AB and BA.

Solution :

In the first matrix there are 3 columns and in the second matrix these are 3 columns. There force both can be multiplied. This a matrix of type 1 × 3 and 3 × 2.

Now $AB = [2\ \ 3\ \ 4]_{1\times 3} \times \begin{bmatrix} 5 & 2 \\ 6 & 8 \\ 7 & 1 \end{bmatrix}_{3\times 2}$

$$= [2\times5+3\times6+4\times7 \quad 2\times2+3\times8+4\times1]$$

$$= [10+18+28 \quad 4+24+4]$$

$$= [56 \quad 32]$$

and $BA = \begin{bmatrix} 5 & 2 \\ 6 & 8 \\ 7 & 1 \end{bmatrix}_{3\times 2} \times [2\ \ 3\ \ 4]_{1\times 3}$

Since in the first matrix there are two columns and in the second matrix there is one row, therefore, these matrices cannot be multiplied.

Example (ii) :

Multiply A and B if :

$A = \begin{bmatrix} 3 \\ 2 \\ 1 \end{bmatrix}$, and $B = [14\ \ 10\ \ 6]$.

Solution :

Here A is a 3 × 1 matrix and B is a 1 × 3 matrix.

$$AB = \begin{bmatrix} 3 \\ 2 \\ 1 \end{bmatrix} [14\ \ 10\ \ 6]$$

$$\therefore\ AB = \begin{bmatrix} 3\times14 & 3\times10 & 3\times6 \\ 2\times14 & 2\times10 & 2\times6 \\ 1\times14 & 1\times10 & 1\times6 \end{bmatrix} = \begin{bmatrix} 42 & 30 & 18 \\ 28 & 20 & 14 \\ 14 & 10 & 6 \end{bmatrix}$$

Example (iii) :

Multiply A and B if :

$A = [2\ \ 4\ \ 6]$ and $B = \begin{bmatrix} 2 \\ 4 \\ 6 \end{bmatrix}$

Solution :

Here order of A is 1 × 3 and that of B is 1 × 1.

$$AB = [2\ \ 4\ \ 6] \times \begin{bmatrix} 2 \\ 4 \\ 6 \end{bmatrix}$$

$$= [2^2 + 4^2 + 6^2]$$

$$= [4+16+36] = [56] \text{ or } 56.$$

Example (iv) :

If $A = \begin{bmatrix} 1 & -2 & 3 \\ -4 & 2 & 5 \end{bmatrix}$ and $B = \begin{bmatrix} 2 & 3 \\ 4 & 5 \\ 2 & 1 \end{bmatrix}$ then what will be AB : BA ?

Solution :

Since A is a 2 × 3 matrix and B is a 3 × 2 matrix.

So AB is defined and this is a matrix of the type 2 × 2.

Now $$AB = \begin{bmatrix} 1 & -2 & 3 \\ -4 & 2 & 5 \end{bmatrix} \begin{bmatrix} 2 & 3 \\ 4 & 5 \\ 2 & 1 \end{bmatrix}$$

$$= \begin{bmatrix} 2-8+6 & 3-10+3 \\ -8+8+10 & -12+10+5 \end{bmatrix}$$

$$= \begin{bmatrix} 0 & -4 \\ 10 & 3 \end{bmatrix}$$

Since B is a 3 × 2 matrix and A is a 2 × 3 matrix, so BA is defined and BA will be a matrix of the type 3 × 3.

Again $$BA = \begin{bmatrix} 2 & 3 \\ 4 & 5 \\ 2 & 1 \end{bmatrix} \begin{bmatrix} 1 & -2 & 3 \\ -4 & 2 & 5 \end{bmatrix}$$

$$= \begin{bmatrix} 2-12 & -4+6 & 6+15 \\ 4-20 & -8+10 & 12+25 \\ 2-4 & -4+2 & 6+5 \end{bmatrix}$$

$$= \begin{bmatrix} -10 & 2 & 21 \\ -16 & 2 & 37 \\ -2 & -2 & 11 \end{bmatrix}$$

∴ $AB \neq BA$

Similarly AB is not equal to BA.

Multiplication of a Matrix by a Scalar

Let A is any $m \times n$ matrix, and K is any scalar, then the scalar multiple of matrix A by K is denoted by KA or AK and is defined as $m \times n$ matrix obtained by multiplying each element of A by scalar K.

Example :

Let $A = \begin{bmatrix} 1 & 2 & 3 \\ 0 & 1 & -2 \end{bmatrix}$ then $3A = \begin{bmatrix} 3 & 6 & 9 \\ 0 & 3 & -6 \end{bmatrix}$

If A is a $m \times n$ matrix, then KA will be also a $m \times n$ matrix.

Properties of Scalar Multiplication

(1) If A and B are any two $m \times n$ matrices and K is a scalar, then

$$K(A+B) = KA + KB$$

(2) If A is any $m \times n$ matrix and a and b are any two scalars, then

$$(a+b)\,A = aA + bA$$

(3) If A is any $m \times n$ matrix and K is any scalar, then

$$(-K)A = -(KA) = K(-A)$$

Associative Law for Multiplication of Matrices

If A, B and C be $m \times n$, $n \times p$ and $p \times q$ matrices respectively, *i.e.*, AB is conformal and BC is conformal, then

$$(AB)C = A(BC)$$

Distributive Law

If A, B and C are $m \times n$, $n \times p$ and $n \times p$ matrices respectively, then

$$A(B+C) = AB + AC$$

Similarly $$(B+C)A = BA + CA$$

7.4.4 Transpose of Matrix

Let A is any matrix, then the matrix obtained by interchanging its corresponding rows and columns is called the transpose of A and is denoted by A′ or A^T.

Thus if A is a $m \times n$ matrix then A′ will be $n \times m$ matrix.

Example : Let $A = \begin{bmatrix} 1 & 5 & 7 \\ 8 & 7 & 4 \end{bmatrix}$ then $A' = \begin{bmatrix} 1 & 8 \\ 5 & 7 \\ 7 & 4 \end{bmatrix}$

If $A = (a_{ij})_{m \times n}$ then $A' = (a_{ji})_{n \times m}$

Properties of Transpose of Matrices

Property (i) : If A and B are two $m \times n$ matrices, then $(A+B)' = A' + B'$.

Proof : Let $A = (a_{ij})_{m \times n}$

$B = (b_{ij})_{m \times n}$

then $A' = (a_{ji})_{n \times m}$ and $B' = (b_{ji})_{m \times n}$

∴ $A + B = (a_{ij} + b_{ij})_{m \times n}$

Now $(A+B)' = [(a_{ij} + b_{ij})_{m \times n}]'$

$= (a_{ji} + b_{ji})_{n \times m}$

$= (a_{ji})_{n \times m} + (b_{ji})_{n \times m}$

$= A' + B'$

Property (ii) : If A is any matrix, then $(A')' = A$

Proof : Let $A = (a_{ji})_{m \times n}$

then $A' = (a_{ij})_{n \times m}$

Now $(A')' = [(a_{ji})_{n \times m}]'$

$= (a_{ij})_{m \times n} = A$

Property (iii) : If K is any scalar and A is any matrix, then $(KA)' = KA'$.

Proof : Let $A = (a_{ij})_{m \times n}$

then $KA = (Ka_{ij})_{m \times n}$

Now $(KA)' = [(Ka_{ji})_{n \times m}]$

$= K(a_{ji})_{n \times m}$

$= KA'$

Proverty (iv) : If A is a $m \times n$ matrix and B is a $n \times p$ matrix, then

$$(AB)' = B'A'$$

7.4.5 Some Special Forms of Square Matrix

1. Singular Matrix :

If A is a square matrix, then if the value of the determine formed by the corresponding elements of A is zero.

i.e., $|A| = 0$, then matrix A is said to be singular.

Example : Let $A = \begin{bmatrix} 6 & 3 \\ 4 & 2 \end{bmatrix}$, then $|A| = 12 - 12 = 0$.

So A is a singular matrix.

2. Non-singular Matrix

A square matrix A is said to be a non-singular matrix if $|A| \neq 0$.

Example : Let $A = \begin{bmatrix} 4 & 8 \\ 5 & 7 \end{bmatrix}$, then $|A| = \begin{vmatrix} 4 & 8 \\ 5 & 7 \end{vmatrix}$

$$= 28 - 40 = -12 \neq 0$$

So A is a non-singular matrix.

3. Orthogonal Matrix

A square matrix A is said to be orthogonal if $A'A = I$, where I is the unit matrix.

Example : Let $A = \frac{1}{3}\begin{bmatrix} -1 & 2 & 2 \\ 2 & -1 & 2 \\ 2 & 2 & -1 \end{bmatrix}$ is orthogonal matrix.

then $A' = \frac{1}{3}\begin{bmatrix} -1 & 2 & 2 \\ 2 & -1 & 2 \\ 2 & 2 & -1 \end{bmatrix}$

$$\therefore \quad A'A = \frac{1}{9}\begin{bmatrix} 1+4+4 & -2-2+4 & -2+4-2 \\ -2-2+4 & 4+1+4 & 4-2-2 \\ -2+4-2 & 4-2-2 & 4+4+1 \end{bmatrix}$$

$$= \frac{1}{9}\begin{bmatrix} 9 & 0 & 0 \\ 0 & 9 & 0 \\ 0 & 0 & 9 \end{bmatrix} = \frac{1}{9}\begin{bmatrix} 1 & 0 & 0 \\ 0 & 1 & 0 \\ 0 & 0 & 1 \end{bmatrix} = I$$

So A is an orthogonal matrix.

4. Symmetric Matrix

A square matrix $A = (a_{ij})$ is said to be a symmetric matrix if $a_{ij} = a_{ji}$ for all i and j or $A' = A$.

Example : $A = \begin{bmatrix} a & h & g \\ h & b & f \\ g & f & c \end{bmatrix}$, then $A' = \begin{bmatrix} a & h & g \\ h & b & f \\ g & f & c \end{bmatrix}$

$\because \quad A' = A$

So A is a symmetric matrix.

5. Skew Symmetric Matrix

A square matrix $A = (a_{ij})$ is said to be a skew symmetric matrix if $a_{ij} = -a_{ji}$ for all i and j.

or $\quad A' = -A$

Example : $\quad A = \begin{bmatrix} o & h & -g \\ -h & o & f \\ g & -f & o \end{bmatrix}$

then $\quad A' = \begin{bmatrix} o & -h & g \\ h & o & -f \\ -g & f & o \end{bmatrix}$

$$= -\begin{bmatrix} o & h & -g \\ -h & o & f \\ g & -f & o \end{bmatrix}$$

$$A' = -A$$

Thus A is a skew symmetric matrix.

Explanation : Let $A = (a_{ij})$ is a skew symmetric matrix, then by the definition

$$a_{ij} = -a_{ji} \text{ for all } i \text{ and } j$$

$\therefore \quad a_{ii} = -a_{ii}$ (Putting $j = i$)

or $\quad 2a_{ii} = 0$

$$a_{11} = 0, a_{22} = 0, \text{ etc.}$$

or the principal diagonal of a skew symmetric matrix is zero.

Property of Symmetric and Skew Symmetric Matrices

(i) If A is a square matrix, then $A + A'$ is symmetric and $A - A'$ is skew symmetric matrix.

Proof : $\quad (A + A')' = A' + (A')' = A' + A = A + A'$

So $A + A'$ is a symmetric matrix.

Now $\quad (A - A')' = A' - (A')' = A' - A = -(A - A')$

So $A - A'$ is a skew symmetric matrix.

(ii) Every square matrix can be uniquely expressed as the sum of a symmetric matrix and a skew symmetric matrix.

Proof : Let A is any square matrix, then $\frac{1}{2}(A + A')$ is a symmetric matrix and $\frac{1}{2}(A - A')$ is a skew symmetric matrix.

Now $\quad A = \frac{1}{2}(2A)$

$$= \frac{1}{2}(A + A' + A - A')$$

$$= \frac{1}{2}(A + A') + \frac{1}{2}(A - A')$$

So A = symmetric matrix + skew symmetric matrix.

Now we have to prove that the representation is unique.

$\because \quad A = \frac{1}{2}(A + A') + \frac{1}{2}(A - A')$

Let $\quad A = B + C, \quad$ ...(i)

where B is symmetric and C is skew symmetric matrix.

$\therefore \quad B' = B$ and $C' = -C$

Now $\quad A' = (B + C)' = B' + C'$

$$= B - C$$

$\therefore \quad A' = B - C \quad$ ...(ii)

By eqns. (i) + (ii),

$$A + A' = 2B$$

$\therefore \quad B = \frac{1}{2}(A + A')$

By (i) – (ii), $A - A' = 2C$

$\therefore \quad C = \frac{1}{2}(A - A')$

So the representation is unique.

6. Adjoint Matrix

Let A is a square matrix and B is a matrix whose elements are co-factors of the corresponding elements of A. Then transpose of B (B') is called adjoint of A. Adjoint of matrix A is denoted by *adj.* A.

Example : $\quad A = \begin{bmatrix} a_{11} & a_{12} & a_{13} \\ a_{21} & a_{22} & a_{23} \\ a_{31} & a_{32} & a_{33} \end{bmatrix}$

Let B is the matrix whose elements are co-factors of the corresponding elements of A, then

$$B = \begin{bmatrix} A_{11} & A_{12} & A_{13} \\ A_{21} & A_{22} & A_{23} \\ A_{31} & A_{32} & A_{33} \end{bmatrix}$$

$$\therefore \quad adj.A = B' = \begin{bmatrix} A_{11} & A_{21} & A_{31} \\ A_{12} & A_{22} & A_{32} \\ A_{13} & A_{23} & A_{33} \end{bmatrix}$$

Only square matrix has its adjoint matrix.

Example : Let $A = \begin{bmatrix} 0 & 1 & 2 \\ 1 & 2 & 3 \\ 3 & 1 & 1 \end{bmatrix}$, then we have to find *adj.* A.

For this let is the matrix whose elements are co-factors of the corresponding elements of A.

then $$B = \begin{bmatrix} +(2-3) & -(1-9) & +(1-6) \\ -(1-2) & +(0-6) & -(0-3) \\ +(3-4) & -(0-2) & +(0-1) \end{bmatrix}$$

$$= \begin{bmatrix} -1 & 8 & -5 \\ 1 & -6 & 3 \\ -1 & 2 & -1 \end{bmatrix}$$

$$\therefore \quad adj.\ A = B' = \begin{bmatrix} -1 & 1 & -1 \\ 8 & -6 & 2 \\ -5 & 3 & -1 \end{bmatrix}$$

7.4.6 Reciprocal or Inverse Matrix

Let A is a non-singular matrix and B is a matrix such that

$$B = A^{-1} = \frac{adj.A}{|A|}$$

Example : Let $A = \begin{bmatrix} 1 & 2 & 5 \\ 2 & 3 & 1 \\ -1 & 1 & 1 \end{bmatrix}$, then we have to find A^{-1}.

For this let B is the matrix whose elements are co-factors of the corresponding elements of A

then $$B = \begin{bmatrix} +(3-1) & -(2+1) & +(2+3) \\ -(2-5) & +(1+5) & -(1+2) \\ +(2-15) & -(1-10) & +(3-4) \end{bmatrix}$$

$$= \begin{bmatrix} 2 & -3 & 5 \\ 3 & 6 & -3 \\ -13 & 9 & -1 \end{bmatrix}$$

$$\therefore \quad adj\,A = B' = \begin{bmatrix} 2 & 3 & -13 \\ -3 & 6 & 9 \\ 5 & -3 & -1 \end{bmatrix}$$

$$|A| = \begin{vmatrix} 1 & 2 & 5 \\ 2 & 3 & 1 \\ -1 & 1 & 1 \end{vmatrix}$$

$$= 1(3-1) - 2(2-5) - 1(2-15)$$
$$= 2 + 6 + 13 = 21$$

$$\therefore \quad A^{-1} = \frac{adj.A}{|A|} = \frac{adj.A}{21}$$

$$= \begin{bmatrix} \frac{2}{21} & \frac{3}{21} & -\frac{13}{21} \\ -\frac{3}{21} & \frac{6}{21} & \frac{9}{21} \\ \frac{5}{21} & -\frac{3}{21} & -\frac{1}{21} \end{bmatrix}$$

Properties of Inverse Matrix

(i) AA^{-1} (Unit Matrix) = I

(ii) $(AB)^{-1} = B^{-1}A^{-1}$

To find the solution of linear equations by Matrix Method

Let three linear equations in three variables are :

$$a_1x + b_1y + c_1z = d_1 \quad ...(i)$$
$$a_2x + b_2y + c_2z = d_2 \quad ...(ii)$$
and $$a_3x + b_3y + c_3z = d_3 \quad ...(iii)$$

Let $$A = \begin{bmatrix} a_1 & b_1 & c_1 \\ a_2 & b_2 & c_2 \\ a_3 & b_3 & c_3 \end{bmatrix},$$

$$X = \begin{bmatrix} x \\ y \\ z \end{bmatrix} \text{ and } B = \begin{bmatrix} d_1 \\ d_2 \\ d_3 \end{bmatrix}$$

and $|A| \neq 0$ or A is non-singular. Then we can write the matrix equation of the above three equations as

$$AX = B = A^{-1}(AX) = A^{-1}B,$$
$$\Rightarrow \quad (A^{-1}A) = A^{-1}B$$
$$\Rightarrow \quad IX = A^{-1}B$$
$$\Rightarrow \quad X = A^{-1}B; \quad (\because IX = X)$$

from this equation we can find the value of x, y and z. This solution is unique.

SOLVED EXAMPLES

❒ Short Answer Type Questions

Example 1

If $\begin{bmatrix} 1 & 2 \\ x & 3 \end{bmatrix} = \begin{bmatrix} y & z \\ 5 & 3 \end{bmatrix}$, then find x, y, z. *(JAC, 2016)*

Solution :

The two matrix will be equal if their corresponding elements are also equal.

$$x = 5, y = 1, z = 2$$ **Ans.**

Example 2

If $Y = \begin{bmatrix} 3 & 2 \\ 1 & 4 \end{bmatrix}$ and $2X + Y = \begin{bmatrix} 1 & 0 \\ -3 & 2 \end{bmatrix}$, find X.

Solution :

$$2X = (2X + Y) - Y = \begin{bmatrix} 1 & 0 \\ -3 & 2 \end{bmatrix} - \begin{bmatrix} 3 & 2 \\ 1 & 4 \end{bmatrix}$$

$$= \begin{bmatrix} 1-3 & 0-2 \\ -3-1 & 2-4 \end{bmatrix}$$

$$= \begin{bmatrix} -2 & -2 \\ -4 & -2 \end{bmatrix}$$

$$\therefore \quad X = \frac{1}{2}\begin{bmatrix} -2 & -2 \\ -4 & -2 \end{bmatrix} = \begin{bmatrix} -1 & -1 \\ -2 & -1 \end{bmatrix}$$ **Ans.**

Example 3

If $A = \begin{bmatrix} 1 & 2 & 3 \\ -1 & 0 & 2 \\ 0 & -3 & 1 \end{bmatrix}$, $B = \begin{bmatrix} 4 & 5 & 6 \\ -1 & 0 & 1 \\ 2 & 1 & 2 \end{bmatrix}$ then find 4A – 3B.

Solution :

$$4A - 3B = 4\begin{bmatrix} 1 & 2 & 3 \\ -1 & 0 & 2 \\ 0 & -3 & 1 \end{bmatrix} - 3\begin{bmatrix} 4 & 5 & 6 \\ -1 & 0 & 1 \\ 2 & 1 & 2 \end{bmatrix}$$

$$= \begin{bmatrix} 4 & 8 & 12 \\ -4 & 0 & 8 \\ 0 & -12 & 4 \end{bmatrix} - \begin{bmatrix} 12 & 15 & 18 \\ -3 & 0 & 3 \\ 6 & 3 & 6 \end{bmatrix}$$

$$= \begin{bmatrix} 4-12 & 8-15 & 12-18 \\ -4+3 & 0-0 & 8-3 \\ 0-6 & -12-3 & 4-6 \end{bmatrix}$$

$$= \begin{bmatrix} -8 & -7 & -6 \\ -1 & 0 & 5 \\ -6 & -15 & -2 \end{bmatrix}$$ **Ans.**

Example 4

Find X and Y, if $X + Y = \begin{bmatrix} 7 & 0 \\ 2 & 5 \end{bmatrix}$ and $X - Y = \begin{bmatrix} 3 & 0 \\ 0 & 3 \end{bmatrix}$.

Solution :

$$2X = (X + Y) + (X - Y)$$

$$= \begin{bmatrix} 7 & 0 \\ 2 & 5 \end{bmatrix} + \begin{bmatrix} 3 & 0 \\ 0 & 3 \end{bmatrix} = \begin{bmatrix} 10 & 0 \\ 2 & 8 \end{bmatrix}$$

$$\therefore \quad X = \frac{1}{2}\begin{bmatrix} 10 & 0 \\ 2 & 8 \end{bmatrix} = \begin{bmatrix} 5 & 0 \\ 1 & 4 \end{bmatrix}$$ **Ans.**

Again $2Y = (X + Y) - (X - Y)$

$$= \begin{bmatrix} 7 & 0 \\ 2 & 5 \end{bmatrix} - \begin{bmatrix} 3 & 0 \\ 0 & 3 \end{bmatrix} = \begin{bmatrix} 4 & 0 \\ 2 & 2 \end{bmatrix}$$

$$\therefore \quad Y = \frac{1}{2}\begin{bmatrix} 4 & 0 \\ 2 & 2 \end{bmatrix} = \begin{bmatrix} 2 & 0 \\ 1 & 1 \end{bmatrix}$$ **Ans.**

Example 5

Write down the matrix $A = (a_{ij})_{2 \times 3}$, where $a_{ij} = 2j - 3j$.

Solution :

$$a_{ij} = 2i - 3j$$

$$\therefore \quad a_{11} = 2.1 - 3.1 = -1$$

$$a_{12} = 2.1 - 3.2 = -4$$

$$a_{13} = 2.1 - 3.3 = -7$$

$$a_{21} = 2.2 - 3.1 = 1$$

$$a_{22} = 2.2 - 3.2 = -2$$

$$a_{23} = 2.2 - 3.3 = -5$$

$$\therefore \quad A = (a_{ij})_{2 \times 3} = \begin{bmatrix} a_{11} & a_{12} & a_{13} \\ a_{21} & a_{22} & a_{23} \end{bmatrix}$$

$$= \begin{bmatrix} -1 & -4 & -7 \\ 1 & -2 & -5 \end{bmatrix}$$

Example 6

How many matrices are there having 12 elements ?

Solution :

(i) 1 × 12, (ii) 2 × 6, (iii) 3 × 4,
(iv) 4 × 3, (v) 6 × 2, (iv) 12 × 1

So there are 6 matrices having 12 elements.

Its order are 1 × 12, 2 × 6, 3 × 4, 4 × 3, 6 × 2, 12 × 1.

❑ Long Answer Type Questions

Example 7

If $A = \begin{bmatrix} 1 & -2 & 3 \\ -5 & 2 & 5 \end{bmatrix}$, $B = \begin{bmatrix} 2 & 6 \\ 4 & 5 \\ 3 & 1 \end{bmatrix}$, find AB and BA and show that AB ≠ BA.

Solution :

A is a 2 × 3 matrix and B is a 3 × 2 matrix so AB is defined and this will be a matrix of the type 2 × 2.

$$\therefore \text{ Now} \quad AB = \begin{bmatrix} 1 & -2 & 3 \\ -5 & 2 & 5 \end{bmatrix} \cdot \begin{bmatrix} 2 & 6 \\ 4 & 5 \\ 3 & 1 \end{bmatrix}$$

$$= \begin{bmatrix} 2-8+9 & 6-10+3 \\ -10+8+15 & -30+10+5 \end{bmatrix}$$

$$= \begin{bmatrix} 3 & -1 \\ 13 & -15 \end{bmatrix}$$

Since B is a 3 × 2 matrix and A is a 2 × 3 matrix so BA is defined and this will be a matrix of the type 3× 3.

$$\text{Again} \quad BA = \begin{bmatrix} 2 & 6 \\ 4 & 5 \\ 3 & 1 \end{bmatrix} \cdot \begin{bmatrix} 1 & -2 & 3 \\ -5 & 2 & 5 \end{bmatrix}$$

$$= \begin{bmatrix} 2-30 & -4+12 & 6+30 \\ 4-25 & -8+12 & 12+25 \\ 3-5 & -6+2 & 9+5 \end{bmatrix}$$

$$= \begin{bmatrix} -28 & 8 & 36 \\ -21 & 2 & 37 \\ -2 & -4 & 14 \end{bmatrix}$$

Thus, $AB \neq BA$

Example 8

If A, B and C are three matrices such that : *(JAC., 2014)*

$A = [x\ y\ z]$, $B = C = \begin{bmatrix} x \\ y \\ z \end{bmatrix}$, find ABC.

Solution :

Since multiplication of matrices obey associative law so A (BC) = (AB) C which can be written by ABC.

$$\text{Now} \quad BC = \begin{bmatrix} a & h & g \\ h & b & f \\ g & f & c \end{bmatrix}\begin{bmatrix} x \\ y \\ z \end{bmatrix}$$

$$= \begin{bmatrix} ax+hy+gz \\ hx+by+fz \\ gx+fy+cz \end{bmatrix}$$

$$\therefore \quad A(BC) = [x\ y\ z]\begin{bmatrix} ax+hy+gz \\ hx+by+fz \\ gx+fy+cz \end{bmatrix}$$

$$= [x(ax+hy+gz) + y(hx+by+fz) + z(gx+fy+cz)]$$

$$= (ax^2 + by^2 + cz^2 + 2hxy + 2gzx + 2fyz)$$

Example 9

If $A = \begin{bmatrix} 3 & -5 \\ -4 & 2 \end{bmatrix}$, find $A^2 - 5A - 14I$, where I is a unit matrix.

Solution :

$$A^2 = \begin{bmatrix} 3 & -5 \\ -4 & 2 \end{bmatrix}\cdot\begin{bmatrix} 3 & -5 \\ -4 & 2 \end{bmatrix}$$

$$= \begin{bmatrix} 9+20 & -15-10 \\ -12-8 & 20+4 \end{bmatrix}$$

$$= \begin{bmatrix} 29 & -25 \\ -20 & 24 \end{bmatrix}$$

$$5A = 5\begin{bmatrix} 3 & -5 \\ -4 & 2 \end{bmatrix}$$

$$= \begin{bmatrix} 15 & -25 \\ -20 & 10 \end{bmatrix}$$

$$14\,I = 14\begin{bmatrix} 1 & 0 \\ 0 & 1 \end{bmatrix} = \begin{bmatrix} 14 & 0 \\ 0 & 14 \end{bmatrix}$$

$$\text{Now } A^2 - 5A - 14\,I$$

$$= \begin{bmatrix} 29 & -25 \\ -20 & 24 \end{bmatrix} - \begin{bmatrix} 15 & -25 \\ -20 & 10 \end{bmatrix} - \begin{bmatrix} 14 & 0 \\ 0 & 14 \end{bmatrix}$$

$$= \begin{bmatrix} 29-15-14 & -25+25-0 \\ -20+20+0 & 24-10-14 \end{bmatrix}$$

$$= \begin{bmatrix} 0 & 0 \\ 0 & 0 \end{bmatrix} = 0$$

where 0 is null matrix.

Example 10

Find the transpose of the matrix, where

$$A = \begin{bmatrix} 1 & 2 & 3 \\ 0 & 5 & 0 \\ 2 & 4 & 3 \end{bmatrix}$$

Solution :

Transpose Matrix of

$$A = A' = \begin{bmatrix} 1 & 0 & 2 \\ 2 & 5 & 4 \\ 3 & 0 & 3 \end{bmatrix} \qquad \textbf{Ans.}$$

Example 11

Transpose of Matrix A is :

$$A = \begin{bmatrix} 1 & 3 & 5 \\ 7 & 2 & 9 \end{bmatrix} \qquad (JAC, 2016)$$

(a) $\begin{bmatrix} 1 & 3 & 7 \\ 7 & 2 & 9 \end{bmatrix}$ (b) $\begin{bmatrix} 1 & 7 \\ 3 & 2 \\ 5 & 9 \end{bmatrix}$

(c) $\begin{bmatrix} 6 & 8 \\ 5 & 7 \\ 1 & 2 \end{bmatrix}$ (d) None of these

Solution :

$$\text{Transpose Matrix of } A^T = \begin{bmatrix} 1 & 7 \\ 3 & 2 \\ 5 & 9 \end{bmatrix}$$

Example 12

Find the adjoint of the matrix A, where

$$A = \begin{bmatrix} 1 & 2 & 3 \\ 0 & 5 & 0 \\ 2 & 4 & 3 \end{bmatrix}$$

Solution :

Let B is the matrix whose elements are co-factors of the corresponding elements of A.

$$\text{Then} \quad B = \begin{bmatrix} +(15-0) & -(0-0) & +(0-10) \\ -(6-12) & +(3-6) & -(4-4) \\ +(0-15) & -(0-0) & +(5-0) \end{bmatrix}$$

$$= \begin{bmatrix} 15 & 0 & -10 \\ 6 & -3 & 0 \\ -15 & 0 & 5 \end{bmatrix}$$

$$\therefore \quad adj.\ A = B' = \begin{bmatrix} 15 & 6 & -15 \\ 0 & -3 & 0 \\ -10 & 0 & 5 \end{bmatrix} \qquad \textbf{Ans.}$$

Example 13

If $A = \begin{bmatrix} 1 & -2 & 3 \\ -4 & 2 & 5 \end{bmatrix}$ and $B = \begin{bmatrix} 1 & 3 \\ -1 & 0 \\ 2 & 4 \end{bmatrix}$, then verify $(AB)' = B'A'$.

Solution :

A is a 2 × 3 matrix and B is a 3 × 2 matrix. So AB is defined and this will be a 2 × 2 matrix.

$$AB = \begin{bmatrix} 1 & -2 & 3 \\ -4 & 2 & 5 \end{bmatrix}\begin{bmatrix} 1 & 3 \\ -1 & 0 \\ 2 & 4 \end{bmatrix}$$

$$= \begin{bmatrix} 1+2+6 & 3+0+12 \\ -4-2+10 & -12+0+20 \end{bmatrix} = \begin{bmatrix} 9 & 15 \\ 4 & 8 \end{bmatrix}$$

$$\therefore \quad (AB)' = \begin{bmatrix} 9 & 4 \\ 15 & 8 \end{bmatrix}$$

$$B' = \begin{bmatrix} 1 & -1 & 2 \\ 3 & 0 & 4 \end{bmatrix}, A' = \begin{bmatrix} 1 & -4 \\ -2 & 2 \\ 3 & 5 \end{bmatrix}$$

$$B'.A' = \begin{bmatrix} 1 & -1 & 2 \\ 3 & 0 & 4 \end{bmatrix} \begin{bmatrix} 1 & -4 \\ -2 & 2 \\ 3 & 5 \end{bmatrix}$$

$$= \begin{bmatrix} 1+2+6 & -4-2+10 \\ 3+0+12 & -12+0+20 \end{bmatrix} = \begin{bmatrix} 9 & 4 \\ 15 & 8 \end{bmatrix}$$

$$\therefore \quad (AB)' = B'A'$$

Example 14

Find the inverse of the following matrix :

$$A = \begin{bmatrix} 0 & 1 & 2 \\ 1 & 2 & 3 \\ 3 & 1 & 1 \end{bmatrix}.$$

Solution :

Let B is the matrix whose elements are corresponding co-factors of A.

$$\text{Then} \quad B = \begin{bmatrix} +(2-3) & -(1-9) & +(1-6) \\ -(1-2) & +(0-6) & -(0-3) \\ +(3-4) & -(0-2) & +(0-1) \end{bmatrix}$$

$$= \begin{bmatrix} -1 & 8 & -5 \\ 1 & -6 & 3 \\ -1 & 2 & -1 \end{bmatrix}$$

$$\therefore \quad adj.\ A = B' = \begin{bmatrix} -1 & 1 & -1 \\ 8 & -6 & 2 \\ -5 & 3 & -1 \end{bmatrix}$$

$$|A| = 0(2-3) - 1(1-2) + 3(3-4)$$
$$= +1 - 3 = -2$$

$$A^{-1} = \frac{adj.A}{|A|} = \frac{adj.A}{-2} = \begin{bmatrix} \frac{1}{2} & -\frac{1}{2} & \frac{1}{2} \\ -4 & 3 & -1 \\ \frac{5}{2} & -\frac{3}{2} & \frac{1}{2} \end{bmatrix}$$

Example 15

If matrix $A = \begin{bmatrix} 1 & -1 & 1 \\ 2 & 3 & 0 \\ 18 & 2 & 10 \end{bmatrix}$ show that $A(adj\ A) = 0$.

Solution :

$$A = \begin{bmatrix} 1 & -1 & 1 \\ 2 & 3 & 0 \\ 18 & 2 & 10 \end{bmatrix}$$

Let B is the matrix whose elements are co-factors of the corresponding elements of A.

$$\text{Then} \quad B = \begin{bmatrix} +(30-0) & -(20-0) & +(4-54) \\ -(-10-2) & +(10-18) & -(2+18) \\ +(0-3) & -(0-2) & +(3+2) \end{bmatrix}$$

$$= \begin{bmatrix} 30 & -20 & -50 \\ 12 & -8 & -20 \\ -3 & 2 & 5 \end{bmatrix}$$

$$(adj.A) = B = \begin{bmatrix} 30 & 12 & -3 \\ -20 & -8 & 2 \\ -50 & -20 & 5 \end{bmatrix}$$

$$\therefore A(adj.A) = \begin{bmatrix} 1 & -1 & 1 \\ 2 & 3 & 0 \\ 18 & 2 & 10 \end{bmatrix} \begin{bmatrix} 30 & 12 & -3 \\ -20 & -8 & 2 \\ -50 & -20 & 5 \end{bmatrix}$$

$$= \begin{bmatrix} 30+20-50 & 12+8-20 & -3-2+5 \\ 60-60+0 & 24-24+0 & -6+6+0 \\ 540-40-500 & 216-16-200 & -54+4+50 \end{bmatrix}$$

$$= \begin{bmatrix} 0 & 0 & 0 \\ 0 & 0 & 0 \\ 0 & 0 & 0 \end{bmatrix} = 0$$

$$\therefore A(adj.A) = 0$$

Example 16

Find the inverse of $A = \begin{bmatrix} 2 & 6 \\ 3 & 5 \end{bmatrix}$.

Solution :

$$\text{Let} \quad A = \begin{bmatrix} 2 & 6 \\ 3 & 5 \end{bmatrix}$$

$$\therefore \quad |A| = 10 - 18 = -8 \neq 0$$

Let B be the matrix whose elements are co-factors of the corresponding elements of A.

$$B = \begin{bmatrix} 5 & -3 \\ -6 & 2 \end{bmatrix}$$

$$\therefore \quad adj.A = B' = \begin{bmatrix} 5 & -6 \\ -3 & 2 \end{bmatrix}$$

$$\therefore \quad A^{-1} = \frac{adj.A}{|A|} = \frac{1}{8}\begin{bmatrix} 5 & -6 \\ -3 & 2 \end{bmatrix}$$

$$A = \begin{bmatrix} -5/8 & +3/4 \\ +3/8 & -1/4 \end{bmatrix}$$ **Ans.**

Example 17

If $A = \begin{bmatrix} 3 & 1 \\ 4 & 0 \end{bmatrix}, B = \begin{bmatrix} 4 & 0 \\ 2 & 5 \end{bmatrix}$, verify that $(AB)^{-1} = B^{-1}A^{-1}$.

Solution :

$$AB = \begin{bmatrix} 12+2 & 0+5 \\ 16+0 & 0+0 \end{bmatrix} = \begin{bmatrix} 14 & 5 \\ 16 & 0 \end{bmatrix}$$

Let C is the matrix whose elements are corresponding co-factors of AB.

$$\therefore \quad C = \begin{bmatrix} +(0) & -(16) \\ -(5) & +(14) \end{bmatrix} = \begin{bmatrix} 0 & -16 \\ -5 & 14 \end{bmatrix}$$

$$\therefore \ adj\,(AB) = C' = \begin{bmatrix} 0 & -5 \\ -16 & 14 \end{bmatrix}$$

$$AB = \begin{bmatrix} 14 & 5 \\ 16 & 0 \end{bmatrix}$$

$$\therefore \quad |AB| = 0 - 80 = -80$$

$$\therefore \quad (AB)^{-1} = \frac{adj.(AB)}{|AB|} = \begin{bmatrix} 0 & \frac{1}{16} \\ \frac{1}{5} & -\frac{7}{40} \end{bmatrix}$$

$$A = \begin{bmatrix} 3 & 1 \\ 4 & 0 \end{bmatrix}$$

$$\therefore \quad |A| = 0 - 4 = -4 \neq 0$$

Let D is the matrix whose elements are corresponding co-factors of A.

$$D = \begin{bmatrix} 0 & -4 \\ -1 & 3 \end{bmatrix}$$

$$\therefore \quad adj.A = D' = \begin{bmatrix} 0 & -1 \\ -4 & 3 \end{bmatrix}$$

$$\therefore \quad A^{-1} = \frac{adj.A}{|A|} = \begin{bmatrix} 0 & \frac{1}{4} \\ 1 & -\frac{3}{4} \end{bmatrix}$$

$$B = \begin{bmatrix} 4 & 0 \\ 2 & 5 \end{bmatrix}$$

$$\therefore \quad |B| = 20 - 0 = 20 \neq 0$$

Again let E is the matrix whose elements are corresponding co-factors of B.

$$E = \begin{bmatrix} 5 & -2 \\ 0 & 4 \end{bmatrix}$$

$$\therefore \ adj.\,B = E' = \begin{bmatrix} 5 & 0 \\ 2 & 4 \end{bmatrix}$$

$$\therefore \quad B^{-1} = \frac{adj.B}{|B|} = \begin{bmatrix} \frac{1}{4} & 0 \\ -\frac{1}{10} & \frac{1}{5} \end{bmatrix}$$

$$\therefore \quad B^{-1}A^{-1} = \begin{bmatrix} \frac{1}{4} & 0 \\ -\frac{1}{10} & \frac{1}{5} \end{bmatrix} = \begin{bmatrix} 0 & \frac{1}{4} \\ 1 & -\frac{3}{4} \end{bmatrix}$$

$$= \begin{bmatrix} 0+0 & \frac{1}{16}+0 \\ 0+\frac{1}{5} & -\frac{1}{40}-\frac{3}{20} \end{bmatrix} = \begin{bmatrix} 0 & \frac{1}{16} \\ \frac{1}{5} & -\frac{7}{40} \end{bmatrix}$$

$$\therefore \quad (AB)^{-1} = B^{-1}A^{-1}$$ **Proved**

Example 18

A man buys 8 dozen of mangoes, 10 dozen of apples and 4 dozen of bananas. Mangoes cost ₹ 18 per dozen, apples ₹ 9 dozen and bananas ₹ 6 per dozen. Represent the quantities bought by a row matrix and the prices by a column matrix and hence obtain the total cost.

Solution :

The quantity of fruits bought by the man can be written in the form of a row matrix A given by

$$A = [8 \ 10 \ 4]$$

The corresponding prices of fruits can be written in the form of a column matrix B given by

$$B = \begin{bmatrix} 18 \\ 9 \\ 6 \end{bmatrix}$$

$$\therefore \text{ The total cost in ₹} = AB = [8 \ 10 \ 4] \begin{bmatrix} 18 \\ 9 \\ 6 \end{bmatrix}$$

$$= [8 \times 18 + 10 \times 9 + 4 \times 6]$$

$$= [144 + 90 + 24]$$

$$= ₹\,285$$ **Ans.**

Example 19

A trust fund has ₹ 30,000 that is to be invested in two different types of bonds. The bond pays 5% interest per year and the second bond pays 7% interest per year. Using matrix multiplication, determine how to divide ₹ 30,000 among the two types of bonds if the trust fund must obtain an annual total interest of ₹ 2,000.

Solution :

Let the investment in first bond = ₹ x. So the investment in second bond = ₹ (30,000 – x). Again let the row matrix A = [x 30,000 – x] and the column matrix B = interest per year.

$$\therefore \quad B = \begin{bmatrix} \frac{5}{100} \\ \frac{7}{100} \end{bmatrix}$$

By the question, $AB = ₹\,2{,}000$

$$\Rightarrow \quad [x \ \ 30{,}000 - x] \cdot \begin{bmatrix} \frac{5}{100} \\ \frac{7}{100} \end{bmatrix} = 2{,}000$$

$$\frac{5x}{100} + \frac{7(30{,}000 - x)}{100} = 2{,}000$$

$$\Rightarrow \quad 5x + 2{,}10{,}000 - 7x = 2{,}00{,}000$$

$$10{,}000 = 2x$$

$$\therefore \quad x = 5{,}000$$

So the investment in first bond

$$= ₹\,5{,}000$$

and the investment in second bond

$$= ₹\,(30{,}000 - 5{,}000)$$

$$= ₹\,25{,}000$$

Example 20

If $A = \begin{bmatrix} 1 & 2 & 2 \\ 2 & 1 & 2 \\ 2 & 2 & 1 \end{bmatrix}$ prove that $A^2 - 4A - 5I = 0$, hence obtain A^{-1}.

Solution :

$$A^2 = A.A = \begin{bmatrix} 1 & 2 & 2 \\ 2 & 1 & 2 \\ 2 & 2 & 1 \end{bmatrix}\begin{bmatrix} 1 & 2 & 2 \\ 2 & 1 & 2 \\ 2 & 2 & 1 \end{bmatrix}$$

$$= \begin{bmatrix} 1+4+4 & 2+2+4 & 2+4+2 \\ 2+2+4 & 4+1+4 & 4+2+2 \\ 2+4+2 & 4+2+2 & 4+4+1 \end{bmatrix}$$

$$= \begin{bmatrix} 9 & 8 & 8 \\ 8 & 9 & 8 \\ 8 & 8 & 9 \end{bmatrix}$$

Now, $A^2 - 4A - 5I$

$$= \begin{bmatrix} 9 & 8 & 8 \\ 8 & 9 & 8 \\ 8 & 8 & 9 \end{bmatrix} - \begin{bmatrix} 4 & 8 & 8 \\ 8 & 4 & 8 \\ 8 & 8 & 4 \end{bmatrix} - \begin{bmatrix} 5 & 0 & 0 \\ 0 & 5 & 0 \\ 0 & 0 & 5 \end{bmatrix}$$

$$= \begin{bmatrix} 9-4-5 & 8-8-0 & 8-8-0 \\ 8-8-0 & 9-4-5 & 8-8-0 \\ 8-8-0 & 8-8-0 & 9-4-5 \end{bmatrix}$$

$$= \begin{bmatrix} 0 & 0 & 0 \\ 0 & 0 & 0 \\ 0 & 0 & 0 \end{bmatrix} = 0$$

Thus $A^2 - 4A - 5I = 0$, here 0 is a zero matrix.

$$\therefore \quad A^{-1}A^2 - 4A^{-1}A - 5A^{-1}I = A^{-1}.0 = 0;$$

or $\quad (A^{-1}A)A - 4(A^{-1}A) - 5A^{-1}I = 0$

or $\quad IA - 4I - 5A^{-1} = 0$

$\therefore \quad 5A^{-1} = A - 4I$

$$= \begin{bmatrix} 1 & 2 & 2 \\ 2 & 1 & 2 \\ 2 & 2 & 1 \end{bmatrix} - \begin{bmatrix} 4 & 0 & 0 \\ 0 & 4 & 0 \\ 0 & 0 & 4 \end{bmatrix}$$

$$= \begin{bmatrix} -3 & 2 & 2 \\ 2 & -3 & 2 \\ 2 & 2 & -3 \end{bmatrix}$$

$$\therefore \quad A^{-1} = \frac{1}{5}\begin{bmatrix} -3 & 2 & 2 \\ 2 & -3 & 2 \\ 2 & 2 & -3 \end{bmatrix}$$

$$= \begin{bmatrix} -\frac{3}{5} & \frac{2}{5} & \frac{2}{5} \\ \frac{2}{5} & -\frac{3}{5} & \frac{2}{5} \\ \frac{2}{5} & \frac{2}{5} & -\frac{3}{5} \end{bmatrix}$$

Example 21

Solve the following equations by matrix method :

$$5x + 3y + z = 16$$
$$2x + y + 3z = 19$$
$$x + 2y + 4z = 25$$

(*JAC*, 2015)

Solution :

Let $\quad A = \begin{bmatrix} 5 & 3 & 1 \\ 2 & 1 & 3 \\ 1 & 2 & 4 \end{bmatrix}, X = \begin{bmatrix} x \\ y \\ z \end{bmatrix}$ and $B = \begin{bmatrix} 16 \\ 19 \\ 25 \end{bmatrix}$

Thus the matrix equation is :

$$AB = X$$

Now $\quad |A| = \begin{vmatrix} 5 & 3 & 1 \\ 2 & 1 & 3 \\ 1 & 2 & 4 \end{vmatrix}$

$$= 5(4-6) - 3(8-3) + 1(4-1)$$
$$= -22 \neq 0$$

So $\quad X = A^{-1}B$

Let C is the matrix whose elements are co-factors of the corresponding elements of A.

Then $\quad C = \begin{bmatrix} -2 & -5 & 3 \\ -10 & 19 & -7 \\ 8 & -13 & -1 \end{bmatrix}$

$$adj.A = C' = \begin{bmatrix} -2 & -10 & 8 \\ -5 & 19 & -13 \\ 3 & -7 & -1 \end{bmatrix}$$

$$\therefore A^{-1} = \frac{adj.A}{|A|} = \frac{1}{-22}\begin{bmatrix} -2 & -10 & 8 \\ -5 & 19 & -13 \\ 3 & -7 & -1 \end{bmatrix}$$

$$= \begin{bmatrix} \frac{2}{22} & \frac{10}{22} & -\frac{8}{22} \\ \frac{5}{22} & -\frac{19}{22} & \frac{13}{22} \\ -\frac{3}{22} & \frac{7}{22} & \frac{1}{22} \end{bmatrix}$$

$$\therefore \quad X = A^{-1}B = \begin{bmatrix} \frac{2}{22} & \frac{10}{22} & -\frac{8}{22} \\ \frac{5}{22} & -\frac{19}{22} & \frac{13}{22} \\ -\frac{3}{22} & \frac{7}{22} & \frac{1}{22} \end{bmatrix}\begin{bmatrix} 16 \\ 19 \\ 25 \end{bmatrix}$$

$$\Rightarrow \quad X = \begin{bmatrix} \frac{32+190-200}{22} \\ \frac{80-361+325}{22} \\ \frac{-48+133+25}{22} \end{bmatrix} = \begin{bmatrix} 1 \\ 2 \\ 5 \end{bmatrix}$$

$$\Rightarrow \quad \begin{bmatrix} x \\ y \\ z \end{bmatrix} = \begin{bmatrix} 1 \\ 2 \\ 5 \end{bmatrix}$$

$\therefore \quad x = 1, y = 2, z = 5$ **Ans.**

Example 22

Find the product of two matrices A and B, where A $= \begin{bmatrix} -5 & 1 & 3 \\ 7 & 1 & -5 \\ 1 & -1 & 1 \end{bmatrix}$, B $= \begin{bmatrix} 1 & 1 & 2 \\ 3 & 2 & 1 \\ 2 & 1 & 3 \end{bmatrix}$ and use it for solving the equations :

$$x + y + 2z = 1$$
$$3x + 2y + z = 7$$
$$2x + y + 3z = 2$$

Solution :

$$AB = \begin{bmatrix} -5 & 1 & 3 \\ 7 & 1 & -5 \\ 1 & -1 & 1 \end{bmatrix}\begin{bmatrix} 1 & 1 & 2 \\ 3 & 2 & 1 \\ 2 & 1 & 3 \end{bmatrix}$$

$$= \begin{bmatrix} -5+3+6 & -5+2+3 & -10+1+9 \\ 7+3-10 & 7+2-5 & 14+1-15 \\ 1-3+2 & 1-2+1 & 2-1+3 \end{bmatrix}$$

$$= \begin{bmatrix} 4 & 0 & 0 \\ 0 & 4 & 0 \\ 0 & 0 & 4 \end{bmatrix} = 4\begin{bmatrix} 1 & 0 & 0 \\ 0 & 1 & 0 \\ 0 & 0 & 1 \end{bmatrix} = 4 I_3 \quad ...(i)$$

The matrix form of the given equation is :

$$BX = C \quad ...(ii)$$

where $X = \begin{bmatrix} x \\ y \\ z \end{bmatrix}$ and $C = \begin{bmatrix} 1 \\ 7 \\ 2 \end{bmatrix}$

From (ii), $X = B^{-1}C$

From (i),

$$AB = 4 I_3$$

$$\therefore \quad \frac{A}{4}.B = I_3$$

$$\therefore \quad I_3 B^{-1} = \frac{A}{4}$$

$$\therefore \quad B^{-1} = \frac{A}{4} = \begin{bmatrix} -\frac{5}{4} & \frac{1}{4} & \frac{3}{4} \\ \frac{7}{4} & \frac{1}{4} & -\frac{5}{4} \\ \frac{1}{4} & -\frac{1}{4} & \frac{1}{4} \end{bmatrix}$$

$$\therefore \quad \begin{bmatrix} x \\ y \\ z \end{bmatrix} = X = B^{-1}C$$

$$= \begin{bmatrix} -\frac{5}{4} & \frac{1}{4} & \frac{3}{4} \\ \frac{7}{4} & \frac{1}{4} & -\frac{5}{4} \\ \frac{1}{4} & -\frac{1}{4} & \frac{1}{4} \end{bmatrix}\begin{bmatrix} 1 \\ 7 \\ 2 \end{bmatrix}$$

$$= \begin{bmatrix} -\frac{5}{4} + \frac{7}{4} + \frac{6}{4} \\ \frac{7}{4} + \frac{7}{4} - \frac{10}{4} \\ \frac{1}{4} - \frac{7}{4} + \frac{2}{4} \end{bmatrix} = \begin{bmatrix} 2 \\ 1 \\ -1 \end{bmatrix}$$

$\therefore \quad x = 2, y = 1, z = -1$ **Ans.**

Example 23

If $A = \begin{bmatrix} 3 & -4 \\ 1 & -1 \end{bmatrix}$, show that $A^n = \begin{bmatrix} 1+2n & -4n \\ n & 1-2n \end{bmatrix}$, where n is a positive interger.

Solution :

Let $\quad P(n) : A^n = \begin{bmatrix} 1+2n & -4n \\ n & 1-2n \end{bmatrix}$

Step (i) : for $n = 1$

$$\text{L.H.S.} = A^1 = A = \begin{bmatrix} 3 & -4 \\ 1 & -1 \end{bmatrix}$$

$$\text{R.H.S.} = \begin{bmatrix} 1+2.1 & -4.1 \\ 1 & 1-2.1 \end{bmatrix} = \begin{bmatrix} 3 & -4 \\ 1 & -1 \end{bmatrix}$$

$\therefore \quad$ L.H.S. = R.H.S

So $P(n)$ is true for $n = 1$

Step (ii) : Let P (n) is true for $n = m$,

$$\therefore \quad A^m = \begin{bmatrix} 1+2m & -4m \\ m & 1-2m \end{bmatrix}$$

Then we have to prove that P (n) is true for $n = m + 1$ or we have to prove that

$$A^{m+1} = \begin{bmatrix} 1+2(m+1) & -4(m+1) \\ m+1 & 1-2(m+1) \end{bmatrix}$$

$$= \begin{bmatrix} 2m+3 & -4(m+1) \\ m+1 & -2m-1 \end{bmatrix}$$

Now $A^{m+1} = A^m.A = \begin{bmatrix} 1+2m & -4m \\ m & 1-2m \end{bmatrix}\begin{bmatrix} 3 & -4 \\ 1 & -1 \end{bmatrix}$

$$= \begin{bmatrix} 3+6m-4m & -4-8m+4m \\ 3m+1-2m & -4m-1+2m \end{bmatrix}$$

$$= \begin{bmatrix} 2m+3 & -4(m+1) \\ m+1 & -2m-1 \end{bmatrix}$$

$\because$ Here we see that if $P(m)$ is true, then $P(m + 1)$ is also true.

So P (n) is true for all natural numbers n.

Example 24

If $A = \begin{bmatrix} 1 & a \\ 0 & 1 \end{bmatrix}$, then prove that :

$$A^n = \begin{bmatrix} 1 & na \\ 0 & 1 \end{bmatrix}$$

Solution :

$$P(n) : A^n = \begin{bmatrix} 1 & na \\ 0 & 1 \end{bmatrix}$$

Step (i) : $n = 1$ L.H.S. $= A^1 = A = \begin{bmatrix} 1 & a \\ 0 & 1 \end{bmatrix}$

R.H.S. $= \begin{bmatrix} 1 & 1a \\ 0 & 1 \end{bmatrix} = \begin{bmatrix} 1 & a \\ 0 & 1 \end{bmatrix}$

$\therefore$ L.H.S. = R.H.S.

So P(n) is true for $n = 1$.

Step (ii) : Let P(n) is true for $n = m$.

$$\therefore \quad A^m = \begin{bmatrix} 1 & ma \\ 0 & 1 \end{bmatrix} \quad ...(i)$$

Then we have to prove that P(n) is true for $n = m + 1$, or we have to prove that

$$A^{m+1} = \begin{bmatrix} 1 & (m+1)a \\ 0 & 1 \end{bmatrix}$$

Now $A^{m+1} = A^m.A = \begin{bmatrix} 1 & ma \\ 0 & 1 \end{bmatrix} \cdot \begin{bmatrix} 1 & a \\ 0 & 1 \end{bmatrix}$

$= \begin{bmatrix} 1+0 & a+ma \\ 0+0 & 0+1 \end{bmatrix}$

$= \begin{bmatrix} 1 & (m+1)a \\ 0 & 1 \end{bmatrix}$

$\because$ Here we see that if P(m) is true, then P(m + 1) is also true.

Since P(n) is true for n = 1, so on this basis we can say that P(n) is true for all natural numbers.

Example 25

If $A = \begin{bmatrix} 2 & 3 & 5 \\ 6 & 8 & 9 \end{bmatrix}$ find 5A. [*Mock Test Paper (JAC)*]

Solution :

$\because \quad A = \begin{bmatrix} 2 & 3 & 5 \\ 6 & 8 & 9 \end{bmatrix}$

then $5A = 5\begin{bmatrix} 2 & 3 & 5 \\ 6 & 8 & 9 \end{bmatrix} = \begin{bmatrix} 10 & 15 & 25 \\ 30 & 40 & 49 \end{bmatrix}$

Example 26

If $A = \begin{bmatrix} 5 & 6 & 7 \\ 1 & 2 & 3 \end{bmatrix}$. What type of matrix is A ?

[*Mock Test Paper (JAC)*]

(a) Vertical (b) Horizontal
(c) Square (d) Null

Solution :

Option (b) is correct. Because no. of rows is less than 2 and no. of columns is less then 3.

Example 27

If $A = \begin{bmatrix} 1 & 2 & 3 \\ 3 & 4 & 5 \end{bmatrix}$ and $B = \begin{bmatrix} 2 & 3 & 1 \\ 5 & 4 & 3 \\ 2 & 1 & 1 \end{bmatrix}$. Find AB and BA. Is AB = BA ? [*Mock Test Paper (JAC)*]

Solution :

$\because \quad A = \begin{bmatrix} 1 & 2 & 3 \\ 3 & 4 & 5 \end{bmatrix}$ and $B = \begin{bmatrix} 2 & 3 & 1 \\ 5 & 4 & 3 \\ 2 & 1 & 1 \end{bmatrix}$

$\therefore \quad AB = \begin{bmatrix} 2+10+6 & 3+8+3 & 1+6+3 \\ 6+20+10 & 9+16+5 & 3+12+5 \end{bmatrix}$

$= \begin{bmatrix} 18 & 14 & 10 \\ 36 & 30 & 20 \end{bmatrix}$

BA is not possible because order of B is 3 × 3 where as order of A is 3 × 2 and multiple of B with A is only possible when number of columns of B are equal to the number of rows of A

$\therefore \quad AB \neq BA$

Example 28

If $A = \begin{bmatrix} 5 & 7 \\ 2 & 3 \end{bmatrix}$ and $B = \begin{bmatrix} 1 & 3 \\ 2 & 7 \end{bmatrix}$, find AB (*JAC, 2024*)

Solution :

$AB = \begin{bmatrix} 5 & 7 \\ 2 & 3 \end{bmatrix} \times \begin{bmatrix} 1 & 3 \\ 2 & 7 \end{bmatrix}$

$= \begin{bmatrix} 5\times1+7\times2 & 5\times3+7\times7 \\ 2\times1+3\times2 & 2\times3+3\times7 \end{bmatrix}$

$= \begin{bmatrix} 5+14 & 15+49 \\ 2+6 & 6+21 \end{bmatrix}$

$= \begin{bmatrix} 19 & 64 \\ 8 & 27 \end{bmatrix}$ **Ans.**

Exercise 7 (A)

❒ Short Answer Type Questions

1. If $A = \begin{bmatrix} 2 & 4 & 6 \\ 3 & 5 & 7 \end{bmatrix}$, $B = \begin{bmatrix} 5 & 6 & 7 \\ 7 & 8 & 9 \end{bmatrix}$, then find A + B.
2. If $A = \begin{bmatrix} 3 & 6 \\ 5 & -4 \end{bmatrix}$ and $B = \begin{bmatrix} 7 & 8 \\ 5 & 6 \end{bmatrix}$, then find 2A + 3B.
3. If $A = \begin{bmatrix} 3 & 6 \\ 5 & -4 \end{bmatrix}$ and $B = \begin{bmatrix} 7 & 8 \\ 5 & 6 \end{bmatrix}$, then find 6A – 5B. (*JAC, 2020*)
4. If $A + B = \begin{bmatrix} 1 & 0 & 2 \\ 2 & 2 & 2 \\ 1 & 1 & 2 \end{bmatrix}$ and $A - B = \begin{bmatrix} 1 & 4 & 4 \\ 4 & 2 & 0 \\ -1 & -1 & 2 \end{bmatrix}$, then find A and B.
5. If $A = \begin{bmatrix} 5 & 4 \\ 3 & -1 \end{bmatrix}$, $B = \begin{bmatrix} 2 & 1 \\ 0 & 4 \end{bmatrix}$ and $C = \begin{bmatrix} -3 & 2 \\ 1 & 0 \end{bmatrix}$, then find A + B – C.
6. If $A = \begin{bmatrix} 5 & 4 \\ 3 & -1 \end{bmatrix}$ and $C = \begin{bmatrix} -3 & 2 \\ 1 & 0 \end{bmatrix}$ then find 3A – 4C.
7. $A = \begin{bmatrix} 1 & 3 & 9 \\ 4 & -3 & 5 \end{bmatrix}$ $B = \begin{bmatrix} 4 & -9 & 2 \\ 4 & -3 & 5 \end{bmatrix}$ find 3A – 2B. (*JAC, 2023*)
8. If $A = \begin{bmatrix} 3 & 2 \\ 0 & 5 \end{bmatrix}$ and $B = \begin{bmatrix} 1 & 0 \\ 1 & 2 \end{bmatrix}$, then find (A + B) (A – B).

9. If $A = \begin{bmatrix} 2 & 1 & 3 \\ 4 & -3 & 2 \end{bmatrix}$, then find A′.

10. If $A = \begin{bmatrix} 0 & -2 & 3 \\ 0 & 4 & 2 \end{bmatrix}$, then prove that (2A)′ = 2A′.

11. Find the value of AB :

if $A = \begin{bmatrix} 6 \\ 4 \\ 2 \end{bmatrix}$ and $B = [14 \quad 10 \quad 6]$.

12. If $A = \begin{bmatrix} 1 & 2 & 3 \\ 4 & 5 & 6 \end{bmatrix}_{2\times3}$ and $B = \begin{bmatrix} 7 & 8 \\ 9 & 10 \\ 11 & 12 \end{bmatrix}_{3\times2}$, find the value of AB.

13. If $A = \begin{bmatrix} 9 & 10 \\ 12 & 11 \end{bmatrix}$, $B = \begin{bmatrix} 5 & 8 \\ 4 & 8 \end{bmatrix}$ then find (A + B) (A – B).

(JAC, 2025)

Answers

1. $A + B = \begin{bmatrix} 7 & 10 & 13 \\ 10 & 13 & 16 \end{bmatrix}$ 2. $2A + 3B = \begin{bmatrix} 27 & 36 \\ 25 & 10 \end{bmatrix}$

3. $\begin{bmatrix} -17 & -4 \\ 5 & -54 \end{bmatrix}$ 4. $A = \begin{bmatrix} 1 & 2 & 3 \\ 3 & 2 & 1 \\ 0 & 0 & 2 \end{bmatrix}$, $B = \begin{bmatrix} 0 & -2 & -1 \\ -1 & 0 & 1 \\ 1 & 1 & 0 \end{bmatrix}$

5. $\begin{bmatrix} 10 & 3 \\ 2 & 3 \end{bmatrix}$ 6. $\begin{bmatrix} 27 & 4 \\ 5 & -3 \end{bmatrix}$ 7. $\begin{bmatrix} -5 & 27 & 23 \\ 4 & -3 & 5 \end{bmatrix}$

8. $\begin{bmatrix} 6 & 14 \\ -5 & 23 \end{bmatrix}$ 9. $\begin{bmatrix} 2 & 4 \\ 1 & -3 \\ 3 & 2 \end{bmatrix}$ 11. $\begin{bmatrix} 84 & 60 & 36 \\ 56 & 40 & 24 \\ 28 & 20 & 12 \end{bmatrix}$

12. $\begin{bmatrix} 58 & 64 \\ 139 & 154 \end{bmatrix}$ 13. $\begin{bmatrix} 200 & 82 \\ 216 & 89 \end{bmatrix}$

Exercise 7 (B)

❑ Long Answer Type Questions

1. If $A = \begin{bmatrix} 1 & -2 & 3 \\ -4 & 2 & 5 \end{bmatrix}$, $B = \begin{bmatrix} 2 & 3 \\ 4 & 5 \\ 2 & 1 \end{bmatrix}$ find AB, BA and show that AB ≠ BA.

2. If $A = \begin{bmatrix} 1 & 0 & 0 \\ 0 & 1 & 0 \\ a & b & -1 \end{bmatrix}$, find A^2.

3. If $A = \begin{bmatrix} 2 & 3 & 4 \\ -3 & 0 & 2 \end{bmatrix}$, $B = \begin{bmatrix} 3 & -4 & -5 \\ 1 & 2 & 1 \end{bmatrix}$ and $C = \begin{bmatrix} 5 & -1 & 2 \\ 7 & 0 & 3 \end{bmatrix}$ find the matrix X such that 2A + 3B = X + C.

[**Hint :** X + C = 2A + 3B

⇒ X = 2A + 3B – C]

4. If $A = \begin{bmatrix} -1 & 1 \\ 0 & 4 \end{bmatrix}$ and $B = \begin{bmatrix} -3 & 2 \\ 0 & -1 \end{bmatrix}$ then show that $(A + B)^2 \neq A^2 + 2AB + B^2$.

5. Verify that $A = \begin{bmatrix} 2 & 3 \\ 1 & 2 \end{bmatrix}$ satisfies the equation $A^3 - 4A^2 + A = 0$.

6. If $A = \begin{bmatrix} 1 & -1 \\ -1 & 1 \end{bmatrix}$, show that $A^3 = 4A$.

7. If $A = \begin{bmatrix} 3 & 1 \\ -1 & 2 \end{bmatrix}$, find f (A), where $f(x) = x^2 - 5x + 7$.

[**Hint :** $f(A) = A^2 - 5A + 7 = A^2 - 5A + 7I$]

8. Given the matrices A, B, C :

$A = \begin{bmatrix} 2 & 3 & -1 \\ 3 & 0 & 2 \end{bmatrix}$, $B = \begin{bmatrix} 1 \\ 1 \\ 2 \end{bmatrix}$, $C = [1 \; -2]$, prove that (AB)C = A(BC).

9. If $A = \begin{bmatrix} 1 & 2 \\ 2 & 1 \end{bmatrix}$, show that $A^2 - 3I = 2A$.

10. If $A = \begin{bmatrix} 3 & 1 \\ -1 & 2 \end{bmatrix}$, show that $A^2 - 5A + 7I = 0$.

11. If $A = \begin{bmatrix} 1 & 2 & 3 \\ 4 & 5 & 6 \end{bmatrix}$ and $B = \begin{bmatrix} 7 & 8 & 9 \\ 10 & 11 & 12 \end{bmatrix}$, then prove that (A + B)′ = A′ + B′

12. Without using the concept of inverse of a matrix, find the matrix $\begin{bmatrix} x & y \\ z & u \end{bmatrix}$ such that

$$\begin{bmatrix} 5 & -7 \\ -2 & 3 \end{bmatrix} \begin{bmatrix} x & y \\ z & u \end{bmatrix} = \begin{bmatrix} -16 & -6 \\ 7 & 2 \end{bmatrix}$$

Hint: $\begin{bmatrix} 5x-7z & 5y-7u \\ -2x+3z & -2y+3u \end{bmatrix} = \begin{bmatrix} -16 & -6 \\ 7 & 2 \end{bmatrix}$

∴ $5x - 7z = -16$ ...(i)

$-2x + 3z = 7$ ...(ii)

Get the value of x, z from it,

$5y - 7u = -6$ ...(iii)

$-2y + 3u = 2$ ...(iv)

Then get the value of y, u

Then get the value of $\begin{bmatrix} x & y \\ z & u \end{bmatrix}$.

13. Under what conditions is the matrix equation $A^2 - B^2 = (A - B)(A + B)$ true ?

14. A manufacturer produces three products A, B and C which are sold in Agra and Ranchi. The annual sales are as follows :

Centre	*Product* A	B	C
Agra	4,000	7,000	9,000
Ranchi	10,000	8,000	8,500

If the sale prices of the three products A, B, and C per unit be ₹ 3, ₹ 4, ₹ 5 respectively, calculate the total revenue in each centre by using matrices.

[**Hint:** $S = \begin{bmatrix} 4,000 & 7,000 & 9,000 \\ 10,000 & 8,000 & 8,500 \end{bmatrix}$ and $P = \begin{bmatrix} 3 \\ 4 \\ 5 \end{bmatrix}$

then $SP = \begin{bmatrix} 4,000 & 7,000 & 9,000 \\ 10,000 & 8,000 & 8,500 \end{bmatrix} \begin{bmatrix} 3 \\ 4 \\ 5 \end{bmatrix}$

$= \begin{bmatrix} 12,000+28,000+45,000 \\ 30,000+32,000+42,500 \end{bmatrix}$

$= \begin{bmatrix} 85,000 \\ 1,04,500 \end{bmatrix}$

So Revenue from Agra = ₹ 85,000
and Revenue from Ranchi = ₹ 1,04,500]

15. A manufacturer produces three products A, B, C which are sold in Mumbai and Chennai centres. The annual sales are as under :

Centre	Product		
	A	B	C
Mumbai	5,000	6,000	8,000
Chennai	9,000	10,000	12,000

If the sale price of the products A, B, C per unit be ₹ 2, ₹ 3, ₹ 4 respectively, calculate the total revenue at each centre by using matrices.

16. If $A = \begin{bmatrix} 1 & 2 & 3 \\ 2 & 3 & 2 \\ 3 & 3 & 4 \end{bmatrix}$ find *adj.* A.

17. Find the inverse of the following matrices :

(i) $\begin{bmatrix} 1 & 3 & 3 \\ 1 & 4 & 3 \\ 1 & 3 & 4 \end{bmatrix}$ (ii) $\begin{bmatrix} 3 & -2 & 1 \\ 2 & 1 & -3 \\ -1 & 2 & 1 \end{bmatrix}$

18. Solve the following system of linear equations by matrix method :

(i) $3x - 2y = 7$, $5x + 3y = 1$ (ii) $5x - 7y = 2$, $7x - 5y = 3$

(iii) $x + y + z = 3$, $2x - y + z = 2$, $x - 2y + 3z = 2$

19. Find the inverse of the following matrix :

$$\begin{bmatrix} 2 & 3 & 1 \\ 3 & 4 & 1 \\ 3 & 7 & 2 \end{bmatrix}$$

20. If $A = \begin{bmatrix} 3 & 1 \\ -1 & 2 \end{bmatrix}$, show that $A^2 - 5A + 7I = 0$.

21. Find the value of Y so that A + 2Y = 5B. Given that :

$A = \begin{bmatrix} 1 & 2 & 7 \\ 3 & 2 & 5 \end{bmatrix}$, $B = \begin{bmatrix} 3 & -2 & 5 \\ 6 & 2 & 8 \end{bmatrix}$

22. If A, B, and C are three Matrices such that $A = [x, y, z]$, $B = \begin{bmatrix} a & h & g \\ h & b & f \\ g & f & c \end{bmatrix}$ and $C = \begin{bmatrix} x \\ y \\ z \end{bmatrix}$, find the value of ABC.

23. Find matrix A, where $2A - 3B + 5C = 0$, $B = \begin{bmatrix} -2 & 2 & 0 \\ 3 & 1 & 4 \end{bmatrix}$ and $C = \begin{bmatrix} 2 & 0 & -2 \\ 7 & 1 & 6 \end{bmatrix}$

Answers

2. I_3 3. $\begin{bmatrix} 8 & -5 & 9 \\ -10 & 6 & 4 \end{bmatrix}$ 7. $\begin{bmatrix} 0 & 0 \\ 0 & 0 \end{bmatrix}$

10. $A^{-1} = \frac{adj.A}{(A)} = \frac{1}{2}\begin{bmatrix} 1 & 1 & -1 \\ -3 & 1 & 1 \\ 9 & -5 & -1 \end{bmatrix}$

12. $\begin{bmatrix} x & y \\ z & u \end{bmatrix} = \begin{bmatrix} 1 & -4 \\ 3 & -2 \end{bmatrix}$ 13. AB = BA

14. Agra : ₹ 85,000; Ranchi ₹ 1,04,500

15. Mumbai : ₹ 60,000; Chennai : ₹ 96,000

16. $\begin{bmatrix} 6 & 1 & -5 \\ -2 & -5 & 4 \\ -3 & 3 & -1 \end{bmatrix}$

17. (i) $\begin{bmatrix} 7 & -3 & -3 \\ -1 & 1 & 0 \\ -1 & 0 & 1 \end{bmatrix}$ (ii) $\begin{bmatrix} 7/24 & 4/24 & 5/24 \\ 1/24 & 4/24 & 11/24 \\ 5/24 & -4/24 & 7/24 \end{bmatrix}$

18. (i) $x = \frac{23}{19}, = -\frac{32}{19}$ (ii) $x = \frac{11}{24}, y = \frac{1}{24}$

(iii) $x = 1, y = 1, z = 1$

19. $A^{-1} = \frac{adj.A}{|A|} = \frac{1}{2}\begin{bmatrix} 1 & 1 & -1 \\ -3 & 1 & 1 \\ 9 & -5 & -1 \end{bmatrix}$

21. $Y = \frac{1}{2}\begin{bmatrix} 14 & -12 & 18 \\ 27 & 8 & 35 \end{bmatrix}$

22. $ax^2 + by^2 + cz^2 + 2hxy + 2gzx + 2fyz$

23. $\begin{bmatrix} 2 & 3 & -5 \\ 22 & 4 & 21 \end{bmatrix}$

Exercise 7 (C)

Objective Type Questions

❑ Multiple Choice Questions

1. A matrix with single column and any number of rows in known as :
(a) Singular Matrix (b) Row Matrix
(c) Diagonal Matrix (d) Column Matrix

2. In a row matrix, the number of row is :
(a) 1 (b) 2 (c) 3 (d) None of these

3. In a scalar matrix if all the diagonal elements are equal, then it is known as :
(a) Unit Matrix (b) Symmetric Matrix
(c) Skew-symmetric Matrix (d) None of these

4. Adjoint of matrix may be :
(a) Row Matrix (b) Column Matrix
(c) Square Matrix (d) Any other Matrix

5. If A, B and C are three matrices such that C = A + B, then the number of elements of C is :
(a) More than A (b) Less than A
(c) Same as A (d) Different number

6. If A is a matrix of the type $m \times n$ and B is a matrix of the type $n \times p$, then AB is a matrix of the type :
(a) $m \times n$ (b) $n \times p$ (c) $p \times m$ (d) $m \times p$

7. If $A = \begin{bmatrix} -1 & 0 \\ 0 & 1 \end{bmatrix}$ then the value of A^2 is :

(a) $\begin{bmatrix} 1 & 0 \\ 0 & 1 \end{bmatrix}$ (b) $\begin{bmatrix} 0 & 1 \\ 0 & 1 \end{bmatrix}$

(c) $\begin{bmatrix} -1 & 0 \\ 1 & 0 \end{bmatrix}$ (d) $\begin{bmatrix} 1 & 0 \\ 0 & 1 \end{bmatrix}$

8. If $A = \begin{bmatrix} 0 & 0 \\ 2 & 0 \end{bmatrix}$ then A^2 is :

(a) Unit Matrix (b) Null Matrix
(c) Diagonal Matrix (d) None of these

9. If $A = \begin{bmatrix} 1 & 1 \\ 0 & 1 \end{bmatrix}$, $B = \begin{bmatrix} 0 & 1 \\ 1 & 0 \end{bmatrix}$ then AB :

(a) $\begin{bmatrix} 1 & 1 \\ 1 & 0 \end{bmatrix}$ (b) $\begin{bmatrix} 0 & 1 \\ 0 & 0 \end{bmatrix}$

(c) $\begin{bmatrix} 0 & 0 \\ 0 & 0 \end{bmatrix}$ (d) $\begin{bmatrix} 1 & 2 \\ 2 & 0 \end{bmatrix}$

10. $\begin{bmatrix} 8 & 0 & 0 \\ 0 & 8 & 0 \\ 0 & 0 & 8 \end{bmatrix}$ is *a* :

(a) Diagonal Matrix (b) Square Matrix
(c) Symmetric Matrix (d) Scalar Matrix

11. If $A = \begin{bmatrix} 4 & 1 \\ 2 & 3 \end{bmatrix}$, then $A^2 = ?$

(a) $\begin{bmatrix} 9 & 7 \\ 4 & 11 \end{bmatrix}$ (b) $\begin{bmatrix} 18 & 7 \\ 14 & 11 \end{bmatrix}$

(c) $\begin{bmatrix} 18 & 17 \\ 14 & 11 \end{bmatrix}$ (d) $\begin{bmatrix} 17 & 18 \\ 11 & 14 \end{bmatrix}$

12. $\begin{bmatrix} 3 & 4 \\ 4 & 5 \end{bmatrix} - \begin{bmatrix} -1 & 3 \\ 2 & -3 \end{bmatrix}$ is equal to :

(a) $\begin{bmatrix} 4 & 1 \\ 0 & 8 \end{bmatrix}$ (b) 10

(c) 4 (d) $\begin{bmatrix} 2 & 1 \\ 0 & 2 \end{bmatrix}$

13. If $A = \begin{bmatrix} 2 & 3 \\ 4 & 5 \end{bmatrix}$ and $B = \begin{bmatrix} -1 & -3 \\ -4 & -5 \end{bmatrix}$ then the value of A – B will be : *(JAC, 2018)*

(a) $\begin{bmatrix} 1 & 0 \\ 0 & 0 \end{bmatrix}$ (b) $\begin{bmatrix} 3 & 6 \\ 8 & 10 \end{bmatrix}$

(c) $\begin{bmatrix} -2 & -9 \\ -16 & -25 \end{bmatrix}$ (d) $\begin{bmatrix} -1 & 0 \\ 0 & 1 \end{bmatrix}$

14. If $X = \begin{bmatrix} 3 & 9 & 6 \\ 7 & 8 & 4 \end{bmatrix}$ and $Y = \begin{bmatrix} 1 & 6 & 10 \\ 4 & 5 & 7 \end{bmatrix}$ then value of X + Y is : *(JAC, 2018)*

(a) $\begin{bmatrix} 2 & 3 & 16 \\ 11 & 3 & 3 \end{bmatrix}$ (b) $\begin{bmatrix} 3 & 9 & 6 \\ 7 & 8 & 4 \end{bmatrix}$

(c) $\begin{bmatrix} 3 & 54 & 60 \\ 28 & 40 & 28 \end{bmatrix}$ (d) $\begin{bmatrix} 4 & 15 & 16 \\ 11 & 13 & 11 \end{bmatrix}$

15. If $A = \begin{bmatrix} 3 & 1 \\ 7 & 6 \end{bmatrix}$, $B = \begin{bmatrix} 4 & 7 \\ 5 & 2 \end{bmatrix}$, then A + B = *(JAC, 2019, 24)*

(a) $\begin{bmatrix} 12 & 7 \\ 35 & 12 \end{bmatrix}$ (b) $\begin{bmatrix} 7 & 8 \\ 12 & 8 \end{bmatrix}$

(c) $\begin{bmatrix} -1 & -6 \\ -2 & 4 \end{bmatrix}$ (d) $\begin{bmatrix} 3 & 7 \\ 5 & 6 \end{bmatrix}$

16. In diagonal matrix, the number of row and column is :
(a) more (b) equal (c) less (d) zero

17. The number of elements in 3 × 4 matrix is :
(a) 12 (b) 7 (c) 6 (d) 3

18. Which of the following matrices is not a scalar matrix ?

(a) $\begin{bmatrix} 3 & 0 \\ 0 & 3 \end{bmatrix}$ (b) $\begin{bmatrix} 5 & 0 \\ 0 & 5 \end{bmatrix}$

(c) $\begin{vmatrix} 2 & 0 & 0 \\ 0 & 2 & 0 \\ 0 & 0 & 2 \end{vmatrix}$ (d) $\begin{bmatrix} 0 & 0 & 0 \\ 0 & 0 & 0 \\ 0 & 0 & 0 \end{bmatrix}$

19. The number of all possible matrices of order 3 × 3 with each entry 0 or 1 is :
(a) 27 (b) 18 (c) 81 (d) 512

20. A row matrix has only :
(a) one element
(b) one row with one or more columns
(c) one column with one or more rows
(d) one row and one column

21. A matrix with single column and more than one row is known as :
(a) Single matrix (b) Row matrix
(c) Diagonal matrix (d) Column matrix

22. If $A = \begin{bmatrix} 2 & 5 \\ 7 & -8 \end{bmatrix}$ then A′ is : *(JAC, 2022)*

(a) $\begin{bmatrix} 2 & -8 \\ 5 & 7 \end{bmatrix}$ (b) $\begin{bmatrix} 5 & 2 \\ -8 & 7 \end{bmatrix}$

(c) $\begin{bmatrix} 2 & 7 \\ 5 & -8 \end{bmatrix}$ (d) $\begin{bmatrix} 7 & -8 \\ 2 & 5 \end{bmatrix}$

23. If $\begin{bmatrix} 2 & x \\ y & 0 \end{bmatrix} = \begin{bmatrix} 2 & 1 \\ 4 & 0 \end{bmatrix}$, then the value of x and y : *(JAC, 2022)*

(a) $x = -1, y = 4$ (b) $x = 2, y = 0$
(c) $x = 4, y = 2$ (d) $x = 1, y = 4$

24. If A = [3 5 7], B = [4 3 2], then (A + B) is :
(a) [7 8 9] (b) [3 5 7] (c) [4 3 2] (d) [1 2 5]

25. If $A = \begin{bmatrix} 5 & 3 \\ 2 & 8 \end{bmatrix}$, $B = \begin{bmatrix} 2 & 1 \\ 1 & 6 \end{bmatrix}$, then A – B is :

(a) $\begin{bmatrix} 5 & 3 \\ 2 & 8 \end{bmatrix}$ (b) $\begin{bmatrix} 3 & 2 \\ 1 & 2 \end{bmatrix}$

(c) $\begin{bmatrix} 2 & 1 \\ 1 & 6 \end{bmatrix}$ (d) $\begin{bmatrix} 1 & 2 \\ 4 & 5 \end{bmatrix}$

26. If $A = \begin{bmatrix} 8 & 2 & 3 \\ 4 & 5 & 6 \end{bmatrix}$, than the value of 5A is : *(JAC, 2024)*

(a) $\begin{bmatrix} 40 & 15 & 10 \\ 20 & 25 & 30 \end{bmatrix}$ (b) $\begin{bmatrix} 40 & 10 & 15 \\ 20 & 25 & 30 \end{bmatrix}$

(c) $\begin{bmatrix} 20 & 25 & 30 \\ 40 & 15 & 10 \end{bmatrix}$ (d) $\begin{bmatrix} 10 & 8 & 15 \\ 20 & 25 & 10 \end{bmatrix}$

27. If A = [1 2 3], B = [2 3 5] then A + B is : (*JAC, 2025*)
(a) [4 5 6] (b) [1 2 3] (c) [6 5 4] (d) [3 5 8]

28. If $\begin{bmatrix} x & 1 \\ 2 & 3 \end{bmatrix} = \begin{bmatrix} 4 & 1 \\ 2 & 3 \end{bmatrix}$ then x is : (*JAC, 2025*)
(a) 2 (b) 4 (c) 1 (d) 3

Answers

1. (d)	2. (a)	3. (a)	4. (c)	5. (c)	6. (d)	7. (a)
8. (b)	9. (a)	10. (d)	11. (b)	12. (a)	13. (b)	14. (d)
15. (b)	16. (b)	17. (a)	18. (d)	19. (d)	20. (b)	21. (d)
22. (c)	23. (d)	24. (a)	25. (b),	26. (b)	27. (d)	28. (b).

❑ Fill in the blanks

1. If A is an $m \times n$ matrix and B is an $n \times p$ matrix, then the product BA can be found out when p = ...
2. A matrix whose each element is zero, is called .... matrix.
3. A matrix having equal number of rows and columns is called .... matrix.
4. $\begin{bmatrix} 5 \\ 6 \\ 7 \end{bmatrix}$ is the example of a .... matrix.
5. $4\begin{bmatrix} 1 & 2 \\ 3 & 4 \end{bmatrix} = \begin{bmatrix} 4 & 8 \\ 12 & .... \end{bmatrix}$

Answers

1. m 2. 0 (Null) 3. Square
4. Column 5. 16.

❑ Write True or False

1. The product of matrix and its transposed matrix is symmetric.
2. Matrix is a representation whereas determinant has a value.
3. If A and B is two matrices that AB = 0, then A = 0 or B = 0
4. If A, B, C be three matrices and A = B then A + C = B + C.
5. A square matrix is such that its number of rows and columns are unequal.

Answers

1. True 2. True 3. False 4. True
5. False.

❖❖

8 SET THEORY

LEARNING OBJECTIVES

After studying this chapter, you will be able to know :

- **8.1 Meaning and Definition of Set**
- **8.2 Representation of a Set—Methods of Representation**
- **8.3 Set Notations**
- **8.4 Meaning of the Symbol ∈ and ∉**
- **8.5 Types of Sets :**
  1. **Finite Set**
  2. **Infinite Set**
  3. **Null Set or Empty Set or Void Set**
  4. **Singleton Set**
  5. **Pair Set**
  6. **Set of Sets**
  7. **Equivalent Sets**
  8. **Sub-set**
  9. **Proper Sub-set**
  10. **Super Set**
  11. **Equal Sets**
  12. **Power Set**
  13. **Universal Set**
  14. **Disjoint Sets**
  15. **Family or Class of Sets**
- **8.6 Algebra of Sets : Basic Set Operations**
  - **(i) Union of Sets**
  - **(ii) Intersection of Sets**
  - **(iii) Difference of Two Sets**
- **8.7 Venn Diagram**
- **8.8 Applications of Sets**

SOLVED EXAMPLES AND PRACTICAL PROBLEMS : AT A GLANCE

No. of Examples		*No. of Problems*
1 to 4	Representation of a Set	Exercise 8 (A) 1 to 9
1 to 6	Types of Sets	Exercise 8 (B) 1 to 15
1 to 17	Algebra of Sets—Theorem	Exercise 8 (C) 1 to 14
1 to 5	Venn Diagram	Exercise 8 (D) 1 to 5
1 to 10	Applications of Sets	Exercise 8 (E) 1 to 26
1 to 7	Miscellaneous	Exercise 8 (F) 1 to 3
	Objective Type Questions	Exercise 8 (G) 17 + 5 + 5
49	Total	72 + 27

(8.1) MEANING AND DEFINITION OF SET

The concept of set is very important in modern mathematics. George Cantor (1845–1918), a German Mathematician, is regarded as the father of the Set Theory. An elementary idea of this theory is given here to meet the needs of the commerce students.

A set is a collection of objects according to *Cantor*, "A set is a collection of definite will distinguished objects of perception or thought."

Another definition of a set is given as under :

"Set is a well defined collection of objects." By a "well defined we mean that there is a rule (or rules) by means of which it is possible to say, whether the given object belongs to that set or not. For example, if we are given the set of vowels *i.e.* a, e, i, o, u we can say that the letter 'b' does not belong to this set.

Here the term 'objects' has been used is broad sense. In mathematics letter, figure, numbers, symbols etc. are objects. Each of the objects of collection is called a member or an element of the set.

Hence from above we conclude that the classification of objects with respect to a given set is subject to two rules, *viz*.

(i) The objects in the set should not be alike and

(ii) It should be possible to distinguish between the objects in the set and those not in the set.

(8.2) REPRESENTATION OF A SET—METHODS OF REPRESENTATION

A set is described by the following two methods :

(i) Tabular Form or Roaster Method,

(ii) Set-builder Form or Symbolic Method.

(i) Tabular Form : This method is also known as Listing Method or Roaster Method.

If the elements are enclosed in curly brackets or braces { } after separating then by commas, a set consists of 7 natural number, then

$$A = \{1, 2, 3, 4, 5, 6, 7\}$$

Similarly, a set B consisting of integral figures less than 5 will be written as :

$$B = \{0, 1, 2, 3, 4\}$$

Important Note : (a) The tabular form is useful only when the number of elements are not large.

(b) The order of writing the lements of a set is immaterial.

So, {Ram, Shyam, Mohan} and {Mohan, Ram and Shyam} or {Shyam, Ram and Mohan} all denotes the same set. Similarly $\{a, b, c\}$, $\{b, a, c\}$, $\{b, c, a\}$ all denotes the same set.

(c) Also an element of a set is not written more than once *i.e.* the set {1, 5, 7, 7, 9} is identical with the set {1, 5, 7, 9}.

Similarly from the words follow, wolf and flow, we get only one set {f, l, o, w}.

(ii) Set-builder Form : This method is also known as a property method or symbolic method or rule method. Under this method a set is defined by stating properties which its element are to satisfy. Here we express the element or arbitrary member of a set by the method word x. If p be the property of x, then the set will be written as :

$$A = \{x : p(x)\} \text{ or } \{x\}\ x\ p(x)$$

It will be read as :

"A is the set of elements x such that x has the property p".

Here we should remember that

(a) "A = {'x'}" means A is the set of elements x,

(b) "/" or ":" means such that, and

(c) After "/" or ":" is written the condition or property $p(x)$ which are satisfied by the element x of the set.

(8.3) SET NOTATIONS

Sets are usually denoted by Capital letters A, B, C, ..., X, Y, Z.

Elements or members are usually denoted by small letters $a, b, c, \ldots\ldots, x, y, z$.

Notation for Some Familiar Sets

(i) Set of natural numbers (positive integers) is denoted by N.

So $N = \{1, 2, 3, 4, 5, \ldots\ldots\}$

or $N = \{x/x \text{ is a natural number}\}$

(ii) The set of whole number is denoted by W.

So $W = \{0, 1, 2, 3, \ldots\ldots\}$

or $W = \{x/x \text{ is whole number}\}$

(iii) The set of integers is denoted by I or Z.

So $I = \{\ldots\ldots, -3, -2, -1, 0, 1, 2, 3, \ldots\ldots\}$

or $I = \{x/x\ a \text{ is an integer}\}$

(iv) The set of rational numbers is denoted by Q.

So $Q = \{\frac{p}{q} : p \text{ and } q \text{ are integers and } q \neq 0\}$

(v) The set of real numbers is denoted by R.

So $R = \{x/x \text{ is a real number}\}$

Note : It is not possible to represent every set by above two methods.

(8.4) MEANING OF THE SYMBOL ∈ AND ∉

Membership Symbol (∈)

The symbol ∈ indicates that an object or quantity is an element of a set.

(i) If A is a set and x is its element or member, then this fact is indicated by writing $x \in A$. This is read as 'x belongs to A' or x is in A'.

The symbol ∈ stands for 'is in', "are in belongs to" belong to according to the context.

(ii) $A = \{a, e, i, o, u\}$ If a and e are elements of a set, then write $a, e \in A$ instead of $a \in A$ and $e \in A$. Here $a, e \in A$ is read as 'a' and 'e' are in A or 'a' and 'e' belongs to A.

(iii) If x does not belong to A, *i.e.* x is not an element of A. Then we write $x \notin A$ which is read as 'x' is not in A or 'x' does not belong to A.

Example : A = {1, 3, 5, 7}

Then $3 \in A$ *i.e.* 3 is in A or 3 belongs to A.

$2 \notin A$ or 2 is not in A or 2 does not belong to A.

(iv) $\frac{7}{9}$ is a vulgar fraction. If S be the set of all vulgar fraction S, $\frac{7}{9}$ is a member of the set S and is expressed as $\frac{7}{9} \in S$.

Symbol		Meaning
: or /	$\longrightarrow$	such that
$\in$	$\longrightarrow$	is an element of
$\notin$	$\longrightarrow$	is not an element of
ϕ	$\longrightarrow$	the Null Set
Ω	$\longrightarrow$	Universal Set
$\subseteq$	$\longrightarrow$	Sub-set
$\supseteq$	$\longrightarrow$	Super set
$\subset$	$\longrightarrow$	Proper sub-set
$\Rightarrow$	$\longrightarrow$	Implies
$\Leftrightarrow$	$\longrightarrow$	if and only if
$\cup$	$\longrightarrow$	Union
$\cap$	$\longrightarrow$	Intersection
$-$	$\longrightarrow$	Difference
Δ	$\longrightarrow$	Symmetric difference
$\forall$	$\longrightarrow$	for every

SOLVED EXAMPLES

Example 1

Write the following in tabular form :

(i) A = {x/x is a letter of word MATHEMATICS}
(ii) R = {x/x is a natural number less than 6}
(iii) M = {x/x is a natural number of two digits and the sum of the digits of 8}

Solution :

(i) A = {M, A, T, H, E, I, C, S}
(ii) R = {1, 2, 3, 4, 5}
(iii) M = {17, 26, 35, 44, 53, 62, 71, 80}

Example 2

Write the following sets in set builder form :

(i) T = {1, 3, 5, ...}
(ii) M = {2, 4, 8, 16, 32}
(iii) C = {3, 6, 9, 12}
(iv) P = {a, e, i, o, u}

Solution :

(i) T = {1, 3, 5, ...}
T = {x/x is an odd natural number}
(ii) M = {2, 4, 8, 16, 32}
M = {$x : x = 2^n$; where $n \in$ N and $n \le 5$}
(iii) C = {3, 6, 9, 12}
C = {$x : x$, 3 Positive multiple of 3 and $x \le 12$}
(iv) P = {a, e, i, o, u}
P = {x/x is a vowel alphabet}

Example 3

Write the following in notation :

(i) 5 is a member of set P.
(ii) m is a member of set M.
(iii) {x} is a member of set A.
(iv) x is not a member of set X.

Solution :

(i) $5 \in P$ (ii) $m \in M$
(iii) $\{x\} \in A$ (iv) $x \notin X$

Example 4

If A = {1, 2 {3, 4}, 5} then which of the following is 'true' and 'false', give also the reasons :

(i) $1 \in A$ (ii) $4 \in A$
(iii) $5 \notin A$ (iv) $\{1, 2\} \in A$

Solution :

(i) True; as 1 is the element of set A.
(ii) False; as 4 is not the element of set A but {3, 4} $\in$ A
(iii) False; as $5 \in A$
(iv) False; as $\{1, 2\} \notin A$ but $1 \in A$ and $2 \in A$

Exercise 8 (A)

1. Express the following sets in tabular form :
(a) {$x : x$ = integer and $1 \le x \le 9$}
(b) {$x : x$ = odd integer and $5 < x \le 15$}
(c) {$x : x$ = set of even positive integers}
(d) Set of all odd positive integers between 4 and 16.
(e) A = {x/x is a letter of the word ARITHMETIC}
(f) T = {x/x is a positive integer and $x^2 \le 100$}
(g) B = {x/x is an odd positive integer less than 10}
(h) A = {$x/x^2 + x - 6 = 0$}
[**Hint :** $x^2 + x - 6 = 0$
$\Rightarrow x^2 + 3x - 2x - 6 = 0$
$\Rightarrow x(x + 3) - 2(x + 3) = 0$
$\Rightarrow (x - 2)(x + 3) = 0$]
(i) M = {x/x is letter of the word 'LULL'}
(j) T = Set of all letters used in the word 'SETS'
2. If A is set of the letters of the word eat, then which one of the following is true ? (*JAC*, 2016, 22)
(i) $e \in A$ (ii) $A \in a$
(iii) $t \notin A$ (iv) $at \in A$
3. If A = {x/x, even number less than 10} which one of the following is false :
(i) A = {2, 4, 6}
(ii) A = {2, 4, 6, 8}
(iii) $4 \in A$
(iv) $10 \in A$
4. Write the following sets in set builder form :
(a) A = {1, 3, 5}
(b) S = {2, 4, 6, 8}
(c) A = {5, 10, 15, ...}
(d) B = {2, 3, 5, 7, 11, 13, 17, ...}
5. If C is set of the capital of states of India, then fill in the blanks with $\in$ and $\notin$:
(i) Jaipur .... C (ii) Mysore C
(iii) Srinagar .... C (iv) Shimla C
(v) Meerut .... C (vi) Patna C

6. If A = {1, 2, 3, 4,} and B = {5, 6, 7}, then fill in the blanks with ∈ or ∉ :
   (i) 3 ... A (ii) 5 ... A
   (iii) 10 ... B (iv) {1, 2 .... A}
   (v) 7 .... B (vi) {1... 5}
   (vii) 4 ... A (viii) 6 ... A
   (ix) 6 3
7. Write the following in language :
   (i) $4 \in A$ (ii) $5 \in P$
   (iii) $x \notin A$ (iv) $-7 \in Q$
   (v) $\{1, 2\} \notin A$ (vi) Chair ∈ B
8. The set of positive integers less than 4 is : (*JAC*, 2022)
   (a) {– 1, 0, 1, 2} (b) {– 2, – 1, 0, 3}
   (c) {1, 2, 3} (d) {1, 4}
9. Two sets are disjoint if and only if : (*JAC*, 2022)
   (a) $A \cap B = \phi$ (b) $A \cap B \neq \phi$
   (c) $A - B \neq \phi$ (d) $A - B = B$

Answers

1. (a) {1, 2, 3, 4, 5, 6, 7, 8, 9}, (b) {7, 9, 11, 13, 15}, (c) {2, 4, 6, 8, ...}, (d) {5, 7, 9, 11, 13, 15}, (e) A = {A, R, I, T, H, M, E, C}, (f) T = {1, 2, 3, 4, 5, 6, 7, 8, 9, 10}, (g) B = {1, 3, 5, 7, 9}, (h) A = {2, – 3}, (i) M = {L, U}, (j) T = {S, E, T}].
2. (i) $e \in A$
3. (i) A = {2, 4, 6}.
4. (a) A = {x/x, 7 is less odd positive integer};
   (b) S = {x/x, 10 is less even positive number};
   (c) A = {x : x, 5 its multiple is positive number};
   (d) B = {x : x, is positive indivisible number}.
5. (i) ∈, (ii) ∉, (iii) ∈, (iv) ∈, (v) ∉, (vi) ∈.
6. (i) ∈, (ii) ∉, (iii) ∉, (iv) ∉, (v) ∈, (vi) ∉, (vii) ∈, (viii) ∉, (ix) ∈.
7. (i) 4 is the element of set A., (ii) 5 belongs of set P., (iii) *x* does not belong to set A., (iv) – 7 belongs to set Q., (v) {1, 2} does not belong to set A., (vi) Chair belongs to set B.
8. {1, 2, 3}
9. $A \cup B = \phi$

(8.5) TYPES OF SETS

1. Finite Set : A set is said to be a finite set if it contains definite number of elements in it.

Example :

(i) {x/x is a letter of English alphabet}
(ii) {a, e, i, o, u}
(iii) {4, 5, 7}

are finite sets as it contains definite number of elements in it.

2. Infinite Set : The set whose elements cannot be counted is called an infinite set.

In other words "A set is said to be an infinite set if it is not a finite set."

Example :

(i) {x/x is a natural number}
(ii) Set of straight lines in a plane.

3. Null Set or Empty Set or Void Set : "A set is said to be a null set if it contains no elements. Null set is denoted by ϕ or { }.

Example :

(i) set of immortal men.
(ii) $\phi = \{x : x$ is a positive integer and $x < 0\}$
(iii) $\phi = \{x : x$ is an odd integer whose square is even$\}$

4. Singleton Set : A set is said to be a singleton set if it contains one and only one element in it.

Example :

(i) {a} (ii) {g} (iii) {x/x – 7 = 0}

5. Pair Set : A set is said to be a pair set if it contains two elements.

Example :

(i) {a, b}, (ii) {x/x is a letter of the word "it".}

6. Set of Sets : If all the elements of a set are also sets themselves, then the set is called set of sets.

Example :

(i) {5, 7}, {8, 4}, {1, 3, 5}
(ii) {ϕ} is a singleton set.

7. Equivalent Sets : If two sets have same number of elements, then they are said to be equivalent sets.

Equivalent sets are denoted by the symbol ↔ or ~ or ≡.

Example :

(i) {8, 7, 4} ↔ {a, b, c} (ii) {5, 4} ~ {6, 8}
(iii) {x, z} ≡ {3, 4}

8. Sub-set : If A and B are two sets such that all elements of set A are also in set B, then set A is called the sub-set of set B.

Example :

(i) A = {3, 5, 7}; B = {7, 5, 3} Here $A \subseteq B$ as all elements of set A are also in set B.

(ii) A = {a, b, c}; B = {a, b, c, d, e}, then $A \subseteq B$ as all elements of set A are also in set B.

9. Proper Sub-set : If A and B are two sets such that $A \subseteq B$ and $A \neq B$ then A is said to be proper sub-set of B.

In other words we can say that "If A and B are two sets a such that all the members (or elements) of set A are members of set B and atleast one member of B be such that it is not a member of A, then A will be the proper sub-set of B."

Example :

(i) A = {5, 8, 9}, B = {5, 8, 9, 10}
then $A \subset B$
(ii) A = Set of Biharies, B = Set of Indians
then $A \subset B$

The symbol ⊂ denotes proper sub-set.

10. Super Set : If A is the sub-set of set B, then set B is called the super set of A.

Example :

$A = \{5, 7, 9\}$, $B = \{5, 7, 9, 10\}$

then $B \supset A$

11. Equal Sets : If A and B are two sets such that $A \subseteq B$ and $B \subseteq A$, then A and B are said to be equal sets.

In other words, two sets A and B are said to be equal if each element of set A is also an element of set B and each element of set B is also an element of A.

Example :

$A = \{a, b, c\}$, $B = \{b, c, a\}$

then $A \subseteq B$ and $B \subseteq A$

So $A = B$

*** Prove that Null set is unique.**

Proof :

Let ϕ is not unique (one and only one). Let ϕ' is another null set.

So $\phi \neq \phi'$

It means that for some element

(i) $x \in \phi$

$\Rightarrow$ $x \notin \phi'$

or (ii) $x \in \phi'$

$\Rightarrow$ $x \notin \phi$

but ϕ and ϕ' are null sets. So statements (i) and (ii) both are false. So our supposition $\phi = \phi'$ was wrong.

So $\phi = \phi'$

or the null set ϕ is unique.

*** Prove that the null set ϕ is sub-set of every set.**

Proof :

If possible let null set ϕ is not the sub-set of any set A.

$\phi \not\subset A$

It means that there exists at least one element $x \in \phi \Rightarrow x \notin A$ but ϕ is a null set which has no element. Thus we get a contradiction. So our supposition was wrong. Thus the null set ϕ is the sub-set of every set.

12. Power Set : The set of all possible sub-sets of a set is called power set of the set.

The power set of set A is denoted by P(A) or P^A. Thus $P(A) = \{B/B \subseteq A\}$

Note : Each element of a power set is a set.

Example :

(i) If $A = \phi$, then $P(A) = \{\phi\}$.

(ii) If $A = \{a\}$, then $P(A) = \{\phi, \{a\}\}$

(iii) If $A = \{x, y\}$, then $P(A) = \{\phi, \{x\}, \{y\}, \{x, y\}\}$

*** Prove that the power set of a set having *n* element has 2^n elements.**

Proof :

Let $A = \phi$

Then sub-set of $A = \phi$

Number of Sub-sets of $A = 1 = 2^0$

Again Let $B = \{a\}$

Then sub-set of B $B = \phi, \{a\}$

Number of sub-sets of $B = 2 = 2^1$

Again let $C = \{a, b\}$

Then sub-set of $C = \phi, \{a\}, \{b\}, \{a, b\}$

Number of sub-set of $C = 4 = 2^2$

Again let $D = \{a, b, c\}$

Then subset of $D = \phi, \{a\}, \{b\}, \{c\}, \{a, b\}, \{b, c\}, \{c, a\}, \{a, b, c\}$

So number of sub-sets of $D = 8 = 2^3$

Thus we can say that *a* set having *n* elements has 2^n sub-sets.

*** Distinguish between ϕ, {0} and {ϕ}**

Solution :

(i) ϕ is null set which has no element.

(ii) {0} represents a singleton set which has the element 0.

(iii) {ϕ} represents set of a set which has only one element ϕ. Thus the above three sets are different to each other.

13. Universal Set : If all the sets under investigation are sub-set of a particular set, then the particular set is called the universal set

Universal set is generally denoted by $\cup$ or Ω or S or E.

Example 1

$I = \{\ldots\ldots, -3, -2, -1, 0, 1, 2, \ldots\ldots\}$

$N = \{1, 2, 3, 4, 5, \ldots\ldots\}$

$O = \{1, 3, 5, 7, \ldots\ldots\}$

$E = \{0, 2, 4, 6, 8, \ldots\ldots\}$

Here we see that

$N \subseteq I$, $O \subseteq I$, $E \subseteq I$

So I is the universal set of sets N, O, E.

Example 2

Let A = {Set of Studens of Arts faculty of R.D.S. College, Muzaffarpur}

B = {Set of Students of Commerce faculty of R.D.S. College, Muzaffarpur}

C = {Set of Students of Science faculty of R.D.S. College, Muzaffarpur}

U = {Set of Students of R.D.S. College, Muzaffarpur}

Which we have to consider sets A, B and C, set U has been imagined. U is arbitrary set in which the condition $A \subseteq U$, $B \subseteq U$ and $C \subseteq U$ is fulfilled. So U is the Universal set of A, B and C.

14. Disjoint Sets : Two sets A and B are said to be disjoint sets or mutually exclusive sets if there is no common elements of $A \cap B = \phi$.

Example :

$A = \{a, b, c, d\}$;

$B = \{e, f, g, h, i, j, k\}$

then $A \cap B = \phi$

So A and B are disjoint sets.

15. Family or Class of Sets : If elements of a set are itself a set, then the set is called family of sets.

Thus power set is a family of sets.

As $\{A = \{\{1\}, \{2\}, \{1, 2\}\}$

is a family of sets.

SOLVED EXAMPLES

Example 1

Every set is the sub-set of itself.

Solution

If possible let any set A is not the sub-set of itself.

i.e. $A \not\subset A$

So by the definition of sub-set there exist atleast one element $x \in A$ and $x \notin A$ which is impossible together. So our supposition that $A \subseteq A$ was wrong.

Thus $A \subseteq A$

Again A is arbitrary set. So every set is the sub-set of itself.

Example 2

Fill in the blanks selecting from null, singleton pair so that the statements may be true :

(i) $\{x / x^2 + 1 = 0, x$ is real number$\}$ is .... set.

(ii) {0} is .... set.

(iii) {x / x is a letter of English alphabets which comes after Z} is ..... set.

(iv) {x / x is a letter of word 'no'} is .... set.

Solution

(i) Null

Explanation : $x^2 + 1 = 0 \Rightarrow x^2 = -1$

Which is not true for any real number.

(ii) Singleton

Explanation : The set has only one element 0.

(iii) Null

Explanation : There is no letter after Z in English alphabet.

(iv) Pair

Explanation : There are two elements n, o.

Example 3

State finite and infinite sets in the following :

(i) Set of people living in India

(ii) {1, 2, 3, 4, ...}

(iii) {3, 6, 9, 12, ...}

(iv) {x / x is an integer and $x \leq 4$}

(v) {x/x is a positive integer and $x \leq 4$}

Solution

(i) Finite Set

Explanation : Number of people living in India can be counted.

(ii) Infinite set

Explanantion : There are infinite natural number.

(iii) Infinite set

Explanation : All natural numbers are elements of the set which are divisible by 3.

(iv) Infinite set

Explanation : The values of x are 4, 5, 6, 7, 8, ..., to ∞

(v) Finite Set

Explanation : The values of x are 1, 2, 3, 4.

Example 4

Let A = {1, 2, {3, 4}, 5} then which of the following is false ?

(i) $1 \in A$ (ii) $\{3, 4\} \notin A$

(iii) $\{1, 2, 5\} \subset A$ (iv) $\{1\} \subset A$

Solution

(ii)

Explanation : (i) is true as $1 \in A$

(ii) is false as $\{3, 4\} \in A$

(iii) is true as {1, 2, 5} is proper sub-set of A.

(iv) is true as {1} is the proper sub-set of A.

Example 5

(i) Write all sub-sets of {1, 2, 3}.

(ii) Write all proper sub-sets of {2 ,3, 4}.

(iii) If there are 5 elements in a set, then find out its number of sub-sets.

(iv) If a set consists of 3 elements, then find out the number of its proper sub-sets.

Solution :

(i) Sub-set of {1, 2, 3} are

ϕ {1}, {2}, {3}, {1, 2}, {1, 3}, {2, 3}, {1 ,2, 3}

(ii) Proper sub-set of {2, 3, 4} are

ϕ {2}, {3}, {4}, {2, 3}, {2, 4}, {3, 4}

(iii) Number of element $n = 5$

So number of sub-set $= 2^n = 2^5 = 32$

(iv) Number of elements $n = 3$

So number of proper sub-sets $= 2^n - 1 = 2^3 - 1 = 8 - 1 = 7$

Example 6

Fill in the blanks with $\subset$ and $\not\subset$:

(i) {2, 3, 4} ..... {6, 2, 8, 12, 10, 4}

(ii) {2, 3} ..... {5, 6}

(iii) {a, e, i, o, u} .... {x / x is a letter of English alphabets}

(iv) {x / x, is a multiple of 10} .... {x/x is a multiple of 5}

(v) $\{x / x$ is a student of class IX of your school$\}$ ....
$\{x/x$ is a student of your school$\}$

Solution

(i) $\subset$ (ii) $\not\subset$ (iii) $\subset$ (iv) $\subset$ (v) $\subset$

Exercise 8 (B)

1. Which of the following sets is finite set ?
   (i) Set of people living on the earth
   (ii) $\{x/x$ is even integer$\}$
   (iii) Set of positive integers less than 50
   (iv) Set of those lines which moves through a certain points of the surface.
2. (a) Which is null set in the following ? (*JAC*, 2022, 23, 26)
   (i) 0 (ii) $\{0\}$ (iii) $\{\phi\}$ (iv) ϕ
   (b) (i) A = $\{x/x$, is positive undivisible even integer$\}$
   (ii) C = $\{x/x, + 8 = 8\}$
   (iii) D = $\{x / x \neq x$, x is a real number$\}$
3. Fill in the blanks with appropriate word selecting from singleton or null or pair :
   (i) $\{0, 1\}$ is a ... set.
   (ii) $\{\phi\}$ is a .... set.
   (iii) $\{x/x^2 - 1 = 0\}$ is a ..... set.
   (iv) ϕ is a ..... set.
   (v) $\{x/x$ integer whose square is negative$\}$ is a ....set.
4. Which of the following statement is true ?
   (a) $\{\phi\} = \{0\}$ (b) $3 \subset \{2, 3, 4\}$
   (c) $\{0\} = \phi$ (d) $\{p, q, m\} = \{q, m, p\}$
5. Fill in the blanks :
   (a) Every set is a .... of itself.
   (b) If there are no members in a set then the number of its sub-set is ....
   (c) If all the elements of set X have elements, then X is .... of Y.
   (d) Null set is a ...... of all sets.
6. Which are the following sub-sets of set A = $\{0, 3\}$:
   (i) $\{0\}$, $\{3\}$ (b) $\{0\}$, $\{3\}$, $\{0, 3\}$
   (iii) $\{0\}$, $\{3\}$, $\{0, 3\}$, $\{\phi\}$ (d) $\{0\}$, $\{3\}$, $\{0, 3\}$, ϕ
7. If A = $\{a, b\}$, then which one is not sub-set of A : (*JAC*, 2016, 24)
   (a) $\{0\}$ (b) $\{a\}$ (c) $\{b\}$ (d) ϕ
8. Which of the following is true ? (*JAC*, 2022)
   (i) $\phi = \{\phi\}$
   (ii) $\{1, 2, 3\} \subset \{2, 3, 4, 5\}$
   (iii) $\{a, \{b\}, c\} \subset \{a, \{b\}, 1, 2, c\}$
   (iv) $\{1, 2, 3\} = \{1, \{2\}, 3\}$
9. Which of the following is equal ?
   ϕ, $\{\phi\}$, $\{0\}$, 0
10. Which of the following statements are true and which are false ?
    (i) $\{a, b\} \notin \{b, c, a\}$ (ii) $\{1, 2, 3\} \subseteq \{1, 2, 3\}$
    (iii) $\{a\} \subset \{a, b, c\}$ (iv) $\{a\} \in \{a, b, c\}$
    (v) $\{a, e\} \subset \{x/x$ is a vowel of English alphabet$\}$
    (vi) $\{x/x$, is even natural number which is less than 6$\}$ $\subset \{x / x$ is a natural number which is divisor of 36$\}$
11. Write all sub-sets of the following sets :
    (i) A = $\{a, b\}$ (ii) $\{3, 4, 5\}$ (iii) ϕ
    (iv) $\{1, 2, 3\}$ (v) $\{a\}$
12. Which of the following is equal ?
    ϕ, $\{0\}$, $\{\phi\}$, 0, $\{ \{\phi\} \}$
13. Whether the statement $\phi = \{\phi\}$ is 'true' ? Give reasons.
14. Find power set, if :
    (i) A = $\{b, c\}$ (ii) B = $\{5, 8, 9\}$
15. Null set is a .... of all sets. (*JAC*, 2026)
    (a) Subset (b) Power set
    (c) Universal set (d) All of these

Answers

1. (i), (iii) 2. (a) (iv), (b) (iii)
3. (i) pair, (ii) singleton, (iii) pair, (iv) null, (v) null
4. (d)
5. (i) Sub-set, (ii) 2^n, (iii) Sub-set, (iv) Sub-set
6. (iv)
7. (a) 8. (iii) 9. None of these
10. (i) True, (ii) True, (iii) True, (iv) False, (v) True, (vi) True
11. (i) ϕ, $\{a\}$, $\{b\}$, $\{a, b\}$, (ii) ϕ, $\{3\}$, $\{4\}$, $\{5\}$, $\{3, 4\}$, $\{4, 5\}$, $\{3, 5\}$, $\{3, 4, 5\}$, (iii) ϕ, (iv) $\{1\}$, $\{2\}$, $\{3\}$, $\{1, 2\}$, $\{1, 3\}$, $\{2, 3\}$, $\{1, 2, 3\}$, ϕ, (v) $\{a\}$, ϕ.
12. None of these,13. No, as $\{\phi\}$ is a singleton set when ϕ is an null set.
14. (i) P(A) = ϕ, $\{b\}$, $\{c\}$, $\{b, c\}$; (ii) P(B) = ϕ, $\{5\}$, $\{8\}$, $\{9\}$, $\{5, 8\}$, $\{5, 9\}$, $\{8, 9\}$, $\{5, 8, 9\}$.
15. (a)

(8.6) ALGEBRA OF SETS

Basic Set Operations

(i) Union of Sets (ii) Intersection of Sets
(iii) Difference of Two Sets

(i) Union of Sets : The union of two sets A and B, is the set of those elements which belongs to A or B or both A and B.

We use the symbol U to represent union.

The union of two sets A and B is denoted by $A \cup B$ and we read it A union B.

In symbolic form we write

$$A \cup B = \{x/x \in A \text{ or } x \in B\}$$

For 'or' we write $\cup$.

Example :

(i) If $A = \{1, 3, 5, 7, 9\}$
$B = \{3, 7, 11, 12\}$
then $A \cup B = \{x : x \in A \text{ or } x \in B\}$
$= \{1, 3, 5, 7, 9, 11, 12\}$
thus $A \subseteq A \cup B$, $B \subseteq A \cup$

(ii) If $A = \{1, 3, 5, 7, 9, ...\}$
$B = \{2, 4, 6, 8, ...\}$
then $A \cup B = \{x : x \in A \text{ or } x \in B\}$
$= \{1, 2, 3, 4, 5, 6, 7, 8, 9, ... \}$

*** General Form of Union of Sets**

If $A_1, A_2, A_3, ..., A_n$ are sets, then

$$A_1 \cup A_2 \cup A_3 \cup ..... \cup A_n = \bigcup_{n=1}^{n} A_n$$

$= \{x : x \in A_n$ for at least one value of $n = 1, 2, 3, 4, ..., n\}$

Example :

If $A = \{a, b, c\}$

$B = \{a, p, q\}$

$C = \{p, q, r\}$ and $D = \{x, y, z\}$

then $A \cup B \cup C \cup D = \{x : x \in A$ or $x \in B$ or $x \in C$ or $x \in D\}$

$= \{a, b, c, p, q, r, x, y, z\}$

(ii) Intersection of Sets : Intersection of two sets A and B is the set of those elements which are common to A and B.

In symbol intersection is denoted by $\cap$. The intersection of two sets A and B is denoted by $A \cap B$. We read it A intersection B.

In set builder method we write

$$A \cap B = \{x/x \in A \text{ and } x \in B\}$$

Example :

(i) If $A = \{0, 1, 3, 5\}$

and $B = \{0, 2, 4, 6\}$

then $A \cap B = \{x : x \in A \text{ and } x \in B\} = \{0\}$

(ii) If $A = \{x, y, z\}$

and $B = \{a, b, c\}$

then $A \cap B = \{x : x \in A \text{ and } x \in B\} = \phi$

(iii) If $A = \{1, 2, 3, 4, 5, 6, 7\}$

and $B = \{2, 4, 6\}$

then $A \cap B = \{x : x \in A \text{ and } x \in B\}$

$= \{2, 4, 6\} = B$

By the definition of intersection and subjects $A \cap B \subseteq A$ and $A \cap B \subseteq B$.

General form of intersection of sets. If $A_1, A_2, A_3, ..., A_n$ are sets then

$$A_1 \cap A_2 \cap A_3 \cap .... \cap A_n = \bigcap_{n=1}^{n} A_n$$

(iii) Difference of Two Sets : The difference of two sets A and B is the set of those elements which belongs to A but not in B.

Thus $A - B = \{x : x \in A \text{ and } x \notin B\}$

Similarly $B - A = \{x : x \in B \text{ and } x \notin A\}$

So $A - B \neq B - A$

Hence the difference of two sets is not commutative.

Example :

(i) If $A = \{1, 2, 3, 4, 5\}$

and $B = \{2, 3, 4, 6\}$

then $A - B = \{x : x \in A \text{ and } x \notin B\} = \{1, 5\}$

and $B - A = \{x : x \in B \text{ and } x \notin A\} = \{6\}$

$\therefore$ $A - B \neq B - A$

(ii) If $A = \{1, 2, 3, 4\}$

$B = \{2, 4\}$

then $A - B = \{x : x \in A \text{ and } x \notin B\} = \{1, 3\}$

and $B - A = \{x : x \in B \text{ and } x \notin A\} = \phi$

as all elements of B are also in A.

Complementary Set : The complement of a set A is the set of those elements which belong to the universal set but not in set A.

The complement of a set A is denoted by A' or A^c.

Thus if $x \in A'$ then

Clearly $A' = U - A$

In set builder form A'

$= \{x/x \in U \text{ and } x \in A\}$

Example :

(i) If $U = \{1, 2, 3, 4, 5, 5, 6\}$

$A = \{1, 2, 3\}$

then $A' = U - A = \{4, 5, 6\}$

(ii) If $U = \{x/x \text{ is a natural number}\}$

$B = \{x/x \text{ is an even positive integer}\}$

then $B' = U - B$

$= \{x/x \text{ is an odd positive integer}\}$

Complementary Set of B relative to A : If $B \subseteq A$, then $A - B$ is the set of all those elements of A which are not in B. This set is called the complementary set of B related to A. It is symbolically written by B'.

If $A = \{1, 2, 3, 4, 5\}$

$B = \{1, 4, 5\}$

then B' w.r.t. $A = A - B = \{2, 3\}$

since $A \not\subseteq B$ so we cannot write A' w.r.t. B.

Disjoint Sets or Non-intersection Sets : Two sets A and B are said to be disjoint sets if they have no elements in common *i.e.,* $A \cap B = \phi$.

Example :

(i) $A = \{1, 2, 3\}$

$B = \{4, 5, 6\}$

then $A \cap B = \phi$

or A and B have no element in common.

So A and B are disjoint sets.

(ii) Since $\{a, b\} \cap \{e, f, g\} = \phi$

So $\{a, b\}$ and $\{e, f, g\}$ are disjoint sets.

Symmetric Difference : Symmetric difference is represented by 'Δ' (delta) and can be defined as follows :

If A and B are two sets, then the symmetric difference of A and B will be :

$$A \Delta B = (A - B) \cup (B - A)$$

Example : (i) If $A = \{1, 2. 3, 4, 5\}$

$B = \{4, 5, 8\}$

then $A \Delta B = (A - B) \cup (B - A)$

$= \{1, 2, 3\} \cup \{8\}$

$= \{1, 2, 3, 8\}$

(ii) If $A = \{1, 2, 3, 4, 5, 6, 7\}$ and $B = \{3, 4, 5, 6, 7, 8, 9\}$, find $A - B$, $B - A$, $A \Delta B$.

Solution :

$$A - B = \{1, 2\}$$
$$B - A = \{8, 9\}$$
$$A \Delta B = (A - B) \cup (B - A) = \{1, 2\} \cup \{8, 9\} = \{1, 2, 8, 9\}$$

SOME THEOREMS RELATED TO UNION AND INTERSECTION OF SETS

De-Morgan's Laws

(i) $D - (A \cup B) = (D - A) \cap (D - B)$

(ii) $D - (A \cap B) = (D - A) \cup (D - B)$

Proof : (i) Let $x \in D - (A \cup B)$

$\Leftrightarrow$ $x \in D$ and $x \notin (A \cup B$

$\Leftrightarrow$ $x \in D$ and $(x \notin A)$ and $(x \notin B)$

$\Leftrightarrow$ $x \in D$ and $(x \notin A)$ and $(x \in D)$ and $(x \notin B)$

$\Leftrightarrow$ $x \in D - A$ and $x \in (D - B)$

$\Leftrightarrow$ $x \in (D - A) \cap (D - B)$

$\therefore$ $D - (A \cup B) = (D - A) \cap (D - B)$ **Proved**

(ii) Let $x \in D - (A \cap B)$

$\Leftrightarrow$ $x \in D$ and $x \notin (A \cap B)$

$\Leftrightarrow$ $x \in D$ and $(x \notin A$ or $x \notin B)$

$\Leftrightarrow$ $x \in D$ and $(x \notin A)$ or $(x \in D)$ and $(x \notin B)$

$\Leftrightarrow$ $x \in (D - A)$ or $x \in (D - B)$

$\Leftrightarrow$ $x \in (D - A) \cup (D - B)$

$\therefore$ $D - (A \cap B) = (D - A) \cup (D - B)$ **Proved**

De-Morgan's Laws (Second Form)

For any two sets A and B

(i) $(A \cup B)' = A' \cap B'$

(ii) $(A \cap B)' = A' \cup B'$

Proof. (i) Let $x \in (A \cup B)'$

$\Leftrightarrow$ $x \notin (A \cup B)$

$\Leftrightarrow$ $x \notin A$ and $x \notin B$

$\Leftrightarrow$ $x \in A'$ and $x \in B'$

$\Leftrightarrow$ $x \in A' \cap B'$

$\because$ $x \in (A \cup B)'$

$\Leftrightarrow$ $x \in A' \cap B'$

$\therefore$ $(A \cup B)' = A' \cap B'$ **Proved**

(ii) Let $x \in (A \cap B)'$

$\Leftrightarrow$ $x \notin (A \cap B)$

$\Leftrightarrow$ $x \notin A$ or $x \notin B$

$\Leftrightarrow$ $x \in A'$ or $x \in B'$

$\Leftrightarrow$ $x \in A' \cup B'$

$\because$ $x \in (A \cap B')$

$\Leftrightarrow$ $x \in A' \cup B'$

$\therefore$ $(A \cap B)' = A' \cup B'$ **Proved**

SOLVED EXAMPLES

Example 1

If $A \subseteq B$, then prove that $P(A) \subseteq P(B)$.

Solution :

Let $\{x\} \in P(A)$

$\Rightarrow$ $x \in A$

$\Rightarrow$ $x \in B$ $(\because A \subseteq B)$

$\Rightarrow$ $\{x\} \in P(B)$

$\therefore$ $P(A) \subseteq P(B)$ **Proved**

Example 2

For any two sets 'A' and 'B', prove that :

$$P(A) \cap P(B) = P(A \cap B)$$

Solution :

Let $\{x\} \in P(A) \cap P(B)$

$\Leftrightarrow$ $\{x\} \in P(A)$ and $\{x\} \in P(B)$

$\Leftrightarrow$ $x \in A$ and $x \in B$

$\Leftrightarrow$ $x \in (A \cap B)$

$\Leftrightarrow$ $\{x\} \in P(A \cap B)$

$\therefore$ $P(A) \cap P(B) = P(A \subseteq B)$ **Proved**

Example 3

For any two sets A and B, prove that

$$P(A) \cup P(B) \subseteq P(A \cup B)$$

Solution :

Let $\{x\} \in P(A) \cup P(B)$

$\Rightarrow$ $\{x\} \in P(A)$ or $\{x\} \in P(B)$

$\Rightarrow$ $x \in A$ or $x \in B$

$\Rightarrow$ $x \in A \cup B$

$\Rightarrow$ $\{x\} \in P(A \cup B)$

$\therefore$ $P(A) \cup P(B) \subseteq P(A \cup B)$

Comment : It is not necessarily true that

$$P(A) \cup P(B) = P(A \cup B)$$

Example : Let $A = \{1, 2\}; B = \{2, 3\}$

then $P(A) = \{\phi, \{1\}, \{2\}, \{1, 2\}\}$

$P(B) = \{\phi, \{2\}, \{3\}, \{2, 3\}\}$

$A \cup B = \{1, 2, 3\}$

$P(A \cup B) = \{\phi, \{1\}, \{2\}, \{3\}, \{1, 2\}, \{1,3\}, \{2, 3\} \{1, 2, 3\}\}$

Now $P(A) \cup P(B) = \{\phi, \{1\}, \{2\}, \{3\}, \{1, 2\}, \{2, 3\}\}$

$\therefore$ $P(A) \cup P(B) \neq P(A \cup B)$

Example 4

If $A = \{3, 5, 7, 9\}; B = \{6, 8, 10\}$, then find

(a) $A \cup B$ (b) $A \cap B$

Solution :

(a) $A \cup B = \{3, 5, 7, 9\} \cup \{6, 8, 10\} = \{3, 5, 6, 7, 8, 9, 10\}$

(b) $A \cap B = \{3, 5, 7, 9\} \cap \{6, 8, 10\} = \phi$

Example 5 (A)

If A = {1, 2, 3, 4}; B = {2, 4, 6, 8} and C = {3, 4, 5, 6}, then find :

(i) $(A \cup B) \cap C$ (ii) $(A \cap B)(A \cap C)$

Solution :

(i) $A \cup B = \{1, 2, 3, 4,\} \cup \{2, 4, 6, 8\} = \{1, 2, 3, 4, 6, 8\}$

$\therefore (A \cup B) \cap C = \{1, 2, 3, 4, 6, 8\} \cap \{3, 4, 5, 6\} = \{3, 4, 6\}$

(ii) $A \cap B = \{1, 2, 3, 4\} \cap \{2, 4, 6, 8\} = \{2, 4\}$

$A \cap C = \{1, 2, 3, 4\} \cap \{3, 4, 5, 6\} = \{3, 4\}$

$\therefore (A \cap B) \cup (A \cap C) = \{2, 4\} \cup \{3, 4\} = \{2, 3, 4\}$

Example 5 (B)

If A = {1, 2, 3, 4, 5}, B = {2, 4, 6, 8}, C = {3, 5, 7}, then find :

(i) $A \cup (B \cup C)$ (ii) $(A \cup B) \cap C$ (iii) $A - (B - C)$
(iv) $A \cap (B \cap C)$ (v) $(A \cap B) \cup C$

Solution :

(i) $A = \{1, 2, 3, 4, 5\}$

$(B \cup C) = \{2, 3, 4, 5, 6, 7, 8\}$

$\therefore A \cup (B \cup C) = \{1, 2, 3, 4, 5, 6, 7, 8\}$

(ii) $C = \{3, 5, 7\}$

$A \cup C = \{1, 2, 3, 4, 5, 6, 8\}$

$\therefore (A \cup B) \cap C = \{3, 5\}$

(iii) $A = \{1, 2, 3, 4, 5\}$

$B - C = \{2, 4, 6, 8\} - \{3, 5, 7\} = \{2, 4, 6, 8\}$

$\therefore A - \{B - C\} = \{1, 2, 3, 4, 5\} - \{2, 4, 6, 8\} = \{1, 3, 5\}$

(iv) $A = \{1, 2, 3, 4, 5\}$

$B \cap C = \phi$

$\therefore A \cap (B \cap C) = A \cap \phi = \phi$

(v) $A \cap B = \{2, 4\}$

$\therefore (A \cap B) \cup C = \{2, 3, 4, 5, 7\}$

Example 5(C)

If A = {1, 2, 3, 7), B = {2, 3, 5, 7}
C = {2, 4, 6, 8}. Find $(A \cap B) \cup (A \cap C)$

(JAC, 2024)

Solution :

$(A \cap B) = \{1, 2, 3, 7\} \cap \{2, 3, 5, 7\} = \{2, 3, 7\}$

$(A \cap C) = \{1, 2, 3, 7\} \cap \{2, 4, 6, 8\} = \{2\}$

$(A \cap B) \cup (A \cap C) = \{2, 3, 7\} \cup \{2\} = \{2, 3, 7\}$. **Ans.**

Example 6

If A = {x/x is an even integer}, B = {x/x is an odd integer}, then find $A \cup B$.

Solution :

$A \cup B$ = {x/x is an even integer} ∪ {x/x is an odd integer}
= {x/x is even or odd integer}
= {x/x is an integer}

Example 7

If A = {x/x is a factor of 12}, B = {x/x is a factor of 20}, then find $A \cap B$.

Solution :

$A \cap B$ = {x/x is a factor of 12}, ∩ {x/x is a factor of 20}
= {1, 2, 3, 4, 6, 12} ∩ {1, 2, 4, 5, 10, 20}
= {1, 2, 3}

Example 8

If {A = x/x is a rational number}, {B = x/x is an irrational number}, then find $A \cup B$.

Solution :

$A \cup B$ = {x/x is a rational number} ∪ {x/x is an irrational number}
= {x/x is a real number}

Example 9

If A = {x/x is a multiple of 2}, B = {x/x is a multiple of 3} then find $A \cap B$.

Solution :

$A \cap B$ = {x/x is multiple of 2} ∩ {x/x is a multiple of 3}
= {x/x is a multiple of 2 or 3}
= {x/x is a multiple of 6}

Example 10

If F(n) denotes the set of factors of the whole number n then find :

(i) F(16), F(40), $F(16) \cap F(40)$, $F(16) \cup F(40)$

(ii) For what value of x; $F(16) \cap F(40) = F(x)$

Solution :

(i) F(16) = {x/x is a positive factor of 16}
= {1, 2, 4, 8, 16}

F(40) = {x/x is a positive factor of 40}
= {1, 2, 4, 5, 8, 10, 20, 40}

$F(16) \cap F(40) = \{1, 2, 4, 8\}$

$F(16) \cup F(40) = \{1, 2, 4, 5, 8, 10, 16, 20, 40\}$

(ii) $F(x) = F(16) \cap F(40)$
= {1, 2, 4, 8}
= {x/x is a positive factor of 8}
= F(8)

$\therefore x = 8$ **Ans.**

Example 11

Show with proper reason that which of the following statement is true or false :

(i) {1, 2, 3, 4} and {2, 4, 6, 8, 10} are disjoint sets.

(ii) {x/x is an even integer} and {x/x is an odd integer} are disjoint sets.

(iii) $\{x/x$ is a prime number$\}$ and $\{x/x$ is an odd integer$\}$ are disjoint sets.

Solution :

(i) False

Reason : $\{1, 2, 3, 4\} \cap \{2, 4, 6, 8, 10\} = \{2, 4\}$

(ii) True

Reason : The two sets has no element in common.

(iii) False

Reason : Some positive integers are also a prime number.

$\therefore \{x/x \text{ is a prime number}\} \cap \{x/x \text{ is an odd integer}\} \neq \phi$

Example 12

If $A = \{p, q, r\}$, $B = \{l, m\}$, $C = \{r, l\}$ then show that :

$A \cap (B \cup C) = (A \cap B) \cup (A \cap C)$.

Solution :

$$\begin{aligned} \text{L.H.S.} &= A \cap (B \cup C) \\ &= A \cap (\{l, m\} \cup \{r, l\}) \\ &= \{p, q, r\} \cup \{l, m, r\} \\ &= \{r\} \\ \text{R.H.S.} &= (A \cap B) \cup (A \cap C) \\ &= (\{p, q, r\} \cap \{l, m\}) \cup (\{p, q, r\} \cup \{r, l\}) \\ &= \phi \cup \{r\} = \{r\} \end{aligned}$$

$\therefore$ L.H.S. = R.H.S. **Proved**

Example 13

If $A = \{1, 2, 3, 4\}$, $B = \{2, 4, 6, 8\}$ and $C = \{3, 4, 5, 6\}$ then prove that :

$A \cap (B \cap C) = (A \cap B) \cap C$

Solution :

$$\begin{aligned} \text{L.H.S.} &= A \cap (B \cap C) \\ &= A \cap (\{2, 4, 6, 8\} \cap \{3, 4, 5, 6\}) \\ &= \{1, 2, 3, 4\} \cap \{4, 6\} = \{4\} \\ \text{R.H.S.} &= (A \cap B) \cap C \\ &= (\{1, 2, 3, 4\} \cap \{2, 4, 6, 8\}) \cap C \\ &= \{2, 4\} \cap \{3, 4, 5, 6\} = \{4\} \end{aligned}$$

$\therefore$ L.H.S. = R.H.S. **Proved**

Some Results related to Algebraic Laws of Sets

(I) **Idempotent Laws :**

(i) $A \cup A = A$ (ii) $A \cap A = A$

(II) **Identity Laws :**

(i) $A \cup \phi = A$

(ii) $A \cap X = A$, where X is the universal Set.

(III) **Commutative Laws :**

(i) $A \cup B = B \cup A$ (ii) $A \cap B = B \cap A$

(IV) **Associative Laws :**

(i) $A \cup (B \cup C) = (A \cup B) \cup C$

(ii) $A \cap (B \cap C) = (A \cap B) \cap C$

(V) **Distributive Laws :**

(i) $A \cup (B \cap C) = (A \cup B) \cap (A \cup C)$

(ii) $A \cap (B \cup C) = (A \cap B) \cup (A \cap C)$

(VI) **De-Morgan's Laws :**

(i) $A - (B \cup C) = (A - B) \cap (A - C)$

(ii) $A - (B \cap C) = (A - B) \cup (A - C)$

Second Form of De-Morgan's Law

(De-Morgan's Complementary Laws) :

(i) $(A \cup B)' = A' \cap B'$ (ii) $(A \cap B)' = A' \cup B'$

(VII) **Complement Laws :**

If ϕ is a null set and x is a universal set, then

(i) $A \cup A' = X$ (ii) $A \cap A' = \phi$

(iii) $(A')' = A$ (iv) $X' = \phi$

(v) $\phi' = X$

Some Other Results :

(i) $A \cup X = X$; where X is a universal set.

(ii) If $A \subseteq B$, then $A \cap B = A$ and $A \cup B = B$.

(iii) $A - B = A \cap B$

(iv) If $A \subseteq B$ and $A \subseteq C$, then $A \subseteq B \cap C$.

(v) $A \subseteq A \cup B$.

(vi) $B \subseteq A \cup B$.

(vii) $A \cap B \subseteq A$.

(viii) $A \cap B \subseteq B$.

(ix) $\phi \subseteq A$, where A is any set.

(x) $A \cap B \subseteq A \cup B$.

Example 14

If $A = \{10, 11, 12, 15\}$, $B = \{12, 13, 15, 16\}$ $C = \{10, 15, 16\}$, Find $(A \cup B) \cap C$ *(JAC, 2024)*

Solution :

$$\begin{aligned} A \cup B &= \{10, 11, 12, 15\} \cup \{12, 13, 15, 16\} \\ &= \{10, 11, 12, 13, 15, 16\} \\ (A \cup B) \cap C &= \{10, 11, 12, 13, 15, 16\} \cap \{10, 15, 16\} \\ &= \{10, 15, 16\} \end{aligned}$$

Ans.

Example 15

For any two sets A and B, prove that :

(i) $(A \cap B) \cup (A \cap B') = A$

(ii) $(A \cap B) \cup (A - B) = A$

Solution :

(i) L.H.S. $= (A \cap B) \cup (A \cap B')$

$= D \cup (A \cap B')$, where $D = A \cap B$

$= (D \cup A) \cap (D \cup B')$ (By distribution Law)

$= [(A \cap B) \cup A] \cap [(A \cap B) \cup B']$

$= A \cap [(A \cup B')] \cap (B \cup B')]$ $(\because A \cap B \subseteq A)$

$= A \cap [(A \cup B') \cap X]$, where X is a universal Law

$= A \cap A \cup B'$ $(\because A \cup B' \subseteq X)$

$= A$

$=$ R.H.S. $(\because A \subseteq A \cup B')$

(ii) L.H.S. $= (A \cap B) \cup (A - B)$

$= (A \cap B) \cup (A \cap B')$

$= A =$ R.H.S. [As in(i)]

Example 16

For any two sets A and B, prove that :

$(A - B) \cap (B - A) = \phi$

Solution :

$$\text{L.H.S.} = (A - B) \cap (B - A)$$
$$= (A \cap B') \cap (B \cap A')$$
$$= (A \cap A') \cap (B \cap B')$$
$$= \phi \cap \phi = \phi$$

Example 17

Prove that :

$A \cap (B - C) = (A \cap B) - (A \cap C)$

Solution :

Let $x \in A \cap (B - C)$

$\Rightarrow x \in A \text{ and } x \in (B - C)$

$\Rightarrow x \in A \text{ and } x \in B \text{ and } x \notin C)$

$\Rightarrow x \in A \text{ and } x \in B) \text{ and } (x \notin C)$

$\Rightarrow x \in (A \cap B) \text{ and } x \notin (A \cap C);$ ...(i)

$\therefore A \cap (B - C) \subseteq (A \cap B) - (A \cap C)$

$(\because x \notin C \therefore x \notin A \cap C)$

Again Let $x \in (A \cap B) - (A \cap C)$

$\Rightarrow x \in A \cap B \text{ and } x \notin A \cap C$

$\Rightarrow (x \in A \text{ and } x \in B) \text{ and } (x \notin C)$

$\Rightarrow x \in A \text{ and } (x \in B \text{ and } x \notin C)$

$\Rightarrow x \in A \text{ and } x \in (B - C)$

$\Rightarrow x \in A \cap (B - C)$

$\therefore A \cap B - (A \cap C) \subseteq A \cap (B - C)$ ...(ii)

From (i) and (ii),

$A \cap (B - C) = (A \cap B) - (A \cap C)$ **Proved.**

Exercise 8 (C)

1. If A = {1, 2, 3, 4, 5, 6, 7} and B = {3, 4, 5, 6, 7, 8, 9}, then find :
   (i) $A \cup B$ (ii) $A \cap B$ (*JAC*, 2020)
2. If A = {11, 12, 13, 14, 15, 16} and B = {11, 12, 15, 16, 17, 18, 19} then find :
   (i) $A \cup B$ (ii) $A \cap B$
   (iii) $A - B$ (iv) $B - A$
3. If A = {0, 1, 2}, B = {1, 3, 4, 5} and C = {0, 4, 5, 6}, then find the following :
   (a) $A \cup (B \cap C)$ (b) $(A \cap B) \cup C$
   (c) $A \cap (B \cap C)$ (d) $(A \cup B) \cap C$
   (e) $(A \cap B) \cup (A \cap C)$
4. Which is disjoint set in the following set pairs ?
   (i) {1, 2, 3, 4} and {*x*/*x*, are natural numbers and $4 < x < 6$}
   (ii) {*a*, *e*, *i*, *o*, *u*} and {*c*, *d*, *e*, *f*}
   (iii) {*x*/*x*, is an even integer, and {*x*/*x* is an odd integer}
5. If $A \cap B = \phi$, then A and B are called which type of set ?
6. If A = {1, 2, 3, 4}, B = {2, 4, 6, 8} and C = {3, 4, 5, 6}, then find the following sets :
   (a) $A \cap (B \cup C)$ (b) $A \cap (B \cap C)$ (c) $A \cup (B \cap C)$
7. Fill up the blanks from the given number such that each pair set becomes disjoint set :
   (a) {2, 4, 6, 8, 10} and {3, —, 7, —, 11} (selecting from 2, 5, 7, 9)
   (b) {5, 8, 11, 14, 17} and {3, —, 6, 12, 16} (selecting from 4, 5, 10, 12)
8. If A = {1, 2, 3, 4} and B = {2, 1, 5, 9}, then the value of A – B will be equal to ?
   (a) {1, 1} (b) {3, 4}
   (c) {5, 9} (d) {1, 2, 4, 5, 9}
9. If universal set Ω = {1, 2, 3, 4, 5, 6, 7} and A = {1, 3, 5, 6, 7}, then find A'. (*JAC*, 2024)
10. If A = {*a*, *b*, *c*, *d*}, B = {*b*, *d*, *e*, *f*} then the value of $A \cup B$ will be : (*JAC*, 2022, 26)
    (a) {*a*, *b*, *c*, *d*, *e*, *f*} (b) {*b*, *d*}
    (c) {*a*, *e*, *f*} (d) {*c*, *d*, *e*}
11. If A = {5, 6, 8, 9}, B = {6, 7, 8, 10} then A – B is : (*JAC*, 2022)
    (a) {5, 9} (b) {7, 10}
    (c) {5, 6, 8, 9} (d) {6, 7, 8, 10}
12. If A = {1, 3, 4, 5}, B = {1, 5, 6, 7}, then $A \cup B$ is : (*JAC*, 2023)
    (a) {1, 3} (b) {1, 3, 4, 5, 6, 7}
    (c) {1, 3, 4, 5} (d) {1, 5, 6, 7}
13. If A = {1, 2, 3, 4}, B = {5, 6, 7} then $A \cap B$ is : (*JAC*, 2023)
    (a) {1, 2, 3, 4, 5, 6, 7} (b) {4, 5}
    (c) {4} (d) {ϕ}
14. If universal set Ω = {1, 2, 3, 4, 5, 6, 7} and A = {1, 3, 4, 5} : (*JAC*, 2026)
    (a) {1, 3, 5, 6, 7} (b) {2, 6, 7}
    (c) {1, 3, 4, 5} (d) {4, 6, 7}

Answers

1. (i) {1, 2, 3, 4, 5, 6, 7, 8, 9}, (ii) {3, 4, 5, 6, 7}
2. (i) {11, 12, 13, 14, 15, 16, 17, 18, 19}, (ii) {11, 12, 15, 16} (iii) {17, 18, 19}, (iv) {13, 14}
3. (a) {0, 1, 2, 4, 5}, (b) {1, 0, 4, 5, 6}, (c) ϕ, (d) {0, 4, 5}, (e) {1, 0}
4. (i), (iii)
5. Disjoint
6. (a) {2, 3, 4}, (b) {4}, (c) {1, 2, 3, 4, 6}
7. (a) 5, 9; (b) 4, 10,
8. (b)
9. {2, 4}
10. {*a*, *b*, *c*, *d*, *e*, *f*}
11. {5, 9}
12. {1, 3, 4, 5, 6, 7}
13. {ϕ}
14. {2, 6, 7}

(8.7) VENN DIAGRAM

There are many relations among sets which involve the operations of union, intersection, difference and complementation such relationships often may be tested by means of Venn diagrams.

English mathematician and logician John Venn (1834-1883) evolved a diagrammatic method of describing sets and their relations. These diagrams are called Venn diagram. However, they are useful visual aids to understand the relations between sets and helpful to discern what must be or has been proved.

In a Venn diagram the universal set is represented by a rectangle and its sub-sets are represented by areas bounded by closed curves (usually circles) inside the rectangle. The elements of the sets are represented by interior points of the region.

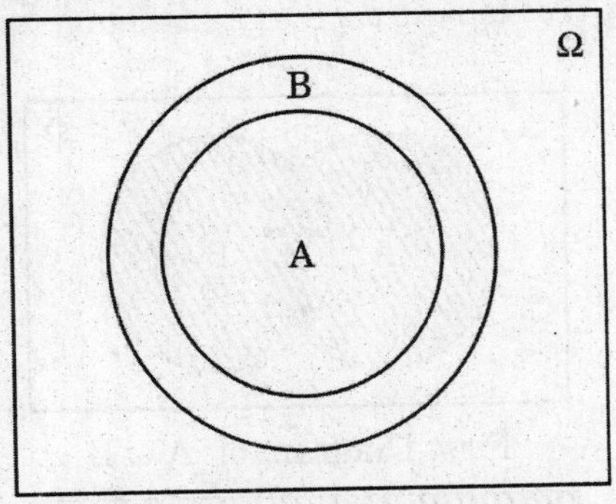

$A \subseteq B$

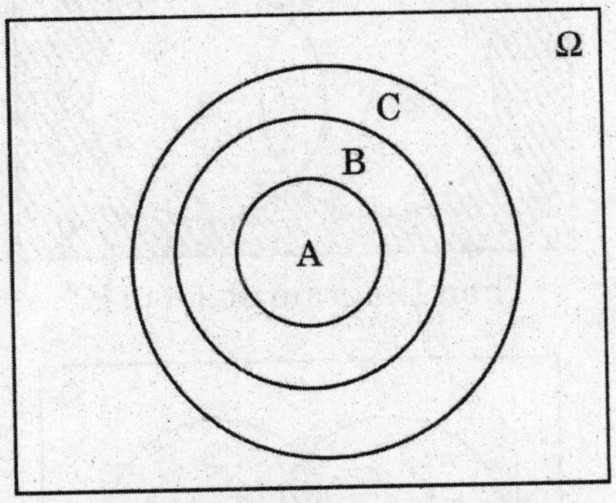

$A \subseteq B, B \subseteq C \Rightarrow A \subseteq C$

UNION Diagram of $A \cup B$

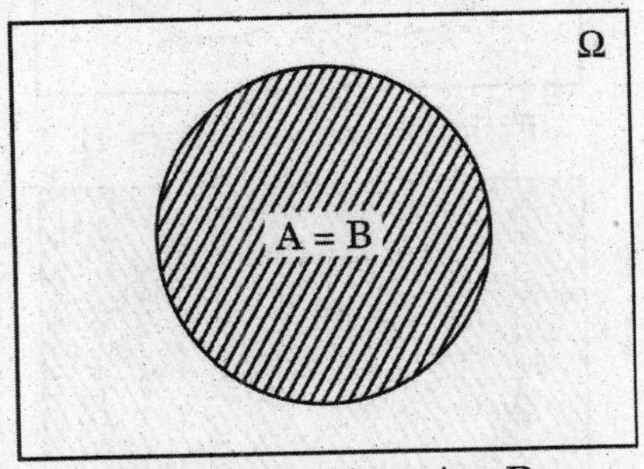

$A \subseteq B, B \subseteq A \Rightarrow A = B$

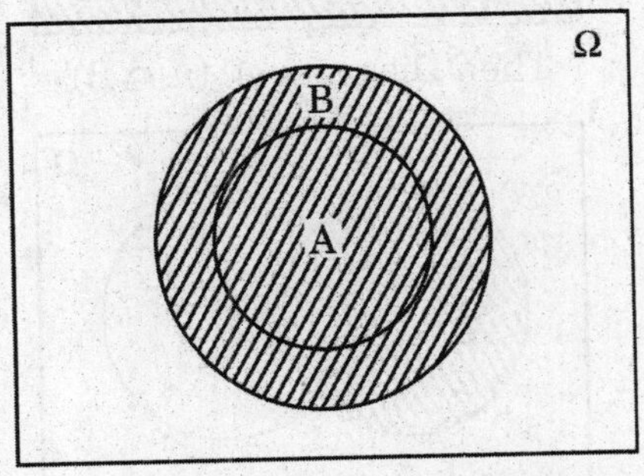

$A \cup B = B$ Comparable

$A \cup B = A$ Incomparable

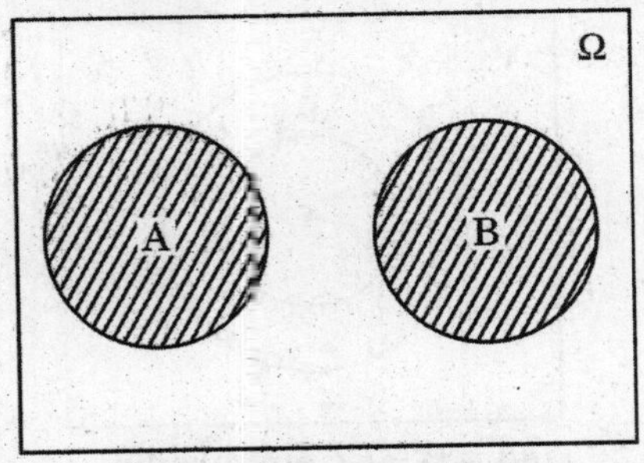

$A \cup B$ Disjoint, Incomparable

INTER-SECTION

Diagram of $A \cap B$

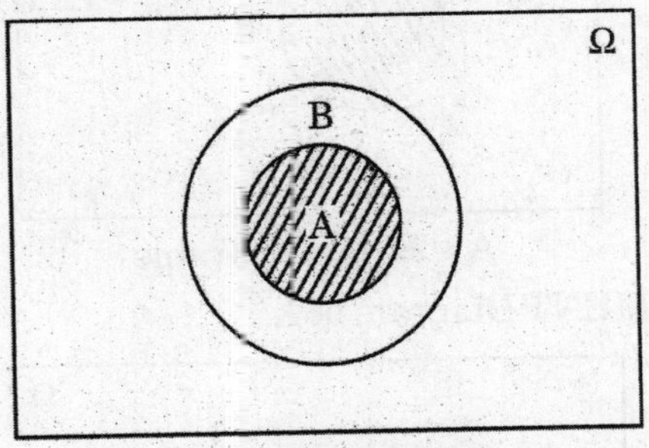

$A \cap B = A$ Comparable

Diagram of Difference $A - B$

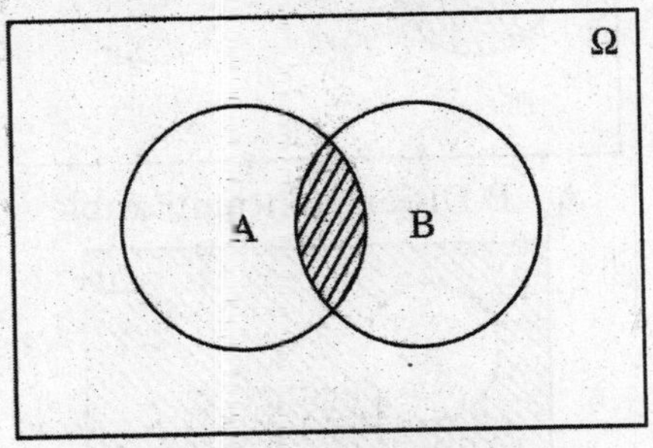

$A \cap B$ Incomparable

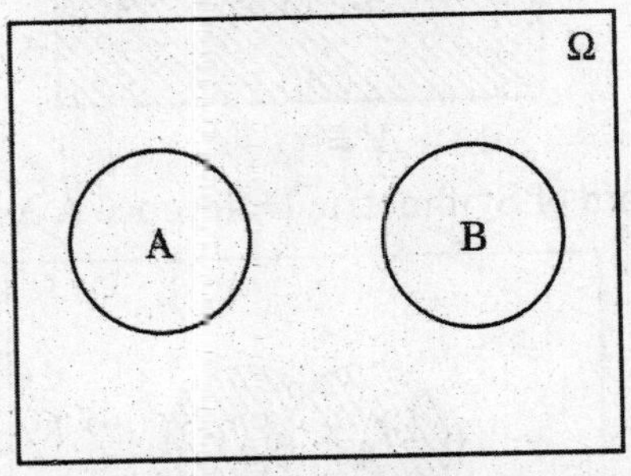

$A \cap B = \phi$ Disjoint, Imcomparable

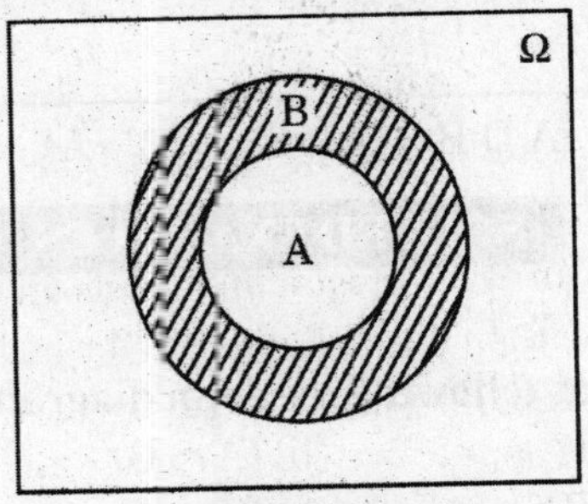

$A - B$ Comparable

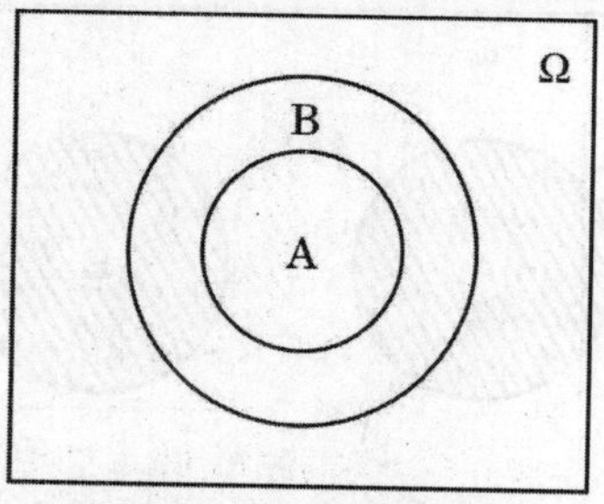

A – B = ϕ Comparable

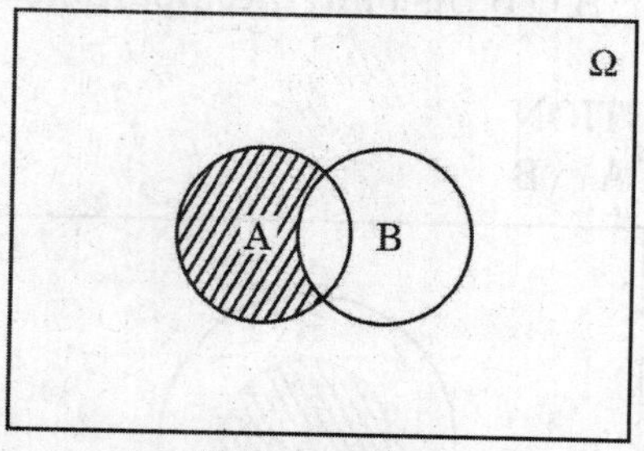

A – B Incomparable

COMPLEMENT Diagram of A′

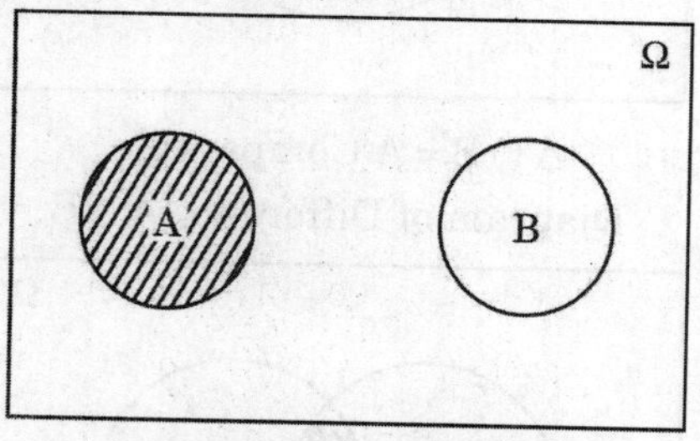

A – B Disjoint, Incomparable

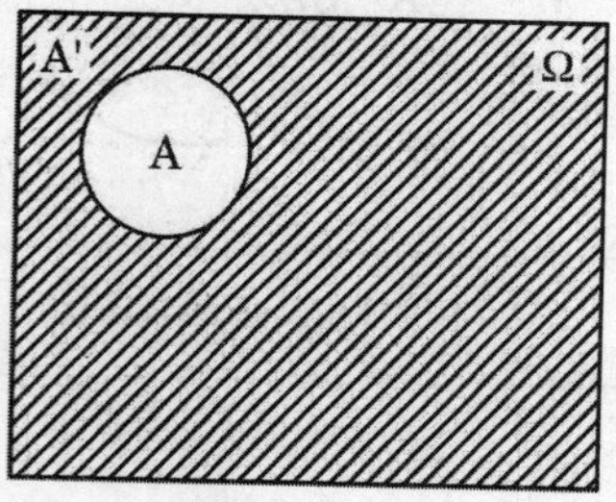

A′ = Ω – A

Diagram of Symmetric Difference A Δ B

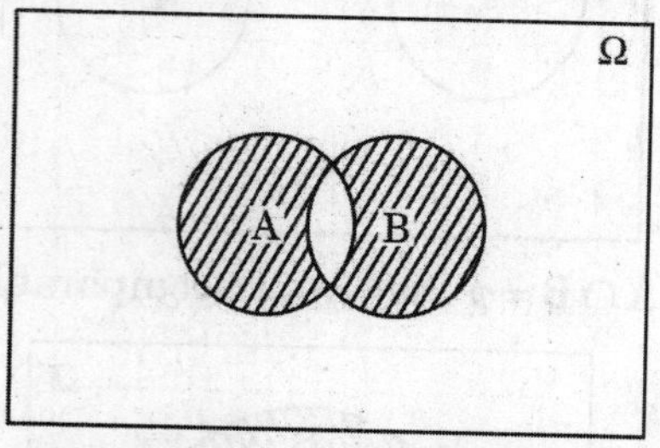

A D B = (A – B) ∪ (B – A)

SOLVED EXAMPLES

Example 1

Show that following by Venn diagram :

(i) $(A \cup B)'$ (ii) $(A \cap B)'$

(iii) $(A - B)'$ (iv) $(B - A)$

Solution

(i)

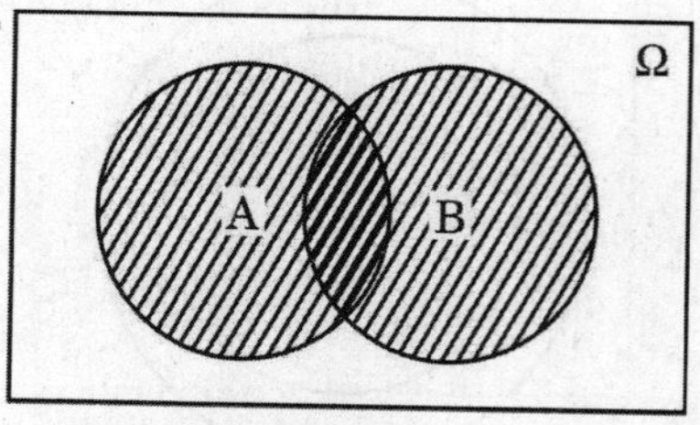

First Diagram of $A \cup B$

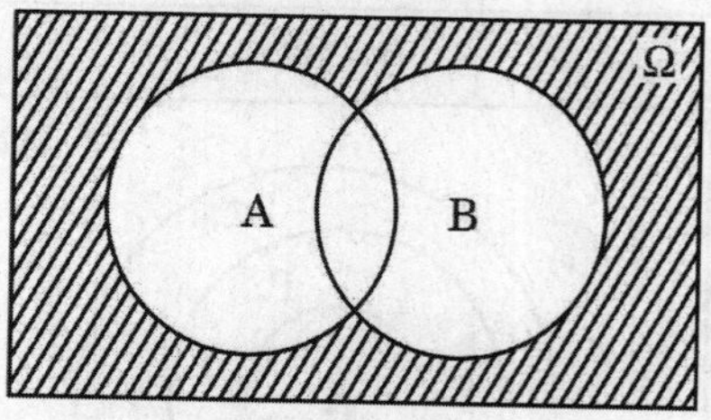

Then Diagram of $(A \cup B)'$

(ii)

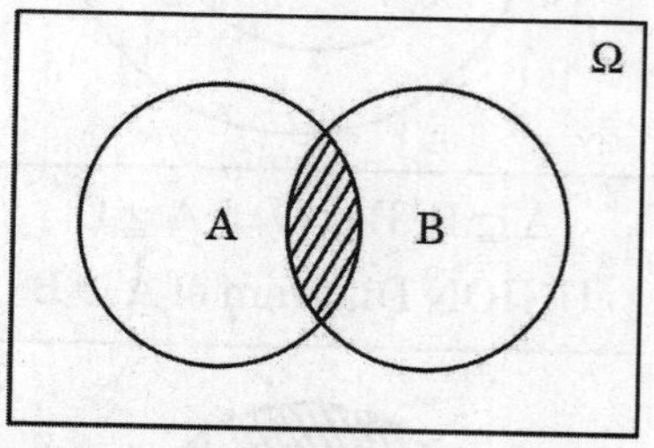

First Diagram of $A \cap B$

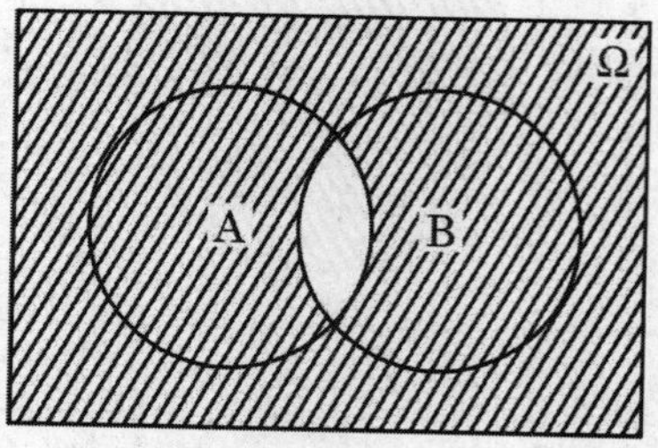

Then Diagram of $(A \cap B)'$

(iii)

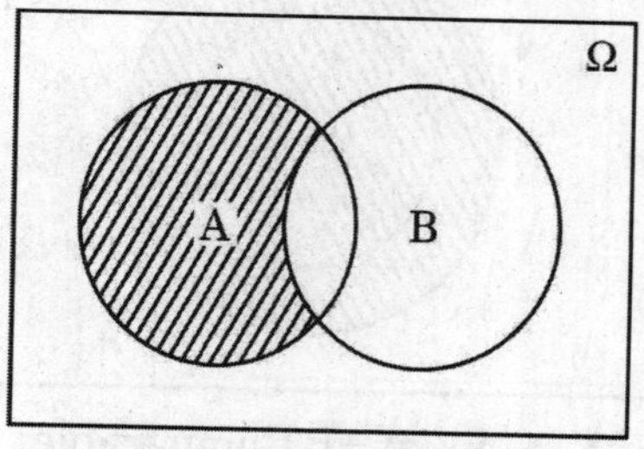

Firs Diagram of $A - B$

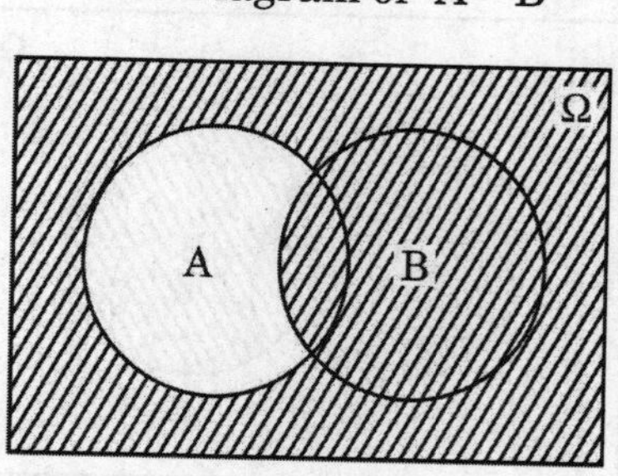

Then Diagram of $(A - B)'$

(iv)

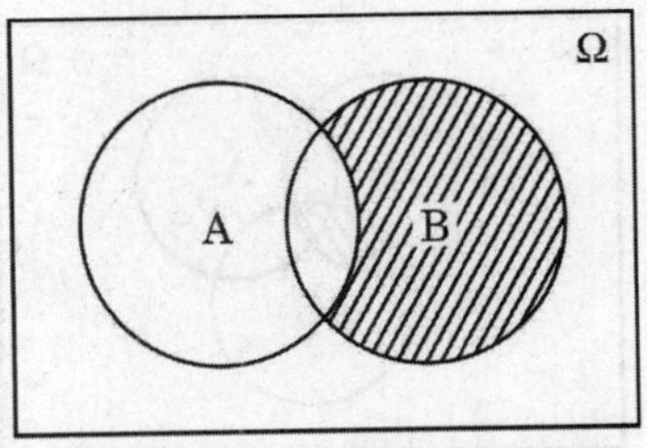

First Diagram of B – A

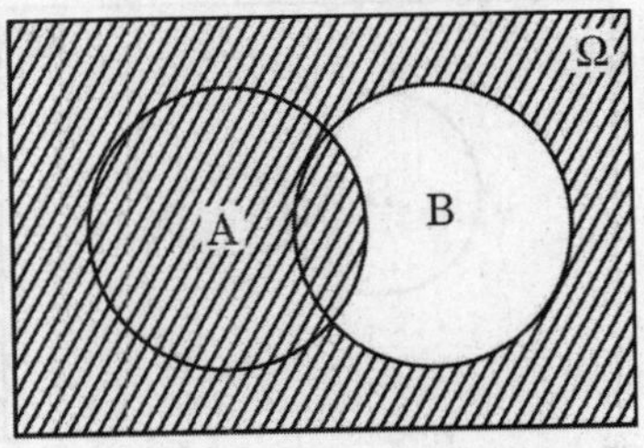

Then Diagram of (B – A)'

Example 2

With the help of Venn diagram show that :

(i) (A ∩ B) ∪ (A – B) = A

(ii) A ∪ (A ∩ B) = A

(iii) (A – B) ∪ (B – A) = (A ∪ B) – (A ∩ B)

Solution

(i)

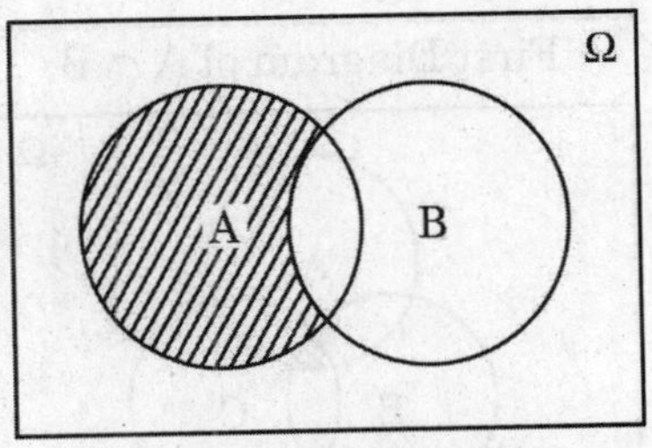

Diagram of A – B

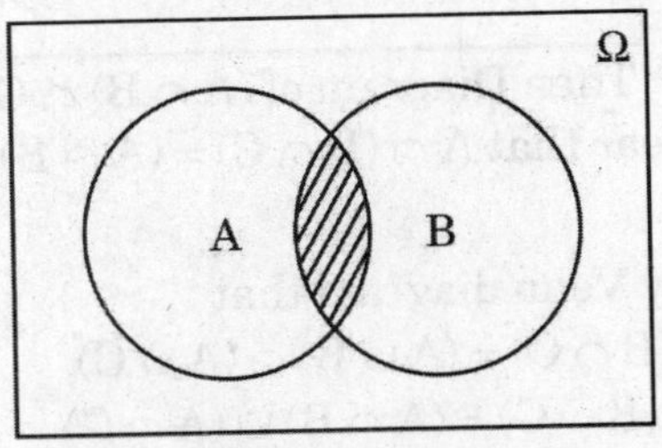

First Diagram of A ∩ B

(ii)

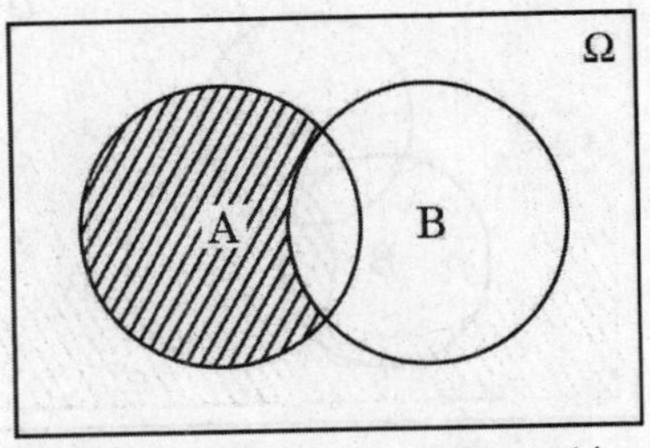

Then Diagram of (A ∩ B) ∪ (A– B)

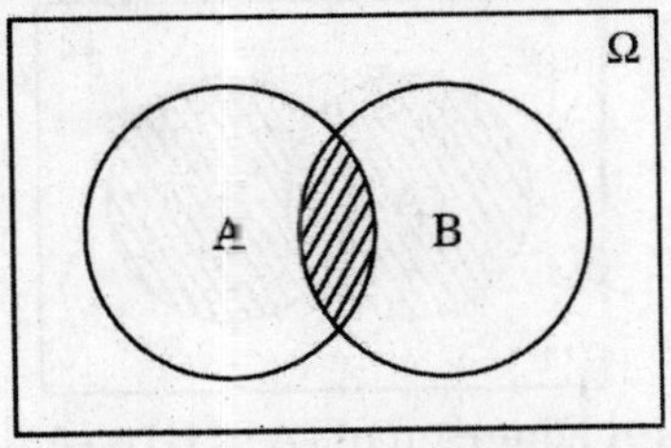

First Diagram of A ∩ B

(iii) L.H.S.

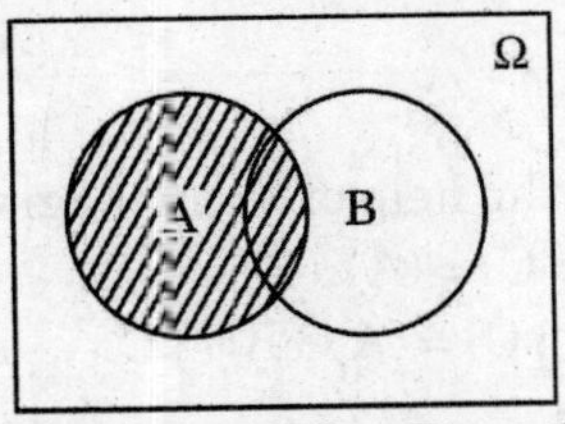

Then Diagram of (A – B) ∪ (B – A)

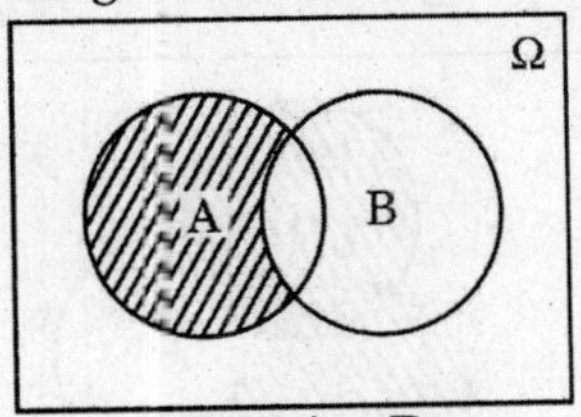

First A – B

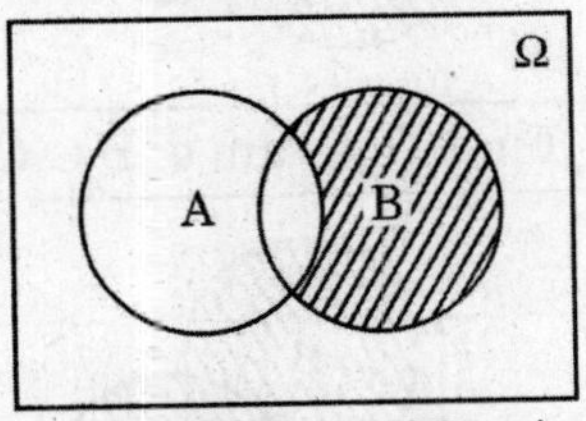

and Diagram of B – A

who is equal to A.

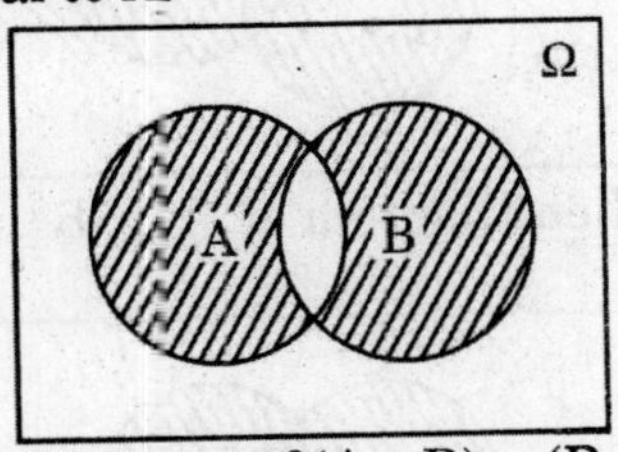

The Diagram of (A – B) ∪ (B – A)

Again R.H.S.

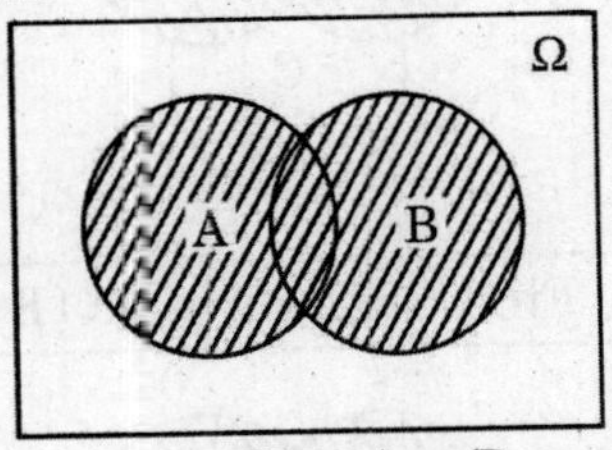

First A ∪ B

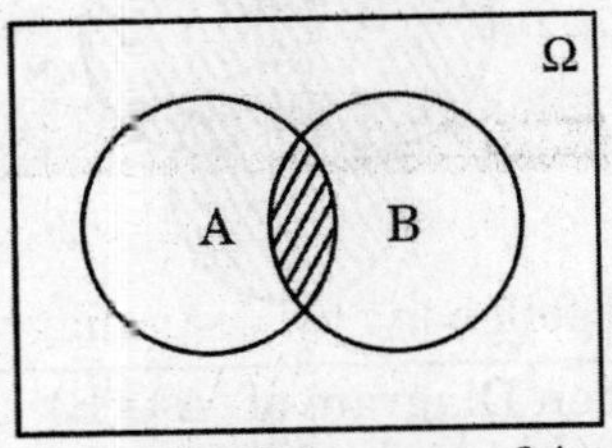

and the Diagram of A ∩ B

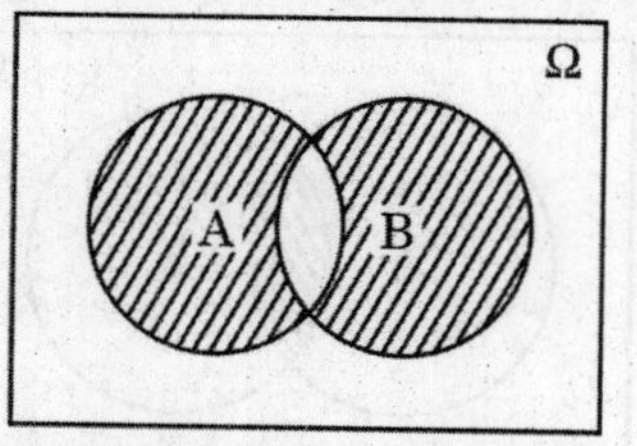

Then Diagram of (A ∪ B) – (A ∪ B)

Here clear by diagram (A – B) ∪ (B – A) = (A ∩ B) – (A ∩ B)

Example 3

Show with the help of Venn diagram that :

(i) A ∪ (B ∪ C) = (A ∪ B) ∪ C

(ii) A ∩ (B ∩ C) = (A ∩ B) ∩ C

Solution

(i) L.H.S.

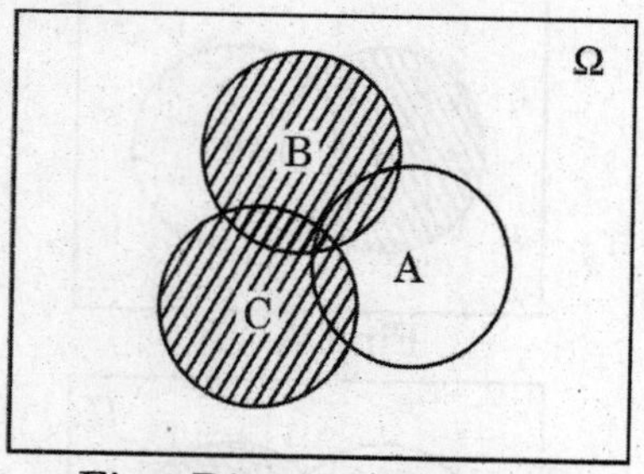

First Diagram of B ∪ C

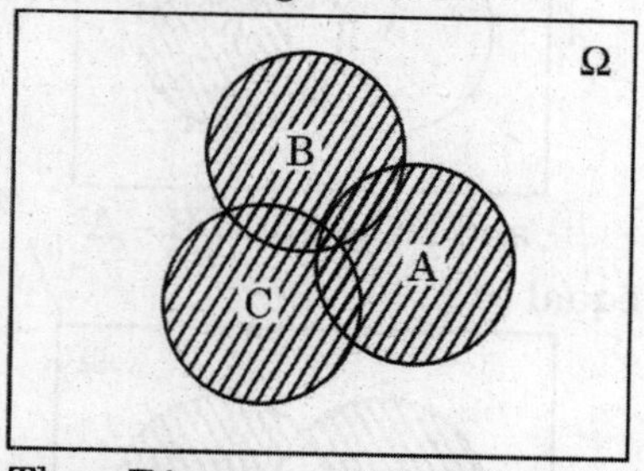

Then Diagram of A ∪ (B ∪ C)

R.H.S.

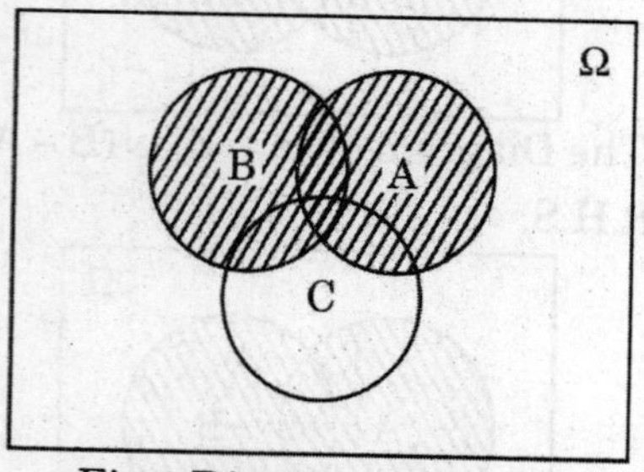

First Diagram of A ∪ B

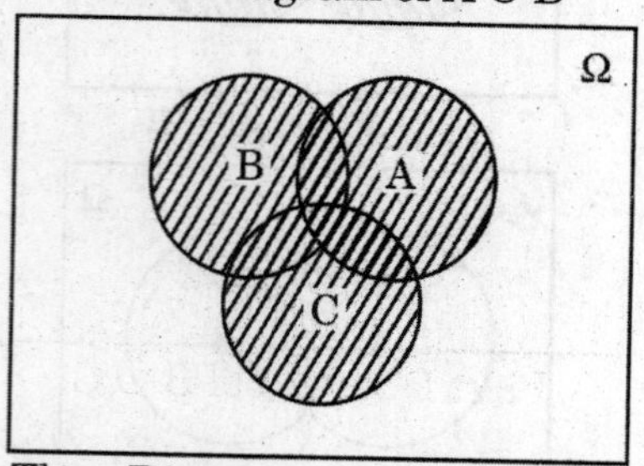

Then Diagram of (A ∪ B) ∪ C

Here clear with diagram of A ∪ (B ∪ C) = (A ∪ B) ∪ C

(ii) L.H.S.

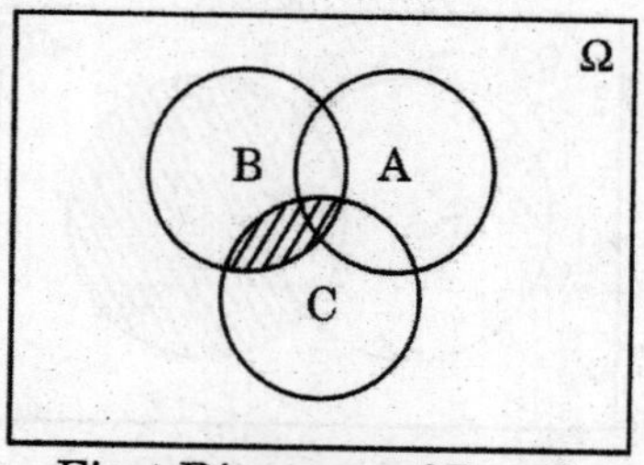

First Diagram of B ∪ C

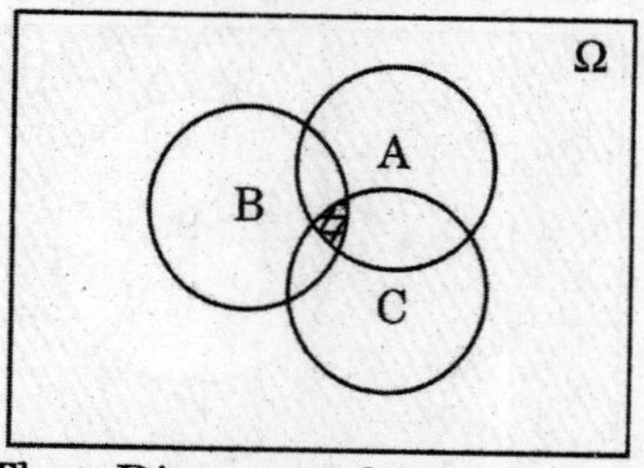

Then Diagram of A ∩ (B ∩ C)

Again R.H.S.

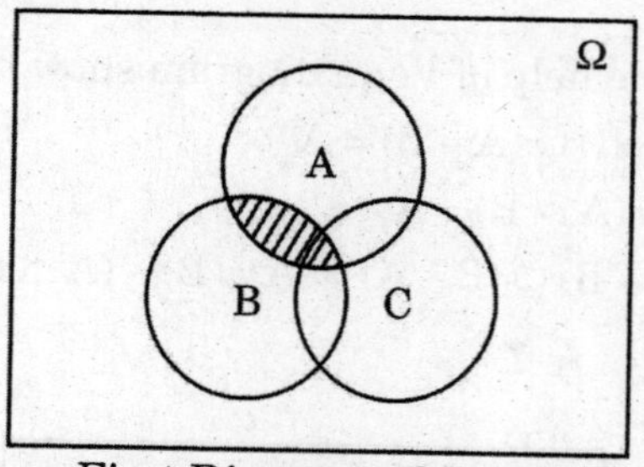

First Diagram of A ∩ B

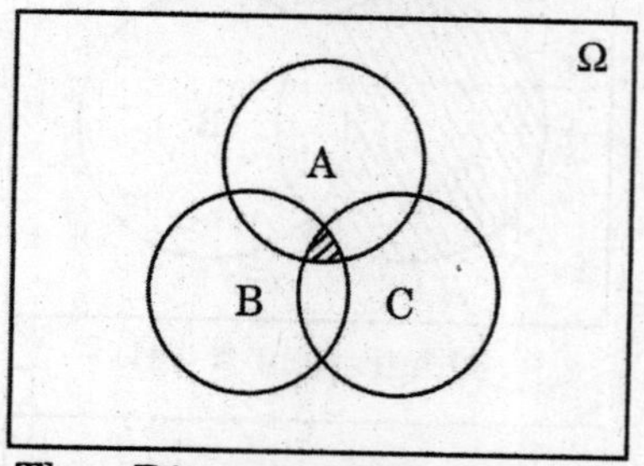

Then Diagram of (A ∩ B) ∩ C

Here clear that A ∩ (B ∩ C) = (A ∩ B) ∩ C

Example 4

Show by Venn diagram that :

(i) A ∪ (B ∩ C) = (A ∪ B) ∩ (A ∪ C)

(ii) A ∩ (B ∪ C) = (A ∩ B) ∪ (A ∩ C)

Solution

(i)

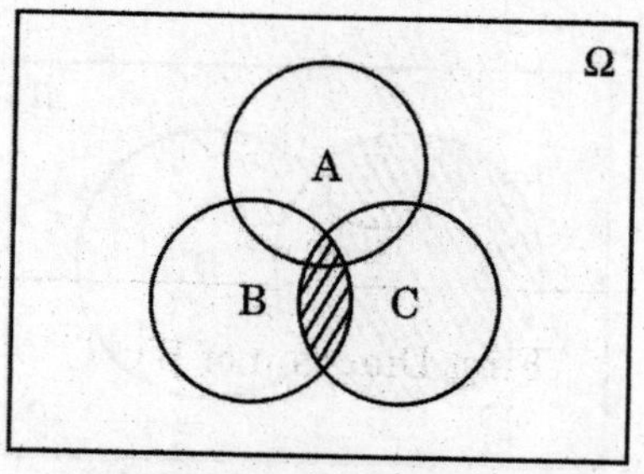

First Diagram of B ∩ C

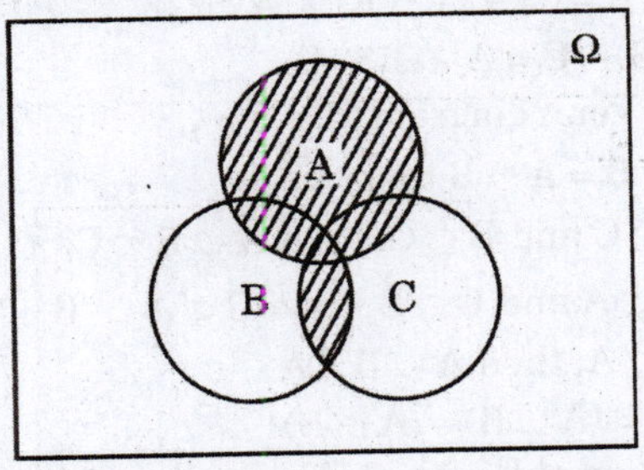

Then Diagram of (A ∩ B) ∩ C

Again R.H.S.

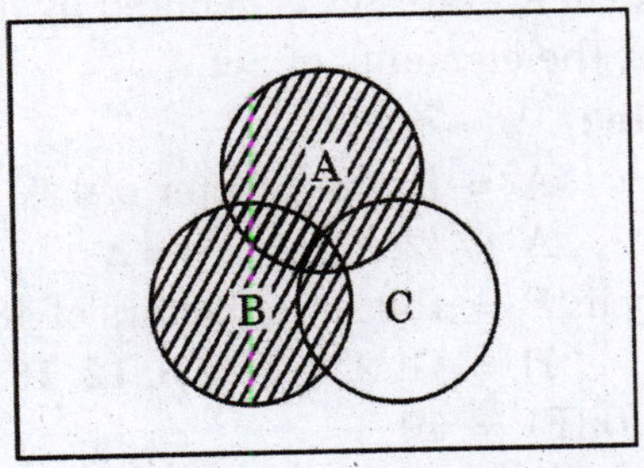

First Diagram of A ∪ B

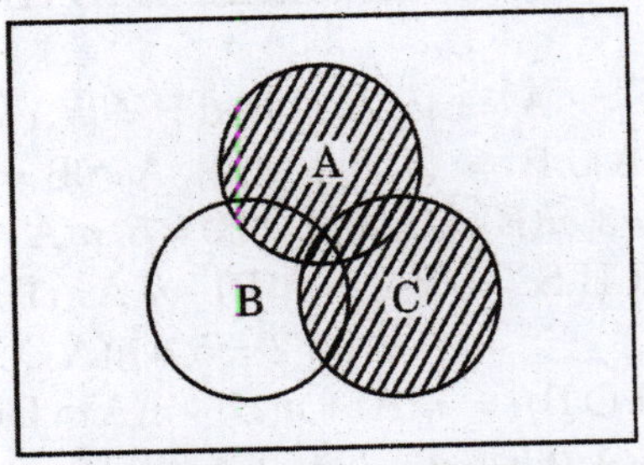

and Diagram of A ∪ C

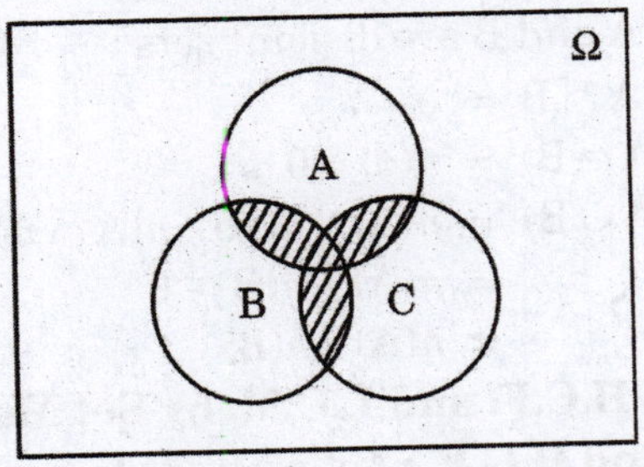

Then Diagram of (A ∪ B) ∩ (A ∪ C)

∴ A ∪ (B ∩ C) = (A ∪ B) ∩ (A ∪ C)

(ii) L.H.S.

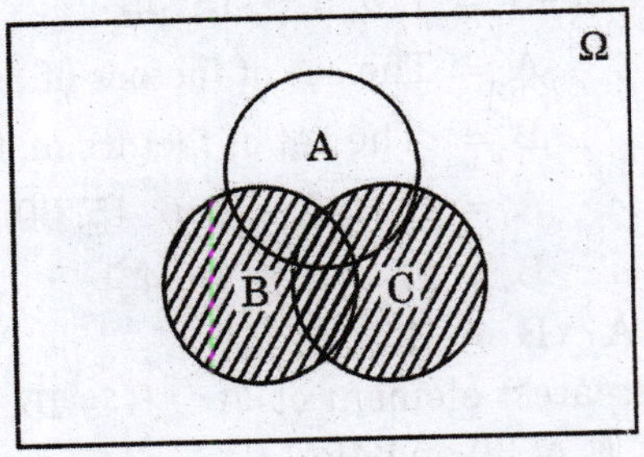

First Diagram of B ∪ C

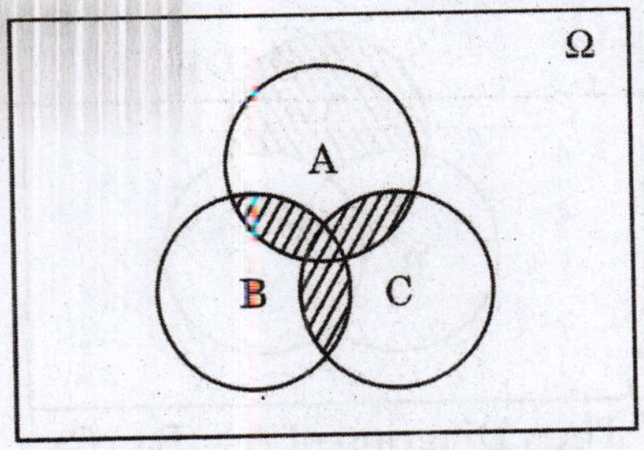

Then Diagram of A ∩ (B ∪ C)

Again R.H.S.

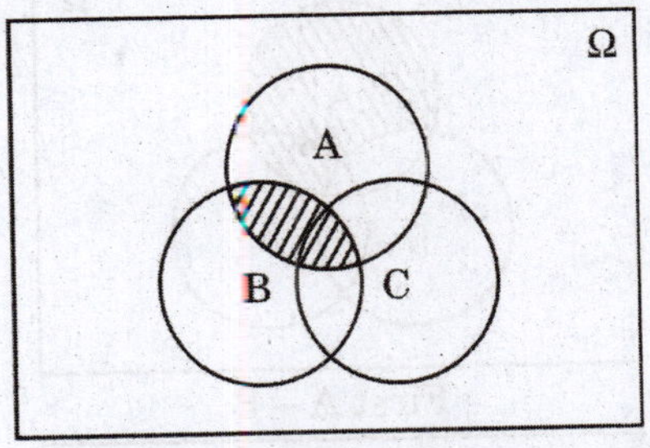

First A ∩ B

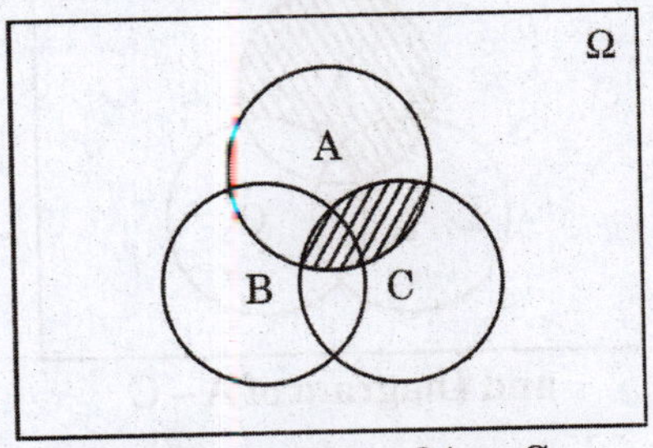

and Diagram of A ∩ C

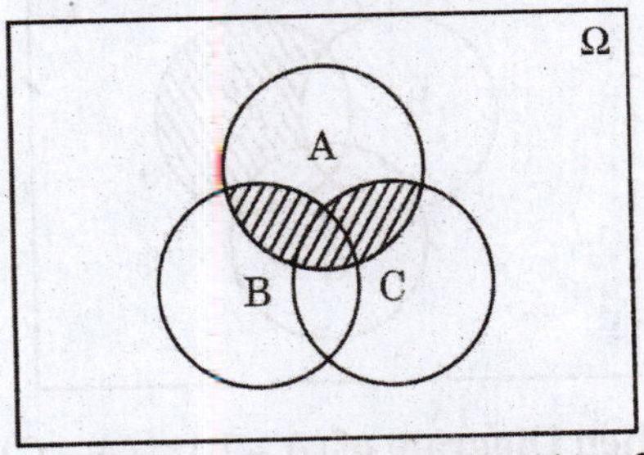

Then Diagram of (A ∩ B) ∪ (A ∩ C)

∴ A ∩ (B ∪ C) = (A ∩ B) ∪ (A ∩ C)

Example 5

Show with the help of Venn diagram that :

A – (B ∪ C) = (A – B) ∪ (A – C)

Solution

L.H.S.

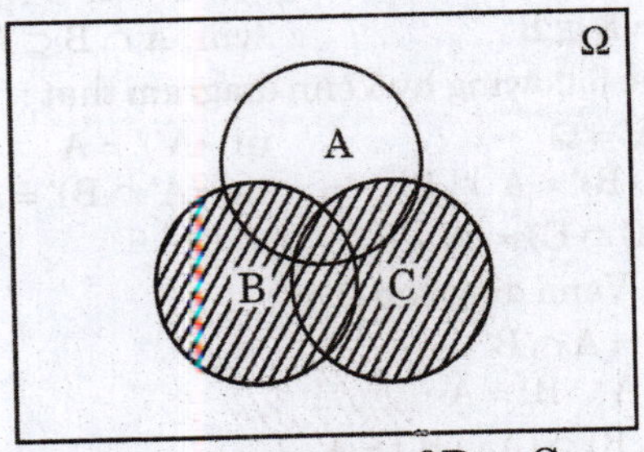

First Diagram of B ∪ C

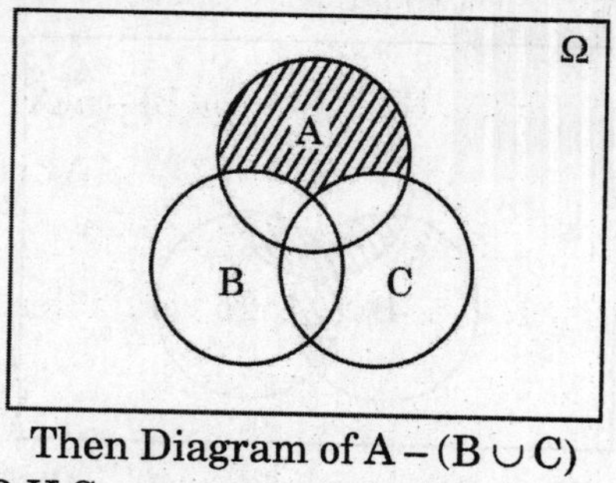

Then Diagram of $A - (B \cup C)$

Again R.H.S.

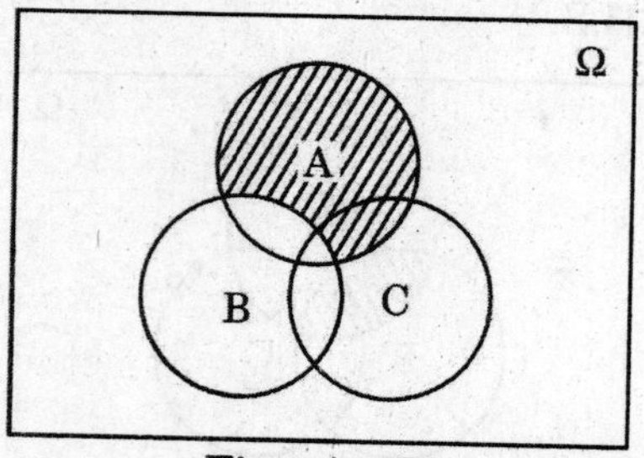

First $A - B$

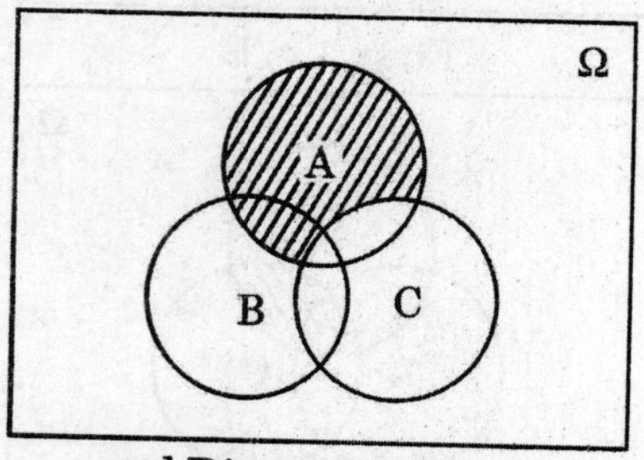

and Diagram of $A - C$

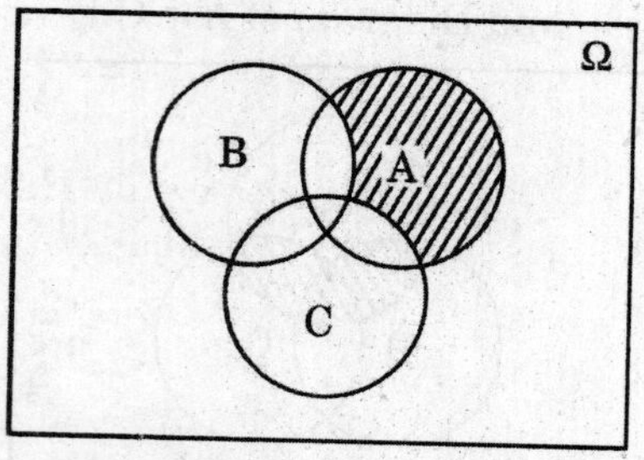

Then Diagram of $(A - B) \cap (A - C)$

Here clear by diagram that $A - (B \cup C) = (A - B) \cap (A - C)$

Exercise 8 (D)

1. Show the following by Venn diagram :
   (i) $A' \cup B'$ (ii) $A' \cap B$
   (iii) $(A - B)'$ (iv) $A' - B$
   (v) $A - A'$ (vi) $C - (B \cup A)$
   (vii) $A \cap B \subseteq B$ (viii) $A \cap B \subseteq A$
2. Show the following by Venn diagram that :
   (i) $A \cup A' = \Omega$ (ii) $(A')' = A$
   (iii) $(A \cup B)' = A' \cap B'$ (iv) $(A' \cap B)' = A' \cup B'$
   (v) $A - (B \cap C) = (A - B) \cup (A - C)$
3. Show by Venn diagram that :
   (i) $A - B = A \cap B'$
   (ii) $A \cap (A \cup B) = A$
   (iii) $(A \cup B) \cap (A \cup B') = A$
   (iv) $A \cap (B - C) = (A \cap B) - (A \cap C)$
   (v) $(A - B) - C = A - (B \cup C)$
4. Show by Venn diagram that :
   (i) If $A \cup B = A \cap B$ then $A = B$
   (ii) If $A \subseteq C$ and $B \subseteq C$, then $A \cup B \subseteq C$
   (iii) If $C \subseteq A$ and $C \subseteq B$, then $C \subseteq A \cup B$
   (iv) If $B \subseteq A$, then $A \cup B = A$
   (v) $A \Delta B = (A \cup B) - (A \cap B)$
5. If A, B, C are sub-sets of universal set Ω, then show $(A' \cap B' \cap C') \cup (A' \cap B \cap C)$ by Venn diagram.

(8.8) APPLICATIONS OF SETS

Elements of a finite set is denoted by $n(A)$. To find $n(A)$ we count the elements of Set A.

Example :

If $A = \{x/x \text{ is a factor of } 12\}$

then $A = \{2, 3\} \Rightarrow n(A) = 2$

Similarly if F = the set of factors of 48

then $F = \{1, 2, 3, 4, 6, 8, 12, 16, 24, 48\}$

$\therefore \quad n(F) = 10$

*** If A and B are two disjoint sets, then**

$$n(A \cup B) = n(A) + n(B) - n(A \cap B)$$

Proof :

Let $A = \{a, b, c\}$ and $B = \{b, c, d, e\}$

then $A \cup B = \{a, b, c, d, e\}$, $A \cap B = \{b, c\}$

$\therefore n(A) = 3, n(B) = 4, n(A \cup B) = 5, n(A \cap B) = 2$

R.H.S. $= n(A) + n(B) - n(A \cap B)$

$= 3 + 4 - 2 = 5 = n(A \cup B) =$ L.H.S.

$\therefore \quad n(A \cup B) = n(A) + n(B) - n(A \cap B)$ **Proved**

*** If A and B are two disjoint sets, then**

$$n(A \cup B) = n(A) + n(B)$$

Proof : A and B are disjoint sets

$\therefore \quad A \cap B = \phi$

$\Rightarrow \quad n(A \cap B) = n(\phi) = 0$

$\therefore \quad n(A \cup B) = n(A) + n(B) - n(A \cap B)$

$= n(A) + n(B) - 0$

$= n(A) + n(B)$ **Proved**

To Find the H.C.F. and L.C.M. by Set Method

(i) **To Find H.C.F. :** Let we want to find the H.C.F. of 30 and 45. For this at first we will find the factors of 30 and 45 which are follows :

Factors of 30 = 1, 2, 3, 5, 6, 15, 30

Factors of 45 = 1, 3, 5, 9, 15, 45

Let A = The set of factors of 30.

B = The set of factors of 45.

$\therefore \quad A = \{1, 2, 3, 4, 5, 6, 15, 30\}$

and $B = \{1, 3, 5, 9, 15, 45\}$

then $A \cap B = \{1, 3, 5, 15\}$

$\therefore$ The greatest element of $A \cup B$ is 15.

The H.C.F. of 30 and 45

so the required H.C.F. = 15

(ii) **To Find L.C.M. :** Let we want to find the L.C.M. of 6 and 21. For this at first we will find the multiple of 6 and 21 which are follows :

Multiples of 6 = 6, 12, 18, 24, 30, 36, 42, 48, ...

Multiple of 21 = 21, 42, 63, 84, ...

Let A = the set of multiples of 6

B = the set of multiples of 21

A = {6, 12, 18, 24, 30, 36, 42, 48, ..., 72, 78, 84, 90}

B = {21, 42, 63, 84......}

$\therefore$ $A \cap B = \{42, 84\}$

The lowest number of $A \cap B$ is the L.C.M. of 6 and 21.

So the required L.C.M. = 42.

SOLVED EXAMPLES

Example 1.

If $n(A) = 25$, $n(A \cup B) = 47$ and $n(A \cap B) = 9$ then fixed $n(B - A)$. *(JAC, 2022)*

Solution :

$n(B - A) = n(A \cup B) - n(A)$

$= 47 - 25$

$= \mathbf{22}$

Example 2

The total membership of Mathematical Society and Science Club is 122. If 50 students are the members of Mathematical Society and 28 students are members of both the organisation, find how many students are the members of Science Club ?

Solution :

Let A = {x/x is the member of Mathematics Society}

B = {x/x is the member of Science Club}

By the question,

$n(A \cup B) = 122, n(A) = 50, n(A \cap B) = 28,$

$n(B) = ?$

By the formula,

$n(A \cup B) = n(A) + n(B) - n(A \cap B)$

or $122 = 50 + n(B) - 28$

or $n(B) = 122 - 50 + 28 = 100$

$\therefore$ So number of members of Science Club = 100 **Ans.**

Example 3

In a group of 26 persons, 8 persons take tea instead of coffee and 16 persons take tea. How many persons take only coffee, not taking tea ? *(JAC, 2015)*

Solution :

Let A = {x/x is the person takes tea}

B = {x/x is the person takes coffee}

By the question,

$n(A \cup B) = 26, n(A) - n(A \cap B) = 8$

$n(A) = 16, n(B) - n(A \cap B) = ?$

By the formula,

$n(A \cup B) = n(A) + n(B) - n(A \cap B)$

or $26 = 16 + n(B) - n(A \cap B)$

$\therefore$ $n(B) - n(A \cap B) = 26 - 16 = 10$

So the number of persons take only coffee, not taking tea = 10 **Ans.**

Example 4

In a class there are 50 students. Of them each student study neither Hindi or Urdu or both. If 21 students study Hindi and 10 students Hindi and Urdu both, then state how many students study Urdu, how many study Urdu only and how many study Hindi only ?

Solution :

Let H = {x/x is the person study Hindi}

U = {x/x is the person study Urdu}

By the question,

$n(H \cup U) = 50, n(H) = 21, n(U) = ?$

$n(H \cap U) = 10$

By the formula,

$n(H \cup U) = n(H) + n(U) - n(H \cap U)$

or $50 = 21 + n(U) - 10$

$\therefore$ $n(U) = 39$

So number of students study Urdu only

$= n(U) - n(H \cap U) = 39 - 10 = 29$

Number of students study Hindi only

$= n(H) - n(H \cap U) = 21 - 10 = 11$

Example 5

Out of 600 persons, 350 speak only Hindi and 115 only English. How many persons speak both Hindi and English ?

Solution :

Let H = {x/x is the person speaks Hindi}

E = {x/x is the person speaks English}

By the question,

$n(H \cup E) = 600, n(H) - n(H \cap E) = 350$

$n(E) - n(H \cap E) = 115, n(H \cap E) = ?$

By the formula,

$n(H \cup E) = n(H) + n(E) - n(H \cap E)$

or $600 = 350 + n(H \cap E) + 115 + n(H \cap E) - n(H \cap E)$

or $n(H \cap E) = 600 - 465$

$\therefore$ $n(H \cap E) = 135$

$\because n(H) - n(H \cap E) = 350$
$\therefore n(H) = 350 + n(H \cap E)$
and $n(E) - n(H \cap E) = 115$
$\therefore n(E) = 115 + n(H \cap E)$

So the number of persons speak both Hindi and English = 135 **Ans.**

Example 6

In a town population 5,000 persons read Hidustan, 2,300 read Prabhat and 400 read both. How many do not read any newspaper.

Solution :

Only read of Hindustan = 2,800 − 400 = 2,400

Only read of Prabhat = 2,300 − 400 = 1,900

Total Person of read Newspaper

= 2,400 + 1,900 + 400

= 4,700

Do not read Newspaper = 5,000 − 4,700 = 300

Example 7

In a group of 520 persons, 360 can speak only Hindi and 130 only English. How many persons can speak both Hindi and English ?

Solution :

Let A = {*x*/*x* is the person can speak Hindi}

B = {*x*/*x* is the person can speak English}

So by the question,

$$n(A \cup B) = 520$$
$$n(A) - n(A \cap B) = 360$$
$$n(B) - n(A \cap B) = 130$$
$$n(A \cap B) = ?$$

By the formula,

$$n(A \cup B) = n(A) + n(B) - n(A \cap B)$$

or $520 = n(A) + 130$

$\therefore$ $n(A) = 520 - 130 = 390$

$\therefore$ By the question,

$$n(A) - n(A \cap B) = 360$$

or $390 - n(A \cap B) = 360$

or $n(A \cap B) = 390 - 360$

$\therefore$ $n(A \cap B) = 30$

So number of persons can speak both Hindi and English = 30 **Ans.**

Example 8

In a school 60% students contributed in National Defence Fund and 70% students contributed in National Savings Scheme. How many students contributed in both the schemes ?

Solution :

Let A = {*x*/*x* is the student contributed in National Defence Fund}

B = {*x*/*x* is the student contributed in National Saving Scheme}

By the question,

$$n(A \cup B) = 100, n(A) = 60, n(B) = 70,$$
$$n(A \cap B) = ?$$

By the formula,

$$n(A \cup B) = n(A) + n(B) - n(A \cap B)$$

or $100 = 60 + 70 - n(A \cap B)$

$\therefore$ $n(A \cap B) = 130 - 100 = 30$

So percentage of students contributed in both the schemes = 30% **Ans.**

Example 9

Find the H.C.F. of 18, 24 and 30 by using set. (*JAC*, 2016)

Solution :

Let factors of A = 18 {1, 2, 3, 6, 9, 18}

factors of B = 24 {1, 2, 3, 4, 6, 8, 12, 24}

factors of C = 30 {1, 2, 3, 5, 6, 10, 15, 30}

$\therefore$ $A \cap B \cap C = \{1, 2, 3, 6\}$

$\therefore$ The greatest digit in

$A \cap B \cap C = 6$

So the required H.C.F. = 6 **Ans.**

Example 10.

Calculate the L.C.M. of 4, 6, 8 by set method. (*JAC*, 2015)

Solution :

A = the set of multiple of 4

B = the set of multiple of 6

C = the set of multiple of 8

then A = {4, 8, 12, 16, 20, 24, 28, 32, 36, 40, 44, 48, ...}

B = {6, 12, 18, 24, 30, 36, 42, 48, ...}

C = {8, 16, 24, 32, 40, 48, ...}

$\therefore$ $A \cap B \cap C = \{24, 48, ...\}$

So least integer of $A \cap B \cap C = 24$

So the required L.C.M. = 24 **Ans.**

Exercise 8 (E)

1. If $A \cap B = \phi$, then $n(A \cup B)$ is equal to which of the following : (*JAC*, 2015, 19)
   (a) $n(A) - n(B)$ (b) $n(A) + n(B)$
   (c) $n(A) \times n(B)$ (d) $n(A \times B)$
2. If $n(A) = 20$, $n(B) = 30$ and $n(A \cap B) = 10$, then find the value of $n(A \cup B)$. (*JAC*, 2023)
3. If $n(A \cup B) = 50$, $n(A) = 28$ and $n(B) = 32$, then find the value of $n(A \cap B)$. (*JAC*, 2017, 22)
4. If $n(A) = 40$, $n(A \cup B) = 60$ and $n(A \cap B) = 10$, then calculate the value of $n(B)$.
5. If $n(A) = 17$, $n(B) = 23$ and $n(A \cup B) = 38$, then find the value of $n(A \cap B)$.
6. If $n(A \cup B) = 80$, $n(B) = 15$ and $n(A \cap B) = 5$, then find the value of $n(A)$ and $n(A) - n(A \cap B)$.
7. In a school there are 20 teachers who teach Mathematics and Physics. Out of them 12 teaches Mathematics and 4 Physics and Mathematics. State how many teachers teach Physics ? (*JAC*, 2026)
8. In a group each person knows atleast one language out of Hindi and Urdu. 100 persons know Hindi, 50 Urdu and of

them 25 knows both Hindi and Urdu, find by set method how many person are there in the group ?

9. In a group of 70 persons, 37 persons like coffee, 52 likes tea and each persons likes atleast one of the two drinks. Find how many persons like both coffee and tea ?

10. Out of a survey of 500 car owners 400 gets the report of car A, 200 of car B and 50 of car A and B both. Is this report correct ?

[**Ans.** No]

[**Hint :** $n(A \cup B) = 500$
$n(A) = 400$
$n(B) = 200$
$n(A \cap B) = 50$
Again $n(A \cup B) = n(A) + n(B) - n(A \cap B)$
or $500 = 400 + 200 - 50$
$\therefore$ $500 = 550$, which is not true.]

11. Out of 560 persons speaking Hindi, English of both languages, 390 can speak only Hindi and 130 only English. How many persons can speak both English and Hindi ?

12. 19 boys play Kabbaddi out of which 11 boys put on shoes and 14 boys socks. Here are no such boy who neither puts on socks nor shoes. How many boys put on both shoes and socks ?

13. In a class of 30 students, 20 likes to play cricket and 15 football. Every student likes atleast one of the two plays. Find how many students like to play both cricket and football ?

14. By using set, find out H.C.F. of the following :
(i) 12 and 18 (ii) 30 and 84
(iii) 24, 36 and 48

15. Find L.C.M. of the following by method of set :
(i) 12, 18 (ii) 3, 6 and 15
(iii) 4, 8 and 12

16. If 63% persons like orange and 76% like apple, then find the percentage of persons who like both orange and apple. (*JAC*, 2019)

17. If 65% students know Bangla and 85% students know Hindi, what the percentage of students know both Hindi and Bangla ?

18. If 75% boys preferred mangoes and 53% boys prefer bananas, what the percentage of such students who prefer both mango and banana ? (*JAC*, 2024)

19. Out of a group of 45 students, 22 students can speak only Hindi and 12 can speak only English. How many students can speak Hindi and English both ?

20. In a town, having population of 5,000; 2,800 persons read Hindustan Times, 2,300 persons Dainik Jagran and 400 persons read both the newspapers. How many persons do not read any newspaper ?

21. The population of a village is 5,000 out of which 2,800 eat eggs, 2,500 eat mutton and 1,200 persons eat eggs and mutton both. How many persons are vegetarian in the village ?

22. In a class there are 30 students who studies Mathematics or Geography. If out of them 13 studies Mathematics and out of them 7 studies both Mathematics and Geography, then find out how many of them study Geography ?

23. Out of a group of 60 persons, 40 persons like cricket, 10 persons like both cricket and tennis. Find out how many persons like only tennis and how many cricket only ?

24. Out of 60 students, 35 students play Hockey, 20 students play both Hockey and Cricket. Find out how many students play Cricket only ?

25. If $A = \{1, 2, 3, 4, 5\}$, $B = \{4, 5, 6, 7\}$ and $C = \{6, 7, 8, 9, 10\}$, prove that $A \cap (B \cup C) = (A \cap B) \cup (A \cap C)$.

26. 50 students of a class study either Accountancy or Statistics or both; 12 students take both subjects and 18 study only Statistics. How many students study Accountancy ?

Answers

1. (b)	2. 40	3. 10	4. 30	5. 2
6. 70, 65	7. 12	8. 125	9. 19	10. No
11. 40	12. 6	13. 5	14. (i) 6 (ii) 6, (iii) 12	
15. (i) 36, (ii) 30, (iii) 24		16. 39%	17. 50%	18. 28%
19. 11	20. 300	21. 900	22. 24	23. 20, 30
24. 45	26. 44.			

MISCELLANEOUS SOLVED EXAMPLES

Example 1

In a class of 42 students. Each student plays atleast one of the three games Cricket, Hockey and Football. 14 students play Cricket, 20 play Hockey, 24 play Football, 3 play both Cricket and Football, 2 play both Hockey and Football and none plays all the three games. Find the number of students who play Cricket but not Hockey ?

Solution :

C = {The set of students play Cricket}
H = {The set of students play Hockey}
F = {The set of students play Football}

$n(C) = 14$
$n(H) = 20$
$n(F) = 24$
$n(C \cap F) = 3$
$n(H \cap F) = 2$
$n(C \cap H \cap F) = 0$
$n(C \cup H \cup F) = 42$
$\therefore n(C) - n(C \cap H) = ?$

$n(C \cup H \cup F) = n(C) + n(H) + n(F) - n(C \cap H) - n(H \cap F) - n(C \cap F) + n(C \cap H \cap F)$

or $42 = 14 + 20 + 24 - n(C \cap H) - 2 - 3 - 0$

or $42 = 53 - n(C \cap H)$

$\therefore$ $n(C \cap H) = 11$

So number of those students who play Cricket but not Hockey

$= n(C) - n(C \cap H)$
$= 14 - 11 = 3$ **Ans.**

Example 2

Out of members of three teams of sports of a school, 21 are in basketball team, 26 in hockey team and 29 in football team of which 14 plays hockey and basketball, 15 plays hockey and football, 2 plays football and basketball and 8 are in all (three) the teams. How many members in all the teams ?

Solution :

Let B = {The set of persons play basket-ball}

H = {The set of persons play hockey}

F = {The set of persons play football}.

So by the question,

$n(B) = 21, n(H) = 26, n(F) = 29$

$n(H \cap B) = 14$

$n(H \cap F) = 15$

$n(F \cap B) = 12$

$n(H \cap B \cap F) = 8$

$n(H \cup F \cup B) = ?$

Now,

$n(B \cup H \cup F) = n(B) + n(H) + n(F) - n(B \cap H) - n(H \cap F) - n(F \cap B) + n(H \cap F \cap B)$

$= 21 + 26 + 29 - 14 - 15 - 12 + 8$

$= 84 - 41 = 43$ **Ans.**

Example 3

A college gives 30 medal Football (F), 15 in Basketball (B) and 20 in Cricket (C). These medals goes to 58 persons out of which 3 persons get 3 medals in 3 games. How many persons get 2 and only 2 medals ?

Solution :

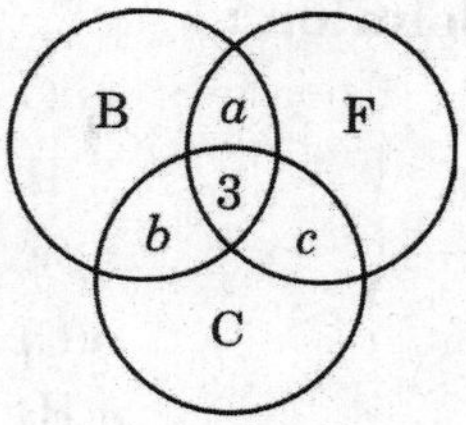

$n(F) = 38$

$n(B) = 15$

$n(C) = 20$

$n(F \cup B \cup C) = 58$

and $n(F \cap B \cap C) = 3$

By the formula,

$n(F \cup B \cup C) = n(F) + n(B) + n(C) - n(F \cap B) - n(B \cap C) - n(C \cap F) + n(F \cap B \cap C)$

or $58 = 38 + 15 + 20 - n(F \cap B) - n(B \cap C) - n(C \cap F) + 3$

$\therefore n(F \cap B) + n(B \cap C) + n(C \cap F) = 76 - 58 = 18$ ...(i)

As shown in the Venn diagram

$n(F \cap B) = a + 3$

$n(B \cap C) = b + 3$

and $n(C \cap F) = c + 3$

By the equation (i),

$(a + 3) + (b + 3) + (c + 3) = 18$

$\Rightarrow a + b + c = 18 - 9 = 9$

So number of persons get two and only two medal = 9

Example 4

If A = {1, 3, 5, 7} B = {2, 3, 4, 5} C = {2, 4, 6, 8} are three sets then find $A \cap (B \cup C)$.

[Mock Test Paper (JAC)]

Solution :

$\because$ A = {1, 3, 5, 7}

B = {2, 3, 4, 5}

C = {2, 4, 6, 8}

$\therefore$ $B \cup C$ = {2, 3, 4, 5, 6, 8}

and $A \cap (B \cup C)$ = {3, 5}

Example 5

If the two sets are A = {11, 12,13, 14, 15, 16} B = {11, 12, 15, 16, 17, 18, 19} find A – B.

[Mock Test Paper (JAC)]

Solution :

$\because$ A = {11, 12, 13, 14, 15, 16}

and B = {11, 12, 15, 16, 17, 18, 19}

$\therefore$ A – B = {13, 14}

Example 6

If $n(A \cup B) = 50$, $n(A) = 28$ and $n(B) = 32$. Find $n(A \cap B)$. *[Mock Test Paper (JAC)]*

Solution :

If $n(A \cup B) = 50$

$n(A) = 28$

and $n(B) = 32$

$\because n(A \cup B) = n(A) + n(B) - n(A \cap B)$

$50 = 28 + 32 - n(A \cap B)$

$n(A \cap B) = 60 - 50 = 10$

Example 7

Out of 560 persons speaking Hindi or English or both languages, 390 can speak only Hindi and 230 can speak only English. How many persons can speak both Hindi an English ? *[Mock Test Paper (JAC)]*

Solution :

If $n(H \cup E) = 560$

$n(H) = 390$

and $n(E) = 230$

then $n(H \cup E) = n(H) + n(E) - n(H \cap E)$

$560 = 390 + 230 - n(H \cap E)$

$n(H \cap E) = 620 - 560$

$= 60$

So, 60 Persons Speak Hindi and English.

Exercise 8 (F)

1. In a school all boys play one or more games out of cricket, tennis and football. Out of which 60% of the boys play cricket, 75% tennis and 70% football. If 45% boys play cricket and tennis, 40% cricket and football, 50% tennis and football, then what is the percentage of the boys who play all the three games ?
2. In a group of boys 35 play football, out of which 20 boys play only football, 20 boys play hockey and 25 boys play cricket, out of which 11 plays only cricket. Out of them 7 boys play cricket and football but not hockey, 3 football and hockey but not cricket, 12 boys plays football and cricket both. Find out how many boys play three games.

3. An investigator collects the following data in respect of liking drinks—Milk (M), Coffee (C) and Tea (T) of 100 students. 10 likes all the three drinks, 20 M and C, 30 C and T, 25 M and T, 12 M only, 5 only C and 8 only T. State by Venn diagram by any other method how many students do not like any of the three drinks ?

[Hint :

$n(M \cap C \cap T) = 10$

$n(M \cap C) = 20$

$n(C \cap T) = 30$

$n(M \cap T) = 25$

$n(M - C - T) = 12$

$n(C - T - M) = 5$

$n(T - M - C) = 8$

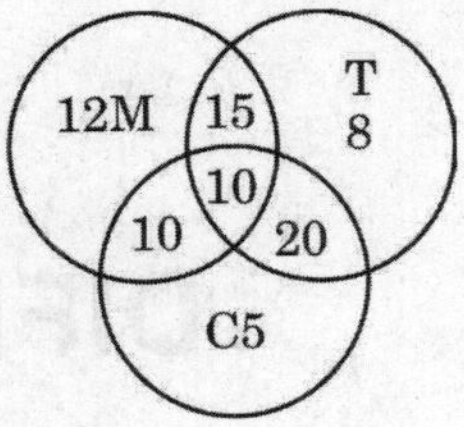

$n(M \cup C \cup T) = n(M - C - T) + n(C - T - M) + n(T - M - C) + n(M \cap C) + n(M \cap T) + n(C \cap T) - n(M \cap C \cap T) - n(M \cap C \cap T)$

$= 12 + 5 + 8 + 20 + 25 + 30 - 10 - 10$

$= 80$

So the number of students do not like any of three drinks

$= 100 - 80 = 20$]

Answers

1. 30% 2. 5 3. 20

Exercise 8 (G)

Objective Type Questions

❑ Multiple Choice Questions

1. If $A \cup B = \phi$ then :
   (a) $A = \phi$ or $B = \phi$ (b) $A = \phi$ and $B = \phi$
   (c) $A = \phi$ and $B \neq \phi$ (d) $A \neq \phi$ and $B = \phi$
2. If X and Y are two sets and X' denotes the complement of X then $X \cap (X \cup Y)'$ equals :
   (a) X (b) Y
   (c) ϕ (d) None of these
3. $A - (B \cup C) =$
   (a) $(A - B) \cup (A - C)$ (b) $(A - B) \cap (A - C)$
   (c) $(A - B) \cup C$ (d) $(A - C) \cup B$
4. The number of elements in the power set of {1, 2, 3, 4, 5} is :
   (a) 16 (b) 32 (c) 64 (d) 80
5. The number of non-empty sub-sets of the set {1, 2, 3, 4} is :
   (a) 14 (b) 15 (c) 16 (d) 18
6. If A = {*a, b, c, d*}, B = {*b, d, e, f*} then the value of $A \cap B$ will be : (*JAC*, 2018)
   (a) {*a, b, c, d, e, f*} (b) {*b, d*}
   (c) {*d, e, f*} (d) {*c, d, e*}
7. If universal set X = {1,2,3 .... 20} A = {1, 2, 3, 4, 5} the value of (A')' will be (*JAC*, 2018)
   (a) {1, 2, 3, 4, 5} (b) {6,7,8,9 ... 20}
   (c) {1,2,3} (d) {5,6,7,8}
8. If A = {*p, q, r, s*}, B = {*q, s, t*}, C = {*m, q, n*}, find $C - (A \cap B)$: (*JAC*, 2019)
   (a) {*m, n*} (b) {*p, q*} (c) {*r, s*} (d) {*p, r*}
9. $A \subset B$, then which one of the following is true :
   (a) $A \cap B = B$ (b) $A \cup B = B$
   (c) $A \cap B = A'$ (d) $A \cap B = \phi$
10. Out of 20 members in a family, 11 like to take tea and 14 like coffee. Assume that each one likes at least one of the two drinks. Find how many like both coffee and tea ?
    (a) 2 (b) 3 (c) 4 (d) 5
11. For any two sets A and B, $A \cap (A' \cup B) =$ ...., where A' represents the complement of the set A :
    (a) $A \cap B$ (b) $A \cup B$
    (c) $A' \cup B$ (d) None of these
12. Null set is a............ of all sets :
    (a) set (b) sub-set
    (c) super set (d) single ton set
13. If $\cup$ = {1, 2, 3,.......9}, A = {1, 2, 4, 5}, B = {6, 7, 8}, then {3, 6, 7, 8, 9} is) : (*JAC*, 2022)
    (a) A' (b) B' (c) A (d) B
14. What is singleton set (*JAC*, 2024)
    (a) It is a single set. (b) It is a singular matrix.
    (c) It is a null set
    (d) It is a set with a single element.
15. If A = {1, 2, 4, 5} and B = {4, 5, 6, 8} then $A \cap B$ is : (*JAC*, 2025)
    (a) {1, 2, 4, 5} (b) {4, 5, 6, 8}
    (c) {4, 5} (d) {1, 2, 4, 5, 6, 8}
16. Two sets are disjoint if and only if : (*JAC*, 2025)
    (a) $A \cap B = \phi$ (b) $A \cap B \neq \phi$
    (c) $A - B \neq \phi$ (d) $A - B \neq B$
17. If A is the set of the word 'eat' then which one of the following is true ? (*JAC*, 2025)
    (a) $e \in A$ (b) $A \in a$ (c) $t \notin A$ (d) $at \in A$

Answers

1. (b)	2. (c)	3. (b)	4. (b)	5. (b)	6. (b)	7. (a)
8. (a)	9. (b)	10. (d)	11. (a)	12. (b)	13. (c)	14. (d)
15. (c)	16. (a)	17. (a).				

❑ Fill in the blanks

1. A set having no element is called .... set.
2. A set having finite number of elements is called .... set.
3. Null set is a .... of all sets.
4. $(A \cup B)^C$ = ...
5. $\phi \cap A$ = ...

Answers

1. Null set 2. Finite set 3. Sub-set
4. $A^C \cap B^C$, 5. ϕ

❑ Write True or False

1. If $A \cap B = \phi$ then $A \cap \phi = B$.
2. If $A \in B$ and $B \cap C = \phi$ then $A \cap C = \phi$.
3. If $A \subseteq B$ then $B \subseteq A^C$.
4. 1, 2, 5 ⊂, 9, 11, 5, 6, 12.
5. $\phi \in$ 2, 5.

Answers

1. False 2. True 3. False 4. True
5. False.

❖❖

9 DIFFERENTIATION

LEARNING OBJECTIVES

After studying this chapter, you will be able to know :

- **9.1 Introduction**
- **9.2 Definition of a Function**
- **9.3 Limit of a Function**
- **9.4 Some Important Theorem Related to Limit**
- **9.5 Some Rules of Differentiation**
- **9.6 Differential Coefficient of Function of Function**
  - **9.6.1 Meaning of Function of Function**
  - **9.6.2 Differential Coefficient of Inverse Functions**
- **9.7 Differentiation of Implicit Functions**
- **9.8 Logarithmic Differentiation**

SOLVED EXAMPLES AND PRACTICAL PROBLEMS : AT A GLANCE

No. of Examples		*No. of Problems*
1 to 12	Type I : To find the Differential Coefficient	Exercise 9(A) : 1 to 22
1A to 5	Type II : Differential Coefficient of Function	Exercise 9(B) : 1 to 10
1 to 12	Type III : Differentiation of Implicit Functions	Exercise 9(C) : 1 to 17
1 to 16	Type IV : Logarithmic Differentiation	Exercise 9(D) : 1 to 13
	Objective Type Questions	Exercise 9(E) : 12 + 5 + 5
45	**Total**	**62 + 22**

(9.1) INTRODUCTION

Calculus is that branch of mathematics in which we study changes or analysis related to Business Mathematics. Mathematics is the key of science. Calculus is developed by Sir Isaac Newton and Gottfried Leibnitz in 17th century. Newton developed calculus of solving problems in Physics while Leibnitz developed calculus for solving problems in Geometry.

Calculus

Differentiation   Integration

In this chapter we want to know about differentiaton for which at first we should know the basic idea of function.

A function always explains the nature of correspodence between some variables which can be indicated by some formula or graph or mathematical equation.

The work 'function' is derived from a latin word meaning operation."*A function is a rule, which assigns to every element of the first set a unique element of the second set B.*"

(9.2) DEFINITION OF A FUNCTION

Let A and B be two non-empty sets, then a rule 'f', which associates each element of A with a unique element of B is called a mapping or function from A to B. If it is a mapping from A to B we write $f : A \rightarrow B$ (read as f is mapping from A to B).

If f associates $x \in A$ to $y \in B$, then we say that y is the image of the element x is called the pre-image or inverse image of y.

- If two variables x and y are so related that for every value of x there is a definite value of y, then y is said to be a function of x.
- General form of function i.e., $y = f(x)$. Here x is called independent variable and y is called dependent variable.
- Function is denoted by $f(x), g(x), \phi(x), f_1(x)$ or $f_2(x)$ etc.

Domain, Codomain and Range of a Function : Let f be a function from A to B, then the set A is called the domain of a map 'f' and the set B is called the co-domain. The set of the images of all the elements of A under the map f is called the range of f and is denoted by $f(A)$. Thus range of A *i.e.*, $f(A) = \{f(x) : x \in A\}$ clearly $f(A) \subseteq B$.

Some Examples of Functions

Example 1.

Let $A = \{1, -1, 2, 3, -3\}$

$B = \{1, 4, 9, 10, 11\}$.

The rule f given by

$f(x) = x^2$ is a map form A to B.

Domain $f = A = \{1, -1, 2, 3, -3\}$

Range $f = \{1, 4, 9\}$

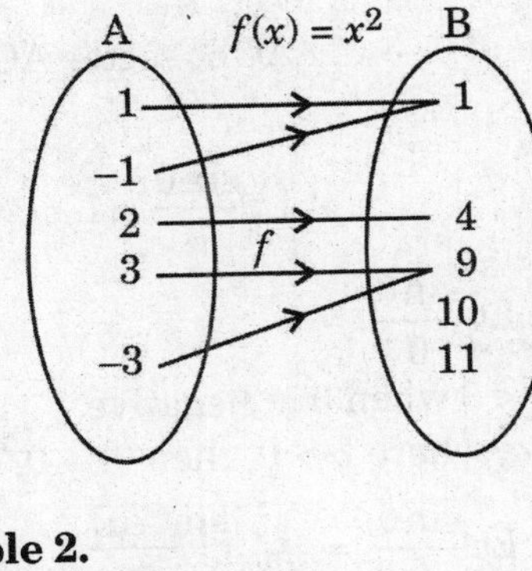

Example 2.

Let $A = \{1, -1, 2, 3\}$

$B = \{2, -2, 4, 6\}$.

The rule f given by

$f(x) = 2x$ is a map from A to B.

Domain $f = A = \{1, -1, 2, 3\}$

Range $f = \{2, -2, 4, 6\}$

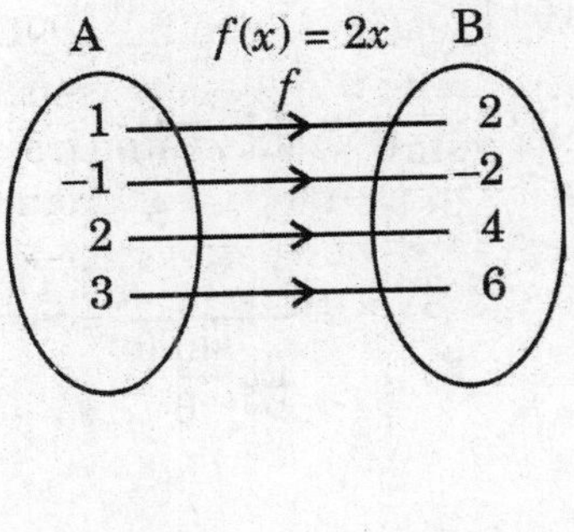

(9.3) LIMIT OF A FUNCTION

Definition : 'l' is said to be the limit of function $f(x)$ at $x = a$ if $\underset{x \to a}{\text{Lt}} f(x) = l$.

$\underset{x \to a}{\text{Lt}} f(x)$ means that the value of x is nearly to a.

i.e. x is nearly to a.

i.e. x is very-very near to a.

Example 1

Find the value of $\underset{x \to 2}{\text{Lt}} \dfrac{x^2 - 4}{x - 2}$.

Solution :

If we put $x = 2$, then $\dfrac{4-4}{2-2} = \dfrac{0}{0}$

which is indeterminate form so at first we should remove this form.

Now, $$\underset{x \to 2}{\text{Lt}} \frac{x^2 - 4}{x - 2} = \underset{x \to 2}{\text{Lt}} \frac{(x+2)(x-2)}{(x-2)}$$
$$= \underset{x \to 2}{\text{Lt}} (x+2)$$
$$= 2 + 2 = 4$$

Example 2

Find the value of $\underset{x \to 1}{\text{Lt}} (x^2 + 1)$.

Solution :

Here the function is not in indeterminate form $\dfrac{0}{0}$, so to find the value of the limit of the function we should put $x = 1$

So $$\underset{x \to 1}{\text{Lt}} (x^2 - 1) = (1)^2 + 1 = 1 + 1 = 2$$

INDETERMINATE FORMS OR MEANINGLESS FORMS OF FUNCTION

(1) $\dfrac{0}{0}$ (2) $\dfrac{\infty}{\infty}$ (3) $0 \times \infty$ (4) $\infty - \infty$

(5) 1^∞ (6) 0^0 (7) ∞^0

(9.4) SOME IMPORTANT THEOREMS RELATED TO LIMIT

1. $\underset{x \to 0}{\text{Lt}} \dfrac{x^n - a^n}{x - a} = na^{n-1}$, where n is a rational number.

Proof : Let $x = a + h$, then as $x \to a, h \to 0$

Now $$\underset{x \to a}{\text{Lt}} \frac{x^n - a^n}{x - a} = \underset{h \to 0}{\text{Lt}} \frac{(a+h)^n - a^n}{a + h - a}$$
$$= \underset{h \to 0}{\text{Lt}} \frac{a^n\left(1 + \frac{h}{a}\right)^n - a^n}{h}$$
$$= \underset{h \to 0}{\text{Lt}} \frac{a^n\left[\left(1 + \frac{h}{a}\right)^n - 1\right]}{h}$$

$$= \begin{cases} \underset{h\to 0}{\text{Lt}} \dfrac{a^n\left[\left\{1+\dfrac{n}{|\underline{1}}\left(\dfrac{h}{a}\right)+\dfrac{n(n-1)}{|\underline{2}}\left(\dfrac{h}{a}\right)^2+\ldots+\left(\dfrac{h}{a}\right)^n\right\}-1\right]}{h} & \text{when } n \text{ is positive integer.} \\ \underset{h\to 0}{\text{Lt}} \dfrac{a^n\left[\left\{1+\dfrac{n}{|\underline{1}}\left(\dfrac{h}{a}\right)+\dfrac{n(n-1)}{|\underline{2}}\left(\dfrac{h}{a}\right)^2+\ldots to\ \infty\right\}-1\right]}{h} & \text{when } n \text{ is negative integer.} \end{cases}$$

$$= \underset{h\to 0}{\text{Lt}} \frac{a^n - n.\dfrac{h}{a}\left[1+\dfrac{n-1}{|\underline{2}}.\dfrac{h}{a}+\text{Sum of high power terms of } h\right]}{h}$$

$$= a^n.n.\frac{1}{a} = na^{n-1}$$

2. $\underset{h\to 0}{\text{Lt}} \cos\theta = 1.$

Proof : As x approaches 0, cos θ approaches cos θ *i.e.* 1.

Hence $\underset{\theta\to 0}{\text{Lt}} \cos\theta = 1$

3. $\underset{\theta\to 0}{\text{Lt}} \dfrac{\sin\theta}{\theta} = 1$, where θ is in radian.

Proof : Case I. When θ > 0 Let $0 < \theta \frac{\pi}{2}$ let 0 be the centre of a circle whose redius is r. Let ∠AOB = θ radian, where $0 < \theta < \frac{\pi}{2}$.

Let the tangent to the circle at point A cut OB at C. From B draw BD on OA.

Now Area of Δ AOB

$$= \frac{1}{2}.\text{OA.BD}$$

$$= \frac{1}{2}.r.r \sin\theta$$

$$= \frac{1}{2} r^2 \sin\theta$$

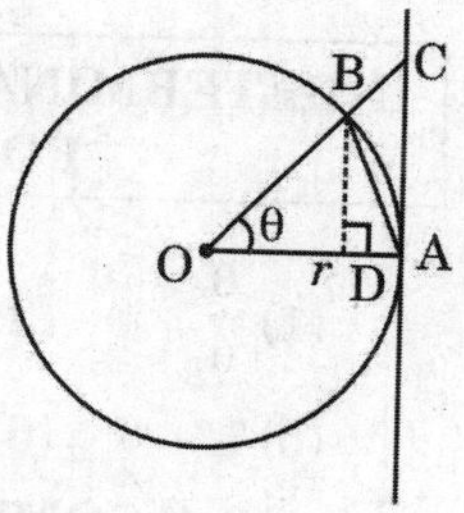

Area of sector AOB

$$= \frac{\theta}{2\pi}.\pi r^2$$

$$= \frac{1}{2} r^2\theta$$

Area of Δ AOC

$$= \frac{1}{2}.\text{OA.AC}$$

$$= \frac{1}{2}.r.r \tan\theta \qquad \left[\because \sin\theta = \frac{\text{BD}}{r} \quad \therefore \text{BD} = r\sin\theta\right]$$

$$= \frac{1}{2} r^2 \tan\theta \qquad \left[\because \text{in } \Delta\text{AOC } \tan\theta = \frac{\text{AC}}{\text{OA}} = \frac{\text{AC}}{r}\right]$$

$$\Rightarrow \quad \text{AC} = r\tan\theta$$

It is clear from figure that area of Δ AOB < area of sector AOB < area of Δ AOC

$$\therefore \quad \frac{1}{2} r^2 \sin\theta < \frac{1}{2} r^2\theta < \frac{1}{2} r^2 \tan\theta$$

or
$$1 < \frac{\theta}{\sin\theta} < \frac{1}{\cos\theta} \qquad \left[\text{dividing by } \frac{1}{2} r^2 \sin\theta\right]$$

or
$$1 > \frac{\sin\theta}{\theta} > \cos\theta$$

$$\therefore \quad \underset{\theta\to 0}{\text{Lt}}\, 1 \geq \underset{\theta\to 0}{\text{Lt}} \frac{\sin\theta}{\theta} \geq \underset{\theta\to 0}{\text{Lt}} \cos\theta$$

when area of θ → 0, ΔAOB, sector AOB and ΔAOC will be equal.

or
$$1 \geq \underset{\theta\to 0}{\text{Lt}} \frac{\sin 0}{\theta} \geq 1 \quad \left(\because \underset{\theta\to 0}{\text{Lt}} \cos\theta = 1\right)$$

Hence
$$\underset{\theta\to 0}{\text{Lt}} \frac{\sin 0}{\theta} = 1 \qquad \text{(i)}$$

Case II. θ < 0 when θ in negative.

Let θ = – α, where $\alpha > 0$, then θ → 0, $\alpha \to 0$

Now
$$\underset{\theta\to 0}{\text{Lt}} \frac{\sin\theta}{\theta} = \underset{\alpha\to 0}{\text{Lt}} \frac{\sin(-\alpha)}{-\alpha}$$

$$= \underset{\alpha\to 0}{\text{Lt}} \frac{-\sin\alpha}{-\alpha}$$

$$= \underset{\alpha\to 0}{\text{Lt}} \frac{\sin\alpha}{\alpha} = 1$$

4. $\underset{\theta\to 0}{\text{Lt}} \dfrac{\theta}{\sin\theta} = 1$

Proof :
$$\underset{\theta\to 0}{\text{Lt}} \frac{\theta}{\sin\theta} = \underset{\theta\to 0}{\text{Lt}} \frac{1}{\dfrac{\sin\theta}{\theta}}$$

$$= \frac{1}{\underset{\theta\to 0}{\text{Lt}} \dfrac{\sin\theta}{\theta}} = \frac{1}{1} = 1$$

5. $\underset{\theta\to 0}{\text{Lt}}\frac{\tan\theta}{\theta} = 1$, where θ is in radian.

Proof : $\underset{\theta\to 0}{\text{Lt}}\frac{\tan\theta}{\theta} = \underset{\theta\to 0}{\text{Lt}}\frac{\sin\theta}{\cos\theta}.\frac{1}{\theta}$

$$= \underset{\theta\to 0}{\text{Lt}}\left(\frac{\sin\theta}{\theta}-\frac{1}{\cos\theta}\right)$$

$$= \underset{\theta\to 0}{\text{Lt}}\frac{\sin\theta}{\theta}.\underset{\theta\to 0}{\text{Lt}}\left(\frac{1}{\cos\theta}\right)$$

$$= 1.\frac{1}{\underset{\theta\to 0}{\text{Lt}}\cos\theta} = 1.\frac{1}{1} = 1$$

$$\left[\because \underset{\theta\to 0}{\text{Lt}}\frac{\sin\theta}{\theta} = 1\right]$$

6. $\underset{\theta\to 0}{\text{Lt}}\frac{\theta}{\tan\theta} = 1$

Proof : $\underset{\theta\to 0}{\text{Lt}}\frac{\theta}{\tan\theta} = \underset{\theta\to 0}{\text{Lt}}\frac{1}{\frac{\tan\theta}{\theta}}$

$$= \frac{1}{\underset{\theta\to 0}{\text{Lt}}\frac{\tan\theta}{\theta}} = \frac{1}{1} = 1$$

7. Use the following formula if necessary :

(a) $\log(1+x) = x - \frac{x^2}{2} + \frac{x^3}{3} - \frac{x^4}{4} + \ldots \text{to}\,\infty$, where $-1 < x \le 1$

(b) $\log(1-x) = -x - \frac{x^2}{2} - \frac{x^3}{3} - \frac{x^4}{4} \ldots \text{to}\,\infty$, where $-1 \le x < 1$

(c) $e^x = 1 + \frac{x}{\lfloor 1} + \frac{x^2}{\lfloor 2} - \frac{x^3}{\lfloor 3} + \ldots \text{to}\,\infty$, for all x

(d) $e^{-x} = 1 - \frac{x}{\lfloor 1} + \frac{x^2}{\lfloor 2} - \frac{x^3}{\lfloor 3} + \ldots \text{to}\,\infty$, valid for all x.

Derivability : Let $y = f(x)$ be a function of x, then corresponding to each value x of domain of definition of $f(x)$ there will be unique value of y depending on x.

Now $y = f(x)$ ...(i)

Let δx be a small change in x and δy be the corresponding change in y, then

$y + \delta y = f(x + \delta x)$ ...(ii)

Subtracting (i) from (ii), we get

$$\delta y = f(x+\delta x) - f(x)$$

$$\therefore \quad \frac{\delta y}{\delta x} = \frac{f(x+\delta x)-f(x)}{\delta x}$$

$$\underset{\delta x\to 0}{\text{Lt}}\frac{\delta y}{\delta x} = \underset{\delta x\to 0}{\text{Lt}}\frac{f(x+\delta x)-f(x)}{\delta x}$$

$$= \underset{n\to 0}{\text{Lt}}\frac{f(x+h)-f(x)}{n}$$

where $n = \delta x$

If $\underset{\delta x\to 0}{\text{Lt}}\frac{\delta y}{\delta x}$ *i.e.* $\underset{\delta x\to 0}{\text{Lt}}\frac{f(x+\delta x)-f(x)}{\delta x}$ exists (*i.e.* its value is a definite unique number, then we say that $f(x)$ is differentiable or derivable with respect to x and in this case $\underset{\delta x\to 0}{\text{Lt}}\frac{\delta y}{\delta x}$ is called the d.c. or derivative of y of $f(x)$ w.r.t. x and is denoted by $\frac{dy}{dx}$ or $\frac{df(x)}{dx}$, $f'(x)$ or D $f(x)$ or y' or y_1.

$$\text{Thus} \quad \frac{dy}{dx} = \underset{\delta x\to 0}{\text{Lt}}\frac{\delta y}{\delta x}$$

$$\text{i.e.} \quad f'(x) = \underset{\delta x\to 0}{\text{Lt}}\frac{f(x+\delta x)-f(x)}{\delta x}$$

Provided the limit exists.

We say that $\frac{dy}{dx}$ is the differential coefficient of y with respect to x.

Differential Coefficient or Derivative of a Function

By definition d.c. of $f(x)$ w.r.t. x *i.e.*

The differential coefficient of $f(x)$ for any particular value a of x is denoted by $f'(a)$.

Hence d.c. of $f(x)$ at $x = a$

$$\text{i.e.} \quad f'(a) = \underset{h\to 0}{\text{Lt}}\frac{f(a+h)-f(a)}{h}$$

Provided the limit exists.

If $h < 0$ and $h \to 0$, then $\underset{h\to 0-0}{\text{Lt}}\frac{f(a+h)-f(a)}{h}$ is called left hand derivative of $f(x)$ at $x = 0$ and is denoted by $f'(a-0)$.

If $h > 0$ and $h \to 0$, then $= \underset{h\to 0^+}{\text{Lt}}\frac{f(a+h)-f(a)}{h}$ is called right hand derivative of $f(x)$ at $x = a$ and is denoted by $f'(a+0)$.

$$\text{Thus} \quad f'(a-0) = \underset{h\to 0^-}{\text{Lt}}\frac{f(a+h)-f(a)}{h}$$

$$\text{and} \quad f'(a+0) = \underset{h\to 0^+}{\text{Lt}}\frac{f(a+h)-f(a)}{h}$$

Clearly $f(x)$ is differentiable at $x = a$ if and only if (iii)

$$f'(a-0) = f'(a+0) = l_1$$

An Important Formula

To find the Differential Coefficient of x^n w.r.t. x

or Prove that $\frac{d(x^n)}{dx} = nx^{n-1}$

Proof : Let $y = x^n$ ...(i)

Let δx be a small change in x and δy be the corresponding change in y

then $y + \delta y = (x + \delta x)^n$ ...(ii)

Subtracting (i) from (ii), we get

$$\delta y = (x+\delta x)^n - x^n$$

$$= x^n\left(1+\frac{\delta x}{x}\right)^n - x^n$$

$$= x^n\left[\left\{1+\frac{n}{\underline{|1}}\cdot\frac{\delta x}{x}+\frac{n(n-1)}{\underline{|2}}\left(\frac{\delta x}{x}\right)^2+\ldots\right\}-1\right]$$

(From Binomial Theorem)

or $$\delta y = n.\frac{\delta x}{x} - x^n\left(\frac{1}{\underline{|1}}+\frac{n-1}{\underline{|2}}\cdot\frac{\delta x}{x}+\ldots\right)$$

$$\therefore \quad \frac{\delta y}{\delta x} = nx^{n-1}\left(1+\frac{n-1}{\underline{|2}}\cdot\frac{\delta x}{x}+\ldots\right)$$

$$\therefore \quad \underset{\delta x\to 0}{\text{Lt}}\frac{\delta y}{\delta x} = \underset{\delta x\to 0}{\text{Lt}}\, nx^{n-1}\left(1+\frac{n-1}{\underline{|2}}\cdot\frac{\delta x}{x}+\ldots\right)$$

Hence $\dfrac{dy}{dx} = nx^{n-1}$ or $\dfrac{d'(x^n)}{dx} = nx^{n-1}$

Some Important Results

To find the differential coefficient of x^n w.r.t. x :

Formula : $\boxed{\dfrac{d}{dx}(x^n) = nx^{n-1}}$

1. $\dfrac{d}{dx}(x^3) = 3.x^{3-1} = 3x^2$
2. $\dfrac{d}{dx}(x^2) = 2.x^{2-1} = 2x$
3. $\dfrac{d}{dx}(x) = \dfrac{d}{dx}(x^1) = 1.x^{1-1} = 1.x^0 = 1\times 1 = 1$
4. $\dfrac{d}{dx}\left(\dfrac{1}{x}\right) = \dfrac{d}{dx}(x^{-1}) = -1.\,x^{-1-1} = 1.x^{-2} = \dfrac{-1}{x^2}$
5. $\dfrac{d}{dx}(\sqrt{x}) = \dfrac{d}{dx}(x^{1/2}) = \dfrac{1}{2}x^{1/2-1} = \dfrac{1}{2}x^{-1/2}$

$$= \frac{1}{2x^{1/2}} = \frac{1}{2\sqrt{x}}$$

$\boxed{a^x = e^{x\log_e a}}$

Proof :

Let $\log_e a^x = y$

$\Rightarrow \quad a^x = e^y$

$\Rightarrow \quad a^x = e^{\log_e a^x} = e^{x\log_e a}$ **Proved**

If	$\log x_a = \text{N}$
then	$x = \log_a \text{N}$

To Find the Differential Coefficient of e^x w.r.t. x

Or prove that

$$\frac{d(e^x)}{dx} = e^x$$

Proof :

Let $\quad y = e^x \qquad \ldots$ (i)

Let δx be small change in x and δy be the corresponding change in y, then

$$y+\delta y = e^{x+\delta x} \qquad \ldots\text{(ii)}$$

Subtracting (i) from (ii), we get

$$\delta y = e^{x+\delta x} - e^x$$

$$= e^x.e^{\delta x} - e^x$$

$$= e^x(e^{\delta x}-1)$$

$$= e^x\left[\left\{1+\frac{\delta x}{\underline{|1}}+\frac{\delta x^2}{\underline{|2}}+\frac{\delta x^3}{\underline{|3}}+\ldots\right\}-1\right]$$

$$= e^x\delta x\left(\frac{1}{\underline{|1}}+\frac{\delta x}{\underline{|2}}+\frac{\delta x^2}{\underline{|3}}+\ldots\right)$$

$$\left(\because e^x = 1+\frac{x}{\underline{|1}}+\frac{x^2}{\underline{|2}}+\frac{x^2}{3}\right)$$

$$\therefore \quad \frac{\delta y}{\delta x} = e^x\left(\frac{1}{\underline{|1}}+\frac{\delta x}{\underline{|2}}+\frac{\delta x^2}{\underline{|3}}+\ldots\right)$$

$$\therefore \quad \underset{\delta x\to 0}{\text{Lt}}\frac{\delta y}{\delta x} = \underset{\delta x\to 0}{\text{Lt}}\, e^x\left(\frac{1}{\underline{|1}}+\frac{\delta x}{\underline{|2}}+\frac{\delta x^2}{\underline{|3}}+\ldots\right)$$

$$= e^x$$

$$\therefore \quad \frac{dy}{dx} = e^x$$

or $$\frac{d(e^x)}{dx} = e^x$$

To Find Differential Coefficient of $\log_e x$ w.r.t. x

or prove that $\dfrac{d\,(\log x)}{dx} = \dfrac{1}{x}$

Proof : Let $\quad y = \log x \qquad \ldots$(i)

Let δx be a small change in x and δy be the corresponding change in y, then

$$y+\delta y = \log(x+\delta x) \qquad \ldots\text{(ii)}$$

Subtracting (i) form (ii), we get

$$\delta y = \log(x+\delta x) - \log x$$

$$= \log\left(\frac{x+\delta x}{x}\right)$$

$$= \log\left(1+\frac{\delta x}{x}\right)$$

$$= \frac{\frac{\delta x}{x}}{1} - \frac{\left(\frac{\delta x}{x}\right)^2}{2} + \frac{\left(\frac{\delta x}{x}\right)^3}{3} - \ldots$$

$$\because \log(1+x) = x - \frac{1}{2}x^2 + \frac{1}{3}x^3 + \ldots$$

$$\therefore \quad dy = \frac{\delta x}{x}\left\{\frac{1}{1} - \frac{1}{2}\frac{\delta x}{x} + \frac{1}{3}\left(\frac{\delta x}{x}\right)^2 \ldots\right\}$$

$$\Rightarrow \quad \frac{\delta y}{\delta x} = \frac{1}{x}\left\{\frac{1}{1} - \frac{1}{2}\frac{\delta x}{x} + \frac{1}{3}\left(\frac{\delta x}{x}\right)^2 \ldots\right\}$$

$$\therefore \quad \underset{x\to 0}{\text{Lt}}\frac{\delta y}{\delta x} = \underset{\delta x\to 0}{\text{Lt}}\frac{1}{x}\left\{\frac{1}{1} - \frac{1}{2}\cdot\frac{\delta x}{x} + \frac{1}{3}\left(\frac{\delta x}{x}\right)^2 \ldots\right\}$$

$$= \frac{1}{x}$$

$$\therefore \quad \frac{dy}{dx} = \frac{1}{x} \text{ or } \frac{d(\log x)}{dx} = \frac{1}{x}$$

FORMULA : AT A GLANCE

1. $\frac{dx^n}{dx} = nx^{n-1}$ 2. $\frac{de^x}{dx} = e^n$ 3. $\frac{d \log x}{dx} = \frac{1}{x}$
4. $\frac{da^x}{dx} = a^x \log a$ [where a = constant]
5. $\frac{d(c)}{dx} = 0$, where c = Constant 6. $\frac{dv}{dx} = 1$
7. $\frac{d(u \pm v)}{dx} = \frac{du}{dx} \pm \frac{dv}{dx}$
8. $\frac{du \times v}{dx} = \frac{udv}{dv} + \frac{vdu}{dx}$
9. $\frac{d\frac{u}{v}}{dx} = \frac{\frac{vdu}{dv} - \frac{udv}{dx}}{v^2}$

SOLVED EXAMPLES

✎ Type I

Example 1

Find the differential coefficient of $5x^3$ from the first principle.

Solution :

Let $y = 5x^3$ ...(i)

Let δx be a small change in x and δy be the corresponding change in y,

then $y + \delta y = 5(x + \delta x)^3$ ...(ii)

Subtracting (i) from (ii), we get

$$\delta y = 5[(x + \delta x)^3 - x^3]$$
$$= 5(x^3 + 3x^2 \delta x + 3x\delta x^2 + \delta x^3 - x^3)$$
$$= 5\delta x(3x^2 + 3x\delta x + \delta x^2)$$
$$\therefore \quad \frac{\delta y}{\delta x} = 5(3x^2 + 3x\delta x + \delta x^2)$$
$$\therefore \quad \underset{\delta x \to 0}{\text{Lt}} \frac{\delta y}{\delta x} = \underset{\delta x \to 0}{\text{Lt}} 5(3x^2 + 3x\delta x + \delta x^2)$$
$$\therefore \quad \frac{dy}{dx} = \mathbf{15x^2}$$ **Ans.**

Example 2

Find the differential coefficient of $\frac{1}{\sqrt{x}}$ from definition.

Solution :

Let $y = \frac{1}{\sqrt{x}}$ ...(i)

Let δx be a small change in x and δy be the corresponding change in y

then $y + \delta y = \frac{1}{\sqrt{x + \delta x}}$ ...(ii)

Subtracting (i) from (ii), we get

$$\delta y = \frac{1}{\sqrt{x+\delta x}} - \frac{1}{\sqrt{x}} = \frac{\sqrt{x} - \sqrt{x+\delta x}}{\sqrt{x}\sqrt{x+\delta x}}$$
$$= \frac{(\sqrt{x} - \sqrt{x+\delta x})(\sqrt{x} + \sqrt{x+\delta x})}{\sqrt{x}\sqrt{x+\delta x}(\sqrt{x} + \sqrt{x+\delta x})}$$
$$= \frac{x - (x + \delta x)}{\sqrt{x}\sqrt{x+\delta x}(\sqrt{x} + \sqrt{x+\delta x})}$$
$$\therefore \quad \frac{\delta y}{\delta x} = \frac{-1}{\sqrt{x}\sqrt{x+\delta x}(\sqrt{x} + \sqrt{x+\delta x})}$$
$$\therefore \quad \underset{\delta x \to 0}{\text{Lt}} \frac{\delta y}{\delta x} = \underset{\delta x \to 0}{\text{Lt}} \frac{-1}{\sqrt{x}\sqrt{x+\delta x}\,(\sqrt{x} + \sqrt{x+\delta x})}$$
$$= \frac{-1}{\sqrt{x}.\sqrt{x}(\sqrt{x} + \sqrt{x})}$$
$$\text{Hence} \quad \frac{dy}{dx} = -\frac{1}{x.\,2\sqrt{x}}$$
$$= -\frac{\mathbf{1}}{\mathbf{2x^{3/2}}}$$ **Ans.**

9.5 SOME RULES FOR DIFFERENTIATION

Find the Differential Coefficient of a Constant

Or Prove that $\frac{d(c)}{dx} = 0$, where c is constant

Proof : Let $y = f(x) = c$ for every value of x ...(i)

Let δx be a small change in x and δy be the corresponding chnage in y, then since for each value of x, y has the same value c.

$\therefore \quad y + \delta y = c$ ...(ii)

Subtracting (i) from (ii), we get

$$\delta y = 0$$
$$\therefore \quad \frac{\delta y}{\delta x} = \frac{0}{\delta x} = 0$$
$$\because \quad \underset{\delta x \to 0}{\text{Lt}} \frac{\delta y}{\delta x} = 0$$
$$\text{Hence} \quad \frac{dy}{dx} = 0$$
$$\therefore \quad \frac{d(c)}{dx} = 0$$

Thus the differential coefficient of constant is zero.

Find the d.c. of the product of a Constant and a Differentiable Function

Or Prove that $\frac{d}{dx}(cu) = c.\frac{du}{dx}$

Where u is a function of x and c be a constant.

Proof : Let $y = cu$ ...(i)

Therefore y will be also a function of x, let δx be a small change in x and δu and δy be the corresponding changes in u and y respectively, then

$y + \delta y = c(u + \delta u)$ ...(ii)

Subtracting (i) from (ii) we get

$$\delta y = c\delta u$$

$$\therefore \quad \frac{\delta y}{\delta x} = c.\frac{\delta u}{\delta x}$$

$$\therefore \quad \underset{\delta x\to 0}{\text{Lt}} \frac{\delta y}{\delta x} = \underset{\delta x\to 0}{\text{Lt}}\, c.\frac{\delta u}{\delta x} = c.\underset{\delta x\to 0}{\text{Lt}} \frac{\delta u}{\delta x}$$

Hence $\frac{dy}{dx} = c.\frac{du}{dx}$

$$\Rightarrow \quad \frac{d}{dx}(cu) = c.\frac{du}{dx}$$

Example 3

If $y = 3x^5$, then find $\frac{dy}{dx}$.

Solution :

$$y = 3x^5$$

$$\therefore \quad \frac{dy}{dx} = 3\frac{d}{dx}(x^5)$$

$$= 3\,(5x^{5-1})$$

$$= 15x^4 \quad \textbf{Ans.}$$

$\left[\textbf{Formula}: \frac{d}{dx}(cu) = c.\frac{du}{dx} \text{ and } \frac{d}{dx}(x^n) = nx^{n-1}\right]$

Example 4

If $y = 2\sqrt{x}$, then find $\frac{dy}{dx}$.

Solution :

$$y = 2\sqrt{x} = 2x^{1/2}$$

$$\therefore \quad \frac{dy}{dx} = 2\frac{d}{dx}(x^{1/2})$$

$$= 2.\left(\frac{1}{2}x^{\frac{1}{2}-1}\right) = x^{-1/2} = \frac{1}{x^{1/2}}$$

$$= \frac{1}{\sqrt{x}}$$

Find Differential Coefficient of the Sum of two Differentiable Functions

Prove that $\frac{d(u+v)}{dx} = \frac{du}{dx} + \frac{dv}{dx}$

Or, Since u and v are functions of x, therefore y is also a function of x.

Proof : Let $y = u + v$ ...(i)

Let δx be a small change in x and δu, δv and δy be the corresponding changes in u, v and y respectively, then

$$y + \delta y = (u + \delta u) + (v + \delta v) \quad ...(ii)$$

Subtracting (i) from (ii), we get

$$\delta y = \delta u + \delta v$$

$$\frac{\delta y}{\delta x} = \frac{\delta u}{\delta x} + \frac{\delta v}{\delta x}$$

$$\therefore \quad \underset{\delta x\to 0}{\text{Lt}} \frac{\delta y}{\delta x} = \underset{\delta x\to 0}{\text{Lt}} \frac{\delta u}{\delta x} + \underset{\delta x\to 0}{\text{Lt}} \frac{\delta v}{\delta x}$$

$$\frac{dy}{dx} = \frac{du}{dx} + \frac{dv}{dx}$$

Hence $\frac{d(u+v)}{dx} = \frac{du}{dx} + \frac{dv}{dx}$

Corollary :

(i) If $y = u - v$ then $\frac{dy}{dx} = \frac{du}{dx} - \frac{dv}{dx}$.

(ii) If $y = u \pm v \pm w \pm$ ....,where u, v, w are all differentiable functions of x, then

$$\frac{dy}{dx} = \frac{du}{dx} \pm \frac{dv}{dx} \pm \frac{dw}{dx} \pm ...$$

Example 5

If $y = x^4 + 4x^3 + 5x - 6$, then find $\frac{dy}{dx}$.

Solution :

$$y = x^4 + 4x^3 + 5x - 6$$

$$\therefore \quad \frac{dy}{dx} = \frac{d}{dx}(x^4 + 4x^3 + 5x - 6)$$

$$= \frac{d}{dx}(x^4) + \frac{d}{dx}(4x^3) + \frac{d}{dx}(5x) - \frac{d}{dx}(6)$$

$$= \frac{d}{dx}(x^4) + 4.\frac{d}{dx}(x^3) + 5.\frac{d}{dx}(x) - \frac{d}{dx}(6)$$

$$= 4x^3 + 4.3x^2 + 5.1 - 0$$

$$= \mathbf{4x^3 + 12x^2 + 5} \quad \textbf{Ans.}$$

Find Differential Coefficient of the Product of Two Differentiable Functions

Prove that $\frac{d(uv)}{dx} = v.\frac{du}{dx} + u\frac{dv}{dx}$

Or, When u and v be two differentiable functions of x.

Proof : Let $y = uv$ ...(i)

Since u and v are functions of x therefore, y is also a function of x.

Let δx be a small change in x and δu, δv and δy be the corresponding changes in u, v and y respectively, then

$$y + \delta y = (u + \delta u)(v + \delta v)$$

$$= uv + v\delta u + u\delta v + \delta u\,\delta v \quad ...(ii)$$

Subtracting (i) form (ii), we get

$$\delta y = v\delta u + u\delta v + \delta u\,\delta v$$

$$\therefore \quad \frac{\delta y}{\delta x} = \frac{\delta u}{\delta x} + u.\frac{\delta v}{\delta x} + \frac{\delta u.\delta v}{\delta x}$$

$$\therefore \underset{\delta x\to 0}{\text{Lt}} \frac{\delta y}{\delta x} = \underset{\delta x\to 0}{\text{Lt}}\, v.\frac{\delta u}{\delta x} + \underset{\delta x\to 0}{\text{Lt}}\, u.\frac{\delta v}{\delta x} + \underset{\delta x\to 0}{\text{Lt}} \frac{\delta u}{\delta x}.\frac{\delta v}{\delta x}$$

$$= \underset{\delta x\to 0}{\text{Lt}}\, v.\frac{\delta u}{\delta x} + \underset{\delta x\to 0}{\text{Lt}}\, u.\frac{\delta v}{\delta x} + \underset{\delta x\to 0}{\text{Lt}} \frac{\delta u}{\delta x}.\underset{\delta x\to 0}{\text{Lt}} \frac{\delta v}{\delta x}$$

$$= v.\frac{du}{dx} + u.\frac{dv}{dx} + \frac{du}{dx}.\frac{dv}{dx} = 0$$

$$\therefore \quad \frac{dy}{dx} = v.\frac{du}{dx} + u.\frac{dv}{dx}$$

$$\Rightarrow \quad \frac{d(uv)}{dx} = v.\frac{du}{dx} + u.\frac{dv}{dx}$$

$$= u.\frac{dv}{dx} + v.\frac{du}{dx}$$

Thus d.c. of the product of two functions

= First Function × d.c. of second function

+ Second function × d.c. of first function.

Example 6

If $y = x^4 \log x$, then find $\frac{dy}{dx}$.

Solution :

$$y = x^4 \log x$$

$$\therefore \quad \frac{dy}{dx} = x^4 \frac{d}{dx}(\log x) + \log x \times \frac{d}{dx}(x^4)$$

$$= x^4\left(\frac{1}{x}\right) + \log x\,(4x^{4-1})$$

$$= x^3 + 4x^3 \log x \qquad \textbf{Ans.}$$

Example 7

If $y = (x^2 + 1)\,x^3$, then find $\frac{dy}{dx}$.

Solution :

$$y = (x^2 + 1)x^3$$

$$\therefore \quad \frac{dy}{dx} = (x^2+1)\frac{d}{dx}(x^3) + x^3\frac{d}{dx}(x^2+1)$$

$$= (x^2 + 1)(3x^{3-1}) + x^3(2x^{2-1} + 0)$$

$$= 3x^2(x^2 + 1) + 2x^3.x$$

$$= 3x^4 + 3x^2 + 2x^4 = 5x^4 + 3x^2 \quad \textbf{Ans.}$$

Find Differential Coefficient of the Quotient of Two Differentiable Functions

Prove that $\frac{d\left(\frac{u}{v}\right)}{dx} = \frac{v.\frac{du}{dx} - u.\frac{dv}{dx}}{v^2}$

Or, where u and v are two functions of x.

Proof : Let $\quad y = \frac{u}{v} \qquad$ ...(i)

Let δx be a small change in x and δu, δv and δy respectively

then $\quad y + \delta y = \frac{u+\delta u}{v+\delta v} \qquad$ ...(ii)

Subtracting (i) from (ii), we get

$$\delta y = \frac{u+\delta u}{v+\delta v} - \frac{u}{v}$$

$$= \frac{v(u+\delta u) - u(v+\delta v)}{v(v+\delta v)}$$

$$= \frac{v\delta u - u\delta v}{v^2 + v\delta v}$$

$$\therefore \quad \frac{\delta y}{\delta x} = \frac{v.\frac{\delta u}{\delta x} - u.\frac{\delta v}{\delta x}}{v^2 + v\delta v}$$

$$\Rightarrow \quad \underset{\delta x \to 0}{\text{Lt}} \frac{\delta y}{\delta x} = \underset{\delta x \to 0}{\text{Lt}} \frac{v.\frac{\delta u}{\delta x} - u.\frac{\delta v}{\delta x}}{v^2 + v\delta v}$$

$$\Rightarrow \quad \underset{\delta x \to 0}{\text{Lt}} \frac{\delta y}{\delta x} = \frac{\underset{\delta x \to 0}{\text{Lt}}\, v.\frac{\delta u}{\delta x} - \underset{\delta x \to 0}{\text{Lt}}\, u.\frac{\delta v}{\delta x}}{v^2 + \underset{\delta x \to 0}{\text{Lt}}\, v.\frac{\delta v}{\delta x}.\delta x}$$

$$= \frac{v.\frac{du}{dx} - u.\frac{dv}{dx}}{v^2}$$

$$\frac{dy}{dx} = \frac{v.\frac{du}{dx} - u.\frac{dv}{dx}}{v^2}$$

Thus the differential coefficient of the quotient of two differentiable funtion

$$= \frac{\text{Denominator} \times (\text{d.c. of numerator}) - \text{Number} \times (\text{d.c. of denominator})}{(\text{Denominator})^2}$$

Example 8

Find the d.c. of $\frac{e^x}{\log x}$ w.r.t. x.

Solution :

$$y = \frac{e^x}{\log x}$$

$$\therefore \quad \frac{dy}{dx} = \frac{d}{dx}\left(\frac{e^x}{\log x}\right)$$

$$= \frac{\log x\frac{d}{dx}(e^x) - e^x\frac{d}{dx}(\log x)}{(\log x)^2}$$

$$= \frac{\log x.e^x - e^x.\frac{1}{x}}{(\log x)^2}$$

$$= \frac{x.e^x \log x - e^x}{x(\log x)^2}$$

$$= \frac{e^x(x\log x - 1)}{x(\log x)^2}$$

Example 9

If $y = \frac{x^2 - x + 1}{x^2 + x + 1}$, then find $\frac{dy}{dx}$.

Solution :

$$y = \frac{x^2 - x + 1}{x^2 + x + 1}$$

$$\therefore \quad \frac{dy}{dx} = \frac{(x^2 - x + 1).\frac{dy}{dx}(x^2 - x + 1) - (x^2 - x + 1)\frac{d}{dx}(x^2 + x + 1)}{(x^2 + x + 1)^2}$$

$$= \frac{(x^2+x+1)(2x-1)-(x^2-x+1)(2x+1)}{(x^2+x+1)^2}$$

$$\Rightarrow \frac{dy}{dx} = \frac{(2x^3-x^2-x+2x-1)-(2x^3+x^2-2x^2-x+2x+1)}{(x^2+x+1)^2}$$

So $\frac{dy}{dx} = \frac{2x^2-2}{(x^2+x+1)^2}$ **Ans.**

Example 10

Find $\frac{d}{dx}\left(\frac{x+1}{x-1}\right)$.

Solution :

$$\frac{d}{dx}\left(\frac{x+1}{x-1}\right) = \frac{(x-1)\frac{d}{dx}(x+1)-(x+1)\frac{d}{dx}(x-1)}{(x-1)^2}$$

$$= \frac{(x-1)(1)-(x+1)(1)}{(x-1)^2}$$

$$\therefore \frac{d}{dx}\left(\frac{x+1}{x-1}\right) = \frac{x-1-x-1}{(x-1)^2} = \frac{-2}{(x-1)^2}$$

Example 11

Find $\frac{dy}{dx}$ if $y = \frac{3-x}{(x^2-3)}$.

Solution :

$$\therefore y = \frac{3-x}{(x^2-3)}$$

$$\therefore \frac{dy}{dx} = \frac{d(3-x)}{dx(x^2-3)}$$

$$= \frac{(x^2-3)\frac{d}{dx}(3-x)-(3-x)\frac{d}{dx}(x^2-3)}{(x^2-3)^2}$$

$$= \frac{(x^2-3)(0-1)-(3-x)(2x-0)}{(x^2-3)^2}$$

$$= \frac{-x^2+3-(6x-2x^2)}{(x^2-3)^2}$$

$$= \frac{-x^2+3-6x+2x^2}{(x^2-3)^2} = \frac{x^2-6x+3}{(x^2-3)^2}$$

Example 12

Differentiate $y = 5x^4 - 3x^3 + 1$ with respect to x. (*JAC*, 2023)

Solution :

$$\frac{dy}{dx} = 20x^3 - 9x^2$$

Exercise 9 (A)

Find the differential coefficient of the following from the first principle :

✎ Type I

1. $4x^5$
2. x^3
3. $3x^{-5}$
4. $5x^4$
5. $4x$
6. (A) $x^{1/3}$

(B) (i) $6\sqrt{x}$, (ii) x^{-3}, (iii) x^{m+n} (iv) $\frac{1}{x^{m+1}}$.

✎ Type II

7. $3x^5 + 3x^3 - 5$
8. $2x^2 - 3x^3$
9. $5x^4 - 3x^3 + 1$
10. $(1 + 3x^2)(2x^3 - 1)$
11. $(3x - 4)(x^2 - 6x + 7)$
12. $(x^3 + 6x^2)(x^2 - x)$
13. $\frac{(x+1)(2x-1)}{x-3}$
14. $\frac{x^2-7x}{x-5}$
15. $\frac{x-1}{\sqrt{x+1}}$
16. If $y = (x-a)(x-b)$, then find the value of x for which $\frac{dy}{dx} = 0$.

[**Hint:** $y = (x-a)(x-b)$

$$\therefore \frac{dy}{dx} = (x-a)\frac{d}{dx}(x-b) + (x-b)\frac{d}{dx}(x-a)$$

or $0 = (x-a)(1-0) + (x-b)(1-0)$

or $0 = (x-a) + (x-b)$

or $a + b = 2x$

$\Rightarrow x = \frac{a+b}{2}$]

17. If $f(x) = \frac{x-4}{21\sqrt{x}}$, then find $f'(4)$.

[**Hint:** $\because f(x) = \frac{x-4}{21\sqrt{x}} = \frac{1}{21}\left\{\frac{x-4}{\sqrt{x}}\right\}$

$$\therefore f'(x) = \frac{1}{21}\left[\frac{\sqrt{x}\frac{d}{dx}(x-4)-(x-4)\frac{d}{dx}(\sqrt{x})}{(\sqrt{x})^2}\right]$$

$$= \frac{1}{21}\left[\frac{\sqrt{x}(1-0)-(x-4)\frac{1}{2\sqrt{x}}}{x}\right]$$

Putting $x = 4$

$$\therefore f'(4) = \frac{1}{21}\left[\frac{2-(4-4)\times\frac{1}{2\times 2}}{4}\right]$$

$$= \frac{1}{21}\left[\frac{2}{4}\right] = \frac{1}{42}]$$

18. Differentiate with respect to x of the following function : $\frac{x^2+1}{x^2}$ (*JAC*, 2019)
19. Differentiate with respect to x : $\frac{x^2}{x^2+1}$
20. Differentiate with respect to x of the following function :
    (i) $(x^2 - 5x + 6)(x - 3)$ (*JAC*, 2020)
    (ii) $\left(\sqrt{x}\times\frac{1}{\sqrt{x}}\right)^2$
21. Differentiate with respect to x : $\frac{(x-3)(x+2)}{x}$
22. Differentiate $y = 5x^6 + x^2$ with respect to x) (*JAC*, 2025)

Answers

1. $20x^4$ 2. $3x^2$ 3. $-15x^{-6}$ 4. $20x^3$ 5. 4

6. (A) $\frac{1}{3}x^{-2/3}$

(B) (i) $\frac{3}{\sqrt{x}}$, (ii) $\frac{-3}{x^4}$, (iii) $(m+n)x^{m+n-1}$, (iv) $\frac{-(m+1)}{x^{m+2}}$

7. $15x^4+9x^2$ 8. $4x-9x^2$ 9. $20x^3-9x^2$

10. $6x(5x^3+x-1)$ 11. $9x^2-44x+45$

12. $5x^4+20x^3-18x^2$ 13. $\frac{2(x^2-6x-1)}{(x-3)^2}$ 14. $\frac{x^2-10x+35}{(x-5)^2}$

15. $\frac{x+3}{2(x+1)^{3/2}}$ 16. $\frac{a+b}{2}$ 17. $\frac{1}{42}$

18. $\frac{-2}{x^3}$ 19. $\frac{2x}{(x^2+1)^2}$

20. (i) $3x^2-16x+21$ (ii) $1-\frac{1}{x^2}$ 21. $1+\frac{6}{x^2}$

22. $30x^5+2x$

(9.6) DIFFERENTIAL COEFFICIENT OF FUNCTION OF FUNCTION

9.6.1 Meaning of Function of Function

To understood the meaning of function of function we take the following example :

Let $y = (x^3+1)^5$

Here x^3+1 is a function of x and if we take $x^3+1 = u$, then $y = u^5$

So y is a function of u and u is the function of x.

Thus y is a function of function.

Example 1. Let

$$y = \cos^3 x = (\cos x)^3$$

Here y is function of $\cos x$ and $\cos x$ is a function of x.

So y is a function of function.

Differential Coefficiential of Function of Function

Let y be the differentiable function of u and u be the differentiable function of x, then

$$\frac{dy}{dx} = \frac{dy}{du}\times\frac{du}{dx}$$

Proof. Let $y = f(u)$ and $u = \phi(x)$, then y is a function of x. Let δx be a small change in x and δu and δy be the corresponding changes in u and y respectively, then

$$\delta x \to 0$$

$$\Rightarrow \quad \delta u \to 0 \qquad [\because \delta u = \phi(x+dx)-\phi(x)]$$

Now $$\frac{\delta y}{\delta x} = \frac{\delta y}{\delta u}\times\frac{\delta u}{\delta x}$$

$$\therefore \quad \underset{\delta x\to 0}{\text{Lt}}\frac{\delta y}{\delta x} = \underset{\delta x\to 0}{\text{Lt}}\left(\frac{\delta y}{\delta u}\times\frac{\delta u}{\delta x}\right)$$

$$= \underset{\delta x\to 0}{\text{Lt}}\frac{\delta y}{\delta x}.\underset{\delta x\to 0}{\text{Lt}}\frac{\delta u}{\delta x} \qquad (\because \delta x\to 0, \delta u\to 0)$$

$$\therefore \quad \boxed{\frac{\delta y}{\delta x} = \frac{\delta y}{\delta x}.\frac{\delta u}{\delta x}}$$

Corollary : If $y = f(u)$, $u = \phi(v)$ and $u = \psi(x)$

Then $$\boxed{\frac{dy}{dx} = \frac{dy}{du}\times\frac{dy}{dv}\times\frac{dv}{dx}}$$

9.6.2 Differential Coefficient of Inverse Function

Let $y = f(x)$ be a differentiable function in its domain of defnition. Let inverse function of $y = f(x)$ exist and let it be $x = \phi(y)$.

Let δx be a small change in x and δy be the corresponding change in y. Change in x determined by $x = \phi(y)$ will be δx.

Now $\quad y = f(x) \quad$ ...(i)

$\therefore \quad y+\delta y = f(x+\delta x) \quad$ ...(ii)

By (ii) – (i), $\quad \delta y = f(x+\delta x)-f(x)$

When $\delta x \to 0$, then $\delta y \to 0$

Now $$\frac{\delta y}{\delta x}.\frac{\delta x}{\delta y} = 1$$

$$\Rightarrow \quad \frac{\delta x}{\delta y} = \frac{1}{\left(\frac{\delta y}{\delta x}\right)}$$

$$\Rightarrow \quad \underset{\delta y\to 0}{\text{Lt}}\frac{\delta x}{\delta y} = \frac{1}{\underset{\delta x\to 0}{\text{Lt}}\frac{\delta y}{\delta x}} \quad (\text{when } \delta x\to 0, \delta y\to 0)$$

$$\Rightarrow \quad \frac{dx}{dy} = \frac{1}{\frac{dy}{dx}}$$

SOLVED EXAMPLES

✎ Type II

Example 1(A)

If $y = (x^3+3x)^2$, then find $\frac{dy}{dx}$.

Solution :

Method I :

Let $\quad u = x^3+3x$

then $\quad y = u^2$ and $u = x^3+3x$

$$\therefore \quad \frac{dy}{du} = 2u \text{ and } \frac{du}{dx} = 3x^2+3$$

$$\because \quad \frac{dy}{dx} = \frac{dy}{du}.\frac{du}{dx}$$

$$= 2u(3x^2+3)$$

$$= 2(x^3+3x)(3x^2+3)$$

$$= 2(3x^5+3x^3+9x^3+9x)$$

$$= 6x^5+24x^3+18x \qquad \textbf{Ans.}$$

Method II :

$$y = (x^3+3x)^2$$

$$\therefore \quad \frac{dy}{dx} = \frac{d(x^3+3x)^2}{dx}$$

$$= \frac{d(x^3+3x)^2}{d(x^3+3x)} \times \frac{d(x^3+3x)}{dx}$$
$$= 2(x^3+3x) \times (3x^2+3)$$
$$= 2(3x^5+3x^3+9x^3+9x)$$
$$= 6x^5+24x^3+18x$$ **Ans.**

Example 1(B)

Differentiate with respect to x : $y = 30 - 4x - x^3$. (*JAC, 2024*)

Solution :

Differentiating each term

$$\frac{dy}{dx} = \frac{d}{dx}(30-4x-x^3)$$
$$= \frac{d(30)}{dx} - 4.\frac{d(x)}{dx} - \frac{d(x^3)}{dx}$$
$$= 0 - 4 \times 1 - 3x^{3-1}$$
$$= -4 - 3x^2$$
$$= -(3x^2+4)$$ **Ans.**

Example 2

If $y = \sqrt{1+x^2}$, then find $\frac{dy}{dx}$. (*JAC, 2016*)

Solution

Method I :

$$y = \sqrt{1+x^2}$$

Let $u = 1+x^2$ then $y = \sqrt{u}$ and $u = 1+x^2$

$$\frac{dy}{dx} = \frac{dy}{du}.\frac{du}{dx}$$
$$= \frac{d}{du}(\sqrt{u})\frac{d}{dx}(1+x^2) \quad \left(\because \frac{d}{x}(x) = \frac{1}{2\sqrt{x}}\right)$$
$$= \left(\frac{1}{2}u^{-1/2}\right)(2x)\frac{1}{2\sqrt{u}}(2x)$$
$$= \frac{1}{2\sqrt{1+x^2}}.2x = \frac{x}{\sqrt{1+x^2}}$$ **Ans.**

Method II :

$$y = \sqrt{1+x^2}$$
$$\therefore \frac{dy}{dx} = \frac{d\sqrt{1+x^2}}{dx}$$
$$= \frac{d\sqrt{1+x^2}}{d(1+x^2)} \times \frac{d(1+x^2)}{dx}$$
$$= \frac{1}{2\sqrt{1+x^2}} \times 2x = \frac{x}{\sqrt{1+x^2}}$$ **Ans.**

Example 3

If $y = \log(\sqrt{x+a}+\sqrt{x+b})$, then find $\frac{dy}{dx}$.

Solution :

Method I :

$$y = \log(\sqrt{x+a}+\sqrt{x-b})$$

Let $u = \sqrt{x+a}+\sqrt{x-b}$

$\therefore$ $y = \log u$, and $u = (x+a)^{1/2} + (x-b)^{1/2}$

$$\therefore \frac{dy}{du} = \frac{1}{u}$$

and $$\frac{du}{dx} = \frac{1}{2}(x+a)^{-1/2} + \frac{1}{2}(x-b)^{-1/2}$$

$$\therefore \frac{dy}{dx} = \frac{dy}{du} \times \frac{du}{dx}$$
$$= \frac{1}{u} \times \frac{1}{2}\left[\frac{1}{\sqrt{x+a}} + \frac{1}{\sqrt{x-b}}\right]$$
$$= \frac{1}{\sqrt{x+a}+\sqrt{x-b}} \times \frac{1}{2}\left[\frac{1}{\sqrt{x+a}} + \frac{1}{\sqrt{x-b}}\right]$$
$$= \frac{1}{\sqrt{x+a}+\sqrt{x-b}} \times \frac{1}{2}\left\{\frac{\sqrt{x-b}+\sqrt{x+a}}{\sqrt{x+a}-\sqrt{x-b}}\right\}$$
$$= \frac{1}{2\sqrt{(x+a)(x-b)}}$$ **Ans.**

Method II :

$$y = \log(\sqrt{x+a}+\sqrt{x-b})$$
$$\therefore \frac{dy}{dx} = \frac{d}{dx}\log(\sqrt{x+a}+\sqrt{x-b})$$
$$= \frac{d\log(\sqrt{x+a}+\sqrt{x-b})}{d(\sqrt{x+a}+\sqrt{x-b})} \times \frac{d(\sqrt{x+a}+\sqrt{x-b})}{dx}$$
$$= \frac{1}{\sqrt{x+a}+\sqrt{x-b}} \times \left[\frac{d\sqrt{x+a}}{dx} + \frac{d\sqrt{x-b}}{dx}\right]$$
$$= \frac{1}{\sqrt{x+a}+\sqrt{x-b}}$$
$$\times \left[\frac{d\sqrt{x+a}}{d(x+a)} \times \frac{d(x+a)}{dx} + \frac{d\sqrt{x-b}}{d(x-b)} \times \frac{d(x-b)}{dx}\right]$$
$$= \frac{1}{\sqrt{x+a}+\sqrt{x-b}} \times \left[\frac{1}{2\sqrt{x+a}} \times 1 + \frac{1}{2\sqrt{x-b}} \times 1\right]$$
$$= \frac{1}{\sqrt{x+a}+\sqrt{x-b}} \times \left[\frac{\sqrt{x-b}+\sqrt{x+a}}{2\sqrt{x+a}.\sqrt{x-b}}\right]$$
$$= \frac{1}{2\sqrt{(x+a)(x-b)}}$$ **Ans.**

Example 4

If $y = \sqrt{x^2+ax+1}$, $\frac{dy}{dx}$, then find $\frac{dy}{dx}$.

Solution :

$$y = \sqrt{x^2+ax+1}$$
$$\therefore \frac{dy}{dx} = \frac{d}{dx}(\sqrt{x^2+ax+1})$$
$$= \frac{d(\sqrt{x^2+ax+1})}{d(x^2+ax+1)} \times \frac{d(x^2+ax+1)}{dx}$$

$$= \frac{1}{2\sqrt{x^2+ax+1}}(2x+a)$$

$$= \frac{2x+a}{2\sqrt{x^2+ax+1}}$$ **Ans.**

Example 5

Differentiate with respect to x :

$(1 + x^3)^7$.

Solution :

$$y = (1 + x^3)^7$$

Let $u = 1 + x^3$ then $y = u^7$

$\therefore \quad \frac{du}{dx} = 3x^2$ and $\frac{dy}{dx} = 7u^6$

$$\therefore \quad \frac{dy}{dx} = \frac{dy}{du}.\frac{du}{dx}$$

$$= 7u^6.3x^2$$

$$= 7(1 + x^3)^6 \times x^2$$

$$= 21x^2 (1 + x^3)^6$$ **Ans.**

Exercise 9 (B)

1. If $y = \log(x^2\sqrt{x^2+1})$, then find $\frac{dy}{dx}$.

2. If $y = \log\left(\frac{x+\sqrt{x^2+a^2}}{x-\sqrt{x^2+a^2}}\right)$, then find $\frac{dy}{dx}$.

3. If $y = (x^2 + 5x + 1)^5$ then find $\frac{dy}{dx}$.

4. If $y = (5x^2 + 7x + 3)^{2/5}$ then find $\frac{dy}{dx}$.

5. If $y = \sqrt{3x^3 - 7x}$, then find $\frac{dy}{dx}$.

6. If $y = (ax^n + b)^p$, then find $\frac{dy}{dx}$.

7. If $y = (3x^2 + 6x + 5)^{7/2}$, then find $\frac{dy}{dx}$.

8. If $y = \sqrt{5+2x-4x^5}$, then find $\frac{dy}{dx}$.

9. If $y = \frac{1}{\sqrt[3]{6x^5 - 7x^3 - 9}}$, then find $\frac{dy}{dx}$.

[**Hint:** $y = \frac{1}{\sqrt[3]{6x^5 - 7x^3 - 9}}$

$= (6x^5 - 7x^3 - 9)^{-1/3}$

$\therefore \quad \frac{dy}{dx} = \frac{d(6x^5-7x^3-9)^{-1/3}}{d(6x^5-7x^3-9)} \times \frac{d(6x^5-7x^3-9)}{dx}$

$= -\frac{1}{3}(6x^5 - 7x^3 - 9)^{-4/3} \times (30x^4 - 21x^2)$

$= -\frac{1}{3(6x^5-7x^3-9)^{4/3}} \times (3x^4 - 21x^2)$]

10. If $y = \sqrt{ax^2+bc+c}$ then find $\frac{dy}{dx}$.

Answers

1. $\frac{3x^2+2}{x(x^2+1)}$
2. $\frac{2}{\sqrt{x^2+a^2}}$
3. $5(x^2 + 5x + 1)^4 (2x + 5)$
4. $\frac{2}{5}(5x^2+7x+3) - \frac{3}{5}(10x+7)$
5. $\frac{9x^2-7x}{2\sqrt{3x^3-7x}}$
6. $anpx^{n-1}(ax^n + b)^{n-1}$
7. $21(x + 1)(3x^2 + 6x + 5)^{5/2}$
8. $\frac{1-10x^4}{\sqrt{5+2x-4x^5}}$
9. $-\frac{1}{3}\frac{30x^4-21x^2}{(6x^5-7x^3-9)^{4/3}}$
10. $2\frac{2ax+b}{\sqrt{ax^2+bx+c}}$

(9.7) DIFFERENTIATION OF IMPLICIT FUNCTIONS

Implicit Functions

If a relation between x and y is such that y cannot be expressed in terms of x, then y is called an implicit function of x.

Example : $x^3 + y^3 = xy$

Working Rules

(i) Differentiate the given relation w.r.t. x.

(ii) Bring all the terms containing $\frac{dy}{dx}$ on left side and remaining terms on right side and then find $\frac{dy}{dx}$.

(iii) Use the given relation between x and y to get the result.

SOLVED EXAMPLES

✎ Type III

Example 1

If $ax^2 + 2hxy + by^2 = 1$, then find $\frac{dy}{dx}$.

Solution :

$$ax^2 + 2hxy + by^2 = 1$$

Differentiating both sides w.r.t. x, we get

$$a\frac{d(x^2)}{dx} + 2h\frac{d(xy)}{dx} + b\frac{d(y^2)}{dx} = 0$$

or $$a.2x + 2h\left(x.\frac{dy}{dx} + y.1\right) + b.2y\frac{dy}{dx} = 0$$

or $$2(hx + by)\frac{dy}{dx} = -2(ax + hy)$$

$$\therefore \quad \frac{dy}{dx} = -\frac{ax+hy}{hx+by}$$

Ans.

Example 2

If $xy = x^3 + y^3$, then find $\frac{dy}{dx}$.

Solution :

$$xy = x^3 + y^3$$

Differentiating with respect to x,

$$\frac{d}{dx}(xy) = \frac{d}{dx}(x^3) + \frac{d}{dx}(y^3)$$

or $$1.y + x.\frac{dy}{dx} = 3x^2 + 3y^2\frac{dy}{dx}$$

or $$(x - 3y^2)\frac{dy}{dx} = 3x^2 - y$$

$\therefore$ $$\frac{dy}{dx} = \frac{3x^2 - y}{x - 3y^2}$$ **Ans.**

Example 3

If $x^2 + y^2 = 1$, then find $\frac{dy}{dx}$.

Solution :

$$x^2 + y^2 = 1$$

Differentiating with respect to x,

$$2x + 2y\frac{dy}{dx} = 0 \quad \left(\because \frac{d}{dx}(y^n) = ny^{n-1}\frac{dy}{dx}\right)$$

or $$2y.\frac{dy}{dx} = -2x$$

$\therefore$ $$\frac{dy}{dx} = -\frac{x}{y}$$ **Ans.**

Example 4

If $x^2 + 3xy + y^2 = 4$, then find $\frac{dy}{dx}$.

Solution :

$$x^2 + 3xy + y^2 = 4$$

Differentiating with respect to x,

$$\frac{d}{dx}(x^2) + 3\frac{d}{dx}(xy) + \frac{d}{dx}(y^2) = 0$$

$$\Rightarrow 2x + 3\left(x\frac{dy}{dx} + y.1\right) + 2y\frac{dy}{dx} = 0$$

$$\Rightarrow 2x + 3x\frac{dy}{dx} + 3y + 2y\frac{dy}{dx} = 0$$

$$\Rightarrow (3x + 2y)\frac{dy}{dx} = -(2x + 3y)$$

$\therefore$ $$\frac{dy}{dx} = \frac{-(2x + 3y)}{3x + 2y}$$ **Ans.**

Example 5

If $\log xy = x^2 + y^2$, then find $\frac{dy}{dx}$.

Solution :

$$\log xy = x^2 + y^2$$

Differentiating with respect to x,

$$\frac{1}{x} + \frac{1}{y}\frac{dy}{dx} = 2x + 2y\frac{dy}{dx}$$

$$\Rightarrow \left(\frac{1}{y} - 2x\right)\frac{dy}{dx} = 2x - \frac{1}{x}$$

$$\Rightarrow \left(\frac{1 - 2y^2}{y}\right)\frac{dy}{dx} = \frac{2x^2 - 1}{x}$$

$\therefore$ $$\frac{dy}{dx} = \frac{y(2x^2 - 1)}{x(1 - 2y^2)}$$ **Ans.**

Example 6

If $xy + \frac{x}{y} = x^2 - y$, then find $\frac{dy}{dx}$.

Solution :

$$xy + \frac{x}{y} = x^2 - y$$

Differentiating with respect to x,

or $$x.\frac{dy}{dx} + y.1 + \frac{y(1) - x.\frac{dy}{dx}}{y^2} = 2x - \frac{dy}{dx}$$

or $$x.\frac{dy}{dx} + y + \frac{1}{y} - \frac{x}{y^2}\frac{dy}{dx} = 2x - \frac{dy}{dx}$$

or $$\frac{dy}{dx}\left[x - \frac{x}{y^2} + 1\right] = 2x - y - \frac{1}{y}$$

$\therefore$ $$\frac{dy}{dx} = \frac{y(2xy - y^2 - 1)}{xy^2 + y^2 - x}$$ **Ans.**

Example 7

If $xy + xe^{-y} + ye^x = x^2$, then find $\frac{dy}{dx}$.

Solution :

$$xy + xe^{-y} + ye^x = x^2$$

Differentiating with respect to x,

$$x.\frac{dy}{dx} + y.1 + xe^{-y}\left(-\frac{dy}{dx}\right) + e^{-y}.1 + ye^x + e^x\frac{dy}{dx} = 2x$$

or $$(x - xe^{-y} + e^x)\frac{dy}{dx} = 2x - y - e^{-y} - ye^x$$

$\therefore$ $$\frac{dy}{dx} = \frac{2x - y - e^{-y} - ye^x}{x - xe^{-y}e^x}$$ **Ans.**

Example 8

If $x\sqrt{1+y} + y\sqrt{1+x} = 0$, then show that $\frac{dy}{dx} = -\frac{1}{(1+x)^2}$.

Solution :

$$x\sqrt{1+y} + y\sqrt{1+x} = 0$$

or $$x\sqrt{1+y} = -y\sqrt{1+x}$$

By squaring both sides,

$$(x\sqrt{1+y})^2 = (-y\sqrt{1+x})^2$$

or $$x^2(1 + y) = y^2(1 + x)$$

or $$x^2 + x^2y = y^2 + xy^2$$

or $$x^2 + x^2y - y^2 - xy^2 = 0$$

or $$(x - y)(x + y) + xy(x - y) = 0$$

By dividing $(x - y)$,

$$x + y + xy = 0$$

or $y(1+x) = -x$

or $y = \frac{-x}{1+x}$

Differentiating with respect to x,

$$\therefore \quad \frac{dy}{dx} = \frac{(1+x)\frac{d}{dx}(x) - x.\frac{d}{dx}(1+x)}{(1+x)^2}$$

$$= -\frac{(1+x).1 - x.1}{(1+x)^2}$$

$$= -\frac{1}{(1+x)^2}$$ **Proved**

Example 9

If $y = \frac{1}{x}$, prove that $\frac{dy}{\sqrt{1+y^4}} + \frac{dx}{\sqrt{1+x^4}} = 0.$

Solution :

$$y = \frac{1}{x} \quad \text{...(i)}$$

Differentiating with respect to x,

$$\frac{dy}{dx} = -\frac{1}{x^2} \quad \text{...(ii)}$$

then $$\frac{\sqrt{1+y^4}}{\sqrt{1+x^4}} = \frac{\sqrt{1+\frac{1}{x^4}}}{\sqrt{1+x^4}} \quad \left(\because y = \frac{1}{x}\right)$$

$$= \frac{\sqrt{x^4+1}}{x^2} \times \frac{1}{\sqrt{1+x^4}}$$

$$= \frac{1}{x^2} \quad \text{...(iii)}$$

From equations (ii) and (iii),

$$\frac{\sqrt{1+y^4}}{\sqrt{1+x^4}} = -\frac{dy}{dx}$$

By writing in differentiation,

$$\frac{dx}{\sqrt{1+x^4}} = -\frac{dy}{\sqrt{1+y^4}}$$

$$\therefore \quad \frac{dx}{\sqrt{1+y^4}} + \frac{dy}{\sqrt{1+y^4}} = 0$$ **Proved**

Example 10

If $y = \sqrt{x+\sqrt{x+\sqrt{x+\ldots\text{to}\infty}}}$, prove that $\frac{dy}{dx} = \frac{1}{2y-1}$.

(*JAC*, 2018)

Solution :

$$y^2 = x + \sqrt{x+\sqrt{x+\ldots\text{to}\infty}}$$

$$y^2 = x + y$$

Differentiating with respect to x,

$$2y.\frac{dy}{dx} = 1 + \frac{dy}{dx}$$

$$\Rightarrow \quad (2y-1)\frac{dy}{dx} = 1$$

$$\Rightarrow \quad \frac{dy}{dx} = \frac{1}{2y-1}$$ **Proved**

Example 11

If $t = \sqrt{x+\sqrt{x+\sqrt{x\infty}}}$ then prove that $\frac{dt}{dx} = \frac{1}{2t-1}$

(*JAC.*, 2018)

Solution :

$$t = \sqrt{x+\sqrt{+x\sqrt{x.....\infty}}}$$

$$\Rightarrow \quad t^2 = x + \sqrt{x+\sqrt{+x.....\infty}}$$

$$\Rightarrow \quad t^2 = x + t$$

By writing in differentiation,

$$\frac{d}{dx}t^2 = \frac{d}{dx}.x + \frac{dt}{dx}$$

$$\Rightarrow \quad 2t\frac{dt}{dx} = 1 + \frac{dt}{dx}$$

$$\Rightarrow \quad 2t\frac{dt}{dx} - \frac{dt}{dx} = 1$$

$$\Rightarrow \quad \frac{dt}{dx}(2t-1) = 1$$

$$\Rightarrow \quad \frac{dt}{dx} = \frac{1}{2t-1}$$ **Proved**

Example 12

If $y = x + \cfrac{1}{x + \cfrac{1}{x + \cfrac{1}{x} + ...\infty}}$

prove that $(x^2 - y^2 + 3)\frac{dy}{dx} = 1.$

Solution :

$$\because \quad y = x + \frac{1}{y} \quad \text{...(i)}$$

$$\Rightarrow \quad y^2 = xy + 1$$

$$\Rightarrow \quad y^2 - 1 = xy \quad \text{...(ii)}$$

Differentiating with respect to x,

$$\frac{dy}{dx} = 1 - \frac{1}{y^2}.\frac{dy}{dx}$$

$$\Rightarrow \quad \left(1+\frac{1}{y^2}\right)\frac{dy}{dx} = 1$$

From (i) $$y = x + \frac{1}{y}$$

or $$y - x = \frac{1}{y}$$

or $$(y-x)^2 = \frac{1}{y^2}$$

$$\Rightarrow \quad \{1 + (y - x)^2\}\frac{dy}{dx} = 1$$

$$\Rightarrow \quad (1 + x^2 + y^2 - 2xy)\frac{dy}{dx} = 1$$

From (ii) $\quad xy = y^2 - 1$

$$\Rightarrow \{1 + x^2 + y^2 - 2(y^2 - 1)\}\frac{dy}{dx} = 1$$

$$\Rightarrow \quad (1 + x^2 + y^2 - 2y^2 + 2)\frac{dy}{dx} = 1$$

$$\Rightarrow \quad (x^2 - y^2 + 3)\frac{dy}{dx} = 1$$

Proved

Exercise 9 (C)

Find $\frac{dy}{dx}$ if :

1. $x^n + y^n = a^n$
2. $x + y = xy^3$
3. $xy + x^2y^2 = c$
4. $x^3y^4 = (x - y)^7$
5. $2x + y = 7$
6. $x^2y = 75$
7. $x^2y + xy^2 = a$
8. $x^3 + y^3 = 3axy$ (*JAC*, 2018)
9. $(x - y)y^n = 2\sqrt{x}$
10. $x^m.y^n = (x - y)^{m+n}$
11. $(x^3 + y^3)\,xy = x^5 - y^5$
12. $x^2y^3 + 2xy + y + 2 = 0$
13. $xy = x^2 + y^2$
14. $x\sqrt{y} + y\sqrt{x} = 1$
15. $x^3 + y^3 - 3axy = 0$
16. $x^5 + y^5 + 5xy - c = 0$
17. If $y\sqrt{1-x^2} + x\sqrt{1-y^2} = 1$, prove that $\frac{dy}{dx} = -\sqrt{\frac{1-y^2}{1-x^2}}$.

Answers

1. $-\frac{x^{n-1}}{y^{n-1}}$
2. $\frac{y}{x(1-3xy^2)}$
3. $-\frac{y}{x}$
4. $\frac{y}{x}$
5. -2
6. $-\frac{2y}{x}$
7. $-\frac{y}{x}.\frac{2x+y}{x+2y}$
8. $\frac{ay-x^2}{y^2-ax}$
9. $\frac{1-\sqrt{xy^n}}{2n\sqrt{x}-y^{n+1}}.\frac{y}{\sqrt{x}}$
10. $\frac{y}{x}$
11. $\frac{5x^4-4x^3y-y^4}{x^4+4xy^3+5y^4}$
12. $-\frac{2xy^3+2y}{2x^2y^2+2x+1}$
13. $\frac{2x-y}{x-2y}$
14. $\frac{y}{x}.\frac{2\sqrt{x}+\sqrt{y}}{2\sqrt{y}+1\sqrt{x}}$
15. $\frac{ay-x^2}{y^2-ax}$
16. $\frac{x^4+y}{y^4+x}$

(9.8) LOGARITHMIC DIFFERENTIATION

Properties of Logarithm

(i) $\log_a mn = \log_a m + \log_a n$

(ii) $\log_a \left(\frac{m}{n}\right) = \log_a m - \log_a n$

(iii) $\log_a m^n = n \log_a m$

(iv) $\log_n m = \frac{\log_a m}{\log_a n}$

Working Rules

(1) If variable power occurs, then differentiate after taking logarithm.

But if y is of the form $f(x) \pm g(x)$, where $f(x)$ and $g(x)$ contain variable powers, then let $u = f(x)$ and $v = g(x)$ and find $\frac{du}{dx}$ and $\frac{dy}{dx}$ separately.

Then use $\quad \frac{dy}{dx} = \frac{du}{dx} \pm \frac{dv}{dx}$

(2) If the function whose d.c. is to be found, is the product or quotient of several functions, then take logarithm and then differentiate.

SOLVED EXAMPLES

✎ Type IV

Example 1

If $y = x^x$, find $\frac{dy}{dx}$.

Solution :

$$y = x^x \quad ...(i)$$

Logarithms both sides,

$$\log y = x \log x$$

Differentiating with respect to x,

$$\frac{d(\log y)}{dx} = \frac{d(x \log x)}{dx}$$

or $\quad \frac{d(\log y)}{dx} = \frac{d(x)}{dx}.\log x + x\frac{d(\log x)}{dx}$

or $\quad \frac{1}{y}\frac{dy}{dx} = 1.\log x + x.\frac{1}{x} = \log x + 1$

$\therefore \quad \frac{dy}{dx} = y(1 + \log x)$

$= x^x(1 + \log x)$ ($\because$ From eq. (i) $y = x^x$)

Ans.

Example 2

If $x^y = y^x$, find $\frac{dy}{dx}$.

Solution :

$$x^y = y^x$$

Logarithms both sides

$$y \log x = x \log y$$

Differentiating with respect to x,

$$\log x.\frac{dy}{dx} + y.\frac{1}{x} = 1 \log y + x.\frac{1}{y}\frac{dy}{dx}$$

or $\quad \left(\log x - \frac{x}{y}\right)\frac{dy}{dx} = \log y - \frac{y}{x}$

or $\quad \frac{y \log x - x}{y}.\frac{dy}{dx} = \frac{x \log y - y}{x}$

$\therefore \quad \frac{dy}{dx} = \frac{y(x \log y - y)}{x(y \log x - x)}$ **Ans.**

Example 3

If $y = (1 + 2x)^{3x}$ then find $\frac{dy}{dx}$.

Solution :

$$y = (1 + 2x)^{3x}$$

Logarithms both sides,

$$\log y = 3x \log (1 + 2x)$$

Differentiating with respect to x,

$$\text{or} \quad \frac{1}{y}.\frac{dy}{dx} = 3x.\frac{d}{dx}\{\log (1 + 2x) + \log (1 + 2x).\frac{d}{dx}(3x)$$

$$= 3x\frac{1}{1+2x}(2) + \log(1+2x)(3)$$

$$\therefore \quad \frac{dy}{dx} = (1 + 2x)^{3x}\left[\frac{6x}{1+2x} + 3\log(1+2x)\right]$$

Ans.

Example 4

If $x^y = e^{x-y}$, prove that :

$$\frac{dy}{dx} = \frac{\log x}{(1+\log x)^2}.$$

Solution :

$$x^y = e^{x-y}$$

Logarithms both sides,

$$y \log x = (x - y) \log e$$

$$\text{or} \quad y \log x = x - y \qquad (\because \log_e e = 1)$$

$$\text{or} \quad y (\log x + 1) = x$$

$$\therefore \quad y = \frac{x}{1+\log x}$$

$$\therefore \quad \frac{dy}{dx} = \frac{(1+\log x).1 - x\left(0+\frac{1}{x}\right)}{(1+\log x)^2}$$

$$= \frac{\log x}{(1+\log x)^2}$$

Ans.

Example 5

If $y = x^{\log x}$ then find $\frac{dy}{dx}$.

Solution :

$$y = x^{\log x}$$

Logarithms both sides,

$$\log y = \log x^{\log x} = \log x \,.\, \log x$$

$$\Rightarrow \quad \log y = (\log x)^2$$

Differentiating with respect to x,

$$\frac{1}{y}.\frac{dy}{dx} = \frac{d(\log x)^2}{d(\log x)} \times \frac{d(\log x)}{dx}$$

$$= 2 \log x \times \left(\frac{1}{x}\right) = \frac{2}{x}\log x$$

$$\therefore \quad \frac{dy}{dx} = y.\left(\frac{2}{x}\log x\right)$$

$$= x^{\log x}\left(\frac{2}{x}\log x\right)$$

Ans.

Example 6

If $x^m y^n = (x + y)^{m+n}$, then find $\frac{dy}{dx}$.

Solution :

$$\because \quad x^m y^n = (x + y)^{m+n}$$

Logarithms both sides,

$$m \log x + n \log y = (m + n) \log (x + y)$$

Differentiating with respect to x,

$$m.\frac{1}{x} + n.\frac{1}{y}\frac{dy}{dx} = (m+n)\frac{d\log(x+y)}{d(x+y)} \times \frac{d(x+y)}{dx}$$

$$\text{or} \quad \frac{m}{x} + \frac{n}{y}.\frac{dy}{dx} = (m+n).\frac{1}{x+y} \times \left(1 + \frac{dy}{dx}\right)$$

$$\text{or} \quad \frac{m}{x} + \frac{n}{y}.\frac{dy}{dx} = \frac{m+n}{x+y}\left(1 + \frac{dy}{dx}\right)$$

$$\text{or} \quad \frac{m}{x} + \frac{n}{y}.\frac{dy}{dx} = \frac{m+n}{x+y} + \frac{m+n}{x+y}.\frac{dy}{dx}$$

$$\text{or} \quad \left(\frac{n}{y} - \frac{m+n}{x+y}\right)\frac{dy}{dx} = \frac{m+n}{x+y} - \frac{m}{x}$$

$$\text{or} \left\{\frac{nx + ny - my - ny}{y(x+y)}\right\}\frac{dy}{dx} = \frac{mx + nx - mx - my}{x(x+y)}$$

$$\text{or} \quad \frac{(nx - my)}{y}.\frac{dy}{dx} = \frac{(nx - my)}{x(x+y)}$$

$$\text{or} \quad \frac{1}{y}.\frac{dy}{dx} = \frac{1}{x}$$

$$\therefore \quad \frac{dy}{dx} = \frac{y}{x}$$

Ans.

Example 7

If $y = a^x$, then find $\frac{dy}{dx}$.

Solution :

$$\because \quad y = a^x$$

Logarithms both sides,

$$\log y = x \log a$$

Differentiating with respect to x,

$$\frac{1}{y}.\frac{dy}{dx} = 1. \log a$$

$$\frac{dy}{dx} = y \log a$$

$$= a^x \log a$$

$$\therefore \quad \frac{d}{dx}(a^x) = a^x \log a$$

Remember above Formula.

Example 8

If $y = 5^{x+1}$, then find $\frac{dy}{dx}$.

Solution :

$$\because \quad y = 5^{x+1}$$

Logarithms both sides,

$$\log y = (x+1)\log 5$$

Differentiating with respect to x.

$$\frac{1}{y}\frac{dy}{dx} = \log 5 . \frac{d}{dx}(x+1)$$

$$= \log 5\,(1+0)$$

$$\Rightarrow \quad \frac{dy}{dx} = y \log 5 = 5^{x+1}\log 5 \quad \textbf{Ans.}$$

Example 9

If $y = \log_a x$, then find $\frac{dy}{dx}$.

Solution :

$$y = \log_a x = \log_e x \times \log_a e$$

$$= k \log_e x, \quad \text{where } \log_a e = k \text{ (say)}$$

$$= k \log x$$

$$\therefore \quad \frac{dy}{dx} = k.\frac{d}{dx}(\log x)$$

$$= k.\frac{1}{x} = \frac{1}{x}k = \frac{1}{x}\log_a e \quad \textbf{Ans.}$$

Example 10

If $y = \log_a (x^2+1)$, then find $\frac{dy}{dx}$.

Solution :

$$y = \log_a (x^2+1)$$

$$= \log_e (x^2+1) \times \log_a e$$

$$= k \log_e (x^2+1), \text{ where } \log_a e = k \text{ (let)}$$

$$= k \log (x^2+1)$$

$$\therefore \quad \frac{dy}{dx} = \frac{k\,d\log(x^2+1)}{d(x^2+1)} \times \frac{d(x^2+1)}{dx}$$

$$= k.\frac{1}{x^2+1} \times (2x+0)$$

$$= \frac{2x}{x^2+1}.k = \frac{2x}{x^2+1}\log_a e \quad \textbf{Ans.}$$

Example 11

If $y = e^{x+e^{x+e^{x+\ldots\ldots to\,\infty}}}$ prove that $\frac{dy}{dx} = \frac{y}{1-y}$.

Solution :

$$y = e^{x+e^{x+e^{x+\ldots\ldots to\,\infty}}}$$

$$\therefore \quad y = e^{x+y} \quad \ldots(i)$$

Logarithms both sides,

$$\log y = (x+y)\log_e e \quad (\because \log_e e = 1)$$

Differentiating with respect to x,

$$\frac{1}{y} \cdot \frac{dy}{dx} = 1 + \frac{dy}{dx}$$

$$\text{or} \quad \left(\frac{1}{y} - 1\right)\frac{dy}{dx} = 1$$

$$\text{or} \quad \left(\frac{1-y}{y}\right)\frac{dy}{dx} = 1$$

$$\therefore \quad \frac{dy}{dx} = \frac{y}{1-y} \quad \textbf{Proved}$$

Example 12

If $y = a^x + x^a$, then find $\frac{dy}{dx}$.

Solution :

$$y = a^x + x^a$$

Differentiating with respect to x,

$$\frac{dy}{dx} = \frac{d}{dx}(a^x + x^a)$$

$$= \frac{d}{dx}(a^x) + \frac{d}{dx}(x^a) \quad \left(\because \frac{d}{dx}(a^x) = a^x.\log a\right)$$

$$\frac{d}{dx}(a^x) = \frac{d}{dx}(a^{x\log a})$$

$$= e^{x\log a} \times \frac{d(x\log a)}{dx}$$

$$= a^x \times (1 \log a)$$

$$= a^x \log a$$

$$\therefore \quad \frac{dy}{dx} = a^x \log a + a x^{a-1} \quad \textbf{Ans.}$$

Example 13

If $y = x^{x^x}$ find $\frac{dy}{dx}$.

Solution :

$$y = x^{x^x} \quad \ldots(i)$$

$$\therefore \quad \log y = \log(x^{x^x}) = \log[(x)^{x^x}]$$

$$= x^x \log x \quad \ldots(ii)$$

Logarithms both sides,

$$\log(\log y) = \log(x^x) + \log(\log x)$$

$$= x\log x + \log(\log x)$$

Differentiating with respect to x,

$$\frac{1}{\log y} - \frac{1}{y}\frac{dy}{dx} = 1.\log x + x.\frac{1}{x} + \frac{1}{\log x}.\frac{1}{x}$$

$$\therefore \quad \frac{dy}{dx} = y\log y\left(\log x + 1 + \frac{1}{x\log x}\right)$$

$$= x^{x^x}.\,x^x \log x\left(\log x + 1 + \frac{1}{x\log x}\right)$$

Ans.

Example 14

If $y = \log\sqrt{\dfrac{x+1}{x-1}}$, then find $\dfrac{dy}{dx}$.

Solution :

$$y = \log\sqrt{\frac{x+1}{x-1}}$$

$$\Rightarrow \quad y = \log\left(\frac{x+1}{x-1}\right)^{1/2}$$

$$= \frac{1}{2}\log\left(\frac{x+1}{x-1}\right)$$

$$= \frac{1}{2}[\log(x+1) - \log(x-1)]$$

Differentiating with respect to x,

$$\frac{dy}{dx} = \frac{1}{2}\left[\frac{1}{x+1} - \frac{1}{x-1}\right]$$

$$= \frac{1}{2}\left[\frac{x-1-(x+1)}{(x-1)(x+1)}\right]$$

$$= \frac{1}{2}\left[\frac{-2}{x^2-1}\right] = \frac{-1}{x^2-1} \quad \textbf{Ans.}$$

Example 15

If $y = x^x + x^{1/x}$, then find $\dfrac{dy}{dx}$.

Solution :

Let $u = x^x$ and $v = x^{1/x}$

$\because \quad y = u + v$

$\because \quad u = x^x$ ...(i)

$\therefore \quad \log u = x \log x$

Differentiating with respect to x,

$$\frac{1}{u}.\frac{du}{dx} = x\left(\frac{1}{x}\right) + \log x(1)$$

$$\Rightarrow \quad \frac{du}{dx} = u(1+\log x) = x^x(1+\log x) \quad ...(ii)$$

then $v = x^{1/x}$

$$\therefore \quad \log v = \frac{1}{x}\log x$$

Differentiating with respect to x,

$$\frac{1}{v}.\frac{dv}{dx} = \frac{1}{x}\left(\frac{1}{x}\right) + \log x\left(-\frac{1}{x^2}\right)$$

$$\frac{dv}{dx} = v\left[\frac{1}{x^2} - \frac{1}{x^2}\log x\right]$$

$$= x^{1/x}\frac{(1-\log x)}{x^2} \quad ...(iii)$$

From eq. (i), $y = u + v$

$$\therefore \quad \frac{dy}{dx} = \frac{du}{dx} + \frac{dv}{dx}$$

$$= x^x(1+\log x) + \frac{x^{1/x}(1-\log x)}{x^2}.$$

Ans.

Example 16

Solve : $3x^5 + 3x^3 - 5$ *[Mock Test Paper (JAC)]*

Solution :

$$y = 3x^5 + 3x^3 - 5$$

Differentiating with respect to x,

$$\frac{dy}{dx} = 3 \times 5x^4 + 3 \times 3x^2 - 5 \times 0$$

$$= 15x^4 + 9x^2$$

$$y = (2x^2+1)^2 4x$$

Exercise 9 (D)

Find $\dfrac{dy}{dx}$ if :

1. $y = x^y$
2. $y = x^{1/x}$
3. $y = 2x$
4. $x^a . y^b = (x-y)^{a+b}$
5. $y = \log(\log x)$
6. $y = e^{x^x}$
7. $y = e^{x^2}$
8. $y = a^{2x}$
9. $y = a^{x^2+x}$
10. $y = 3^{x+2}$
11. $y = e^{1/x}$
12. $y = \dfrac{1}{4^{5x}}$
13. $y = e^{3\log x}$

[**Hint :** $y = e^{3\log x}$

$= e^{\log x^3} = x^3$

$\therefore \quad \dfrac{dy}{dx} = 3x^2 \quad \boxed{e^{\log x} = x}$

Answers

1. $\dfrac{y^2}{x(1-y\log x)}$
2. $\dfrac{x^{1/x}(1-\log x)}{x^2}$
3. $2^x \log 2$
4. $\dfrac{y}{x}$
5. $\dfrac{1}{x\log x}$
6. $e^{x^x}.x^x(1+\log x)$
7. $2x = e^{x^2}$
8. $2.a^{2x}.\log a$
9. $(2x+1).a^{x^2+x}.\log a$
10. $3^{x+2}\log 3$
11. $-\dfrac{1}{x^2}e^{1/x}$
12. $\dfrac{-5}{4^{5x}}.\log 4$
13. $3x^2$

Exercise 9 (E)

Objective Type Questions

❑ Multiple Choice Questions

1. The differential coefficient of $3x^4$ w.r.t. x will be : *(JAC, 2024)*

(a) $16x$ (b) $16x^2$ (c) $12x^3$ (d) $4x^3$

2. If $y = 2\log_2 x$, then $\dfrac{dy}{dx}$ is equal to :

(a) x (b) 1 (c) 0 (d) y

3. If $y = \sqrt{x} + \frac{1}{\sqrt{x}}$, then $\frac{dy}{dx}$ at $x = 1$:

(a) 1 (b) $\frac{1}{2}$ (c) $\frac{1}{\sqrt{2}}$ (d) 0

4. If x^2e^x, then $\frac{dy}{dx}$ is equal to :

(a) x^{e^x} (b) $x(x + 2)$
(c) $(x + 2)e^x$ (d) $x(x + 2)e^x$

5. If $y = \log_a x$, then $\frac{dy}{dx}$ is :

(a) $\log_a e$ (b) $\frac{1}{x}\log_a e$ (c) $x \log_a e$ (d) $\frac{1}{x}$

6. The derivative of the function $y = x^5$ will be :
(a) $5x^4$ (b) $4x^4$ (c) $5x^3$ (d) $5x^6$

7. $\frac{dx}{dy}$ of $x^4 + y^4 = 4ax^2$ will be :

(a) $\frac{4ax - x^4}{y^4}$ (b) $\frac{2ax - x^3}{y^3}$
(c) $\frac{4ax - x^3}{y^3}$ (d) $\frac{2ax - x^4}{y^3}$

8. $\frac{d(\log_e x)}{dx}$ is : (*JAC, 2023*)

(a) x^2 (b) $\frac{1}{x}$ (c) $\log x$ (d) x

9. If $y = x^3$, then $\frac{dy}{dx}$ is : (*JAC, 2023*)
(a) $3x^2$ (b) $3x$ (c) $3x^3$ (d) $5x$

10. If $y = \sqrt{x}$ then $\frac{dy}{dx}$ (*JAC, 2024*)

(a) $\frac{1}{\sqrt{x}}$ (b) $\frac{1}{2\sqrt{x}}$ (c) $\sqrt{x}$ (d) x

11. Differential coefficient of $\log x$ with respect to x is : (*JAC, 2025*)

(a) $\frac{1}{x^2}$ (b) $\frac{1}{x}$ (c) $\frac{1}{x^3}$ (d) $\log x$

12. The differential coefficient of $4x^4$ with respect to x will be : (*JAC, 2026*)

(a) $16x^4$ (b) $16x^3$ (c) $9x^3$ (d) $15x^3$

Answers

1. (c) 2. (b) 3. (d) 4. (d) 5. (b) 6. (a) 7. (b)
8. (b) 9. (a) 10. (b) 11. (b) 12. (b).

❐ Fill in the blanks

1. The process of finding out rate of change in function is called .... (*JAC, 2024*)
2. Differentiation is also called ....
3. The derivative of the function $y = x^5$ is ....
4. The differentiation of $\frac{7}{x}$ w.r.t. x is ....
5. The differential coefficient for the function $y = \frac{1}{x^2}$ or x^{-2} is ....

Answers

1. Differentiation 2. Differential Coefficient
3. $5x^4$ 4. $-7.x^{-2}$ 5. $-\frac{2}{x^3}$

❐ Write True or False

1. Differentiation is the mathematical process to find the derivative of $f(x)$.
2. If $y = \log_{10} x$ then $\frac{dy}{dx} = \frac{1}{x}$.
3. The derivative of a function does not involve the application of limit.
4. When a variable changes from one value to another, the difference between the new value of the initial value is called increment.
5. The process of finding the differential coefficient of a function $f(x)$ w.r.t. x in independent variable is called differentiation.

Answers

1. True 2. False 3. False 4. True
5. True

❖❖

10

INTEGRATION

LEARNING OBJECTIVES

After studying this chapter, you will be able to know :

- **10.1 Introduction**
- **10.2 Integration of a Function**
  - **10.2.1 Integration or Integrand**
  - **10.2.2 Indefinite Nature of Integral**
- **10.3 Basic Rules of Integration**
- **10.4 Integration by Transformation and Substitution**
- **10.5 Integration of Some Rational Functions**
- **10.6 Integration by Parts**

SOLVED EXAMPLES AND PRACTICAL PROBLEMS : AT A GLANCE

No. of Examples		*No. of Problems*
1 (A) to 8		Exercise 10 (A) : 1 to 22
1 to 9	Type I : Integration by Transformation and Substitution	
1 to 24	Type II : Substitution Method	Exercise 10 (B) : 1 to 28
1 to 6	Integration of Some Rational Functions	Exercise 10 (C) : 1 to 8
	Partial Integration	
1 to 7	Type I	Exercise 10 (D) : 1 to 8
8 to 12	Type II	Exercise 10 (D) : 9 to 15
	Objective Type Questions	Exercise 10 (E) : 9 + 3 + 4 + 4
59	**Total**	**73 + 20**

(10.1) INTRODUCTION

The concept of integration organised in course of finding the area of plan figure. It is based on the limit of the sum of the series whose each term tends to zero and number of terms tends to infinity. In fact, it is called integration because of process of summation as integration means summation. But later on it was observed that integration is just the inverse process of differentiation.

In this book first of all we will define integration as the inverse process of the differentiation.

We have already read in previous chapters how to find the differential coefficient of a given function. Now we wish to know what is that function whose d.c is a given function whose d.c. w.r.t. to x is $5x^4$. One such function is x^5 since d.c. of x^5. Again since d.c. of $x^5 + c$ is $5x^4$, where c is an arbitrary constant.

(10.2) INTEGRATION OF A FUNCTION

If d.c. of a function F(x) is $f(x)$ *i.e.* if $F(x) = f(x)$, then we will say that one integral or primitive of $f(x)$ is F(x) and in symbols we write :

$$\int f(x)\,dx = F(x)$$

Example :

$$\frac{d(e^x)}{dx} = e^x$$

$$\int e^x\,dx = e^x$$

10.2.1 Integration or Integrand

The process of finding integral of a function is called integration and the function which is integrated is called the integral. The function whose d.c. is the integral, is called the integral of the integrand.

10.2.2 Indefinite Nature of Integral

If $\frac{d\{F(x)\}}{dx} = f(x)$, then also $\frac{d\{F(x)+c\}}{dx} = f(x)$, where c is an arbitrary constant.

Thus here general value of $\int f(x)dx$ is F(x) + C, where C is an arbitrary constant. C is called constant of integration.

Clearly integral will change if one integral of $f(x)$ is F(x), then F(x) + C will be also an integral of $f(x)$, where C is a constant.

Thus $\int f(x)dx$ will have infinite number of values and hence it is called indefinite integral of $f(x)$.

Particular Integral : If $\frac{d[F(x)+c]}{dx} = f(x)$, then $\int f(x) = F(x) + C$.

$\int f(x)dx$ will have different values for different values of c. For a defined value of C $\int f(x)dx$ will have a definite value F(x) + C.

Hence F(x) + C is a particular integral of $f(x)$.

SOME IMPORTANT FORMULAE

(i) $\frac{d}{dx}\left(\frac{x^{n+1}}{n+1}\right) = \frac{(n+1)x^n}{(n+1)} = x^n$ $\quad \left[\because \frac{d}{dx}(x^n) = nx^{n-1}\right]$

$\therefore \quad \int x^n dx = \frac{x^{n+1}}{n+1}$

Example

(a) $\int x^2 dx = \frac{x^{2+1}}{2+1} = \frac{x^3}{3}$

(b) $\int x\, dx = \frac{x^{1+1}}{1+1} = \frac{x^2}{2}$

(ii) $\int dx = \int 1 dx = \int x^0 dx = \frac{x^{0+1}}{0+1} = \frac{x}{1} = x$

(iii) $\because \frac{d(\log x)}{dx} = \frac{1}{x}$

$\therefore \quad \int \frac{1}{x} dx = \log x$

(iv) $\because \frac{d(a^x)}{dx} = a^x \log_e a$

$\therefore \quad \int a^x dx = \frac{a^x}{\log_e a}$

(v) $\because \frac{d(e^x)}{dx} = e^x$

$\therefore \quad \int e^x dx = e^x$

(10.3) BASIC RULES OF INTEGRATION

Rule I. The integral of the product of a constant and a function is equal to the product of the constant and the integral of the function, *i.e.*

$$\int K f(x)dx = K \int f(x)dx$$

In other words, constant can be taken outside of signs.

Proof :

$$\frac{d}{dx}\left[K \int f(x)dx\right] = K.\frac{d}{dx}[f(x)dx] = K f(x)$$

$\because$ Integration is inverse process of differentiation.

$\therefore \quad \boxed{\int K f(x)dx = K \int f(x)dx}$

Rule II. The integral of the sum (or difference) of two functions is equal to the sum (or difference) of the integrals of the functions, *i.e.*

$$\int[f(x) \pm g(x)]dx = \int f(x) \pm \int g(x)dx$$

Proof :

$$\frac{d}{dx}\left[\int f(x)dx \pm \int g(x)dx\right]$$

$$= \frac{d}{dx}\left\{[f(x)dx] \pm \left[\int g(x)dx\right]\right\}$$

$$= f(x) \pm g(x)$$

$$\left(\because \frac{d}{dx}\left[\int f(x)dx\right] = f(x)\right)$$

Since integration is inverse process of differentiation.

$\boxed{\therefore \int[f(x) \pm g(x)]dx = \int f(x)dx \pm \int g(x)dx}$

General form of the above rule is

$$\int[f_1(x) \pm f_2(x) \pm \ldots\ldots \pm f_n(x)]dx$$

$$= \int f_1(x)dx \pm \int f_2(x) \pm \ldots\ldots \pm \int f_n(x)dx$$

Proof : $\frac{d}{dx}\left[\int f_1(x)dx \pm \int f_2(x) \pm \ldots\ldots \pm \int f_n(x)dx\right]$

$$= \frac{d}{dx}\left[\int f_1(x)dx\right] \pm \frac{d}{dx}[f_2(x)dx] \pm \ldots\ldots \pm \frac{d}{dx}[f_n(x)dx]$$

$$= f_1(x) \pm f_2(x) \pm \ldots\ldots \pm f_n(x)$$

$$\therefore \int[f_1(x) \pm f_2(x) \pm \ldots\ldots \pm f_n(x)]dx$$

$$= \int f_1(x)dx \pm \int f_2(x)dx \pm \ldots\ldots \pm \int f_n(x)dx$$

FORMULA : AT A GLANCE

1. $\int x^n dx = \frac{x^{n+1}}{n+1} + C$
2. $\int e^x dx = e^x + C$
3. $\int \frac{1}{x} dx = \log x + C$
4. $\int dx = x + C$

5. $\int (u+v)dx = \int u\, dx + \int v\, dx$

6. $\int (u-v)dx = \int u\, dx - \int v\, dx$

7. $\int u.v\, dx = u\int v\, dx - \int\left[\frac{du}{dv}\int v\, du\right]dx$

SOLVED EXAMPLES

Example 1(A)

Find : $\int x^6\, dx$.

Solution :

Let $I = \int x^6\, dx$

$= \frac{x^{6+1}}{6+1} + C = \frac{x^7}{7} + C$ **Ans.**

Example 1(B)

Find : $\int x^{99}\, dx$.

Solution :

Let $I = \int x^{99}\, dx = \frac{x^{99+1}}{99+1} + C$

$= \frac{x^{100}}{100} + C$ **Ans.**

Example 2(A)

Find : $\int (4x^3+3x^2+2x+4)dx$. *(JAC, 2019)*

Solution :

Let $I = \int (4x^3+3x^2+2x+4)dx$

$= 4\int x^3\, dx + 3\int x^2\, dx + 2\int x\, dx + 4\int 1 dx$

$= 4.\frac{x^4}{4} + 3.\frac{x^3}{3} + 2.\frac{x^2}{2} + 4x + C$

$= x^4 + x^3 + x^2 + 4x + C$ **Ans.**

Example 2(B) *(JAC, 2024)*

Integrate with respect to X : $\int 2x^6 - 9x^3 + 3$

Solution :

$\int (.2x)^6 - 9x^3 + 3)\, dx$

$= 2\int x^6 dx - 9.\int x^3 dx + 3\int dx$

$= 2.\frac{x^{6+1}}{6+1} - 9.\frac{x^{3+1}}{3+1} + 3x + c$

$= \frac{2}{7}x^7 - \frac{9}{4}x^4 + 3x + c$ **Ans.**

Example 3

Find : $\int \frac{(1+x)^3}{\sqrt{x}}dx$.

Solution :

Let $I = \int \frac{(1+x)^3}{\sqrt{x}}dx = \int \frac{1+3x+3x^2+x^3}{\sqrt{x}}dx$

$= \int\left(\frac{1}{\sqrt{x}} + \frac{3x}{\sqrt{x}} + \frac{3x^2}{\sqrt{x}} + \frac{x^3}{\sqrt{x}}\right)dx$

$= \int (x^{-1/2} + 3x^{1-1/2} + 3x^{2-1/2} + x^{3-1/2})dx$

$= \int x^{-1/2}\, dx + 3\int x^{1/2}\, dx + 3\int x^{3/2}\, dx + \int x^{5/2}\, dx$

$= \frac{x^{1/2}}{1/2} + 3.\frac{x^{3/2}}{3/2} + 3.\frac{x^{5/2}}{5/2} + \frac{x^{7/2}}{7/2} + C$

$= 2\sqrt{x} + 2x^{3/2} + \frac{6}{5}x^{5/2} + \frac{2}{7}x^{7/2} + C$ **Ans.**

Example 4

Find : $\int 10^{x+3}\, dx$.

Solution :

Let $I = \int 10^{x+3}\, dx = \int 10^x.10^3\, dx$

$= 10^3 \int 10^x\, dx = 10^3.\frac{10^x}{\log_e 10} + C$

$= 10^{x+3}\log_{10}{}^e + C$ $\left[\because \frac{1}{\log_a b} = \log_b a\right]$

Ans.

Example 5

Find : $\int \sqrt{x}(x^{3/2} - 7x^{5/2} + 9x^{7/2})dx$

Solution :

Let $I = \int \sqrt{x}(x^{3/2} - 7x^{5/2} + 9x^{7/2})dx$

$= \int x^{1/2}(x^{3/2} - 7x^{5/2} + 9x^{7/2})dx$

$= \int x^{1/2}.x^{3/2} - 7x^{5/2}.x^{1/2} + 9x^{7/2}.x^{1/2})dx$

$= \int (x^2 - 7x^3 + 9x^4)dx$

$= \int x^2\, dx - 7\int x^3\, dx + 9\int x^4\, dx$

$= \frac{x^3}{3} - 7.\frac{x^4}{4} + 9.\frac{x^5}{5} + C$ **Ans.**

Example 6

Find : $\int \frac{(x^3+5x^2+4x+1)}{x^2}dx$

Solution :

Let $I = \int \frac{(x^3+5x^2+4x+1)}{x^2}dx$

$= \int\left(\frac{x^3}{x^2} + \frac{5x^2}{x^2} + \frac{4x}{x^2} + \frac{1}{x^2}\right)dx$

$= \int\left(x + 5 + \frac{4}{x} + \frac{1}{x^2}\right)dx$

$= \int x dx + 5\int 1.dx + 4\int \frac{1}{x}dx + \int \frac{1}{x^2}dx$

$= \frac{x^2}{2} + 5x + 4\log x + \frac{x^{-2+1}}{(-2+1)} + C$

$= \frac{x^2}{2} + 5x + 4\log x - \frac{1}{x} + C$ **Ans.**

Example 7

Evaluate : $\dfrac{(x^3+8)(x-1)}{x^2-2x+4}dx.$

Solution :

Let $I = \dfrac{(x^3+8)(x-1)}{x^2-2x+4}dx$

$= \int \dfrac{(x^3+2^3)(x-1)}{x^2-2x+4}dx$

$= \int \dfrac{(x+2)(x^2-2x+4)(x-1)}{x^2-2x+4}dx$

$= \int (x+2)(x-1)dx$

$= \int (x^2+x-2)dx$

$= \int x^2dx + \int xdx - 2\int x^0 dx$

$= \dfrac{x^3}{3}+\dfrac{x^2}{2}-2x+C$ **Ans.**

Example 8

Find : $\int \dfrac{x^4+5x^2+3}{\sqrt{x}}dx.$

Solution :

Let, $I = \int \dfrac{x^4+5x^2+3}{\sqrt{x}}dx$

$= \int \left(\dfrac{x^4}{\sqrt{x}}+\dfrac{5x^2}{\sqrt{x}}+\dfrac{3}{\sqrt{x}}\right)dx$

$= \int (x^{4-1/2}+5x^{2-1/2}+3x^{-1/2})dx$

$= \int (x^{7/2}+5x^{3/2}+3x^{-1/2})dx$

$= \int x^{7/2}dx+5\int x^{3/2}dx+3\int x^{-1/2}dx$

$= \dfrac{x^{7/2+1}}{7/2+1}+5.\dfrac{x^{2/3+1}}{3/2+1}+3.\dfrac{x^{-1/2+1}}{-1/2+1}+C$

$= \dfrac{2}{9}x^{9/2}+2x^{5/2}+6\sqrt{x}+C$ **Ans.**

Exercise 10 (A)

1. (A) Find : $\int x^4\,dx$ (JAC, 2023)

(B) Find : $\int \dfrac{1}{x^{7/2}}dx$ or $\int x^{-7/2}dx$ (JAC, 2020)

2. Find : $\int (x^2-5x+7)dx$

3. Find : $\int dx$

4. Find : $\int (x+\dfrac{1}{x}+3)dx$

5. Find : $\int (x^{1/3}+2x^{1/2}+x^{3/2})dx$

6. (A) Find : $\int \dfrac{(x-3)^2}{\sqrt{x}}dx$

(B) Find : $\int \left(\sqrt{x}-\dfrac{1}{x^2}\right)^2 dx$

7. Find : $\int \dfrac{(x^3+1)(x-2)}{x^2-x-2}dx$

8. Find : $\int (2x+5)^3dx$

9. Find : $\int \sqrt{x}(x^{3/2}+x+5)dx$

10. Find : $\int \dfrac{(1-x)^2}{\sqrt{x}}dx$

11. Find : $\int \dfrac{(x+3)(x-5)}{x^{3/2}}dx$

12. Find : $\int (ax^3+bx^2+cx+d)$

13. Find : $\int (2x^2+1)^2 4x\,dx$

14. Find : $\int (4x^3-3x^2+2x+1)dx$

15. Find : $\int (2x^5-3x^2+2)dx$

16. Find : $\int \dfrac{ax^2+bx+c}{\sqrt{x}}dx$

17. Find : $\int (x+4)(2x+5)dx$

18. Find : $\int (1+3^x+x^3)dx$

19. Find : $\int \dfrac{1+x+x^2}{x^2(1+x)}dx$

[**Hint:** $I = \int \left\{\dfrac{(1+x)}{x^2(1+x)}+\dfrac{x^2}{x^2(1+x)}\right\}dx$

$= \int \left(\dfrac{1}{x^2}+\dfrac{1}{1+x}\right)dx$

$= \int \left(x^{-2}+\dfrac{1}{1+x}\right)dx$

$= \int x^{-2}dx+\int \dfrac{1}{1+x}dx$

$= \dfrac{-1}{x}+\log(1+x)+C$]

20. Find : $\int \dfrac{5x^4+12x^3+7x^2}{x^2+x}dx$.

[**Hint:** $\int \dfrac{5x^4+5x^3+7x^3+7x^2}{x(x+1)}dx$

$= \int \dfrac{5x^3(x+1)+7x^2(x+1)}{x(x+1)}dx$

$= \int \dfrac{x^2(5x+7)(x+1)}{x(x+1)}dx$

$= \int (5x^2+7x)dx$

$= \int x^2dx+7\int x\,dx$

$= \dfrac{5x^3}{3}+\dfrac{7x^2}{2}+C$]

21. If $f(x)=\dfrac{1}{x}+x$ and $f(1)=\dfrac{5}{2}$, then find $f(x)$.

[Hint : ∵ $f'(x) = \frac{1}{x}+x$

∴ $f(x) = \int\left(\frac{1}{x}+x\right)dx$

$= \int\frac{1}{x}dx+\int xdx$

$f(x) = \log x + \frac{x^2}{2} + C$ ...(i)

∴ $f(1) = \log 1 + \frac{1}{2} + C$ (Putting $x = 1$)

or $\frac{5}{2} = 0 + \frac{1}{2} + C$ [∵ log 1 = 0]

or $\frac{5}{2}-\frac{1}{2} = C$

∴ $C = 2$

So from equation (i),

$f(x) = \log x+\frac{x^2}{2}+2$] **Ans.**

22. Integrate $2x + \frac{1}{x} + 7$ with respect to x. (*JAC, 2025*)

Answers

1. (A) $\left[\frac{x^5}{5}+C\right]$ (B) $\left[\frac{-2}{5.x^{5/2}}+C\right]$
2. $\left[\frac{x^3}{3}-5\frac{x^2}{2}+7x+C\right]$ 3. $x + C$
4. $\left[\frac{x^2}{2}+\log x+3x+C\right]$ 5. $\left[\frac{3}{5}x^{4/3}+\frac{4}{3}x^{3/2}+\frac{2}{5}x^{5/2}+C\right]$
6. (A) $\left[\frac{2}{5}x^{5/2}-4x^{3/2}+18x^{1/2}+C\right]$ (B) $\left[\frac{x^2}{2}-\frac{1}{3x^3}+\frac{4}{\sqrt{x}}+C\right]$
7. $\left[\frac{x^3}{2}-\frac{x^2}{2}+x+C\right]$ 8. $\left[\frac{(2x+5)^4}{8}+C\right]$
9. $\left[\frac{x^3}{2}+\frac{2}{5}x^{5/2}+\frac{10}{3}x^{3/2}+C\right]$ 10. $\left[2\sqrt{x}+\frac{2}{5}x^{5/2}-\frac{4}{3}x^{3/2}+C\right]$
11. $\left[\frac{2}{3}x^{3/2}-4\sqrt{x}+\frac{30}{\sqrt{x}}+C\right]$ 12. $\left[a.\frac{x^4}{4}+b.\frac{x^3}{3}+c.\frac{x^2}{2}+dx+C\right]$
13. $\left[8.\frac{x^6}{3}+4x^4+2x^2+C\right]$ 14. $x^4-x^3+x^2+x+C$
15. $\left[\frac{1}{3}x^6-x^3+2x+C\right]$ 16. $\left[\frac{2}{5}ax^{5/2}+\frac{2}{3}bx^{3/2}+2cx^{1/2}+c\right]$
17. $\left[\frac{2}{3}x^3+\frac{13}{2}x^2+20x+c\right]$ 18. $\left[x+\frac{x^4}{4}+\frac{3^x}{\log 3}+c\right]$
19. $\frac{-1}{x}+\log(1+x)+C$, 20. $\frac{5x^3}{3}+\frac{7x^2}{2}+C$
21. $\log_e x + \frac{x^2}{2} + 2$ 22. $x^2+\frac{x}{x}+7x+c$

(10.4) INTEGRATION BY TRANSFORMATION AND SUBSTITUTION

Method of Transformation : In this method of integration given function is expressed as the algebraic sum of such functions whose integral can be written down with the help of standard formulae.

SOLVED EXAMPLES

✎ Type I

Example 1

Find the value of $\int\frac{dx}{\sqrt{x}+\sqrt{x+1}}$.

Solution :

$$\int\frac{dx}{\sqrt{x}+\sqrt{x+1}} = \int\frac{1}{\sqrt{x}+\sqrt{x+1}}\times\frac{\sqrt{x+1}-\sqrt{x}}{\sqrt{x+1}-\sqrt{x}}$$

$$= \int\frac{\sqrt{x+1}-\sqrt{x}}{x+1-x}dx$$

$$= \int(x+1)^{1/2}dx-\int x^{1/2}dx$$

$$= \frac{(x+1)^{3/2}}{\frac{3}{2}}-\frac{x^{3/2}}{\frac{3}{2}}+C$$

$$= \frac{2}{3}\left\{(x+1)^{3/2}-x^{3/2}\right\}+C$$ **Ans.**

Example 2

Find the value of $1\frac{3x+5}{\sqrt{7x+9}}dx$.

Solution :

Here we will write $3x + 5$ in the form $a(7x + 9) + b$

Let $3x + 5 = a(7x + 9) + b$

or $3x + 5 = 7ax - 9a + b$ ...(i)

Equation the coefficients of similar powers of x from both sides, we get

$7a = 3$

∴ $a = \frac{3}{7}$

and $9a + b = 5$

∴ $b = 5 - 9a$

$= 5 - 9.3/7 = 8/7$

Hence from (1),

$$3x + 5 = \frac{3}{7}(7x+9)+\frac{8}{7} \quad ...(ii)$$

$$\therefore \int\frac{3x+5}{\sqrt{7x+9}}dx = \int\frac{\frac{3}{7}(7x+9)+\frac{8}{7}}{\sqrt{7x+9}}dx$$

$$= \frac{3}{7}.\int\frac{7x+9}{\sqrt{7x+9}}dx+\frac{8}{7}\int\frac{dx}{\sqrt{7x+9}}$$

$$= \frac{3}{7}\int\sqrt{7x+9}\,dx+\frac{8}{7}\int(7x+9)^{-1/2}\,dx$$

$$= \frac{3}{7}\frac{(7x+9)^{1/2+1}}{(1/2+1).7}+\frac{8}{7}.\frac{(7x+9)^{-1/2+1}}{(-1/2+1).7}+C$$

$$= \frac{2}{49}(7x+9)^{3/2}+\frac{16}{49}(7x+9)^{1/2}+C$$

$$= \frac{2}{49}\sqrt{7x+9}\,(7x+9+8)+C$$

$$= \frac{2}{49}(7x+17)\sqrt{7x+9}+C \quad \textbf{Ans.}$$

Example 3

Evaluate : $\int (x-1)\sqrt{x+1}\,dx$.

Solution :

Here we will have to express $x - 1$ in the form $a(x + 1) + b$.

Let $x - 1 = a(x + 1) + b$

or $x - 1 = ax + (a + b)$ ...(i)

Equation the coefficients of similar powers of x we get

$a = 1$ and $a + b = -1$

$\therefore$ $b = -1 - a = -2$

From (1), $x - 1 = (x + 1) - 2$

Now $\int (x-1)\sqrt{x+1}\,dx$

$$= \int [(x+1)-2]\sqrt{x+1}\,dx$$

$$= \int \left[(x+1)^{3/2}-2\sqrt{x+1}\right]dx$$

$$= \int (x+1)^{3/2}\,dx - 2\int \sqrt{x+1}\,dx$$

$$= \frac{(x+1)^{5/2}}{5/2} - 2.\frac{(x+1)^{3/2}}{3/2}+C$$

$$= \frac{2}{5}(x+1)^{5/2}-\frac{4}{3}(x+1)^{3/2}+C$$

$$= 2(x+1)^{3/2}\left(\frac{x+1}{5}-\frac{2}{3}\right)+C$$

$$= 2(x+1)^{3/2}.\frac{3x+3-10}{15}+C$$

$$= \frac{2}{15}(x+14)^{3/2}(3x-7)+C \quad \textbf{Ans.}$$

Example 4

Find the value of $\int \frac{x+1}{x-1}dx$. (*JAC*, 2015, 16)

Solution :

$$\int \frac{x+1}{x-1}dx = \int \frac{x+1-1+1}{x-1}dx$$

$$= \int \frac{x-1+2}{x-1}dx$$

$$= \int \left(\frac{x-1}{x-1}+\frac{2}{x-1}\right)dx$$

$$= \int \left(1+\frac{2}{x-1}\right)dx$$

$$= \int 1\,dx + 2\int \frac{1}{x-1}dx$$

$$= x + 2\log(x-1) + C \quad \textbf{Ans.}$$

Example 5

Find the value of $\int \frac{x^2+1}{x-1}dx$.

Solution :

$$\int \frac{x^2+1}{x-1}dx = \int \frac{x^2+2-1}{x-1}dx$$

$$= \int \left(\frac{x^2-2+1}{x-1}\right)dx$$

$$= \int \left\{\frac{(x-1)(x+1)}{x-1}+\frac{2}{x-1}\right\}dx$$

$$= \int \left\{(x+1)+\frac{2}{(x-1)}\right\}dx$$

$$= \int x\,dx + \int 1\,dx + 2\int \frac{dx}{x-1}$$

$$= \frac{x^2}{2}+x+2\log(x-1)+C \quad \textbf{Ans.}$$

Example 6

Find the value of $\int a^x dx$.

Solution : $I = \int a^x dx$

$$= \int e^{\log_e a^x}dx = \int e^{x\log_e a}dx$$

$$= \frac{e^{x\log_e a}}{\frac{d}{dx}(x\log_e a)} = \frac{a^x}{\log_e a}+C \quad \textbf{Ans.}$$

Example 7

Evaluate : $\int a^{3x+3}\,dx; a \neq -1$.

Solution : $I = \int a^{3x+3}\,dx = \int e^{\log e\, a^{3x+3}}\,dx$

$$= \int e^{(3x+3)\log e\, a}\,dx$$

$$= \frac{e^{(3x+3)\log_e a}}{\int \frac{d}{dx}(3x+3)\log a}$$

$$= \frac{a^{3x+3}}{(3.1+0)\log a}+C = \frac{a^{3x+3}}{3\log a} \quad \textbf{Ans.}$$

Example 8

Evaluate : $\int 2^x\,dx$.

Solution : $I = \int 2^x\,dx = \int e^{\log_e 2^x}\,dx$

$$= \int e^{x\log e^2}\,dx$$

$$= \frac{e^{x\log e\,2}}{\int \frac{d}{dx}(x\log 2)}$$

$$= \frac{2^x}{\log 2}+C \quad [\because 2^x = e^{x\log e\,2}] \quad \textbf{Ans.}$$

Example 9

Evaluate : $\int \frac{e^{\log_e \sqrt{x}}}{x} dx$.

Solution :

$$e^{\log\sqrt{x}} = e^{\log_e \sqrt{x}} = \sqrt{x}$$

$$I = \int \frac{e^{\log_e \sqrt{x}}}{x} dx = \int \frac{\sqrt{x}}{x} dx \quad \text{...(i)}$$

$$= \int x^{-1/2} dx = \frac{x^{-1/2+1}}{-1/2+1} + C$$

$$= 2x^{1/2} + C$$

$$= 2\sqrt{x} + C \quad \textbf{Ans.}$$

Method of Substitution : In this method we change the integral in which independent variable z is different from x, where x and z are related by $x = \phi(z)$:

SOLVED EXAMPLES

✎ **Type II**

Example 1

Find the value of : $\int e^{4x} dx$.

Solution :

Let $z = 4x$

$\therefore$ $dz = 4dx$

or $dx = \frac{dz}{4}$

$$\therefore \int e^{4x} dx = \int e^z \frac{dz}{4} = \frac{1}{4}\int e^z dz$$

$$= \frac{1}{4}e^z + C$$

$$= \frac{1}{4}e^{4x} + C \quad \textbf{Ans.}$$

Example 2

Evaluate : $\int (5x+3) + \sqrt{2x-1} dx$

Solution :

Let $z = 2x - 1$

or $dz = 2dx$

or $dx = \frac{dz}{2}$

Again $z = 2x - 1$

$\therefore$ $x = \frac{z+1}{2}$

$$\therefore \int (5x+3)\sqrt{2x-1}\, dx = \int \left[5\frac{(z+1)}{2}+3\right]\frac{\sqrt{z}}{2} dz$$

$$= \int \left[\frac{(5z+5)}{2}+3\right]\frac{\sqrt{z}}{2} dz = \int \frac{5z+5+6}{4}\sqrt{z}\, dz$$

$$= \int \frac{5z+11}{4}\sqrt{z}\, dz = \int \frac{(5z^{3/2}+11z^{1/2})}{4} dz$$

$$= \frac{5}{4}\int z^{3/2} dz + \frac{11}{4}\int z^{1/2} dz$$

$$= \frac{5}{4}.\frac{z^{5/2}}{5/2} + \frac{11}{4}.\frac{z^{3/2}}{3/2} + C$$

$$= \frac{5}{4}.\frac{2}{5}z^{5/2} + \frac{11}{4}.\frac{2}{3}z^{3/2} + C$$

$$= \frac{1}{2}z^{5/2} + \frac{11}{6}z^{3/2} + C$$

$$= \frac{z^{3/2}}{2}\left[z + \frac{11}{3}\right] + C$$

$$= \frac{z^{3/2}}{2}\left[(2x-1) + \frac{11}{3}\right] + C$$

$$= \frac{(2x-1)^{3/2}}{2}\left[\frac{6x-3+11}{3}\right] + C$$

$$= \frac{(2x-1)^{3/2}}{2}.(6x+8) + C$$

$$= \frac{(2x-1)^{3/2}(3x+4)}{3} + C \quad \textbf{Ans.}$$

Example 3(a)

Evaluate : $\int \frac{4x-6}{x^2-3x+7} dx$.

Solution :

$$\int \frac{4x-6}{x^2-3x+7} dx = \int \frac{2(2x-3)}{x^2-3x+7} dx$$

Let $z = x^2 - 3x + 7$

$dz = 2x - 3$

$$\therefore \int \frac{2dz}{z} = 2\int \frac{1}{z} dz$$

$$= 2 \log z + C$$

$$= 2 \log (x^2 - 3x + 7) + C \quad \textbf{Ans.}$$

Example 3(b)

Evaluate : $\int (x^3 - 5x + 8) dx$. .

Solution :

$$\frac{x^4}{4} - \frac{5x^2}{2} + 8x + c$$

Example 4

Evaluate : $\int \frac{3x^5+1}{x^6+2x} dx$.

Solution :

$$\int \frac{3x^5+1}{x^6+2x} dx = \frac{1}{2}\int \frac{(6x^5+2)}{x^6+2x} dx$$

Let $z = x^6 + 2x$

or $dz = (6x^5 + 2)dx$

or $dz = 2(3x^5 + 1)dx$

or $\frac{dz}{2} = (3x^5 + 1)dx$

$$\therefore \int \frac{3x^5+1}{x^6+2x} dx = \int \frac{dz}{2z}$$

$$= \frac{1}{2}\log z + C$$

$$= \frac{1}{2}\log(x^6 + 2x) + C \quad \textbf{Ans.}$$

Example 5

Evaluate : $\int \frac{2ax+b}{(ax^2+bx+c)^4} dx$.

Solution :

Let $ax^2 + bx + c = z$

or $(2ax + b)\, dx = dz$

$\therefore \quad dx = \frac{dz}{2ax+b}$

$$\therefore \int \frac{2ax+b}{(ax^2+bx+c)^4} dx = \int \frac{(2ax+b)}{z^4} dx$$

$$= \int \frac{dz}{z^4}$$

$$= \int z^{-4}\, dz$$

$$= d\frac{z^{-3}}{-3} + C$$

$$= -\frac{1}{3}(ax^2+bx+c)^{-3} + C \quad \textbf{Ans.}$$

Example 6

Evaluate : $\int \frac{x^3}{(4-x^4)^2} dx$.

Solution :

Let $4 - x^4 = z$

or $-4x^3\, dx = dz$

or $x^3\, dx = \frac{1}{4} dz$

$$\therefore \int \frac{x^3}{(4-x^4)^2} dx = \frac{1}{4z^2} dz$$

$$= \frac{1}{4}\int \frac{1}{z^2} dz$$

$$= \frac{1}{4}\int z^{-2}\, dz$$

$$= -\frac{1}{4}\frac{z^{-1}}{-1} + C$$

$$= +\frac{1}{4}.z^{-1} + C$$

$$= \frac{1}{4}.\frac{1}{z} + C$$

$$= \frac{1}{4.(4-x^4)} + C \quad \textbf{Ans.}$$

Example 7

Evaluate : $\int 4x\sqrt{x^2+8}\, dx$.

Solution :

Let $x^2 + 8 = z$

$\therefore \quad 2x\, dx = dz$

or $xdx = \frac{dz}{2}$

$$\therefore \int 4x\sqrt{x^2+8}\, dx = \int 4.\sqrt{z}\frac{dz}{2}$$

$$= 2\int z^{1/2}\, dz$$

$$= 2\frac{z^{3/2}}{3/2} + C$$

$$= \frac{4}{3}.z^{3/2} + C$$

$$= \frac{4}{3}(x^2+8)^{3/2} + C \quad \textbf{Ans.}$$

Example 8

Evaluate : $\int \frac{1}{a-bx} dx$.

Solution :

Let $a - bx = z$

$\therefore \quad -bdx = dz$

or $dx = -\frac{1}{b} dz$

$$\int \frac{1}{a-bx} dx = \int \frac{1}{z}.\left(-\frac{1}{b}\right) dz$$

$$= -\frac{1}{b}\int \frac{1}{z} dz = -\frac{1}{b}\log z + C$$

$$= -\frac{1}{b}\log(a-bx) + C \quad \textbf{Ans.}$$

Example 9

Evaluate : $\int xe^{-x^2} dx$.

Solution :

Let $-x^2 = z$

$-2xdx = dz$

Let $x\, dx = -\frac{dz}{2}$

$$\therefore \int xe^{-x^2} dx = \int e^z\left(-\frac{dz}{2}\right)$$

$$= -\frac{1}{2}\int e^z\, dz$$

$$= -\frac{1}{2}e^z + C$$

$$= -\frac{1}{2}e^{-x^2} + C \quad \textbf{Ans.}$$

Example 10

Evaluate : $\int e^{ax+b} dx$.

Solution :

Let $ax + b = z$

$\Rightarrow \quad adx = dz$

or $dx = \frac{dz}{a}$

$$\therefore \int e^{ax+b} dx = \int e^z.\frac{dz}{a}$$

$$= \frac{1}{a}\int e^z\, dz$$

$$= \frac{1}{a}\int e^z + C$$

$$= \frac{1}{a}.e^{(ax+b)} + C$$ **Ans.**

Example 11

Evaluate : $\int \frac{e^{3x}}{e^{3x}+6}dx$.

Solution :

Let $e^{3x} + 6 = z$

$3\, e^{3x}\, dx = dz$

or $e^{3x}\, dx = dz/3$

$$\therefore \int \frac{e^{3x}}{e^{3x}+6}dx = \int \frac{1}{z}.\frac{dz}{3}$$

$$= \frac{1}{3}\int\left(\frac{1}{z}dz\right)$$

$$= \frac{1}{3}\log z + C$$

$$= \frac{1}{3}\log\left(e^{3x}+6\right) + C$$ **Ans.**

Example 12

Evaluate : $\int \frac{e^x + e^{-x}}{e^x - e^{-x}}\, dx.$

Solution :

Let $e^x - e^{-x} = z$

$(e^x + e^{-x})\, dx = dz$

$$\therefore \int \frac{\left(e^x + e^{-x}\right)}{e^x - e^x}dx = \int \frac{dz}{z}$$

$$= \log z + C$$

$$= \log\,(e^x - e^{-x}) + C$$ **Ans.**

Example 13

Evaluate : $\int \frac{1}{x}.\log x\, dx$.

Solution :

Let $\log x = z$

$\Rightarrow \frac{1}{x}dx = dz$

$$\therefore \int \frac{1}{x}.\log x\, dx = \int z dz$$

$$= \frac{z^2}{2} + C$$

$$= \frac{(\log x)^2}{2} + C$$ **Ans.**

Example 14

Evaluate : $\frac{e^{3x}+e^{4x}}{e^x}dx$.

Solution :

$$\frac{e^{3x}+e^{4x}}{e^x}dx = \int\left(\frac{e^{3x}}{e^x}+\frac{e^{4x}}{e^x}\right)dx$$

$$= \int\left(e^{2x}+e^{3x}\right)dx$$

$$= \int e^{2x}\, dx + \int e^{3x}\, dx$$

$$= \frac{e^{2x}}{\frac{d}{dx}(2x)} + \frac{e^{3x}}{\frac{d}{dx}(3x)}$$

$$= \frac{e^{2x}}{2} + \frac{e^{3x}}{3} + C$$ **Ans.**

Example 15

Evaluate : $\int x\sqrt{x-1}\, dx$.

Solution :

Let $\sqrt{x-1} = z$

$z - 1 = z^2$

$\Rightarrow x = z^2 + 1$

$dx = 2\,zdz$

$$\therefore \int x\sqrt{x-1}\, dx = \int\left(z^2+1\right)z\,2z\, dz$$

$$= \int\left(z^2+1\right).2z^2 dz$$

$$= \int\left(2z^4+2z^2\right)dz$$

$$= \int 2z^4\, dz + 2\int z^2 dz$$

$$= 2.\frac{z^5}{5} + \frac{2z^3}{3} + C$$

$$= \frac{6z^5+10z^3}{15} + C$$

$$= \frac{2}{15}z^3\left(3z^2+5\right) + C$$

$$= \frac{2}{15}(x-1)^{3/2}(3x-3+5) + C$$

$$= \frac{2}{15}(x-1)^{3/2}(x+2) + C$$ **Ans.**

Example 16

Evaluate : $\int x^3\sqrt{x^2-3}\, dx$.

Solution :

Let $\sqrt{x^2-3} = z$

$x^2 - 3 = z^2 \Rightarrow x^2 = z^2 + 3$

or $2xdx = 2zdz$

or $xdx = zdz$

$$\therefore \int x^3\sqrt{x^2-3}\, dx = \int x^2.x\sqrt{x^2-3}\, dx$$

$$= \int\left(z^2+3\right)z.zdx$$

$$= \int\left(z^2+3\right)z^2\, dz$$

$$= \int\left(z^4+3z^2\right)z^2\, dz$$

$$= \int\left(z^4\, dz+3\right)z^2\, dz$$

$$= \frac{z^5}{5} + \frac{3z^3}{3} + C$$

$$= \left(\frac{z^5}{5} + z^3\right) + C$$

$$= \left(\frac{z^5+5z^3}{5}\right)+C$$
$$= \frac{1}{5}z^3\left[z^2+5\right]+C$$
$$= \frac{1}{5}\left(x^2-3\right)^{3/2}\left[x^2-3+5\right]+C$$
$$= \frac{1}{5}\left(x^2-3\right)^{3/2}\left(x^2+2\right)+C \quad \textbf{Ans.}$$

Example 17

Evaluate : $\int \frac{x^2-1}{x^3-3x+2}dx$.

Solution :

Let $x^3 - 3x + 2 = z$

$\Rightarrow (3x^2 - 3)dx = dz$

$\Rightarrow (x^2 - 1)dx = \frac{dz}{3}$

$$\therefore \int \frac{x^2-1}{x^3-3x+2}dx = \int \frac{1}{z}.\frac{dz}{3}$$
$$= \frac{1}{3}\int \frac{1}{z}dz$$
$$= \frac{1}{3}\log z+C$$
$$= \frac{1}{3}\log\left(x^3-3x+2\right)+C \quad \textbf{Ans.}$$

Example 18

Find : $\int x^2\sqrt{(ax+b)}\,dx$.

Solution :

Let $ax + b = z$

and $adx = dz$

or $dx = dz/a$

Again $ax + b = z$

or $ax = z - b$

or $x = \frac{z-b}{a}$

$$\int x^2\sqrt{(ax+b)}\,dx = \int\left(\frac{z-b}{a}\right)^2.\sqrt{z}.\frac{dz}{a}$$
$$= \int\frac{\left(z^2-2bz+b^2\right)}{a^2}.\sqrt{z}.\frac{dz}{a}$$
$$= \frac{1}{a^3}\int\left(z^2-2bz+b^2\right)z^{1/2}\,dz$$
$$= \frac{1}{a^3}\int\left(z^{5/2}-2bz^{3/2}+b^2z^{1/2}\right)dz$$
$$= \frac{1}{a^3}\left[\frac{z^{7/2}}{7/2}-2b\frac{z^{5/2}}{5/2}+b^2.\frac{z^{3/2}}{3/2}+C\right]$$
$$= \frac{1}{a^3}\left[\frac{2}{7}z^{7/2}-\frac{4}{5}bz^{5/2}+\frac{2}{3}b^2z^{3/2}\right]+C$$
$$= \frac{2}{a^3}\left[\frac{1}{7}z^{7/2}-\frac{2}{5}bz^{5/2}+\frac{1}{3}b^2z^{3/2}\right]+C$$
$$= \frac{2}{a^3}z^{3/2}\left[\frac{z^2}{7}-\frac{bz}{5}+\frac{1}{3}b^2\right]+C$$
$$= \frac{2}{a^3}z^{3/2}\left[\frac{15z^2-42bz+35b^2}{105}\right]+C$$
$$= \frac{2}{105}.\frac{(ax+b)^{3/2}}{a^3}[15(ax+b)^2$$
$$-42b(ax+b)+35b^2]+C$$
$$= \frac{2}{105}\frac{(ax+b)^{3/2}}{a^3}[15a^2x^2-12abx$$
$$+8b^2]+C \quad \textbf{Ans.}$$

Example 19

Find the value of : $\frac{x^2}{\sqrt{x+2}}dx$.

Solution :

Let $x + 2 = z$

$\Rightarrow x = z - 2$

and $dx = dz$

$$\therefore \int\frac{x^2}{\sqrt{x+2}}dx = \int\frac{(z-2)^2}{\sqrt{x}}dz$$
$$= \int\frac{\left(z^2-4z+4\right)}{\sqrt{z}}dz$$
$$= \int\left(\frac{z^2}{\sqrt{z}}-\frac{4z}{\sqrt{z}}+\frac{4}{\sqrt{z}}\right)dz$$
$$= \int\left(z^{3/2}-4\sqrt{z}+4z^{-1/2}\right)dz$$
$$= \frac{z^{5/2}}{5/2}-4.\frac{z^{3/2}}{3/2}+\frac{4z^{1/2}}{1/2}+C$$
$$= \frac{2}{5}z^{5/2}-8.\frac{z^{3/2}}{3}+8\sqrt{z}+C$$
$$= 2\sqrt{z}\left[\frac{z^2}{5}-4.\frac{z}{3}+4\right]+C$$
$$= 2\sqrt{z}\frac{\left(3z^2-20z+60\right)}{15}+C$$
$$= \frac{2}{15}\sqrt{x+2}\left[3(x+2)^2-20(x+2)+60\right]+C$$
$$= \frac{2}{15}\sqrt{x+2}\left[3\left(x^2+4x+4\right)-20x-40+60\right]+C$$
$$= \frac{2}{15}\sqrt{x+2}\left(3x^2+12x+12-20x-40+60\right)+C$$
$$= \frac{2}{15}\sqrt{x+2}\left(3x^2-8x+32\right)+C \quad \textbf{Ans.}$$

Example 20

Evaluate : $\int\frac{2-3x}{\sqrt{1+3x}}dx$.

Solution :

Let $1 + 3x = z$

$\Rightarrow 3x = z - 1$

$$\Rightarrow \qquad x = \frac{z-1}{3}$$

and $$dx = \frac{1}{3}dz$$

$$\therefore \int \frac{2-3x}{\sqrt{1+3x}}dx = \int \frac{2-3\left(\frac{z-1}{3}\right)}{\sqrt{z}} - dz/3$$

$$= \frac{1}{3}\int \frac{2-z+1}{\sqrt{z}}dz$$

$$= \frac{1}{3}\int \left(\frac{3}{\sqrt{z}} - \frac{z}{\sqrt{z}}\right)dz$$

$$= \frac{1}{3}\int \left(3z^{-1/2} - \sqrt{z}\right)dz$$

$$= \frac{1}{3}\left[\frac{3z^{1/2}}{1/2} - \frac{z^{3/2}}{3/2}\right] + C$$

$$= \frac{1}{3}\left(6\sqrt{z} - \frac{2}{3}z^{3/2}\right) + C$$

$$= \frac{2}{3}\sqrt{z}\left(3 - \frac{1}{3}z\right) + C$$

$$= \frac{2}{3}\sqrt{z}.\frac{(9-z)}{3} + C$$

$$= \frac{2}{3}\sqrt{1+3x}\left[\frac{9-(1+3x)}{3}\right] + C$$

$$= \frac{2}{3}\sqrt{1+3x}\left(\frac{8-3x}{3}\right) + C$$

$$= \frac{2}{9}(8-3x)\sqrt{1+3x} + C$$ **Ans.**

Example 21

Integrate : $\int \frac{x^3}{\sqrt{x^4+1}}dx$.

Solution :

Let $x^4 + 1 = z$

and $4x^3\, dx = dz$

$$\Rightarrow \qquad x^3\, dx = \frac{dz}{4}$$

$$\therefore \int \frac{x^3}{\sqrt{x^4+1}}dx = \int \frac{1}{\sqrt{z}}.\frac{dz}{4}$$

$$= \frac{1}{4}\int \frac{1}{\sqrt{z}}.dz$$

$$= \frac{1}{4}\int z^{-1/2}.dz$$

$$= \frac{1}{4}\frac{z^{1/2}}{1/2} + C$$

$$= \frac{1}{2}.\sqrt{x^4+1} + C$$ **Ans.**

Example 22

Integrate : $\int \frac{(1+\log x)^2}{x}dx$.

Solution :

Let $1 + \log x = z$

and $\frac{1}{x}dx = dz$

$$\therefore \int \frac{(1+\log x)^2}{x}dx = \int z^2.dz$$

$$= \frac{z^3}{3} + C$$

$$= \frac{(1+\log x)^3}{3} + C$$ **Ans.**

Example 23

Integrate : $\int \frac{e^{2x}}{1+e^x}dx$.

Solution :

Let $z = 1 + e^x$

$\Rightarrow$ $e^x = z - 1$

or $dz = e^x\, dx$

$$\therefore \int \frac{e^{2x}}{1+e^x}dx = \int \frac{e^x}{1+e^x}e^x\, dx$$

$$= \int \frac{(z-1)}{z}dz$$

$$= \int \left(1 - \frac{1}{z}\right)dz$$

$$= z - \log z + C$$

$$= 1 + e^x - \log(1 + e^x) + K$$

$$= e^x - \log(1 + e^x) + K$$

where K = C + 1 **Ans.**

Example 24

Integrate with respect to x : $\frac{2x}{1+x^2}$

Solution :

Let $1 + x^2 = z$

$\Rightarrow$ $2xdx = dz$

$$\therefore \int \frac{2x}{1+x^2}dx = \int \frac{1}{z}dz$$

$$= \log z + C$$

$$= \log(1 + x^2) + C$$ **Ans.**

Exercise 10 (B)

Evaluate :

1. $\int 4x^2\sqrt{x^3+3}\,dx$ (*JAC*, 2018)
2. $\int \frac{(\log x)^3}{x}dx$
3. $\int \frac{2x}{\sqrt{x^2+4}}dx$
4. $\int x.e^{x^2}\,dx$
5. $\int x\left(1+3x^2\right)^{5/2}dx$
6. $\int \frac{x^2}{x^3+1}dx$

7. $\int x^3\sqrt{x^2+5}\,dx$

8. $\int x^2\sqrt{a^3+x^3}\,dx$

9. $\int \frac{x^3}{\sqrt{x^2+3}}dx$

10. $\int \frac{x^3}{\sqrt{x^4+1}}dx$

11. $\int (2x+3)\sqrt{x^2+3x}\,dx$

12. $\int x\sqrt{1+x^2}\,dx$

13. $\int 3x^2(x^3+5)^4\,dx$

14. $\int x^4 ex^5\,dx$

15. $\int \frac{x}{\sqrt{2x^2+3}}dx$

16. $\int x\sqrt{2x^2+3}\,dx$

17. $\int \frac{1}{x}.e^{\log x}\,dx$

18. $\int \frac{x^2}{\sqrt{1-x}}dx$

19. $\int \frac{2ax+b}{ax^2+bx+c}dx$

20. $\int \frac{e^x}{e^{x+2}}dx$

21. $\int (x-1)\sqrt{x^2-2x\,dx}$

22. $\int (4x+3)\sqrt{4x^2+6x+1}\,dx$

23. $\int \frac{dx}{x\sqrt{\log_e x}}$

24. $\int \frac{dx}{x(1+\log_e x)^2}$

25. $\int x^2\sqrt{x+2}\,dx$

26. $\int \frac{x^2+3x+1}{(x+1)^2}dx$

27. $\int \frac{2x-1}{(x+1)^2}dx$

28. Evaluate : $\int_0^1 \frac{x}{\sqrt{1+x^2}}dx$

Answers

1. $\left[\frac{8}{9}(x^3+3)^{3/2}+C\right]$

2. $\left[\frac{(\log x)^4}{4}+C\right]$

3. $\left[2(x^2+4)^{1/2}+C\right]$

4. $\left[\frac{1}{2}e^{x^2}+C\right]$

5. $\left[\frac{1}{21}(1+3x)^{7/2}+C\right]$

6. $\left[\frac{1}{3}\log(x^3+1)+C\right]$

7. $\left[\frac{1}{15}(3x^2-10)(x^2+5)^{3/2}+C\right]$

8. $\left[\frac{2}{9}(a^3+x^3)^{3/2}+C\right]$

9. $\left[\frac{1}{3}\sqrt{x^2+3}(x^2-6)+C\right]$

10. $\left[\frac{1}{4}\log(x^4+1)+C\right]$

11. $\left[\frac{2}{3}(x^2+3x)^{3/2}+C\right]$

12. $\left[\frac{1}{3}(1+x^2)^{3/2}+C\right]$

13. $\left[\frac{1}{5}(x^3+5)5+C\right]$

14. $\left[\frac{1}{5}ex^5+C\right]$

15. $\left[\frac{\sqrt{2x^2+3}}{2}+C\right]$

16. $\left[\frac{1}{6}(2x^2+3)^{3/2}+C\right]$

17. $e^{\log x}+C$,

18. $\left[-\frac{2}{15}\sqrt{1-x}(3x^2+4x+8)\right]+C$

19. $\log(ax^2+bx+c)+C$

20. $\log(e^x+2)+C$

21. $\left[\frac{1}{3}(x^2-2x)^{3/2}+C\right]$

22. $\left[\frac{(4x^2+6x+1)^{3/2}}{3}+C\right]$

23. $\left[2\sqrt{\log_e x}+C\right]$

24. $\left[-\frac{1}{1+\log_e x}+C\right]$

25. $\left[2(x+2)^{3/2}\left[\frac{(x+2)^2}{7}-\frac{4}{5}(x+2)+\frac{4}{3}\right]+C\right]$

26. $\left[x+\log(x+1)+\frac{1}{(x+1)}+C\right]$

27. $\left[2\log(x-1)-\frac{1}{x-1}+C\right]$

28. $\left[\frac{1}{\sqrt{2}}-1+C\right]$

(10.5) INTEGRATION OF SOME RATIONAL FUNCTIONS

SOLVED EXAMPLES

Example 1

Integrate : $\int \frac{dx}{a^2-x^2}$, where $x < a$.

Solution :

$$\therefore \quad \int \frac{dx}{a^2-x^2} = \int \frac{dx}{(a-x)(a+x)} \quad ...(i)$$

Let $\frac{1}{(a-x)(a+x)} = \frac{A}{a-x}+\frac{B}{a+x}$

$= A(a+x) + B(a-x)$ ...(ii)

Putting $x = a$ in (ii),

$A(a+a) + B.0 = 1$

$\therefore \quad A = \frac{1}{2a}$

Again putting $x = -a$ in (ii),

$B(a+a) = 1$

$\therefore \quad B = \frac{1}{2a}$

$$\therefore \quad \frac{1}{(a-x)(a+x)} = \frac{A}{a-x}+\frac{B}{a+x} = \frac{1}{2a}\left(\frac{1}{a-x}\right)+\frac{1}{2a}\left(\frac{1}{a+x}\right)$$

From equation (i),

$$I = \frac{1}{2a}\int\left(\frac{1}{a-x}+\frac{1}{a+x}\right)dx$$

$$= \frac{1}{2a}\left[\frac{\log(a-x)}{-1}+\log(a+x)\right]+C$$

$$= \frac{1}{2a}\left[\log(a+x)-\log(a-x)\right]+C$$

$$= \frac{1}{2a}\log\frac{a+x}{a-x}+C$$ **Ans.**

Example 2

Integrate : $\int \frac{dx}{x^2-a^2}, x>a$.

Solution :

$$\frac{1}{x^2-a^2} = \frac{1}{(x-a)(x+a)} \quad ...(i)$$

Let $\dfrac{1}{(x-a)(x+a)} = \dfrac{A}{x-a}+\dfrac{B}{x+a}$

$\Rightarrow$ A $(x + a)$ + B $(x - a) = 1$ ...(ii)

Putting $x = -a$,

$B(-a-a) = 1$

$\therefore B = \dfrac{1}{2a}$

Again putting $x = a$,

$A.2a = 1$

$\therefore A = \dfrac{1}{2a}$

$\therefore$ From equation (i),

$$\frac{1}{(x-a)(x+a)} = \frac{1}{2a}\left(\frac{1}{x-a}-\frac{1}{x+a}\right)$$

$$\therefore I = \int\frac{dx}{a^2-x^2}=\int\frac{dx}{(x-a)(x+a)}$$

$$= \frac{1}{2a}\int\left(\frac{1}{x-a}-\frac{1}{x+a}\right)dx$$

$$= \frac{1}{2a}\left[\log(x-a)-\log(x+a)\right]+C$$

$$= \frac{1}{2a}\log\left(\frac{x-a}{x+a}\right)+C \quad \textbf{Ans.}$$

Example 3

Integrate : $\int\dfrac{dx}{3+2x-x^2}, x<3$.

Solution :

$$\because 3 + 2x - x^2 = -(x^2 - 2x - 3)$$
$$= -(x^2 - 3x + x - 3),$$
$$= -[x(x-3) + 1(x-3)]$$
$$= -(x-3)(x+1)$$
$$= (3-x)(x+1)$$

$$\therefore \frac{1}{3+2x-x^2} = \frac{1}{(x+1)(3-x)}$$

Let $\dfrac{1}{(x+1)(3-x)} = \dfrac{A}{(x+1)}+\dfrac{B}{(3-x)}$ ...(i)

$$= \frac{A(3-x)+B(x+1)}{(x+1)(3-x)}$$

$\Rightarrow$ A $(3 - x)$ + B $(x + 1) = 1$ ...(ii)

Putting $x = -1$,

$4A = 1$

$\Rightarrow A = \dfrac{1}{4}$

Again Putting $x = 3$,

$4B = 1$

$B = 1/4$

Now $I = \int\dfrac{dx}{3+2x-x^2}=\int\dfrac{dx}{(x+1)(3-x)}$

$$= \frac{1}{4}\int\left(\frac{1}{x+1}+\frac{1}{3-x}\right)dx$$

$$= \frac{1}{4}\left[\log(x+1)-\log(3-x)\right]+C$$

$$= \frac{1}{4}\log\left(\frac{x+1}{3-x}\right)+C \quad \textbf{Ans.}$$

Example 4

Integrate : $\int\dfrac{x\,dx}{(x^2-a^2)(x^2-b^2)}$.

Solution :

Let $z = x^2$

$\Rightarrow dz = 2xdx$

$\Rightarrow \dfrac{dz}{2} = xdx$ ...(i)

$$\therefore I = \int\frac{xdx}{(x^2-a^2)(x^2-b^2)}$$

$$= \frac{1}{2}\int\frac{dz}{(z-a^2)(z-b^2)} \quad ...(ii)$$

Let $\dfrac{1}{(z-a^2)(z-b^2)} = \dfrac{A}{z-a^2}+\dfrac{B}{z-b^2}$

$$\therefore \frac{1}{(z-a^2)(z-b^2)} = \frac{A(z-b^2)+B(z-a^2)}{(z-a^2)(z-b^2)}$$

$\Rightarrow$ A $(z - b^2)$ + B $(z - a^2) = 1$

Putting $z = a^2$,

$A(a^2 - b^2) = 1$

$\Rightarrow A = \dfrac{1}{a^2-b^2}$

Again $z = b^2$, B $(b^2 - a^2) = 1$

$\Rightarrow B = \dfrac{-1}{a^2-b^2}$

$\therefore$ From equation (i),

$$I = \frac{1}{2(a^2-b^2)}\int\left(\frac{1}{z-a^2}-\frac{1}{z-b^2}\right)dz$$

$$= \frac{1}{2(a^2-b^2)}\left[\log(z-a^2)-\log(z-b^2)\right]+C$$

$$= \frac{1}{2(a^2-b^2)}\log\left(\frac{z-a^2}{z-b^2}\right)+C$$

$$= \frac{1}{2(a^2-b^2)}\log\left(\frac{x^2-a^2}{x^2-b^2}\right)+C \quad (\because z = x^2)$$

Example 5

Integrate : $\int \frac{x+5}{(x+1)(x+2)^2}dx$.

Solution :

Here the given fraction is proper because degree numerator is less than degree of denominator. Let the pratial fractions be,

$$\frac{x+5}{(x+1)(x+2)^2} = \frac{A}{(x+1)} + \frac{B}{(x+2)} + \frac{C}{(x+2)^2}$$

or $x + 5 = A(x+2)^2 + B(x+1)(x+2) + C(x+1)$

Put $x = -2$

$3 = C(-2+1)$

$\Rightarrow C = -3$

Put $x = -1$

$4 = A$

Now put $x = 0$

$5 = 4A + 2B + C$

or $5 = 16 + 2B - 3$

$\therefore B = -4$

$$\therefore \int \frac{x+5}{(x+1)(x+2)^2}$$

$$= \int \left[\frac{4}{(x+1)} - \frac{4}{(x+2)} - \frac{3}{(x+2)^2}\right]dx$$

$$= 4\int \frac{dx}{x+1} - 4\int \frac{dx}{x+2} - 3\int \frac{dx}{(x+2)^2}$$

$$= 4\log(x+1) - 4\log(x+2) + \frac{3}{x+2} + C$$

Example 6

Integrate : $\int \frac{x^3-5x}{(x^2-9)(x^2+1)}dx$

Solution :

Here the given fraction is proper, because degree of numerator is less than degree of denominator.

$$\frac{x^3-5x}{(x^2-9)(x^2+1)} = \frac{x^3-5x}{(x-3)(x+3)(x^2+1)}$$

$$= \frac{A}{(x-3)} + \frac{B}{(x+3)} + \frac{Cx+D}{(x^2+1)}$$

$\Rightarrow A(x+3)(x^2+1) + B(x-3)(x^2+1) + (Cx+D)(x^2-9) = x^3 - 5x$

Put $x = 3$,

$27 - 15 = 6A$

$\Rightarrow A = 1/5$

Put $x = -3$,

$-12 = -60B$

$\Rightarrow B = 1/5$

Comparing the cofficients of x^3 and x^2,

$1 = A + B + C$

$\Rightarrow 1 = \frac{1}{5} + \frac{1}{5} + C$

$\Rightarrow C = 3/5$

$0 = 3A - 3B + D$

$\Rightarrow D = 0$

Now, $\int \frac{x^3-5x}{(x^2-9)(x^2+1)}dx$

$$= \frac{1}{5}\int \frac{1}{x-3}dx + \frac{1}{5}\int \frac{1}{x+3}dx + \frac{3}{5}\int \frac{x}{x^2+1}dx$$

$$= \frac{1}{5}\log(x-3) + \frac{1}{5}\log(x+3) + \frac{3}{10}\log(x^2+1) + C$$

Exercise 10 (C)

Integrate :

1. $\int \frac{dx}{x^2-9} (x>3)$
2. $\int \frac{dx}{25-x^2} (x<5)$
3. $\int \frac{dx}{(x+1)(x+2)}$
4. $\int \frac{x\,dx}{(x-1)(x-2)}$
5. $\int \frac{x-1}{(x-2)(x-3)}dx$
6. $\int \frac{dx}{(x+a)(x+b)(x+c)}$
7. $\int \frac{dx}{x(1+x^4)}$ **[Hint :** Put $z = x^4$]
8. Integrate with respect to x : $\frac{x^4+3x^2+1}{x^3}$

Answers

1. $\left[\frac{1}{6}\log\left(\frac{x-3}{x+3}\right)+C\right]$
2. $\left[\frac{1}{10}\log\left(\frac{5+x}{5-x}\right)+C\right]$
3. $\left[\log\left(\frac{x+1}{x+2}\right)+C\right]$
4. $\left[\log\left[\frac{(x-2)^2}{x-1}\right]+C\right]$
5. $\left[\log\left[\frac{(x-3)^2}{x-2}\right]+C\right]$
6. $\left[\frac{1}{(b-a)(c-a)}\log(x+a) + \frac{1}{(a-b)(c-b)}\log(x+b) + \frac{1}{(b-c)(c-b)}\log(x+c)+C\right]$
7. $\left[\frac{1}{4}\log\frac{x^4}{x^4+1}+C\right]$
8. $\left[\frac{x^2}{2}+3\log x-\frac{1}{2x^2}+C\right]$

(10.6) INTEGRATION BY PARTS

Formula for Integration by Parts : If u and v be two functions of x, then

$$\int uvdx = u\int udx - \int\left(\frac{du}{dx}\int udx\right)dx \quad ....(i)$$

In words : Integral of product of two functions = First function × Integral of second function – Integral of [d.c. of first function × Integral of second function]

Proof : If u and w be two functions of x, then

$$\frac{d(uw)}{dx} = u.\frac{dw}{dx}+w.\frac{du}{dx}$$

Integrating both sides w.r.t. x, we get

$$uw = \int\left(u.\frac{dw}{dx}\right)dx+\int\left(w.\frac{du}{dx}\right)dx$$

$$\therefore \quad \int u.\frac{dw}{dx}dx = uw-\int\left(\frac{du}{dx}w\right)dx \quad ...(i)$$

Let $\frac{dw}{dx}=v$ then $w=\int vdx$

$\therefore$ From eq.(i),

$$\int uvdx = u\int vdx-\int\left(\frac{du}{dx}\int vdx\right)dx$$

Working Rules

(i) Integration of functions of the form uv may be found by method of integration by part when u and v are two different functions not cannected by their derivatives.

If u and v are connected by their derivatives, then first use method of substitution and then if needed use integration by parts. Some functions are such that they are not product of two functions nervertheless, their integrals may be found by integration by parts taking 1 as the second function, logarithmic and inverse trigonometrical functions are example of such functions.

(ii) In finding integrals by this method proper choice of functions u and v is essential. Although there is no fixed law for taking u and v their choice is possible by practice, yet following rule is helpful in the choice of function u and v :

(a) If the two functions are of diiferent types, take that function as u, which comes first in the word LIATE

L $\rightarrow$ Logarithmic function
I $\rightarrow$ Inverse trigonometric function
A $\rightarrow$ Algebraic function
T $\rightarrow$ Trigonometrical function
E $\rightarrow$ Exponential function

(b) If both the functions are trigonometrical take that function as v whose integral is simpler.

(c) If both the functions are algebraic take that function as u whose d.c. is simpler.

SOLVED EXAMPLES

✎ Type I

Example 1

Integrate : $\int xe^x\, dx$.

Solution :

$$\int xe^x\,dx = x\int e^x\,dx-\int\left(\frac{d(x)}{dx}.\int e^x\,dx\right)dx$$
$$= xe^x - \int 1.e^x\,dx$$
$$= xe^x - e^x + C$$
$$= e^x\,(x-1) + C$$

Ans.

Example 2

Integrate : $\int \log x\,dx$.

Solution :

$$I = \int \log x\,dx$$
$$= \int 1\ \log x\,dx$$
$$= (\log x).x-\int\left(\frac{1}{x}.x\right)dx$$
$$= x\log x - \int dx$$
$$= x\log x - x + C$$

Ans.

Example 3

Integrate : $\int(\log x)^2\,dx$.

Solution :

$$I = \int(\log x)^2\,dx$$
$$= \int\left\{1.(\log x^2)\right\}dx$$
$$= (\log x)^2.x-\int\left(2\log x\frac{1}{x}.x\right)dx$$
$$= x(\log x)^2 - 2\int \log x\,dx$$
$$= x(\log x)^2 - 2.\int 1.\log x\,dx$$
$$= x(\log x)^2 - 2\left[(\log x)x-\int\left(\frac{1}{x}x\right)dx\right]$$
$$= x.(\log)^2 - 2x\log x + 2\int dx$$
$$= x(\log x)^2 - 2x\log x + 2x + C$$

Ans.

Example 4

Integrate : $\int x^n \log x\,dx, n\neq-1$.

Solution :

$$I = \int x^n \log x$$
$$= \log x\left(\frac{x^n+1}{n+1}\right)-\int\left(\frac{1}{x}.\frac{x^{n+1}}{n+1}\right)dx$$
$$= \frac{x^{n+1}}{n+1}\log x-\frac{1}{n-1}\int x^n\,dx$$
$$= \frac{x^{n+1}}{n+1}\log x-\frac{1}{n+1}\left(\frac{x^{n+1}}{n+1}\right)+C$$
$$= \frac{x^{n+1}}{n+1}\log x-\frac{x^{n+1}}{(n+1)^2}+C$$

Ans.

Example 5

Evaluate : $\int x^2 e^{3x}\,dx$.

Solution :

$$I = \int x^2 e^{3x}\,dx$$

$$= x^2 \int e^{3x} dx - \int \left\{ \frac{d}{dx} x^2 \int e^{3x} dx \right\} dx$$

$$= x^2 . \frac{e^{3x}}{3} - \int 2x \frac{e^{3x}}{3} dx$$

$$= \frac{x^2 . e^{3x}}{3} - \frac{2}{3} \int x e^{3x} dx$$

$$= x^2 \frac{e^{3x}}{3} - \frac{2}{3} \left[x \int e^{3x} dx - \int \left\{ \frac{d}{dx} x \int e^{3x} dx \right\} dx \right]$$

$$= x^2 . \frac{e^{3x}}{3} - \frac{2}{3} \left[x . \frac{e^{3x}}{3} - \int \frac{e^{3x}}{3} dx \right]$$

$$= x^2 . \frac{e^{3x}}{3} - \frac{2xe^{3x}}{9} + \frac{2}{9} . \frac{e^{3x}}{3} + C$$

$$= \frac{x^2 e^{3x}}{3} - \frac{2}{9} x e^{3x} + \frac{2e^{3x}}{27} + C$$

Ans.

Example 6

Prove that : $\int (\log x^2) dx = x \left[(\log x - 1)^2 + 1 \right]$.

Solution :

$$I = \int (\log x)^2 dx$$

$$= \int (\log x)^2 . 1 dx$$

$$= (\log x)^2 . x - \int \left[\frac{d}{dx} (\log x)^2 . \int 1 dx \right] dx$$

$$= x (\log x)^2 . - \int 2 \log x . \frac{1}{x} . x dx$$

$$= x (\log x)^2 - 2 \int \log x . 1 dx$$

$$= x (\log x)^2 - 2 \left[\log x \int 1 dx - \int \left\{ \frac{d}{dx} (\log x) \int 1 dx \right\} dx \right]$$

$$= x (\log x)^2 - 2 \left[x \log x - \int \frac{1}{x} . x \, dx \right]$$

$$= x (\log x)^2 - 2x \log x + 2 \int 1 dx$$

$$= x (\log x)^2 - 2x \log x + 2x + C$$

$$= x [(\log x)^2 - 2 \log x + 1 + 1] + C$$

$$= x [\log x - 1)^2 + 1] + C$$

Proved

Example 7

Evaluate : $\int e^x (1+x) \log (x e^x) dx$.

Solution :

$$I = \int e^x (1+x) \log (x e^x) dx$$

Let $xe^x = z$

or $(xe^x + e^x) dx = dz$

or $e^x (1 + x) dx = dz$

$$\therefore \quad I = \int \log z \, dz$$

$$= \int \log z . 1 dz$$

$$= \log z \int 1 dz - \int \left[\frac{d}{dz} (\log z) \int 1 . dz \right] dz$$

$$= z \log z - \int \frac{1}{z} . z \, dz$$

$$= z \log z - \int dz$$

$$= z \log z - z + C$$

$$= z (\log z - 1) + C$$

$$= xe^x \left\{ \log (x e^x) - 1 \right\} + C$$

One Important Formula :

$$\int e^x [f(x) + f'(x)] dx = e^x f(x)$$

Proof :

$$\int e^x [f(x) + f'(x)] dx = \int e^x f(x) dx + \int e^x f'(x) dx$$

$$= f(x) \int e^x dx - \int \left[\frac{d\{f(x)\}}{dx} \int e^x dx \right] dx + \int e^x f'(x) dx$$

$$= f(x) . e^x - \int f'(x) . e^x dx + \int e^x f'(x) dx$$

$$= e^x f(x)$$

Proved

✎ Type II

Example 8

Evaluate : $\int \frac{e^x (x-1)}{x^2} dx$

Solution :

$$I = \int \frac{e^x (x-1)}{x^2} dx$$

or
$$I = \int e^x \left(\frac{1}{x} - \frac{1}{x^2} \right) dx \quad ...(i)$$

Let $f(x) = \frac{1}{x}$ Then $f'(x) = -\frac{1}{x^2}$

$\therefore$ From equation (i),

$$I = \int e^x \{ f(x) + f'(x) \} dx = e^x f(x) + C$$

$$= e^x f(x) + C$$

$$= e^x . \frac{1}{1+x} + C = \frac{e^x}{1+x} + C$$ **Ans.**

Example 9

Evaluate : $\int \frac{xe^x}{(1+x)^2} dx$.

Solution :

$$I = \int \frac{(1+x-1)e^x}{(1+x)^2} dx$$

$$I = \int e^x \left\{ \frac{1}{1+x} - \frac{1}{(1+x)^2} \right\} dx \quad ...(i)$$

Let $f(x) = \frac{1}{1+x}$ then $f'(x) = -\frac{1}{(1+x)^2}$

∴ From equation (i),

$$I = \int e^x \{f(x)+f'(x)\} dx$$

$$= e^x f(x)+C$$

$$= e^x \cdot \frac{1}{1+x} + c = \frac{e^x}{1+x} + C$$

Example 10

Evaluate : $\int \frac{x+1}{(x+2)^2} e^x dx$.

Solution :

$$I = \int e^x \frac{(x+2-1)}{(x+2)^2} dx$$

or

$$I = \int e^x \left\{ \frac{1}{x+2} - \frac{1}{(x+2)^2} \right\} dx \quad ...(i)$$

Let $f(x) = \frac{1}{x+2}$

∴ $f'(x) = \frac{1}{(x+2)^2}$

∴ From equation (i),

$$I = \int e^x \{f(x)+f'(x)\} dx$$

$$= e^x f(x) + C$$

$$= e^x \times \frac{1}{x+2} + C$$

$$= \frac{e^x}{x+2} + C$$ **Ans.**

Example 11

Evaluate : $\int \left(\frac{1+x \log x}{x} \right) e^x dx$.

Solution :

$$I = \int \left(\frac{1+x \log x}{x} \right) e^x dx$$

$$= \int e^x \left(\frac{x \log x}{x} + \frac{1}{x} \right) dx$$

$$= \int e^x \left(\log x + \frac{1}{x} \right) dx \quad ...(i)$$

Let $f(x) = \log x$

∴ $f'(x) = \frac{1}{x}$

∴ from equation (i),

$$I = \int e^x \{ f(x) + f'(x) \} dx$$

$$= e^x f(x) + C$$

$$= e^x \log x + C$$ **Ans.**

Example 12

Integrate with respect to x : $(2x^2 + 1)^2 4x$.

[*Mock Test Paper (JAC)*]

Solution :

$y = (2x^2 + 1)^2 . 4x$

Let, $t = 2x^2 + 1$

$dt = 4x\, dx$

then $\int y\, dx = \int (2x^2+1)^2 4x\, dx$

$$= \int t^2 dt = \frac{t^3}{3} + C$$

$$= \frac{(2x^2+1)^3}{3} + C$$

Exercise 10 (D)

✎ Type I

Integrate the following :

1. $\int x^2 e^x dx$
2. $\int x^2 (\log x)^2 dx$
3. $\int x^5 . e^{x^2} dx$
4. $\int x^n (\log x)^2 dx$
5. $\int x^3 e^{-x} dx$
6. $\int x^2 \log x\, dx$
7. $\int \frac{\log(\log x)}{x} dx$
8. $\int x^2 \log x\, dx$

✎ Type II

9. $\int e^x \frac{(1-x)^2}{(1+x^2)^2} dx$ **Hint :** $(1-x)^2 = 1 + x^2 - 2x$]
10. $\int \frac{x-1}{(x+1)^3} e^x dx$
11. $\int e^x (2x + x^2) dx$
12. $\int e^x \left(\frac{2-x}{(1-x)^2} \right) dx$
13. $\int e^{2x} \left(\frac{2x-1}{4x^2} \right) dx$
14. $\int x^3 e^{x^2} dx$
15. Find y, if $\frac{dy}{dx} = 5x^2 + 2$.

Answers

1. $(x^2 - 2x + 2)e^x + C$
2. $\left[\frac{1}{3} x^3 (\log x)^2 - \frac{2}{3} x^3 (\log x) + \frac{2}{27} x^3 + C \right]$
3. $\left[\frac{1}{2} x^4 e^{x^2} - x^2 e^{x^2} + e^{x^2} + C \right]$
4. $\left[\frac{x^{n+1}}{n+1} (\log x)^2 - \frac{2 \log x}{(n+1)^2} x^{n+1} + 2 \frac{x^{n+1}}{(n+1)^3} + C \right]$
5. $e^{-x} (x^3 + 3x^2 + 6x + 6) + C$

6. $\left[\frac{x^3}{3}\left(\log x-\frac{1}{3}\right)+C\right]$ 7. $\log x(\log x)-1]+C$

8. $\left[\frac{x^3}{27}\left[9(\log x)^2-6\log x+2\right]+C\right]$

9. $\left[\frac{e^x}{1+x^2}+C\right]$ 10. $\left[\frac{e^x}{(x+1)^2}+C\right]$

11. x^2e^x+C 12. $\left[\frac{e^x}{1-x}+C\right]$

13. $\left[\frac{e^{2x}}{4x}+C\right]$ 14. $\left[\frac{1}{2}e^{x^2}(x^2-1)+C\right]$

15. $\left[\frac{5x^3}{3}+2x+C\right]$

Exercise 10 (E)

Objective Type Questions

Multiple Choice Questions

1. $\int(2x+3)^5\,dx=?$

(a) $\frac{(2x+3)^6}{6}$ (b) $\frac{(2x+3)^4}{8}+C$

(c) $\frac{(2x+3)^6}{12}+C$ (d) None of these

2. $\int_1^2 x^2(3-x)\,dx=?$

(a) $\frac{13}{4}$ (b) $\frac{4}{13}$

(c) $\frac{25}{4}$ (d) None of these

3. $\int 10^{x+3}\,dx=?$

(a) $10^{x+3}\log_{10}e$ (b) $10^{x+3}\log_{10}e+C$

(c) $10^{x+3}\log_{10}d+x$ (d) None of these

4. $\int e^6\,dx=?$

(a) $7x^7+C$ (b) $\frac{x^7}{7}+C$ (c) $6x^5+C$ (d) $6x^7+C$

5. $\int e^x\,dx$ is :

(a) x (b) e (c) e^x (d) e^x+C

6. The value of $6\int x^2.dx$ is : (*JAC*, 2023)

(a) $2x^3+c$ (b) $6x^2+c$ (c) $5x^4+c$ (d) $7x+c$

7. Integration of $4x^3$ with respect of x is (*JAC*, 2024)

(a) $4x^2+c$ (b) x^4+c (c) $\frac{x^5}{5}+c$

(d) None of these

8. The value of $\int x^5\,dx$ is : (*JAC*, 2025)

(a) x^6 (b) x^7+c (c) $\frac{x^5}{5}+c$ (d) $\frac{x^6}{6}+c$

9. The value of $\int\frac{1}{x}\,dx$ is : (*JAC*, 2025)

(a) $\log x+c$ (b) $\frac{x^2}{2}+c$ (c) $\frac{x^3}{3}+c$ (d) $\log x^2$

Answers

1. (c) 2. (a) 3. (b) 4. (b) 5. (d) 6. (a) 7. (b)
8. (d) 9. (a)

[Hints to the given objective questions

1. Put $(2x+3)=t$
and $2dx=dt$

2. $\int_1^2 x^2(3-x)\,dx=\int_1^2(3x^2-x^3)\,dx$

$$=\left|\frac{3x^3}{3}-\frac{x^4}{4}\right|_1^2$$

$$=\left(2^3-\frac{2^4}{4}\right)-\left(1^3-\frac{1^4}{4}\right)$$

$$=4-\frac{3}{4}=\frac{13}{4}$$

3. $\int 10^{x+3}\,dx$

Let $I=\int 10^{x+3}\,dx$

$$=\int 10^x.10^3\,dx$$

$$=10^3\int 10^x\,dx$$

$$=10^3.\frac{10x}{\log_e 10}+C$$

$$=10^{x+3}\log 10^{\,e}+C]$$

Fill in the blanks

1. Integration is the .... process of differentiation.
2. Integration is the inverse process of ....
3. In $\int f(x)\,dx=F(x)+C$, C is called........ .
4. $\int uv\,dx=u\int v.dx-\int(..........)\int v\,dx+C$

Answers

1. Inverse 2. Differentiation
3. Constant of Integration 4. $\frac{du}{dx}$

Write True or False

1. Integration is the inverse process of differentiation.
2. The arbitrary constant C is called the constant of integration.
3. $\int\log x\,dx=x\log(x/e)+C$
4. $\int e^x\log a\,dx=\frac{a^x}{2x}+C$

Answers

1. True 2. True 3. True 4. True

(B) STATISTICS

Unit 1 : Measures of Central Tendency : Arithmetic Mean, Median, Mode

Unit 2 : Geometric Mean and Harmonic Mean

Unit 3 : Time Series

Unit 4 : Theory of Probability

Unit 5 : Interpolation and Extrapolation

1

MEASURES OF CENTRAL TENDENCY : ARITHMETIC MEAN

LEARNING OBJECTIVES

After studying this chapter, you will be able to know :

- **1.1 Meaning of Measures of Central Tendency or Average**
- **1.2 Essentials of a Good Average**
- **1.3 Objectives and Functions of Averages**
- **1.4 Importance of Uses of Average**
- **1.5 Kinds of Statistical Averages**
- **1.6 Arithmetic Mean**
  - **1.6.1 Meaning**
  - **1.6.2 Types of Arithmetic Mean**
- **1.7 Combined Arithmetic Mean**
- **1.8 Important Properties of the Mean**
- **1.9 Merits or Advantages of Arithmetic Mean**
- **1.10 Demerits or Disadvantages or Limitations of Arithmetic Mean**
- **Theoretical Questions : Long Answer Questions, Short Answer Questions, Very Short Answer Questions**
- **Practical Problems**

ILLUSTRATIONS AND PRACTICAL PROBLEMS : AT A GLANCE

No. of Illustration		*No. of Problems*
1(A) to 3(A), (B)	Individual Series	1(A) to 6
4(A) to 6	Discrete Series	7, 8
7 to 13	Continuous Series	9 to 18
14 to 16	To Find out an Unknown Value or Frequency	19 to 20
17, 18	Calculation of Weighted Mean	21, 22
19 to 23	To Find and mean after Preparing Table	23 to 25
24 to 25	Correcting Incorrect Mean	26 to 29
26	Combined Arithmetic Mean	30 to 34
27, 28	Miscellaneous Illustrations/Problems	35 to 52
29 to 31	Based on Properties of A.M.	
31	**Total**	**52**

(1.1) MEANING OF MEASURES OF CENTRAL TENDENCY OR AVERAGE

An average is used to summarise a mass of individual observation in much more concise fashion. An average reduces the large number of observations to one figure. It is thus the process of condensation. The purpose for computing an average value for a set of observations is to obtain a single value which is representative of all the items. It lies somewhere between the smallest and the largest observations of the distribution. An average is, generally the central part of the distribution and, therefore, it is also called the Measure of *Central Tendency*. It is also known as the Measure of Location. In short, an average is a figure that represents the whole group.

According to *Croxton* and *Cowden*, "*An Average value is a single value within the range of the data which is used to represent all of the values in the group/series/ data.*"

According to *Simpson* and *Kafka*, "A Measure of Central Tendency is a typical value around which other figures congregate (cluster)."

(1.2) ESSENTIALS OF A GOOD AVERAGE

A good average should possess the following properties :

(1) It should be rigidly defined so that different people may not interpret it differently.

(2) It should be easy to calculate so that it can be widely used.

(3) It should be easy to understand, since average are designed to simplify complexity.

(4) It should be based on all the observations *i.e.* average should depend upon each and every item of the series.

(5) It should be least affected by the fluctuations of sampling/sampling stability treatments.

(6) It should be capable of further algebraic and arithmetical analysis so that its utility is enhanced.

(7) A good average should be able to represent as many characteristics of the series as possible.

(8) It should not be unduly affected by the extreme values.

(9) It should be easy to interpret.

(1.3) OBJECTIVES AND FUNCTIONS OF AVERAGES

The main objects and functions of an averge are :

(1) To present the salient features of a mass of complex data.

(2) To facilitate comparison for different large groups.

(3) To provide a condensed picture of a large group.

(4) To know about universe from a sample.

(5) To trace mathematical relationship.

(6) To help in decision-making or in the process of experimentation and research.

(1.4) IMPORTANCE OR USES OF AVERAGE

The averages play an important role in Statistics. Many other techniques of statistical analysis depend upon this measure. Averages are widely used than any other statistical measures, because of their many applications. This is the reason that *Dr. Bowley* defines Statistics as "The Science of Average", *Prof. L. C. Tippet* says, "The average has its limitations but provided they are recognised, there is no single statistical quantity more valuable than an average."

In short, an Average has the following uses :

(1) One important use of averages is to reduce two or more aggregates to a common denominator in order to make comparisons.

(2) A second important use of averages is to provide one summary figure that is typical of all the items in a distribution of individual items that are essentially different. When using an average as a typical of all the values of a variable, the data should be homogeneous for the purpose at hand.

(3) An average helps in tracing out mathematical relationship between different groups or classes. It is extensively used in practical problems of statistics.

(4) An average also helps in decision-making, research and experiments.

(5) Businessman uses it to find out the operation cost, profit per unit of article, output per man and per machine, average monthly income and expenditure etc.

(1.5) KINDS OF STATISTICAL AVERAGES

There are five types of measures of central tendency or averages which are commonly used :

(1) Arithmetic Mean (A.M.)

(2) Median

(3) Mode

(4) Geometric Mean (G.M.)

(5) Harmonic Mean (H.M.).

Mathematical Average

(1) Arithmetic Mean (2) Geometric Mean

(3) Harmonic Mean

Positional Average

(1) Median (2) Mode

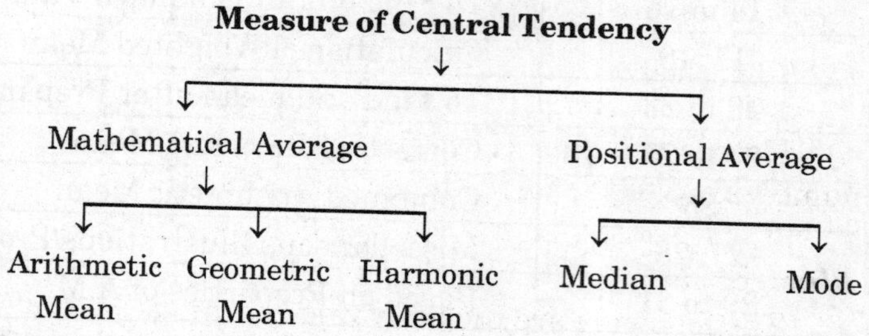

It should be noted that the *Arithmetic Mean, The Median and The Mode* are the three most common averages in general use. The *Geometric Mean* and *the Harmonic Mean* have important specialised uses.

(1.6) ARITHMETIC MEAN

1.6.1 Meaning

Arithmetic Mean (or Simply Mean) is the most widely used average. For this reason, when the term 'Mean' is used alone, it almost always refers to the Arithmetic Mean. The Arithmetic Mean or Average is the value obtained by adding the numbers of a set of ovservations divided by their number of observations.

Thus, Arithmetic mean or Mean is the quantity obtained by dividing the sum of observations values of observations variable by their number of observations.

1.6.2 Types of Arithmetic Mean

The Arithmetic Mean is of two types :

(A) Simple Arithmetic Mean,

(B) Weighted Arithmetic Mean.

(A) Calculation of Simple Arithmetic Mean

(i) *Calculation of Arithmetic Mean in Individual Series (Ungrouped Data)* **:** The Arithmetic Mean of individual series or ungrouped data can be computed either by (a) Direct Method, or (b) Short-cut Method.

The results from both the methods will be the same.

(a) ***Direct Method*** **:** The Arithmetic Mean of a series of observations of a variable $x_1, x_2, x_3, ..., x_n$ is the sum of the values divided by the number of items.

Symbolically it may be expressed as :

(1) $\quad \text{A. M.} = \left[\dfrac{\text{Sum of observation}}{\text{No. of observation}}\right]$

(2) $\quad \overline{X} = \dfrac{x_1 + x_2 + x_3 + ... + x_n}{n}$

or $\quad \overline{X} = \dfrac{\Sigma x}{n}$

$\therefore \quad \overline{X} = \dfrac{1}{n}\sum_{i=1}^{n} x_i$

where $\overline{X}$ = Arithmetic Mean, $\overline{x}$ (It is read as x bar)

Σ = Summation or the sum of, Symbol Σ is a Greek letter called capital sigma

n = Number of Items or Values

X represents observation of a variable.

In normal use only Σx is written in place of $\sum_{i=1}^{n} x_i$.

Unless the sum is confined to a given range of numbers out of the total, then it becomes to specify.

(3) The formula $\overline{X} = \dfrac{\Sigma x}{n}$ may be written as $a = \dfrac{\Sigma m}{n}$

where, a = Arithmetic Mean

Σ = Total Value of Items

n = Total Number of Items.

✎ Type 1

Individual Series : By Direct Method

Illustration **1(A)**

Calculate the average weight of a student from the following weights given in kg of 8 students :

60, 50, 62, 55, 58, 65, 56, 54

Solution :

$\Sigma x = 60 + 50 + 62 + 55 + 58 + 65 + 56 + 54 = 460$

$n = 8$

$\therefore \quad \overline{X} = \dfrac{\Sigma x}{n} = \dfrac{460}{8} = \mathbf{57.5\ kg}$ **Ans.**

Illustration **1(B)**

The Mean of 10 values are 19. If further 5 values are included, the Mean becomes 20. What is the Mean of these 5 additional values ?

Solution :

Given $\quad n = 10, \overline{X} = 19;$

where $\quad \overline{X} = \dfrac{\Sigma x}{n}$

$\therefore \quad \Sigma x = n \times \overline{X}$

or $\quad 10 \times 19 = 190$

5 further values are included, hence new $n = 10 + 5 = 15$

Arithmetic Mean of 15 items = 20

$\therefore$ Thus, New $\Sigma x = 15 \times 20 = 300$

New Sum (15 items) – Old Sum (10 items) $= 300 - 190 = 110$

Thus, Sum of 5 additional values = 110

Hence, Mean of 5 additional value $= \dfrac{110}{5}$

$= \mathbf{22}$ **Ans.**

Illustration **1(C)**

Find the Arithmetic Mean of – 1, 0, 1, 8 and – 3.

Solution :

$\Sigma x = -1 + 0 + 1 + 8 - 3 = 5$

$n = 5$

$\therefore$ Arithmetic Mean $(\overline{X}) = \dfrac{\Sigma x}{n} = \dfrac{5}{5} = 1$

A.M. = 1

Illustration **2**

The following are the daily wage earnings (in ₹) of 12 families. Calculate the Arithmetic Mean :

S. No.	1	2	3	4	5	6	7	8	9	10	11	12
Income	280	180	96	98	104	75	80	94	100	75	600	200

Solution :

(a) We have $\Sigma x = 280 + 180 + 96 + 98 + 104 + 75 + 80 + 94 + 100 + 75 + 600 + 200$

$= 1{,}982$

$n = 12$

$\therefore \quad \overline{X} = \dfrac{\Sigma x}{n}$

or $\quad \overline{X} = \dfrac{1{,}982}{12} = ₹\ \mathbf{165.16}$ **Ans.**

(b) **Short-cut Method :** The Arithmetic Mean may be computed by short-cut method. The following process should be adopted in computing Arithmetic Mean by short-cut method :

(1) Take any item of the series, preferably the middle one, as the *Assumed Mean* or *Provisional Mean.* Denote it by *'A'.*

(2) Take the difference x – *'A'* and denote it by d or d_x, where d or d_x is the deviations from any variable from A. d_x may be positive or negative.

(3) Find the sum Σd_x or Σd.

(4) Use the following formula to calculate Arithmetic Mean :

of the variable x from the Assumed Mean (A)

$$\overline{X} = A + \frac{\Sigma d_x}{n} \text{ or } \overline{X} = A + \frac{\Sigma d}{n}$$

✎ Type 2

Individual Series : By Short-cut Method

***Illustration* 3(A)**

Find the Average marks of a class by using short-cut method in which 10 students scored 50, 25, 45, 30, 35, 20, 15, 48, 42 and 52 marks.

Solution :

Calculation of Arithmetic Mean
(By Short-cut Method, A = 35)

S. No.	*Marks* x	*Deviation* $(X - 35)$ $d_x = (x - A)\ d_x$
1	50	$(50 - 35) = +15$
2	25	$(25 - 35) = -10$
3	45	$(45 - 35) = +10$
4	30	$(30 - 35) = -5$
5	35	$(35 - 35) = 0$
6	20	$(20 - 35) = -15$
7	15	$(15 - 35) = -20$
8	48	$(48 - 35) = +13$
9	42	$(42 - 35) = +7$
10	52	$(52 - 35) = +17$
$n = 10$	$\Sigma x = 362$	$+62$ -50 $\Sigma d_x = +12$

Let $A = 35$ (Assumed Mean)

Short-cut Method :

$$\overline{X} = A + \frac{\Sigma d_x}{n}$$

$$= 35 + \frac{12}{10}$$

$$= 35 + 1.2$$

$\therefore \quad \overline{X} = \mathbf{36.2}$

Direct Method :

$$\overline{X} = \frac{\Sigma x}{n}$$

$$= \frac{362}{10}$$

$$= 36.2$$

$\therefore \quad \overline{X} = \mathbf{36.2}$

Alternatively : The calculation of Arithmetic Mean may sometimes be facilitated by subtracting a quantity, say A, from each value. In other words, by shifting the value from 0 to A.

Let $\quad u_i = x_i - A \quad$ (So that $x_i = A + u_i$)

$\sum^{n} u_i \ \sum^{n} x_i$

Then, $\quad \sum_{i=1}^{n} u_i = \sum_{i=1}^{n} x_i - nA$ or $\sum_{i=1}^{n} u_i = \dfrac{\sum_{i=1}^{n} x_i}{n} - \dfrac{nA}{n}$

or $\quad \bar{u} = \bar{x} - A$ Arithmetic Mean of u $(\bar{u})$

Thus, to get the Arithmetic Mean $\bar{x}$ of x, we just to add *'A'* to the Arithmetic Mean $(\bar{u})$ of u.

***Illustration* 3(B)**

The total marks obtained by 5 students at degree level examinations are 1058, 1100, 1200, 1082 and 1060. What is the mean marks per student ?

Solution :

Let x_1, x_2, x_3, x_4 and x_5 denote the marks of 5 students and let $A = 1{,}000$

Hence $\quad u_i = x_i - 1000$

Thus, $\quad u_1 = 1058 - 1000 = 58$

$u_2 = 1100 - 1000 = 100$

$u_3 = 1200 - 1000 = 200$

$u_4 = 1082 - 1000 = 82$

$u_5 = 1060 - 1000 = 60$

Hence $\quad \bar{u} = \dfrac{58 + 100 + 200 + 82 + 60}{5}$

$$= \frac{500}{5} = 100$$

Thus $\quad \bar{x} = A + \bar{u}$

$= 1{,}000 + 100 = 1{,}100$

(ii) *Calculation of Arithmetic Mean in Discrete Series :* In a discrete series items are grouped according to their size. In such a case, the Arithmetic Mean will be calculated as ahead :

(a) **Direct Method :**

Step 1. Each size of item is multiplied by its frequency (*i.e.*, $f \times x$).

Step 2. Products so obtained are then added (*i.e.*, Σfx).

Step 3. The total value, obtained then, is divided by the total number of frequencies, that is N to find out Arithmetic Mean.

$$\overline{X} = \frac{\Sigma fx}{\Sigma f} \quad \text{or} \quad \frac{\Sigma fx}{N}$$

where $\overline{X}$ = Arithmetic Mean

f = Frequency

x = The concerned variable

Σfx = Total of Products of f and x values

Sum of frequencies or $\sum_{i=1}^{n} f$

In frequency distribution $N = \Sigma f$

Let $x_1, x_2, x_3, \ldots\ldots, x_n$ be the variates and let $f_1, f_2, f_3, \ldots\ldots, f_n$ be their corresponding frequencies, then their Mean $\bar{x}$ is given by

$$\bar{x} = \frac{f_1x_1 + f_2x_2 + f_3x_3 + \ldots\ldots + f_nx_n}{f_1 + f_2 + f_3 + \ldots\ldots + f_n} = \frac{\sum_{i=1}^{n} f_i.x_i}{\sum_{i=1}^{n} f_i} = \frac{\sum_{i=1}^{n} f_i.x_i}{N}$$

where $N = f_1 + f_2 + f_3 \ldots\ldots + f_n$

✎ Type 3

Discrete Series : By Direct Method

***Illustration* 4(A)** (JAC, 2026)

Calculate Arithmetic Mean for the following data :

Size	0	1	2	3	4	5	6	7	8
Frequency	1	9	26	59	72	52	29	7	1

Solution :

Calculation of Arithmetic Mean (Direct Method)

Size (x)	0	1	2	3	4	5	6	7	8	Total
Frequency (f)	1	9	26	59	72	52	29	7	1	$\Sigma f = 256$
fx	0	9	52	177	288	260	174	49	8	$\Sigma fx = 1017$

$$\bar{x} = \frac{\Sigma fx}{\Sigma f} = \frac{1017}{256} = 3.97$$

$\therefore$ $\bar{x}$ = **3.97** **Ans.**

***Illustration* 4(B)**

Present the following marks obtained by 30 students in the form of a discrete series and then calculate the Mean of the marks obtained :

7 8 3 5 3 7 5 3 7 9 2 4 5 2 4
3 2 7 3 6 3 8 4 4 2 3 6 2 4 7

Solution :

Marks x	*Tally Marks* T.M.	*No. of Students* f	*Product* fx
2	卌	5	10
3	卌 II	7	21
4	卌	5	20
5	III	3	15
6	II	2	12
7	卌	5	35
8	II	2	16
9	I	1	9
Total		Σf or $N = 30$	$\Sigma fx = 138$

$$\bar{x} = \frac{\Sigma fx}{N}$$

$$= \frac{138}{30} = 4.6$$

$\therefore$ Mean = **4.6** marks) **Ans.**

(b) **Short-cut Method** : To calculated Arithmetic Mean in a Discrete Series by short-cut method, the following steps should be taken :

Step 1. Denote the variable by X or x and the corresponding frequency by f.

Step 2. Any value of distribution (x series) may be taken as 'Assumed Mean', or 'Provisional Mean'. Generally middle value of the frequency distribution is taken as assumed mean. Assumed Mean is denoted by 'A'.

Step 3. Deviations of the variable X from the Assumed Mean $(X - A)$ is formed out denoted by 'd_x' or 'd'.

Step 4. Multiply each item in the d_x or 'd' column by its respective frequency (f) and denote the products by 'fd_x' or fd or $f \times d_x$ or $f \times d$.

Step 5. Obtain the sum of fd or fd_x, that is, Σfd or Σfd_x.

Step 6. Use the following formula to obtain Arithmetic Mean :

$$\overline{X} = A + \frac{\Sigma fd_x}{\Sigma f} \text{ or } A + \frac{\Sigma fd_x}{N}$$

or $$\overline{X} = A + \frac{\Sigma fd}{N}$$

Type 4

Calculation of Arithmetic Mean in Discrete Series by Short-cut Method

Illustration 5

In a Carnival 10 ladies ate lollipops as follows :

No. of Ladies	:	1	2	3	4
No. of Lollipops	:	3	4	5	8

Find the Average number of lollipops eaten by a lady.

(*JAC*, 2016)

Solution :

Calculation of Arithmetic Mean

No. of Lollipops x	*No. of Ladies* f	*Deviation from* A (5) $d_x = x - 5$	*Product* $f \times d_x$
3	1	− 2 (3 − 5)	− 2
4	2	− 1 (4 − 5)	− 2
5	3	0 (5 − 5)	0
8	4	+ 3 (8 − 5)	+ 12
Total	$\Sigma f = 10$		+ 12 − 4
			$\Sigma f \times d_x = +8$

$$\overline{X} = A + \frac{\Sigma fd_x}{\Sigma f} = 5 + \frac{8}{10} = 5 + 0.8 = \mathbf{5.8} \text{ (lollipops)}$$

Illustration 6

From the following frequency distribution, find the Mean height of the students by Direct and Short-cut Methods :

Heights (in inch)	62	63	64	65	66	67	68
No. of Students	4	4	8	10	15	14	5

Solution :

Calculation of Arithmetic Mean

Height (in inch) X	*Direct Method*		*Short-cut Method*	
	No. of Students f	*Product* fx	*Deviation from* A (X − 65) d_x	*Product* $f \times d_x$
62	4	248	− 3 (62 − 65)	− 12
63	4	252	− 2 (63 − 65)	− 8
64	8	512	− 1 (64 − 65)	− 8
65	10	650	0 (65 − 65)	0
66	15	990	+ 1 (66 − 65)	+ 15
67	14	938	+ 2 (67 − 65)	+ 28
68	5	340	+ 3 (68 − 65)	+ 15
Total	$N = 60$	$\Sigma fx = 3930$		+ 58 − 28 $\Sigma f \times d_x = 30$

Direct Method :

$$\text{Mean Height or } \overline{X} = \frac{\Sigma fx}{N} = \frac{3930}{60} = \mathbf{65.5} \text{ inch}$$ **Ans.**

Short-cut Method :

$$\overline{X} = A + \frac{\Sigma f \times d_x}{N} = 65 + \frac{30}{60} = 65 + 0.5 = \mathbf{65.5} \text{ inch}$$ **Ans.**

(iii) Calculation of Arithmetic Mean in a Continuous Series : In a continuous frequency distribution, Arithmetic Mean can be calculated by any of the following methods :

(A) Direct Method, (B) Short-cut Method, and (C) Step Deviation Method.

(a) Direct Method : The following procedure is adopted for calculating Arithmetic Mean in a Continuous Series by Direct Method :

(i) Mid-values of each class-interval is found out. This is denoted by '*m*'.

(ii) Each mid-value (*m*) is multiplied by its respective frequency (*f*). The product is denoted by $f \times m$.

(iii) All the products are then added and denoted by Σfm.

(iv) All the frequencies are added-up, to obtain Σf or N.

(v) The sum of the products Σfm is divided by the total frequencies (Σf or N). The result is Arithmetic Mean.

Symbolically, $\overline{X} = \frac{\Sigma fm}{\Sigma f}$ or $\overline{X} = \frac{\Sigma fm}{N}$

✎ Type 5

Calculation of Arithmetic Mean in continuous Series by Direct Method

Illustration 7

From the following data, Calculate the Arithmetic Mean :

Weekly Wages (in ₹)	32.5—37.5	37.5—42.5	42.5—47.5	47.5—52.5
No. of Workers (f)	20	15	12	3

Solution : **Calculation of Arithmetic Mean**

Weekly Wages in (₹)	*No. of Workers (f)*	*Mid-value (m)*	*Product f × m*
32.5—37.5	20	35	700
37.5—42.5	15	40	600
42.5—47.5	12	45	540
47.5—52.5	3	50	150
Total	Σf or $N = 50$		$\Sigma fm = 1990$

$$\overline{X} = \frac{\Sigma fm}{N} = \frac{1990}{50} = \mathbf{39.80} \quad \textbf{Ans.}$$

∴ Arithmetic Mean = ₹ 39 and 80 paise

(b) Short-cut Method : The following procedure is adopted for computing Arithmetic Mean in a Continuous Series by *Short-cut* Method :

Step 1. Obtain the mid-values of class-intervals, denoted by '*m*'.

Step 2. Assume one of the mid-values (preferably in the middle of the distribution) as Assumed Mean (*A*).

Step 3. From each mid-point deduct the Assumed Mean ($m - A$) denoted by d_x or d.

Step 4. Multiply each d_x or d by its corresponding frequency and denote the product by $f \times d_x$ or '$f \times d$'.

Step 5. Add all the products to find out $\Sigma f \times d_x$ or $\Sigma f \times d$.

Step 6. Use the following formula to calculate the Arithmetic Mean :

$$\overline{X} = \frac{\Sigma f \times d_x}{N} \text{ or } A + \frac{\Sigma fd_x}{\Sigma f} \text{ or } \overline{X} = A + \frac{\Sigma fd}{N}$$

✎ Type 6

Calculation of Arithmetic Mean in Continuous Series by Short-cut Method

Illustration 8

Calculate the Arithmetic Mean of the following by the Short-cut Method :

Size of the Items	0—10	10—20	20—30	30—40	40—50	Total
Frequency	1	3	6	2	3	15

Solution : **Calculation of Arithmetic Mean**

$A = 25$

Size of the Items	*Frequency (f)*	*Mid-value (m)*	*Deviations (d_x) = (m − 25)*	$f \times d_x$
0—10	1	(0 + 10) ÷ 2 = 5	− 20	− 20
10—20	3	(10 + 20) ÷ 2 = 15	− 10	− 30
20—30	6	(20 + 30) ÷ 2 = 25	0	0
30—40	2	(30 + 40) ÷ 2 = 35	+ 10	+ 20
40—50	3	(40 + 50) ÷ 2 = 45	+ 20	+ 60
				+ 80
Total	N = 15			− 50
				$\Sigma f \times d_x = 30$

Hence, $\overline{X} = A + \frac{\Sigma f \times d_x}{N}$

$= 25 + \frac{30}{15} = 25 + 2 = 27$

$\therefore \quad \overline{X} = \mathbf{27}$ **Ans.**

✎ Type 7

***Illustration* 8(A)**

Find the value of A if $\sum_{i=1}^{10}(X_i - A) = 25$ and $\overline{X} = 30$.

Solution :

$\because$ Given

$\sum_{i=1}^{10}(X_i - A) = 25$

$\therefore$ Sum of 10 Observations

$- 10A = 25$

We have, $\overline{X} = 30 \quad \because \overline{X} = \frac{\sum_{i=1}^{n} X_i}{n}$

$\therefore \quad \frac{\sum_{i=1}^{10} X_i}{10} = 30$

$\therefore \quad \sum_{i=1}^{10} X_i = 30 \times 10 = 300$ (Sum of 10 obs.)

$300 - 10A = 25$

$\Rightarrow \quad 300 - 25 = 10A$

$\Rightarrow \quad 10A = 275$

$\Rightarrow \quad A = \frac{275}{10} = 27.5$

$\therefore \quad A = \mathbf{27.5}$ **Ans.**

***Illustration* 8(B)**

If $\sum_{i=1}^{10}(x_i - 8) = 32$, find $\overline{X}$.

Solution :

Given $\sum_{i=1}^{10}(x_i - 8) = 32$

$\sum_{i=1}^{10} x_1 - 10 \times 8 = 32 + 80 = 32$

or $\sum_{i=1}^{10} x_1 - 10 \times 6 = 32$

or $\sum_{i=1}^{10} x_1 = 112$ (Sum of 10 obs.)

Now $\overline{X} = \frac{\sum_{i=1}^{n} x_i}{n} = \frac{112}{10}$

$\overline{X} = \mathbf{11.2}$ **Ans.**

***Illustration* 8(C)**

If $\sum_{i=1}^{10} x_i = 141$, then find $\sum_{i=1}^{10}(x_i - 2)$.

Solution :

Given (Sum of 10 obs.)

$\sum_{i=1}^{10} x_i = 141$

Now $\sum_{i=1}^{10}(x_i - 2) = \sum_{i=1}^{10} x_i - 10 \times 2$

$= 141 - 20 = \mathbf{121}$ **Ans.**

Inclusive Series : If the class-intervals under inclusive method are given, they need not be adjusted, that is, they should not be transformed into exclusive series.

✎ Type 8

Calculation of Arithmetic Mean in Inclusive Series

***Illustration* 9**

The following table shows the age (in years) distribution of males. Find the Mean Age.

Age-group	0—9	10—19	20—29	30—39	40—49	50—59
Males	25	60	100	220	150	45

Solution :

Calculation of Mean Age

(Short-cut Method) Let $A = 24.5$

Age-group	*Males* (*f*)	*Mid-value* (*m*)	*Deviations* $(d_x) = (m - A)$	*Product* fd_x
0—9	25	4.5	– 20	– 500
10—19	60	14.5	– 10	– 600
20—29	100	24.5	0	0
30—39	220	34.5	+ 10	+ 2200
40—49	150	44.5	+ 20	+ 3000
50—59	45	54.5	+ 30	+ 1350
Total	$N = 600$			+ 6550 – 1100 $\Sigma fd_x = 5450$

$$\overline{X} = A + \frac{\Sigma fd_x}{N} = 24.5 + \frac{5450}{600} = 24.5 + 9.08 = \mathbf{33.58\ years}$$ **Ans.**

Cumulative Series : Sometimes we are given the cumulative frequencies. Frequencies may also be given in terms of (i) '*More Than*' or '*Above*', or (ii) '*Less Than*' or '*Below*'. In such a case, we shall have to determine the frequencies of the class-intervals. Now simple frequency table will be available to find the Arithmetic Mean. The procedure of calculation will be the same as discussed earlier.

✎ Type 9

Calculation of Arithmetic Mean in Cumulative Series

***Illustration* 10(A)**

Determine the Arithmetic Mean of the following series :

Marks below	10	20	30	40	50	60	70	80
Frequency	25	40	60	75	95	125	190	240

Solution :

In this question cumulative frequencies are given. So we should first determine the frequencies of the class-intervals (0—10), (10—20),..................,(70—80).

Calculation of Arithmetic Mean Let (A = 45)

Marks	*Frequency (f)*	*Mid-value (m)*	*Deviation* d_x $(m - A)$	fd_x
0—10	25	5	– 40	– 1000
10—20	40 – 25 = 15	15	– 30	– 450
20—30	60 – 40 = 20	25	– 20	– 400
30—40	75 – 60 = 15	35	– 10	– 150
40—50	95 – 75 = 20	45	0	0
50—60	125 – 95 = 30	55	+ 10	+ 300
60—70	190 – 125 = 65	65	+ 20	+ 1300
70—80	240 – 190 = 50	75	+ 30	+ 1500
				+ 3100
				– 2000
Total	N = 240			Σfd_x = 1100

$$\overline{X} = A + \frac{\Sigma fd_x}{N} = 45 + \frac{1100}{240} = 45 + 4.58 = 49.58$$

Arithmetic Mean = **49.58** **Ans.**

***Illustration* 10(B)**

Calculate Arithmetic Mean from the following frequency distribution :

More than	10	25	40	55	70	85
No. of Persons	100	94	74	30	4	1

Solution :

Calculation of Mean (A = 47.5)

Class	*Mid-value (m)*	*Frequency (f)*	*Deviation* $d_x(x - A)$	fd_x
10—25	17.5	6	– 30	– 180
25—40	32.5	20	– 15	– 300
40—55	47.5	44	0	0
55—70	62.5	26	+ 15	+ 390
70—85	77.5	3	+ 30	+ 90
85—100	92.5	1	+ 45	+ 45
Total		N = 100		Σfd_x = + 45

$$\overline{X} = A + \frac{\Sigma fd_x}{N}$$

$$= 47.5 + \frac{45}{100}$$

$= 47.5 + 0.45 =$ **47.95** **Ans.**

(c) Step Deviation Method : In case of grouped or continuous frequency distribution, *Step Deviation method* can also be adopted for reducing the calculation work further. In the step deviation method, the method of calculating mean is carried one step further than in the short-cut method. In this method, we take a common factor from the deviations. The common factor is equal to the width of class-interval, that is, $L_2 - L_1$. The deviations from the assumed mean, as calculated in the short-cut method, are divided by the common factor. The result is denoted by d'_x or d'.

Thus

$$d_x' \text{ or } d' = \frac{x-A}{C} \text{ or } \frac{m-A}{C} \text{ or } \frac{x-A}{i} \text{ or } \frac{d}{i} \text{ or } \frac{d_x}{i}$$

d'_x or d' so obtained is multiplied by respective frequency of each class-interval. The arithmetic mean is then obtained by using the following formula :

$$\overline{X} = A + \left(\frac{\Sigma fd'}{N} \times i\right)$$

or $$\overline{X} = A + \left(\frac{\Sigma fd'_x}{N} \times i\right)$$

or $$\overline{X} = A + (\Sigma fd' \times C)$$

or $$\overline{X} = A + \left(\frac{\Sigma fd'_x}{N} \times C\right)$$

where d' or $d'_x = \frac{d_x}{i}$

$\Sigma fd'_x$ = Total of the Products

N = Total Frequencies

i or C = Common Factor or Size of the Class-intervals.

✎ Type 10

Calculation of Arithmetic Mean by Step Deviation Method

***Illustration* 11**

Calculate the Arithmetic Mean of the following data by using step deviation method :

Class	0—10	10—20	20—30	30—40	40—50
Frequency (f)	14	23	27	21	15

Solution :

Calculation of Mean

Let $A = 25$, i (or C) = 10

Class	*Mid-value (m)*	*Frequency (f)*	$d_x = m - 25$	$d'_x = \frac{d_x}{i}$	$f \times d'_x$
0—10	5	14	– 20	– 20/10 = – 2	– 28
10—20	15	23	– 10	– 10/10 = – 1	– 23
20—30	25	27	0	0	0
30—40	35	21	+ 10	+ 10/10 = + 1	+ 21
40—50	45	15	+ 20	+ 20/10 = + 2	+ 30
Total		$N = 100$			$\Sigma f \times d'_x = 0$

$$\overline{X} = A + \frac{\Sigma fd'_x}{N} \times i = 25 + \frac{0}{100} \times 10 = 25$$

∴ Arithmetic Mean = **25** **Ans.**

***Illustration* 12**

Given below is the distribution of 140 students obtaining marks x or higher in a certain examination. All marks are given in the whole numbers :

x	10	20	30	40	50	60	70	80	90	100
cf	140	133	118	100	75	45	25	9	2	0

Calculate the mean marks obtained by the candidate.

Solution :

The given data is in the form of a cumulative frequency distribution. For calculating Arithmetic Mean, the series has to be re-arranged in class-intervals of (10—20), (20—30),.................. .

Simple Frequency Distribution (Exclusive Series)

Marks (x or more)	*Cum. Freq. (cf)*	*Class-intervals*	*Frequency (f)*
10	140	10—20	140 − 133 = 7
20	133	20—30	133 − 118 = 15
30	118	30—40	118 − 100 = 18
40	100	40—50	100 − 75 = 25
50	75	50—60	75 − 45 = 30
60	45	60—70	45 − 25 = 20
70	25	70—80	25 − 9 = 16
80	9	80—90	9 − 2 = 7
90	2	90—100	2 − 0 = 2
100	0		

Calculation of Mean

Let $A = 55$, and $i = 10$

Class-intervals	*m*	*f*	d_x	$d'_x = \frac{d_x}{10}$	fd'_x
10—20	15	7	− 40	− 4	− 28
20—30	25	15	− 30	− 3	− 45
30—40	35	18	− 20	− 2	− 36
40—50	45	25	− 10	− 1	− 25
50—60	55	30	0	0	0
60—70	65	20	+ 10	+ 1	+ 20
70—80	75	16	+ 20	+ 2	+ 32
80—90	85	7	+ 30	+ 3	+ 21
90—100	95	2	+ 40	+ 4	+ 08
Total		N = 140			$\Sigma fd'_x = -53$

$$\overline{X} = A + \frac{\Sigma fd'_x}{N} \times i = 55 + \left(\frac{-53}{140} \times 10\right) = 55 - 3.7857 = 51.2143$$

$\therefore$ $\overline{X}$ = **51.21 Marks.** **Ans.**

Calculations of Arithmetic Mean in Series having Open-end Classes

In some frequency distribution, lower limit of the first class-interval and the upper limit of the last class-interval are not known. Such class-intervals are called open-end classes. In such cases, some figures will have to be put there to compute Arithmetic Mean. The placing of the figures depend upon the pattern of class-intervals. If all the class-intervals are of equal magnitude, then first and the last classes will be made accordingly.

***Illustration* 13 (Open-end Series)**

Find the Mean of the following series :

Marks	Below 20	20—40	40—60	60—80	More than 80
No. of Students (f)	8	12	20	40	20

Solution :

Calculation of Mean

Let $A = 50$

Marks	*No. of Students (f)*	*Mid-values (m)*	*Deviations* $d_x = x - A$	*Step Deviation* (d'_x) $\frac{d_x}{20}$	fd'_x
0—20	8	10	− 40	− 2	− 16
20—40	12	30	− 20	− 1	− 12
40—60	20	50	0	0	0

60—80	40	70	+ 20	+ 1	+ 40
80—100	20	90	+ 40	+ 2	+ 40
Total	N = 100				+ 80 − 28
					$\Sigma fd'_x$ = + 52

$$\overline{X} = A + \left(\frac{\Sigma fd'_x}{N} \times i\right)$$

$$= 50 + \left(\frac{52}{100} \times 20\right)$$

or $\overline{X}$ = 50 + 10.4 = **60.4 Marks.** **Ans.**

To Find out Unknown Value or Frequency

If in some frequency distribution any value or frequency is not known but Arithmetic Mean is given, the unknown value or frequency can be found out. The following illustration makes it clear :

✎ Type 11

To Find out Unknown Item

***Illustration* 14**

Find out the missing item in the following series :

Size	0	1	x	3	4	5
Frequency	46	76	38	25	10	5

The Mean of the series is 1.46.

***Solution* :**

Let missing item be x

Location of Mising Item

Size (m)	*Frequency (f)*	*Product (mf)*
0	46	0
1	76	76
? (x)	38	$38x$
3	25	75
4	10	40
5	5	25
Total	N = 200	$\Sigma fm = 216 + 38x$

Where $\overline{X} = \frac{\Sigma fm}{N}$

By substituting the given values :

$$1.46 = \frac{216 + 38x}{200}$$

or $1.46 \times 200 = 216 + 38x$

or $292 = 216 + 38x$

or $-38x = 216 - 292$

or $-38x = -76$

$\therefore$ $x = -\frac{76}{-38} = 2$

Thus missing item is **2.** **Ans.**

✎ Type 12

To Find out Unknown Frequency

***Illustration* 15**

In the following frequency distribution locate the missing frequency if the Arithmetic Mean of the series is 22 :

Size of the Items	0—10	10—20	20—30	30—40
Frequency (f)	1	3	?	2

***Solution* :**

Let missing frequency of class-interval 20—30 be f

Size of Items (x)	*Mid-Value (m)*	*Frequency (f)*	*Product (fm)*
0—10	5	1	5
10—20	15	3	45
20—30	25	(f)	$25f$
30—40	35	2	70
Total		N = 6 + f	Σfm = 120 + $25f$

where $\overline{X} = \frac{\Sigma fm}{N}$

or $22 = \frac{120 + 25f}{6 + f}$

or $22(6 + f) = 120 + 25f$

or $132 + 22f = 120 + 25f$

or $22f - 25f = 120 - 132$

or $-3f = -12$ or $3f = 12$

$\therefore$ $f = \frac{12}{3} = 4$

$\therefore$ Unknown Frequency = 4 **Ans.**

***Illustration* 16**

(To locate two unknown class-frequencies)

For a certain frequency table with total frequency 150, the Mean was found to be ₹ 56.47. But while copying out the table, a typist left out two of the class frequencies, say f_3 and f_5 so that the table is given to you in the following form :

Daily Wages (in ₹) (Mid-value)	*Frequency*
45	5
50	48
55	f_3
60	30
65	f_5
70	8
75	6
Total	150

Find the value of f_3 and f_5.

Solution :

Determination of Missing Frequencies Let $A = 55$

Wages (in ₹) (m)	Frequency (f)	d_x ($m-55$)	$d'_x = \left(\frac{m-55}{5}\right)$	fd'_x
45	5	− 10	− 2	− 10
50	48	− 5	− 1	− 48
55	f_3	0	0	0
60	30	+ 5	+ 1	+ 30
65	f_5	+ 10	+ 2	$2f_5$
70	8	+ 15	+ 3	24
75	6	+ 20	+ 4	24
Total	$N = 97 + f_3 + f_5$			$\Sigma fd'_x = 20 + 2f_5$

We have $N = 97 + f_3 + f_5 = 150$

$\therefore \quad f_3 + f_5 = 150 - 97 = 53$

Now, $\overline{X} = A + \left(\frac{\Sigma fd'_x}{N} \times i\right)$

or $56.47 = 55 + \left(\frac{20 + 2f_5}{150} \times 5\right)$

or $56.47 = 55 + \frac{20 + 2f_5}{30}$ or $1.47 = \frac{20 + 2f_5}{30}$

$1.47 \times 30 = 20 + 2f_5$

or $44.1 = 20 + 2f_5$

$\therefore \quad f_5 = \frac{44.1 - 20}{2} = \frac{24.1}{2} = 12$ (Approx.)

Now, $f_3 + f_5 = 53$ and $f_5 = 12$

$\therefore \quad f_3 = 53 - 12 = 41$

$f_3 = \mathbf{41}, f_5 = \mathbf{12}$ **Ans.**

(B) Calculation of Weighted Arithmetic Mean

In simple Arithmetic Mean, equal importance is given to all items. (But there are some situations when the relative importance of the different items is not the same in such situation we apply weighted A.M.)

Note : Where "Weights" show the relative importance of the different items.

Here weights may be assigned to the values according to their relative importance for calculating Arithmetic Mean. Arithmetic Mean computed on the basis of weights to different items, is called *Weighted Arithmetic Mean*.

If $w_1, w_2, w_3, ..., w_n$ are the weights assigned to the values $x_1, x_2, x_3, ..., x_n$ respectively, then the weighted average is defined as :

Weighted Arithmetic Mean

$$= \frac{w_1x_1 + w_2x_2 + ... + w_nx_n}{w_1 + w_2 + ... + w_n}$$

Method of Calculation of Weighted Mean :

The formulas for computing weighted arithmetic mean are as ahead :

(A) Direct Method :

$$\overline{X}_w = \frac{\Sigma WX}{\Sigma W}$$

Where, $\overline{X}_w$ = Weighted A.M.

W = Weights

X = Variable

ΣW = Summation of Weights

ΣWX = Summation of Weights and Values WX (Total of Weighted Products)

Working Rule :

Step 1 : Multiply weights by the Variable and add up the products (ΣWX).

Step 2 : Add up the Weights (ΣW).

Step 3 : Divide the Total Weighted Products by the Total Weights $\left(\frac{\Sigma WX}{N}\right)$.

(B) Short-cut Method :

$$\overline{X}_w = A + \frac{\Sigma Wd_x}{\Sigma W}$$

Where, $\overline{X}_w$ = Weighted Mean

A = Assumed Mean / Assumed Weighted Mean

W = Weights

d_x = Deviation of the Variable from Assumed Mean

ΣW = Total Weights

ΣWd_x = Total of Wd_x

Working Rule :

Step 1 : Assume any value as the Assumed Weighted Mean.

Step 2 : Calculate deviation (A) from the Assumed Mean (d_x).

Step 3 : Multiply the deviations with the respective wieghts to find out Wd_x.

Step 4 : Add up Wdx i.e. find ΣWd_x

Step 5 : Divide ΣWd_x by the total weights and add it to the Assumed Weighted Mean (A).

✎ Type 14

Weighted Arithmetic Mean

***Illustration* 17**

Calculate the Weighted Average Price per ton of coal purchased by an industry for the half-year :

(₹ in hundred)

Month	*Price Per Ton (X)*	*Ton Purchased (W)*
Jan.	520	25
Feb.	500	30
March	600	40
April	650	50
May	625	10
June	700	45

Solution :

Caluculation of Weighted Mean

Month	*Price* (X)	*Weight* (W)	*WX*
Jan.	520	25	13,000
Feb.	500	30	15,000
March	600	40	24,000
April	650	50	32,500
May	625	10	6,250
June	700	45	31,500
Total		$\Sigma W = 200$	$\Sigma WX = 1,22,250$

$$\overline{X}_w = \frac{\Sigma WX}{\Sigma W}$$

$$= \frac{122250}{200} \text{ hundred}$$

$$= 611.25 \text{ hundred}$$

$$\therefore \quad \overline{X}_w = ₹\mathbf{611.25} \text{ hundred}$$

Ans.

***Illustration* 18**

The Monthly Salary and the number of staff of a glass factory are given below. Calculate the Weighted Arithmetic Mean of salaries by Direct method as well as by Short-cut Method :

	Monthly Salary (in ₹)	*No. of Persons*
Manager	1000	1
Clerical Staff	200	8
Skilled Labour	250	20
Unskilled Labour	140	11

Solution :

Computation of Weighted Mean

	Direct Method			*Short-cut Method* A = 250	
	X	W	WX	d_x	Wd_x
Manager	1000	1	1000	+ 750	+ 750
Clerical Staff	200	8	1600	− 50	− 400
Skilled Labour	250	20	5000	0	0
Unskilled Labour	140	11	1540	− 110	− 1210
Total		$\Sigma W = 40$	$\Sigma WX = 9140$		$\Sigma Wd_x - 860$

Direct Method :

$$\overline{X}_w = \frac{\Sigma WX}{\Sigma W} = \frac{9140}{40}$$

$$= 228.50$$

$$\overline{X}_w = ₹\mathbf{228.50}$$

Ans.

Indirect Method :

$$\overline{X}_w = A + \frac{\Sigma Wd_x}{\Sigma W} = 250 + \frac{-860}{40}$$

$$= 250 - 21.50 = 228.50$$

$$\therefore \quad \overline{X}_w = ₹\mathbf{228.50}$$

Ans.

***Illustration* 19**

(a) Prepare a frequency distribution from the following data taking the class-interval as 7 by inclusive method :

24	26	28	32	37	9	17	15	13	14
18	29	31	32	9	18	27	36	9	15
21	27	33	8	12	16	20	10	8	9
12	18	27	23	21	29	22	15	17	28

(b) Calculate the Mean of the above distribution.

Solution :

We have Smallest Value = 8, Largest Value = 37

Frequency Distribution Table of Calculation of Mean

Class-intervals	*Tally Marks (T.M.)*	*Frequency (f)*	*Mid-value (m)*	*Product (f × m)*
8—14	𝍸𝍸 I	11	11	121
15—21	𝍸𝍸 II	12	18	216
22—28	𝍸 IIII	9	25	225
29—35	𝍸 I	6	32	192
36—42	II	2	39	78
Total		$N = 40$		$\Sigma fm = 832$

$$\overline{X} = \frac{\Sigma fm}{N} = \frac{832}{40} = 20.8 \qquad \therefore \text{ Mean} = \mathbf{20.8}$$ **Ans.**

***Illustration* 20**

From the following table, Calculate the Arithmetic Mean :

Marks	More than 70	More than 60	More than 50	More than 40	More than 30	More than 20
No. of Students	7	18	40	40	63	65

Solution :

In this case we are given a cumulative series. All the 65 students scored more than 20 marks but 63 students have scored more than 30 marks and so on. It means that 2 students (65 – 63) have secured marks between 20 and 30. We can rearrange the distribution and then A.M. will be calculated.

Calculation of Arithmetic Mean

Marks	*No. of Students (cf)*	*Class-interval*	*Frequency (f)*	*Mid-value (m)*	*Product (fm)*
More than 70	7	70—80	7	75	525
More than 60	18	60—70	18 – 7 = 11	65	715
More than 50	40	50—60	40 – 18 = 22	55	1210
More than 40	40	40—50	40 – 40 = 0	45	0
More than 30	63	30—40	63 – 40 = 23	35	805
More than 20	65	20—30	65 – 63 = 2	25	50
Total			$N = 65$		$\Sigma fm = 3305$

$$\overline{X} = \frac{\Sigma fm}{N} = \frac{3305}{65} = \mathbf{50.8}$$ **Ans.**

***Illustration* 21 (Mean in Case of Mixed Series)**

Calculate Mean from the following data :

Size	0	1	3	5—7	8—14	15—24	25—45
Frequency	5	7	10	25	40	30	23

Solution :

This problem will be solved by Direct Method.

Calculation of Arithmetic Mean

Class	*Frequency (f)*	*Mid-value (m)*	*fm*
0	5	0	0
1	7	1	7
3	10	3	30
5—7	25	6	150
8—14	40	11	440
15—24	30	19.5	585
25—45	23	35	805
Total	$N = 140$		$\Sigma fm = 2017$

$$\overline{X} = \frac{\Sigma fm}{N} = \frac{2017}{140} = \mathbf{14.407}$$ **Ans.**

Mean in Unequal Class-Intervals

Illustration 22

Calculate the Average Income per head from the following data :

Income per day (₹)	0-10	10-20	20-30	30-50	50-100	100-250	250-500	500-1000	1000-10000
No. of Persons	13	80	70	100	29	15	8	3	2

Solution :

Calculation of Average Income

Income per day (₹)	*Mid-point* (*m*)	*No. of Persons* (*f*)	*fm*
0—10	5	13	65
10—20	15	80	1,200
20—30	25	70	1,750
30—50	40	100	4,000
50—100	75	29	2,175
100—250	175	15	2,625
250—500	375	8	3,000
500—1000	750	3	2,250
1000—10000	5,500	2	11,000
Total		$N = 320$	$\Sigma fm = 28{,}065$

$$\text{Average Income } (\overline{X}) = \frac{\Sigma fm}{N} = \frac{28{,}065}{320} = \textbf{₹ 87.70}$$ **Ans.**

Calculation of Arithmetic Mean in a Mid-value Series

Illustration 23

The following marks have been obtained in Business Economics by 50 students. Calculate its Arithmetic Mean :

Mid-value (Marks) (*m*)	5	15	25	35	45	55
No. of Students (*f*)	4	6	10	20	6	4

Solution :

Mid-values have been given in the question. Hence, the question will be solved without converting it into exclusive series.

Let A = 25

Calculation of Arithmetic Mean by Short-cut Method

Mid-value (*m*)	*No. of Students* (*f*)	$d = m - A$ or $d = m - 25$	*fd*
5	4	− 20	− 80
15	6	− 10	− 60
25	10	0	0
35	20	+ 10	+ 200
45	6	+ 20	+ 120
55	4	+ 30	+ 120
Total	$N = 50$		$\Sigma fd = + 300$

$$\overline{X} = A + \frac{\Sigma fd}{N} = 25 + \frac{300}{50} = 25 + 6 = 31$$

∴ Arithmetic Mean = **31 Marks** **Ans.**

Correcting Incorrect Mean

Formula : Correct Mean = $(N\overline{X}$ – Misread Score + Correct Score) ÷ N

✎ Type 14

Correcting Incorrect Mean

Illustration 24

The Average Marks scored by 100 students was 40. Later on it was discovered that a score of 74 of a student was misread as 14. Find the Correct Average Marks scored.

Solution :

Given, $n = 100$, $\overline{X} = 40$, Correct Marks = 74, Incorrect Marks = 14 (Misread)

Now, Arithmetic Mean of marks of 100 students,

$$\overline{X} = \frac{\Sigma x}{n} = 40$$

∴ Sum of the marks of 100 students (Incorrect)

$$\because \quad \overline{X} = \frac{\sum_{i=1}^{n} x_i}{n}$$

$$\therefore \quad \sum_{i=1}^{n} x_i = n\overline{X}$$

$$= 100 \times 40 = 4000$$

Now correct sum of the marks of 100 students

$$= 4000 - \text{Misread Score} + \text{Correct Score}$$

$$= 4000 - 14 + 74 = 4060$$

$$\therefore \text{Correct Average Marks} = \frac{4060}{100} = 40.6$$

Correct Average Marks. = **40.6 Marks.** **Ans.**

Illustration 25

Mean of 200 items was 50. Later on it was found that two items were misread as 92 and 8 instead of 192 and 88. Find the Correct Mean.

Solution :

Given :

$\overline{X} = 50$ (Incorrect Mean)

$n = 200$

Misread Items : 92 and 8

Correct Items : 192 and 88

Correct Mean

$$= \frac{n.\overline{X} - \text{Misread Score} + \text{Correct Score}}{n}$$

$$= \frac{(200 \times 50) - (92 + 8) + (192 + 88)}{200}$$

Correct Mean

$$= \frac{10000 - 100 + 280}{200} = \frac{10180}{200}$$

Thus Correct Mean = **50.9** **Ans.**

(1.7) COMBINED ARITHMETIC MEAN

If we are given the Mean of two series and their seizes, then the Combined Mean for two series can be obtained. In such a case the following formula should be used for obtaining the Combined Mean :

Combined Mean $\overline{X}_C$ or $\overline{X}_{1,2,\ldots\ldots k}$

$$= \frac{n_1\overline{X}_1 + n_2\overline{X}_2 \ldots\ldots + n_k\overline{X}_k}{n_1 + n_2 + \ldots\ldots + n_k}$$

where n_1 = Size of the First Series

n_2 = Size of the Second Series

n_k = Size of nth Series

$\overline{X}_1$ = Mean of the First Series

$\overline{X}_2$ = Mean of the Second Series

= Combined Mean of the Series

....

....

$\overline{X}_k$ = Mean of the kth series

✎ Type 15

Calculation of Combined Arithmetic Mean

Illustration 26

There are 45 students in a class out of which 15 are girls. The average weight of 15 girls is 45 kg and that of 30 boys 52 kg Find the Average Weight of the whole class.

Solution :

Given $n_1 = 15$, $n_2 = 30$,

$\overline{X}_1 = 45$ kg, $\overline{X}_2 = 52$ kg

∴ Combined Agerage

$$(\overline{X}_c) = \frac{(15 \times 45) + (30 \times 52)}{(15 + 30)} \text{kg}$$

$$= \frac{675 + 1560}{45} \text{kg}$$

$$\text{Combined Average} = \frac{2235}{45} = 49.67 \text{ kg}$$

∴ Combined Average Weight = **49.67 kg** **Ans.**

Miscellaneous Illustrations

Illustration 27

(i) Given : $\overline{X} = 28$, $\Sigma fd'_x = 30$, $A = 25$, $i = 10$, find out the number of items (N).

(ii) If $\overline{X} = 27.85$, $n = 72$, $\Sigma fd_x = -155$, find the value of Assumed Mean.

(iii) Given : $\overline{X} = 66.5$, $A = 55$, $n = 60$, find out the summations of deviations or Σfd_x.

Solution :

(i) $$\overline{X} = A + \frac{\Sigma fd'_x}{n}$$

or $28 = 25 + \frac{30}{n} \times 10$

or $28 - 25 = \frac{300}{n}$

or $3 = \frac{300}{n}$ or

$3n = 300$

$\therefore$ $n = \frac{300}{3} = \mathbf{100}$ **Ans.**

(ii) $\overline{X} = A + \frac{\Sigma f d_x}{n}$

or $27.85 = A + \frac{-155}{72}$

or $27.85 = A - 2.15$

or $A = 27.85 + 2.15 = 30$

$\therefore$ $A = \mathbf{30}$ **Ans.**

(iii) $\overline{X} = A + \frac{\Sigma f d_x}{n}$

or $66.5 = 55 + \frac{\Sigma f d_x}{60}$

or $66.5 - 55 = \frac{\Sigma f d_x}{60}$

or $11.5 = \frac{\Sigma f d_x}{60}$

or $11.5 \times 60 = \Sigma f d_x$

$\therefore$ $\Sigma f d_x = 11.5 \times 60 = \mathbf{690}$ **Ans.**

Illustration 28

Calculate the Mean from the following data :

(Temperature (°C)	– 40 to – 30	– 30 to – 20	– 20 to – 10	– 10 to 0	0 to 10	10 to 20	20 to 30
(No. of Days)	10	28	30	42	65	180	10

Solution :

Calculation of Mean (Let A = – 5)

Temperature C	*Mid-value* (*m*)	*No. of Days* *f*	*Deviations* $d_x = m - A$	fd_x
– 40 to – 30	– 35	10	– 30	– 300
– 30 to – 20	– 25	28	– 20	– 560
– 20 to – 10	– 15	30	– 10	– 300
– 10 to 0	– 5	42	0	0
0 to 10	+ 5	65	+ 10	+ 650
10 to 20	+ 15	180	+ 20	+ 3600
20 to 30	+ 25	10	+ 30	+ 300
Total		N = 365		$\Sigma f d_x = 3390$

$$\overline{X} = A + \frac{\Sigma f d_x}{N} = -5 + \frac{3390}{365}$$

$$= -5 + 9.287 = 4.287°C$$

$\therefore$ Mean $=$ **4.287°C** **Ans.**

(1.8) IMPORTANT PROPERTIES OF THE MEAN

The following are the algebraic properties of the Mean :

(1) The sum of the deviations of the items from the Arithmetic Mean (taking into account *plus* and *minus* sign) is always zero *i.e.*

(i) $\sum_{i=1}^{n} (x_i - \overline{x}) = 0$ or $\Sigma d = 0$

(ii) $\sum_{i=1}^{n} f_i (x_i - \overline{x}) = 0$

where $\overline{x} = \frac{\Sigma fx}{N}$

Proof : $d_1 = x_1 - \overline{x}$;

$d_2 = x_2 - \overline{x}$

$d_3 = x_3 - \overline{x}$

$d_n = x_n - \overline{x}$

or $d_1 + d_2 + d_3 + \ldots\ldots + d_n$

$= (x_1 - \overline{x}) + (x_2 - \overline{x}) + (x_3 - \overline{x}) + \ldots. + (x_n - \overline{x})$

$\Sigma d_i = \Sigma (x_i - \overline{x}) = \Sigma x_i - n\frac{\Sigma x}{N}$

where $\overline{x} = \frac{\Sigma x}{n}$

or $\sum_{i=1}^{n} d_i = \sum_{i=1}^{n} x_i - \sum_{i=1}^{n} x_i$

or $\Sigma d_i = 0$ (where, d_i = deviations)

Illustration 29

From the following data, calculate Arithmetic Mean and show that the sum of deviations of the following items from arithmetic mean is zero :

100, 200, 300, 400, 500

Solution :

x	$(x - \overline{x})$	
100	– 200	} = – 300
200	– 100	
300	0	
400	+ 100	} = + 300
500	+ 200	
$\Sigma_x = 1{,}500$	$\Sigma(x - \overline{x}) = 0$	

$$\overline{X} = \frac{\Sigma x}{n} \quad \therefore \overline{X} = \frac{1500}{5} = \mathbf{300} \quad \textbf{Ans.}$$

(2) The sum of squares of deviations of a set of observations has the smallest value, when deviations are taken from their *A.M.*

(i) $\Sigma(x - \overline{x})^2$ or Σd^2 is minimum, when $\overline{x}$ = Simple Arithmetic Mean.

(ii) $\Sigma f(x - \overline{x})$ is minimum, when $\overline{x}$ = Arithmetic Mean.

Illustration 30

Explain that the sum of deviations of the items from Arithmetic Mean is minimum : x : 10, 15, 25, 30

Solution :

Assumed Mean $(A) = 15$

x	$(x - \overline{x}) = d$	$(x - \overline{x})^2 = d^2$	$x - 15$	$(x - 15)^2$
10	10 – 20 = – 10	100	10 – 15 = – 5	25
15	15 – 20 = – 5	25	15 – 15 = 0	0
25	25 – 20 = + 5	25	25 – 15 = + 10	100
30	30 – 20 = + 10	100	30 – 15 = + 15	225
$\Sigma x = 80$		$\Sigma d^2 = 250$		$\Sigma(x - 15)^2 = 350$

$$\overline{x} = \frac{\Sigma x}{n} = \frac{80}{4} = \mathbf{20}$$

From the above table, it is clear that sum of squares of deviation from Arithmetic Mean is 250 and from Assumed Mean is 350. Hence, sum of squares of deviations from simple mean $\Sigma(x - \overline{x})^2$ is minimum.

(3) If any two of three values, arithmetic mean $(\overline{x})$, number of items (n) and total of the values (Σx) are known, the third can be found out.

$$\overline{x} = \frac{\Sigma x}{N},$$

$$\Sigma x = (\overline{x} \times n),$$

$$n = \frac{\Sigma x}{\overline{x}} \text{ or } \frac{\Sigma fx}{\overline{x}}$$

(4) The standard error of the arithmetic mean is less than that of any other measure of central tendency.

(5) If arithmetic mean and the number of items of two or more than two related groups are known, then their combined mean can be calculated.

$$\overline{x} = \frac{n_1 \overline{x}_1 + n_2 \overline{x}_2 + \ldots + n_n \overline{x}_n}{n_1 + n_2 + \ldots + n_n}$$

(6) The arithmetic mean of addition or subtraction of the corresponding values of two series, will be equal to the addition or subtraction of the values of the two mean.

For Example,

S. No.	X	Y	$X + Y$	$X - Y$
1	10	4	14	6
2	15	6	21	9
3	25	7	32	18
4	30	11	41	19
Total	80	28	108	52
$\overline{x}$	20	7	27 (20 + 7)	13 (20 – 7)

(7) If a constant is added, multiplied, divided or subtracted from each in a series, the means will increase or decrease by the some amount. If the items in a series are multiplied by a constant, the mean will also be affected that way.

Illustration 31

State the effect on mean of the followng series if 2 is added, subtracted, multiplied and divided in the items :

x : 10, 15, 25, 30

Solution :

x	$x + 2$	$x - 2$	$x \times 2$	$x \div 2$
10	12	8	20	5
15	17	13	30	7.5
25	27	23	50	12.5

30	32	28	60	15
$\Sigma x = 80$	$\Sigma x = 88$	$\Sigma x = 72$	$\Sigma x = 160$	$\Sigma x = 40$
$x = \frac{80}{4} = 20$	New $\bar{x} = \frac{88}{4} = 22$	New $\bar{x} = \frac{72}{4} = 18$	New $\bar{x} = \frac{160}{4} = 40$	New $\bar{x} = \frac{40}{4} = 10$

(1.9) MERITS OR ADVANTAGES OF ARITHMETIC MEAN

1. Arithmetic Mean is easy to understand and easy to calculate.
2. Arithmetic Mean is based on each and every observation of the series.
3. An Arithmetic Mean is an exact or computed figure and is suitable for further mathematical treatment.
4. It is a good basis of comparison of two or more series.
5. It is not necessary to carry or group the items to calculate Arithmetic Mean.
6. It is least affected by sampling fluctuations.
7. Arithmetic Mean is obtained by calculations and does not depend on position in the series.

(1.10) DEMERITS OR DISADVANTAGES OR LIMITATIONS OF ARITHMETIC MEAN

1. Arithmetic Mean is not a representative measure in extremely symetrical (skewed) distribution.
2. It is very much affected by extreme items.
3. It cannot be calculated if all the values are not given.
4. It cannot be determined by inspection nor can it be located graphically.
5. Sometimes Arithmetic Mean may not be an actual item in the series, and as such it is called a fictitious average.

THEORETICAL QUESTIONS

Long Answer Type Questions

1. What is a Statistical Average ? What are the characteristics of an ideal average ?
2. What is meant by measures of central tendency ? State the qualities or essentials of a good average.
3. What do you understand by statistical average ? Describe its objectives and functions.
4. What do you mean by 'Arithmetic Mean' ? Discuss its merits and demerits.
5. What is 'Statistical Average' ? What are the desirable properties for an average to possess ?

Short Answer Type Questions

1. What do you understand by meausres of central tendency ?
2. What is arithmetic mean ? Explain with example.
3. What is meant by statistical average ?
4. State five essentials of an ideal average.
5. State the advantages of arithmetic mean.
6. State the advantages and disadvantages of arithmetic mean.
7. What are the different types of arithmetic mean ? Explain.
8. Compare simple arithmetic mean and weighted arithmetic mean.
9. State any five algebraic properties of the arithmetic mean.

Very Short Answer Type Questions

1. State the name of different types of averages.
2. Mention two characteristics of an ideal average.
3. What is weighted mean ?
4. What is combined arithmetic mean ? Give its formula.
5. State two advantages of arithmetic mean.
6. State two demerits of arithmetic mean.
7. What is average ?
8. Define simple arithmetic mean.
9. Give the formula(s) of calculating arithmetic mean in a continuous series.
10. Distinguish between simple and weighted arithmetic mean.
11. The marks obtained by a student in English, Mathematics and Economics are 75, 92 and 49. Find his average score.
[**Ans.** 72]
12. Find the Arithmetic Mean of – 2, 0, 2, 16 and – 6.
[**Ans.** 2]
13. The average age of 30 children in a class is 9 years. If the teacher's age be included, the average age becomes 10 years. Find the teacher's age.
[**Ans.** 40 years]
14. The average age of 5 children is 8 years. If the age of the father be included, the average increased by 7 years. Find the age of the father.
[**Ans.** 50 years]
15. The average of 6 numbers is 8. What is the 7th number so that average becomes 10 ?
[**Ans.** 22]
16. The average of 8 numbers is 21. If each of the numbers is multiplied by 8, find the average of new set of numbers.
[**Ans.** 168]
[**Hint :** Sum of 8 numbers = $(21 \times 8) = 168$
Sum of new 8 numbers = $(168 \times 8) = 1,344$
$\therefore$ Average of new set of numbers = $\frac{1344}{8} = 168$.]
17. Three years ago the average age of a family of 5 members was 17 years. A baby having been born, the average of the family is the same today, find the age of the baby.
[**Ans.** 2 years]
18. A batsman makes a score of 85 runs in the 13th inning and thus increased his average by 3. Find his average after the 13th inning.
[**Ans.** 49]

19. The monthly income of five persons is as follows :

S. No.	1	2	3	4	5
Income (₹)	4,500	5,800	3,200	8,500	6,500

Find Arithmetic mean.

[**Ans.** ₹ 5,700]

20. Profit and Loss of a firm for the last five years is as follows :

1st year : ₹ 30,000, 2nd year ₹ 40,000; 3rd year ₹ 45,000, 4th year ₹ 25,000 (Loss), 5th year ₹ 36,000.

[**Ans.** ₹ 25,200]

21. The best measure to central tendency is A.M. Is it true ?

(a) Yes (b) No

[**Ans.** (b)]

22. The average income of 100 persons is calculated 20, while the average income of all the 150 persons is 25. Calculate average income of 50 persons. (*JAC*, 2025)

[**Ans.** 35]

PRACTICAL QUESTIONS

Individual Series

1. (A) Find out the mean from the following data :

Income ₹ 50, 100 200, 500, 2,000, 3,000, 4,000.

[**Ans.** ₹ 1,407.14]

(B) Calculate the Simple Arithmetic Mean of the following numbers :

28, 34, 39, 42, 50, 53, 54, 59.

[**Ans.** 44.875]

(C) Find the mean of 14, 3, 0, 4, 5, 6. (*JAC*, 2026)

[**Ans.** $\overline{X} = 5.33$]

2. Find the Arithmetic Mean of 20.35, 15.75, 16.5, 34.95, 25.75, 27.04.

[**Ans.** 23.39]

3. Compute the arithmetic average of the following items :

(i) 25, 0.405, 3.245, 0.0832, (ii) 25, 0.3005, 4.81, 0.1003

[**Ans.** (i) 7.1833, (ii) 7.5527]

4. The following are the ten meausred value of X : 20.6, 19.8, 21.1, 21.8, 21,7, 24.7, 21.4, 21.5, 21.2, 21.0. Find (i) the average of the first six measurements, (ii) the average of the last six measurements.

[**Ans.** (i) $21.61\dot{6}$, (ii) $21.91\dot{6}$]

5. The following are the monthly salaries in rupees of 12 families. Calculate the Arithmetic Mean :

S. No.	1	2	3	4	5	6	7	8	9	10	11	12
Income	280	180	96	98	104	75	80	94	100	75	600	200

[**Ans.** ₹ 165.17]

6. Calculate the Mean of the following data :

S. No.	1	2	3	4	5	6	7	8	9	10	11	12
Size	96	180	98	75	270	80	102	100	94	75	200	610

[**Ans.** 165]

Discrete Series

7. (i) From the following frequency distribution find out Mean height of the students :

Height (in cm)	160	162	164	166	168	170	172
No. of Students	5	10	15	30	25	10	5

[**Ans.** 166.2 cm.]

(ii) The following data relate to sizes of shoes sold at a store during the given week. Find the average size by the short-cut method :

Size of Shoes	4	5	6	7	8	9	10
No. of Shoes	15	30	45	60	55	40	5

[**Ans.** 7]

8. (i) Students of a school contributed towards National Defence Fund as follows :

Students	10	15	24	30	21
Contribution per Student (in ₹)	5	4	3	2	1

Find out the Mean Contribution.

[**Ans.** $\overline{X}$ = ₹ 2.63]

(ii) Find arithmetic mean : (*JAC*, 2023)

Marks	20	30	40	50	60	70
No. of Students	5	15	10	7	8	5

[**Ans.** 42.06]

(iii) Calculate the Mean number of accidents per driver from the following :

No. of Accidents	0	1	2	3	4	5	6	7	8
No. of Drivers	45	36	40	19	12	8	3	2	1

[**Ans.** $\overline{X} = 1.813$]

(iv) A market survey on demands of Modern Bread at a shop in a locality provided the following distribution of daily demand :

Daily Demand	*Frequency*
12	36
17	160
21	92
27	56
30	26
Total	370

Find the average demand per day.

[**Ans.** 19.93 Breads]

Continuous Series

9. Find Mean from the following data :

Class	10—20	20—30	30—40	40—50	50—60	60—70
Frequency	15	18	27	14	9	7

[**Ans.** $\overline{X}$ = 35.55]

10. Calculate mean from the following table :

Class	0—4	5—9	10—14	15—19	20—24	25—29
Frequency	12	17	35	18	8	2

[**Ans.** $\overline{X}$ = 11.95]

11. Find out simple arithmetic mean from the following data :

Profit per Shop (in ₹)	0—10	10—20	20—30	30—40	40—50
No. of Shops	12	18	21	20	9

[**Ans.** ₹ 24.50]

12. Calculate mean from the following table :

Class	8—14	14—20	20—26	26—32	32—38
Frequency	30	40	20	10	5

[**Ans.** ₹ 18.42]

13. Find out the mean of the following data :

Age in Years	20—30	30—40	40—50	50—60	60—70	70—80
No. of Men	12	18	42	54	45	15

14. (A) Calculate the arithmetic mean by short-cut method :

Age in Years	18—22	23—27	28—32	33—37	38—42	43—47	48—52	53—57
No. of Persons	14	28	33	30	20	15	13	7

[**Ans.** $\overline{X}$ = 34.56 years]

(B) Calculate the mean from the following frequency table : (*JAC*, 2017)

x	6—10	11—15	16—20	21—25	26—30
Frequency	20	30	50	40	10

[**Ans.** $\overline{X}$ = 17.67]

15. From the following table, find the mean by step deviation method :

Income (in ₹)	1000—2000	1000—3000	1000—4000	1000—5000	1000—6000
No. of Persons	15	33	63	83	100

[**Ans.** $\overline{X}$ = ₹ 3,560]

16. Calculate the mean :

Marks	Less than 20	Less than 30	Less than 40	Less than 50	Less than 60	Less than 70
Students	5	13	28	46	49	50

[**Ans.** $\overline{X}$ = 36.8 Marks]

17. Calculate the arithmetic mean :

Marks	More than 10	More than 20	More than 30	More than 40	More than 50	More than 60
Students	50	42	36	20	7	3

[**Ans.** $\overline{X}$ = 36.6 Marks]

18. Calculate arithmetic mean of the following data :

Daily Wages (in ₹)	Below 80	80—85	85—90	90—95	95—100	100—105	105—110	Above 110
No. of Workers	10	12	14	11	20	20	11	2

[**Ans.** $\overline{X}$ = ₹ 94.15]

Unknown Value or Frequency

19. In the following frequency distribution locate the missing frequency if the arithmetic mean of the series is 67.45 :
(*JAC*, 2016)

Height	60—62	63—65	66—68	69—71	72—74
Frequency	15	54	?	81	24

[**Ans.** Missing Frequency = 126]

20. In the mean of the following series is 47.95, find out the missing frequency :

Height	10—25	25—40	40—55	55—70	70—85	85—100
Frequency	6	20	44	?	3	1

[**Ans.** Missing Frequency = 26]

Weighted Mean

21. Calculate the weighted mean from the following :

Name of Examination	*Percentage of Result*	*Weight*
I.A.	80	10
I.Sc.	95	4
I. Com.	75	6

[**Ans.** 81.5%]

22. Calculate the weighted arithmetic mean from the following :

Articles of food	*Quantity Consumed* (kg)	*Price* (in ₹) (per kg)
Flour	20	2.50
Rice	25	4.00
Ghee	2	30.00
Sugar	5	5.00
Potatoes	6	2.00
M. Oil	2	16.00

[**Ans.** Weighted Mean = ₹ 4.65]

When Cummulative Frequency is Given

23. From the following cumulative frequency table, prepare a frequency distribution table and calculate the mean of the distribution :

Class-intervals	10—16	16—22	22—28	28—34	34—40
Cumulative Frequency	2	8	18	27	32

[**Ans.** $\overline{X}$ = 26.6875 or 26.69]

Preparation of Frequency Distribution Table and Calculation of Mean

24. Given below are the monthly wages in rupees of 30 employees of a firm :

139	126	114	100	88	62	77	99	103	144
148	63	69	148	132	118	142	61	123	104
95	80	85	106	123	133	140	134	108	129

(a) Prepare a frequency table taking the class-intervals as 60–70 and so on.

(b) Hence or otherwise find the number of employees whose monthly salary is (i) less than ₹ 100, and (ii) more than ₹ 120 but less than ₹ 130.

(c) Compute the average wages of employee.

[**Ans.** (b) (i) 10, (ii) 4, (c) ₹ 110]

25. Daily income of 40 labourers working in a factory are given below ;

Daily Income (in ₹)

25	34	26	38	32	31	36	42	30	34
20	35	35	39	40	28	33	39	44	29
35	30	30	41	35	39	27	22	43	28
38	34	32	32	25	30	31	29	38	44

(a) Prepare a classified frequency distribution table of the above data beginning with the class 20—25 with uniform class-interval 5.

(b) Hence or otherwise find the mean of daily income.

[**Ans.** (a)

X	:	20—25	25—30	30—35	35—40	40—45
f	:	2	8	13	11	6

(b) ₹ 33.875]

Correcting the Result

26. The arithmetic mean of 15 values was calculated as 20.2. Later, it was found that two values 23 and 35 were wrongly taken as 32 and 53. Find the correct mean.

[**Ans.** Correct Mean 18.4]

27. The average marks secured by 50 students was 44. Later on, it was found that a score of 36 was misread as 56. Find the correct average marks obtained by the students.

[**Ans.** Correct Marks 43.6]

28. The arithmetic mean of weekly income of 50 families is ₹ 2,800. But incourse of counting the income of one family of ₹ 2,050 was misread as ₹ 2,500. Find the correct arithmetic mean.

[**Ans.** ₹ 2,791]

29. The average marks secured by 100 students was 80. Later on, it was found that marks of two students 93 and 58 were misread as 39 and 85. Find the correct average marks secured.

[**Ans.** $\overline{X}$ = 80.27]

Combined Arithmetic Mean

30. The means of three samples of sizes 200, 250 and 300 are 25, 10 and 15 respectively. Find out the mean of the combined distribution.

[**Ans.** 16]

31. The average income of 100 labourers is ₹ 50 per day and the average income of 150 labourers is ₹ 60 per day. Find the combined mean of income of 250 labourers.

[**Ans.** ₹ 56]

32. Find the combined mean marks from the following data given below :

$N_1 = 60$, $\overline{X} = 400$ marks; $N_2 = 40$, $\overline{X}_2 = 450$ marks

[**Ans.** 420 Marks]

33. The average income of 100 labourers is ₹ 200. If the average income of all 150 labourers is ₹ 250. Calculate the average income of remaining 50 labourers.

[**Ans.** $\overline{X}$ = ₹ 350]

34. The average run scored by Australian Team in a match consisting of 10 players is 50 and the average run of Indian Team of 11 players is 42. Find the combined average run scored by both the teams.

[**Ans.** Combined Mean = 45.8 Runs]

Miscellaneous Problems

35. The pass out result of 50 students who took up a class test is given below :

Marks	4	5	6	7	8	9
No. of Students	8	10	9	6	4	3

If the average marks for all the 50 students were 5.16, find out the average maks of the students who failed.

[**Ans.** $\overline{X}$ of students who failed = 2.1]

36. Find the mean in the following table :

Class	10—15	15—20	20—25	25—30	30—35
Frequency	10	18	32	18	12

[**Ans.** $\overline{X}$ = 22.72]

37. Find the arithmetic mean in the following table :

Class	0—9	10—19	20—29	30—39	40—49
Frequency	4	6	10	8	2

[**Ans.** $\overline{X}$ = 23.83]

38. Find the arithmetic mean in the following table :

Class	0—5	5—10	10—15	15—20	20—25
Frequency	3	7	15	13	7

[**Ans.** $\overline{X}$ = 14.06]

39. Find the arithmetic mean of 120, 150, 280, 250 and show that the sum of the deviations of the items from mean is 0.

[**Ans.** A. M. 200]

40. From the following data, calculate weighted arithmetic mean :

X	76	74	81	70	88
Weight	3	6	2	3	7

[**Ans.** 79.04]

41. A student obtained the following percentage of marks in an examination : English 60, Economics 75, Business Studies 72, Accountancy 90, Statistics 95. Find the weighted mean if weights are 3, 1, 2, 4, 3 respectively. Also find out A.M.

[**Ans.** A.M. ($\overline{X}$) = 78.4%, $\overline{X}_W$ = 80.3%]

42. Given :

(i) $\overline{X} = 33$, $\Sigma fd'_x = -20$, $A = 35$, $i = 10$

Find out the number of items (n)

(ii) $\overline{X} = 23.5$, $n = 40$, $\Sigma fd_x = -440$

Find the value of assumed mean.

(iii) $\overline{X} = 27, A = 25, n = 15$

Find out the deviations multiplied by frequency of Σfd_x.

[**Ans.** (i) $n = 100$, (ii) A = 34.5, (iii) $\Sigma fd_x = 30$.]

43. Calculate the mean of the following data :

Class	12—18	18—24	24—30	30—36	36—42
Frequency	5	6	4	4	2

[**Ans.** $\overline{X} = 24.71$]

44. Calculate the mean of the following frequency distribution :

Income (₹)	*No. of Workers*
200—300	5
300—400	36
400—500	24
500—600	16
600—700	9
700—800	6
800—900	4

[**Ans.** ₹ 472]

45. Find the mean weekly earnings of a worker from the following data given below :

Weekly Earnings (₹)	*No. of Workers*
0—50	8
50—100	15
100—150	32
150—200	26
200—250	12
250—300	7

[**Ans.** ₹ 145]

46. The number of employees in two branches say A and B of a company are 80 and 65 respectively. Average salary of employees in branch A is ₹ 875 per month and in B ₹ 1,260 per month. Give the formula and calculate the combined salary of the two branches.

[**Ans.** ₹ 1,047.59]

47. From the following data, calculate weighted arithmetic mean :

Marks	*No. of Students*
10—15	3
15—20	6
20—25	8
25—30	10
30—35	7
35—40	6

[**Ans.** Mean 26.25]

48. Marks in Statistics of the students of Class XII are given below. Find out arithmetic mean :

Marks	*Students*
Less than 10	5
Less than 20	17
Less than 30	31
Less than 40	41
Less than 50	49
Less than 60	50

[**Ans.** Mean 26.4]

49. The average income of 100 persons is calculated ₹ 20, while the average income of all the 150 persons is ₹ 25. Calculate the average income of 50 persons.

[**Ans.** Average Income ₹ 35]

50. Find Mean : (*JAC*, 2020)

x	5	10	15	20	25
f	2	4	8	6	3

[**Ans.** $\overline{X} = 15.87$]

51. Calculate Arithmetic mean from he following data :

Size	*Frequency*
10	2
20	5
30	9
40	10
50	12
60	7
70	3
80	2

[**Ans.** $\overline{X} = 43.6$]

52. Find arithmetic mean : (*JAC*, 2025)

Marks (less than)	10	20	30	40	50	60
No. of Students	5	17	31	41	49	50

[**Ans.** $\overline{X} = 26.4$]

OBJECTIVE TYPE QUESTIONS

I. Multiple Choice Questions

1. Mean of 5, 8, 11, 16, 15 is : (*JAC*, 2018)
   (a) 10 (b) 11 (c) 12 (d) 13
2. Daily wages of 12 families are 280, 180, 96, 98, 104, 75, 80, 94, 100, 75, 600 and 200. Respectively what is the Arithmetic mean.
   (a) 165.16 (b) 182 (c) 171 (d) 178
3. For the calculation of arithmetic mean the class intervals should be : (*JAC*, 2016, 17)
   (a) Exclusive (b) Unequal
   (c) Equal (d) All are possible
4. A. M. and Average are the same : (*JAC*, 2015)
   (a) True (b) False
5. The best measure to central tendency is A. M. Is it true ?
   (a) Yes (b) No
6. Which average is affected most by extreme observations ?
   (a) Median (b) Mode
   (c) Arthmatic mean (d) Geometric mean
7. The sum of the deviotions of Individual observations is always zero form :
   (a) Mean (b) G.M. (c) H.M. (d) Mode
8. The A.M. is best measure of central Tendency be cause :
   (a) Most stable measure
   (b) Easy to calculate
   (c) Based on all observation only
   (d) All
9. One advantage of AM is :
   (a) Cannot be determined by Observation
   (b) Is not an unambigicus/indeterminate titration.

(c) Gives more importance to big value and less importance to small values
(d) None of these

10. Mean of – 2, 0, 2, 16 and – 6 is : (*JAC*, 2024)
(a) 1 (b) 3 (c) 4 (d) 2

11. The average of 6 numbers is 8. What is the 7th number so that the average becomes 10 :
(a) 23 (b) 22 (c) 21 (d) 20

12. Weight of 8 students are 60, 50, 62, 55, 58, 65, 56 and 54 kg. What is the mean weight ?
(a) 57.1 kg (b) 57.3 kg
(c) 57.5 kg (d) 57.7 kg

13. Age of 5 students are 15, 18, 16, 17 and 14 years. What is the A. M. ?
(a) 14 years (b) 16 years
(c) 18 years (d) 15 years

14. Monthly income of 5 persons are ₹ 4,500, ₹ 5,800, ₹ 3,200, ₹ 8,500 and ₹ 6,500. What is the mean income ?
(a) ₹ 5,700 (b) ₹ 5,800
(c) ₹ 5,900 (d) ₹ 6,000

15. Mean of – 1, 0, 1, 8 and – 3 is :
(a) 1 (b) 2 (c) 3 (d) 4

16. The arithmetic mean of 5, 10 and 15 : (*JAC*, 2020)
(a) 5 (b) 10 (c) 15 (d) 30

17. If mean of 'x' is 50 then mean of U = 10 + 5x will be : (*JAC*, 2020)
(a) 250 (b) 260
(c) 265 (d) 273

18. The number of measures of central tendency is : (*JAC*, 2023)
(a) 5 (b) 3 (c) 2 (d) 4

19. Arithmetic mean is always more than geometric mean : (*JAC*, 2023)
(a) False (b) True
(c) Both (a) and (b) (d) None of these

20. Average of 2, 5, 6, 8 and 9 is : (*JAC*, 2025)
(a) 5 (b) 8 (c) 6 (d) 2

21. Which of the following is a measure of central tendency? (*JAC*, 2026)
(a) Arithmetic Mean (b) Median
(c) Mode (d) All of these

22. Which of the following is difficult to compute in the measures of central tendency ? (*JAC*, 2026)
(a) Mean (b) Median
(c) Mode (d) Geometric Mean

[**Ans.** 1. (b), 2. (a), 3. (c), 4. (a), 5. (a), 6. (c), 7. (a), 8. (b), 9. (a), 10. (d), 11. (b), 12. (c), 13. (b), 14. (a), 15. (a), 16. (b), 17. (b), 18. (a), 19. (b), 20. (c), 21. (d), 22. (d).]

II. Fill in the Blanks :

1. The arithmatic mean of – 2, 0, 2, 16 and – 6....... .
2. The formula of Arithmatic mean is......... .
3. If $\overline{X} = 27.85$, $n = 72$, $\Sigma fd = -155$ then assumed mean = ...
4. If $\overline{X} = 66.5$, A = 55, $n = 60$,, then sum of deviation = ...
5. There are 45 students in a class out of which 15 are girls. The average weight of 15 girls is 45 kg and that of 30 boys 52 kg the average weght of the whole class is = ...

[**Ans.** 1. – 2; 2. (i) $\frac{\Sigma fx}{\Sigma f}$ – Discreate series, (ii) $\frac{\Sigma x_i}{n}$ – Individual series; 3. 30; 4. 690; 5. 49.67.]

2

MEDIAN

LEARNING OBJECTIVES

After studying this chapter, you will be able to know :
- **2.1 Meaning and Definition of Median**
- **2.2 Determination of Median**
- **2.3 Merits or Advantages of Median**
- **2.4 Demerits or Disadvantages of Median**
- **2.5 Uses of Median**
- **2.6 Graphic Representation of Median**
- **Theoretical Questions : Long Answer Questions, Short Answer Questions, Very Short Answer Questions**
- **Practical Problems**

ILLUSTRATIONS AND PRACTICAL PROBLEMS : AT A GLANCE

No. of Illustration		*No. of Problems*
1, 2(A)	Calculation of Median in Individual Series	1(A) to 4
3	Calculation of Median in Discrete Series	5 to 7(A), (B), (C)
4(A) to 13	Calculation of Median in Continuous Series	8(A) to 16
14, 15	To Find out Mean and Median	17 to 28
16, 17	To Find out Missing Frequency	29 to 31
18, 19	Determination of Median by Graphic Method	32 to 34
—	Miscellaneous Problems	35 to 38
19	**Total**	**38**

(2.1) MEANING AND DEFINITION OF MEDIAN

The Median is the middle most or central value of the given data. When the items are arranged in ascending or descending order, then half of the items lie below the Median and half of the items lie above the Median. In other words, the Median divides the arranged series in two equal parts.

According to "*Connor*", "The Median is that value of the variable which divides the group into two equal parts, one part all comprising values greater and the other values less than the Median."

Thus, Median is the average of position of the numbers. We generally denote Median by *M*.

In the following picture 3 is Median.

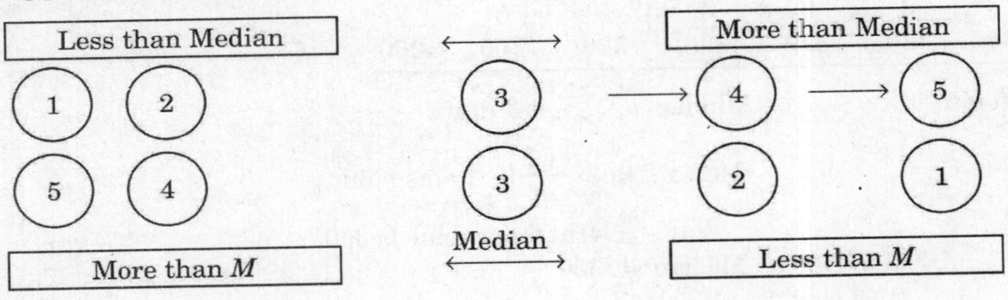

(2.2) DETERMINATION OF MEDIAN

(a) Determination of Median in Individual Series/Ungrouped Data

Step I. Arrange the series in either ascending or descending order of magnitude.

Step II. Case I. *When n is odd* : Use the following formula to locate Median :

$$M = \text{Size of the } \left(\frac{n+1}{2}\right)^{th} \text{ item.}$$

where, M = Median, n = Number of Items.

Case II. *When n is Even* : In this case, there are two middle terms or items. Hance Median is obtained as the Arithmetic Mean of the two middle items. Care should be taken, that the items are first arranged either in ascending or desending order.

$$\text{Symbolically } M = \frac{\left(\frac{n}{2}\right)^{th} \text{ item's value} + \left(\frac{n}{2}+1\right)^{th} \text{ item's value}}{2}$$

Median Formulae at a Glance

Individual Series	*Discrete Series*	*Continuous Series*
Arrange the series. In Ascending (Rising) or Descending (Decreasing) order and then use the formula $M = \left(\frac{n+1}{2}\right)^{th}$ item's value	Find out cum. freq. then use the formula $M = \left(\frac{n+1}{2}\right)^{th}$ item if n is odd. M = Mean of $\left(\frac{n}{2}\right)^{th}$ item and $\left(\frac{n}{2}+1\right)^{th}$ item, if n is even.	(i) Find out *c.f.* and then (ii) Find out the Median class $M = \left(\frac{N}{2}\right)^{th}$ items value, (iii) Use the following formula to find out Median : $M = l_1 + \frac{i}{f}(m-c)$ or $M = l_1 + \frac{i}{f}\left(\frac{N}{2}-c\right)$ or $M = l_1 + \frac{l_2 - l_1}{f}(m-c)$

Note : i may be replaced for C, where $i = l_2 - l_1$.

✎ Type 1

***Illustration* 1 (Odd Numbers)**

Find the Median from the following figures :

250, 400, 350, 380, 370, 300, 320

***Solution* :**

Let us arrange the figures in ascending order :

250,	300,	320,	350	370,	380,	400	here n = 7 obs.
1	2	3	[4]	5	6	7	

$$\text{Median} = \left(\frac{n+1}{2}\right)^{th} \text{ item's value}$$

$$= 4^{th} \text{ item's value}$$

$$= \mathbf{350}$$

Ans.

Alternatively :

Arrangement of data in descending order :

Sl. No.	1	2	3	4	5	6	7	n
Item	400	380	370	[350]	320	300	250	7

3 items ← Middle → 3 items

$$\text{Median} = \left(\frac{n+1}{2}\right)^{th} \text{ items value}$$

$\because$ = 4th items value is 350

$\therefore$ Median = **350**

Ans.

✎ Type 2

***Illustration* 2 (Even Number)**

Obtain the Median from the following data :

200, 160, 75, 110, 225, 150, 170, 185, 180, 220

Solution :

Let us arrange the items in ascending order :

75, 110, 150, 160, 170, 180, 185, 200, 220, 225

here, $n = 10$

$$M = \frac{\left(\frac{n}{2}\right)^{th} \text{item's value} + \left(\frac{n}{2}+1\right)^{th} \text{item's value}}{2}$$

$$= \frac{10+1}{2} = \frac{11}{2} = 5.5^{th} \text{ item}$$

$$= \frac{5^{th} \text{ item} + 6^{th} \text{ item}}{2}$$

∴ Size of 5.5^{th} item

$$M = \frac{5^{th} \text{ item's value} + 6^{th} \text{ item's value}}{2}$$

$$M = \frac{170+180}{2} = \mathbf{175}$$ **Ans.**

***Illustration* 2(A)**

Find the Median in the following data set :

108, 92, – 43, 0, 6, 11, – 2 and 15.

Solution :

Arranging the data in ascending order, we get

Serial No.	1	2	3	4	5	6	7	8
(*X*)	– 43	– 2	0	6	11	15	92	108

here, $n = 8$ (even)

$$M_e = \frac{\left(\frac{n}{2}\right)^{th} \text{item's value} + \left(\frac{n}{2}+1\right)^{th} \text{item's value}}{2}$$

$$= \frac{4^{th} \text{ item's value} + 5^{th} \text{ item's value}}{2}$$

$$M = \frac{6+11}{2} = \frac{17}{2} = \mathbf{8.5}$$ **Ans.**

(b) Determination of Median in Discrete Series (or Unclassified Series)

The following steps are taken while treating Median in the discrete series :

Step 1. The variable is arranged in ascending or descending order, if necessary.

Step 2. A table is prepared showing the corresponding frequencies.

Step 3. Find N, where $N = \Sigma f$ = Sum of the frequencies.

Step 4. Find the cumulative frequencies (*cf*) of each value of the variable.

Step 5. Then determine Median by using the following formula :

$$M = \left(\frac{N+1}{2}\right)^{th} \text{item's value}$$

Finding out the value of middle item : The value of $\left(\frac{N+1}{2}\right)^{th}$ item is ascertained as under :

Find Median item, *i.e.*, 1/2 of (N + 1) and then find out cumulative frequency (*cf*) in which this Median item falls and finally determine the value of the variable corresponding to this total. The value so determined will be the Median.

The following illustration will make it clear :

✎ Type 3

***Illustration* 3 (Number)**

Calculate the Median from the following data :

(*JAC*, 2019)

Income (in ₹)	150	160	180	190	200
No. of Workers	15	40	30	20	10

Solution :

Income (in ₹) (x)	*No. of Workers* (f)	*Cum. Freq* (*c.f.*)
150	15	15
160	40	15 + 40 = 55
Median 180	30	55 + 30 = 85
190	20	85 + 20 = 105
200	10	105 + 10 = 115
Total	N or $\Sigma f = 115$	

$$\text{Median} = \left(\frac{N+1}{2}\right)^{th} \text{item}$$

$$= \frac{115+1}{2}^{th} \text{ item}$$

$$= \frac{116}{2} = 58^{th} \text{ item}$$

58 lies in *c.f.* 85. Its corresponding value is 180.

Hence **Median = ₹ 180** **Ans.**

(c) Determination of Median in Continuous Series

In this case the data is given in the form of a frequency table with class-interval. To compute Median in continuous series the following steps are taken :

Step 1. Cumulative frequencies are calculated.

Step 2. Median item is located by applying the formula $\frac{N}{2}\left(\text{not} \frac{N+1}{2}\right)$ (In continuous series it is $\left(\frac{N}{2}\right)$ which divides the area of the frequency curve into two equal parts.)

Step 3. Median Class : The Median item is located in cumulative frequency (*cf*) column. It lies in the (*c.f*) greater than $\left(\frac{N}{2}\right)$ and lies in its corresponding class-interval. This class-interval is called Median class. Median value lies in this class-interval.

Step 4. The Median value is calculated by applying the following formula :

$$M = l_1 + \frac{l_2 - l_1}{f}(m - c)$$

or $$M = l_1 + \frac{(m-c)}{f} \times i$$

or $$M = l_1 + \frac{i}{f}(m - c)$$

or $$M = l_1 + \frac{i}{f}\left(\frac{N}{2} - c\right)$$

Where M = Median

l_1 = Lower limit of Median class

i = Length of the Median class (that is $l_2 - l_1$)

f = Frequency of the Median class

c = Cumulative frequency of the class just before the Median class (N/2).

$$m = \left(\frac{N}{2}\right)^{th} \text{ item}$$

(d) Determination of Median by taking Upper Limit

The Median can also be computed by taking upper limit of the Median class. In that case, the formula for calculating Median will be :

$$M = l_1 + \frac{i}{f}(m - c)$$

Where l_2 = Upper Class Limit of the Median Class.

c = Cumulative Frequency of the class just before the Median Class.

Note : If the Median class is the first class-interval of the frequency distribution, then 'c' will always be treated as 0 (zero).

When Mid-values are given

Sometimes mid-value of the classes are given in a question. In such a case, mid-values should be converted into class-intervals before calculating the Median.

Procedure for conversion :

(i) Find out the 'Difference' between adjoining mid-values.

(ii) Divide the difference by 2 to get quotient. Thus, if the mid-values are 10, 20, 30... and so on. Then, the difference will be 20 – 10 = 10 and its quotient will be $\frac{10}{2} = 5$.

(iii) Deduct the quotient to each of the mid-values to obtain the lower limits l_1 of the classes. Add the quotient to each of the middle values to obtain upper limits (l_2) of the classes.

✎ Type 4

Median in Continuous Series

***Illustration* 4(A)**

Calculate the value of Median from the following table :

Wages (in ₹)	*No. of Workers*
30—40	50
40—50	54
50—60	85
60—70	45
70—80	30

***Solution* :**

Calculation of Median

Wages (₹)	*No. of Workers (f)*	*Cumulative Frequency (c.f.)*
30—40	50	50
40—50	54	104 (*C*)
50—60 (Median Class)	85	189
60—70	45	234
70—80	30	264
Total	*N* = 264	

$$m = \left(\frac{N}{2}\right)^{th} \text{ item's value}$$

$$= \left(\frac{264}{2}\right)^{th} \text{ (item' value)}$$

$$= 132^{th} \text{ item's value}$$

132 falls in cumulative frequency 189. This lies in interval (50—60).

Therefore,

Median Class = (50—60).

Now, $$M = l_1 + \frac{i}{f}(m - c)$$

$$\therefore \quad M = 50 + \frac{10}{85}(132 - 104)$$

$$\Rightarrow \quad M = 50 + \frac{10 \times 28}{85}$$

$$= 50 + \frac{56}{17}$$

$$\therefore \quad = 50 + 3.29 = 53.29$$

∴ **Median = ₹ 53.29** **Ans.**

***Illustration* 4(B)**

Calculate Median from the following data :

Marks	*No. of Students (f)*
5—10	6
10—15	5
15—20	18
20—25	10
25—30	5
30—35	4
35—40	2
40—45	2

Solution :

Calculation of Median

Wages (₹)	No. of Students (f)	Cumulative Frequency (c.f.)
5—10	6	6
10—15	5	11 (c)
15—20 (Median Class)	18 (f)	29
20—25	10	39
25—30	5	44
30—35	4	48
35—40	2	50
40—45	2	52
Total	N = 52	

$$m = \text{Size of } \left(\frac{N}{2}\right)^{th} \text{ item}$$

$$= \text{Size of } \left(\frac{52}{2}\right)^{th} \text{ item} = \text{Size of } 26^{th} \text{ item}$$

∵ 26th item lies in *c.f.* 29. Hence the corresponding class (15—20) is Median class.

∴ $l_1 = 15, i = 5, c = 11, f = 18, m = 26$

∴ Median, $M = l_1 + \frac{i}{f}(m - c)$

$$= 15 + \frac{5}{18}(26 - 11)$$

$$= 15 + \frac{5}{18} \times 15 = 15 + \frac{25}{6} = 15 + 4.16$$

∴ **M = 19.16 Ans.**

✎ Type 5

When Mid-values are given

Illustration 5

From the following distribution, calculate Median :

Mid-value	50	150	250	350	450
Frequency	50	90	158	68	134

Solution :

Difference between two adjoining values = (150 – 50) = 100, Now 100 ÷ 2 = 50, 50 will be deducted and added in each mid-value.

Calculation of Median

Size of Items	Frequency (f)	Cumulative Frequency (c.f.)
0—100	50	50
100—200	90	140 (c)
200—300 (Median class)	158 (f)	298
300—400	68	366
400—500	34	500
Total	N = 500	

$$\text{The Median item } (m) = \left(\frac{N}{2}\right)^{th} \text{ item}$$

$$= \left(\frac{500}{2}\right)^{th} \text{ item} = 250^{th} \text{ item}$$

Where 250 falls in *c.f.* 298. Its corresponding size is (200—300).

∴ Median Class = 200—300

Thus, $$M = l_1 + \left(\frac{m - c}{f}\right) \times i$$

$$= 200 + \frac{250 - 140}{158} \times 100$$

$$= 200 + \frac{110 \times 100}{158}$$

∴ $M = 200 + 69.62 = 269.62$

∴ **Median = 269.62** **Ans.**

Descending Order of the Series

Sometimes series is given in descending order instead of ascending order. In such cases Median can be calculated by either of the following methods :

(i) Series is changed into ascending order and the problem is solved by applying the following formula :

$$M = l_1 + \frac{i}{f}(m - c)$$

or $$M = l_1 + \frac{i}{f}\left(\frac{N}{2} - c\right)$$

(ii) The problem can be solved on the basis of descending order itself by applying the following formula :

$$M = l_2 - \frac{i}{f}(m - c)$$

or $$M = l_2 + \frac{i}{f}\left(\frac{N}{2} - c\right)$$

✎ Type 6

Median in Cumulative Series

Illustration 6 (A)

The following table gives the marks obtained by 65 candidates in Statistics in a cortain examination :

Marks	No. of Students (f)
More than 70%	7
More than 60%	18
More than 50%	40
More than 40%	50
More than 30%	63
More than 20%	65

Calculate the Median marks.

Solution :

Median marks can be obtained, by arranging in ascending order :

Marks	*No. of Students (f)*	*Cumulative Frequency (c.f.)*
20—30	2	2
30—40	13	15
40—50	10	25 (*c*)
50—60 (Median Class)	22 (*f*)	47
60—70	11	58
70—80	7	65
Total	*N* = 65	

$$m = \text{Size of } \left(\frac{N}{2}\right)^{th} \text{ item}$$

$$= \left(\frac{65}{2}\right)^{th} \text{ item} = 32.5^{th} \text{ item}$$

Which lies in *c.f.* 47, it corresponding class (50—60).

Median Class = (50—60)

$$\text{Median} = l_1 + \frac{i}{f}\left(\frac{N}{2} - c\right)$$

$$= 50 + \frac{10}{22}(32.5 - 25)$$

$$= 50 + \frac{10 \times 7.5}{22} = 50 + \frac{75}{22}$$

$$= 55 + 3.41 = 53.41$$

∴ **Median = 53.41 = 53.40 Marks Ans.**

Alternative Method : Descending Order :

Calculation of Median

Marks	*No. of Students (f)*	*Cumulative Frequency (c.f.)*
70—80	7	7
60—70	11	18 (*c*)
50—60 (Median Class)	22 (*f*)	40
40—50	10	50
30—40	13	63
20—30	2	65
Total	*N* = 65	

$$m = \left(\frac{N}{2}\right)^{th} \text{ item's value}$$

$$= \left(\frac{65}{2}\right)^{th} \text{ item's value}$$

or $m = 32.5^{th}$ item's value

32.5 falls in *c.f.* 40, its Median size is (50—60).

Therefore,

$$\text{Median} = l_2 - \frac{i}{f}\left(\frac{N}{2} - c\right)$$

$$= 60 - \frac{10}{22}\left(\frac{65}{2} - 18\right)$$

$$= 60 - \frac{10 \times 14.5}{22}$$

$$= 60 - 6.59 = 53.41$$

∴ ***M* = 53.41 Marks Ans.**

***Illustration* 6(B)**

Calculate the Median from the following data :

Marks	*No. of Students (f)*
Less than 10	15
Less than 20	35
Less than 30	60
Less than 40	84
Less than 50	96
Less than 60	127
Less than 70	198
Less than 80	250

Solution :

To calculate Median, we have

Class	*Frequency (f)*	*Cumulative Frequency (c.f.)*
0—10	15	15
10—20	20	35
20—30	25	60
30—40	24	84
40—50	12	96 (*c*)
50—60 (Median Class)	31 (*f*)	127
60—70	71	198
70—80	52	250
Total	*N* = 250	

$$m = \left(\frac{N}{2}\right)^{th} \text{ item's value}$$

$$m = \left(\frac{250}{2}\right)^{th} \text{ item's value}$$

or $m = 125^{th}$ item's value

which lies in *c.f.* 127

∴ Median Class = 50—60

Now, $M = l_1 + \frac{i}{f}(m - c)$

where $l_1 = 50,\ i = 60 - 20 = 10, f = 31$

$m = 125,\ c = 96$

$$= 50 + \frac{10}{31}(125 - 96)$$

$$= 50 + \frac{10 \times 29}{31}$$

$$= 50 + \frac{290}{31} = 50 + 9.35 = 59.35$$

∴ **Median = 59.35 Ans.**

Calculation of Median in a Series with Unequal Class-intervals

If the class-intervals with unusual magnitude are given the following procedures may be adopted for calculating the Median :

Step 1. The magnitude of the series or class-interval should be made equal by adding or sub-dividing the frequency, as the case may be. Thus, the frequency distribution table should be amended or re-constructed.

Step 2. Locate the Median Class.

Step 3. Apply the formula to determine the Median.

Note : (i) It should be noted that the class-intervals not be made equal while calculating Median because the Median is the same. Whether it is calculated with unequal class-intervals or with equal class-intervals.

(ii) However, if any instruction is given in the question for restructuring of the frequency distribution table and then to Calculate the Median, in such a case the instruction must be followed, that is, the class-intervals should be made of equal magnitude.

✎ Type 7

Median in Unequal Class-intervals

***Illustration* 7 (A)**

Calculate the Median from the following data after amending the table :

Variable	*(f)*
0—2	3
2—6	6
6—12	17
12—17	17
17—18	10
18—24	10
24—30	8
30—34	5
34—36	2

***Solution* :**

In this table class-intervals with unequal magnitude. So this should be amended on the basis of equal class magnitude. By observation, we find that the maximum magnitude of the class-interval is 6. Hence, the amended frequency table will be as follows :

Determination of Median

Variable	*Frequency (f)*	*Cumulative Frequency (c.f.)*
0—6	3 + 6 = 9	8
6—12	17	26 (*c*)
12—18	17 + 10 = 27 (*f*)	53 (Median)
18—24	10	63
24—30	8	71
30—36	5 + 2 = 7	78
Total	*N* = 78	

$$m = \left(\frac{N}{2}\right)^{th} \text{ item's value}$$

$$m = \left(\frac{78}{2}\right)^{th} \text{ item's value}$$

$$m = 39^{th} \text{ item's value}$$

39 lies in *c.f.* 53. Its corresponding size is (12—18).

$\therefore$ Median Class = (12—18)

Now $$M = l_1 + \frac{l_2 - l_1}{f}(m - c)$$

$$\Rightarrow \quad M = 12 + \frac{18-12}{27}(39-26)$$

$$= 12 + \frac{16 \times 13}{27}$$

$$= 12 + 2.88 = 14.88$$

$\therefore$ M = **14.88** **Ans.**

Median in case of Mixed Series

***Illustration* 7(B)**

Find out Median from the following data :

Size	*Frequency*
0	5
1	7
3	10
5—7	25
8—14	40
15—24	30
25—45	23

***Solution* :**

Calculation of Median

x	*f*	*c.f.*
0	5	5
1	7	12
3	10	22
5—7	25	47 (*c*)
8—14	40 (*f*)	87
15—24	30	117
25—45	23	140
Total	*N* = 140	

$$M = \left(\frac{N}{2}\right)^{th} \text{ item's value}$$

$$= \left(\frac{140}{2}\right)^{th} \text{ item's value}$$

$$= 70^{th} \text{ item's value}$$

Where, 70 lies in *c.f.* 87. Its size is 8—14. (Median)

But its real limits are 7.5—14.5.

Where $l_1 = 7.5,\ i = 14.5 - 7.5 = 7$

$f = 40,\ c = 47,\ m = 70$

Now, Median, $M = l_1 + \frac{i}{f}(m - c)$

$= 7.5 + \frac{7}{40}(70 - 47)$

$= 7.5 + \frac{7 \times 23}{40}$

$= 7.5 + 4.025 = 11.525$

$\therefore$ M = **11.525** **Ans.**

Illustration 7(C)

Find the Median : (*JAC*, 2018)

Marks	*No. of Students (f)*
0—10	10
10—20	15
20—30	30
30—40	32
40—50	7
50—60	6

Solution :

We know that $M_e = l_1 + \frac{N/2 - c}{f}(l_2 - l_1)$

Calculation Table

Marks	*No. of Students (f)*	*Cum. Freq. (c.f.)*
0—10	10	10
10—20	15	25 → c
(l_1) 20—30 (l_2)	30(f)	55 (N/2)
30—40	32	87
40—50	7	94
50—60	6	100
Total	N = 100	—

here, $M_e = \left(\frac{N}{2}\right)$th item's value $= \frac{100}{2} =$ 50th item's value, which lies in the c.f. 55, Hence (20 – 30) will be Median class.

$\therefore \quad M_e = 20 + \frac{50 - 25}{30}(30 - 20)$

$= 20 + \frac{25 \times 10}{30} \Rightarrow$ **28.33**

Determination of the Median in Inclusive Series

If the class-intervals under 'Inclusive Method' are given, the class-intervals should be changed into 'Exclusive Series' to obtain 'Real Class Limits'. However, it should be noted that instead of converting each Inclusive Class-Interval into Exclusive Class-Interval, it will suffice our requirement to convert the 'Median Class' (under Inclusive Series) into Exclusive Series.

✎ Type 8

Median in Inclusive Continuous Series

Illustration 8

Find Median from the following data :

Size	*Frequency*
11—15	7
16—20	10
21—25	13
26—30	26
31—35	35
36—40	22
41—45	11
46—50	5

Solution :

Calculation of Median

Size	*Freq. (f)*	*Cum. Freq. (c.f.)*	*Real Class Limits*
11—15	7	7	10.5—15.5
16—20	10	17	15.5—20.5
21—25	13	30	20.5—25.5
26—30	26	56 (c)	25.5—30.5
31—35	35 (f)	91	30.5—35.5
36—40	22	113	35.5—40.5
41—45	11	124	40.5—45.5
46—50	5	129	45.5—50.5
Total	N = 129		

$m = \left(\frac{N}{2}\right)^{th}$ item's value

$= \left(\frac{129}{2}\right)^{th}$ item's value

$= 64.5^{th}$ item's value

64.5^{th} item lies in the (31—35) class or (30.5—35.5). Thus,

Median $= l_1 + \frac{i}{f}(m - c)$

$= 30.5 + \frac{5}{35}(64.5 - 56)$

$= 30.5 + \frac{5 \times 8.5}{35}$

$= 30.5 + \frac{8.5}{7} = 30.5 + 1.21 = 31.71$

$\therefore$ Median = **31.71** **Ans.**

Calculation of Median when Mid-values are given

When mid-values are given, the following steps need to be taken :

Step 1. From the mid-values, we find respective class-intervals. For this (i) Difference between two consecutive mid-values is taken, (ii) Divide the difference by 2, (iii) Then deduct it from each mid-value to find **Lower Limit** and add it to each mid-value to find the **Upper Limit** of that class.

For example, if mid-values are 10, 15, 20, then

(i) Difference between the two consecutive mid-values : 15 – 10 = 5

(ii) $\frac{5}{2} = 2.5$

(iii)

l_1	l_2	*Class*
10 – 2.5 = 7.5	10 + 2.5 = 12.5	7.5—12.5
15 – 2.5 = 12.5	15 + 2.5 = 17.5	12.5—17.5
20 – 2.5 = 17.5	20 + 2.5 = 22.5	17.5—22.5

Illustration 9

Calculate the Median from the following : (*JAC*, 2016)

Mid-Value (m)	5	10	15	20	25	30
Frequency (f)	4	6	10	7	3	2

Solution :

Size	*Frequency (f)*	*Cum. Freq. (c.f.)*
2.5—7.5	4	4
7.5—12.5	6	10 (c)
12.5—17.5	10 (f)	20 ←
17.5—22.5	7	27
22.5—27.5	3	30
27.5—32.5	2	32
Total	N = 32	

$m = \left(\frac{32}{2}\right)^{th}$ item's value

$m = \left(\frac{N}{2}\right)^{th}$ item's value

= 16th item's value

which lies in the group (12.5—17.5)

Now, $M = l_1 + \frac{i}{f}(m - c)$

$= 12.5 + \frac{5}{10} \times (16 - 10)$

$= 12.5 + \frac{5}{10} \times 6$

$= 12.5 + 3 = 15.5$

∴ Median = **15.5** **Ans.**

For determining Median, there is no nbeed to make equal class-intervals from unequal intervals. However, if Median is required after preparing revised table, then in that case, class-interval should be of equal size. For conveyance, students are advised to make the unequal class-intervals changed into equal class-intervals as far as possible.

Illustration 10

Calculate the Median from the following :

Marks Obtained	*No. of Students*
0—20	10
20—30	10
30—40	5
40—60	62
60—75	10
75—80	3

Solution :

Size		*Frequency (f)*	*Cum. Freq. (cf)*
0—20		10	10
20—40	20—30 30—40	10 5 } 15	25 (c)
40—60		62 (f)	67 ←
60—80	60—75 75—80	10 3 } 13	100
Total		N = 100	

$m = \left(\frac{N}{2}\right)^{th}$ item's value

$= \left(\frac{100}{2}\right)^{th}$ item's value

= 50th item's value

which lies in the group (40–60)

Now, $m = l_1 - \frac{i}{f}(m - c)$

$= 40 + \frac{20}{62}(50 - 25)$

$= 40 + \frac{20}{62} \times 25$

$= 40 + 8.06 = 48.06$ Marks

∴ Median = **48.06 Marks** **Ans.**

Illustration 11

Calculate the Median from the following frequency distribution :

Class	*Frequency*
0—10	5
10—20	15
20—30	30
30—40	0
40—50	35
50—60	15

Solution :

Class	*Frequency (f)*	*Cum. Freq. (c.f.)*
0—10	5	5
10—20	15	20 (c)
20—30	30 (f)	50
30—40	0	50
40—50	35	85
50—60	15	100
Total	N = 100	

On Rearranging the table, we get

Class	*Frequency (f)*	*Cum. Freq. (c.f.)*
0—10	5	5
10—20	15	20
20—35	30	50
35—50	35	85
50—60	15	100
Total	$N = 100$	

$$m = \left(\frac{N}{2}\right)^{th} \text{ item's value}$$

$$= 50^{th} \text{ item's value}$$

Here we find two *c.fs.* being 50. Hence, the median class is uncertain.

By Assuming (20—30) as the Median class.

$$M = l_1 + \frac{i}{f}(m - c)$$

$$= 20 + \frac{10}{30}(50 - 20)$$

$$= 20 + \frac{10}{30} \times 30 = 20 + 10 = 30$$

or Assuming (30—40) as the Median class

$$M = l_1 + \frac{i}{f}(m - c)$$

$$= 30 + \frac{10}{0}(50 - 20)$$

$$= 30 + 0 = 30$$

But 30 is not true Median since class 30—40 has zero (0) frequency. Therefore, we should frame new class-interval by dividing it in two parts and adding the same in two class-intervals.

$$\therefore \quad M = l_1 + \frac{i}{f}(m - c)$$

$$= 20 + \frac{15}{30}(50 - 20)$$

$$= 20 + \frac{15}{30} \times 30$$

$$= 20 + 15 = 35$$

$\therefore$ **M = 35** **Ans.**

If the first class itself is the Median class

***Illustration* 12**

Calculate the Median :

Size	*Frequency*
0—10	80
10—20	44
20—30	20
30—40	6
40—50	4

Solution :

Size	*Frequency (f)*	*Cum. Freq. (c.f.)*
0—10	80	80
10—20	44	124
20—30	20	144
30—40	6	150
40—50	4	154
Total	$N = 154$	

$$m = \left(\frac{N}{2}\right)^{th} \text{ item's value}$$

$$= \left(\frac{154}{2}\right) = 77^{th} \text{ item}$$

which lies in *cf* 80. Its size is (0—10) Median Class, Thus, $l_1 = 0, f = 80, i = 10, N/2 = 77, c = 0$

$$\text{Thus,} \quad M = l_1 + \frac{i}{f}\left(\frac{N}{2} - c\right)$$

$$= 0 + \frac{10}{80}(77 - 0)$$

$$= 0 + \frac{10 \times 77}{80} = 0 + 9.625$$

$\therefore$ **M = 9.625** **Ans.**

Calculation of Median in Open-end Series

In Open-ended Series at Lower Limit of the First Class and Upper Limit of the Last Class, it is not known what are the end values. Therefore, the Mathematical Average, *viz.*, $\overline{X}$, *G.M.*, or *H.M.* cannot be calculated unless some assumptions are made about the extreme values. Median and Mode are suitable averages in such a situation.

✎ Type 9

***Illustration* 13**

Find out the Median from the following frequency distribution :

Value	*Frequency*
Less than 100	40
100—200	85
200—300	150
300—400	66
400 and Above	59

Solution : **Calculation of Median**

Value	*Frequency (f)*	*Cum. Frequency (cf)*
Less than 100	40	40
100—200	85	40 + 85 = 125 (*c*)
200—300	150 (*f*)	125 + 150 = 275
300—400	66	275 + 66 = 341
400 and Above	59	341 + 59 = 400
Total	$N = 400$	

Median Item $(m) = \left(\frac{N}{2}\right)^{th}$ item' value $= \left(\frac{400}{2}\right)^{th}$ item's value = 200th item's value

which falls in the cumulative frequency 275, hence Median class is (200—300).

Thus, Median $= l_1 + \frac{i}{f}(m - c)$

$= 200 + \frac{100}{150}(200 - 125)$

$= 200 + \frac{100 \times 75}{150}$

$= 200 + 50 = 250$

∴ **Median = 250.** **Ans.**

✎ Type 10

To Find out Arithmetic Mean, Median

Illustration 14

Calculate Arithmetic Mean and Median of the following series :

Size	*Frequency*
10—20	6
20—30	20
30—40	44
40—50	26
50—60	3
60—70	1

Solution :

Calculation of Arithmetic Mean and Median

Let $A = 35$

Size	*Frequency (f)*	*Mid-value (m)*	$d_x = m - A$	fd_x	*Cum. Freq. (c.f.)*
10—20	6	15	– 20	– 120	6
20—30	20	25	– 10 (*f*)	– 200	6 + 20 = 26
30—40	44	35	0	0	26 + 44 = 70
40—50	26	45	+ 10	+ 260	70 + 26 = 96
50—60	3	55	+ 20	+ 60	96 + 3 = 99
60—70	1	65	+ 30	+ 30	99 + 1 = 100
Total	$N = 100$			$\Sigma fd_x = +30$	

(i) Arithmetic Mean $(\overline{X}) = A + \frac{\Sigma fd_x}{N}$

$= 35 + \frac{30}{100} = 35 + 0.3$

$= 35.3$

(ii) $(M) = \left(\frac{N}{2}\right)^{th}$ item's value

$= \left(\frac{100}{2}\right)^{th}$ items' value

$= 50^{th}$ item's value

where 50 lies in *cf* 70.

Its corresponding size is (30—40).

Therefore, Median Class = 30—40

Now, Median $(M) = l_1 + \frac{i}{f}\left(\frac{N}{2} - c\right)$

Where, $l_1 = 30, i = 40 - 30 = 10$

$f = 44, c = 26$

$= 30 + \frac{10}{44}\left(\frac{100}{2} - 26\right)$

$= 30 + \frac{10 \times 24}{44}$

$= 30 + 5.45 = 35.45$

(i) Arithmetic Mean = **35.5**

(ii) Median = **35.45** **Ans.**

✎ Type 11

To Find out difference between Mean and Median

Illustration 15

Find out the difference between Mean and Median from the following data :

16, 13, 2.8, 10, 4, 9, 24.2, 22, 12, 23, 7.

Solution :

Given $n = 11$

Thus, $\Sigma x = 16 + 13 + 2.8 + 10 + 4 + 9 + 24.2 + 22 + 12 + 23 + 7 = 143$

∴ or $\overline{X} = \frac{\Sigma x}{n} = \frac{143}{11} = 13$ (Mean)

Calculation of Median

On arranging the data in Ascending order, we get

Serial No.	1	2	3	4	5	6	7	8	9	10	11
(*X*)	2.8	4	7	9	10	12	13	16	22	23	24

$m = \left(\frac{N+1}{2}\right)^{th}$ item's value

$= 6^{th}$ item's value = 12

Thus, Median = 12

Now, Difference between Mean and Median

= 13 – 12 = 1 **Ans.**

Finding out Missing Frequency

When Median value is given and necessary data are also given but frequency of one or more classes is missing.

Then the missing frequency can be obtained by using the formula of Median.

✎ Type 12

To Find out Missing Frequencies

***Illustration* 16**

Find the missing frequency of the following table if Median wages are ₹ 48 :

Wages per day (₹)	*No. of Workers*
0—20	24
20—40	46
40—60	—
60—80	26
80—100	34

Solution :

Let the missing frequency of class (40 – 60) be f :

Daily Wages (₹)	*No. of Workers (f)*	*Cum. Frequency (c.f.)*
0—20	24	24
20—40	46	70
40—60	f	$70 + f$
60—80	28	$96 + f$
80—100	34	$130 + f$
Total	$N = 130 + f$	

$$\text{Median Item } (m) = \left(\frac{130+f}{2}\right)^{th} \text{ item's value}$$

$$= \left(65 + \frac{f}{2}\right)^{th} \text{ item's value}$$

Since Median is 48, Median class will be (40—60) and the value of $\left(65 + \frac{f}{2}\right)$ or $(65 + 0.05 f)$ will lie in class (40—60).

Now, $$M = l_1 + \frac{i}{f}(m - c)$$

$$48 = 40 + \frac{20}{f}(65 + 0.5f - 70)$$

or $$48 - 40 = \frac{20}{f}(65 + 0.5f - 70)$$

or $$8 = \frac{1300 + 10f - 1400}{f}$$

or $$8f = 10f - 100$$

or $$8f - 10f = -100$$

or $$-2f = -100$$

or $$f = 100/2 = 50$$

Therefore the number of workers in the Median class (40—60) is 50. **Ans.**

When frequencies of two class-intervals are missing

***Illustration* 17**

In the following given frequency distribution, some frequencies are missing :

Class	*Frequency*
10—20	185
20—30	—
30—40	34
40—50	180
50—60	136
60—70	—
70—80	50

If the total frequency is 685 and Median is 42.6, find out the missing frequencies.

Solution :

Let the missing frequencies be f_1 (20—30) and f_2 (60—70).

Calculation of Median

Class (X)	*Frequency (f)*	*Cum. Frequency (c.f.)*
10—20	185	185
20—30	f_1	$185 + f_1$
30—40	34	$219 + f_1$ (c)
l_1(40—50)l_2	180 (f)	$399 + f_1$ (Median Class)
50—60	136	$535 + f_1$
60—70	f_2	$535 + f_1 + f_2$
70—80	50	$585 + f_1 + f_2$
Total	$N = 685$	

∵ Median is 42.6. Hence lower limit *i.e.*

$$l_1 = 40, N = 685$$

Thus, $$m = \left(\frac{N}{2}\right)^{th} \text{ item's value}$$

$$= \left(\frac{685}{2}\right)^{th} \text{ item's value}$$

$$= 342.5^{th} \text{ item's value}$$

c = Cumulative freq. of the class (30—40) = $219 + f_1$,

$$f = 180, i = 50 - 40 = 10$$

$$\text{Median} = 42.6 \text{ (given)}$$

Now, $$M = l_1 + \frac{i}{f}\left(\frac{N}{2} - c\right)$$

$$42.6 = 40 + \frac{342.5 - 219 - f_1}{180} \times 10$$

or $$42.6 - 40 = \frac{3425 - 2190 - 10f_1}{180}$$

or $$2.6 \times 180 = 3425 - 2190 - 10f_1$$

or $$468 = 3425 - 2190 - 10f_1$$

or $10f_1 = 1235 - 468$

or $f_1 = \frac{767}{10}$

$= 76.7 = 77$

$\therefore$ $f_1 = 77$

(Since frequency can not be in fraction)

$\because$ $N = 685$

Also $N = 585 + f_1 + f_2;$

putting $f_1 = 77$

$\therefore$ $f_2 = 685 - 585 - 77 = 23$

Thus, $f_1 = \mathbf{77}$

and $f_2 = \mathbf{23}$ **Ans.**

(2.3) MERITS OR ADVANTAGES OF MEDIAN

(1) Median is very easy to calculate. (2) It is easy to understand. (3) It is not affected by the extreme observations as Median is a positional average. (4) It is the best measure for qualitative data such as Beauty, Intelligence. Honesty etc. (5) It can be located graphically. (6) It can be computed while dealing with a distribution with open-end classes.

(2.4) DEMERITS OR DISADVANTAGES OF MEDIAN

(1) The computation of Median requires in certain cases, arranging of the items in ascending or descending order. It is often a tedious job. (2) It is not suitable for further mathematical treatment. (3) It does not take into account the values of all the items in the series. (4) A very little importance is attached to the items on the extremes. (5) A little change in the series may change the value of the median substantially. (6) Since the median is not based on the total, it is not possible to determine the total from the median and the number of observations.

(2.5) USES OF MEDIAN

(1) It is a useful in those cases where numerical measurements are not possible. (2) It is also useful in those cases where mathematical calculations cannot be made in order to obtain the mean. (3) It is used most frequently when we require a measure of location which is not affected by high or low value item.

(2.6) GRAPHIC REPRESENTATION OF MEDIAN

Median can be located graphically. There are two methods of determining median with the help of graph :

(1) By an Ogive : (i) With the help of 'Less than' cumulatiave frequency distributions or ogive. (ii) With the help of 'More than' cumulative frequency distributions or ogive. (2) By drawing two Ogives.

(1) Determining Median by drawing One Ogive

An ogive is a cumulative frequency curve. In 'less than' cumulative frequency distributions, the curve shows a rising trend. In case of 'more than' cumulative frequency distributions, the curve shows a declining trend. The following steps are taken to determine median by graphic method :

Step 1. Variables are taken on X-axis and the cumulative frequencies on Y-axis.

Step 2. Draw a Less Than Type of More Than Type frequency curve.

Step 3. Calculate $N/2$ (since Median item is determined by $N/2$ formula) and locate a point corresponding to $N/2$ along O-Y axis.

Step 4. From the located point along the Y-axis, draw a line paralled to X-axis which will cut the ogive at a point, say 'A' or 'T'.

Step 5. From this point 'A' or 'T', a perpendicular is drawn on X-axis. The point, where perpendicular touches, X-axis, shows Median value (M). Let us explain it with example.

***Illustration* 18**

Find the Median from the following data by Graphic Method :

Daily Wages (in ₹)	*Frequency*
40—50	20
50—60	30
60—70	50
70—80	60
80—90	30
90—100	10

***Solution* :**

1. Computation of Median by 'Less than Method'

Step 1.

Wages (in ₹)	*f*	*c. f.*
40—50	20	20
50—60	30	20 + 30 = 50
60—70	50	50 + 50 = 100
70—80	60	100 + 60 = 160
80—90	30	160 + 30 = 190
90—100	10	190 + 10 = 200
Total	$N = 200$	

Step 2. Plotting cf *c.f.* on graph paper.

Step 3. To find out $\frac{N}{2} = \frac{200}{2} = 100$

Step 4. And locating a point corresponding to $N/2$ along Y-axis which meets the Ogive at point.

Step 5. From the located point, a line paralled to X-axis is drawn. The point (M) where it meets the X-axis, is the Median.

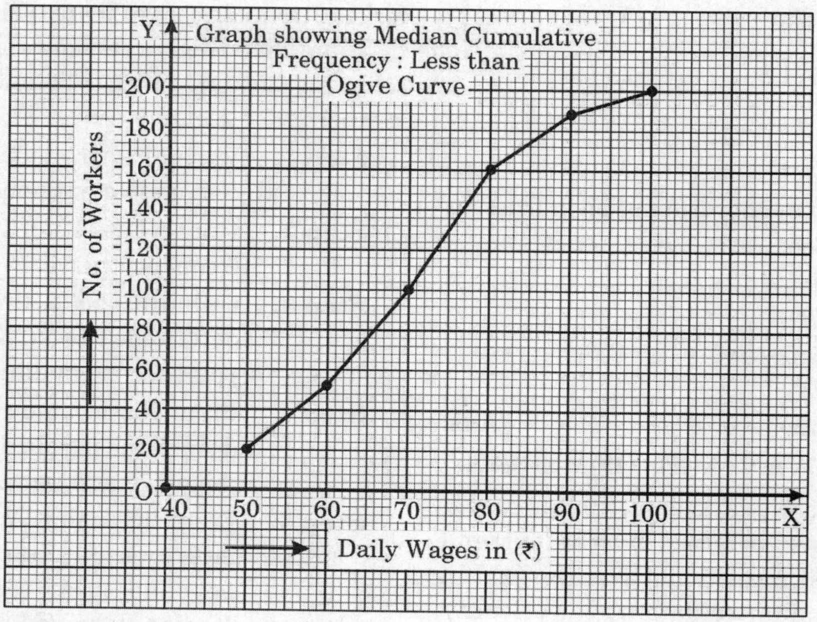

Note : We take Wage on X-axis and Frequency on Y-axis.

2. Determination of Median by 'More than Method'

Wages (₹)	40	50	60	70	80	90	100
c. f.	200	180	150	100	40	10	0

$$\frac{N}{2} = \frac{200}{2} = 100$$

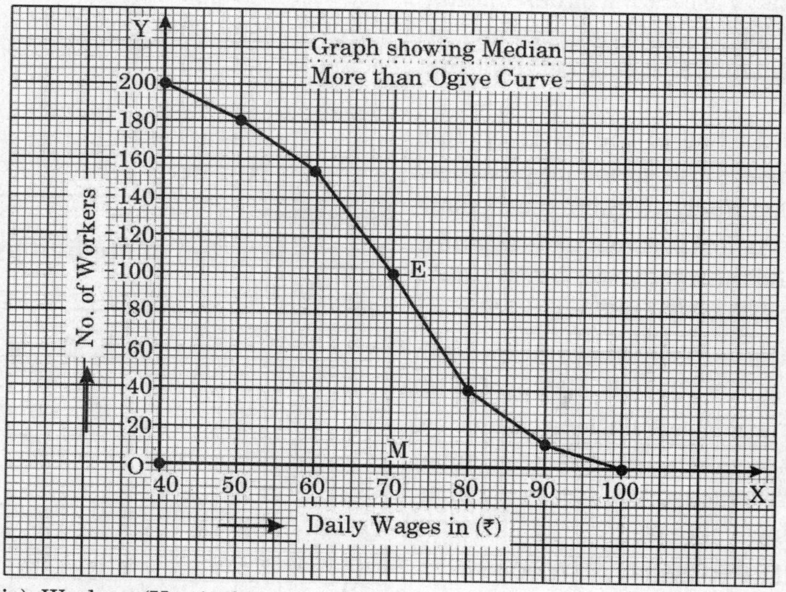

Note : Wages (Horizontal axis), Workers (Vertical axis).

3. Determination of Median by drawing Two Ogives (Less than and More than)

Under this method, both 'less than' and 'more than' ogives (*i.e.* frequency curves) are drawn on the same scale and graph. These two curves intersect at a point, say '*A*' or '*T*'. From the intersection point of these two Ogives, a perpendicular is drawn on the X-axis. The point where perpendicular touches X-axis, denotes Median value. This method is also known as 'Galton Method'.

***Illustration* 19**

Prepare 'Less than' and 'More than' Ogives and find out the Median :

Class	10—20	20—40	40—70	70—100	100—150
Frequency	4	10	26	8	12

Solution :

Class	f	Less than	c.f.	More than	c.f.
10—20	4	20	4	10	60
20—40	10	40	14 (c)	20	56
40—70	26 (f)	70	40 (Median Class)	40	46
70—100	8	100	48	70	20
100—150	12	150	60	100	12
	N = 60				

$$m = \left(\frac{N}{2}\right)^{th} \text{ item's value} = 30^{th} \text{ item's value.}$$

This lies in (40—70) class.

Thus, $\text{Median, } M = l_1 + \frac{i}{f}(m - c)$

$$= 40 + \frac{30}{26}(30 - 14)$$

$$= 40 + \frac{30}{26} \times 16 = 58.46$$ **Ans.**

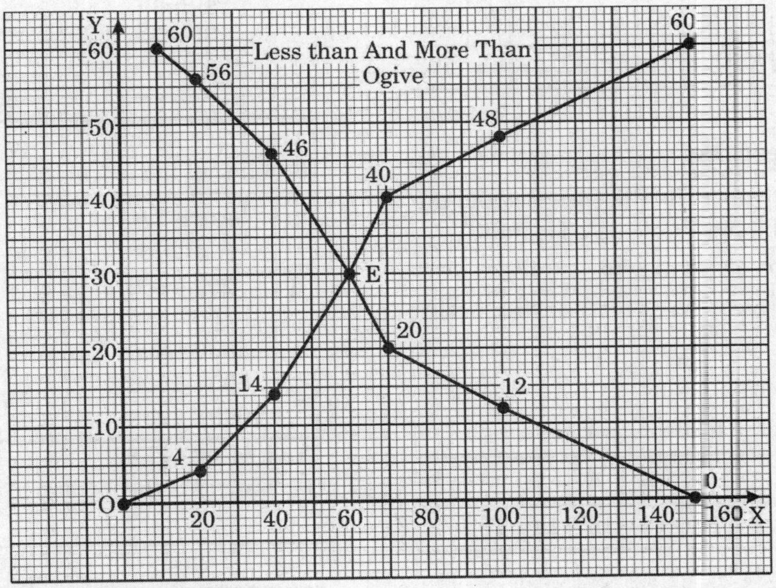

THEORETICAL QUESTIONS

Long Answer Type Questions

1. Define median and state its merits and demerits.
2. Descuss the merits and demerits of median as positional average.

Short Answer Type Questions

1. What is median ?
2. Define median.
3. What are the advantages of median ?
4. Explain the demerits of median.
5. Distinguish between arithmetic mean and median.
6. What are the properties of median ?
7. Explain how median is obtained graphically ?

Very Short Answer Type Questions

1. What do you understand by median ?
2. Give three characteristics of median.
3. State any two advantages of median.
4. State two disadvantages of median.
5. Mention any two differences between arithmetic mean and median.
6. Give the formula of calculating median in a discrete series.
7. Give the formula of calculating median in a continuous series.
8. Formula of median for individual series is : (J.A.C., 2019)

(a) $\frac{(n-1)}{2}$ th term (b) $\frac{(n+2)}{2}$ th term

(c) $\frac{(n+1)}{2}$ th term (d) $\frac{(n)}{2}$ th term

[Ans. (c)**]**

PRACTICAL QUESTIONS

Individual Series

Very Short Answer Type Questions

1. (A) Find the median from the following figures :
15, 45, 37, 50, 53, 65, 46
[**Ans.** $M = 46$]

(B) Find the median from the following data :
8, 3, 0, 1, 12, 6.
[**Ans.** $M = 4.5$]

2. Find the median from the following data :
135, 125, 146, 132, 158, 160, 175, 186, 168
[**Ans.** $M = 158$]

3. (A) Calculate median of the following figures :
(i) 94, 33, 86, 68, 32, 80, 48, 70
(ii) 79, 82, 36, 38, 51, 72, 68, 70, 64, 63
[**Ans.** (i) $M = 69$, (ii) $M = 66$]

(B) From the following figures, calculate the median :

Roll No.	1	2	3	4	5	6	7	8	9	10
Marks Obtain.	43	45	65	57	34	62	37	48	68	59

[**Ans.** $M = 52.5$]

Short Answer Type Questions

4. A class of 16 boys was given an intelligence test and the following marks were obtained. Calculate Median :

15	35	43	46	48	48	49	50
55	56	60	64	71	75	80	85

[**Ans.** $M = 52.5$]

Discrete Series

5. Calculate the median of the following series :

Size of the item	2	3	4	5	6	7	8	9
Frequency	3	8	10	12	16	14	10	8

[**Ans.** Median = 6]

6. (A) Determine the median from the following distribution :

Size	21	22	23	24	25	26	27	28
Frequency	5	7	11	9	8	7	3	2

[**Ans.** 24]

(B) Find the median from the following data :

Size	5	6	7	8	9	10	11	12	13
Frequency	4	10	12	15	18	20	16	15	12

[**Ans.** $M = 10$]

7. (A) Calculate the median of the following data :

Height in inch	60	61	62	63	64	65	66	67
No. of Students	10	12	20	30	40	18	12	10

[**Ans.** $M = 64$ inch]

(B) Find out the median :

Size of Item	*Frequency*	*Size of Item*	*Frequency*
0	1	5	52
1	9	6	29
2	26	7	7
3	59	8	1
4	72		

[**Ans.** $M = 4$]

(C) Compute median from the following table : (*JAC*, 2025)

x	10	15	20	30	40	60
y	8	12	15	10	3	2

[**Ans.** $M = 30$]

Continuous Series

8. (A) Calculate the value of median from the following table :

Wages (₹)	*No. of Workers*
30—40	100
40—50	108
50—60	170
60—70	90
70—80	60

[**Ans.** $M =$ ₹ 53.29]

(B) Find out median of the following distribution :

Income (in ₹)	*No. of Persons*
0—200	80
200—400	165
400—600	230
600—800	80
800—1000	32
1000—1200	13

[**Ans.** $M =$ ₹ 447.82]

(C) Calculate the median of the following series : (*JAC*, 2020)

Size	*Frequency*
10—20	6
20—30	20
30—40	44
40—50	26
50—60	3
60—70	1

[**Ans.** $M = 35.45$]

9. (A) Calculate median from the following :

Marks Obtained	*No. of Students*
0—20	10
20—40	15
40—50	30
50—60	32
60—70	8
70—80	5

[**Ans.** $M = 48.06$ Marks]

(B) Calculate median from the following data :

Variable	*Frequency*	*Variable*	*Frequency*
20—40	6	120—140	15
40—60	9	140—160	10
60—80	11	160—180	8
80—100	14	180—200	7
100—120	20		

[Ans. $M = 110$]

(C) Compute median from the following data :

Wages (₹)	*No. of Labourers*
50—60	5
40—50	10
30—40	20
20—30	8
10—20	7

[Ans. $M =$ ₹ 35]

(D) Calculate median from the following data :

Mid-point	18	25	32	39	46
Frequency	10	15	32	42	26

[Ans. $M = 36.41$]

Long Answer Type Questions

10. Amend the following table and locate the median from the amended table :

Size	*Frequency*
10—15	10
15—17.5	17
17.5—20	17
20—30	25
30—35	28
35—40	30
above 40	40

[Ans. $M = 32.67$]

[**Hint :** Amend the table as follows :

x :	10—20	20—30	30—40	40—50
f :	42	25	58	40]

11. (A) Calculate median of the following series :

Size	*Frequency*
6—10	20
11—15	30
16—20	50
21—25	40
26—30	10

[Ans. $M = 18$]

(B) Find out median from the following series :

Size	*Frequency*
1—10	3
11—20	5
21—30	8
31—40	6
41—50	3

[Ans. $M = 26.125$]

(C) Find the median in the following data :

Class	*Frequency*
0—9	10
10—19	18
20—29	32
30—39	12
40—49	8

[Ans. 23.25]

Calculation of Median in Cumulative Series

12. (A) Calculate median from the following data :

Marks less then	*No. of Students*
80	100
70	90
60	80
50	60
40	32
30	20
20	13
10	5

[Ans. $M = 46.43$

(B) Calculate median from the following data :

Marks less than	*No. of Students*
3	2
5	5
7	10
10	15
13	30
15	35
20	42
25	47
30	50

[Ans. $M = 12$]

[**Hint :** Amend the table and then calculate median.]

13. Calculate median from the following data :

Size	*Frequency*
More than 10	10
More than 20	8
More than 30	6
More than 40	4
More than 50	1

[Ans. $M = 35$]

14. Calculate the median from the following series :

Marks	*No. of Students*
30—35	4
25—30	8
20—25	13
15—20	15
10—15	12
5—10	10
0—5	2

[Ans. 17.67 Marks]

15. (A) Find median in the following table :

Class	Frequency
0—10	8
10—20	12
20—30	20
30—40	10
40—50	5

[Ans. 23.75]

(B) Find median from the following :

Size	Frequency
0—10	44
10—20	66
20—30	36
30—40	44
40—50	8

[Ans. 18.33]

16. The monthly profits of 50 petty retailers of a town in rupees, are recorded below :

57	68	65	53	73	48	52	53
56	59	55	55	66	71	64	61
57	52	63	51	59	57	67	54
58	55	59	58	57	53	59	48
75	58	62	60	55	55	72	53
62	51	56	52	56	46	54	78
54	68						

(a) From a frequency distribution taking the first class-interval as ₹ 45—50.

(b) Find out the median.

(c) Find the number of shops whose monthly income is (i) less than ₹ 60, and (ii) more than ₹ 59 but less than 65.

[Ans. (a)

x	f
45—50	3
50—55	12
55—60	19
60—65	6
65—70	5
70—75	32
75—80	2

(b) ₹ 57 and Paise 63, (c) (i) 34, (ii) 6]

Mean and Median

17. Calculate Mean and Median from the following figures :

375.5	153.4,	28.5	12.01,	4.5,
3.74,	12.79,	35,	41.9	and 58

[Ans. Mean = 72.534, median = 31.75]

18. (A) Calculate the mean age and the median from the following data :

Age (in years)	20	25	30	35	40	45	50	55
No. of Persons	14	28	33	30	20	15	13	7

[Ans. A.M. = 34.56 years, M = 35 years]

(B) Calculate the mean and median from the following data :

Size	2	3	4	5	6	7	8	9
Frequency	3	8	9	10	12	16	14	7

[Ans. $\overline{X}$ = 6.01, M = 6]

19. Calculate the mean and median from the following data :

Size	Frequency
0—5	4
5—10	6
10—15	10
15—20	16
20—25	12
25—30	8
30—35	4

[Ans. A.M. = 18, M = 18.125]

20. Calculate the mean and median from the following data :

Size	Frequency
60	25
65	125
62	400
63	375
66	101
61	140
64	220

[Ans. Mean = 63.01, Median = 63]

21. Find the difference of mean and median of the following data :

6.5	42	11	30	19
34.8	21	43.7		

[Ans. $\overline{X}$ = 26, M = 25.5; Diff. = 0.5]

22. Find the difference of mean and median from the following data :

60	50	62	55	58
65	56	54		

[Ans. $\overline{X}$ = 57.5, M = 57, Diff. = 0.5]

23. Find the difference of mean and median from the following data :

375.5,	153.4,	28.5,	12.01,	4.5,
3.74,	12.79,	35, 41.9	and 58.	

[Ans. 40.784]

24. Find median from the following data :

Wages (₹)	No. of Persons
2.30	6
2.40	4
3.20	3
3.40	4
3.50	4
4.50	4
5.10	4
5.50	1

[Ans. ₹ 3.40]

25. Calculate mean and median from the following data, and also find out the difference between the two :
94, 33, 86, 68, 32, 80, 48, 70
[**Ans.** $\overline{X}$ = 63.875, M = 69, Diff. = 5.125]

26. Find the values of median and median from the following frequency table :

Class	5—9	10—14	15—19	20—24	25—29
Frequency	6	16	27	15	6

[**Ans.** $\overline{X}$ = 16.93 M = 16.9]

27. (A) Calculate median from the following data :

Mid-values	15	25	35	45
Frequency	42	25	58	40

[**Ans.** M = 32.7]

(B) Calculate median : (*JAC*, 2023, 24)

Mid-values	15	25	35	45	55	65
Frequency	5	12	23	35	18	9

[**Ans.** 43.14]

(C) Find median from the following table : (*JAC*, 2026)

Marks	10	20	30	40	50
No. of students	3	7	10	4	6

[**Ans.** Median = 30]

Calculation of Median in Open-end Series

28. From the following data, compute the median weekly expenditure :

Daily Expenditures (in ₹)	*Number of Families*
Less than 10	14
10—20	23
20—30	27
30—40	21
Above 40	15

[**Ans.** M = ₹ 24.81]

To find out Missing Frequencies

29. Find the missing frequency from the following by using the median formula, if the median is 26 :

X	0—10	10—20	20—30	30—40	40—50
Y	4	7	16	10	?

[**Ans.** 4.2]

30. Find the frequency of the class 15—20 in the following table if the value of median is 12.5.

Class	*Frequency*
0—5	4
5—10	6
10—15	10
15—20	—
20—25	2
25—30	1

[**Ans.** Frequency of Class 15—20 = 7]

[**Hint :** $M = l_1 + \frac{i}{f}\left(\frac{N}{2} - c\right)$ or $12.5 + \frac{5}{10}\left(\frac{23+f}{2} - 10\right)$]

31. From the data given below, find the missing frequency if the arithmetic mean is 33. Also find the median of the series :

Loss per Shop	*No. of Shops*
0—10	10
10—20	15
20—30	30
30—40	—
40—50	25
50—60	20

[**Ans.** Missing Freq = 25, Median = 33]

Graphic Determination of Mean

32. From graphical method find the median of the following frequency distribution :

Wages (₹)	*Frequency*
40—50	20
50—60	30
60—70	50
70—80	60
80—90	30
90—100	10

[**Ans.** M = 70]

33. Calculate median from the following data by drawing two ogive curves :

Wages (₹)	*Frequency*
10—20	7
20—30	8
30—40	20
40—50	10
50—60	5

[**Ans.** M = 35]

34. Find median from the following data by using graph paper :

Class	0—10	10—20	20—30	30—40	40—50
Frequency	8	30	40	12	10

[**Ans.** M = 20]

Miscellaneous Problems

35. Below are given in life (in hours) of 50 Philips electric bulbs of 100 watts :

550	500	675	800	700	750
900	925	1000	1100	1200	1380
1400	1600	1575	1800	1920	1980
1300	1260	695	770	756	1225
1180	900	1425	1450	1500	608
840	300	600	690	875	1250
1700	1760	575	500	1050	1700
1600	1612	1312	1115	880	980
1356	475				

(i) From a frequency distribution taking the first class-intervals as 300—600 hrs.
(ii) Compute median from this distribution.

[Ans.

x	f
300—600	6
600—900	13
900—1200	9
1200—1500	11
1500—1800	8
1800—2100	3

M = 1100 hrs.]

36. Compute median from the following series :

Size	*Frequency*
11—14	7
15—19	15
20—24	30
25—29	10
30—34	5
35—39	2

[Ans. $M = 21.58$]

37. Calculate median of the following data :

Salary Group	*No. of Workers*
0—9	14
10—19	10
20—29	8
30—39	12
40—49	6

[Ans. $M = 20.75$]

38. The Median of 80, 100, 90, 170, 60, 50, 40 : (*JAC*, 2018)
(a) 80 (b) 170 (c) 90 (d) 60
[Ans. (a)]

OBJECTIVE TYPE QUESTIONS

I. Multiple Choice Questions

1. 80, 100, 90, 170, 60, 50, 40 of median : (*JAC*, 2018)
(a) 80 (b) 170 (c) 90 (d) 60
2. Values are to be arranged in ascending or descending order of magnitude for computing median. Is it correct ?
(a) Yes (b) No
3. The sum of absolute deviations of items of the series is minimum from :
(a) Arithmetic mean (b) Median
(c) Geometric mean (d) Harmonic mean
4. Which of the following is the measure of Position ?
(a) Median (b) Mean
(c) Mode (d) [Both (a) and (c)]
5. Median is that value which divides the data into :
(a) 2 parts (b) 8 parts (c) 10 parts (d) 50 parts
6. The sum of the diviations from median, is :
(a) Minimum (b) 0
(c) Maximum (d) None of these
7. Median of following figures :
25, 40, 35, 38, 32, 30, 37
(a) 30 (b) 38 (c) 35 (d) 32
8. Median of following figures :
200, 160, 75, 110, 225, 150, 170, 185, 180, 220
(a) 160 (b) 170 (c) 175 (d) 180
9. Median formula for individual series is :
(a) $\frac{(n-1)}{2}$ th term (b) $\frac{(n+2)}{2}$ th term
(c) $\frac{(n+1)}{2}$ th term (d) $\frac{(n)}{2}$ th term
10. In Continuous series median = size of .... :
(a) $\frac{(N-1)}{2}$ th term (b) $\frac{(N+2)}{2}$ th term
(c) $\frac{(N+1)}{2}$ th term (d) $\frac{(N)}{2}$ th term
11. Median of 8, 3, 0, 1, 12, 6 is :
(a) 3 (b) 4 (c) 4.5 (d) 5
12. Median of 108, 92, – 43, 0, 6, 11, –2, 15 is :
(a) 8 (b) 8.5 (c) 9 (d) 9.5
13. Median of continuous series :
(a) $L_1 + \frac{\frac{N}{2} + cf}{f}$ (b) $L_1 + \frac{\frac{N}{2} - cf}{f} \times i$
(c) $A + \frac{\sum fd_x}{\sum f}$ (d) $\frac{\sum fn}{\sum f}$
14. If each value of the given data is multiplied by 2, then the new median :
(a) twice the old median (b) unmoved
(c) five more than the old median
(d) five less than the old median
15. Disadvantage of median is :
(a) Normal (b) Easy to understand
(c) Graphic is displayed (d) Hard to calculate
16. .... divides the total number of observations in two equal parts : (*JAC*, 2023)
(a) Median (b) Mode (c) Mean (d) None of these
17. For an even number of values, the median is the :
(a) Average of two median value
(b) Median value
(c) Both (a) and (b) (d) None of these
18. What is the median of the following variables ?
4, 9, 12, 15, 7, 18 (*JAC*, 2024, 25)
(a) 9 (b) 12 (c) 15 (d) None
19. If the mode is 28 and mean is 25 then median is : (*JAC*, 2026)
(a) 25 (b) 28 (c) 26 (d) 50

[Ans. 1. (a), 2. (a), 3. (b), 4. (d), 5. (a), 6. (a), 7. (c), 8. (c), 9. (c), 10. (d), 11. (c), 12. (b), 13. (b), 14. (a), 15. (d), 16. (a), 17. (a), 18. (d), 19. (c).]

II. Fill in the Blanks :

1. Median of discreate (series) = ...
2. ....is that value of the variable which divides the series into two equal parts.
3. The median of the date 8, 3, 0, 1, 12, 6 is......
4. If arithmatic mean = 25 and mode = 24.83 the median = ...
5. The median of 42, 51, 65, 90, 100, 105, 108, 118, 125 is.....

[Ans. 1. Median = $\left(\frac{n+1}{2}\right)^{th}$ items value; 2. Median; 3. 4.5; 4. 24.81; 5. 100.]

3

MODE

LEARNING OBJECTIVES

After studying this chapter, you will be able to know :

- **3.1 Meaning and Definition of Mode**
- **3.2 Calculation of Mode**
- **3.3 Relationship among Arithmetic Mean, Median and Mode**
- **3.4 Graphic Method of Locating Mode**
- **3.5 Finding the Missing Frequency**
- **3.6 Merits or Advantages of Mode**
- **3.7 Demerits or Disadvantages of Mode**
- **3.8 Uses of Mode**
- **Theoretical Questions : Long Answer Questions, Short Answer Questions, Very Short Answer Questions**
- **Practical Problems**

ILLUSTRATIONS AND PRACTICAL PROBLEMS : AT A GLANCE

No. of Illustration		*No. of Problems*
1(A), (B)	Calculation of Mode in Individual Series	1(A) to (D)
2	Calculation of Mode in Discrete Series	2, 3(D), (E)
3 (A) to 14	Calculation of Mode in Continuous Series	4(A) to 15(A)
15	Graphic Method of Locating Mode	15 (B)
—	Median and Mode	16 to 20
16	Mean and Mode	21
17, 18	Mean, Median and Mode	22 to 29
19	To Find out Missing Frequency	30 to 32
—	Miscellaneous Problems	33 to 40
	Based on Properties of A.M.	
19	**Total**	**40**

(3.1) MEANING AND DEFINITION OF MODE

In French to be "In The Mode" implies to be in fashion. The Mode as a statistical average is that value in a series which occurs most frequently. In a frequency distribution Mode is that variate which has the maximum frequency.

Mode is variously defined. It is the most frequent size of the item. It is a position of greatest density or a point of highest concentration of values. The Modal item is, therefore, the most representative or typical item in distribution.

Important Definitions :

(1) According to *Prof. Kenny*, "The value of the variable which occurs most frequently in the distribution is called the Mode."

(2) According to *Zizek*, "The value occurring most frequently in a series (or group) of item and around which the other items are distributed most densely."

(3) In the words of *Croxton and Cowden*, "The Mode of a distribution is the value at the point around which the items tend to be most heavily concentrated. It may be regarded as the most typical of a series of value."

Example : In the series of 12, 10, 15, 15, 5, 8, 15, 7, 8, 9 we notice that 15 occurrs most frequently, therefore 15 is the Mode.

(3.2) CALCULATION OF MODE

(1) Calculation of Mode in Individual Series : In the case of individual or simple series the value which is repeated maximum number of times is said to be Modal item or Mode. So in individual series Mode is located by inspection or observation.

Some times the data are placed in an array so that items having the same value can be identified and quickly counted. The value of that item which occurs most frequently is the Modal item.

***Illustration* 1(A)**

From the following number of shoes, find out the Modal size :

2, 4, 6, 5, 3, 7, 6, 8, 5, 6, 7, 3, 1

Solution :

By inspection we find that the figure 6 has occurred most frequently. Hence, Modal size = **6**.

Alternately

On arranging the figures in ascending order :

Modal Items

1, 2, 3, 3, 4, 5, 5, 6, 6, 6, 7, 7, 8. Since 6 occurrs thrice and no other items occurrs three times or more than three times, Modal size is 6.

Alternative Method :

The Mode can be located in a series of individual observations by converting it into a discrete series.

In Illustration 1, the Mode can be located as number :

Size (X) :	1	2	3	4	5	[6] ↑ Mode	7	8
No. of Items (f) :	1	1	2	1	2	[3] ↑ Modal Items	2	1

$N = 13$

Value 6 has the largest number of items (3), hence Mode = **6**.

***Illustration* 1(B)**

Find the mode of the following :

5, 2, 3, 1, 2, 8, 6, 2, 3, 2, 4, 2, 9, 2, 5, 2, 3, 6, 2

[*Mock Test Paper (JAC)*]

Solution :

Mode = 2

(2) Discrete Series : In a discrete series, Mode can be determined in two ways :

(i) *By Inspection* **:** If there is regularity and homogeneity in the series, Mode can be determined by inspection of the series alone. The size having the maximum frequency will be treated as the Mode.

***Illustration* 2**

Compute the Mode from the following data :

Size of Item	61	62	63	64	65	66	67	68	69	70
Frequency	5	7	10	8	7	10	11	8	7	6

Solution :

Grouping Table

Size of the Item	*Frequency* 1	*Grouping in Two's* 2	3	*Grouping in Three's* 4	5	6
61	5					
62	7	12		22		
63	10		17			
64	8	18			25	
65	7		15	25		25
66	10	17			28	
67	**11**		**21**			
68	8	**19**				**29**
69	7		15	**26**	21	
70	6	13				

Analysis Table

Column No.	Size Items 61	62	63	64	65	66	67	68	69	70
1							✓			
2							✓	✓		
3						✓	✓			
4							✓	✓	✓	
5					✓	✓	✓			
6						✓	✓	✓		
Frequency	0	0	0	0	1	3	6	3	1	0

By inspection of the data, it is noted that size 67 has the maximum frequency, *viz.*, 11. Therefore **67** is the Mode.

(ii) *By Grouping* : Some times inspection method may give wrong answer. An error of judgement is possible in such cases where the difference between the maximum frequency and the frequency preceding or succeeding it is very small and the items are heavily concentrated on either side. Under such circumstances, the value of the Mode is determined by preparing a Grouping Table and Analysis Table.

A grouping table has six columns apart from the column of size of the item.

Process of Grouping and Analysis :

Column 1 : In the first column, original frequencies are written. The maximum frequency of this column is marked by bold type. In analysis column, the item or size having the maximum frequency is assigned one point.

Column 2 : In the second column, the frequencies of column 1 are grouped in twos, starting from the top. Their totals are found out and the highest total is marked by bold type. The items or sizes having the highest (maximum) combined frequency are assigned one point each in the analysis column.

Column 3 : In the third column, frequencies are again grouped into twos, but the first frequency of column 1 is left out. Thus, the grouping will start from the 2nd frequency of column 1. Now totals of the each group are found out and the highest frequency is marked by bold type. The items having highest total are assigned one point each in the analysis column.

Column 4 : In this column, the frequencies of the first column are grouped (or combined) in threes, starting from the top. Their total are made and the highest total is marked. The items having highest total are assigned one point each in the analysis column.

Column 5 : In this column, frequencies are grouped again in threes, but the grouping starts from the second frequency. (In other words, the first frequency of column 1 is left out.) The totals of each group are made and the highest frequency is marked by bold type. In analysis column 1 point each is given to the items comprising the highest total.

Column 6 : In this column, while making groups in threes, first and second frequencies of column 1 is left out. The totals are done and the highest total is marked. In analysis column assign 1 point each to the items or sizes comprising highest total.

Analysis Column : Now in analysis column the points scored by each size are counted. The item or size getting the highest point is considered as the modal size. Thus, it is obvious that in order to find out the item which repeats largest number of times grouping is analysed.

Remember : There are *six columns* in a grouping table showing frequencies. In the grouping process, grouping is not made in column 1.

Groups of two frequencies are made 2 times (second time leaving the first frequency).

Groups of three frequencies are made 3 times (second time leaving the first frequency and third time leaving the 1st and 2nd frequencies.)

The total points scored by any item or size cannot exceed 6.

Analysis Table may be prepared separately or it can be dispensed with if one more column is added to the grouping table to indicate analysis.

(3) **Determination of Mode in Continuous Series :** The following steps are taken in the computation of Mode in case of continuous series :

(i) *Modal Class* **:** Modal class is that class in grouped or continuous series in which the Mode lies. It is, generally, the class-interval with the greatest number of frequencies in it. The modal class can be determined either by inspection (or observation) or with the help of grouping table in case of irregular distribution.

(ii) *Use of Formula* **:** After finding out the modal class, mode is calculated by applying the following formula :

Formula No. 1 :

$$M_o \text{ (or } Z) = l_1 + \frac{f_1 - f_0}{2f_1 - f_0 - f_2} \times i$$

or $$M_o \text{ (or } Z) = l_1 + \frac{f_1 - f_0}{2f_1 - f_0 - f_2} \times (l_2 - l_1)$$

or $$M_o \text{ (or } Z) = l_1 + \frac{f_1 - f_0}{(f_1 - f_0) + (f_1 + f_2)} \times i$$

Where, M_0 or Z = Mode

also l_1 = Lower limit of the Modal class

f_1 = Frequency of the Modal class

f_2 = frequency of Post-Modal class

f_0 = frequency of Pre-Modal class

i = Magnitude or the width of the Modal class, *i.e.* $(l_2 - l_1)$.

Formula No. 2 :

In case frequency of the class preceding or succeedding the Modal class is more than the frequency of the Modal class, Mode should not be calculated by Formula No. 1. If it is applied, it will give wrong answer. Hence, in such cases following Formula No. 2 should be applied :

$$M_o \text{ (or } Z) = l_1 + \frac{f_2}{f_1 + f_2} \times i \text{ or } l_1 + \frac{f_2}{f_1 + f_2} \times (l_2 - l_1)$$

The notations in this formulae are the same as were in Formula No. 1.

Remarks :

(1) It may be noted that the above formulae for computing Mode is based on the following assumptions :

(a) The frequency distribution must be continuous with exclusive classes without any gaps. If the data are not given in the form of continuous classes, it must first be converted into continuous classes before applying the formula.

(b) The class-interval must be uniform throughout the series, that is, the width of all the class-intervals must be the same. In case of the distribution with unequal class-intervals, they should be made equal.

(2) However, the above technique of locating Mode is not practicable in the following situations :

(a) If the maximum frequency is repeated or approximately equal concentration is found in two or more neighbouring values.

(b) If the maximum frequency occurs either in the very beginning or at the end of the distribution.

(c) If there are irregularities in the distribution, that is, the frequencies of the variable increase or decrease in a haphazard manner.

In the above situations Mode (or Modal class in the case of continuous frequency distribution) is located by the method of grouping.

***Illustration* 3 (A)**

The distribution of wages in a factory is as follows calculate the mode : (*JAC*, 2017, 19)

Wages (in ₹)	0—10	10—20	20—30	30—40	40—50	50—60	60—70
No. of Workers	6	9	10	16	12	8	7

Solution :

Calculation for finding Mode

Wages (in ₹)	*No. of Workers*	*Grouping in Two's*		*Grouping in Three's*			*Analysis*	
0—10	6	15		25				0
10—20	9		19		35		|	1
20—30	10 f_0	**26**				**38**	||||	4
30—40	**16** f_1		**28**	**36**			~~||||~~ ||	7
40—50	12 f_2	20			27		||||	4
50—60	8		15				|	1
60—70	7							0

Analysis Table

Column No.	Size of Item containing Maximum Frequency 0—10	10—20	20—30	30—40	40—50	50—60	60—70
1				✓	✓		
2			✓	✓			
3		✓	✓	✓	✓		
4				✓			
5			✓	✓	✓	✓	
6			✓	✓			
7				✓			
No. of Times	0	1	4	7 (Maximum)	4	1	0

∴ Mode Group = 30—40

Now $M_o = l_1 + \dfrac{f_1 - f_0}{2f_1 - f_0 - f_2} \times i$

$= 30 + \dfrac{16-10}{2 \times 16 - 10 - 12} \times 10$

$= 30 + \dfrac{6 \times 10}{32 - 22}$

$= 30 + \dfrac{60}{10} = 30 + 6 =$ **36 Ans.**

***Illustration* 3(B)**

Calculate mode : [*Mock Test Paper (JAC)*]

Class-interval	*Frequency*
20—25	50
25—30	70
30—35	100
35—40	180
40—45	150
45—50	120
50—55	70
55—60	60

Solution :

$M_0 = l_1 + \dfrac{f_m - f_1}{2f_m - f_1 - f_2}(l_2 - l_1)$

$= 35 + \dfrac{180 - 100}{2 \times 180 - 100 - 150}(40 - 35)$

$= 35 + \dfrac{80 \times 5}{360 - 250}$

$= 35 + \dfrac{400}{110} = 35 + 3.63$

$M_0 = 38.63$

***Illustration* 3(C)**

Calculate the Moce in the following series :

Size	*Frequency*
0—10	5
10—20	7
20—30	19
30—40	18
40—50	16
50—60	10
60—70	5

Solution :

Size	Freq. (f) 1	Grouping in Two's 2	3	Grouping in Three's 4	5	6	Analysis	
0—10	5	12		31				0
10—20	7		26		(44)		|	1
20—30	(19) f_0	(37)				(53)	||||	4
30—40	18 f_1		(34)	(44)			~~||||~~	5
40—50	16 f_2	26			31		|||	3
50—60	10		15				|	1
60—70	5							0

∵ Mode lies in the class (30—40) because frequency of this class is maximum.

∵ Mode is that value which occurs with the largest number of times or most frequent obs, is the Mode.

∴ $M_o = l_1 + \dfrac{f_2}{f_1 + f_2} \times i$

($\because f_0$ is greater than the frequency of the Modal class)

From the question,

$$f_0 = 19, f_1 = 18, f_2 = 16, l_1 = 30$$
$$i = (30 - 20) = 10$$

$$= 30 + \frac{16}{(18+16)} \times 10$$

$$= 30 + \frac{16}{34} \times 10 = 30 + 4.71$$

$\therefore$ $M_0 = 34.70$ **Ans.**

Determination of Mode by Density Method

Sometime, Mode is determined by Density Method. When the analysis of grouping shows that the items have occurred equal number of times, then to determine at which point, there is greater concentration of frequencies, we add three frequencies say, $x + y + z$, where there is greater total, Mode is calculated. When the totals are equal, then the series is Modal or Multimodal.

Remark :

(1) Density Method may be applied without using the Grouping Method. (2) This method should be used when there is a tie in the grouping method.

Let us take an example to make it clear.

***Illustration* 4(A)**

Calculate Modal Income from the following frequency distribution :

Earnings	*No. of Workers*
10—20	10
20—30	14
30—40	16
40—50	14
50—60	11
60—70	13
70—80	17
80—90	13

Solution :

From observation it appears that either (30—40) or (70—80) may be Modal class.

Assumed Modal Class	*Case* I (30—40)	*Case* II (70—80)
1. Frequency of Modal Class (f_1)	16	17
2. Frequency of the class preceding to Modal Class (f_0)	14	13
3. Frequency of the class next to Modal Class (f_2)	14	13
Total	44	43

Here it is obvious that (30–40) is the Modal class.

$$\therefore \quad Z = l_1 + \frac{f_1 - f_0}{(f_1 - f_0) + (f_1 + f_2)} \times i = 30 + \frac{16-14}{(16-14)+(16-14)} \times 10 = 30 + \frac{20}{4} = 30 + 5 = 35$$

$\therefore$ **Mode = ₹ 35** **Ans.**

***Illustration* 4(B)**

Calculate the value of Mode :

Class	10—20	20—30	30—40	40—50	50—60	60—70	70—80	80—90	90—100	100—110
f	4	6	5	10	20	22	24	6	2	1

Solution :

By inspection the mode seems to lie in the class 70—80 but this is not a fact. Therefore Grouping Table will have to be prepared.

Grouping Table

Class	*Freq.* 1	*Grouping in Two's* 2	3	*Grouping in Three's* 4	5	6	*Analysis*	
10—20	4	10		15				0
20—30	6		11		21			0
30—40	5	15				35		0
40—50	10		30	**52**				0
50—60	20	**42**			**66**		|	1
60—70	22		**46**			**52**	|||	3
70—80	24	30		32			~~||||~~	5
80—90	6		8		9		||||	4
90—100	2	3					|	1
100—110	1							0

By grouping method it is ascertained that the Mode lies in the class (60—70). So (60—70) is the Modal class.

Since the frequency of the class following the Modal class is greater than that of the Modal class (*i.e.* f_2 is greater in f_1), we should apply the second formula to determine the Mode.

Here, $$Z = l_1 + \frac{f_2}{f_0 + f_2} \times i$$

or $$Z = 60 + \frac{24}{20+24} \times 10$$

$$= 60 + \frac{240}{44}$$

or $$Z = 60 + 5.45 = 65.45$$

$\therefore$ **Value of Mode = 65.45** **Ans.**

Determination of Mode in Inclusive Series : If inclusive class-intervals are given, the limits of the Modal class should be ascertained under exclusive method of class-interval, that is, inclusive series should be changed into exclusive series. This requires necessary adjustment in lower limit and upper limit of the Modal class.

Illustration 5

Calculate Mode from the following data :

x	*f*
11—15	5
16—20	10
21—25	22
26—30	26
31—35	20
36—40	11
41—45	6

Solution :

By inspection it appears that Mode lies in the class (26—30) as it has maximum frequency. Since the problem related with inclusive series, the Modal class will be changed into exclusive series by making adjustments of $\left(\frac{1}{2}\right) = 0.5$. Thus l_1 will be $(26 - 0.5) = 25.5$, l_2 will be $(30 + 0.5) = 30.5$. Thus, the Modal class – (25.5 – 30.5).

Now, $$\text{Mode} = l_1 + \frac{f_1 - f_0}{2f_1 - f_0 - f_2} \times i$$

$$= 25.5 + \frac{26-22}{2 \times 26 - 22 - 20} \times 5$$

$$= 25.5 + \frac{4 \times 5}{10} = 25.5 + 2 = 27.5$$

Therefore, **Mode = 27.5** **Ans.**

Calculation of Mode when Mid-values are given

Sometimes mid-values of the classes are given. In such a case mid-values should be replaced by class-intervals before calculating the Mode. In order to convert mid-values into class-intervals the following steps should be taken :

(i) Lower limit (l_1) = Mid-value $- \frac{i}{2}$

(ii) Upper limit (l_2) = Mid-value $+ \frac{i}{2}$

where, i = Difference between the two mid-values

Illustration 6

Calculate the Mode from the following :

Mid-value (m)	15	20	25	30	35	40	45	50	55
Frequency (f)	2	22	19	14	3	4	6	1	1

Solution :

First of all mid-values will have to be converted into class-intervals by applying the formula $\left(\pm \frac{i}{2}\right)$. Since the difference between the two mid-values is 5 (20 – 15), i = 5. Now $\left(\frac{5}{2}\right) = 2.5$ will be deducted and 2.5 will be added to find out l_1 and l_2 from mid-values.

Thus,

X	12.5—17.5	17.5—22.5	22.5—27.5	27.5—32.5	32.5—37.5	37.5—42.5	42.5—47.5	47.5—52.5	52.5—57.5
f	2	22	19	14	3	4	6	1	1

Grouping Table

Class-interval	*f*	Grouping					Analysis	
		In Two's		*In Three's*				
	1	2	3	4	5	6		
12.5—17.5	2	24		43			I	1
17.5—22.5	22		41		55		IIII	4
22.5—27.5	19	33				36	~~IIII~~	5
27.5—32.5	14		17	21			III	3
32.5—37.5	3	7			13		I	1
37.5—42.5	4		10			11		0
42.5—47.5	6	7		8				0
47.5—52.5	1		2					0
52.5—57.5	1							0

From inspection it appears that (17.5—22.5) should be the Modal class as it has maximum frequency. But from the grouping table and analysis table it is clear that size (22.5—27.5) occurs maximum number of times. So (22.5—27.5) is the Modal class.

Modal class may also be determined by following concentration method :

	(17.5—22.5)			(22.5—27.5)	
f_0	2		f_0	22	
f_1	22	= 43 (Total)	f_1	19	= 55 (Total)
f_2	19		f_2	14	

where Total = $f_0 + f_1 + f_2$

Therefore, Modal Class = (22.5—27.5)

Since the number of frequencies in the class preceding the Modal class is greater than the frequencies of the Modal class, the following formula can be used :

$$\text{Mode } (Z) = l_1 + \frac{f_2}{f_0 + f_2} \times i$$

$$= 22.5 + \frac{14}{22+14} \times 5$$

$$= 22.5 + \frac{70}{36}$$

$$= 22.5 + 1.94 = 24.44$$

∴ **Mode = 24.44 Ans.**

Calculation of Mode in a Series with Unequal Class-interval : If the class-intervals are of unequal size, we should make them equal before computing Mode and frequencies should be adjusted on the assumption that they are equally distributed throughout the class.

Illustration 7(A)

Calculate Mode from the following :

Class	*Frequency*
2	1
3	2
4	2
5—7	3
7—10	5
10—15	10
15—20	8
20—25	4

Solution :

Here class-intervals are of unequal size, so we shall have to make them equal.

Class	*Frequency*
0—5	1 + 2 + 2 = 5
5—10	3 + 5 = 8 f_0
10—15	10 f_1
15—20	8 f_2
20—25	4

By observation, the Mode lies in class (10—15) having max frequency.

$$\text{Mode} = l_1 + \frac{f_1 - f_0}{2f_1 - f_0 - f_2} \times i$$

$$= 10 + \frac{10-8}{2 \times 10 - 8 - 8} \times 5$$

$$= 10 + \frac{2}{4} \times 5$$

$$= 10 + 2.5 = 12.5$$

∴ Mode = **12.5 Ans.**

Illustration 7(B)

Calculate Mode from the following data :

Marks	0—10	10—20	20—40	40—50	50—70
Frequency	5	15	40	32	28

Solution :

Since the class-intervals are of unequal size, they should be of equal size to calculate Mode :

Revised Table

Marks	*Frequency*
0—10	5
10—20	15
20—30	20
30—40	20
40—50	32
50—60	14
60—70	14

By observation we find that (40—50) is the Modal class having max. freq.

$$Z = l_1 + \frac{f_1 - f_0}{2f_1 - f_0 - f_2} \times i$$

From the question :

$$f_1 = 32, f_2 = 14, f_0 = 20$$
$$i = (50 - 40) = 10$$

$$= 40 + \frac{32-20}{2 \times 32 - 20 - 14} \times 10$$

$$= 40 + \frac{12 \times 10}{64 - 34} = 40 + \frac{120}{30}$$

∴ $Z = 44$ **Ans.**

When Mode lies in the first or last class-interval : Generally first or the last class of the series does not happen to be the Modal class. However, if by inspection, Mode lies in the first or last class-interval, we remember the following :

(1) If the Mode lies in the first class-interval, f_0 is taken as 0 (Zero).

(2) If the Mode lies in the last class-interval, f_2 is taken as 0 (Zero).

But in such case it will be better to determine modal class by grouping method.

Illustration 8

Find Mode from the following table : (*JAC*, 2026)

Size	0—10	10—20	20—30	30—40	40—50	50—60
Freq.	40	30	18	12	10	5

Solution :

By inspection Mode seems to lie in the class (0—10).

$$Z = l_1 + \frac{f_1 - f_0}{2f_1 - f_0 - f_2}(l_2 - l_1)$$

$$= 0 + \frac{40-0}{2 \times 40 - 0 - 30}(10-0)$$

$$= 0 + \frac{40}{80-30} \times 10$$

$$= 0 + \frac{40}{50} \times 10$$

$$= 0 + 8 = 8$$

$\therefore$ Mode = **8** **Ans.**

Alternative Method

Grouping Table

Class	Frequency	Grouping in Two's		Grouping in Three's			Analysis
	1	2	3	4	5	6	
0—10	40	**70**		**88**			‖‖‖
10—20	30		**48**		**60**		‖‖‖‖
20—30	18	30				**40**	‖‖‖‖
30—40	12		22	27			‖‖‖‖
40—50	10	15					‖‖
50—60	5						‖

The application of grouping method shows that the Mode does not lie in class (0—10). From analysis it is clear that the Mode lies in class (10—20), (20—30) and (30—40) as they have got four points each. Thus, here the series is Multi-Modal and Mode is ill defined.

Calculation of Mode in Cumulative Series

Sometimes Mode is to be located in cumulative series. In such a case the following steps should be taken to determine Mode :

Step 1 : Convert the cumulative frequency distribution table into a normal frequency distribution table.

Step 2 : Find out, either by observation or by grouping method, Modal class.

Step 3 : Then use the formula (as explained earlier) to determine the Mode.

Illustration 9

Find out the Modal marks from the following distribution of marks of 22 students : (*JAC*, 2015)

Marks less than	10	20	30	40	50
No. of Students	3	8	17	20	22

Solution :

First of all cumulative frequency distribution should be converted into normal frequency distribution.

Marks	No. of Students (f)
0—10	3
10—20	$8 - 3 = 5\ f_0$
20—30	$17 - 8 = 9\ f_1$
30—40	$20 - 17 = 3\ f_2$
40—50	$22 - 20 = 2$
	$N = 22$

Modal Class (By observation) ⇒ (20—30)

Thus, $$Z = l_1 + \frac{f_1 - f_0}{2f_1 - f_0 - f_2} \times (l_2 - l_1)$$

$$= 20 + \frac{9-5}{(2 \times 9) - 5 - 3} \times (30-20)$$

$$= 20 + \frac{4}{18-5-3} \times 10$$

$$Z = 20 + \frac{40}{10} = 20 + 4 = 24$$

$\therefore$ $Z = \mathbf{24}$ **Ans.**

Illustration 10

Calculate Mode of the following :

Size	Frequency
More than 50	0
More than 40	40
More than 30	98
More than 20	123
More than 10	165

Solution : **Frequency Table**

Size	Frequency
50—60	0
40—50	40 f_0
l_1 30—40	$98 - 40 = 58\ f_1$
20—30	$123 - 98 = 25\ f_2$
10—20	$165 - 123 = 42$

Modal Class by Observation ⇒ (30—40)

$$Z = l_1 + \frac{f_1 - f_0}{2f_1 - f_0 - f_2} \times (l_2 - l_1)$$

$$= 30 + \frac{58-40}{(2\times58)-40-25} \times (40-30)$$

$$= 30 + \frac{18}{116-40-25} \times 10$$

$$= 30 + \frac{18\times10}{51}$$

$$= 30 + 3.529 = 33.529$$

$\therefore$ $Z = \mathbf{33.529}$ **Ans.**

Determination of Mode in case of Descending Series

In case of descending series, either of the following methods should be used to determine Mode :

(1) Arrange the table in ascending order and use the formula of Mode (as explained earlier).

Or

(2) Keep the figures in descending order and use the following formula to determine Mode :

(i) $$Z = l_1 + \frac{f_1 - f_0}{(2f_1 - f_0 - f_2)} \times i (\text{or } l_2 - l_1)$$

or (ii) $$Z = l_1 + \frac{f_2}{f_0 + f_2} \times i$$

***Illustration* 11**

From the data given below, Calculate the Mode :

Size	55—60	50—55	45—50	40—45	35—40	30—35	25—30	20—25
Frequency	5	7	12	15	18	8	7	9

Solution :

Grouping Table

Class-interval	*Frequency*	*Grouping in Two's*		*Grouping in Three's*			*Analysis*
55—60	5	12					
50—55	7		19	24			I
45—50	12 f_0	**27**			**34**		III
40—45	15 f_1		**33**			**45**	𝍸
35—40	**18** f_2	26		**41**			IIII
30—35	8		15		33		I
25—30	7	12				20	
20—25	5						

Therefore, (40—45) is the Modal class.

Since here f_2 (18) is greater than f_0 / f_1

$$Z = l_1 + \frac{f_2}{f_0 + f_2} \times i$$

$$f_1 = 15, f_2 = 18, f_0 = 12$$

$$i = (45-40) = 5$$

$$l_2 = 45$$

$$= 45 - \frac{18}{12+18} \times 5$$

$$= 45 - 3 = 42$$

$\therefore$ **Mode = 42** **Ans.**

Determination of Mode in Bi-Modal or Multi-Modal Distribution

Sometimes there may be two or more values which occur with equal highest frequency. Sometimes concentration method too shows that the total of two or more sizes are equal. Such distribution is called Bi-Modal. Sometimes, Tri-Modal or Multi-Modal may also be noticed. In such a case the Mode cannot be determined by the formula discussed above. It means Mode is ill-defined.

In such a case, mode, if at all is needed, may be computed by using the following formula :

$$\text{Mode } (Z) = l_1 + \frac{f_2}{f_0 + f_2} \times i$$

$$(\text{Mode}) Z = 3M - 2\bar{X}$$

$$(\text{Mode}) Z = 3 \text{ Median} - 2 \text{ Mean}$$

***Illustration* 12**

Find the Mode from the following data :

Marks	*No. of Students*
0—10	4
10—20	2
20—30	18
30—40	22
40—50	21
50—60	19
60—70	10
70—80	3
80—90	1

Solution :

Grouping Table

Class	Frequency	Grouping in Two's		Grouping in Three's			Analysis
	1	2	3	4	5	6	
0—10	4	6					
10—20	2		20	24			
20—30	18	**40**			42		II
30—40	**22**		**43**			**61**	卌
40—50	21	**40**		**62**			卌
50—60	19		29		**50**		III
60—70	10	13				32	I
70—80	3		4	14			
80—90	1						

From the grouping table and analysis it appears that both (30—40) and (40—50) class-intervals have got five points each. So this distribution is bi-modal.

Using Density Method

	(30—40)	(40—50)
Frequency of Modal Class (f_1)	22	21
Frequency of the class preceding to Modal Class (f_0)	18	22
Frequency of the class succeeding to Modal Class (f_2)	21	19
Total	61	62 (Max.)

where Total = $f_1 + f_0 + f_2$

From density table, it appears that mode lies in class (40—50). In this case f_0 is 22 which is greater than f_1 (21). Hence the following formula will be used to determine Mode :

$$M_o = l_1 + \frac{f_2}{f_0+f_2} \times (l_2 - l_1)$$

$$= 40 + \frac{19}{22+19} \times (50-40)$$

$$= 40 + \frac{19 \times 10}{41} = 40 + \frac{190}{41}$$

$\therefore$ $M_o = 40 + 4.63 = \mathbf{44.63}$ **Ans.**

(3.3) RELATIONSHIP AMONG ARITHMETIC MEAN, MEDIAN AND MODE

The relationship among Mean, Median and Mode depends upon the nature of distribution. The distribution may be either symmetrical or asymmetrical.

(i) **In case of Symmetrical Distribution :** A distribution in which Mean, Median and Mode coincide is called Symmetrical Distribution. Therefore,

Mean $(\bar{X})$ = Median (M) = Mode $(Z) = k$ (say)

Such a distribution is Bell-Shaped and its curve is called Normal Curve.

(ii) **In case of Asymmetrical Distribution :** If a series is moderately asymmetrical, the Median lies in between the Arithmetic Mean and the Mode. The difference between Mean $(\bar{X})$ and Mode (M_o) is three times of the difference between Mean $(\bar{X})$ and Median (M)

Symbolically, $(\bar{X} - M_o) = 3(\bar{X} - M)$

or Mean – Mode = 3 (Mean – Median)

In case of a Moderately Aymmetrical Distribution, the following relationship exists among Mean, Median and Mode :

(1) Mode (M_o) = 3 Median – 2 Mean

(2) Median (M) = 1/3 (2 Mean + Mode)

(3) Mean $(\bar{X})$ = 1/2 (3 Median – Mode).

***Illustration* 13(A)**

(i) If the value of Mode and Mean is 8 and 68 respectively. Find the value of Median.

(ii) If the Mode and Median of a Moderately Asymmetrical Series are 50 cm and 56 cm respectively, what would be its most probable Mean?

(iii) If the Mean and Median of a Moderately Asymmetrical Series are 52 years and 48 years respectively, what would be its most probable Mode?

Solution :

(i) Mode (M_o) = 80, Mean $(\bar{X})$ = 68

Median (M) = ?

$$M = \frac{1}{3}(2\bar{X} + M_o)$$

$$= \frac{1}{3}\{(2 \times 68) + 80\}$$

$$= \frac{1}{3}(136 + 80) = \frac{1}{3}(216)$$

$\therefore$ (Median) M = **72** **Ans.**

(ii) Mode (M_o) = 50 cm, Median (M) = 56 cm

Mean $(\bar{X})$ = ?

$\bar{X}\ \frac{1}{2}(3M - M_o) = \frac{1}{2}\{(3 \times 56) - 50)\}$

$= \frac{1}{2}(168 - 50) = \frac{1}{2}(118)$

$\therefore$ (Mean) $\bar{X}$ = **59 cms.** **Ans.**

(iii) Mean $(\bar{X})$ = 52, Median $(M) = 48$

Mode (M_o) = ?

$M_o = 3M - 2X$

$= (3 \times 48) - (2 \times 52) = 144 - 104$

$\therefore$ (Mode) M_o = **40 years.** **Ans.**

Mode on the basis of Mean and Median

Formula : Mode = 3 Median – 2 Mean.

***Illustration* 13(B)**

Mean = 31.25 Median = 31.5. Find Mode.

[*Mock Test Paper (JAC)*]

Solution :

$\because$ Mode = 3 Median – 2 Mean

Now, putting the values

Mode = 3 × 31.5 – 2 × 31.25

= 94.5 – 62.5 = 32

$\therefore$ Mode = **32** **Ans.**

***Illustration* 13(C)**

If the value of mean $\bar{X}$ is 25 and median (M) is 26, then find the value of mode. (*JAC,* 2024)

Solution :

Mode = 3 Median – 2 Mean

= 3 × 26 – 2 × 25

= 78 – 50

= 28 **Ans.**

***Illustration* 14**

Find out Mode of the following data on the basis of Arithmetic Mean and Median :

Marks	0—10	10—20	20—30	30—40	40—50	50—60	60—70	70—80	80—90
No. of Students	4	2	18	22	21	19	10	3	1

Solution :

Let

$A = 45$

$Z = 3$ Median – 2 Mean

Calculation of Mean and Median

Marks	*M.V.(m)*	*Frequency (f)*	$d_x = (m - A)$	$d'_x = \frac{d_x}{i}$	fd'_x	*c.f.*
0—10	5	4	– 40	– 4	– 16	4
10—20	15	2	– 30	– 3	– 6	4 + 2 = 6
20—30	25	18	– 20	– 2	– 36	6 + 18 = 24
30—40	35	22	– 10	– 1	– 22	24 + 22 = 46 (*c*)
40—50	45	21	0	0	0	46 + 21 = 67
50—60	55	19	+ 10	+ 1	+ 19	67 + 19 = 86
60—70	65	10	+ 20	+ 2	+ 20	86 + 10 = 96
70—80	75	3	+ 30	+ 3	+ 9	96 + 3 = 99
80—90	85	1	+ 40	+ 4	+ 4	99 + 1 = 100
Total		$N = 100$			$\Sigma fd'_x = -28$	

Arithmetic Mean $\bar{X} = A + \frac{\Sigma fd'x}{N} \times i$

$= 45 + \frac{-28}{100} \times 10$

$= 45 - 2.8 =$ **42.2 (Marks)**

Median $(M) = \left(\frac{N}{2}\right)^{th}$ item's value

$= \left(\frac{100}{2}\right)^{th}$ item's value

= 50th item's value

and 50 lies in *cf* 67. Its corresponding size is (40—50). Median class.

Hence, median lies in class (40—50).

Now,

$M = l_1 + \frac{i}{f}(m - c)$

$= 40 + \frac{10}{21}(50 - 46)$

$= 40 + \frac{10 \times 4}{21}$

$M = 40 + 1.91$

= **41.91 (Marks)** **Ans.**

Mode :

Mode = 3 Median – 2 Mean

$M_o = (3 \times 41.9) - (2 \times 42.2)$

$= 125.7 - 84.4$

M_o = **41.3 Marks** **Ans.**

(3.4) GRAPHIC METHOD OF LOCATING MODE

In a frequency distribution, Mode can also be located graphically.

Procedure :

(1) Draw a Histogram of the given distribution.

(2) The highest rectangle will be of the Modal class.

(3) Draw a line from the top *right hand* corner of the Modal class rectangle to the point, where top of the next adjacent rectangle to the left touches it.

Draw corresponding line on the opposite diagonal from the top *left hand* corner to the rectangle on the right.

(4) From the point of inter-section of these lines. Draw a perpendicular on the X-axis and read the Modal value.

Illustration 15

Draw a Histogram on the graph paper from the data given below and read the value of Mode :

Production (in Ton)	*No. of Labourers*
0—10	8
10—20	18
20—30	23
30—40	37
40—50	47
50—60	26
60—70	16
70—80	5

Solution :

$$\text{Mode} = l_1 + \frac{f_1 - f_0}{2f_1 - f_0 - f_2} \times i$$

$$= 40 + \frac{47 - 37}{(2 \times 47) - 37 - 26} \times 10$$

$$= 40 + \frac{10 \times 10}{31}$$

$$= 40 + \frac{100}{31}$$

Mode = 40 + 3.2 = **43.22** **Ans.**

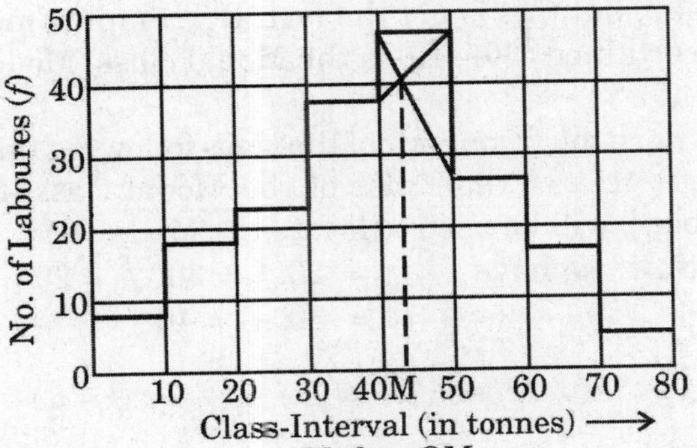

Fig. 1

Calculation of Mean and Mode

Illustration 16

Calculate Mean and Mode of the following distribution :

Age	0—10	10—20	20—30	30—40	40—50	50—60	60—70
Frequency	2	11	20	26	30	10	1

Solution :

Age	*Frequency (f)*	*Mid-value (m)*	$d_x = m - A$	$f \times d_x$
0—10	2	5	− 30	− 60
10—20	11	15	− 20	− 220
20—30	20	25	− 10	− 200
30—40	26	35	0	− 0
40—50	30	45	+ 10	+ 300
50—60	10	55	+ 20	+ 200
60—70	1	65	+ 30	+ 30
				+ 530
				− 480
Total	N = 100			$\Sigma fd_x = 50$

$$\text{Mean } (\bar{X}) = A + \frac{\Sigma fd_x}{N}$$

$$\therefore \quad \bar{X} = 35 + \frac{50}{100}$$

$$= 35 + 0.5$$

= **35.5 Ans.**

Calculation of Mode

Grouping Table

Age	Freq. (f) 1	Grouping in Two's 2	3	Grouping in Three's 4	5	6	Analysis	
0—10	2	13						0
10—20	11		31	33			|	1
20—30	20	**46**			**57**		|||	3
30—40	26		**56**			**76**	|||||	5
40—50	**30**	40		**66**			||||	4
50—60	10		11		41		|	1
60—70	1							0

By inspection the Mode seems to lie in the class (40—50) but this is not the fact. By grouping method it is ascertained (30—40) is the Modal class. Mode lies in (30—40).

Since the frequency of the class following the modal class is greater than that of the Modal class, formula number 2 will be used to locate the Mode.

Now, we have $f_1 = 26, f_2 = 30, f_0 = 20$

$l_1 = 30,\ l_2 = 40$

$$\text{Mode } (Z) = l_1 + \frac{f_2}{f_0 + f_2} \times (l_2 - l_1)$$

$$= 30 + \frac{30}{20+30} \times (40\text{–}30)$$

$$= 30 + \frac{30 \times 10}{50}$$

$\therefore$ $Z = 30 + 6 = \mathbf{36}$ **Ans.**

Calculation of Mean, Median and Mode

***Illustration* 17**

A student received following marks in five papers :

72, 50, 65, 85, 56

Find Mean, Median and Mode.

Solution : $\bar{X} = \dfrac{72+50+65+85+56}{5}$

$\therefore$ $\bar{X} = \dfrac{328}{5} = \mathbf{65.6}$ **Ans.**

Figures in Ascending Order :

50, 56, 65, 72, 85

n = 5 obs. (odd)

$M = \left(\dfrac{n+1}{2}\right)^{th}$ item's value

= 3rd item's value, which is 65

Hence, Median = **65** **Ans.**

Now, Mode = 3 Median – 2 Mean

= 195 – 131.2

= 3 × 65 – 2 × 65.6

$\therefore$ Mode = **63.8** **Ans.**

***Illustration* 18**

Calculate Mean, Median and Mode of the following :

x	f
10—20	4
20—30	12
30—40	40
40—50	41
50—60	27
60—70	13
70—80	9
80—90	4

Solution :

Calculation of Mean *where i* = 10 A = 45

Class	Mid-value (m)	f	$d_x = m - A$	$d_x' = \frac{d_x}{i}$	$f \times d_x'$
10—20	15	4	– 30	– 3	– 12
10—20	25	12	– 20	– 2	– 24
10—20	35	40	– 10	– 1	– 40
40—50	45	41	0	0	0
50—60	55	27	+ 10	+ 1	+ 27
60—70	65	13	+ 20	+ 2	+ 26
70—80	75	9	+ 30	+ 3	+ 27
80—90	85	4	+ 40	+ 4	+ 16
Total		$N = 150$			$\Sigma fd'_x = 20$

$$\text{Mean } (\bar{X}) = A + \left(\frac{\Sigma fd'_x}{N} \times i\right)$$

$$= 45 + \left(\frac{20}{150} \times 10\right)$$

$$= 45 + \frac{4}{3} = 45 + 1\frac{1}{3} = 46\frac{1}{3}$$

$\therefore$ Mean $(\bar{X})$ = **46.33** **Ans.**

Class	Frequency (f)	Cumulative Frequency (c.f.)
10–20	4	4
20–30	12	16
30–40	40	56 (c)
40–50	41 (f)	97 (Median Class)
50–60	27	124
60–70	13	137
70–80	9	146
80–90	4	150

$m = \left(\frac{N}{2}\right)^{th}$ item's value = 75th item's value, which lies in 97 (cf)

Hence, Median class will be (40—50).

Now, Median, $M = l_1 + \frac{i}{f}(m - c)$

$l_1 = 40, \; i = 10, \; f = 41$

$c = 56, \; m = 75$

$$= 40 + \frac{10}{41}(75 - 56)$$

$$= 40 + \frac{10}{41} \times 19$$

$$= 40 + \frac{190}{41}$$

$$= 40 + 4.61$$

$\therefore$ M = **44.63** **Ans.**

Mode : By observations, we find that (40—50) is the Modal class. Since this class has the max. frequency.

Now, Mode, $Z = l_1 + \frac{f_1 - f_0}{2f_1 - f_0 - f_2} \times i$

$$= 40 + \frac{41 - 40}{2 \times 41 - 40 - 27} \times 10$$

$$= 40 + \frac{1}{82 - 40 - 27} \times 10$$

$$= 40 + \frac{1 \times 10}{15}$$

$\therefore$ $Z = 40 + \frac{2}{3} = 40 + 0.6 =$ **40.66**

Thus, Mean $(\bar{X})$ = **46.33**
Median (M) = **44.63**
Mode (Z) = **40.66** **Ans.**

(3.5) FINDING THE MISSING FREQUENCY

***Illustration* 19**

Mode of the following distribution is 48.6. Find the missing frequency :

Class	10—25	25—40	40—55	55—70	70—85
Frequency	6	20	44	?	3

Solution :

Since Mode is 48.6, Modal Class will be (40—55). Assuming that missing frequency of class (55—70) is f_2.

According to question,

$Z = 48.6, f_1 = 44, f_0 = 20,$
$i = 15, f_2 = ?, l_1 = 40$

Now, $Z = l_1 + \frac{f_1 - f_0}{2f_1 - f_0 - f_2} \times i$

$$48.6 = 40 + \frac{40 - 20}{(2 \times 44) - 20 - f_2} \times 15$$

or $48.6 = 40 + \frac{25 \times 15}{68 - f_2}$

or $48.6 - 40 = \frac{360}{68 - f_2}$

or $8.6 = \frac{360}{68 - f_2}$

or $8.6(68 - f_2) = 360$

or $584.8 - 8.6 f_2 = 360$

or $-86 f_2 = 360 - 584.8$

or $8.6 f_2 = 224.8$

$\therefore$ $f_2 = \frac{224.8}{8.6} = 26.13$

Therefore, missing frequency of the class (55—70) is 26.13. **Ans.**

(3.6) MERITS OR ADVANTAGES OF MODE

(1) Mode is easy to understand.

(2) It is easy to calculate. It can be calculated in some cases merely by inspection.

(3) It is capable of being ascertained graphically.

(4) It is not affected by extreme values.

(5) It represents most frequent value. Hence it is there best representative of the data.

(6) It can be calculated from frequency distribution with open-end classes

(3.7) DEMERITS OR DISADVANTAGES OF MODE

(1) Mode is not suitable for further mathematical treatment.

(2) Mode for the series with unequal class-intervals cannot be calculated.

(3) Mode is unsuitable measure as it is affected by sampling fluctuations.

(4) Mode is not based on all the observations of the series.

(5) In many cases Mode is difficult to determine accurately. Some series may have two or more Mode values.

(3.8) USES OF MODE

(1) It is used for the study of most popular fashion.

(2) It is extensively used by Businessmen and Business Managements.

(3) Mode is, perhaps, the average which the ordinary mind seems best to represent the group. Average family income, average size of shirt or shoes sold, usual duration of cold-fever getting cared etc. the most frequently occurring value, that is Mode. Hence Mode is conceptually very useful.

FORMULAE OF MODE : AT A GLANCE

Series	*Determination of Mode*
1. Individual Series	By observation or inspection we find the Mode. The item which is repeated maximum number of times is referred to as Modal item/Modal value or Mode.
2. Discrete Series	(a) The size or item having the maximum frequency is Mode. (b) By grouping and analysis table we ascertain that value which has been repeated maximum number of times and that gives us the mode. (c) By Concetration Method.
3. Continuous Series	

$$1. \text{ Mode } = l_1 + \frac{f_1 - f_0}{(f_1 - f_0) + (f_1 - f_2)} \times i$$

$i = l_2 - l_2$

'*i*' may be replaced by '*c*'

$$\text{or Mode } = l_1 + \frac{f_1 - f_0}{(2f_1 - f_0 - f_2)} \times i$$

$$2. \text{ Mode } = l_1 + \frac{f_2}{f_0 + f_2} \times i$$

(When f_0 or f_2 is more than that of f_1')

3. Mode = 3 Median – 2 Arith. Mean.

THEORETICAL QUESTIONS

Long Answer Type Questions

1. What do you understand by mode? Point out its merits and demerits.
2. Differentiate between mean and mode.
3. What is mode? Distinguish between mode and arithmetic mean.
4. Define arithmetic mean, median and mode and explain their uses.
5. Define mean, mode and median and discuss their merits and demerits.

Short Answer Type Questions

1. What is mode? State its two advantages.
2. State the characteristics of mode.
3. State the advantages of mode.
4. Discuss the merits and demerits of mode.
5. Distinguish between mean and mode.
6. Distinguish between mode and median.
7. Explain the relationship between arithmetic mean, median and mode.
8. Give a relationship among mean, median and mode for a moderately skewed distribution.

Very Short Answer Type Questions

1. Give three characteristics of mode.
2. Give three advantages of mode.
3. Explain two merits and one demerits of mode.
4. Write one demerit each of mean, median and mode.
5. Give three differences between median and mode.
6. Point out any three differences between Arithmetic Mean and Mode.
7. Express the relationship among Mean, Median and Mode.

PRACTICAL QUESTIONS

Short Answer Type Questions

Individual Series

1. (A) The following are the marks secured by 20 students in Statistics. Find the mode :

15, 10, 25, 30, 32, 16, 22, 24, 15, 17, 20, 25, 27, 30, 38, 25, 28, 30, 25, 24.

[**Ans.** Mode = 25.]

(B) Find the mode of the following data :

5, 7, 6, 9, 8, 6, 7, 8, 9, 3, 7, 5, 7, 4.

[**Ans.** Mode = 7.]

(C) Given below are monthly salaries of 12 clerks of an industrial concern.

Find out the modal salary.

Clerk	*Salaries (in ₹)*	*Clerk*	*Salaries (in ₹)*
A	500	G	800
B	650	H	700
C	575	I	750
D	700	J	700
E	600	K	550
F	650	L	950

Ans. Mode = ₹ 700.]

(D) Find the mode from the following data :

5, 6, 7, 9, 8, 6, 7, 8, 9, 3, 5, 7, 9, 8, 6, 7, 8, 9, 3

[**Ans.** Mode : Multi-mode, or Mode Ill defined.]

Discrete Series

2. Find out the mode in the following series :

Size of the Ganjee (in cm)	60	65	70	75	80	85	90	95
Frequency	5	12	20	32	40	30	18	10

[**Ans.** Mode = 80 cm]

3. (A) Compute the mode from the following data :

Size of Items	2	3	4	5	6	7	8	9	10	11	12	13
Frequency	3	8	10	12	16	14	10	8	17	5	4	1

[**Ans.** Mode = 6.]

(B) The following table shows the various sizes of shoes sold at a shop during a month. Find out the mode :

Size	4.0	4.5	5.0	5.5	6.0	6.5	7.0	8.0	9.0	10.0
Pairs	6	10	14	17	15	18	20	16	10	6

[**Ans.** Mode = 7.]

(C) From the following frequency distribution, find out mode :

Size	10	20	30	40	50	60
Frequency	5	9	16	28	12	8

[**Ans.** Mode = 40]

(D) Find mode from the following table :

x	4	6	9	15	18	22
f	20	104	252	282	101	34

[**Ans.** Mode = 15]

(E) In moderately skewed distribution arithmetic mean is 32 and median is 36. Find out the mode. (*JAC*, 2026)

[**Ans.** Mode = 44]

Long Answer Type Questions

Continuous Series

4. (A) Compute the mode from the following table :

Size	0—5	5—10	10—15	15—20	20—25	25—30
Frequency	10	25	50	7	13	5

[**Ans.** Mode = 11.83]

(B) Calculate the value of the mode from the following data :

Marks	5—10	10—15	15—20	20—25	25—30
No. of Students	10	15	25	20	12

[**Ans.** Mode = 18.33]

5. Calculate mode of the following :

X	10—20	20—30	30—40	40—50	50—60	60—70	70—80
f	4	10	25	45	40	15	5

[**Ans.** Mode = 48.]

6. Calculate mode of the following :

Wages (in ₹)	12.5—17.5	17.5—22.5	22.5—27.5	27.5—32.5	32.5—37.5	37.5—42.5	42.5—47.5	47.5—52.5	52.5—57.5
No. of Workers	4	44	38	28	6	8	12	2	2

[**Ans.** Mode ₹ 24.44.]

[**Hint :** By the help of formula No. 2.]

7. From the following frequency distribution, find out mode :

Size	0—3	3—5	5—10	10—15	15—20	20—30	30—40	40—50	50—60	60—70
Frequency	4	3	9	15	17	20	18	15	8	3

[**Ans.** Z = 15.714.]

8. (A) The mid-points and their corresponding frequencies are given below. Find out the mode value :

M.V.	2	3	4	5	6	7
Frequency	4	1	20	16	10	6

[**Ans.** Z = 4.32]

(B) From the following frequency distribution, find out mode :

Central Size	10	20	30	40	50	60
Frequency	5	9	16	28	12	8

[**Ans.** $Z = 39.28$]

(C) Find out the mode of the following series :

Mid Point	5	10	15	20	25	30	35
Frequency	10	15	28	35	16	7	4

[**Ans.** $Z = 18.84$]

9. Calculate mode from the following data :

Age	20—25	25—30	30—35	35—40	40—45	45—50	50—55	55—60
Frequency	50	70	100	180	150	120	70	60

[**Ans.** Mode 38.63.]

10. From the data given below, find the mode :

Age in years	20—25	25—30	30—35	35—40	40—45	45—50	50—55	55—60
No. of Persons	50	70	80	180	150	120	70	50

[**Ans.** Mode = 42 years.]

[**Hint :** By grouping method ascertain the modal class. It is 40—45. Apply formula No. 2 :

$$Z = l_1 + \frac{f_2}{f_0 + f_2} \times l_2 - l_1]$$

11. (A) Calculate mode of the following series :

X	1—5	6—10	11—15	16—20	21—25	26—30	31—35	36—40	41—45
f	7	10	13	32	24	18	10	5	1

[**Ans.** Mode = 19.01.]

(B) Find mode in the following table :

Class	0—4	5—9	10—14	15—19	20—24	25—29
Frequency	11	18	30	42	28	10

[**Ans.** Mode = 16.8.]

12. Calculate the mode from the following :

Marks Above	0	10	20	30	40	50	60	70	80	90
Frequency	80	77	72	65	55	43	28	16	10	8

[**Ans.** Mode = 55.]

13. Calculate mode of the following data :

Marks Below	10	20	30	40	50	60	70	80
Frequency	15	35	60	84	96	127	198	250

[**Ans.** Mode = 66.77]

14. From the following table, find the mode :

Income (Between) in ₹	100—200	100—300	100—400	100—500	100—600
No. of Persons	15	33	63	83	100

[**Ans.** Mode = 354.54.]

15. (A) The marks obtained by 30 students in Economics are given below :

25	30	32	47	50	60	55	52	40	35	43	45
54	47	43	50	56	28	48	47	48	49	50	38
44	39	30	30	48	50						

(a) Form a Frequency table taking first class-interval as 25—30.

(b) Find out the mode from this distribution.

[**Ans.** (a)

x	25—30	30—35	35—40	40—45	45—50	50—55	55—60	60—65
f	2	4	3	4	8	6	2	1

(b) 48.33.]

Caculation of Mode by Graphic Method

(B) Determine the value of mode of the following distribution graphically and verify the result :

Class	0—10	10—20	20—30	30—40	40—50
Frequency	10	15	30	20	5

[**Ans.** Mode = 26.]

Median and Mode

16. Find the median and mode of the following data :

7, 8, 9, 9, 7, 6, 9, 4, 10, 3, 5, 9, 9

[**Ans.** $M = 8, Z = 9.$]

17. The incomes of 16 labourers are given below. Find out the Median and Mode by observation :

Serial Nos.	1	2	3	4	5	6	7	8	9	10	11	12	13	14	15	16
Income (₹)	200	204	206	204	214	198	206	250	220	224	206	200	208	208	214	210

[**Ans.** M = ₹ 207, Z = ₹ 206.]

18. Compute median and mode from the following :

Marks (m)	20	21	22	23	24	25	26	27	28
Frequency (f)	2	4	12	18	30	20	9	2	1

[**Ans.** Median = 24, Mode = 24.]

19. (A) Calculate Median and Mode from the following series : (*JAC*, 2017)

Marks (m)	6—10	11—15	16—20	21—25	26—30
Freq. (f)	20	30	50	40	10

[**Ans.** Median = 18, Mode = 18.83.]

(B) Obtain median and mode of the following distribution :

Marks	10—25	25—40	40—55	55—70	70—85	85—100
Frequency	6	22	44	26	3	1

[**Ans.** $M = 47.84, Z = 48.25.$]

(C) Calculate median and mode in the following table :

Class	5—9	10—19	20—24	25—29	30—34
Frequency	12	18	32	8	3

[**Ans.** $M = 20.515, Z = 21.34.$]

(D) Given below is the distribution of marks obtained by 140 students in an examination :

Marks	10—19	20—29	30—39	40—49	50—59	60—69	70—79	80—89	90—99
No. of Students	7	15	18	22	30	20	16	7	2

Find the Median and Mode.

[**Ans.** Median = 51.16, Mode = 52.83]

20. Calculate Median and Mode from the following :

Income (₹)	100—200	200—300	300—400	400—500	500—600
No. of Persons	15	18	30	20	17

[**Ans.** Median = ₹ 356.66, Mode = ₹ 354.54.]

Mean and Mode

21. Calculate mean from the following data and also compute mode from the same :

Size	0—3	3—6	6—10	10—15	15—20	20—30	30—40	40—50	50—60	60—70
Frequency	4	3	9	15	17	20	18	15	8	3

[**Ans.** $\bar{X} = 26.879, Z = 15.714$]

Mean, Median and Mode

22. Compute Mean, Median and Mode from the following distribution :

Marks	30	31	32	33	34	35	36	37	38	39
Frequency (f)	4	8	23	35	62	44	18	4	1	1

[**Ans.** $\overline{X}$ = 33.9, M = 34, Z = 34.]

23. Obtain the Mean, Median and Mode of the following distribution :

Marks	10—25	25—40	40—55	55—70	70—85	85—100
Frequency	6	22	44	26	3	1

[**Ans.** $\overline{X}$ = 47.647, M = 47.84, Z = 48.25.]

24. Calculate Mean, Median and Mode from the following data :

Marks Below	10	20	30	40	50	60	70	80
No. of Students	5	11	22	37	56	68	75	80

[**Ans.** $\overline{X}$ = 40.75, M = 41.57, Z = 43. 64.]

25. Find the difference of median and mode of the following data :

7 8 9 9 7 6 9 4 10 3 5 9 9

[**Ans.** Diff. = 1]

26. Calculate mean, mode and median of the following data :

Marks	0—10	10—20	20—30	30—40	40—50	50—60	60—70
Frequency	10	25	35	70	90	40	30

[**Ans.** $\overline{X}$ = 39.83, M = 41.1, Z = 42.857.]

27. Find the mean, median and mode of the following data :

Age	20—25	25—30	30—35	35—40	40—45	45—50	50—55	55—60
No. of Employees	8	23	51	81	103	113	117	120

[**Ans.** $\overline{X}$ = 45.5, M = 46.85, Z = 49.58.]

28. Find out mean, median and mode of the following data :

Marks :	1—5	6—10	11—15	16—20	21—25	26—30	31—35	36—40
No. of Students	5	7	12	19	17	19	15	6

[**Ans.** $\overline{X}$ 22.15, M = 22.55, Z = 23.]

29. Calculate mean, median and mode in the following data :

Class	0—5	5—10	10—15	15—20	20—25
Frequency	10	12	20	9	4

[**Ans.** Mean = 13.863, Median = 11.375, Mode = 12.105]

To find out missing frequency when mode is given

30. Find the frequency of the class (20—25) in the following table if the value of mode is 18 :

Class	5—10	10—15	15—20	20—25	25—30
Frequency	8	12	30	?	8

[**Ans.** 18]

31. Find the missing frequency in the following table if the value of mode is 35.5 :

Class	0—14	15—29	30—44	45—59	60—74
Frequency	10	18	—	12	6

[**Ans.** 12.85 = 13 (∵ 'f' can never be a fractional)]

32. Find the missing figure in the following table if its mode is 54 :

Daily Expenditure (₹)	0—20	20—40	40—60	60—80	80—100
No. of Families	10	—	30	—	14

[**Ans.** 16, 24]

Miscellaneous Problems

33. Given below are the daily wages in rupees of 60 employees of a factory :

23	48	51	64	72	82	56	33	50	42	35	88	77
65	39	52	48	64	49	57	41	72	62	42	32	54
67	46	55	50	82	44	75	56	51	63	59	69	53
42	75	85	68	55	52	42	57	20	57	46	45	51
50	16	62	56	54	40	55	71					

(A) From a Frequency Table taking the class-interval as (10—20).

(B) Find the (i) modal class, and (ii) modal daily wages.

[**Ans.** (A)

10—20	20—30	30—40	40—50	50—60	60—70	70—80	80—90
1	2	4	13	21	9	6	4

(B) Model Class = (60—60), Mode = ₹ 54.]

34. From the following set of data, prepare of frequency distribution table in ascending order starting with 100—110 when the class-interval be always 10 :

Daily Income of some Families in Rupees

110	125	108	112	126	132	136	130	149	155
120	130	136	138	125	111	119	125	140	148
147	137	145	150	142	135	137	137	165	154

(i) What is the modal group in the above prepared frquency table ?

(ii) In the above data, how many families have daily income of ₹ 130 at least ?

[**Ans.**

100—110	110—120	120—130	130—140	140—150	150—160	160—170
1	4	5	10	6	3	1

(i) Modal class (130—140), (ii) 20 Families.]

35. Find the mode in the following frequency table :

Class	0—10	10—10	20—30	30—40	40—50
Frequency	19	26	27	45	15

[**Ans.** Mode = 33.75]

36. Find mode in the following table :

Class	0—4	5—9	10–14	15—19	20—24	25—29
Frequency	12	17	32	20	18	9

[**Ans.** M_o = 12.27]

37. Find the mode in the following table :

Class	0—4	5—9	10—14	15—19	20—24
Frequency	12	18	30	12	8

[**Ans.** *Z* = 11.5]

38. Find mode from the following :

Age more than	0	10	20	30	40	50
No. of Persons	100	88	70	43	23	6

[**Ans.** 25.625]

39. Calculate mode of the following data :

Marks	10—19	20—29	30—39	40—49	50—59	60—69	70—79
No. of Stds.	8	19	29	36	25	13	4

[**Ans.** 43.38]

40. Find the mode of the following series :

Wages (in ₹)	0—10	10—20	20—30	30—40	40—50	50—60
No. of Workers	6	10	10	16	12	8

[**Ans.** Mode = 36]

OBJECTIVE TYPE QUESTIONS

I. Multiple Choice Questions

1. Which average is affected most by extreme observations ? (*JAC*, 2020)
   (a) Median (b) Mode
   (c) Arithmetic Mean (d) Geometric Mean
2. Median is :
   (a) Most frequent value (b) Least frequent value
   (c) Centre of gravity (d) Middle most value
3. Mode is :
   (a) Most frequent value (b) Least frequent value
   (c) Middle most value
   (d) Representing majority out of total frequency
4. Which of the following averages is a positional average ?
   (a) Arithmetic Mean (b) Median
   (c) Geometric Mean (d) Harmonic Mean
5. The sum of deviations of individual observations of the series is zero from :
   (a) Median (b) Mode
   (c) Arithmetic Mean (d) Geometric Mean
6. The sum of absolute deviations of items of the series is minimum from :
   (a) Arithmetic Mean (b) Median
   (c) Mode (d) Geometric Mean
7. Which of the following is not a mathematical mean ? (*JAC*, 2024)
   (a) Mode (b) Geometric Mean
   (c) Arithmetic Mean (d) Harmonic Mean
8. Which of the following is true ? (*JAC*, 2016)
   (a) Mean = 3 Median – 2 Mode
   (b) Median = 3 Mode – 2 Mean
   (c) Mode = 3 Median – 2 Mean
   (d) Mode = Mean + Median
9. On what basis the value of Median is calculated ?
   (a) Cumulative Frequency curve
   (b) Histogram
   (c) Frequency curve
   (d) Frequency polygon
10. For the calculation of arithmetic mean the class intervals should be : (*JAC*, 2016)
    (a) Exclusive (b) Unequal
    (c) Equal (d) All are possible
11. The mean of 15 number is 15. If the two numbers 18 and 12 are excluded, then the mean of the remaining number is :
    (a) 15 (b) 10
    (c) 25 (d) 12
12. Which of the following is the most uncertain coverage ?
    (a) Mode (b) Median
    (c) Harmonic Mean (d) Arithmetic Mean
13. Two ogive curves of a distribution intersects at 55, which of the following is correct ?
    (a) Arithmetic mean of the distribution is 55
    (b) Median of the distribution is 55
    (c) Mode of the distribution 55
    (d) Standard deviation of the distribution is 55
14. For any given statistical series which of the following measures many have more than one value ?
    (a) Mean (b) Median
    (c) Mode (d) Geometric Mean
15. The median divides the distribution in :
    (a) Three equal parts (b) Four equal parts
    (c) Two equal parts (d) None of these
16. In a moderately skewed distribution arithmetic mean is 32 and mode is 44. Find out Median :
    (a) 12 (b) 24
    (c) 36 (d) 48
17. Average salary of a group of 40 women workers is ₹ 5,200 per month and whenever average salary of a group of 60 men workers is ₹ 6,800 per month. What is mixed salary ?
    (a) ₹ 6,160 (b) ₹ 6,280
    (c) ₹ 6,890 (d) ₹ 6,920
18. Average salary of 50 men is ₹ 80 but we have found that ₹ 64 and ₹ 82 taking in place of ₹ 46 and ₹ 28 salary of 2 of them, correct average salary is :
    (a) ₹ 80 (b) ₹ 78.56 (c) ₹ 85.26 (d) ₹ 82.92
19. Average weight of 15 students is 110 kg. Average weight of 5 of them is 100 kg and other 5 is 125 kg. Average wieght of remaining students is :
    (a) 120 kg (b) 105 kg
    (c) 115 kg (d) None of these
20. If mean of 'x' is 50 then mean of $u = 10 + 5x$ will be :
    (a) 250 (b) 260 (c) 265 (d) 273
21. Daily wages (in ₹) of 12 families are 280, 180, 96, 98, 104, 75, 80, 94, 100, 75, 600 and 200 respectively. What is arithmetic mean ? (*JAC*, 2015)
    (a) 16.5 (b) 14.5 (c) 10.5 (d) 22.5
    (e) None of these
22. For the calculation of arithmetic mean the class intervals should be : (*JAC*, 2017)
    (a) exclusive (b) unequal
    (c) equal (d) all are possible
23. The arithmetic mean of 5, 10 and 15 is :
    (a) 5 (b) 10 (c) 15 (d) 30
24. The most common and ideal measure of central tendency is :
    (a) Arithmetic Mean (b) Geometric Mean
    (c) Mode (d) Median
25. The best measure to central tendency is A. M. is it true ? (*JAC*, 2019)
    (a) Yes (b) No

26. The mean of 5, 8, 11, 16, 15 is : (*JAC*, 2018)
(a) 10 (b) 11 (c) 12 (d) 13

27. The median of 80, 100, 90, 170, 60, 50, 40 is :
(a) 80 (b) 170 (c) 90 (d) 60

28. The mode of 5, 7, 8, 7, 6 is :
(a) 5 (b) 6 (c) 7 (d) 8

29. Formula of median for individual series is : (*JAC*, 2019)
(a) $\left(\frac{n-1}{2}\right)$th term (b) $\left(\frac{n+1}{2}\right)$th term
(c) $\left(\frac{n+1}{2}\right)$th term (d) $\left(\frac{n}{2}\right)$th term

30. If mean of 'x' is 50 then mean of $\dot{U} = 10 + 5x$ will be : (*JAC*, 2020)
(a) 250 (b) 260
(c) 265 (d) 273

31. Which of the following is the formula of calculating arithmetic mean ?
(a) $\bar{X} = \frac{\Sigma X}{n}$ (b) $\bar{X} = \frac{\Sigma fx}{n}$
(c) $\bar{X} = A + \frac{\Sigma f\,dx}{N}$ (d) All of these

32. The mode of 0, 15, 18, 19, 20, 22, 25, 0, 4 is : (*JAC*, 2023, 24)
(a) – 25 (b) 20
(c) 0 (d) 22

33. The value which occurs with maximum frequency is called : (*JAC*, 2023)
(a) Median (b) Mode
(c) Mean (d) None of these

34. In 5, 7, 6, 7, 8, 6, 7 mode is : (*JAC*, 2025)
(a) 7 (b) 6 (c) 5 (d) 2

35. Mode of 5, 6, 10, 6, 0, 12, 6, 13, 17, 6 is : (*JAC*, 2026)
(a) 6 (b) 0 (c) 12 (d) 5

[Ans. 1. (c), 2. (d), 3. (a), 4. (b), 5. (c), 6. (b), 7. (a), 8. (c), 9. (a), 10. (d), 11. (a), 12. (a), 13. (b), 14. (c), 15. (c), 16. (c), 17. (a), 18. (b), 19. (b), 20. (b), 21. (c), 22. (a), 23.(b), 24. (a), 25. (a), 26. (b), 27. (a), 28. (c), 29. (c), 30. (b), 31. (d), 32. (c), 33. (b), 34. (a), 35. (a).]

II. State whether the following statements are 'True or False' :

1. Mode is affected by extreme items.
2. Arithmetic Mean is not affected by extreme items.
3. Mode is defined as that value in aseries which occurs most frequently.
4. The items are arranged in a scending or descending order to calculate Median.
5. Sum of deviation taken from arithmetic mean is zero.
6. Arithmetic Mean is a positional average.
7. The Median and Mode may be found graphically, but not the Mean.
8. Mode divides the series into two equal parts.
9. In a perfect asymetrical distribution, Mean = Mode = Median.
10. Median is a value having maximum frequency.
11. A measure of central tendency is a typical value around which other figures congregate.
12. Arithmetic Mean and Average are the same (*JAC*, 2015)

[Ans. 1. False, 2. False, 3. False, 4. True, 5. True, 6. False, 7. True, 8. False, 9. False, 10. False, 11. True, 12. True.]

III. Fill in the Blanks

1. Average is the .... figure of the universe.
2. .... mean is maximum affected by extreme observations.
3. For the average salary of a teacher, the suitable average is ....
4. Arithmetic mean is based on .... the observations.
5. The value which divides a series into two parts is called ....
6. Simple frequency distribution should be converted into cumulative frequency distribution to calculate ....
7. The item's value are arranged in ascending or descending order to calculate ....
8. Mode is a value having .... frequencies.
9. The value which occurs for maximum number of times in a series is called ....
10. For the average size of ready-made garments is appropriate measure is ....

[Ans. 1. Representative, 2. Arithmetic, 3. Arithmetic mean. 4. All. 5. Median, 6. Median, 7. Median, 8. Maximum, 9. Mode. 10. Mode.]

❖❖

4

GEOMETRIC MEAN

LEARNING OBJECTIVES

After studying this chapter, you will be able to know :

- **4.1 Meaning and Definition**
- **4.2 Computation of Simple Geometric Mean**
- **4.3 Weighted Geometric Mean**
- **4.4 Special Uses of Geometric Mean**
- **4.5 Combined Geometric Mean**
- **4.6 Properties of Geometric Mean**
- **4.7 Merits of Geometric Mean**
- **4.8 Demerits of Geometric Mean**
- **4.9 Uses of Geometric Mean**
- **Theoretical Questions : Long Answer Questions, Short Answer Questions, Very Short Answer Questions**
- **Practical Problems**

ILLUSTRATIONS AND PRACTICAL PROBLEMS : AT A GLANCE

No. of Illustration		*No. of Problems*
1(A) to 4	Calculation of Geometric Mean in Individual Series	1 to 9
5(A), (B)	Calculation of Geometric Mean in Discrete Series	10 to 12
6(A), (B)	Calculation of Geometric Mean in Continuous Series	13 to 16
7(A), (B)	Weighted Geometric Mean	17, 18
—	Arithmetic Mean and Geometric Mean	19
8 to 14	Special Uses of Geometric Mean	20, 21
15	Combined Geometric Mean	22
—	Miscellaneous Problems	23 to 29
15	**Total**	**3 + 29 = 32**

(4.1) MEANING AND DEFINITION

The *Geometric Mean is the nth root of the product of n numbers*. If there are two terms or values, the square root of the product of the two values is the Geometric Mean. If there are three values, the cube root of their products of 3 values is the Geometric Mean and so on. Geometric Mean is denoted by *G* or G.M. The Geometric Mean is also called Geometric Average.

The G.M. or the Geometric Average is found by obtaining the product of the items and extracting the corresponding root of this product. Geometric Mean is of two types :

1. Simple Geometric Mean, 2. Weighted Geometric Mean.

Formula 1 :

$$\text{G.M.} = \sqrt[n]{(x_1)\times(x_2)\times(x_3)\,........\times(x_n)}$$

x_1, x_2, x_3 ..... refer to the various values in the series.

n = Numbers of items

Example 1. Find out the Geometric Mean of 4 and 16.

Solution :

$$\text{G.M.} = \sqrt[2]{4\times 16}$$

$$= \sqrt[2]{64} = \mathbf{8}$$ **Ans.**

Example 2. The weekly wages of 3 workers are ₹ 20, ₹ 40 and ₹ 80. Find the Geometric Mean.

Solution :

$$\text{G.M.} = \sqrt[3]{20\times 40\times 80}$$

$$= \sqrt[3]{64{,}000} = \sqrt[3]{64\times 1{,}000}$$

$$= 4\times 10 = \mathbf{40}$$ **Ans.**

In order to facilitate calculations, logarithms are used in its calculation. In that case the following formula is used to find out G.M. of an individual series :

(4.2) COMPUTATION OF SIMPLE GEOMETRIC MEAN

(A) Calculation of G.M. in Individual Series

$$\text{G.M.= Anti-log}\left[\frac{\log x_1 + \log x_2 + \,..........\, + \log x_n}{n}\right]$$

$$\text{G.M.= Anti-log}\left\{\frac{1}{n}\sum_{i=1}^{n}\log x_i\right\}$$

Steps :

1. First of all the logarithms of the observations are noted from the log table.
2. Then find $\sum_{i=1}^{n}\log x_i$.
3. Find the Number of Ovservations or Items, that is n.
4. Divide ($\Sigma \log x_i$) by n *i.e.*, $\dfrac{\sum_{i=1}^{n}\log x_i}{n}$
5. Take Anti-log of the quotient as calculated in step 4. This will be required the G.M.

Calculation of G.M. in Individual Series

***Illustration* 1(A)**

Find out the Geometric Mean for the following data :

5, 3, 15, 48, 40

Solution :

x	$\log x_i$
5	0.6990
3	0.4771
15	1.1761
48	1..6812
40	1.6021
$n = 5$	$\Sigma \log x_i = 5.6355$

$$\text{G.M.} = \text{Anti-log}\left\{\frac{\Sigma \log x_i}{n}\right\}$$

$$= \text{Anti-log}\left(\frac{5.6355}{5}\right)$$

$$= \text{Anti-log}\,(1.1271)$$

$$= 13.39$$

G.M. = 13.39 **Ans.**

***Illustration* 1(B)**

What is the Geometric mean of 5 and 20 ? [*Mock Test Paper* (*JAC*)]

Solution :

$$\text{GM} = \sqrt{x_1\times x_2}$$

$$= \sqrt{5\times 20} = \mathbf{10}$$ **Ans.**

***Illustration* 1(C)**

What is the GM of 3, 8, 9 ? [*Mock Test Paper* (*JAC*)]

Solution :

$$\text{GM} = \sqrt[3]{x_1\times x_2\times x_3}$$

$$\text{GM} = \sqrt{3\times 8\times 9}$$

$$= \sqrt{3\times 2\times 2\times 2\times 3\times 3} = \mathbf{6}$$ **Ans.**

***Illustration* 2**

The monthly incomes of ten families in Rupees in a certain locality are given below. Calculate the Geometric Mean :

85, 70, 15, 75, 500, 8, 45, 250, 40 and 36.

Solution :

Geometric Mean

S.No.	*Income* ₹	*Logarithms* ($\log x_i$)
1.	85	1.9294
2.	70	1.8450
3.	15	1.1760
4.	75	1.8750
5.	500	2.6989
6.	8	0.9030
7.	45	1.6532
8.	250	2.3979
9.	40	1.6020
10.	36	1.5563
$n = 10$		$\sum_{i=1}^{n}\log x_i = 17.6367$

$$\text{G.M.} = \text{Antilog}\left\{\frac{1}{n}\sum_{i=1}^{n}\log x_i\right\}$$

$$= \text{Antilog}\left\{\frac{1}{10}\times 17.6367\right\}$$

G.M. = 58.032 **Ans.**

***Illustration* 3**

Calculate Geometric Mean from the following data :

1.2564, 2.0985, 1.0164, 0.4508, 0.6928, 0.0032

Solution :

Calculation of G.M.

S.No.	x	$\log x_i$
1	1.2564	0.0990
2	2.0985	0.3219
3	1.0164	0.0071
4	0.4508	$\bar{1}.6540$
5	0.6928	$\bar{1}.8406$
6	0.0032	$\bar{3}.5051$
$n = 6$		$\Sigma \log x_i = 3.4277$

$$\text{G.M.} = \text{Anti-log}\left(\frac{\Sigma \log x_i}{n}\right)$$

$$= \text{Anti-log}\left(\frac{\bar{3}.4277}{6}\right)$$

$$= \text{Anti-log}\{(\bar{3}.4277) \div 6\}$$

$$= \text{Anti-log}\left(\frac{\bar{6} + 3.4277}{6}\right)$$

$$= \text{Anti-log}\left(\bar{1}.5716\right)$$

G.M. = **0.3727** **Ans.**

***Illustration* 4**

Calculate G.M. of the following series :
0.2039, 0.0162, 0.0038, 0.4805, 0.8914, 0.9206

Solution :

Calculation of G.M.

S.No.	x	$\log x_i$
1	0.2039	$\bar{1}.3094$
2	0.0162	$\bar{2}.2095$
3	0.0038	$\bar{3}.5798$
4	0.4805	$\bar{1}.6816$
5	0.8914	$\bar{1}.9501$
6	0.9206	$\bar{1}.9641$
		$\Sigma \log x_i = 6.6945$

$$\text{G.M.} = \text{Anti-log}\left(\frac{\Sigma \log x}{n}\right)$$

$$= \text{Anti-log}\left(\frac{\bar{6}.6945}{6}\right)$$

$$= \text{Anti-log}\left(\bar{1}.11575\right)$$

= **0.1305** **Ans.**

(B) Calculation of G.M. in Discrete Series

When the date is in the form of 'Discrete series' following steps are taken to find out the G.M.

Steps :

1. Find the logarithms of each observation of item, that is, find ($\log x_i$).

2. Multiply these logarithms by corresponding frequencies *i.e.*, $f_i \times \log x_i$.

3. Add these products, $\sum_{i=1}^{n} f_i \log x_i$.

4. Find n by adding all the frequencies (*i.e.*, $n = \Sigma f$).

5. Divide $\sum_{i=1}^{n} f_i \log x_i$ by n.

6. Lastly take Anti-log of the quotient (as obtained in step 5).

Formula :

$$\text{G.M.} = \frac{\text{Anti-log }(\log x_1 \times f_1 + \log x_2 \times f_2 + \log x_3 \times f_3 + \ldots\ldots + \log x_n \times f_n)}{f_1 + f_2 + f_3 + \ldots\ldots\ldots + f_n}$$

$$\text{G.M.} = \text{Anti-log}\left\{\frac{1}{n}\sum_{i=1}^{n} f_i \log x_i\right\} \left\{\frac{\Sigma(f \log x)}{\text{N}}\right\}$$

$$\text{Anti-log}\left\{\frac{1}{\sum_{i=1}^{n} f_i} \sum_{i=1}^{n} f_i \log x_i\right\}$$

***Illustration* 5(A)**

Find the G.M. of 12, 18, 48, 61 whose frequencies are 5, 3, 2, 8 respectively.

Solution :

Calculation of G.M.

x	$\log x_i$	f	$f_i \log x_i$
12	1.0791	5	5.3955
18	1.2552	3	3.7656
48	1.6812	2	3.3624
61	1.7853	8	14.2824
Total	—	$\Sigma f = 18$	$\sum_{i=1}^{n} f_i \log x_i = 26.8059$

$$\text{G.M.} = \text{Anti-log}\left(\frac{\sum_{i=1}^{n} f_1 \log x_1}{\Sigma f_1}\right)$$

$$= \text{Anti-log}\left(\frac{26.8059}{18}\right)$$

$$= \text{Anti-log } 1.4892$$

$$= 30.8460$$

G.M. = **30.8460** **Ans.**

***Illustration* 5(B)**

Write a benefit from Time series Analysis.

[Mock Test Paper (JAC)]

Solution :

Time Series benefit is that, we can understand, interpret, and evaluate changes in the economic conditions of an organisation or a particular country.

(C) Calculation of G.M. in Continuous Series step

Steps :

1. Find out the mid-vlaues of the class-intervals.
2. Find out the logarithms of the mid-values (*i.e.,* log *m*).
3. Multiply the logs (log *m*) with the corresponding class frequencies (*f* × log *m*).
4. Add these products (Σ*f* log *m*).
5. Divide the total products (Σ*f* log *m*) by the total frequencies (Σ*f* log m or *fm*).
6. Take Anti-log of the quotient to obtain G.M.

Symbolically,

Formula :

$$\text{G.M.} = \text{Anti-log}\left(\frac{\Sigma f \log m}{\Sigma f}\right) \text{ or } \left(\frac{\Sigma f \log m}{N}\right)$$

$$\text{or} \quad \text{G.M.} = \text{Antilog}\left\{\frac{1}{N}\sum_{i=1}^{n} f_i \log m_i\right\}$$

$$\text{or} \quad \text{Antilog}\left\{\frac{1}{\sum_{i=1}^{n} f_i}\sum_{i=1}^{n} f_i \log x_i\right\}$$

***Illustration* 6(A)**

Calculate Geometric Mean from the following data :

Class	0—10	10—20	20—30	30—40	40—50
Frequency	4	6	14	8	4

Solution :

Calculation of Geometric Mean

Class	*Mid-value (m)*	*Frequency (f)*	*log m*	*f × log m*
0—10	5	4	0.6989	2.7956
10—20	15	6	1.1760	7.0560
20—30	25	14	1.3979	19.5706
30—40	35	8	1.5440	12.3528
40—50	45	4	1.6532	6.6128
Total		Σ*f* = 36		Σ*f* log *x* = 48.3878

$$\therefore \quad \text{Geometric Mean (G.M.)} = \text{Anti-log}\left(\frac{\Sigma f \log m}{\Sigma f}\right)$$

$$= \text{Anti-log}\left(\frac{48.3887}{36}\right) = 22.08$$

$$= \text{Anti-log}\,(1.3440) = \mathbf{22.08}$$ **Ans.**

***Illustration* 6(B)**

Find the Geometric Mean of the following frequency table :

Wages more than (₹)	90	80	70	60	50	40
Frequency	3	11	28	43	53	65

Solution :

Calculation of Geometric Mean

Wages (₹)	*Frequency (f)*	*Mid-values (m)*	*log m*	*f × log m*
90—100	3	95	1.9777	5.9331
80—90	11 – 3 = 8	85	1.9294	15.4352
70—80	28 – 11 = 17	75	1.8750	31.875
60—70	43 – 28 = 15	65	1.8129	27.193
50—60	53 – 43 = 10	55	1.7403	17.403
40—50	65 – 53 = 12	45	1.6532	19.8384
	Σ*f* = 65			Σ*f* log *m* = 117.677

$$\text{G.M.} = \text{Anti-log}\left[\frac{\Sigma f \log m}{N}\right]$$

$$\text{G.M.} = \text{Anti-log}\left\{\frac{1}{65} \times 117.677\right\}$$

$$\text{G.M.} = \text{Anti-log}\,(1.8104) = 64.63$$

G.M. = **64.63** **Ans.**

(4.3) WEIGHTED GEOMETRIC MEAN

If the different values $x_1, x_2, \ldots, x_n$ of the variable are not of equal importance and they are assigned different weights, say, $W_1, W_2, \ldots, W_n$ respectively according to their degree of importance then their Weighted Geometric Mean, is given by :

$$GM_w = \text{Anti-log}\left\{\frac{\log x_1 \times W_1 + \log x_2 \times W_2 + \ldots + \log x_n \times W_n}{W_1 + W_2 + \ldots + W_n}\right\}$$

$$= \text{Anti-log}\left(\frac{\Sigma \log x \times W}{\Sigma W}\right)$$

Where, GM_w = Weighted Geometric Mean

$x_1, x_2, \ldots, x_n$ = Values of Items

$W_1, W_2, \ldots, W_n$ = Weights corresponding to the size of items

$\Sigma \log x \times W$ = Products of weights and logs of the size of items

ΣW = Total of weights

***Illustration* 7(A)**

From the following data, calculate Weighted Index Number by Geometric Mean :

Group	*Index Number*	*Weight*
Food	125	6
Clothing	133	5
Fuel and Light	140	4
House Rent	175	2
Miscellaneous Expenses	183	3

Solution :

Calculation of the Weighted Index Number

Group	*Index No.* (*x*)	*Weight* (*w*)	(log *x*)	*w* × log *x*
Food	125	6	2.0969	12.5814
Clothing	133	5	2.1238	10.6190
Fuel and Light	140	4	2.1461	8.5844
House Rent	175	2	2.2430	4.4860
Misc. Expenses	183	3	2.2624	6.7873
Total		*n* = 20		Σ *Wx* log *x* = 43.0581

Weighted Geometric Mean (GM_w)

$$= \text{Anti-log}\left(\frac{\Sigma W \log x}{N}\right)$$

$$= \text{Anti-log}\left(\frac{43.0581}{20}\right)$$

$$= \text{Anti-log}\,(2.1529)$$

GM_w = **142.200** **Ans.**

***Illustration* 7(B)**

Calculate the Geometric Mean of the following :

Expenditure (₹)	*Weight* (*W*)
125—129	84
130—134	124
135—139	58
140—144	22
145—149	32

Solution :

Expenditure	*Mid-Values* (*m*)	*Weights*	log *m*	W × log *m*
125—129	127	84	2.1038	176.7192
130—134	132	124	2.1205	262.942
135—139	137	58	2.1376	123.9808
140—144	142	22	2.1522	47.3484
145—149	147	32	2.1673	69.3536
Total		Σ*W*= 320		Σ*Wx* log *m* = 680.344

$$\text{G.M.} = \text{Anti-log}\left(\frac{\Sigma W \log m}{\Sigma W}\right)$$

$$= \text{Anti-log}\left(\frac{680.3446}{320}\right)$$

$$= \text{Antilog}\,(2.1260)$$

G.M. = **133.6595** **Ans.**

(4.4) SPECIAL USES OF G.M.

Use of Geometric Mean in Finding out Rate of Growth : Geometric Mean may be used in finding out Rate of Growth.

The formulae are :

(i) $P_n = P_0(1+r)^n$ or

(ii) $r = \left(\sqrt[n]{\dfrac{P_n}{P_0}} - 1\right)$

Where, P_n = Variable at the end of the period

P_0 = Variable at the beginning

r = Rate of growth per unit

n = Number of years

To Find out Average Growth Rate

***Illustration* 8**

If the price of commodity doubles in a period of 4 years, what is the average percentage increase per year ?

Solution :

Let price of the commodity at the beginning

(P_0) = ₹ 100

Price at the end of 4 years,

$(P_n) = 100 \times 2 = 200$

$r = ?$

$$r = \sqrt[n]{\left(\frac{P_n}{P_0} - 1\right)} = \sqrt[4]{\frac{200}{100}} - 1$$

$$= \text{Anti-log}\left[\frac{\log 2}{4}\right] - 1$$

$$= \text{Anti-log}\left(\frac{0.3010}{4}\right) - 1$$

$= \text{Anti-log}\,(0.07525 - 1)$

$= 1.190 - 1 = 0.19$

$\therefore$ $r =$ **19% (0.19 × 100)** **Ans.**

Illustration 9

The National Income of India has registered increase of 2.6, 1.9, 5.0 and 7.7 percent respectively during the first four years of the third plan. What was the average rate of National Income during this period ?

Solution :

Year	*Rate of Increase*	*National Income (x)*	log *x*
I	2.6%	100 + 2.6 = 102.6	2.011
II	1.9%	100 + 1.9 = 101.9	2.0081
III	5.0%	100 + 5.0 = 105.0	2.0211
IV	7.7%	100 + 7.7 = 107.7	2.032
Total	$n = 4$		S log x = 8.0725

$$\text{G.M.} = \text{Anti-log}\left(\frac{\Sigma \log x}{n}\right)$$

$$= \text{Anti-log}\left(\frac{8.0725}{4}\right)$$

$= \text{Anti-log}\ 2.0181$

$= 104.2557$

Average Rate of Growth $= 104.2557 - 100$

$=$ **4.2577%** **Ans.**

Illustration 10

The rates of increases in population of country during the last three decades are 10%, 20% and 30%. Find the Average Rate of population growth.

Solution :

Calculation of Geometric Mean

Increase in Population	*Population at the end of the decade (x)*	log *x*
10%	100 + 10 = 110	2.0413
20%	100 + 20 = 120	2.0791
30%	100 + 30 = 130	2.1139
$n = 3$		S log x = 6.2343

$$\text{G.M.} = \text{Anti-log}\left(\frac{6.2343}{3}\right)$$

$= \text{Anti-log}\,(2.0781)$

$= 119.701$

$\therefore$ Average Rate of Growth

$= 119.701 - 100$

$=$ **19.701** **Ans.**

Illustration 11

The Geometric Mean of a series of 4 items is 10.2. Find the product of all the items.

Solution :

Product of n items $= \text{Anti-log}\,(\log \text{G.M.} \times n)$

Here, Product of 4 items $= \text{Anti-log}\,(\log 10.2 \times 4)$

$= \text{Anti-log}\,(1.0086 \times 4)$

$= \text{Anti-log}\,(4.0344)$

$=$ **10824.3044** **Ans.**

Illustration 12

A sum of ₹ 3,000 is invested at 6% p.a. compound interest. Find its amount at the end of 5 years.

Solution :

$P_n = P_0(1 + r)^n$

Given : $P_0 = ₹\,3{,}000$

$$r = \frac{6}{100} = 0.06$$

$n = 5$

$P_n = 3{,}000\,(1 + 0.06)^5$

Taking logs $\log P_n = \log 3{,}000 + 5 \log (1.06)$

$\log P_n = 3.4771 + 5(0.0253)$

$= 3.4771 + 0.1265$

$= 3.6036$

$P_n = \text{Anti-log}\,(3.6036)$

$= 4014.209$

$\therefore$ **P_n or Amount = 4014.209** **Ans.**

To Find out Percentage of Rate of Depreciation

Illustration 13

A machine is assumed to depreciate 40% in value in the first year, 25% in the second year and 10% per annum for the next three year, each percentage being calculted on the diminishing value. What is the average depreciation for the five years ?

Solution :

Year	*Value of the beginning of the year*	*Rate of Depreciation*	*Value at the end of the year (x)*	log *x*
1	100	40	60	1.7781
2	100	25	75	1.8750
3	100	10	90	1.9542
4	100	10	90	1.9542
5	100	10	90	1.9542
$n = 5$				Σ log x = 9.5157

$$\text{G.M.} = \text{Anti-log}\left\{\frac{1}{n}\Sigma \log x\right\}$$

$$= \text{Anti-log}\left\{\frac{1}{5} \times 9.5157\right\}$$

$$\text{G.M.} = \text{Anti-log}\,(1.9301)$$

$$\text{G.M.} = 80.0018$$

∴ Diminishing value of the machine is 80.0018

Hence, the average rate of depreciation

$$= 100 - 80.0018$$

$$= \mathbf{19.99\%}$$ **Ans.**

***Illustration* 14**

In a town the growth of population was 5% during each of the first three decades, 15% during each of the next two decades and 25% in the last decade. Find the "Average Rate" of increase per decade.

Solution :

Population (x)	*Weight* (W)	log x	W × log x
100 + 5 = 105	3	2.0211	6.0633
100 + 15 = 115	2	2.0606	4.1212
100 + 25 = 125	1	2.0969	2.0969
Total	ΣW = 6		ΣWlog x = 12.2814

$$\text{G.M.} = \text{Anti-log}\left(\frac{\Sigma W \log xW}{\Sigma W}\right)$$

$$= \text{Anti-log}\left(\frac{12.2814}{6}\right)$$

$$= \text{Anti-log}\,(2.0469)$$

$$\text{G.M.} = 111.4037$$

Thus, Average Increase = 111.4037 − 100

$$= \mathbf{11.4037\%}$$ **Ans.**

(4.5) COMBINED GEOMETRIC MEAN

Formula :

$$\text{Combined G.M.} = \text{Anti-log}\left[\frac{n_1 \log G_1 + n_2 \log G_2 + ...}{n_1 + n_2 + ...}\right]$$

***Illustration* 15**

There are two sets of 2 figures each and their Geometric Means are 15 and 12. Find the combined Geometric Mean.

Solution :

Given $n_1 = 2,\ n_2 = 2$

$G_1 = 15,\ G_2 = 12$

$$\text{Combined G.M.} = \text{A.L.}\left[\frac{n_1 \log G_1 + n_2 \log G_2}{n_1 + n_2}\right]$$

$$= \text{A.L.}\left[\frac{(2 \log 15) + (2 \log 12)}{2+2}\right]$$

$$= \left[\frac{(2 \times 1.1760) + 2(1.0791)}{4}\right]$$

$$= \left[\frac{2.3520 + 2.1582}{4}\right]$$

$$\text{Combined G.M.} = \left[\frac{4.5102}{4}\right] = 1.1275$$

Combined G.M. = **13.4121** **Ans.**

(4.6) PROPERTIES OF GEOMETRIC MEAN

1. Unlike A.M., G.M. is not affected much by the presence of extermely small or extermely large observations.

2. It is suitable for further mathematical treatment.

3. It is not much affected by the fluctuations of sampling. It gives comparatively more weight to smaller items.

4. It has the property that taking its nth power (that is multiplying together n numbers all equal to the G.M.) gives the same result as multiplying together all of the original observations. If G.M. is placed in place of each value, there will be no difference in the product of the values. For example, the G.M. of 2,4, 8, 16 and 32 is 8 and 2 × 4 × 8 × 16 × 32 = 32,768 = 8 × 8 × 8 × 8 × 8.

5. The sum of deviations of logs of the values from the log of the G.M. is equal to zero.

6. The product of the ratios of the values less than or equal to G.M. to the G.M. is equal to the ratios of the values greater than G.M. to the G.M. :

$$\frac{GM}{X \le GM} \times \frac{GM}{X \le GM} = \frac{X > GM}{GM} \times \frac{X > GM}{GM}$$

where GM = Geometric Mean

$X < GM$ = Value less than geometric mean

$X > GM$ = Value greater than geometric mean

X_m = Value

(4.7) MERITS OF GEOMETRIC MEAN

(i) It is less affected by extreme items.

(ii) It is based on all the observations.

(iii) It is capable of further algebraic treatment.

(iv) It is more balanced than the Arithmetic Mean.

(v) It is an average most suitable when large weights have to be given to a small items and small weight to large items.

(vi) The geometric mean is rigidly defined.

(4.8) DEMERITS OF GEOMETRIC MEAN

(i) It is neither easy to calculate nor simple to understand.

(ii) If any value in a series is zero then geometric mean would also be zero.

(iii) It becomes an imaginary vlaue if any one of the observation is negative.

(iv) The geometric mean may be a figure which is not there in the series.

(v) The property of giving more weight to smaller items may, in some cases, prove to be a drawback of the geometric mean.

(4.9) USES OF GEOMETRIC MEAN

(i) G.M. is specially suitable in averaging rates, percentages and rates of increase between two periods.

(ii) Geometric Mean is used in the construction of Index Number.

(iii) It is most appropriate average when large observations are to be given less weight.

(iv) It is also appropriate when some of the observations are too small and/or too large.

THEORETICAL QUESTIONS

Long Answer Type Question

1. Define Geometric Mean and discuss its merits and demerits.

Short/Very Short Answer Type Questions

1. State the properties of Geometric Mean.
2. Explain merits of Geometric Mean. *(JAC, 2026)*
3. Explain demerits of Geometric Mean.
4. Explain claculation process of Geometric Mean.
5. State any three merits and two demerits of Geometric Mean.

PRACTICAL QUESTIONS

Short Answer Type Questions

Individual Series

1. Find out geometric mean of 3, 8 and 9.
   [Ans. 6]
2. Find geometric mean of 20, 40 and 80 without using log table. *(JAC, 2023, 24, 25)*
   [Ans. 40]
3. What will be the geometric mean of 20, 50, 27 and 30 without using log table? *(JAC, 2026)*
   [Ans. GM = 30]

Long Answer Type Questions

Individual Series

1. Calculate the geometric mean of 3, 6, 24 and 48.
   [Ans. 11.999]
2. Find out geometric mean from the following weight of 5 persons in Ibs. :
   100, 120, 85, 140, 110.
   [Ans. 109.44]
3. Compute the geometric mean for the following data :
   10, 37, 50, 52, 60, 80, 110, 120
   [Ans. G.M. 52.86]
4. From the following table, find out the geometric mean :
   (A) 2574, 475, 75, 5, 0.8, 0.08, 0.005, 0.0009
   [Ans. G.M. 1.841]
   (B) 2574, 475, 75, 5, 0.8, 0.08, 0.005, 0.009
   [Ans. 2.455]
5. Monthly incomes of 8 families are ₹ 240, 500, 180, 250, 120, 1,400, 7,000, 360. Calculate the geometric mean.
   [Ans. 467.51]
6. Find the Geometric Mean of the following numbers correct to two decimal place :
   (i) 90, 25, $\frac{125}{3}$, 81
   [Ans. G.M. 52.49]
   (ii) 125, $\frac{700}{3}$, 450, 87
   [Ans. G.M. 183.82]
7. From the following data, find geometric mean :
   (A) 6.5, 169.0, 130, 75, 10, 45, 5, 0.5, 0.4, 500.
   [Ans. G.M. 17.30]
   (B) 125, 130, 75, 10, 45, 5, 0.5, 0.4, 0.500, 150
   [Ans. 22.982]
8. Calculate the geometric mean of the following series :
   173, 182, 75, 5, 0.8, 0.08, 0.8974
   [Ans. G.M. = 6.80]
9. Calculate the goemetric mean of the following series :
   25.74, 475, 75, 0.8, 0.08, 0.005, 0.0009.
   [Ans. G.M. = 0.8268]

Discrete Series

10. Find the goemetric mean from the following data :

Size	10	11	12	13	14	15	16
Frequency	2	4	5	3	3	2	1

[Ans. G.M. = 12.44]

11. Find out geometric mean from the following data :

Marks	10	15	25	40	50
No. of Students	4	6	10	7	3

[Ans. G.M. 23.88]

12. Calculate the geometric mean for the following :

x	12	13	14	15	16	17
f	5	4	4	3	2	1

[Ans. G.M. = 13.70]

Continuous Series

13. Compute geometric mean of the following series :

Marks	0—10	10—20	20—30	30—40	40—50
No. of Students	5	7	15	25	8

[Ans. G.M. = 25.62]

14. Calculate the geometric mean from the following distribution :

Marks	0—10	10—20	20—30	30—40	40—50
No. of Students	3	4	6	3	2

[Ans. 19.23]

15. Find the geometric mean of the following distribution :

Marks	0—10	10—20	20—30	30—40
No. of Students	5	8	3	4

[Ans. 14.57]

16. Calculate geometric mean of the following data :

Size	0—10	10—20	20—30	30—40	40—50
Weight	4	5	6	3	2

[**Ans.** Gm = 17.780]

Weighted Geometric Mean

17. Find weighted geometric mean from the follwoing data :

Group	Index No.	Weight
Food	125	7
Clothing	133	5
Fuel & Lighting	141	4
Rent	173	1
Miscellaneous Exp.	182	3

[**Ans.** Gm_w = 139.82]

18. Find the weighted geometric mean of the numbers 20, 18, 12 and 4 if their weights are 1, 3, 4 and 2 respectively.
[**Ans.** Gm_w = 11.44]

Arithmetic Mean and Geometric Mean

19. The daily incomes of 5 labourers are ₹ 150, 140, 165, 170 and 180. Calculate the Arithmetic Mean and the Geometric Mean.
[**Ans.** $\overline{X}$ = ₹ 160.36; G.M. = 160.36]

Special Uses of Geometric Mean

20. The population of a country increased by 20% in the first decade, 30% in the second and 45% in the third decade. Find the average rate of increase per decade in the population.
[**Ans.** Average Increase 31.28%]

21. The population of a town increased from 1,00,000 to 1,20,000 in a decade. What is the annual rate of increase ? Is it 2% ?
[**Ans.** 1.8%, It is approximately 2%]

Combined G.M.

22. The geometric mean of 10 items is 8 and of another 5 itmes geometric mean is 27. Find out combined Geometric Mean.
[**Ans.** Combined G.M. = 12]

Miscellaneous Problems

23. Find the geometric mean of the following frequency distribution :

Wages (₹)	Frequency
40—50	12
50—60	10
60—70	15
70—80	17
80—90	8
90—100	3

[**Ans.** 64.62]

24. Calculate geometric mean from the following table :

Marks more than	No. of Students
70	7
60	18
50	40
40	40
30	63
20	70

[**Ans.** 46.34]

25. Calculate geometric mean from the following data :

Size	Frequency
10	2
11	3
12	5
13	4
14	3
15	1

[**Ans.** 12.25%]

26. The annual rates of growth of output of a factory in 5 years are 5%, 7.5%, 2.5%, 5% and 10%, What is the compound rate of growth of output per annum for the period ?
[**Ans.** 5.94%]

27. In a factory indirect expenses went up 20% in the first year, 15% in the second year and 40% in the third year. Find out the average rate of increase per annum.
[**Ans.** Rate of Growth = 24.53%]

28. A machine is assumed to depreciate at the rate of 35.5% p.a. in value in the first year, @ 22.5% p.a. in the second year and @ 9.5% p.a. in the third year. Each percentage being computed on the diminishing value. What is the average percentage of depreciation for the three years ?
[**Ans.** Average Rate of Depreciation = 23.25%]

29. Calculate the G.M. of the following series :

Marks	No. of Students
0—10	5
10—20	7
20—30	15
30—40	25
40—50	8

[**Ans.** 49.02]

OBJECTIVE TYPE QUESTIONS

I. Multiple Choice Questions

1. The G.M. of two numbers 4 and 16 shall be : (*JAC*, 2016, 17, 19)
(a) 8 (b) 10 (c) 9 (d) 12

2. GM is *n*th root of sum of *n* terms : (*JAC*, 2015)
(a) True (b) False

3. G.M. of *a* and *b* is : (*JAC*, 2015)
(a) $\frac{a+b}{2}$ (b) ab^2 (c) $\sqrt{ab}$ (d) None

4. GM is the geometric mean of AM and HM. Is it true ?
(a) Yes (b) No

5. The GM of two numbers 4 and 9 will be : (*JAC*, 2015)
(a) 4 (b) 9 (c) 6 (d) 8

6. The GM of two numbers 8 and 18 will be :
(a) 12 (b) 13 (c) 15 (d) 11.09

7. GM of the series 3, 9, 27 is : (JAC, 2020)
(a) 7 (b) 9 (c) 5 (d) 8

8. The G.M. is used in case of :
(a) Drope in average rate (b) Average rate increase
(c) Mean of percentage (d) All of these

9. The G.M. of 'n' observation :
(a) Square root of the product of observations
(b) n^{th} root of the product of observations
(c) Cube root of the product of observations
(d) None of these

10. The G.M. of the observation 6 and – 6 is :
(a) 36 (b) –36
(c) 0 (d) None of these

11. The G.M. of 1, 5 and 25 is :
(a) 25 (b) 15 (c) 5 (d) 125

12. Which of the following measures of the central tendency is difficult to compute ? (JAC, 2023, 24)
(a) Mean (b) Median (c) G.M. (d) Mode

13. Geometric mean of 25 and 100 is : (JAC, 2025)
(a) 5 (b) 50 (c) 500 (d) 10

14. Geometric mean of a and b is : (JAC, 2025)
(a) $\frac{a+b}{2}$ (b) $\frac{2ab}{a+b}$ (c) $\sqrt{ab}$
(d) none of these

15. If mode is 36 and median is 32 then mean is : (JAC, 2025)
(a) 31 (b) 32
(c) 30 (d) 35

16. The geometric mean of 3 and 75 is : (JAC, 2026)
(a) 15 (b) 20
(c) 25 (d) 30

[Ans. 1. (a), 2. (b), 3. (c), 4. (b), 5. (c), 6. (a), 7. (b), 8. (d), 9. (b), 10. (d), 11. (c), 12. (c), 13. (b), 14. (c), 15. (c), 16. (a).]

II. Fill in the Blanks :

1. Geometric mean of 5 and 20 is ....
2. The formula of geometric mean is........
3. Geometric mean is a .... average of central tendency.
4. For the average rate of growth of population, the suitable average is ....
5. If AM and GM of two numbers 15 and 9 respecrtively, then numbers are.......

[Ans. 1. 10; 2. G.M. = $(x_1 \times x_2 \times \ldots. x_n)^{\frac{1}{n}}$ or Anti-log $\left(\frac{\sum_{i=1}^{n} \log x_i}{n}\right)$; 3. mathematical, 4. geometric mean, 5. 3 and 27.]

5

HARMONIC MEAN

LEARNING OBJECTIVES

After studying this chapter, you will be able to know :

- **5.1 Meaning of Harmonic Mean**
- **5.2 Computation of Simple Harmonic Mean :**
  - **Calculation of H.M. in Individual Series**
  - **Calculation of H.M. in Discrete Series**
  - **Calculation of H.M. in Continuous Series or Grouped Series**
- **5.3 Weighted Harmonic Mean**
- **5.4 Merits of Harmonic Mean**
- **5.5 Demerits of Harmonic Mean**
- **5.6 Relationship among A.M., G.M., and H.M.**
- **5.7 Uses of Harmonic Mean**
- **5.8 Formulae of G.M. and H.M. At a Glance**
- **Theoretical Questions : Long Answer Questions, Short Answer Questions, Very Short Answer Questions**
- **Practical Problems**

ILLUSTRATIONS AND PRACTICAL PROBLEMS : AT A GLANCE

No. of Illustration		*No. of Problems*
1 to 3(B)	Calculation of Harmonic Mean in Individual Series	1 to 7
	Short Answer Type Question, Long Answer Type Questions	1 to 2
4	Calculation of Harmonic Mean in Discrete Series	3 to 6
5(A) & 5(B)	Calculation of H.M. in Continuous Series	7
6	Weighted Harmonic Mean	8
7 to 14 (A)	Special Uses of H.M.	
–	G.M. and H.M.	9 to 13
—	A.M., G.M., & H.M.	14(A) to (C)
15 to 22	Relationship among A.M., G.M., & H.M. Sequence	15 to 17
23, 24	Uses of Harmonic Mean	
	Special uses of H.M.	18 to 26 (C)
24	**Total**	**7 + 26 = 33**

(5.1) MEANING OF HARMONIC MEAN

Harmonic Mean of a series is the reciprocal of the Arithmetic Average of the reciprocal of the values of its various items. In the words of *Dr. B.N. Gupta*, "The Harmonic Mean of a series is the reciprocal of the Arithmetic Mean of the reciprocal of the individual values. In short it is denoted by 'H.M.' or 'H'.

Here the word reciprocal needs to be explained. Reciprocal of any figure is that figure which is obtained by dividing 1 by the given number. For example,

$$\text{Reciprocal of } 3 = \frac{1}{3} = 0.3333$$

$$\text{Reciprocal of } 4 = \frac{1}{4} = 0.25$$

Reciprocal of 5 $= \frac{1}{5} = 0.2$

Reciprocal of 4.50165 $= \frac{1}{4.50165} = 0.2221$

Harmonic Mean is of two types :

1. Simple Harmonic Mean,
2. Weighted Harmonic Mean.

(5.2) COMPUTATION OF SIMPLE HARMONIC MEAN

Calculation of H.M. in Individual Series

Formula : $\text{H.M.} = \dfrac{n}{\frac{1}{x_1}+\frac{1}{x_2}+\frac{1}{x_3}+\ldots+\frac{1}{x_n}}$

or $\text{H.M.} = \dfrac{n}{\sum_{i=1}^{n}\left(\frac{1}{x_i}\right)}$

where H.M. = Harmonic Mean

x_1, x_2, x_3, x_n = Various values in the series

n = Number of Items

H.M. of Individual Series

Steps :

(i) Find out the reciprocals of the observations (*i.e.*, $1/x_i$).

(ii) Add these reciprocals [*i.e.*, $\Sigma(1/x_i)$].

(iii) Now, divide 'n' by $\sum_{i=1}^{n}(1/x_i)$, to obtain H.M. *i.e.*

$$\frac{n}{\sum_{i=1}^{n}\left(\frac{1}{x_i}\right)}$$

H.M. = Reciprocal of $\dfrac{\Sigma(1/x)}{n}$ = Reciprocal of the quotient $\left[i.e., \dfrac{\Sigma\left(\frac{1}{x}\right)}{n}\right]$.

***Illustration* 1**

Find out the Harmonic Mean of the following :

5, 2, 8, 10

Solution :

$$\text{H.M.} = \frac{n}{\frac{1}{x_1}+\frac{1}{x_2}+\frac{1}{x_3}+\frac{1}{x_4}}$$

$$= \frac{4}{\frac{1}{5}+\frac{1}{2}+\frac{1}{8}+\frac{1}{10}}$$

$$= \frac{4}{0.2+0.5+0.125+0.1}$$

$$= \frac{4}{0.925} = \mathbf{4.3243}$$ **Ans.**

***Illustration* 2**

Find out the Harmonic Mean of the following :

1, 1.5, 5, 15, 250, 0.5, 0.05, 0.095, 12450, 0.009

Solution :

Calculation of Harmonic Mean

Value (x)	$1/x$	*Reciprocals*
.0	1/1	1.0000
1.5	1/15	0.6667
5.0	1/5	0.2000
15.0	1/15	0.0667
250.0	1/250	0.0040
0.5	1/0.5	2.0000
0.05	1/0.05	20.0000
0.095	1/.095	10.5263
12450.00	1/12450	0.0008
0.009	1/0.009	111.1111
$n = 10$		Σ Reciprocals = 145.5747

$$\text{H.M.} = \frac{n}{\sum_{i=1}^{n}(1/x_i)}$$

$$= \frac{10}{145.5747}$$

$\therefore$ H.M. = **0.0686** **Ans.**

***Illustration* 3(A)**

Find the Harmonic Mean of the following numbers :

$1, \frac{1}{2}, \frac{1}{3}, \frac{1}{4}$

Solution :

$$\text{H.M.} = \frac{4}{\frac{1}{1}+\frac{1}{\frac{1}{2}}+\frac{1}{\frac{1}{3}}+\frac{1}{\frac{1}{4}}}$$

$$= \frac{4}{1+2+3+4}$$

$$= \frac{4}{10} = \frac{2}{5} = \mathbf{0.4}$$ **Ans.**

***Illustration* 3(B)**

Calculate Harmonic Mean of the following numbers :

32, 35, 36, 58, 61, 73

Solution :

Computation of Harmonic Mean

Value (x)	*Reciprocals* ($1/x$)
32	0.03125
35	0.0285
36	0.0277
58	0.0172
61	0.0163
73	0.0136
$n = 6$	0.13455

$\Sigma(1/x) = 0.13455$

Thus, $\text{H.M.} = \dfrac{n}{\sum_{i=1}^{n}(1/x_i)} = \dfrac{6}{0.13455}$

∴ H.M. = **44.593** **Ans.**

Calculation of H.M. in Discrete Series

Steps :

(i) Find out reciprocal of each observation or item (*i.e.,* 1/x).

(ii) Multiple each reciprocal by corresponding frequency (*i.e.,* 1/x × f).

(iii) Add all the products [(*i.e.,* Σ(f × 1/x)].

(iv) Find the total frequency or N (N = Σf).

(v) Now, divide 'N' by Σ(f × 1/x) to obtain H.M.

$$\text{H.M.} = \frac{\sum_{i=1}^{n} f_i}{\sum_{i=1}^{n}\left(f_i \times \frac{1}{x_i}\right)}$$

Thus, $\text{H.M.} = \dfrac{N}{\Sigma\left(f_i \times \frac{1}{x_i}\right)}$.

Illustration 4

Calculation Harmonic Mean from the following data :

Size	3	5	7	9	Total
Frequency	20	40	30	10	100

Solution :

Calculation of Harmonic Mean

Size (x)	*Frequency (f)*	$(1/x)_i$	$f_i \times 1/x_i$
3	20	0.3333	6.6666
5	40	0.2000	8.0000
7	30	0.1428	4.284
9	10	0.1111	1.1111
Total	N = 100		$\Sigma\left(f \times \frac{1}{x}\right) = 20.0617$

Thus, $\text{H.M.} = \dfrac{N}{\Sigma\left(f \times \frac{1}{x}\right)}$

$= \dfrac{100}{20.0617}$

∴ H.M. = **4.9846** **Ans.**

Calculation of H.M. in Continuous Series or Grouped Series

Steps :

(i) Find the mid-value of each class interval (*i.e., m*).

(ii) Find the reciprocals of all mid-values (*i.e., m*).

(iii) Multiply the reciprocals by corresponding frequency (*i.e., f* × 1/*m*).

(iv) Add the products (*i.e.,* Σf × 1/*m*).

(v) Now, find N = Σf(Sum of all frequencies)

(vi) Now, divide 'N' by $\sum_{i=1}^{n}\left(f \times \frac{1}{m}\right)$ to obtain H.M.

Thus, $\text{H.M.} = \dfrac{N}{\sum_{i=1}^{n}\left(f \times \frac{1}{m}\right)}$.

Illustration 5(A)

Calculate the Harmonic Mean of the following frequency :

Profit per Shop (₹)	*No. of Shops (f)*
0—10	12
10—20	18
20—30	27
30—40	20
40—50	17
50—60	6

Solution :

Calculation of H.M.

Profit per Shop	*Mid-Value* (m_i)	*Frequency* (f_i)	*Reciprocals* $\left(\frac{1}{m_i}\right)$	$f_i \times \frac{1}{m_i}$
0—10	5	12	0.20000	2.40000
10—20	15	18	0.06666	1.1998
20—30	25	27	0.04	1.08000
30—40	35	20	0.02857	0.57140
40—50	45	17	0.02222	0.37774
50—60	55	6	0.01818	0.10908
Total		N = 100		$\Sigma\left(f_i \times \frac{1}{m_i}\right) = 5.738$

Thus, $\text{H.M.} = \dfrac{N}{\Sigma\left(f_i \times \frac{1}{m_i}\right)} = \dfrac{100}{5.738} = 17.4276$

∴ H.M. = **17.4276** **Ans.**

***Illustration* 5(B)**

From the following data, calculate the average output per worker by Harmonic Mean Method :

Output	*No. of Workers*
70—74	3
75—79	5
80—84	15
85—89	12
90—94	7
95—99	6
100—104	2

Solution :

Calculation of Harmonic Mean

Output	*No. of Workers*	*Mid-Values*	*Reciprocal*	$f \times \frac{1}{m}$
70—74	3	72	0.0139	0.0410
75—79	5	77	0.0130	0.065
80—84	15	82	0.0121	0.1815
85—89	12	87	0.0114	0.1368
90—94	7	92	0.0108	0.0756
95—99	6	97	0.0103	0.0618
100—104	2	102	0.0098	0.0196
Total	N = 50			$\Sigma\left(f \times \frac{1}{m}\right)$ = 0.5812

Thus, $\text{H.M.} = \frac{N}{\Sigma f_i\left(\frac{1}{m_i}\right)} = \frac{50}{0.5812}$

H.M. = **86.028** **Ans.**

(5.3) WEIGHTED HARMONIC MEAN

Let $x_1, x_2, ..., x_n$ be the observations with weights $w_1, w_2, ..., w_n$ respectively then Weighted Harmonic Mean (W.H.M. or H_w) is given by

$$HM_w = \frac{\Sigma_w}{\frac{w_1}{x_1} + \frac{w_2}{x_2} + \frac{w_3}{x_3} + ... + \frac{w_n}{x_n}} \quad \text{or} \quad H_w = \frac{\sum_{i=1}^{n} w}{\sum_{i=1}^{n}\left(\frac{w_i}{x_i}\right)}$$

HM_w = Weighted H.M.

w = Weight

$x_1, x_2, x_3, ..., x_n$ = Value of Items

$w_1, w_2, w_3, ..., w_n$ = Weight of items

***Illustration* 6**

Calculate the Weighted Harmonic Mean from the following data :

Items	1.0	0.5	10.0	45.0	174.0	0.01	4.0	11.2
Weight	5	10	20	10	15	2	15	8

Solution :

Calculation of Weighted Harmonic Mean

Item (x)	*Reciprocal* $(1/x_i)$	*Weight* (w_i)	*Weight × Reci.* $(w_i \times 1/x_i)$
1.0	1.0000	5	5.0000
0.5	2.0000	10	20.0000
10.0	0.1000	20	2.0000
45.0	0.0222	10	0.2220
174.0	0.0057	15	0.0855
0.01	100.0000	2	200.0000
4.0	0.2500	15	3.7500
11.2	0.0892	8	0.7136
Total		$\Sigma w_i = 85$	$\Sigma\left(w_i \times \frac{1}{x_i}\right)$ = 231.7711

Thus, $HM_w = \frac{\sum_{i=1}^{n} w_i}{\sum_{i=1}^{n}\left(w_i \times \frac{1}{x_i}\right)}$

$= \frac{85}{231.7711} = 0.3667$

∴ HM_w = **0.3667** **Ans.**

Special Uses of Harmonic Mean

***Illustration* 7**

The interest paid on each of three different sums of money yielding 3%, 4% and 5% simple interest p.a. respectively, is the same. What is the average yield percent on the total sum invested ?

Solution :

$$\text{H.M.} = \frac{3}{\frac{1}{4} + \frac{1}{4} + \frac{1}{5}}$$

$$= \frac{3}{\frac{20 + 15 + 12}{60}}$$

$$= \frac{3}{\frac{47}{60}} = \frac{3 \times 60}{47}$$

$$= \frac{180}{47} = \mathbf{3.829\%}$$ **Ans.**

***Illustration* 8**

A train travels first 300 kilometre at an average rate of 30 km. p.h. and further travels the same distance at an average rate of 40 km. p.h. What is the average speed over the whole distance ?

Solution :

Here, $w_1 = 300$

$w_2 = 300$

Average speed on using

$$\text{H.M.} = \frac{\Sigma w_i}{\Sigma\left(w_i \times \frac{1}{x_i}\right)}$$

$$= \frac{300 + 300}{300 \times \frac{1}{300}} + 300 \times \frac{1}{40}$$

$$= \frac{600}{10 + 7.5} = \frac{600}{17.5} = 34.28$$

Avg. speed = **34.28 km/hour** **Ans.**

***Illustration* 9**

A motorist travels distance 5, 20, 45, 80, 100 kilometre with speed 5, 10, 15, 20, 25 km. per hour. Find the Average Speed.

Solution :

Speed km. / hour (x)	5	10	15	20	25
Distance (km.) (f)	5	20	45	80	100

Required Average is given by

$$\frac{1}{H} = \frac{\Sigma f \times (1/x)}{\Sigma f}$$

$$= \frac{5 \times (1/5) + 20 \times (1/10) + 45 \times (1/15) + 80 \times (1/20) + 100 \times (1/25)}{5 + 20 + 45 + 80 + 100}$$

$$= \frac{14}{250} = \frac{7}{125}$$

∴ Harmonic Mean = 125/7

= **17.86 km/hour** **Ans.**

***Illustration* 10**

A man travels from Hazaribagh to Ranchi at a speed of 30 km. per hour and returns by the same route with a speed of 50 km. per hour. Find the Average Speed for the whole journey.

Solution :

Speed (x)	*Reciprocals (1/x)*
30	0.0333
50	0.0200
$n = 2$	$\sum_{i=1}^{n}(1/x_i) = 0.0533$

Average Speed

$$\text{H.M.} = \frac{n}{\sum_{i=1}^{n}(1/x_i)}$$

$$= \frac{2}{0.0533} = 37.52$$

(Avg. Speed) H.M. = **37.52** **Ans.**

Alternative Method :

$$\text{Average Speed} = \frac{n}{\frac{1}{x_1} + \frac{1}{x_2}}$$

where, $n = 2$

$x_1 = 30, x_2 = 50$

$$= \frac{2}{\frac{1}{30} + \frac{1}{50}} = \frac{2}{\frac{8}{150}} = \frac{2 \times 150}{8}$$

= **37.50 km/hour** **Ans.**

***Illustration* 11**

A cyclist cover his first three km at average speed of 8 km per hour, another two km at 3 km per hour and the last two km at 2 km per hour. Find the average speed for the entire journey.

Solution :

Speed k.p.h. (x)	*Distance (km) (w)*	*Reciprocal of x*	$w_i \times \frac{1}{x_i}$
8	3	0.1250	0.3750
3	2	0.3333	0.6666
2	2	0.5000	1.0000
Total	$\Sigma w = 7$		$\Sigma (w \times 1/x) = 2.0416$

$$\text{Average Speed W.H. M} = \frac{\Sigma w_i}{\Sigma\left(w_i \times \frac{1}{x_i}\right)}$$

$$= \frac{7}{2.0416}$$

= **3.4286 km/hour**

∴ Average Speed = **3.4286 km/hour** **Ans.**

Alternative Method :

Average Speed (W.H.M.)

$$= \frac{\Sigma w}{\frac{1}{x_1}.w_1 + \frac{1}{x_2}.w_2 + \frac{1}{x_3}.w_3}$$

$$= \frac{3 + 2 + 2}{\left(\frac{1}{8} \times 3\right) + \left(\frac{1}{3} \times 2\right) + \left(\frac{1}{2} \times 2\right)}$$

$$= \frac{7}{\left(\frac{3}{8} + \frac{2}{3} + \frac{2}{2}\right)} = \frac{7}{\left(\frac{9 + 16 + 24}{24}\right)} = \frac{7}{\frac{49}{24}}$$

$$= 7 \times \frac{24}{49} = \mathbf{3.428\ km/hour}$$

Hence, Average Speed = 3.428 km/hour

***Illustration* 12**

A man travels first 900 km of his journey by train at an average speed of 80 km per hour, next 2,000 km by plane at an average speed of 300 km per hour and last 20 km by taxi at an average speed of 30 km per hour. What is his average speed for the entire journey ?

Solution :

Calculation of Weighted Harmonic Mean

Speed per hour km (x)	*Distance travelled (w_i)*	$\frac{w_i}{x_i}$
80	900	11.25
300	2000	6.667
30	20	0.666
Total	Σw = 2,920	$\frac{\Sigma w}{x}$ = 18.583

$$H.M_w = \frac{\Sigma w_i}{\Sigma\left(\frac{w_i}{x_i}\right)}$$

$$= \frac{2,920}{18.583} = \mathbf{157.13\ km}$$

or **157.12 km per hour (nearly)**

H.M. = 157.13 km/hr.

Alternatively :

$$\text{Hormonic Mean} = \frac{\Sigma w}{\frac{w_1}{x_1} + \frac{w_2}{x_2} + \frac{w_3}{x_3}}$$

$$= \frac{900 + 2,000 + 20}{\frac{900}{80} + \frac{2,000}{300} + \frac{20}{30}}$$

$$= \frac{2,920}{\frac{223}{12}} = \frac{2,920 \times 12}{223} = \frac{35,040}{223}$$

$= \mathbf{157.13\ km\ /hour}$ **Ans.**

***Illustration* 13**

Ajay can do a work in 4 days, Vijay can do the same work in 5 days and Sanjay in 8 days. If all of them do for equal days, find the average time taken to complete the work.

Solution :

Days (x)	*Reciprocals* $\left(\frac{1}{x_i}\right)$
4	0.2500
5	0.2000
8	0.1250
$n = 3$	$\Sigma(1/x_i) = 0.5750$

$$H.M. = \frac{n}{\Sigma\left(\frac{1}{x_i}\right)} = \frac{3}{0.575}$$

$H.M. = \mathbf{5.217}$ **Ans.**

***Illustration* 14**

A typist types a letter in 5 minute, second in 8 minute and third in 10 minute. What is the average number of letters typed per hour, per typist ?

Solution :

x	*Reciprocals* $\left(\frac{1}{x_i}\right)$
5	0.2000
8	0.1250
10	0.1000
$n = 3$	$\Sigma\left(\frac{1}{x_i}\right) = 0.425$

$$\text{Here,}\quad H.M. = \frac{n}{\Sigma\left(\frac{1}{x_i}\right)}$$

$$= \frac{3}{0.425} = 7.058$$

H.M. = **7.058 per min/paper**

Thus, No. of letters typed/hour per typist

$= \frac{60}{7.058} = \mathbf{8.500}$ **Ans.**

***Illustration* 14 (A)**

A man travels first 500 km of his journey by train at 80 km/hour speed, next 1200 km by plane at a speed of 350 km/hour and last 30 km by car at 40 km/hour speed. What is the average speed for the journey ? (*JAC*, 2018)

Solution :

Let the speed be 'x' km/h and the distance covered is w (km).

The tabular form of the given data will be :

x	W	W/x
80	500	6.25
350	1200	3.42
40	30	0.75
Total	ΣW = 1730	Σ(W/x) = 10.42

$$H.M_W = \frac{\sum W}{\sum\left(\frac{W}{x}\right)} = \frac{1730}{10.42}$$

$H.M_W =$ **166.02 km /hour** **Ans.**

(5.4) MERITS OF HARMONIC MEAN

1. It is rigidly defined.
2. It is based on all the observations.
3. It is capable of further algebraic treatment.
4. It gives greater importance to small items.
5. It is useful in calculating rates and ratios.
6. It is useful in the case of a series having wide Dispersion.

(5.5) DEMERITS OF HARMONIC MEAN

1. It is difficult to calculate and difficult to understand.

2. Harmonic Mean of a series may be a value, which is no item in the series.

3. It is not true representative of the statistical series.

(5.6) RELATIONSHIP AMONG A.M., G.M. & H.M.

(1) In any distribution there would be a difference in the values of Arithmetic Mean (X), Geometric Mean (G.M.) and Harmonic Mean (H.M.). The situation would be that

$$\overline{X} > G.M. > H.M.$$

Which means that Arithmetic Average is greater than Geometric Mean and which is greater than Harmonic Mean.

(2) If all the items in a distribution have the same values, then,

$$\overline{X} = G.M. = H.M.$$

(3) For any two observations

$$G.M. = \sqrt{A.M. \times H.M.}$$

or $$G^2 = (A.M.) \times (H.M.)$$

***Illustration* 15**

A series has two items, *a* and *b*. Find its Arithmetic Mean, Geometric Mean and Harmonic Mean.

Solution :

We know that $\overline{X} = \dfrac{a+b}{2}$

$$G.M. = \sqrt{a.b}$$

$$H.M. = \frac{2}{\frac{1}{a}+\frac{1}{b}}$$ **Ans.**

***Illustration* 16**

Suppose value of two items is 5. Find its Arithmetic Mean, Geometric Mean and Harmonic Mean.

Solution :

We know that $\overline{X} = \dfrac{5+5}{2} = 5$

$$G.M. = \sqrt{5 \times 5} = \mathbf{5}$$

$$H.M. = \frac{2}{1/5 + 1/5}$$

$$= \frac{2}{\frac{2}{5}} = \frac{2 \times 5}{2} = \mathbf{5}$$ **Ans.**

***Illustration* 17**

If Arithmetic Mean of two items is 5 and G.M. is 4, find their H.M. (*JAC*, 2015)

Solution :

Given, $\overline{X} = 5,$

$$G.M. = 4$$

$$H.M. = ?$$

$$\overline{X} \times H.M. = (G.M.)^2$$

$$\Rightarrow \quad 5 \times H.M. = (4)^2$$

or $$5\ H.M. = 16$$

$$\therefore \quad H.M. = \frac{16}{5} = \mathbf{3.2}$$ **Ans.**

***Illustration* 18**

If for a series the arithmetic mean is 36 and the harmonic mean is 4, what is the geometric mean of the series ?

Solution :

We know that $G.M. = \sqrt{\overline{X}.(H.M.)} = \sqrt{36 \times 4}$

$$= \sqrt{144} = 12$$

$$\therefore \quad G.M. = \mathbf{12}$$ **Ans.**

***Illustration* 19**

If G.M. and H.M. of a series are 20 and 10 respectively, find their mean.

Solution :

We know that $G.M. = \sqrt{\overline{X}\,(H.M.)}$

or $$G.M.^2 = \overline{X}\ H.M.$$

$$\therefore \quad \overline{X} = \frac{(G.M.)^2}{H.M.} = \frac{(20)^2}{10}$$

$$= \frac{400}{10} = 40$$

$$\therefore \quad \overline{X} = \mathbf{40}$$ **Ans.**

***Illustration* 20**

Find Arithmetic Mean, Geometric Mean and Harmonic Mean of 2, 4, 8 and state that A.M. > G.M. > H.M.

Solution :

(i) A.M. of 2, 4, 8 : $\overline{X} = \dfrac{2+4+8}{3}$

$$= \frac{14}{3} = \mathbf{4.6}$$

(ii) G.M. of 2, 4, 8 : $G.M. = (2 \times 4 \times 8)^{1/3}$

$$= (64)^{1/3} = (4^3)^{1/3} = 4$$

(iii) H.M. of 2, 4, 8 : $H.M. = \dfrac{3}{\left(\frac{1}{2}+\frac{1}{4}+\frac{1}{8}\right)}$

$$= \frac{3}{\frac{7}{8}} = \frac{24}{7} = \mathbf{3.428}$$

From A.M. (4.6), G.M. (4) and H.M. (3.428)

Thus, A.M. > G.M. > H.M. Verified

4.6 > 4 > 3.428 **Ans.**

***Illustration* 21**

(i) If Arithmetic Mean and Geometric Mean of two values are 10 and 8 respectively, Find its Harmonic Mean.

(ii) If Mean of two items is 90 and their H.M. is 10, find out their G.M.

(iii) If G.M. and H.M. of two values are 12 and 9 respectively, find out their Mean.

Solution :

Let a & b be 2 values

(i) Given, A.M. $(\overline{X}) = 10$

G.M. = 8

H.M. = ?

Thus, $a + b = 20$ ∴

$ab = 64$

$\overline{X} \times \text{H.M.} = (\text{GM})^2$

$10 \times \text{H.M.} = (8)^2$

or $10 \times \text{H.M.} = 64$

∴ $\text{H.M.} = \frac{64}{10} = \mathbf{6.4}$

(ii) Given $\overline{X} = 90$ & H.M. = 10,

G.M. = ?

$\text{G.M.} = \sqrt{(\overline{X}).(\text{H.M.})}$

$= \sqrt{90 \times 10} = \sqrt{900} = \mathbf{30}$

(iii) Given, G.M. = 12

H.M. = 9

A.M. $(\overline{X})$ = ?

We know that, $\text{G.M.} = \sqrt{\overline{X}.(\text{H.M.})}$

or $(\text{G.M.})^2 = \overline{X}.(\text{H.M.})$

∴ $\overline{X} = \frac{(\text{G.M.})^2}{\text{H.M.}} = \frac{(12)^{12}}{9}$

$= \frac{144}{9} = 16$

Hence, Mean = **16** **Ans.**

Illustration 22

If Arithmetic Mean and Geometric Mean of two values are 50 and 48 respectively, find (a) Harmonic Mean, and (b) their values.

Solution :

(a) Given, $\overline{X} = 50$ & G.M. = 48,

H.M. = ?

Thus, $\overline{X} \times \text{H.M.} = (\text{G.M.})^2$

or $(50 \times \text{H.M.}) = (48)^2 = 2304$

∴ Therefore $\text{H.M.} = \frac{2304}{50} = \mathbf{46.08}$ **Ans.**

(b) Assumed that both items are x and y

Then, $\overline{X} = \frac{x + y}{2} = 50$

∴ $x + y = 50 \times 2 = 100$ ...(1)

and $\text{G.M.} = \sqrt{xy} = 48$

∴ $xy = (48)^2 = 2304$ ...(2)

Using algrebraic formula :

$(x + y)^2 - 4xy = (x - y)^2$

Now on using (1) & (2) relation, we get

or $(100)^2 - (4 \times 2304) = (x - y)^2$

or $10{,}000 - 9{,}216 = (x - y)^2$

or $734 = (x - y)^2$

∴ $x - y = \sqrt{784} = 28$ ...(3)

Now, $x + y = 100$ ...(1)

$x - y = 25$ ...(3)

By adding equation (1) and (3), we get

$2x = 128$

∴ $x = \frac{128}{2} = \mathbf{64}$

and $y = 100 - 64 = \mathbf{36}$

Hence, values are **64 & 36** **Ans.**

(5.7) USES OF HARMONIC MEAN

1. Harmonic Mean is better in the calculation of average speed, average price etc.
2. It is useful in the case of series having wide Dispersion.
3. When it is desired to give the largest weight to the smallest item, this average is used.

Illustration 23

Which of the averages will be most suitable in the following conditions and why ?

(i) Average size of oranges on a tree. (ii) Per capita consumption of food in a family consisting of children, women and men. (iii) Average intelligence of students in a factory. (iv) Average size of ready-made garments. (v) Average production for shift in a facatory. (vi) Average height and weight of students. (vii) Average marks obtained by a student in an examination. (viii) Average number of children in a family. (ix) Average size of a coller. (x) Average income of an advocate.

Solution :

(i) **Mode :** For calculating average size of oranges on a tree mode is considered more suitable.

(ii) **A.M. :** For calculating per capita consumption of food, weighted arithmetic mean is used because children, women and mean consume food in different quantities.

(iii) **Median :** For determining average intelligence of students median is considered more suitable because intelligence is a qualitative fact.

(iv) **Mode :** For determining average size of ready-made garments more is used because the graments used by most of the people are kept for sale.

(v) **A.M. :** For determining average production per shift arithmetic mean is the most suitable because there is no much variation in the output made by the workers.

(vi) **A.M. :** For calculating average height and weight of students arithmetic mean is most suitable because there being no much differences in the height and weight of students.

(vii) **A. M. :** For calculating average marks obtained by a student arithmetic mean is most suitable.

(viii) **Mode :** By average number of children in a family we mean number of children in most of the families. Hence, mode will be most suitable.

(ix) **Mode :** For determining average size of coller mode is most suitable.

(x) **A.M. :** For measuring average income of an advocate arithmetic mean is most suitable.

***Illustration* 24**

Which of the average will be most suitable in the following conditions and why :

(i) Average rate of growth of population per decade.

(ii) An average speed of a car driver who drives the car at different speeds to different periods.

Solution :

(i) **G.M. :** Population growth in geometric progression. So geometric mean is used to calculate average rate of growth of population.

(ii) **H.M. :** For determining average speed of a car driver, harmonic mean is used because car is drived at different speed in different periods.

(5.8) FORMULAE OF G.M. AND H.M. : AT A GLANCE

Series	*G.M.*	*H.M.*
1. Individual	$= \text{A.L.}\left[\frac{\Sigma \log X}{n}\right]$	$= \text{Reci.}\left[\frac{\Sigma \text{ Reci.X}}{n}\right]$
2. Discrete	$= \text{A.L.}\left[\frac{\Sigma f \log X}{N}\right]$	$= \text{Reci.}\left[\frac{\Sigma f \text{ Reci. X}}{N}\right]$
3. Continuous	$= \text{A.L.}\left[\frac{\Sigma f \log m}{N}\right]$	$= \text{Reci.}\left[\frac{f \text{ Reci. X}}{N}\right]$
4. Weighted	$= \text{A.L.}\left[\frac{\Sigma w \log X}{\Sigma w}\right]$	$= \text{Reci.}\left[\frac{\Sigma w \text{ Reci. X}}{\Sigma w}\right]$
5. Average Rate of Growth	$P_n = P_0\left(1+\frac{r}{100}\right)^n$ $\frac{r}{100} = \sqrt[n]{\frac{P_n}{P_0}} - 1$ $\Rightarrow \frac{r}{100} = \text{Anti-log}\left[\frac{\log P_n - \log P_0}{n}\right] - 1$	

THEORETICAL QUESTIONS

Long Answer Type Questions

1. Define Harmonic Mean and discuss its merits and demerits.
2. Explain the meaning of Harmonic Mean. Give examples where it is more appropriate than the Arithmetic Mean.

Short/Very Short Answer Type Questions

1. What is Harmonic Mean ?
2. State the characteristics of Harmonic Mean.
3. State the merits and demerits of Harmonic Mean.
4. Explain special uses of Harmonic Mean with example.
5. Explain the relationship between Arithmetic Mean, Geometric Mean and Harmonic Mean.
6. Prove that : A.M. ≥ G.M. ≥ H.M.
7. Define Harmonic Mean and give its formula of calculation.
8. Define Arithmetic Mean, Geometric Mean and Harmonic Mean.
9. State and prove the relation between A.M., G.M. and H.M.

PRACTICAL QUESTIONS

Short Answer Type Numerical Questions

1. Find out harmonic mean of 5 and 15. (*JAC*, 2019)
[**Ans.** 7.5]
2. Find out harmonic mean of 3, 5 and 8.
[**Ans.** 4.58]
3. If arithmetic average is 5 and geometric mean is 4, find the Harmonic Mean.
[**Ans.** 3.2]
4. If mean of two item values is 16 and H.M. is 9, find out their G.M.
[**Ans.** 12]
5. Calculate H.M. from the following data :
6, 10, 15 and 20.
[**Ans.** 10.43]
6. Calculate the H.M. of the following :
2, 4, 7, 12, 19
[**Ans.** 4.86]
7. Find the H.M. of 2, 5 and 10 : (*JAC*, 2025)
[**Ans.** 3.75]

Long Answer Type Numerical Questions

Harmonic Mean

Individual Series

1. Calculate the harmonic mean of the following items :
6, 10, 15 and 20
[**Ans.** 10.42]
2. Find out the harmonic mean of the following :
2, 5, 6, 10
[**Ans.** 4.1]

Discrete Series

3. Calculate the harmonic mean :

Age in years	50	51	52	53	54	55
No. of Persons	2	4	10	6	2	2

[**Ans.** 52.29]

4. Find Harmonic mean of 3, 6, 12, 24 whose weights are 6, 2, 4, 8 respectively.

[**Ans.** $6\frac{2}{3}$]

5. Compute the Harmonic Mean of the following data :

Marks Obtained	20	21	22	23	24	25
No. of Students	4	2	7	1	3	1

[**Ans.** 21.95]

6. Obtain the Harmonic Mean from the following data :

Marks	10	20	30	40	50
No. of Persons	4	5	8	2	1

[**Ans.** 20.33]

Continuous Series

7. Calculate harmonic mean :

Marks	*No. of Students*
0—10	4
10—20	5
20—30	11
30—40	6
40—50	4

[**Ans.** 16.13]

Weighted Harmonic Mean

8. Find weighted harmonic mean :

Size	40	50	120	150	110
Weighted	10	6	4	2	3

[**Ans.** W.H. M. = 56.43]

G.M. & H.M.

9. Find the geometric mean and harmonic mean of the numbers 1, 9, 81.

[**Ans.** G.M. = 9, H.M. = 2.670]

10. Find out G.M. and H.M. from the following series :

5, 15, 25, 50

[**Ans.** G.M. = 17.5, H. M. = 12.23]

11. Find out G.M. and H.M. from the following series :

100, 700, 500, 750, 80, 250, 180, 420

[**Ans.** G.M. = 281.7, H.M. = 204.1]

12. Calculate Geometric Mean and Harmonic Mean of the following item values :

70, 15, 75, 85, 500

[**Ans.** G.M. = 80.34, H.M. = 46.25]

13. Calculate Geometric Mean and Harmonic Mean from the following figures :

x	68	210	460	570
f	3	4	1	2

[**Ans.** G.M. = 197.7, H.M. = 144.72]

A.M., G.M. and H.M.

14. (A) Calculate the Arithmetic Mean, Geometric Mean and Harmonic Mean of the numbers 3, 6, 24 and 48.

[**Ans.** $\bar{X}$ = 20.25, H.M. = 7.11, G.M. = 12]

(B) If $2v = x$ and the harmonic mean of x is 4, find the harmonic mean of v.

[**Ans.** H.M. = 2]

(C) If for a series the arithmetic mean is 25 and the harmonic mean is 9, what is the geometric mean of the series ?

[**Ans.** G.M. = 15]

Relationship among A.M. G.M. and H.M.

15. Taking three numbers 2, 4, 8 explain the relationship between A.M., G.M., and H.M.

[**Ans.** $\bar{X}$ = 4.67, G.M. = 4, H.M. = 3.43]

16. If the arithmetic mean of two numbers is 25 and their geometric mean is 20, find their harmonic mean.

[**Ans.** H.M. = 16]

17. With the help of the two simple figures 2 and 8, explain the relationship between the arithmetic, geometric and harmonic mean.

[**Ans.** $\bar{X}$ = 5, G.M. = 4, H.M.= 3.2]
[$\bar{X}$ > G.M. > H.M., $\bar{X}$ H.M. = G.M.^{2}]

Special Uses of H.M.

18. A train runs 25 km at a speed of 30 km p.h., another 50 km at a speed of 40 km p.h., then due to repair of the track travels for 6 minute at a speed of 10 km p.h. and finally covers the remining distance of 24 km at a speed of 24 km p.h. What is the average speed in km per hour ?

[**Ans.** 31.4 km p.h.]

19. The population of India was 43.9 crore in 1961 which became 68 crore in 1981. Calculate the annual compound percentage of increase.

[**Ans.** 2.2%]

20. You can take a trip which entails travelling 900 km by train at an average speed of 60 km per hour, 300 km by boat at an average of 25 km per hour, 400 km by aeroplane at 350 km per hour and finally 15 km by taxi at 25 km per hour. What is your average speed for the entire distance ?

[**Ans.** 56.19 km per hour]

21. A person travels from Patna to Ranchi at an average speed of 30 km. per hour and returns along the same route at an average speed of 60 km per hour. Find the average speed for the entire trip.

[**Ans.** H.M. = 40 km per hour.]

22. A aeroplane covers the four sides of a square at a speed of 100, 200, 300 400 km p.h. What is the average speed of the aeroplane ?

[**Ans.** 192 km p.h.]

23. A distance of 100 km is covered by a man as follows :

(i) 80 km in a car at a speed of 40 km per hour

(ii) 15 km on a cycle at a speed of 20 km per hour

(iii) 5 km on foot at a speed of 5 km per hour

What was his average speed ?

[**Ans.** H.M. = 26.66 km per hour.]

24. An investor buys ₹ 1,500 worth of shares in a company each month. During the first four months he bought the shares at a price of ₹ 10, ₹ 15, ₹ 20 and ₹ 30 per share. What is the average price paid for the shares bought during these four months ?

[Ans. ₹ 16 per share.]

25. Find out the H.M. of the following :

Value :	1	1.5	5	15	250	0.5	0.009

[Ans. 0.0608]

26. (a) If mean of two item values is 16 and their H.M. is 9, find out their G.M.

(b) If G.M. and H.M. of two values are 12 and 9 respectively, find out their Mean.

(c) If Mean and G.M. of two values are 10 and 8 respectively, find out their H.M.

[Ans. (a) G.M. = 12, (b) $\overline{X} = 16$, (c) H.M = 6.4]

OBJECTIVE TYPE QUESTIONS

I. Multiple Choice Questions

1. Which of the following relationship is correct ? (*JAC,* 2016, 19, 24)

(a) A.M. = $\sqrt{\text{G.M.} \times \text{H.M.}}$ (b) H.M. = $\sqrt{\text{A.M.} \times \text{G.M.}}$

(c) G.M. = $\sqrt{\text{A.M.} \times \text{H.M.}}$ (d) G.M. = $\dfrac{\text{A.M.} + \text{H.M.}}{2}$

2. In the case of unequal size of items : (*JAC,* 2024)

(a) $\overline{X}$ < G.M. < H.M. (b) $\overline{X}$ > G.M. > H.M.

(c) $\overline{X}$ = G.M. = H.M. (d) None of these

3. Average speed can be calculated by : (*JAC,* 2020)

(a) $\overline{X}$ (b) G.M.

(c) H.M. (d) None of these

4. Which of the following fromula is used to calculate the G.M. in an individual series ?

(a) $\log\left[\dfrac{\Sigma \text{ Antilog X}}{\text{N}}\right]$ (b) $\text{Antilog}\left(\dfrac{\Sigma \log \text{X}}{\text{N}}\right)$

(c) $\left(\dfrac{\Sigma \log \text{X}}{\text{N}}\right)$ (d) $\left(\dfrac{\Sigma \text{ Antilog X}}{\text{N}}\right)$

5. The Geometric Mean of two numbers 8 and 18 shall be :

(a) 12 (b) 13 (c) 15 (d) 11.09

6. In a series $\overline{X}$ = G.M. = H.M. is possible only all values of the series are :

(a) Increasing (b) Decreasing

(c) Equal (d) None of these

7. Which of the following is not a mathematical average ?

(a) Geometric Mean (b) Harmonic Mean

(c) Moving Average (d) Quadratic Mean

8. Harmonic mean of 10 and 15 is : (*JAC,* 2025)

(a) 10 (b) 15 (c) 5 (d) 12

9. If the A.M. and H. M. of two numbers are 5 and 3.2 respectively then Geometric Mean will be :

(a) 4.05 (b) 16 (c) 4 (d) 4.10

10. The geometric mean of 4 and 9 is : (*JAC,* 2015)

(a) 6.5 (b) 9.0

(c) 5.5 (d) None of these

11. The G.M. of two numbers 4 and 16 shall be : (*JAC,* 2017)

(a) 8 (b) 10 (c) 9 (d) 12

12. HM of 5, 2, 8, 10 is : (*JAC,* 2018)

(a) 5.32 (b) 4.32 (c) 4 (d) 5

13. HM of 5 and 15 is : (*JAC,* 2019, 26)

(a) 7 (b) 7.2 (c) 7.5 (d) 7.8

14. Harmonic mean is defined when no observation is : (*JAC,* 2023)

(a) 3 (b) 2 (c) 1 (d) 0

15. If A. M. is 2 and G. M. is 4, then H.M. is : (*JAC,* 2023)

(a) 2 (b) 4 (c) 6 (d) 8

16. When no observation is there HM is defined as (*JAC,* 2024)

(a) 3 (b) 2 (c) 1 (d) 0

[Ans. 1. (c), 2. (b), 3. (c), 4. (b), 5. (a), 6. (d), 7. (c), 8. (d), 9. (d), 10. (d), 11. (a), 12. (b), 13. (c), 14. (d), 15. (d), 16. (d).]

II. State whether the following statements are 'True or False' :

1. Geometric Mean measures the relative rate of change in the value of variable over a period.
2. The Harmonic Mean is useful when data are given in the form of rates.
3. Harmonic mean is the reciprocal of arithmetic mean.
4. Geometric Mean is based on all the observations.
5. Geometric Mean is most affected by the extreme values.
6. Generally Arithmetic Mean is the greatest, Geometric Mean is smaller than A.M. and Harmonic Mean is smaller than both.

$\overline{X} = \geq \text{G.M.} \geq \text{H.M.}$

7. Geometric mean is the *n*th root of the sum of *n* items.
8. Geometric mean gives true conclusion for finding average percentage of growth or decline rate.
9. H.M. = Reci. $\left[\dfrac{n}{\Sigma \text{ Reci. } n}\right]$
10. G.M. is more appropriate for dealing with problem of rates and speed.
11. Geometric mean is the root of the product of *n* number.
12. Geometric mean is the *n*th root of the sum of *n* items. (*JAC,* 2015)

[Ans. 1. True, 2. True, 3. False, 4. True, 5. False, 6. True, 7. False, 8. True, 9. False, 10. False, 11. False, 12. False.]

III. Fill in the Blanks

1. Geometric mean is a ....average of central tendency.
2. For the average rate of growth of population the suitable average is.......... .
3. .... is used to find out the average speed.
4. .... and .... table are used to calculate geometric mean.
5. H.M. = Reci[?]
6. G.M. = $\sqrt{\text{A.M.X. ......}}$
7. G.M. = A.L. $\left[\dfrac{\Sigma \log \text{X}}{?}\right]$

[Ans. 1. Mathematical, 2. Geometric Mean, 3. Harmonic mean, 4. Logarithm, and logarithm, 5. $\left[\dfrac{n}{\Sigma \text{ Reci. } x}\right]$, 6. H.M., 7. [N].]

6

ANALYSIS OF TIME SERIES

LEARNING OBJECTIVES

After studying this chapter, you will be able to know :

- **6.1. Meaning and Definition of Time Series**
- **6.2. Objectives of Analysis of Time Series**
- **6.3. Components of Time Series :**
  1. **Trend or Secular Trend**
  2. **Seasonal Variation**
  3. **Cyclical Fluctuations**
  4. **Irregular Movements**
- **6.4. Analysis or Decomposition of Time Series**
- **6.5. Mathematical Models of Time Series :**
  1. **Additive Model**
  2. **Multiplicative Model**
- **6.6. Importance/Utility or Uses of Time Series**
- **6.7. Measurement of Trend or Secular Trend :**
  1. **Freehand Curve Method**
  2. **Methods of Averages :**
     (i) Selected Point Method
     (ii) Semi-average Method
     (iii) Moving Average Method
  3. **Method of Least Squares :**
     (i) Straight Line Method
     (ii) Parabolic Curve or Non-linear Curve
     (iii) Logarithmic Straight Line
- **6.8. Measurement of Short-time (Short-term) Fluctuations**
- **6.9. Measurement of Seasonal Variations**
- **6.10. Measurement of Cyclical Variations**
- **6.11. Measurement of Irregular or Random Movements/Fluctuations**
- **Important Formulae of Time Series**
- **Theoretical Questions :**
  Long Answer Questions, Short Answer Questions, Very Short Answer Questions
- **Practical Problems**

ILLUSTRATIONS AND PRACTICAL PROBLEMS : AT A GLANCE

No. of Illustration		*No. of Problems*
	Measurement of Trend or Secular Trend	
1	1. Freehand Curve Method	1
	2. Methods of Averages	2
2	(i) Method of Selected Points	
3, 4	(ii) Semi-average Method	3 to 5

5(A) to 7	(iii) Moving Average Method	6 to 10(A)
	3. Methods of Least Squares	
8 to 12(A)	(i) Arithmetic Straight Line Method	11 to 18(A)
12(B), 13	(ii) Parabolic Curve	19, 20
14	(iii) Logarithmic Straight Line Method	21
15	Measurment of Short-terms Fluctuations	22 to 25
	Measurment of Seasonal Variation	
16, 17	1. Seasonal Variation Index Method	
18	2. Seasonal Variation through Moving Average	26
19	3. Chain or Link Relative Method	27, 28
20	4. Ratio-to-Trend Method	29
21	5. Ratio-to-moving Average Method	30, 31
—	Miscellaneous Problems	32 to 37
21	**Total**	**37**

(6.1) MEANING AND DEFINITION

Time series refers to the chronologically ordered values of a variable based on time. According to *Kanney* and *Keeping*, "**A set of data depending on the time is called a Time Series.**"

The following are some definitions of "Time Series" :

(i)"A series of values over a period to time is called a Time Series".

—P. G. Moore

(ii) "A Time Series may be defined as a collection of readings belonging to different time periods of some economic variables or composite of variables."

—Ya Loon-Chou

(iii) "A main objective in analysis of Time Series is to understand, interpret and evaluate changes in economic phenomenon in the hop of most correctly anticipating the course of future events." *–W. Z. Hirsh*

A Time Series is also called as '*Historical Series*' or '*Chronological Series*'. Hence a **Time Series is a Hstorical Series of Statistical Data**.

Kinds of Time Series : Time Series data are of two kinds, *viz.*, Period Data and Point Data. *Period Data* refers to the accumulated value of a flow variable during a particular period. For example, wheat production of 200 million tonne during 2008-09. This data refers to total wheat production during the period April 1, 2008 through March 31, 2009.

Point Data refers to the value of a 'Stock Variable' at a point of time. For example, the quantity of money of ₹ 85,000 crore as on last Friday of March, 2009.

Essential Requirements of Time Series : The essential requirements of a Time Series are :

(1) It must consist of a homogeneous set of values.

(2) The data should be available for a sufficient long period.

(3) The time between various values must be equal.

(4) The gaps, if any, in the data should be made up by inter-polation.

(6.2) OBJECTIVES OF ANALYSIS OF TIME SERIES

1. The main objective of Time Series or Analysis of Time Series is understand, interpret and evaluate changes in the economic phenomena.

2. The purpose of analysis of Time Series is to discover and measure all such types of variation which characterises a Time Series.

3. Its central objective is to decompose various elements present in a Time Series and to use them for business decision-making.

(6.3) COMPONENTS OF TIME SERIES

As said earlier, A Time Series is a historical series of statistical data. Since these statistical data are historical, they are subject to the influences of all the changes that may occur in any period of time. The forces affecting time series data generate certain movements or fluctuations in a time series.

Such characteristic movement or fluctuations of a Time Series are called Components of a Time **Series. In short, the components of a Time Series are the various elements which can be segregated (separated) from the observed data.**

The following are the classification of the components of a time series :

Components of Time Series
- (1) Trend or Secular Trend (T)
- (2) Seasonal Variations (S)
- (3) Cyclical Variations (C)
- (4) Random Movements (R)

Broadly speaking, the components of a "Time Series" are first classified into three categories as shown below :

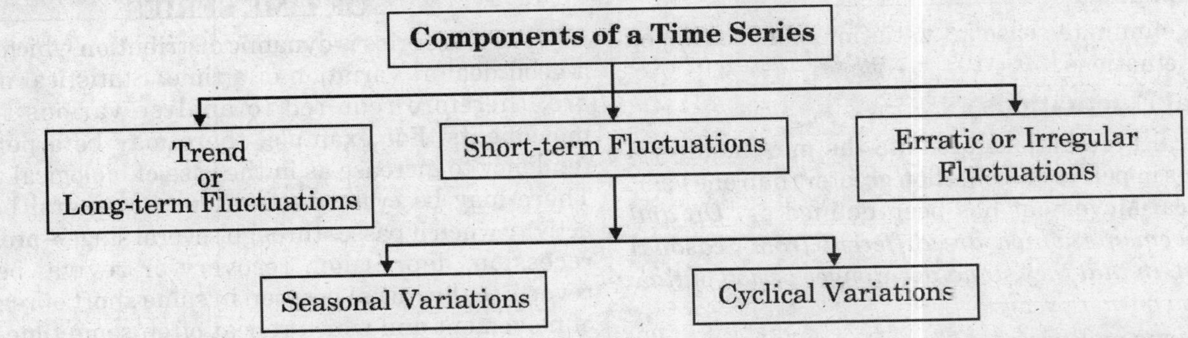

From the above figure it appears that the short time or short-term fluctuations are again divided into two categories, namely, (A) Seasonal Variations, and (B) Cyclical variations.

1. Trend or Secular Trend

Trend is also known as Secular Trend or "Long-Term Trend". Trend is the basic tendency of a series to grow and decline over a period of time. The word 'Secular' is derived from the Latin word 'SAECULUM' which means generation or age. Hence, Secular Trend movements are thought at as long-term movements usually requiring a minimum of 15 to 20 years.

In fact, the concept of Trend does not include short range oscillation, but rather the steady movement over a along time. The Trend thus refers to the general direction and the movements of Time Series considering a fairly long period of time.

The Trend may be **Upward, Downward**

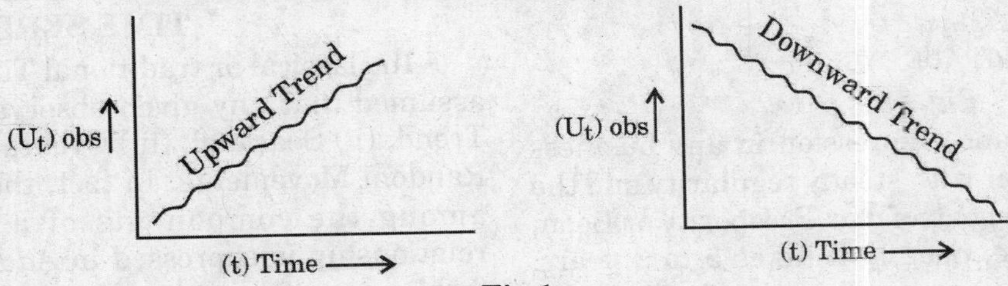

Fig.1

The following two tables show the Upward and Downward trends :

Production of Food Grains showing Upward Trend

Year	1945	1946	1947	1948	1949	1950	1951
Total Food Grains	36	42	51	62	73	82	91

Per Capital Availability of Cotton Cloth (in metres) showing Downward Trend

Year	1980	1981	1982	1983	1984	1985
Consumption	72	56	49	38	26	11

The Purpose of Measuring Trend :

1. The purpose of measuring Trend is to know about the other components such as Seasonal, Cyclical, Irregular variation by eliminating it.
2. To forecast on the basis of Trend.
3. To understand the past behavior of the factors which are responsible for the growth or decline.

2. Seasonal Variation

Seasonal variations are periodic patterns of movement in a Time Series. Seasonal variation has been defined as, "*A recurrent pattern of change to the period that results from the operations of forces connected with climate or custom at different times of the period.*"

The Seasonal Variations are usually measured in an interval within the calendar year. These may be weekly, monthly or quarterly. The following forces are responsible for Seasonal Variation :

(i) **Natural Forces or Factors :** For example, the demand of electric fans and coolers goes up in summer season; the sales of woolens go up in winter, all these being affected by natural forces, the weather conditions.

(ii) **Social Customs and Traditions :** For example, the sales of Jewellery and ornaments goes up in marriage seasons; the sales and profits go up during festivals, like Diwali and Durga Pooja.

Purpose of Measuring Seasonal Variations :

1. To analyse past seasonal behavior.

2. To predict seasonal variations as an aid to short-term planning.

3. To eliminate seasonal variations for measuring cyclical fluctuations.

3. Cyclical Fluctuations

Cyclical Fluctuations oscillate the movement in a Time Series in period of oscillation greater than one year. The Cyclical Movement has been defined as "*Up and Down movements which are different from seasonal fluctuation, in that they stand over longer period of time usually two or more years.*"

Economic or Bussiness Time Series follow a cycle consisting of the following four periods : (i) Prosperity, (ii) Recession, (iii) Depression, and (iv) Recovery (See Fig. 2).

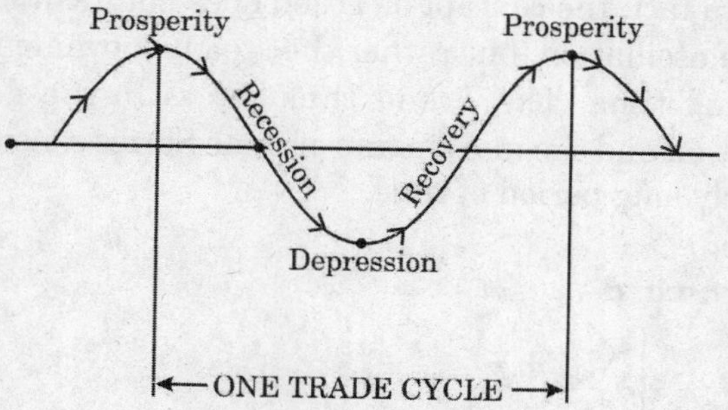

Fig. 2

These Prosperity and Depression in any business activity follow each other with steady regularity and the complete cycle from the peak of one, Prosperity or Boom to the peak at next one, usually it takes 5 to 9 years. This cycle is termed as 'Business Cycle' or 'Trade Cycle.'

Purpose of Measuring Cyclical Fluctuation : The study of cyclical fluctuation in the Time Series serves the following purposes :

1. It helps in predicting the turning points in business activity.

2. Measures of past cyclical behaviour are valuable aids in studying the characteristic fluctuation of a business.

3. The cyclical measures are useful in the formation of policies aimed at stabilizing the level of business activity.

4. Irregular Movements

The fourth component of Time Series is Irregular Movements. Irregular Movements are also known as Erratic, Random or Unpredictable Variations.

These movements are due to accidental changes which are purely random, unforeseen and unpredictable. They turn the series in one way or the other way purely by change. These variations are usually caused by numerous non-recurring factors like floods, famines, wars, earthquakes, strikes and lockouts, epidemics, revolution. etc., which behave in a very erratic and unpredictable manner. Normally, they are short-term variations but sometimes their effect are so intense that they may give rise to new cyclical or other movements.

(6.4) ANALYSIS OR DECOMPOSITION OF TIME SERIES

A Time Series is dynamic distribution which reveals a good deal at variation of a time. Statistical methods are, therefore required to analyse various types of movements. For example, there may be a persistent tendency to increase as in the case of biological growth. There may be cyclical variations in general business activity when it passes through several stages–prosperity, recession, depression, recovery or revival before it reverts to the initial position in same short of regularity of movement and which repeat often some time. Hence analysis of Time Series consists of discovering, measuring and isolating the components of the time series. In other words, *the process of studying, interpreting and isolating the forces that influence a Time Series is called the Analysis of Time Series.*"

Analysis of Time Series is also known as '*Decomposition of Time Series*'. Decomposition refers to the segregation of various components of a Series. Therefore, Decomposition of Time Series data means the study of components of a Time Series individually.

(6.5) MATHEMATICAL MODELS OF TIME SERIES

In classical or traditional Time Series analysis it is assumed that any given observation is made up of (i) Trend, (ii) Seasonal, (iii) Cyclical, and (iv) Irregular or Random Movements. In fact, there exists relationship among the components of a Time Series. These relationship is expressed in *Additive* or *Multiplicative* fashion to produce the observed value in Time Series. *The two relationship are often called 'Mathematical Models of Time Series'.*

1. Additive Model

This model assumes that the observed value is the sum of four components. Symbolically :

$$O \text{ or } Y = T + S + C + I$$

Where O or Y = Original data or observed value in the Time Series

T = Trend or Trend Value
S = Seasonal Variations
C = Cyclical Variations or Fluctuations
I = Irregular Variations

Important Note

1. In additive model S, C and I are absolute quantity deviations about trend.
2. It assumes that all the four components of the Time Series operate independently of one another.
3. It assumes that the behavior of components is of an additive character.

2. Multiplicative Model

This model assumes that the observed value is obtained by multiplying the trend (T) by the rates of three other components. Symbolically,

O or Y = T × S × C × I

Where O or Y = Original Data

S = Seasonal Variations

C = Cyclical Variations

I = Irregular Movements or Variations

Important Note

1. Here S, C and I are relative variations expressed as rates, percentages or index numbers.
2. It assumes that the behaviour of components is of a multiplicative character.

Remarks : Most of the Time Series relating to Economic and Business phenomena conform to the Multiplicative Model.

1. Multiplicative model is the most commonly used model in the decomposition of the Time Series.

2. A Multiplicative Model can be converted into an Additive Model by the use of logarithms, as shown below

$$Y = T \times S \times C\ I$$

$$\log Y = \log T + \log S + \log C + \log I$$

(6.6) IMPORTANCE UTILITY OR USES OF TIME SERIES

1. It helps in studying fluctuations in the field of economic and business activities.
2. It helps in understanding past behaviour of the variable.
3. It helps in forecasting and planning.
4. It helps in evaluating the present accomplishment or achievements.
5. Time series analysis helps in the comparison of the behaviour of different 'Time Series;'.
6. It helps in the estimation of trade cycle on the basis of cyclical fluctuation which helps the businessmen to plan and regulate their activities.

(6.7) MEASUREMENT OF TREND OR SECULAR TREND

The following are the principal methods of determining trend :

(1) Freehand Curve Method

(2) Methods of Averages :
- (i) Selected Point Method
- (ii) Semi-average Method
- (iii) Moving Averages Method

(3) Method of Least Squares :
- (i) Straight Line Method
- (ii) Parabolic Curve or Non-linear Curve
- (iii) Logarithmic Straight Line

1. Freehand Curve Method

The term 'Freehand' is used to any non-mathematical curve in statistical analysis, even when it is drawn with the aid of drafting instruments. This is the simplest method of studying trend of a Time Series.

Procedure : (i) Under this method the original data are plotted on a graph paper. The time is shown on the horizontal axis (X-axis) and the values of the variable on the variable on the vertical axis (Y-axis).

(i) The direction of the plotted points is clearly observed.

(ii) A smooth line based on observation, is drawn through the plotted points.

The fitting of the Trend may be a straight line or curved line and it may be done freehand or by other the Trend may be a straight line or curved line and it may be done freehand or by other aids. Often a straight line trend is fitted because it is less exposed to individual biases of the person fitting it.

Guidelines : The following guidelines must be carefully observed while fitting a trend line by the freehand method :

(a) The curve should be smooth.

(b) As far as possible there must be equal number of points above or below the trend line.

(c) The vertical deviations of the data above the trend line must total the same as vertical deviations below the line.

(d) If there are cycles, equal number of cycles should be above or below the trend line.

(e) The sum of the squares of the vertical deviations of the observations from the trend should be as small as possible.

Merits of Freehand Curve Method : (1) Freehand method of estimating trend is the simplest method.

(2) This method does not require any complex mathematical techniques.

(3) It is more flexible than rigid mathematical function.

Hence, due to these reasons this method is widely used in business.

Demerits : (1) This method is highly subjective. The results depend mainly upon the judgement of the person drawing the line.

(2) Because of the subjective element, the freehand curve is not as accurate as the results obtained from mathematical methods.

(3) Freehand method of curve fitting has little value as a bias or projection for future.

Illustration 1

Find out Secular Trend by Freehand Curve Method from the following data : (In Million Tons)

Year	*Production*	*Year*	*Production*
2000	126	2005	130
2001	132	2006	140
2002	131	2007	135
2003	130	2008	148
2004	133	2009	144

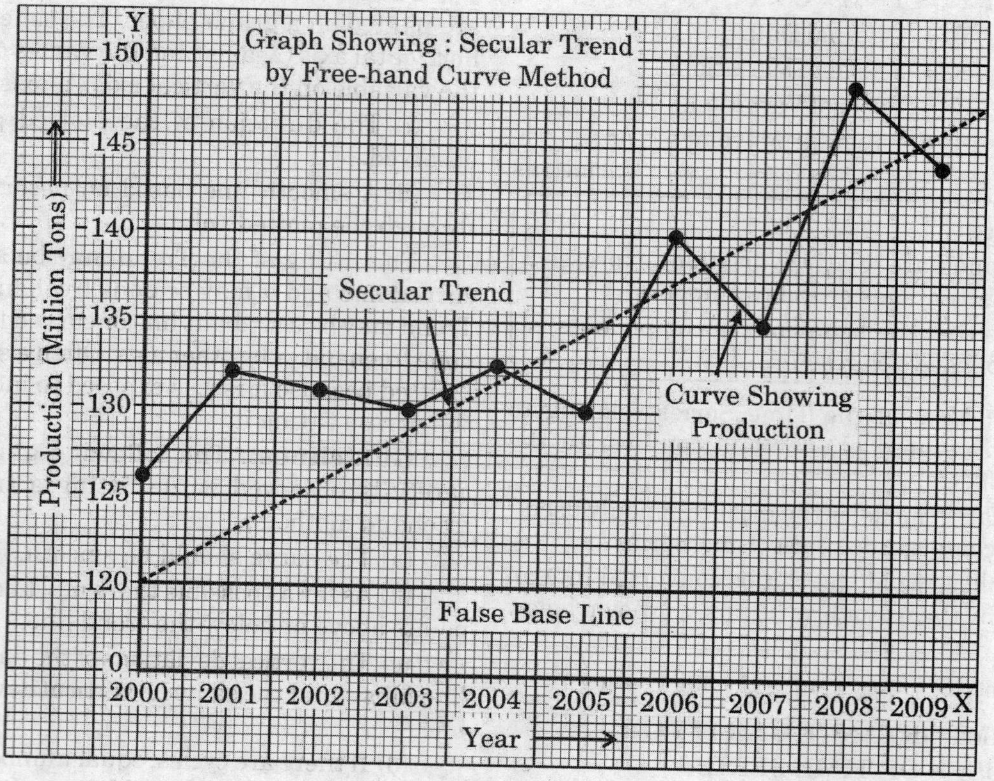

Fig. 3

The graph shows that there is an "Upward Trend"

2. Methods of Averages

There are three methods of measuring Trend with the help of methods of averages :

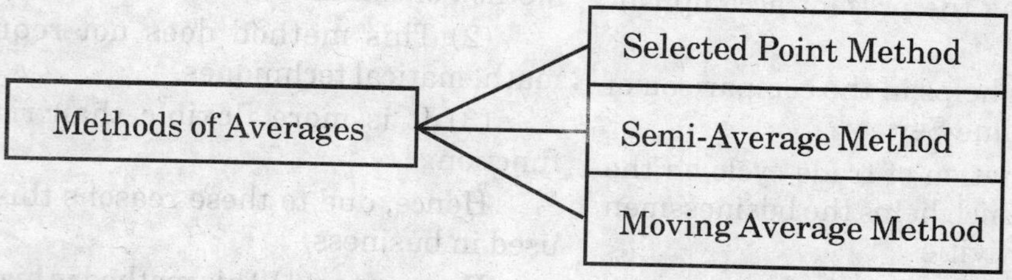

(i) **Selected Point Method** : Under this method *two points* are considered to be the most *representative* or *Normal*. These points are determined and plotted on the graph paper and then they are joined to get the trend line. Prior to that original data are also plotted on the graph paper as it is done in the case of Freehand Curve Method.

This method is not a satisfactory method. The reason is that in the selection of 'points' opinions may differ. Further, what is considered by one as 'normal year' may be treated as abnormal by the another.

Illustration 2

Find out Trend by Selected Point Method from the following data :

Year	*Production (Tons)*
2000	126
2001	132
2002	131
2003	130
2004	133
2005	130
2006	140
2007	135
2008	148
2009	144

Solution :

Let us select 2002 and 2007 as the two points.

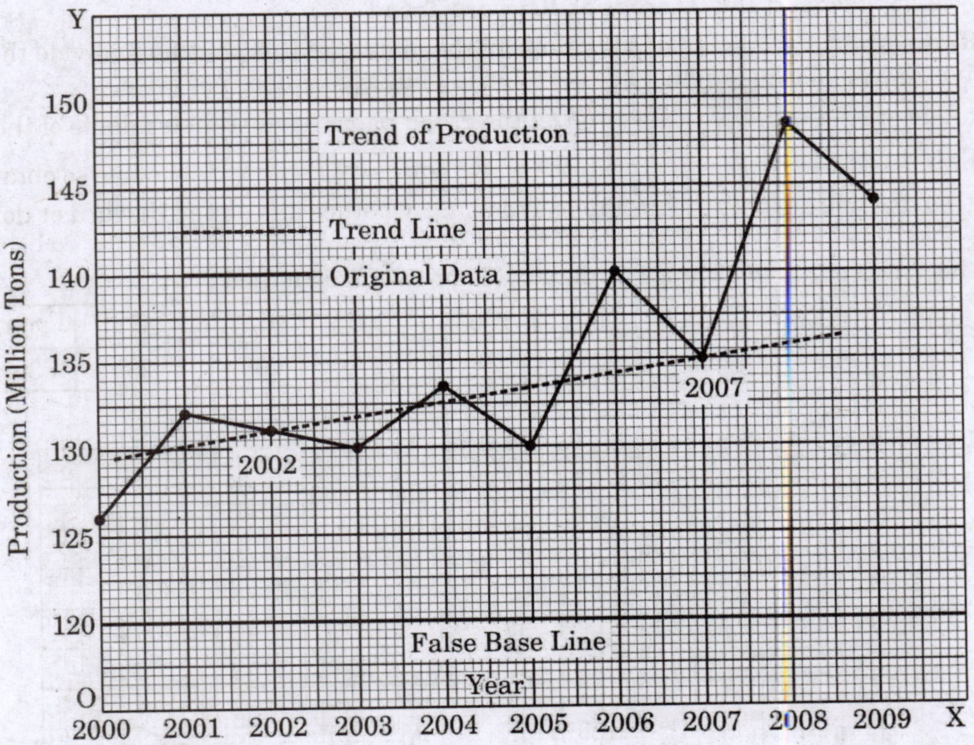

Fig. 4

(ii) **Semi-Average Method :** Under this method data is divided into 2 equal parts then averages are calculated for both the parts. Each average is then centred in the period of time which has been computed. These 2 averages are plotted on graph paper. If there is odd number of years, the value of the middle year is omitted. A straight line is drawn through these two points. This is the required Trend line. Let us illustrate this fact by taking examples.

***Example* (i)**

When the number of items (years) is odd : When the number of years is odd, the value of the middle year is omitted to divide the Time Series into two equal parts as shown in the following table :

Year	*Production (Tons)*
2004	3000
2005	4000
2006	5000
2007	7000
2008	10000

Year	*Production (Tons)*
2004	3000 }
2005	4000 }
2006	5000 }
2007	7000 }
2008	10000

$$\text{Average } (\overline{X}_1) = \frac{3000 + 4000}{2} = 3{,}500$$

(Avg. of first 2 years)

$$\text{Average } (\overline{X}_2) = \frac{7{,}000 + 10{,}000}{2} = 8{,}500$$

(Avg. of last 2 years)

Note : These averages $\overline{X}_1$ and $\overline{X}_2$ suggest that there is an "Upward Trend".

In this case there are five items, so first part will consist of first two years, *i.e.*, 2004 and 2005 third year will be left out and the second part will consist of next two years, *i.e.*, 2007 and 2008.

***Example* (ii)**

If the number of items or years is even : In this case "Time Series" is divided into two parts. Then total of each part is averaged. Each average is then centred in the period of time from which it has been computed and plotted on the graph paper.

Year	*Production (Tons)*
2003	3,000 }
2004	4,000 }
2005	5,000 }
2006	7,000 }
2007	10,000 }
2008	13,000 }

$$\text{I Part} \quad \overline{X}_1 = \frac{3{,}000 + 4{,}000 + 5{,}000}{3}$$

$= ₹\ 4{,}000$ (Avg. of first 3 years)

$$\text{II Part} \quad \overline{X}_2 = \frac{7{,}000 + 10{,}000 + 13{,}000}{3}$$

$= ₹\ 10{,}000$ (Avg. of last 3 years)

Note : These $\overline{X}_1, \overline{X}_2$ suggest that there is an 'Upward Trend'.

Points to Remember : (1) In case of odd numbers the middle year is omitted to divide the Time Series into two equal parts but in case of even number the question of middle year does not arise.

(2) Each average (*i.e.*, $\overline{X}_1$ and $\overline{X}_2$) is plotted on the graph paper against their middle of the time periods.

(3) A straight line is drawn passing through these two points ($\overline{X}_1$ and $\overline{X}_2$). The line so obtained is Trend Line and direction of this line will suggest the nature of Trend, *i.e.* whether it is either Upward or downward.

Illustration 3

Determine the Trend of the following T.S. data by Semi-Average Method : (₹ Crores)

Year	1999	2000	2001	2002	2003	2004	2005	2006	2007	2008
Grants	240	230	220	270	290	270	230	280	300	270

Solution

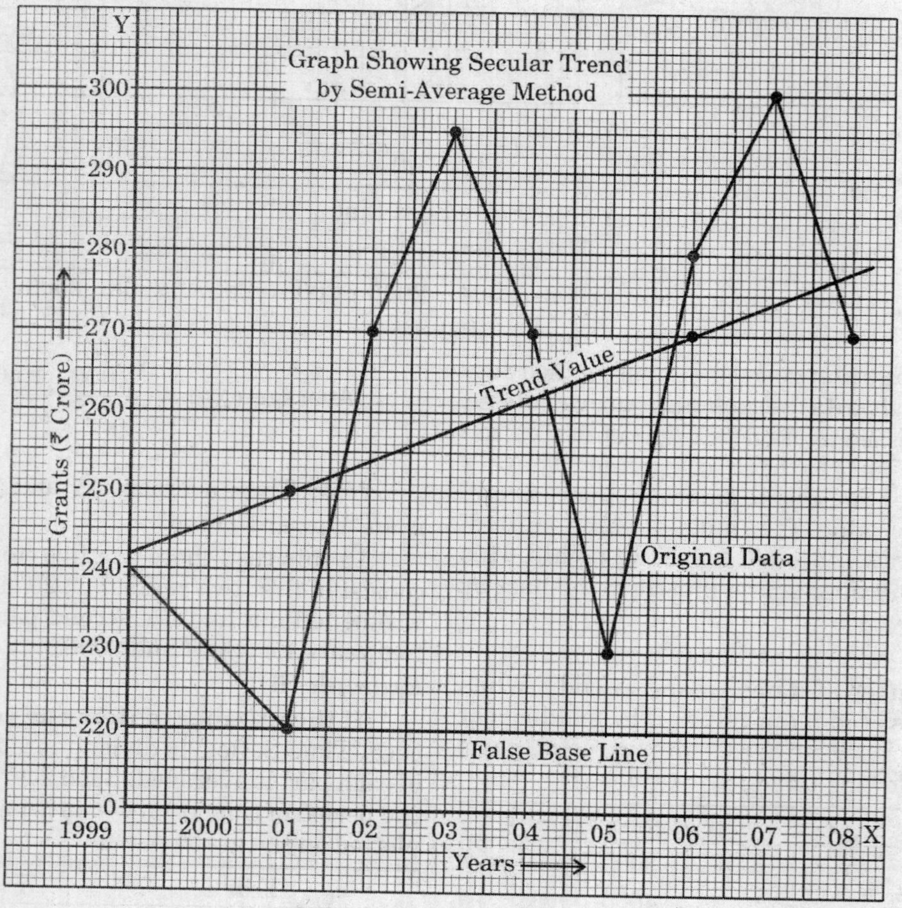

Fig 5

Year	*Grants* (₹ Crore)
1999	240
2000	230
2001	220
2002	270
2003	290
2004	270
2005	230
2006	280
2007	300
2008	270

Mean

I Part $\overline{X}_1 = \frac{1250}{5} = 250$ (Avg. of first 5 years)

II Part $\overline{X}_2 = \frac{1350}{5} = 270$ (Avg. of last 5 years)

Note : Here $\overline{X}_1$, $\overline{X}_2$ suggest an "Upward Trend"

Illustration 4

Determine the Trend of the following by Semi-Average Method : (million tons)

Year	2001	2002	2003	2004	2005	2006	2007	2008	2009
Production of Oil Seeds	10.0	9.6	10.1	8.3	9.4	12.0	10.4	12.6	13.0

Solution :

In this case values of 9 years are given. So this is a case of odd number. Hence, year 2005 will be left out.

Calculation of Trend Value by Semi-average Method

Year	2001	2002	2003	2004	2005	2006	2007	2008	2009
Production of Oil Seeds	10.0	9.6	10.1	8.3	9.4	12.0	10.4	12.6	13.0

Average of the First Half $(\overline{X}_1)$

$$\overline{X}_1 = \frac{\Sigma x_i}{n_1}$$

$$\Sigma x_i = 10 + 9.6 + 10.1 + 8.3 = 38.0$$

$$n_1 = 4$$

$$\overline{X}_1 = \frac{38.0}{4} = 9.5 \text{ (million tons.)}$$

Average of the Second Half $(\overline{X}_2)$

$$\overline{X}_2 = \frac{\Sigma x_j}{n_2}$$

$$\Sigma x_j = 12 + 10.4 + 12.6 + 13 = 48$$

$$n_2 = 4$$

$$\therefore \quad \overline{X}_2 = \frac{48}{4} \quad 12 \text{ (million tons.)}$$

Note : These $\overline{X}_1$ & $\overline{X}_2$ indicate that there is an Upward Trend.

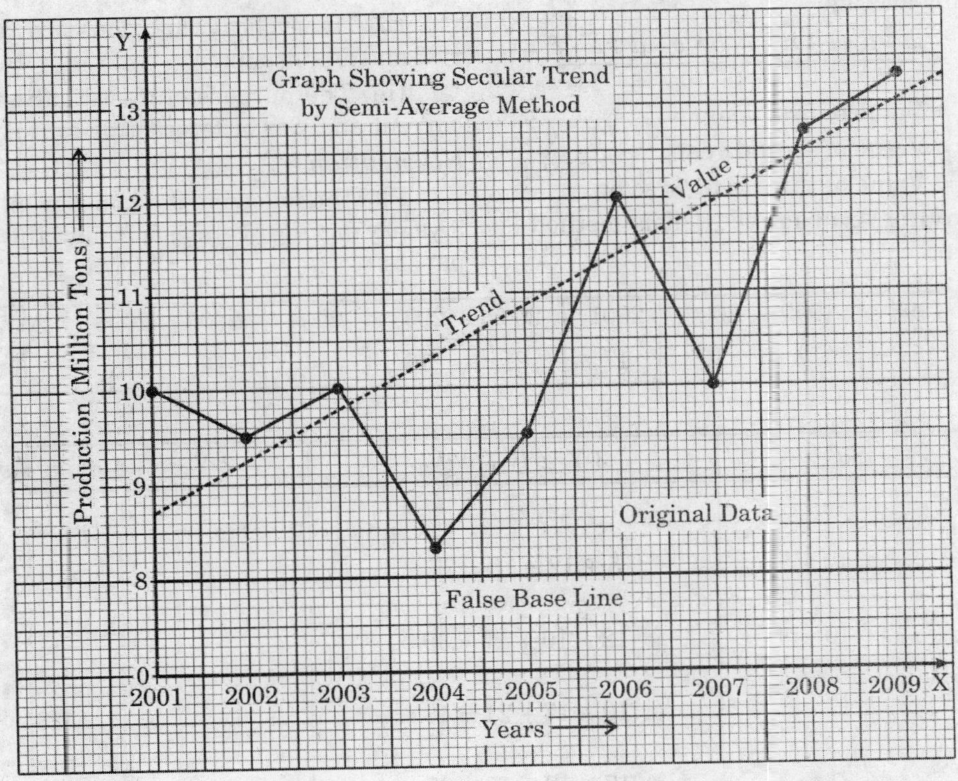

Fig. 6

Merits of Semi-Average : (i) This method is easy to understand and simple to calculate.

(ii) This is an objective method of measuring Trend.

(iii) The line can be extended both ways to obtain future or past estimates.

Demerits of Semi-Average : (i) This method assumes the presence of linear trend in the value of Time Series which may not be true.

(ii) This method has an inbult limitation of Arithmetic Mean.

(iii) There is no assurance that the influence of cycle is eliminated.

(iii) **Moving Average Method :** This method also is based on Arithmetic Means of items. But in this case there are as many averages as there are items in the series except at the two ends of the series (*i.e.*, beginning & the end) where averages can not be computed.

Procedure of Computing Moving Average : (i) First decide the number of years for which Moving Averages are to be computed. It may be 3, 4, 5, 6, 7, 8 or 9 years. The number of years taken is called the time interval or period for computing the moving average.

(ii) The number of years may be either *Odd* or *Even*.

(iii) Then averages are taken from overlapping periods.

(iv) In case of odd period moving average the Arithmetic Mean is written at the middle of the period covered in the computation of average. But when the time period is even, the moving average falls mid-way between the two observations. The reason is that the mid-term will not coincide with the series.

In case of even numbers we calculate further two item moving averages so that mid-points now may coincide with the given time period. The process is known as *centering of the moving averages*.

Formula of Calculating Moving Averages

3-yearly moving average

$$= \frac{a+b+c}{3}, \frac{b+c+d}{3}, \frac{c+d+e}{3}$$

5-yearly moving average

$$= \frac{a+b+c+d+e}{5}, \frac{b+c+d+e+f}{5}$$

where a = Value of first year

b = Value of second year

c = Value of third year & so on.

Merits of Moving Averages : (i) This method is simple to understand.

(ii) This method is better than freehand curve method because it is objective.

(iii) This method is flexible.

(iv) The moving averages method eliminates periodic variations and thus the analysis becomes simple.

Demerits of Moving Averages : (i) The selection of the period for computing moving averages poses another problem. There is no mathematical formula for this.

(ii) Trend value can not be computed for all the years of the series.

(iii) This method is not useful for comparison of the trend.

(iv) If the trend is not linear (a straight line). Then moving averages lie either above or below the curve of the actual data.

(v) This method can not be used for forecasting future trend.

Uses of Moving Averages : The method of moving averages for fitting a trend is useful when

(i) The trend is linear.

(ii) The cyclical variations are regular both in period and amplitude.

(iii) The purpose of investigation does not involve current analysis or forecasting for future.

***Illustration* 5(A)**

Plot the following data on a graph paper. Calculate 3-yearly moving average and show the trend on the same paper :

Year	1998	1999	2000	2001	2002	2003	2004	2005	2006	2007	2008	2009
Sales (qtl.)	5	12	10	17	21	16	14	18	13	8	21	16

Solution :

Year	*Sales*	*3-Yearly Total*	*3-Yearly Moving Average*
1998	5	—	—
1999	12	5 + 12 + 10 = 27	$\frac{27}{3} = 9$
2000	10	12 + 10 + 17 = 39	$\frac{39}{3} = 13$
2001	17	10 + 17 + 21 = 48	$\frac{48}{3} = 16$
2002	21	17 + 12 + 10 = 27	$\frac{54}{3} = 18$
2003	16	21 + 16 + 14 = 51	$\frac{51}{3} = 17$
2004	14	16 + 14 + 18 = 48	$\frac{48}{3} = 16$
2005	18	14 + 18 + 13 = 45	$\frac{45}{3} = 15$
2006	13	18 + 13 + 8 = 39	$\frac{39}{3} = 13$

2007	8	13 + 8 + 21 = 42	$\frac{42}{3} = 14$
2008	21	8 + 21 + 16 = 45	$\frac{45}{3} = 15$
2009	16	—	—

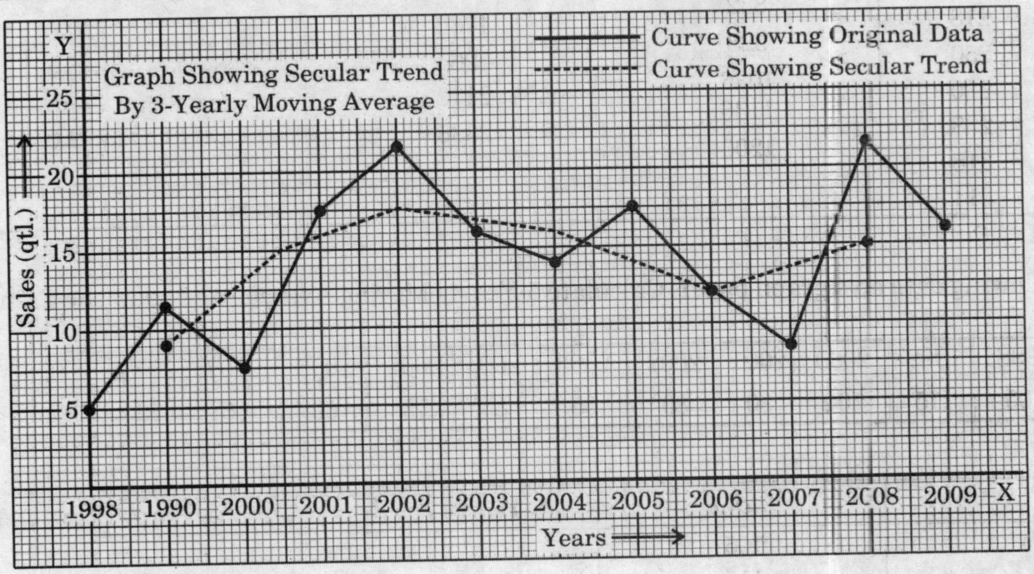

Fig. 7

***Illustration* 5(B)**

Find out the value of the trend by three-yearly moving average : (*JAC*, 2017)

Year	1985	1986	1987	1988	1989	1990	1991	1992	1993	1994	1995	1996	1997
Value	10	15	12	18	15	22	19	24	20	26	22	30	25

Sollution :

Calculation Table

Year	*Value*	*3 Yearly Totals*	*Trend Values* (T)
1985	10		
1986	15	37	12.33
1987	12	45	15.00
1988	18	45	15.00
1989	15	55	18.34
1990	22	56	18.67
1991	19	65	21.67
1992	24	63	21.00
1993	20	70	23.34
1994	26	68	22.67
1995	22	78	26.00
1996	30	77	25.67
1997	25		

***Illustration* 6**

Using Four Yearly Moving Average, determine the Trend of Index Numbers of wholesale prices (Base 2004 = 100)

Year	2001	2002	2003	2004	2005	2006	2007	2008
Index Number	184	180	218	250	280	288	318	314

Solution :

Year	*Value*	*4-Yearly Moving Totals*	*Centered Sum*	*4-Yearly Moving Average or Trend Values*
2001	184			
2002	180			
2003	218	832	1760	220.0
2004	250	928	1964	245.5
2005	280	1036	2172	271.5
2006	288	1136	2336	292.0
2007	318	1200		
2008	314			

Illustration 7

Plot the following data on a graph paper. Calculate 5-Yearly Moving Average and show the Trend on the graph paper :

Year	1998	1999	2000	2001	2002	2003	2004	2005	2006	2007	2008	2009
Index	105	115	100	90	80	95	85	75	60	65	70	55

Solution :

Year	*Index*	*5-Yearly Totals*	*5-Yearly Moving Average*
1998	105	—	—
1999	115	—	—
2000	100	490	98
2001	90	480	96
2002	80	450	90
2003	95	425	85
2004	85	395	79
2005	75	380	76
2006	60	355	71
2007	65	325	65
2008	70	—	—
2009	55	—	—

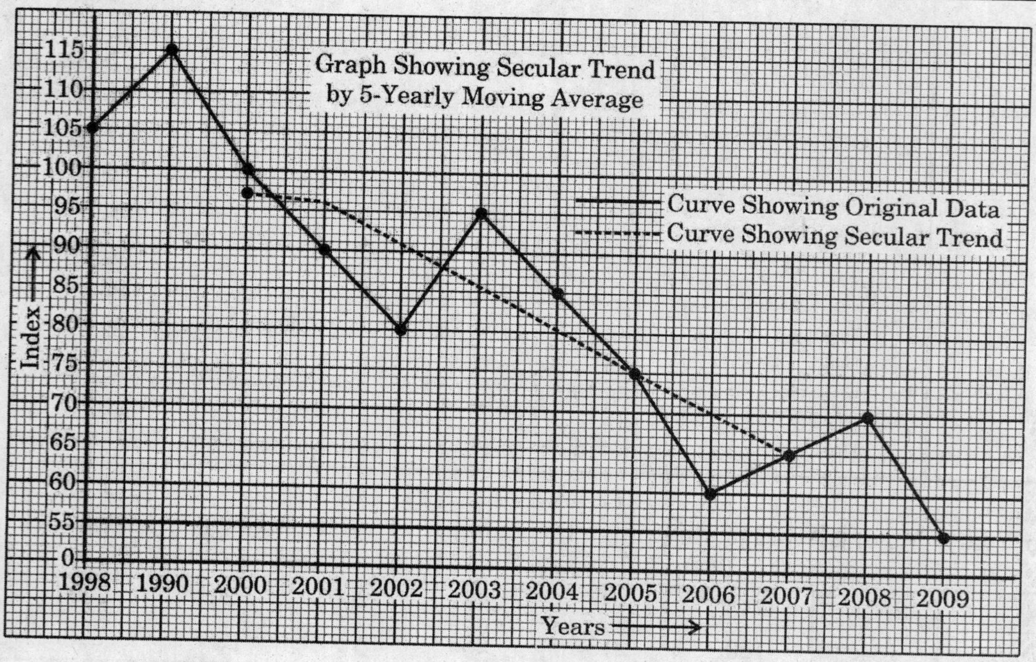

Fig. 8

3. Method of Least Squares

The Method of Least Squares provides a convenient basis for obtaining line of best fit in a series. It accomplishes the following objectives :

(i) The algebraic sum of deviations of individual observations (above or below) from their respective trend values is zero. *i.e.*, $\Sigma (y - y_e) = 0$.

(ii) The sum of the squares of the above deviations is the least, *i.e.*, $\Sigma (y - y_e) = a$.

Time Series data are generally interdependent. On the basis of these interdependence a Trend is calculated.

On the basis of method of least squares the determination of trend can be classified into three categories :

(i) Straight Line Method
(ii) Parabolic Curve or Non-linear Trends
(iii) Logarithmic Straight Line

(i) **Straight Line Method : Fitting a Straight Line Trend :** For fitting a straight line trend the following equation is used :

$$y_e = a + bx$$

or $$y = a + bx$$

or $$y' = a + bx$$

Where, y_e or y or y' = Required trend value

x = Unit of time

a and b = Two constants

a = The constant indicating the arithmetic mean of dependent variable or the constant 'a' is the y intercept *i.e.*, the difference between the point of the origin (O) and the point where the trend line touches the y-axis.

b = The constant indicating the rate of change or slope of the line, *i.e.*, the change in Y for each unit change in X.

Steps : (Direct Method)

The following steps are involved in finding the trend values of straight line method :

(i) The points of time, *i.e.*, years are denoted by natural numbers like 1, 2, 3, ... The summation of X is obtained, *i.e.*, (ΣX).

(ii) The natural numbers assigned to X's are squared up and their total, ΣX^2, is obtained.

(iii) The X's are multiplied with the corresponding values of Y and the total of the product is found out.

(iv) Values of Y are added to get (ΣY).

(v) The values are placed in two Normal Equations and the values of 'a' and 'b' are found out.

(vi) Values so obtained of 'a' or 'b' are placed in the Trend Equation. Then Trend values Y_e are found for various values of X.

(See Illustration 9 Alternative Method)

Steps : (Short-cut Method)

(i) Assume any year as the base year (*i.e.*, zero) and find the time deviation. The deviation may be either positive (+ ve) or negative (– ve). The deviation is treated as X.

(ii) The deviations are squared up (*i.e.*, X^2) and added to get ΣX^2.

(iii) Assume dependent variable as Y and multiply the deviations (X) with the value of Y.

(iv) Find out the total of the product to get ΣXY.

(v) Find the value of 'a' by applying the formula

$$a = \frac{\Sigma Y}{n}$$

(vi)Find the value of 'b' by applying the following formula :

$$b = \frac{\Sigma XY}{\Sigma X^2}$$

(vii)Place the value of $a\,\overline{Y}$, against the year of origin in the trend column (*i.e.*, $\overline{Y}$, or Y_e). By multiplying the value of 'b' different Xs, the other trend value will be computed.

If the values of 'a' and 'b' are known, the value of y can be obtained by applying the following Algebraic *Equations* :

$$\Sigma Y = na + b\Sigma X \quad \text{...(i)}$$

and $$\Sigma XY = a\Sigma X + b\Sigma X^2 \quad \text{...(ii)}$$

where ΣY = Total of the values of Y

ΣX = Total of the values of X

XY = The total of the product of X and Y

ΣX^2 = The total of the square of the values of X

n = Number of items

***Illustration* 8**

Find the Trend of the following values by Least Square Method :

Year	2005	2006	2007	2008	2009
Price (₹)	83	92	71	90	169

Solution :

Year	*X = Year – 2007*	X^2	*Price (Y)*	*XY*	*Trend*
2005	– 2	4	83	– 166	101 – 2 × 17 = 67
2006	– 1	1	92	– 92	101 – 1 × 17 = 84
2007	0	0	71	0	101 – 0 × 17 = 101
2008	+ 1	1	90	90	101 + 1 × 17 = 118
2009	+ 2	4	169	338	101 + 2 × 17 = 135
n = 5		ΣX^2 = 10	ΣY= 505	ΣXY = 170	ΣY' 505

Here $a = \frac{\Sigma Y}{n} = \frac{505}{5} = 101$;

$b = \frac{\Sigma XY}{\Sigma X^2} = \frac{170}{10} = 17$

On putting the values of 'a' & 'b' ; we can find trend

$$Y = 101 + 17X$$

Illustration 9

Fit a straight line trend by the method of least squares of the following data :

Year (X)	2004	2005	2006	2007	2008	2009
Price (₹) (Y)	107	110	114	112	115	113

(*JAC*, 2011)

Solution : **Calculation of Trend Values (By Least Square Short-cut Method)**

Year	*Prices* (Y)	d_x = year – (2006 + 1/2)	$d_x \times 2$	X^2	*XY*	*Trend Values* $a + bx + y$
2004	107	– 2.5	– 5	25	– 535	111.83 + (0.61 × – 5) = 108.78
2005	110	– 1.5	– 3	9	– 330	111.83 + (0.61 × – 3) = 110.00
2006	114	– 0.5	– 1	1	– 114	111.83 + (0.61 × – 1) = 111.22
	0		0	0	0	0 0
2007	112	– 0.5	– 1	1	+ 112	111.83 + (0.61 × – 1) = 112.44
2008	115	– 1.5	+ 3	9	+ 345	111.83 + (0.61 × – 3) = 113.66
2009	113	– 2.5	+ 5	25	+ 565	111.83 + (0.61 × – 5) = 114.88
$n = 6$	$\Sigma Y = 671$			$\Sigma X^2 = 70$	$\Sigma XY = 43$	ΣY = 670.98 or 671

$$Y_e = a + bX$$

$$a = \frac{\Sigma Y}{N} = \frac{671}{6} = 111.83$$

$$b = \frac{\Sigma XY}{\Sigma X^2} = \frac{43}{70} = 0.61$$

Thus, required fitted equation of straight line trend

$$Y = 111.83 + 0.61X$$

Ans.

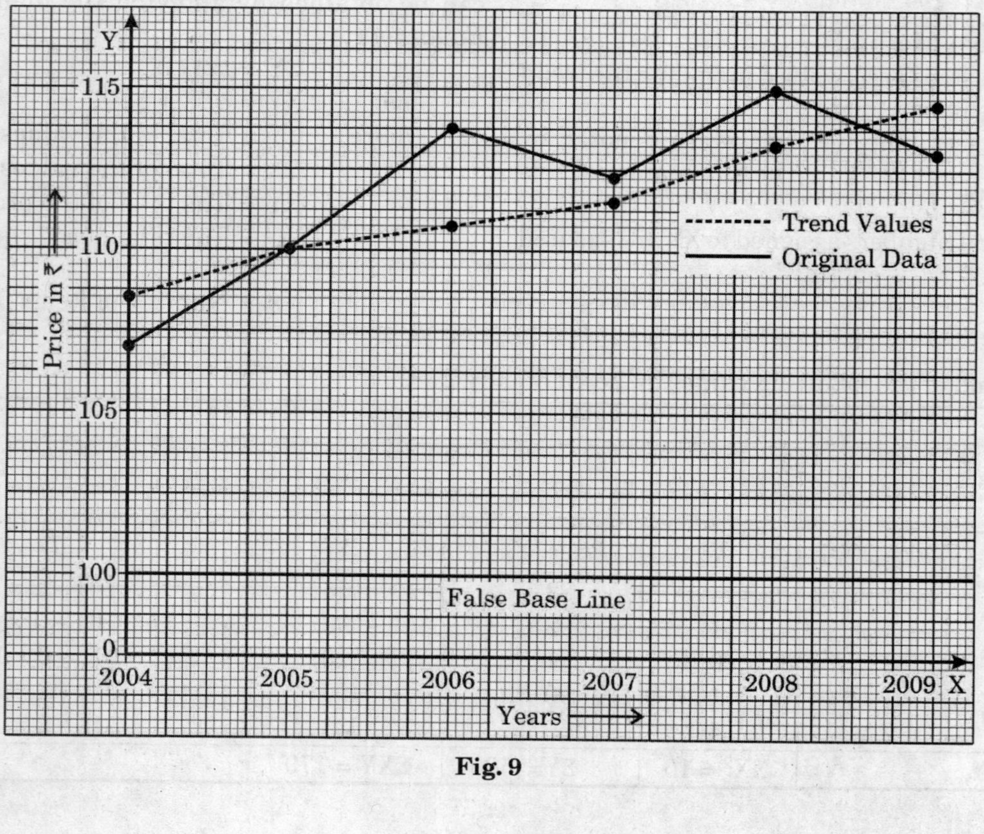

Fig. 9

***Illustration* 10**

Year	1971	1972	1973	1974	1975	1976	1977	1978
Frequency	80	90	92	83	94	99	92	110

Fit the Straight Line Trend to the above by Least Square Method. (*JAC*, 2009)

***Solution* :**

Calculation of Trend Values by the Method of Least Square

Year	*Production* (*Y*)	d_x = {Year – (1974 + 1/2)}	*X* = 2*dx*	X^2	*XY*	*Trend Values* ($Yc = a + bX$)
1971	80	– 3.5	– 7	49	– 560	92.5 + 1.5 × – 7 = 82
1972	90	– 2.5	– 5	25	– 450	92.5 + 1.5 × – 5 = 85
1973	92	– 1.5	– 3	9	– 276	92.5 + 1.5 × – 3 = 88
1974	83	– 0.5	– 1	1	– 83	92.5 + 1.5 × – 1 = 91
	0	0	0	0	0	0
1975	94	– 0.5	+ 1	1	+ 94	92.5 + 1.5 × 1 = 94
1976	99	– 1.5	+ 3	9	+ 297	92.5 + 1.5 × 3 = 97
1977	92	– 2.5	+ 5	25	+ 460	92.5 + 1.5 × 5 = 100
1978	110	– 3.5	+ 7	49	+ 770	92.5 + 1.5 × 7 = 103
Total *n* = 8	ΣY = 740		ΣX = 0	X^2 = 168	ΣXY = 252	ΣY_c = 740

$$Y_c = a + bX$$

$$a = \frac{\Sigma Y}{n} = \frac{740}{8} = 92.5 \qquad \therefore Y_c = 92.5 + 1.5\,X$$

$$b = \frac{\Sigma XY}{\Sigma X^2} = \frac{252}{168} = 1.5$$

The trend can be obtained by applying algebraic equations. (See Illus. 11)

***Illustration* 11**

Given below are the figures of the manufacture of cloth in million metre. Calculate the values of Trend by method of Least Square and plot them on the graph paper :

Year	2005	2006	2007	2008	2009
Production (Ten Million)	4	6	3	5	7

***Solution* :**

Calculation of Trend Values (By Least Square Short-cut Method)

Year	*Production* (Y)	X = *Year* – 2007	X^2	XY	Trend Value $Y_C = a + bx$
2005	4	– 2	4	– 8	[5 + (.5 × - 2) = 4.0
2006	4	– 1	1	– 6	[5 + (.5 × - 1) = 4.5
2007	3	0	0	0	[5 + (.5 × 0) = 5.0
2008	5	+1	1	+ 5	[5 + (.5 × 1) = 5.5
2009	7	+2	4	+ 14	[5 + (.5 × 2) = 6.0
n = 5	ΣY = 25	ΣX = 0	ΣX^2 = 10	ΣXY = 5	ΣY = 25

Now, $Y = a + bX$

Normal equations for finding out the values of '*a*' and '*b*' are

$$\Sigma Y = na + b\,\Sigma X \quad \ldots(i)$$

and

$$\Sigma XY = a\,\Sigma X + b\,\Sigma Y^2 \quad \ldots(ii)$$

Substituting the various values, we have

$$25 = 5a + b(0)$$

$$\therefore \quad a = \frac{25}{5} = 5$$

Now, $5 = a(0) + b(10)$

$$b = \frac{5}{10} = 0.5$$

and

The values of 'Y' will be obtained on the basis of the value of 'X' as given in the above table :

X	– 2	– 1	0	+ 1	+ 2
Y	4	4.5	5	5.5	6

$Y = a + bX = 5 + 0.5X$

When $X = -2$

$Y = 5 + 0.5(-2) = 4.0$

When $X = -1$

$Y = 5 + 05(-1) = 4.5$

When $X = 0$

$Y = 5 + 0.5(0) = 5.0$

When $X = 1$

$Y = 5 + 0.5(1) = 5.5$

When $X = 2$

$Y = 5 + 0.5(2) = 6.0$

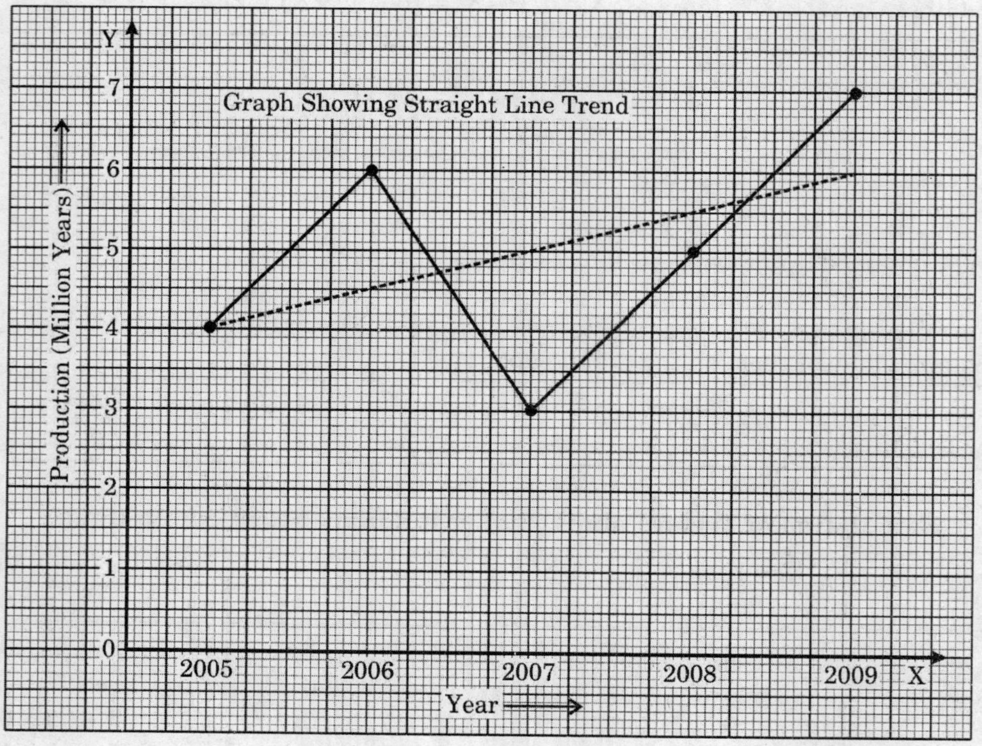

Fig. 10

Alternative Method

Calculation of Trend Values

Year	*S. N. of Year (x)*	*Production (y)*	*xy*	x^2	*Trend Values of y*
2005	1	4	4	1	4.0
2006	2	6	12	4	4.5
2007	3	3	9	9	5.0
2008	4	5	20	16	5.5
2009	5	7	35	25	6.0
$n = 5$	15	25	80	55	25

$\because \quad y = a + bx$

Hence $\quad \Sigma y = na + b\ \Sigma x \quad$ ...(i)

Normal Equations are

$\Sigma xy = ax + b\ \Sigma x^2 \quad$ (ii)

By substituting the value, we get

$25 = 5a + b\,(15) \quad$ ...(i)

$80 = 15a + 55\,(b) \quad$ ...(ii)

or $\quad 25 = 5a + 15\,(b) \quad$ ..(i)

$80 = 15a + 55\,(b) \quad$ ...(ii)

Multiplying (i) by 3 and deducting it from the (ii), we have

$80 = 15(a) + 55(b)$

$75 = 15(a) + 45(b)$

$- \quad - \quad -$

$5 = 10\,(b)$

or $\quad b = \dfrac{5}{10} = 0.5$

$\boxed{b = 0.5}$

Substituting the value of 'b' in equation (i),

$25 = 5a + 15 \times 0.5$

or $\quad 5a = 25 - 7.5$

or $\quad 5a = 17.5$

or $\quad a = \dfrac{17.5}{5} = 3.5$

Calculation of the Trend Values for Different Values of *x* are,

$y = a + bx$

$\Rightarrow \quad y = 3.5 + 0.5\,x$

Thus, if $\quad x = 1$ then $\quad y = 4$

$x = 2$ then $\quad y = 4.5$

$x = 3$ then $\quad y = 5$

$x = 4$ then $\quad y = 5.5$

$x = 5$ then $\quad y = 6$

***Illustration* 12(A) (Using Short-cut Method)**

The following table gives the number of employees in a medium firm as on July 1 for the last five years. Fit a Linear Trend and find the Trend Values. Also estimate the number of employees on 1st July, 2010 :

Year	2011	2012	2013	2014	2015
No. of Employees	100	120	130	140	160

Solution :

Calculation of Trend Values (By Least Square Method)

Year	*Employees*	*x = year – 2013*	x^2	*xy*	*Trend Values* $y_c = a + bx$
2011	100	– 2	4	– 200	130 + (14 × – 2) = 102
2012	120	– 1	1	– 120	130 + (14 × – 1) = 116
2013	130	0	0	0	130 + (14 × 0) = 130
2014	140	+ 1	1	+ 140	130 + (14 × 1) = 144
2015	160	+ 2	4	+ 320	130 + (14 × 2) = 158
$n = 5$	$\Sigma y = 650$	$\Sigma x = 0$	$\Sigma x^2 = 10$	$\Sigma xy = 140$	$y_e = 650$

$y = a + bx$

$a = \dfrac{\Sigma y}{n} = \dfrac{650}{5} = 130$

$b = \dfrac{\Sigma xy}{\Sigma x^2} = \dfrac{140}{10} = 14$

Trend Equation

$y = 130 + 14x$, Origin 2013, Unit : one year

Estimated No. of Employees (2010) = 130 + 14 × (– 3) = 88

(ii) **Parabolic Curves or Non-linear Curve :** When the Time Series data do not confirm with the linear trend then movements are best represented by non-linear trends. The non-linear trends can be parabolic. The second, third and fourth degree parabola provides greater flexibility. However, we shall confine our study only to the second degree parabola.

Fitting a Parabolic Trend by the Method of Least Squares : Parabolas are non-linear but they form smooth curves. The slope of these curves depends upon the values of constants *a*, *b*, *c* etc. The second degree parabola curve equation is

$y = a + bx + cx^2$

The values of *a*, *b* and *c* can be determined by solving three normal equation given below :

Normal Equations

(i) $\quad \Sigma y = na + b\Sigma x + c\Sigma x^2$

(ii) $\quad \Sigma xy = a\Sigma x + b\Sigma x^2 + c\Sigma x^3$

(iii) $\quad \Sigma x^2 y = a\Sigma x^2 + b\Sigma x^3 + c\Sigma x^4$

In practice the all equations are further simplified by letting the sum of X values, which are assigned to represent the number of year in a tie series, be zero.

When $\quad \Sigma x = 0,\ \Sigma x^2 = 0$

The above normal equations now become as under :

(i) $\quad \Sigma y = na + c\Sigma x^2$

(ii) $\quad \Sigma xy = b\Sigma x^2$

(iii) $\quad \Sigma x^2 y = a\Sigma x^2 + c\Sigma x^4$

The value of constant '*b*' can now be directly obtained from equation (ii) and that of '*a*' and '*c*' solving equation (i) and (iii) simultaneously.

$$a = \frac{(\Sigma y - c\Sigma x^2)}{n},$$

$$b = \frac{\Sigma xy}{\Sigma x^2},$$

$$c = \frac{(n\Sigma x^2 y) - (\Sigma x^2 \Sigma y)}{(n\Sigma x^4) - (\Sigma x^2)^2}$$

In order to make $\Sigma x = 0$, the origin of X variable is located in the middle of the period included in the time series. Now when the Time Series has an odd number of years, the (x) values of the series are – 3, – 2, – 1, ..., 1, 2, 3, ... If the x unit is 1 year, when the series has an even number of years, the x values are – 5, – 3, – 1 .... 1, 3, 5 .... If the x unit is 1/2 year.

Illustration 12(B)

The population of a district is given below for different year. Find the population for the year 2016.

Year	2011	2012	2013	2014	2015
Population (in lakhs)	7	9	36	14	16

Solution :

Calculation Table

Time (Year)	*Population* (U_t)	$t' = t - 2013$	t'^2	$t'.U_t$
2011	7	– 2	4	– 14
2012	9	– 1	1	– 9
2013	36	0	0	0
2014	14	1	1	14
2015	16	2	4	32
Total	$\Sigma U_t = 82$	$\Sigma t' = 0$	$\Sigma t'^2 = 10$	$\Sigma t' U_t = 23$

Normal Equations are

$$\Sigma U_t = na + b\Sigma t' \quad ...(i)$$

$$82 = 5a + 0 \times b$$

$$a = \frac{82}{5} = 16.4$$

$$a = 16.4$$

$$\Sigma t' U_t = a\Sigma t' + b\Sigma t'^2 \quad ...(ii)$$

$$23 = a \times 0 + 10b$$

$$b = \frac{23}{10} = 2.3$$

$$b = 2.3$$

Thus, required fitted equation of Trend Line for which we estimated Population for the year 2016 can be obtained, is given below

$$U_t = 16.4 + 2.3t'$$

Now $U_{2016} = 16.4 + 2.3 \times 3$

$$= 16.4 + 6.9$$

$$U_{2016} = 23.3$$ **Ans.**

Illustration 13

Fit a Parabola of the second degree to the following data :

Year	2011	2012	2013	2014	2015
Values of y	5	7	4	9	12

Solution :

Year	*Value (y)*	*x = year – 2013*	*xy*	x^2	x^2y	x^3	x^4	*Trend Values on using* $y = 6 + 1.6x + 0.7x^2$
2011	5	– 2	– 10	4	20	– 8	16	5.6
2012	7	– 1	– 7	1	7	– 1	1	5.1
2013	4	0	0	0	0	0	0	6.0
2014	9	+ 1	+ 9	1	9	1	1	8.3
2015	12	+ 2	+ 24	4	48	8	16	12.0
$n = 5$	$\Sigma y = 37$	$\Sigma x = 0$	$\Sigma xy = 16$	$\Sigma x^2 = 10$	$\Sigma x^2 y = 84$	$\Sigma x^2 = 0$	$\Sigma x^4 = 34$	

Equation of Parabola of the Second Degree $= y = a + bx + cx^2$

Normal Equations of the above equation of parabola are :

$$\Sigma y = na + b\Sigma x + c\Sigma x^2 \quad \text{...(i)}$$
$$\Sigma xy = a\Sigma x + b\Sigma x^2 + c\Sigma x^3 \quad \text{...(ii)}$$
$$\Sigma x^2 y = a\Sigma x^2 + b\Sigma x^3 + c\Sigma x^4 \quad \text{...(iii)}$$

By substituting the values of the above table in the normal equations, we have,

$$37 = 5a + 0 \times b + 10 \times c \quad \text{...(i)}$$

or, $5a + 10c = 37$

$$16 = 0 \times a + 10b + 0 \times c \quad \text{...(ii)}$$

or, $10b = 16$

or, $b = \frac{16}{10} = 1.6$

$$\boxed{b = 1.6}$$

$$84 = 10a + 0b + 34c \quad \text{...(iii)}$$

or $10a + 34c = 84$

Multiplying equation (i) by 2, we have

$$10a + 20c = 74 \quad \text{...(iv)}$$

Now, subtracting (iv) from equation (iii), we have

$$10a + 34c = 84$$
$$10a + 20c = 74 \quad \text{...(iii)}$$
$$- \quad - \quad -$$
$$14c = 10$$

$\Rightarrow$ $c = \frac{10}{14}$

$$\boxed{c = 0.71}$$

$\therefore$ $c = 0.71$ or 0.7 (approx.)

By substituting the value of c in equation (i),

$$5a + 10 \times 0.7 = 37 \text{ or } 5a = 37 - 7$$

or $5a = 30$ or $a = 6$

$$\boxed{a = 6}$$

By substituting the above values of a, i and c in the equation of the parabola of the second degree, *viz.*

$$y = a + bx + cx^2$$
$$y = 6 + 1.6\,x + 0.7\,x^2$$

Now, we can get the value of y for the various values of x, as below :

x	y
-2	$6 + (1.6 \times -2) + 0.7\,(-2)^2 = 5.6$
-1	$6 + (1.6 \times -1) + 0.7\,(-1)^2 = 5.1$
0	$6 + (1.6 \times 0) + 0.7\,(0)^2 = 6.0$
1	$6 + (1.6 \times 1) + 0.7\,(1)^2 = 8.3$
2	$6 + (1.6 \times 1) + 0.7\,(2)^2 = 12.0$

(iii) Logarithmic Straight Line : The logarithmic straight line is used as an expression of the secular movement when the series is increasing or decreasing by a constant percentage rather than a constant absolute amount. The equations of this curve is :

Where the curve is $y = a.bx$

on taking log both sides. Normal Equations can be obtained.

$$\log y = \log a + x \log b$$

or $y = ab^x$

Normal Equation are :

$$\Sigma\,(\log y) = n \log a + \Sigma\,(x) \log b$$
$$\Sigma\,(x.\log y) = \log a\;\; \Sigma\,(x) + \Sigma\,(x^2).\log b$$

If middle year is taken as origin, then Normal Equation are :

$$\Sigma \log y = n \log a$$

$\therefore$ $\log a = \frac{\Sigma \log y}{n}$

$$\Sigma\,(x \log y) = \Sigma\,(x^2) \log b$$

$\therefore$ $\log b = \frac{\Sigma(x, \log y)}{\Sigma(x^2)}$

***Illustration* 14**

The sales of a company in lakh of rupees for the year 2009 to 2015 are given below :

Estimate sales figures for the year 2016 using an equation of the form $y = ab^x$, where x = years and y = sales :

Year	2009	2010	2011	2012	2013	2014	2015
Sales	32	47	65	92	132	190	275

***Solution* :**

Year	*Sales* (y) (₹ in lakh)	x = year – 2012	log y	x^2	x (log y)	log y'	A. L. of log y'
2009	32	– 3	1.5051	9	– 4.5153	1.5084	32.24
2010	47	– 2	1.6721	4	– 3.3442	1.6624	45.96
2011	65	– 1	1.8129	1	– 1.8129	1.8164	65.52
2012	92	– 0	1.9638	0	0	1.9704	93.42
2013	132	– 1	2.2106	1	+ 2.1206	2.1244	133.10
2014	190	– 2	2.2788	4	+ 4.5576	2.2784	189.90
2015	275	– 3	2.4393	9	+ 7.3179	2.4324	270.60
Total	ΣY = 833		Σ log Y = 13.7926	ΣX² = 28	ΣX log y = + 4.3237		

Normal Equations

$$\Sigma (\log y) = n \log a$$

or $$\log a = \frac{\Sigma(\log y)}{n}$$

$$= \frac{13.7926}{7}$$

$$= 1.9704$$

$$\Sigma(x \log y) = (\log b)\, \Sigma x^2$$

or $$\log b = \frac{\Sigma(x.\log y)}{\Sigma x^2}$$

or $$\log b = \frac{4.3237}{28}$$

$$= 0.1544$$

for year 2016

$\therefore$ $x = 4$

Thus we have $\log a = 1.9704$,

$\log b = 0.1544$

Estimates for the year 2016

$\therefore$ $x = 4$

$y = ab^x$ = Antilog $[\log a + x \log b]$

= A.L. $[1.9704 + 4 \times 0.1544]$

= A.L. $[1.9704 + 0.6176]$

$\therefore$ y = A.L. $[2.5888]$

= **387.25** lakh **Ans.**

Merits of Least Square Method : (i) It is a scientific method of determining Trend.

(ii) The line obtained by the method of least squares is the line of best fit.

(iii) It is free from bias, subjectivity does not enter into it.

(iv) Trend value can be estimated or predicted for any other time periods.

Demerits of Least Square Method : (i) It is quite tedious method and involves more calculations.

(ii) The method of least square is not flexible.

(iii) The trend can estimate a value only for immediate future and not for distant future.

(6.8) MEASUREMENT OF SHORT-TIME (SHORT-TERM) FLUCTUATIONS

A Time Series is affected by Secular Trend as well as Short Time Fluctuations. After the computation of Trend Values, we deduct (eliminate) Trend from the original values. The result so obtained is short-time (short-term) fluctuations. In short-time fluctuations both seasonal and cyclical variations are included.

The measurement of short-time fluctuations has been explained in Illustration 15.

Illustration 15

Find the short-time fluctuation of the following Time Series, assuming a Three-Yearly Moving Average :

Year	*Price*
2000	10
2001	8
2002	12
2003	16
2004	14
2005	12
2006	10
2007	20
2008	12
2009	10

Solution :

Measurement of Short-time Fluctuations by 3-yearly Moving Average

Year	*Price* (₹)	*3-Yearly Moving Totals*	*3-Yearly Moving Average* (T)	*Short Time Fluctuations*
2000	10	—	—	—
2001	8	30	10	− 2
2002	12	36	12	0
2003	16	42	14	+ 2
2004	14	42	14	0
2005	12	36	12	0
2006	10	42	14	− 4
2007	20	42	14	+ 6
2008	12	42	14	− 2
2009	10	—	—	—

Graph showing Short-time Fluctuations

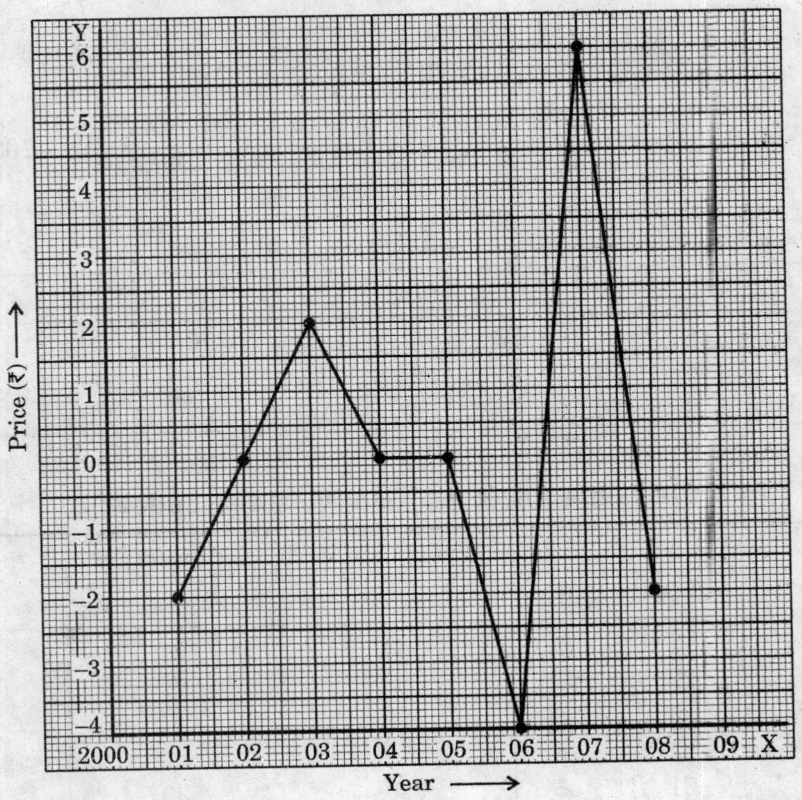

Fig. 11

(6.9) MEASUREMENT OF SEASONAL VARIATIONS

Seasonal Variations

The Seasonal Variations in a Time Series refer to those variations which occur regularly and periodically within a period of less than one year.

Purposes : The following are the purposes of studying seasonal variations :

(i) To study the pattern of seasonal variation themselves.

(ii) To isolate the effect of seasonal factors on a time series.

(iii) To eliminate seasonal variation from the time series.

(iv) To compare changes in seasonal patterns, year after year.

(v) To aid in short-term forecasting and planning.

Methods of Measuring Seasonal Variations : There are five methods of measuring seasonal variations. They are as follows :

(i) Seasonal Variation Index Method or Seasonal Average Method,

(ii) Seasonal Variation through Moving Average,

(iii) Chain or Link Relative Method,

(iv) Ratio to Trend Method,

(v) Ratio to Moving Average Method.

(i) Seasonal Variation Index Method or Seasonal Average Method : This method involves the following steps :

Steps

(i) Arrange the data by years, months or quarters, as the case may be.

(ii) Obtain the totals of each month for all the years. In case of quarterly data obtain the number of quarters.

(iii) Compute the Arithmetic Mean for each month (For example. January, February, ...) from the monthly data or for each quarter say (First, second ...) from the quarterly data for the whole period covered.

(iv) Obtain the over all average ($\overline{X}$) for a month or quarter from all the monthly or quarterly averages as obtained in step (iv). This is given by :

$$\bar{x} = \frac{\bar{x}_1 + \bar{x}_2 + \dots + \bar{x}_{12}}{12} \text{ Monthly or}$$

$$\bar{x} = \frac{\bar{x}_I + \bar{x}_{II} + \bar{x}_{III} + \bar{x}_{IV}}{4} \text{ Quarterly}$$

(v) Lastly obtain seasonal indices for different months expressing each month by (or quarter by) average as a percentage of the over all average.

The following formula should be used for calculating seasonal index for a month (or quarter) :

(i) $$\text{Seasonal Index (Monthly)} = \frac{\text{Monthly Average for the Month}}{\text{Average of Monthly Averages}} \times 100$$

(ii) $$\text{Seasonal Index (Quarterly)} = \frac{\text{Quarterly Average for the Quarter}}{\text{Average of Quarterly Averages}} \times 100$$

***Illustration* 16**

Compute the Seasonal Variation Indices for the following Time Series :

Year	*Jan.*	*Feb.*	*Mar.*	*April*	*May*	*June*	*July*	*Aug.*	*Sept.*	*Oct.*	*Nov.*	*Dec.*
2013	15	16	18	18	23	23	20	28	29	33	33	38
2014	23	22	28	27	31	28	22	28	32	37	34	44
2015	25	25	35	36	36	30	30	34	38	47	41	53

***Solution* :**

Calculation of Seasonal Variation Index

Month	*year*			*3 years Total*	*Monthly Average*	*Index No. of Seasonal Variation*
	2013	2014	2015			
January	15	23	25	63	21	70
February	16	22	25	63	21	70
March	18	28	35	81	27	90
April	18	27	36	81	27	90
May	23	31	36	90	30	100
June	23	31	36	81	27	90
July	20	22	30	72	24	80
August	28	28	34	90	30	100
September	29	32	38	99	33	100
October	33	37	47	117	39	130
November	33	34	41	108	36	120
December	38	44	53	135	45	150
	Total			1,080	360	1,200
	General Average			90[1]	30[2]	100

Working Notes : (1) $\frac{1,080}{12} = 90$

(2) $\frac{360}{12} = 30$

(3) $$\text{Seasonal Variation Index} = \frac{\text{Average of January}}{\text{General Average}} \times 100$$

$$= \frac{21}{30} \times 100 = 70$$

The same procedure has been followed to find out seasonal variation indices for the remaining months.

***Illustration* 17**

Compute the average seasonal movement for the following data relating to the revenue expenditure, Government of Jharkhand :

Years	*April-June*	*July-Sept.*	*Oct.-Dec.*	*Jan.-March*
2012	36	43	44	102
2013	39	44	57	98
2014	47	53	58	104
2015	47	56	60	130

Solution :

Calculation of Quarterly Seasonal Variation Indices

Year	Quarters			
	April-June	*July-Sept.*	*Oct.-Dec.*	*Jan-March*
2012	36	43	44	102
2013	39	44	57	98
2014	47	53	58	104
2015	47	56	60	130
Total	169	196	219	434
Qtly. Average	42.25	49	54.75	108.5
Quarterly Seasonal Variation Indices	$\frac{42.25 \times 100}{63.6}$ = 66.43	$\frac{49 \times 100}{63.6}$ = 77.04	$\frac{54.75 \times 100}{63.6}$ = 86.08	$\frac{108.5 \times 100}{63.6}$ = 170.59

$$\text{General Average} = 42.25 + 49 + 54.75 + 108.5$$

$$= \frac{254.5}{4}$$

$$= 63.625 = 63.6 \text{ (Approx).}$$

1st Quarterly Seasonal Variation Index

$$= \frac{\text{Qtly Average}}{\text{General Average}} \times 100$$

$$\therefore \quad = \frac{42.25 \times 100}{63.6} = 66.4$$

(ii) **Seasonal Variation through Moving Averages :** Among all the methods of measuring seasonal variation, moving average method is the more satisfactory and in widely used. This method analyses all types of variations Trend, Short-Term, Cyclical and Irregular variations. This is based on the Additive Model of time series analysis.

Procedure of Measurement :

Steps :

(i) First of all the *moving averages* of the data are computed. If the data are monthly, then 12 monthly moving averages should be computed. If the data are quarterly, then 4 quarterly moving averages should be computed.

(ii) From each original value (0) the corresponding to moving average figure should be subtracted (deducted) to find out short-term fluctuations.

We know that O or $Y = T + S + C + I$

Therefore, O or $Y - T = S + C + I$

(iii) By preparing a separate table, monthly or quarterly short-term fluctuations are added for each month or (quarter) and their average or mean is calculated. The averages are known as seasonal variations for each month or quarter.

(iv) If we want to isolate or measure irregular variations, the mean of the respective month or quarter is deduted from the short-term variations.

(See Illustration 18)

Advantages : We can analyse the components of trend, short-terms fluctuations, seasonal variations, irregular fluctuations by using this method. But cyclical fluctuations are not measured by this method.

Illustration 18

Find out Seasonal Fuctuations by the Method of Moving Averages :

Year	*1st Quarter*	*2nd Quarter*	*3rd Quarter*	*4th Quarter*
2011	60	80	72	68
2012	68	104	100	88
2013	80	116	108	96
2014	108	152	116	124
2015	160	184	172	164

Solution :

Year	*Quarters*	*Original Data(0)*	*Quarterly Total*	*Total Centered*	*Qtly. Moving Average (T)*	*Short Time Fluctua. (iii) (vi)*	*Seasonal Variation (S)*	*Irregular Fluctuations(I) (vii)–(viii)*
(i)	(ii)	(iii)	(iv)	(v)	(vi)	(vii)	(vii)	(ix)
2011	I	60						
	II	80	280					
	III	72	288	568	71.0	+ 1.0	– 0.4	+ 1.4
	IV	68	312	600	75.0	– 7.0	– 11.8	+ 4.8

2012	I	68	340	652	81.5	– 13.5	– 8.1	– 5.4
	II	104	360	700	87.5	+ 16.5	20.8	– 4.3
	III	100	372	732	91.5	+ 8.5	– 0.4	+ 8.9
	IV	88	384	756	94.5	– 6.5	– 11.8	+ 5.3
2013	I	80	392	776	97.0	– 17	– 8.1	– 8.9
	II	116	400	792	99.0	+ 17	20.8	– 3.8
	III	108	428	828	103.5	+ 4.5	– 0.4	+ 4.9
	IV	96	464	892	111.5	– 15.5	– 11.8	– 3.7
2014	I	108	472	936	117.0	– 9.0	– 8.1	– 0.9
	II	152	500	972	121.5	+ 30.5	20.8	+ 9.7
	III	116	552	1,052	131.5	– 15.5	– 0.4	– 15.1
	IV	124	584	1.136	142.0	– 18.0	– 11.8	– 6.2
2015	I	160	640	1,224	153.0	+ 7.0	– 8.1	+ 15.1
	II	184	680	1,320	165.0	+ 19.0	20.8	– 1.8
	III	172						
	IV	164						

Calculation of Average Seasonal Variation

Years	*Quarters*			
	I	II	III	IV
2011	—	—	+ 1.0	– 7.0
2012	– 13.5	+ 16.5	+ 8.5	– 6.5
2013	– 17.0	+ 17.0	+ 4.5	– 15.5
2014	– 9.0	+ 30.5	– 15.5	– 18.0
2015	+ 7.0	+ 19.0	—	—
Total	– 32.5	83.0	– 1.5	– 47.0
Average	– 8.125	20.75	– 0.375	– 11.75

Working Notes :

1. Add in fours—*e.g.*, (60 + 80 + 72 + 68) = 280
   (80 + 72 + 68 + + 68) = 288 and so on.
2. Add in pairs—*e.g.* (280 + 288) = 568
   (288 + 312) = 600 and so on.
3. Divide by 8—*e.g.*, 568 ÷ 8 = 71

(iii) **Chain or Link Relative Method :** This method involves following steps :

Step :

(i) Link Relative of the seasonal figures are calculated :

Link Relative (L. R.)

$$= \frac{\text{Current season's value (or figure)}}{\text{Previous season's value (or figure)}} \times 100$$

For example : L. R. for April

$$= \frac{\text{Value (fig). for April}}{\text{Value (fig.) for March}} \times 100$$

Note :

(a) Current season's value may be either monthly or quarterly.

(b) There shall be no link relative corresponding to the first month/quarter.

(ii) Average of link relatives is computed for each month or season/quarter.

Mean or Median may be used for averaging.

(iii) Convert the average link relatives into chain relatives (C.R.). Assume the figure of first month or quarter equal to 100. The chain relatives should be calculated by applying following formula :

(1) $$\text{C.R. for any month} = \frac{\text{L. R. of that month} \times \text{C. R. of preceding month}}{100}$$

(2) $$\text{C. R. for any quarter} = \frac{\text{L. R. of that quarter} \times \text{C. R. of preceding quarter}}{100}$$

or

For Example :

The chain relative for the third quarter will be :

$$\frac{\text{L. R. Arithmetic Mean of the 3rd Quarter} \times \text{C. R. of the 2nd Quarter}}{100}$$

The chain relative for the fourth quarter will be :

$$\frac{\text{L. R. Arithmetic Mean of the 4th Quarter} \times \text{C. R. of the 3rd Quarter}}{100}$$

(iv) The second chain relative of 1st month or quarter (season) is computed on the basis of chain relatives of the last (month/quarter/season).

$$\text{Chain relative of the first quarter} = \frac{\text{Average Link Relative of the first} \times \text{Chain Relative of the Last}}{100}$$

Example 1. The second chain relative for January next year on the basis of December (previous year)

$$\text{C. R.} = \frac{\text{L. R. of January} \times \text{C. R. for December of the preceding year}}{100}$$

Example 2.

$$= \frac{\text{1st quarter (of the next year) L.R.} \times \text{4th quarter Cr.}}{100}$$

This chain relative may or may not be 100. It is not equal to 100 due to secular trend.

Note : Usually this chain relative is not equal to 100. It is, therefore, necessary to adjust the chain relatives for the effect of trend.

(v) **Correction Factor :** This adjustment is done by subtracting a correction factor from each chain relative.

For correction find out the difference (d) between the new chain relatives of first as obtained in step (iv) and chain relative assume as 100. Difference (d) is divided by the number of seasons. The resulting figure is multiplied by 1, 2, 3. The product is deducted respectively from the chain relatives of second, third and fourth quarters. These are known as correct chain relatives.

(vi) The corrected chain relatives are expressed as percentages of their averages to give the required seasonal indices, *i.e.*, adjusted chain relatives.

Seasonal Index (S.I.) on the basis of Corrected Chain Relatives

Formula :

$$\text{S.I.} = \frac{\text{Corrected Chain Relative}}{\text{General Average}} \times 100$$

Where : General Average

$$= \frac{\text{Sum of Corrected Chain Relatives (of } Q_1, Q_2, Q_3 \text{ and } Q_4)}{4}$$

***Illustration* 19**

From the following data, calculate the index of Seasonal Variation through "Link Relatives Method".

Prices in seasons

Year	*Summer*	*Monsoon*	*Autumn*	*Winter*
2012	20	40	60	80
2013	30	30	40	90
2014	40	60	30	120
2015	50	50	70	150

***Solution* :**

Computation of Seasonal Variation by Link Relatives Method

	Link Relatives			
Year	I *Quarter*	II *Quarter*	III *Quarter*	IV *Quarter*
2012		200	160.0	133.3
2013	37.5	100	133.3	225.0
2014	44.4	150	50.0	400.0
2015	41.6	100	140.0	214.2
Total L.R.	123.5	550	483.3	972.5
Average of L.R.	$\frac{123.5}{3} = 41.66$	$\frac{550}{4} = 137.5$	$\frac{483.3}{4} = 120.82$	$\frac{972.5}{4} = 243.12$
Chain Relatives (C.R.)	100	$\frac{100 \times 137.5}{100} = 137.5$	$\frac{137.5 \times 120.82}{100} = 166.12$	$\frac{166.2 \times 243.12}{100} = 404.06$
Adjusted Chain Relatives	100	137.5 – 17.08 = 120.42	166.12 – 34.16 = 31.96	404.06 – 16.8 = 378.9
Seasonal Indices	$\frac{100}{176.3} \times 100 = 56.27$	$\frac{120.42}{176.3} \times 100 = 68.30$	$\frac{131.96}{176.3} \times 100 = 78.84$	$\frac{352.82}{176.3} \times 100 = 200.12$

Working Notes :

(i) L.R. :

2012 : (I) —, (II) $\frac{40 \times 100}{20} = 200$

(III) $\frac{60 \times 100}{40} = 150$, (IV) $\frac{80 \times 100}{60} = 133.3$

2013 : (I) $\frac{30 \times 100}{80} = 37.5$ and so on, ...

(II) $$\text{Adjusted C.R.} = \frac{\text{L.R. of 1st Quarter} \times \text{C.R. of the last Quarter}}{100}$$

$$= \frac{41.66 \times 404.06}{100} = 168.33$$

$$\text{Difference } (d) = 168.33 - 100 = 68.33$$

$\therefore$ Correction Factor $= \frac{68.33}{17.08} = 17.08$ (approx.)

or Difference per Quarter

$$= \frac{68.33}{4} = 17.08$$

$\therefore$ Adjusted Chain Relatives

I Quarter = 100

II Quarter = 137.5 – 17.08 = 120.42

III Quarter = 166.12 – 34.16 = 131.96

IV Quarter = 404.06 – 51.24 = 352.82

(iii) Average of Adjusted Chain Index

$$= \frac{100 + 120.42 + 131.96 + 352.82}{4}$$

$$= \frac{705.2}{4} = 176.3$$

(iv) **Ratio to Trend Method : Procedure :**

Steps :

1. First of all Trend values are obtained for seasonal period (month or quarter) by applying least square method. For determining trend values monthly or quarterly average should be calculated and then other steps of measuring of trend by least square method should be followed.
2. Divide the original data month by month or quarter by quarter corresponding to trend values. Multiply the quotient by 100.
   Now cyclical and irregular variations have to be eliminated.
3. For every seasonal time period (month or quarter) of all the years arithmetic mean will be calculated.
4. Adding all the averages of all the seasonal time period, a general average is calculated.
5. Assuming this general average [as obtained in step (iv)] equal to 100, seasonal indices for all the seasonal time period will be computed.

Seasonal Index

$$= \frac{\text{Seasonal Average of Ratio Trend}}{\text{General Average of Ratio to Trend}} \times 100$$

Ratio to trend method is also known as percentage trend value.

Illustration 20

Calculate Seasonal Variation by Ratio-to-Trend method from the following data :

Year	*Quarters*			
	1st	*2nd*	*3rd*	*4th*
2011	30	40	36	34
2012	34	52	50	44
2013	40	57	54	48
2014	54	76	68	62
2015	80	92	86	82

Solution :

In year (2011) (30 + 40 + 36 + 34) = 140

$\therefore$ A. M. or $\overline{X} = 140 \div 4 = 35$

Let Annual Value be *Y* then Trend values by the Least squares Method :

Calculation of Annual Trend Values

Year	*Yearly Totals*	*Average Quarterly Values (y)*	*x*	*xy*	x^2	*Trend Values* $y = a + bx$	$y = 56 + 12x$
2011	140	35	– 2	– 70	4	32	56 + 12 (– 2) = 32
2012	180	45	– 1	– 45	1	44	56 + 12(– 1) = 44
2013	200	50	0	0	0	56	56 + 12(0) = 56
2014	260	65	+ 1	+ 65	1	68	56 + 12 × 1 = 68
2015	340	85	+ 2	+ 170	4	80	56 + 12 × 2 = 80
Total	1120	$\Sigma y = 280$	$\Sigma x = 0$	$\Sigma xy = 120$	$\Sigma x^2 = 10$	$\Sigma y = 280$	$\Sigma y = 280$

Here

$$y = a + bx$$
$$\Sigma y = na$$

$\therefore \quad a = \frac{\Sigma y}{n} = \frac{280}{5} = 56$

and $\quad \Sigma xy = b\Sigma x^2$

$\therefore \quad b = \frac{\Sigma xy}{\Sigma x^2} = \frac{120}{10} = 12$

Computation of Quarterly Trend Values

The Annual Trend Value of the million quarter, *i.e.*, 2011 is 32. It should come between 2nd and 3rd quarter.

Quarterly rate of increase

$= \frac{\text{Annual Increase}}{4} = \frac{12}{4}$

$= 3$

Therefore,Trend value of the second quarter

$= 32 - (3/2) = 32 - 1.5$

$= 30.5$

Trend Value of the third quarter

$= 32 + (3/2) = 32 + 1.5$

$= 33.5$

Trend Value first quarter

$= 30.5 - 3 = 27.5$

Trend Value of the fourth quarter

$= 33.5 + 3 = 36.5$

Similarily trend values for all quarters of the years will be calculated.

Quarterly Trend Values

Year	1st *Qtr.*	2nd *Qtr.*	3rd *Qtr.*	4th *Qtr.*	*Total*
2011	27.5	30.5	33.5	36.5	128
2012	39.5	42.5	45.5	48.5	176
2013	51.5	54.5	57.5	60.5	224
2014	63.5	66.5	69.5	72.5	272
2015	75.5	78.5	81.5	84.5	320
Total					1,120

De-Trend Values

or

Trend Eliminated Values

Year	*1st Qtr.*	*2nd Qtr.*	*3rd Qtr.*	*4th Qtr.*
2011	109.09	131.14	107.46	93.15
2012	86.07	122.35	109.89	90.72
2013	77.66	104.58	93.91	79.33
2014	85.03	114.28	97.84	85.51
2015	105.96	117.19	105.52	97.04
Total	463.31	589.54	514.62	445.75
Average	92.66	117.90	102.92	89.15
Seasonal Indices	92.06	117.13	102.25	88.57

Working Note :

$\frac{O}{T} \times 100 = \frac{30}{27.5} \times 100$

$= 109.09$

Where, O = Original Time Series data.
T = Trend Values (obtained by Least Squares Method)

$\frac{40 \times 100}{30.5} = \frac{8\,000}{61} = 131.14$ and so on.

$\text{Seasonal Indices} = \frac{\text{Quarterly Average}}{\text{General Average}} \times 100$

$\text{1st Qtr.} = \frac{92.66}{100.65} \times 100 = 92.06$

$\text{2nd Qtr.} = \frac{117.9}{100.65} \times 100 = 117.13$

$\text{3rd Qtr.} = \frac{102.92}{100.65} \times 100 = 102.25$

$\text{4th Qtr.} = \frac{89.15}{100.65} \times 100 = 88.57$

$\text{General Average} = \frac{92.66 + 117.90 + 102.9 + 89.15}{4}$

$= 100.65$

Note : The total of seasonal indices should be equal to 400 and that for monthly indices should be 1,200.

(v) **Ratio to Moving Average Method :** This method is the most commonly used method of measuring seasonal variations. This method consists of the following steps :

Steps :

(i) Calculate the moving averages four quarterly, 12 monthly, as the case may be.

(ii) Divide the original value (O or Y) by the corresponding moving average (T) and express it as percentage. The trend and cyclical elements tend to be persent in the moving averages. In that case 'O' should be divided by 'T' and 'C' multiplied by 100.

Thus the formula will be as under :

$$\frac{O}{T \times C} \times 100 = \frac{T \times S \times C \times I}{T \times C}$$

$$= S \times I \times 100$$

Ratio to moving average represents the seasonal and irregular components. Trend and cyclical components are eliminated in the division by moving average.

(iii) The ratio to moving average is arranged season-wise and average for each season over all years is obtained. Average may be computed either by arithmetic mean or median.

(iv) Lastly seasonal indices are obtained on the basis of general average of averages as percentage.

Illustration 21

Calculate Seasonal Indices by the Ratio-to-Moving Average Method from the following data :

Year	*1st Qtr.*	*2nd Qtr.*	*3rd Qtr.*	*4th Qtr.*
2013	68	62	61	63
2014	65	58	66	61
2015	68	63	63	67

Solution :

Calculation of Seasonal Indices by Ratio-to-Moving Average Method

Year	*Qtr.*	*(O)*	*4-Quarterly Moving Total*	*Centred Total*	*4-Quarterly Moving Average (T)*	*Ratio-to Moving Average* $\left(\frac{O}{T} \times 100\right)$
2013	I	68				
	II	62	254			
	III	61	251	505	63.12	96.64
	IV	63	247	498	62.25	101.20
2014	I	65	252	499	62.37	104.21
	II	58	250	502	62.75	92.43
	III	66	253	503	62.87	104.97
	IV	61	258	511	63.87	95.50
2015	I	68	255	513	64.12	106.05
	II	63	261	516	64.5	97.67
	III	63				
	IV	67				

Year	Quarter I	II	III	IV
2013	—	—	96.64	101.20
2014	104.21	92.43	104.97	95.50
2015	106.05	97.67	—	—
Total	210.26	190.10	201.61	196.70
Average	105.13	95.0	100.80	93.35
Seasonal Indices	105.23	95.09	100.90	98.44

Working Note :

Average of Averages : General Average $= \frac{105.13 + 95.0 + 100.8 + 98.35}{4} = \frac{399.63}{4} = 99.90$

Computation of Seasonal Indices :

1st Quarter $= \frac{105.13}{99.90} \times 100 = 105.23$

2nd Quarter $= \frac{95.0}{99.90} \times 100 = 95.09$

3rd Quarter $= \frac{100.8}{99.90} \times 100 = 100.90$

4th Quarter $= \frac{98.35}{99.90} \times 100 = 98.44$

(6.10) MEASUREMENT OF CYCLICAL VARIATIONS

Meaning : Cyclical variations extend over a comparatively long period than the Seasonal variations. It may be defined as Recurrent but not necessarily periodic fluctuations in business activity over a period of years.

Measurement of Cyclical Variations : No complete satisfactory method of measuring directly the cyclical variations in the Time Series has been developed. However, Croxton has suggested four method for the measurement of Cyclical Fuctuations. They are :

(i) The Residual Method,

(ii) Direct Method,

(iii) Harmonic Analysis Method,

(iv) Method of Cyclical Averages.

For convenience, we shall discuss only the resident method.

The residual method attempts to remove the variation in the series that results from seasonal forces or serular trend. The remaining fluctuations are considered to be cyclical and irregular movements.

The Residual method involves the following steps :

(i) First of all Trend Values (T) and seasonal indices (S) are obtained by applying appropriate method.

(ii) The original values are divided by the respective Trend Value and the results are multiplied by 100. This is Ratio-to-trend in percentages.

In case of multiplicative model

$$Y \text{ or } O = T \times S \times C \times I$$

$$\text{Obtain } \frac{O}{T} \times 100 \text{ or } S \times C \times I \times 100$$

$$\text{or} \quad \frac{T \times S \times C \times I}{T} \times 100$$

(iii) To obtain cyclical variations the ratio to trend figures are divided by seasonal indices, *viz.*,

$$\frac{S \times C \times I}{S} = CI$$

$$\text{or} \quad \frac{S \times C \times I}{S} \times 100 \text{ or } C \times I \times 100$$

The original values can be divided by the product of trend and seasonal index figure to find cyclical variations.

$$\text{Thus, } \frac{T \times S \times C \times I}{T \times S} \times 100 = C \times I \times 100$$

Remarks : (i) If the series is not influenced by Random Variations or Irregular Variations, then the figures obtained by the step (ii) will be Cyclical Variations.

(ii) If the Time Series is affected by Random Variations, then they may be eliminated by taking moving averages or appropriate time period.

Additive Model :

In case of additive model

$$O \text{ or } Y = T + S + C + I$$

$$O \text{ or } Y - T = S + C + I$$

and then, $O \text{ or } Y - T - S = C + I$

(6.11) MEASUREMENT OF IRREGULAR OR RANDOM MOVEMENTS/FLUCTUATIONS

There is no specific method for the measurement of irregular or random fluctuations. It represents the residual variation after trend, seasonal variations and cyclical fluctuations have been calculated for. Therefore, the residual method is applied.

(1) On the basis of Additive Model :

$$\because \quad O = T + S + C + I$$

$$\therefore \quad C + I = O - T - S$$

$$\text{or} \quad I = O - T - S - C$$

(2) On the basis of Multiplicative Model :

$$O = T \times S \times C \times I$$

$$\therefore \quad I = \frac{O}{T \times S \times C}$$

Important Formulae of Time Series :

Additive Model

$O = T + S + C + I$

$T = O - S - C - I$

Multiplicative Model

$O = T \times S \times C \times I$

$O = \dfrac{O}{S \times C \times I}$

METHOD OF LEAST SQUARES

Linear Trend :

Key Equation $= Y_c = a + bx$

Direct Method

$\Sigma y = na + b\Sigma x$ ...(i)

$\Sigma xy = a\,\Sigma x + b\,\Sigma x^2$ ...(ii)

Short-cut Method

$\Sigma y = na$ ...(i)

$\Sigma xy = b\,\Sigma x^2$ ...(ii)

Non-Linear Trend or Parabolic Trend :

$Y : a + bx + c\,x^2 + dx^3$

Direct Method

$\Sigma y = na + b\Sigma x + cx^2$ ...(i)

$\Sigma xy = a\Sigma x + b\,\Sigma x^2 + \Sigma x^3$ ...(ii)

$\Sigma x^2 y = a\Sigma x^2 + c\,\Sigma x^4$ ...(iii)

Short-cut Method

$\Sigma y = na + c\,\Sigma x^2$ ...(i)

$\Sigma xy = b\,\Sigma x^2$ ...(ii)

$\Sigma x^2 y = a\,\Sigma x^2 + c\,\Sigma x^4$ ...(iii)

SHORT TIME FLUCTUATIONS

$S = O - T$

$S = \dfrac{O}{T \times C \times I}$

CYCLICAL AND IRREGULAR FLUCTUATIONS

$C + I = O - T - S$

$C \times I = \dfrac{O}{T \times S}$

$I = O - T - S - C$

$I = \dfrac{O}{T \times S \times C}$

THEORETICAL QUESTIONS

Long Answer Type Questions

1. What is a time series ? Show its importance.
2. What is meant by Time Series Analysis ? Indicate fully the importance of such analysis in business.
3. What are the components of time series ? Analyse the different methods of estimating the trend components of time series.
4. What is a time series ? What are its main components ?
5. What is a time series ? Explain the moving average method of estimating trend.
6. What are the components of time series ? How would you find out the trend values in a time series by a method of least squares ? Illustrate by numerical example.
7. Distinguish between secular trend, seasonal variation and cyclical fluctuations. How would you measure secular trend in any given data ?
8. What is a secular trend ? Critically examine the various methods of measuring trend.
9. Define a time series. What are the main constitutents of an economic time series ?
10. What do you mean by seasonal components of a time series ? Describe the various methods of isolating components from a time series and examine them critically.

Short/Very Short Answer Type Questions

1. What do you understand by analysis of time series ? *Or*, What is the time series ? (*JAC*, 2026)
2. Describe the components of time series.
3. State the importance of analysis of time series.
4. What do you understand by trend ?
5. State the merits and limitations of semi-average method.
6. Describe the moving average method of trend.
7. State the merits of least square method.
8. Explain the following :
   (i) Ratio-to-Moving Average Method
   (ii) Ratio-to-Trend Method
   (iii) Measurement of Seasonal Variation
   (iv) Irregular Fluctuations
9. Explain in brief the least squares method of finding out trend.
   Or, How would trend be determined in a time series ?

PRACTICAL PROBLEMS

Measurement of Trend or Secular Trend

Freehand Curve Method

1. Plot the following data on a graph showing Secular Trend by Freehand Curve Method :

Year	1999	2000	01	02	03	04	05	06	07	08	09
Production (000 ton)	5	10	8	12	15	10	18	20	15	25	20

2. Find out Secular Trend by Freehand Curve Method from the following data : (₹ in crores)

Year	2000	01	02	03	04	05	06	07	08	09
Profit	2	3	2.5	3.5	4	3.5	4	6	5	8

Semi-average Method

3. Find the trend of the following values by semi-average method :

Year	2004	2005	2006	2007	2008	2009
Sales (000 units)	20	24	22	30	28	32

[**Ans.** 2005 = 22; 2008 = 30]

4. Find the long-term trend from the following data by semi-average method :

Year	2003	2004	2005	2006	2007	2008	2009
Production of Rice (Lakh ton)	45	40	44	40	49	42	53

[**Ans.** Av. of the 1st. Part 43, Av. of the 2nd Part 48]

5. Find the trend of the following values by semi-average method :

Year	1998	1999	2000	01	02	03	04	05	06	07	08	09
Profit (₹ in Lakh)	5	7	6	9	8	10	12	11	16	15	14	20

[**Ans.** 7.5, 14.7]

Moving Average Method

6. Represent graphically the following numbers of labours in a factory :

Year	2001	2002	2003	2004	2005	2006	2007	2008	2009
No. of Labours	2412	2440	2486	2424	2458	2513	2409	2488	2528

Calculation 3-yearly moving averages from the above and plot them also.
[**Ans.** 2002 : 2446, 2003 : 2450, 2004 : 2456, 2005 : 2465, 2006 : 2460, 2007 : 2470, 2008 : 2475.]

7. Find out the value of the trend by three yearly moving average and plot them on a graph paper : (*JAC*, 2007 Modified)

Year	1985	86	87	88	89	90	91	92	93	94	95	96	97
Value	10	15	12	18	15	22	19	24	20	26	22	30	25

[**Ans.** (—), 12, 15, 15, 18, 19, 22, 21, 23, 23, 26, 26]

8. Find the centred 4-yearly moving average for the following time series data : (*JAC*, 2014)

Year	2002	2003	2004	2005	2006	2007	2008	2009
Units	30.1	45.4	39.3	41.4	42.4	46.4	46.6	49.2

[**Ans.** 2004—40.56, 2005—42.2, 2006—43.23, 2007—45.12]

9. From the following table calculate trend values by the 4-yearly moving average :

Year	1998	1999	2000	01	02	03	04	05	06	07	08	09
Value	100	105	115	90	95	85	80	65	75	70	75	80

[**Ans.** 101.87, 98.75, 91.87, 84.37, 78.75, 74.37, 71.87, 73.12] (*JAC*, 2015)

10. In the following series, find the five-yearly moving averages :

Year	2003	2004	2005	2006	2007	2008	2009
Index	110	125	135	140	150	195	210

[**Ans.** 2005 : 132, 2006 : 149, 2007 : 166]

10A. Calculate trend by 3 yearly moving average method : (*JAC*, 2025)

2000	2001	2002	2003	2004	2005	2006
20	10	30	80	40	50	60

[**Ans.** 2001—20, 2002—40, 2003—50, 2004—56.67, 2005—50]

Least Squares Method

11. Calculate by the method of least squares the trend values of the following :

Year	2011	2012	2013	2014	2015
Sales (000 ₹)	35	56	79	80	48

[**Ans.** Trend 49.6, 54.6, 59.6, 64.6, 69.6]

12. Find the trend values in the following series by Least Squares Method : (*JAC*, 2024)

Year	2009	2010	2011	2012	2013	2014	2015
Production (000 ton)	77	88	94	85	91	98	90

[**Ans.** Trend Values : 83, 85, 87, 89, 91, 93, 95] (*JAC*, 2007)

13. Apply the method of least squares to obtain trend values from the following data :

Year	2011	2012	2013	2014	2015
Sales (Lakh ton)	100	120	110	140	80

[**Ans.** T—114, 112, 110, 108, 106]

14. Find the trend values by least squares method from the following time series data : (*JAC*, 2020)

Year	2010	2011	2012	2013	2014	2015
Production (lakh ton)	5	7	9	10	12	17

[**Ans.** 4.5, 6.7, 8.9, 11.1, 13.3, 15.5]

15. Find the trend values by the method of least squares :

Year	2009	2010	2011	2012	2013	2014	2015
Export (₹ in crore)	80	90	92	83	94	99	92

[**Ans.** $y = 90 + 2x$, Origin 2012, 84, 86, 88, 90, 92, 94, 96.]

16. Fit a straight line trend equation by method of least squares and estimate the values of 2011 :

Year	2002	2003	2004	2005	2006	2007	2008	2009
Values	380	400	650	720	690	600	870	930

[**Ans.** Trend Equation : $Y = 655 + 35.58X$; $Y_{2011} = 1048.8$]

17. The following are the annual profit in thousand rupees in a certain business :

Year	2003	2004	2005	2006	2007	2008	2009
Profit (000)	60	72	75	65	80	85	95

By the method of least squares fit a straight line. Using that estimate the profit for 2010.
[**Ans.** Y = 76 + 4.857X, Estimate for 2010 ₹ 95.428 thousand.]

18. The following data relate to the number of passenger cars (in million) sold from 2002 to 2009 :

Year	2002	2003	2004	2005	2006	2007	2008	2009
Number	6	8	12	10	14	16	15	18

(i) Fit a straight line trend to the above data.
(ii) Plot the above figures and draw the line.
(iii) Also make an estimate of sales for the year 2010.
[**Ans.** $a = 12.4$, $b = 0.8$, T = 6.8, 8.4 ... , Estimate for 2010 = 19.6]

18A. Calculate trend by least square method : (*JAC*, 2025)

Year	2000	2001	2002	2003	2004
Production	45	74	89	92	106

[**Ans.** $a = 81.2$, $b = 14.7$, trend equation = $y = a + bx$]

Fitting a Parabolic or Non-linear Trend

19. Fit a second degree of parabola of the following data

Year	2011	2012	2013	2014	2015
y	8	7	14	19	12

[Y = 6, 11, 14, 15, 14]

20. Fit a parabola of the second order to the following data and estimate the figure for 2016 :

Year	2009	2010	2011	2012	2013	2014	2015
y	13	13	22	21	54	60	83

[**Ans.** y = 12, 14, 20, 30, 44, 62, 84, Figure for 2016 = 110]

Logarithmic Straight Line

21. Find the trend values by Logarithmic Straight Line Method : (*JAC*, 2023)

Year	2011	2012	2013	2014	2015
Value	34	50	67	75	85

Estimate the values for 2019.
[**Ans.** 115.7, $\log a = 1.7722$, $\log b = 0.0097$]

Short-term Fluctuation

22. Compute the seasonal variation indices for the following data :

Quarter/Year	2012	2013	2014	2015
1st (Jan-March)	75	86	90	100
2nd (April-June)	60	65	73	78
3rd (July-Sept.)	54	63	66	72
4th (Oct.-Dec.)	59	80	85	93

[**Ans.** Seasonal Index for I—117.10, II—92.08, III—85.07, IV—105.76]

23. Calculate the quarterly seasonal indices from the data given below :

Year	*1st Quarter*	*2nd Quarter*	*3rd Quarter*	*4th Quarter*
2012-13	5.2	5.7	5.4	5.8
2013-14	5.3	4.8	5.7	5.6
2014-15	6.2	6.5	5.3	4.8
2015-16	3.5	5.0	5.4	5.2

[**Ans.** 94.61, 103.04, 102.10, 100.23]

24. Using the data given below, calculate the seasonal variation :

Year	*Summer*	*Monsoon*	*Autumn*	*Winter*
1	30	81	62	199
2	30	104	85	171
3	42	153	99	221
4	56	172	129	235
5	67	201	136	302

[**Ans.** Seasonal Vari. : $Q_1 = -75$, $Q_2 = 25$, $Q_3 = -19$, $Q_4 = 68$]

25. Construct the index of seasonal variations from the following data :

Year	Jan.	Feb.	Mar.	Apr.	May	June	July	Aug.	Sep.	Oct.	Nov.	Dec.
2013	18	20	18	17	15	16	17	19	21	23	23	24
2014	20	22	19	18	16	20	24	23	23	24	24	26
2015	22	19	20	18	17	18	24	25	26	24	25	27

[**Ans.** 95.41, 96.99, 90.64, 84.25, 76.33, 85.87, 103.33, 106.53, 111.3, 112.88, 114.50, 122.42]

Seasonal Variation through Moving Averages

26. Find out the seasonal fluctuations by the method of moving averages :

Year	1st *Qtr.*	2nd *Qtr.*	3rd *Qtr.*	4th *Qtr.*
2011	30	40	36	34
2012	34	52	50	44
2013	40	58	54	48
2014	54	76	58	62
2015	80	92	86	82

[**Ans.** Av. Seasonal Variation—I Qtr. = – 4.06, II Qtr. = 10.37, III Qtr. = – 0.18, IV Qtr. = – 5.87]

Link Relative Method

27. Find out the seasonal variation by the link relative method from the following data :

Year	*Ist Quarter*	*IInd Quarter*	*IIIrd Quarter*	*IVth Quarter*
2011	45	54	72	60
2012	48	56	63	56
2013	49	63	70	65
2014	52	65	75	72
2015	60	70	84	77

[**Ans.** 82.67, 98,75, 115.69, 102.86]

28. From the following data, calculate the index of seasonal variation through Link Relatives Method :

Value of Production (in thousand ₹)

Year	I*st Qtr.*	II*nd Qtr.*	III*rd Qtr.*	IV*th Qtr.*
2011	136	124	122	126
2012	130	116	113	122
2013	136	126	126	134
2014	140	118	112	124
2015	120	110	102	116

[**Ans.** 107.02, 96.67, 93.89, 102.44]

Ratio-to-Trend Method

29. Calculate seasonal indices by ratio-to-trend method from the following data :

Year	*1st Quarter*	*2nd Quarter*	*3rd Quarter*	*4th Quarter*
2011-12	36	34	38	32
2012-13	38	48	52	42
2013-14	42	56	50	52
2014-15	56	74	68	62
2015-16	82	90	88	80

[**Ans.** 100.13, 109.55, 103.09, 87.21]

Ratio-to-moving Average

30. From the following table, calculate seasonal variations by ratio to moving average method :

Season	2011	2012	2013	2014	2015
I Quarter	40	42	41	45	44
II Quarter	35	37	35	36	38
III Quarter	38	39	38	36	38
IV Quarter	40	38	42	41	42

[**Ans.** I Qtr. = 108.96, II Qtr. = 92.35, III Qtr. = 96.46, IV Qtr. = 102.23]

31. Calculate seasonal indices by the ratio to moving average method from the following data :

Rice Prices in Rupees per quintal Quarter

Year	I	II	III	IV
2012	300	240	216	236
2013	344	260	252	320
2014	360	288	264	340
2015	400	312	288	372

[**Ans.** Seasonal Indices 122.31, 92.39, 84.83, 100.47]

Miscellaneous Problems

32. Using four-yearly moving average determine the trend :

Year	2008	2009	2010	2011	2012	2013	2014	2015
Production	80	90	92	83	89	99	92	110

[**Ans.** 87.37, 89.62, 90.75, 94.12]

33. Fit a traversed line by the method of least squares :

Year	1969	1979	1989	1999	2009
Value	34	50	67	75	85

Estimate Value for 2019.

[**ANs.** 100.3, $a = 62.2$, $b = 12.7$]

34. Fit a trend line to the following data by the least square method and estimate the production for 2006 and 2011 :

Year	2001	2003	2005	2007	2009
Production (000 ton)	18	21	23	27	16

[**Ans.** 2006 : 21.1 ('000 ton); 2011 : 21.6 ('000 ton) $a = 21$, $b = 0.1$]

35. The population of a town at successive census years is given below :

Year (x)	1949	1959	1969	1979	1989	1999	2009
Population Y (in thousand)	193	209	216	235	263	301	337

Fit a curve of the form $y = ab^x$.

[**Ans.** $\log y = 2.3911 + 0.0403x$, 1979 origin 186.29, 204.4, 224.28, 246.09, 270.02, 296.27, 325.08]

36. Present the straight line rule by least square method from the following table :

Time	1991	1992	1993	1994	1995
Variable	15	21	25	33	40

[**Ans.** 1991 1992 1993 1994 1995
14.4 20.6 26.8 33.0 39.2, $a = 26.8$ $b = 6.2$]

37. Fit the trend to the data by least square method and estimate the production for 2007 :

Year	1998	1999	2000	2001	2001	2003	2004
Production ('000 tons)	80	90	92	83	99	92	110

[**Ans.** 113.95 (000 ton), $a = 92.29$ $b = 3.61$]

OBJECTIVE TYPE QUESTIONS

I. Multiple Choice Questions

1. Trend analyse refers to long-term tendency to :
(a) Increasing only
(b) Decrease only
(c) Eighter increase or decrease
(d) None of these
2. Time series analysis following to related for :
(a) Seasonal variation (b) Secular Trend
(c) Cyclical Variation (d) All of these
3. Y or O = *(JAC, 2024)*
(a) T × S × C – I (b) T × S × C × I
(c) T ÷ S × C × I (d) T – S + C – I
4. The most important factor causing seasonal variations are : *(JAC, 2024)*
(a) Growth of population
(b) Change in fashion
(c) Weather and Social Customs
(d) Technological Improvement
5. The most used method of measuring seasonal variation is :
(a) Trend method
(b) Ratio-to-moving average method
(c) Link relative method
(d) Method of simple averages
6. The seasonal fluctuations are : *(JAC, 2016, 23, 24)*
(a) Periodic and irregurlar
(b) Periodic and regular
(c) Not periodic (d) Cyclical
7. Time series data are analysed to :
(a) Understand the past behaviour
(b) Make predictions on the basis of past experience
(c) Eliminate the causes of fluctuations
(d) None of the above
8. A time series is an arrangement of :
(a) Statistical data chronologically
(b) Data not arranged chronologically
(c) Both
(d) None of these
9. Least square method is used for calculating trend. *(JAC, 2020)*
(a) True (b) False
10. Irregular movement occurs periodically. *(JAC, 2020)*
(a) True (b) False
11. Time series is a combination of four components parts.
(a) True (b) False
12. There is no difference between seasonal and cyclical variations.
(a) True (b) False
13. The sum of squares of difference between original values and trend values under least squares method is minimum.
(a) True (b) False
14. Increase is sales of sweets on Deepawali is attributed to secular trend.
(a) True (b) False
15. In a yearly data, we have no seasonal and cyclical fluctuation.
(a) True (b) False
16. Cyclic fluctuation is caused by : *(JAC, 2023)*
(a) Floods (b) Wars
(c) Strikes and Lockout (d) None of these
17. Which of the following components is used for a short-term forecast ? *(JAC, 2023)*
(a) Seasonal (b) Cyclic
(c) Trend (d) None of these
18. The trend is linear when : *(JAC, 2025)*
(a) Growth is not constant
(b) Growth rate is constant
(c) Rate of growth is positive
(d) None of these
19. Trend refers to a long term tendency to : *(JAC, 2025)*
(a) increase only
(b) decrease only
(c) either increase or decrease
(d) None of these

[**Ans.** 1 (c), 2. (d), 3. (b), 4. (c), 5. (b), 6. (b), 7. (b), 8. (a), 9. (a), 10. (b), 11. (a), 12. (b), 13. (b), 14. (b), 15. (b), 16. (d), 17. (a), 18. (b), 19. (c).]

II. State whether the following statements are 'True' or 'False' :

1. Time series is a combination of four components parts.
2. A time series is affected by economic factors.
3. Secular trend can be curve-linear.
4. Cyclical fluctuations are due to trade cycle.
5. Irregular movements occur periodically.
6. The multiplicative model assumes that the four components of time series are independent of each other.
7. In shifting the trend origin the value of '*b*' remain unchanged.
8. The fluctuations having no regularity are called seasonal fluctuations.
9. The additive theory of time series is based on the assumption that different components are residuals.
10. Secular trend cannot be curve-linear.

[**Ans.** 1. True, 2. False 3. False, 4. True, 5. False, 6. False, 7. True, 8. False 9. True, 10. False.]

III. Fill in the blanks

1. The additive model of a time series is expressed as ....
2. The line obtained by the method of least squares method is known as the line of ....
3. Trend refers to long-term tendency to ....
4. The multiplicative model of time series of expressed as ....
5. A set of data depending on the time is called a ....

[**Ans.** 1. O = T + S + C + 1, 2. best fit, 3. either increase or decrease, 4. O = T × S × C × 1, 5. time series.]

7

THEORY OF PROBABILITY

LEARNING OBJECTIVES

After studying this chapter, you will be able to know :

- **7.1 Introduction**
- **7.2 Importance of the Theory of Probability**
- **7.3 Terminology used in Probability :**
  1. Random Experiment, 2. Sample Space, 3. Event, 4. Favourable Events, 5. Mutually Exclusive Events, 6. Independent Events, 7. Dependent Events, 8. Complementary Events, 9. Exhaustive Events, 10. Equally Likely Events
- **7.4 Meaning and Definitions of Probability**
- **7.5 Measurement of Probability or Definitions of Probability :**
  1. Classical or Mathematical or a Priori Approach
  2. Empirical Approach or Statistical Approach
  3. Subjective Approach
  4. Modern Approach or Axiomatic Approach
- **7.6 Probability Theorems or Basic Rules of Probability :**
  1. Addition Theorem or Rule
  2. Multiplication Theorem or Multiplication Law of Probability
  3. Conditional Probability or Theorem of Conditional Probability
  4. Bayes' Theorem (Inverse Probability)
- **7.7 Application of Permutation and Combination in the Theory of Probability**
- **7.8 Bernoulli's Trials or Bernoulli's Theorem**
- **Theoretical Questions : Long Answer Questions, Short Answer Questions, Very Short Answer Questions**
- **Objective Type Questions**

ILLUSTRATIONS AND PRACTICAL PROBLEMS : AT A GLANCE

No. of Illustration		*No. of Problems*
1 to 9 (A)	Solved Illustrations/Problems based on Definition	Exersice 7(A) 1 to 14
10(A) to 17 (B)	**Based on Addition Theorem** I. When Events are Mutually Exclusive II. When Events are not Mutually Exclusive	Exersice 7(B) 1 to 18
18 to 26	**Based on Multiplication Theorem** Independent Events Dependent Events	Exersice 7(C) 1 to 7
27 to 29	Probability of happening atleast one Event Conditional Probability	Exersice 7(D) 1 to 7

30, 31	Inverse Probability (Based on Bayes' Theorem)	Exersice 7(E) 1, 2
32 to 47	Application of Permutation and Combination in the Theory of Probabilities	Exersice 7(F) 1 to 9
48 to 51	Bernoulli Theorem	Exersice 7(G) 1 to 3
52 to 58	Miscellaneous Illustrations/Problems	Exersice 7(H) 1 to 17
58	**Total**	**77**

(7.1) INTRODUCTION

In our life, we often come across events which are concerned with the idea of the *Livelihood* or the *Chance* of occurrence of future events. Infact, two types of phenomena have usually been observed in nature and in every day life. These are :

(i) Deterministic, and (ii) Probabilistic.

If the first type, the hypothesis are stated exactly and no chance elements are involved subsequently during the analysis of the pehnomenon. Consequently, in such a prediction of complete reliability can be made, *e.g.*, if we are given that a train is running at a uniform speed of 80 km per hour we can predict with 100% surety that it will cover one hundred sixty km after two hours. Assuming of course, that it never stopped during these two hours.

Most of the phenomena in physical and chemical sciences are of deterministic nature. However, there exists a number of phenomena where we cannot make predictions with certainty or complete reliability and are known as unpredictable or probabilistic phenomena. Such phenomena are frequently observed in business, economic and socaial sciences or even in our day to day life. For example,

(i) In toss of a uniform coin we are not sure of getting the head or tail.

(ii) A manufacturer cannot ascertain the future demand of his product with certainty.

(iii) A sales manager cannot predict with certainty about the sales target next year.

(iv) If an electric tube has lasted for one year, nothing can be predicted about its future life.

Probability is also used informally in day to day life. We daily come across the sentences like :

(i) Possibly it will rain tonight.

(ii) There is a high chance of your getting the job next year.

(iii) This year's demand for the product is likely to exceed that of the last year.

(iv) The odds are 2 : 1 in favour of getting the contract applied for.

All the above sentences with words like 'possibly', 'high chance', 'likely' and 'odds' are expressions indicating a degree of uncertainty about the happening of the event. *A numerical measure of uncertainty is provided by a very important branch of statistics called the theory of probability.* Broadly there are three possible status of expectation, certainty, impossibility and uncertainty. The probability theory describes certainty by impossibility by 0 and the various grades of uncertainties by coefficients ranging between 0 and 1.

(7.2) IMPORTANCE OF THE THEORY OF PROBABILITY

Many *unpredictable* or *probabilistic* phenomenon are observed in economic, business and social science and even in our day-to-day life. The importance of theory of probability may be outlined as under :

(i) **Importance in Statistics :** Probability is important in statistics because many principles and procedures are based on this concept. The fundamental laws of statistics, *viz.*, "*Law of Statistical Regularity*" and the "*Law of Inertia of Large Number*" are based on the theory of probability.

(ii) **In Decision Theory :** Decision theories are based on fundamental laws of probability and expected value. *Marris Hamburg* opines that "Probability measures provide the decision-maker in business and in Governement with the means for quantifying the uncertainity which affect his choice of appropriate actions.

(iii) **In Economic Decision :** Values of probabilities theory is increasing in economic decision-making. The theory of probability is very useful in situations of uncertainity and risk. For example, management may like to know the probability of success of a new product. A sales manager may want to know the probability of doubling the sales of a particular product.

(iv) **Importance in Day-to-Day Life :** The probability concept based on experimental text provides scope for its application to real life situations.

In fact, there is not even a single discipline in social, physical or natural sciences where the probability theory is not used.

No doubt this theory originated from gambling. But now this theory has become so rich and developed that it is being used in different branches of engineering, statistical analysis of complex economic and business problems.

Solved Problems Based on Definition

Illustration 1

What is the chance of drawing a Queen in a draw from a pack of 52 cards ?

Solution :

Total number of cases that can happen = 52 (n)

No. of favourable cases. *i.e.*, Total No. of Queens in pack of cards = 4(m)

Therefore, The probability $= \frac{m}{n} = \frac{4}{52} = \frac{1}{13}$ **Ans.**

Illustration 2

A bag contains 20 Red and 40 Black balls. What is probability of drawing (i) a Red ball, and (ii) a Black ball ?

Solution :

(i) $P = \frac{\text{No. of Red Balls}}{\text{Total No. of Balls}}$

$= \frac{20}{20+40} = \frac{20}{60} = \frac{1}{3}$ **Ans.**

(ii) $P = \frac{\text{No. of Black Balls}}{\text{Total No. of Balls}}$

$= \frac{40}{20+40} = \frac{40}{60} = \frac{2}{3}$ **Ans.**

Illustration 3

Find the probability of drawing a Red card in a single draw from a well shuffled pack of ordinary playing cards.

Solution :

Total No. of outcomes = 52

No. of favourable outcomes = 13 + 13 = 26

Hence P(drawing a Red card) $= \frac{26}{52} = \frac{1}{2}$ **Ans.**

Illustration 4

Find the probability of drawing a face card in a single random draw from a well shuffled pack of ordinary playing cards.

Solution :

Face card : Jack, Queen and King

Thus, Face cards = 12

The number of favourable outcomes = 12

Total Number of Cards = 52

$\therefore \quad p = \frac{12}{52}$

$= \frac{3}{13}$ **Ans.**

Illustration 5

What is probability that a vovel selected at random in any English books is an '*a*' ?

Solution :

Vowels : *a*, *e*, *i*, *o* and *u*.

$\therefore$ Total number of equally likely events = 5

Number of favourable events = 1

$\therefore \quad P = \frac{\text{Number of favourable events}}{\text{Total no. of equally likely events}}$

$= \frac{1}{5}$ **Ans.**

Illustration 6(A)

(i) Find the probability of getting a number greater than 3 when a die is thrown.

(ii) A dice is thrown twice, find the probability of getting a sum of 9. (*JAC*, 2015)

Solution :

(i) Dots appeared on the face of a die are 1, 2, 3, 4, 5, 6

Favourable members 4, 5, 6 (which are greater than 3)

Thus, $P = \frac{m}{n} = \frac{3}{6} = \frac{1}{2}$ **Ans.**

(ii) Sample space in throw of

$S = \{1, 2, 3, 4, 5, 6\} \times \{1, 2, 3, 4, 5, 6\}$

Fav. Points (Sum is 9)

= (3, 6), (4, 5), (5, 4), (6, 3),

= 4 points

Thus, $P = \frac{m}{n} = \frac{4}{36} = \frac{1}{9}$ **Ans.**

Illustration 6(B)

A die is thrown. Find the probability of getting a digit more than 4. [*Mock Test Paper (JAC)*]

Solution :

A dice contains 6 digits, *i.e.*, 1, 2, 3, 4, 5, 6,

$\therefore \quad n = 6$

Digits more than 4 = 5, 6,

$\therefore \quad m = 2$

P (No. > 4) $= \frac{2}{6}$ **Ans.**

Illustration 7

What is the chance that a leap year, selected at random, will contain 53 Sundays ? (*JAC*, 2015)

Solution :

Leap year = 366 days

In Leap year, we have 52 weeks and 2 days.

Each day comes 52 times, 2 days remain. These two days may come, as under (7 pairs) :

(i) Monday and Tuesday
(ii) Tuesday and Wednesday
(iii) Wednesday and Thursday
(iv) Thursday and Friday
(v) Friday and Saturday
(vi) Saturday and Sunday
(vii) Sunday and Monday

No. of total permutations of 2 days

= 7 (*i.e.*, 7 outcomes)

No. of Permutations of Sunday

= 2 (*i.e.*, Favourable to the 53rd Sunday)

∴ Required Probability

$P(A) = \frac{2}{7}$ **Ans.**

***Illustration* 8**

A dice is thrown. Find the probability of getting a digit 5 or less than 5. (*JAC*, 2017)

***Solution* :**

$$\text{Probability of 5 digit} = \frac{1}{6}$$

$$\text{Probability of less than 5 digit} = \frac{1}{6}+\frac{1}{6}+\frac{1}{6}+\frac{1}{6}=\frac{4}{6}$$

$$\text{Probability of digit 5 or less than 5} = \frac{1}{6}+\frac{4}{6} = \frac{5}{6} \quad \textbf{Ans.}$$

***Illustration* 9**

If 4 coins are tossed, find the chance that there should be two tails.

***Solution* :**

Let E = The events of being two tails

Then $n(E) = {}^4C_2 = 6$

∴ Required Probability

$$= \frac{6}{2^4} = \frac{6}{2\times 2\times 2\times 2}$$

$$= \frac{\mathbf{6}}{\mathbf{16}} \textbf{ or } \frac{\mathbf{3}}{\mathbf{8}} \quad \textbf{Ans.}$$

***Illustration* 9(A)**

A coin is tossed three times. Find the probability of getting at least one head.

***Solution* :**

Sample space : S = {(HHH), (HHT), (HTH), (HTT), (THT), (TTH), (TTT)}.

⇒ $n(S) = 8$

Event A : getting at least one head so that

$\bar{A}$: getting no head at all = {TTT} = $n(\bar{A}) = 1$

$$P(\bar{A}) = \frac{1}{8}$$

Therefore, $P(A) = 1 - P(\bar{A}) = 1 - \frac{1}{8} = \frac{7}{8}$

(7.3) TERMINOLOGY USED IN PROBABILITY

In order to have knowledge of theory of probability we must begin with basic or fundamental concept. This will help us in knowing the theory in a better way.

A randum experiment is an experiment in which :

(i) All the possible outcomes of the experiment are known in advance, and

(ii) The exact outcome of any specific performance of the experiment is unpredictable, *i.e.*, depends on chance.

Examples :

(I) Suppose a coin is tossed. There are two possible outcomes of the experiment-Head (*H*) and Tail (*T*). We cannot say whether Head or Tail will appear. So tossing a coin is a random experiment. Because it is impossible to say which number will occur.

(II) Rolling an unbiased Die or a Homogenous Cube is a "Random Experiment". "No. of Dots" appeared on the face of the dice may be 1, 2, 3, 4, 5, 6. There is no rule to known it.

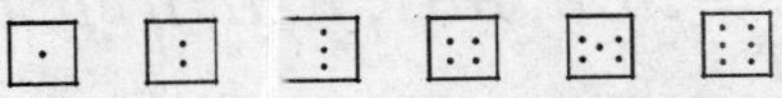

1 2 3 4 5 6

How many dots it will actually throw up is unpredictable and is subject to chance.

(III) Drawing a card from a pack of card is also a "Random Experiment".

(IV) Drawing balls from a bag or box containing a given number of white and red balls is another example of "Random Experiment".

(2) **Sample Space :** A Sample Space is the set of all possible outcomes of a Random Experiment. It is generally devoted by gree letter Ω (Omega) or S and its number of elements by $n(\Omega)$ or $n(S)$.

Example :

(i) If a coin is tossed, either Head (*H*) or Tail (*T*) will appear. So, in this case the sample space S = (*H*, *T*) and $n(S) = 2$.

(ii) In throwing a die, the number that appears is any one of 1, 2, 3, 4, 5, 6. So, in this the sample space : S = (1, 2, 3, 4, 5, 6) and $n(S) = 6$.

(iii) In tossing two coins the sample sapce is : $S = \{HH, HT, TH, TT\}$

Where,

HH means that on both the coins head appears, *TH* means that tail (*T*) appears on the first coin and head (*H*) on the second. Clearly $n(S) = 4$.

In tossing two coins, the simple way of forming the sample space is given below.

		COIN-2	
		H	T
COIN-1	H	HH	HT
	T	TH	TT

The Sample Space of this experiment = {*HH*, *HT*, *TH*, *TT*} or (*HT*) × (*HT*).

(iv) In drawing two cards out of 52, the number of elements in the sample space = $n(S)$ = total number of ways in which 2 cards can be selected from 52 cards = 52_{C2}

Sample Point or Event Point : The elements of the sample space are called the sample points.

Sample Point : The elements of the sample space are called the sample point. Hence, each possible outcome, of a sample space is called "Sample point" or 'Event point'.

Example :

(i) If S = (*HT*), then H and T are sample points.

(ii) If S = {1, 2, 3, 4, 5, 6} then 1, 2, 3, 4, 5 and 6 are sample points.

> If the same coin is tossed twice, then S_2 = (*HH, HT, TH, TT*)
>
> In case the coin is tossed three times, the sample space will be S3 = *HHH, HHT, HTH, HTT, THH, THT, TTH, TTT*
>
> - Incase of a *single* toss the sample space consists of 2 points.
> - In case of *two* tosses, it consists of $2 \times 2 = 2^2 = 4$ points.
> - In case of *three* tosses, it consists $2 \times 2 \times 2 = 2^3 = 8$ points.

(3) **Events :** Any subset of a sample space is called an event. A sample space S serves as the universal set for all questions related to an experiment 'S' and an element A with respect to it is a set of all possible outsomes favourable to the *element* A. In short, an event is any element or point of the sample space (S).

Event is denoted by 'E' or A, B, etc.

Example :

(i) In tossing of a coin → Trial/Experiment

↓

Possible outcome → Head (*H*), Tail (*T*) → Event

(ii) In throwing of a dice → Trial

↓

Possible outcome → [1, 2, 3, 4, 5, 6] → Event

Appearance of an even number be the event E then E = the event of appearing even number = {2, 4, 6}

Types of Events : Following are the main types of elements.

(I) **Simple Event or Elementary Event :** An event is called simple event if it contains one element. "Simple event is also known as *"Elementary Event."* In other words, single element subsets of sample space associated with a randum experiment are known as simple or elementary events.

Example :

Consider the experiment of throwing a dice. The sample space associated with this experiment is $S = \{1, 2, 3, 4, 5, 6\}$. Events $E_1 = (1)$, $E_2 = (2)$, $E_3 = (3)$, $E_4 = (4)$, $E_5 = (5)$, $E_6 = (6)$ are simple events.

(II) **Compound Event :** A subset of the sample space which has more then one element is called compound event. In other words, those sub-sets of sample space *S* associated to an experiment which are disjoint union of single element subset of sample space *S* are known as compound events. Compound event is also called as *"Complex"* or *Composit Event*.

Example :

(i) In tossing of a single dice, the event of getting 6 is a single event but A_1 (Odd Number) : [1, 3, 5], A_2 (Even Number) : [2, 4, 6] are compound events.

(III) **Mutually Exclusive Events :** Two or more events are said to be "Mutually Exclusive" if the happening of any one of them prevent happening of the other in the same experiment. In short, two events are called "Mutually Exclusive" if they cannot occur simultaneously. For example, in toss of a coin the events 'Head' and 'Tail' are "Mutually Exclusive". If Head comes, we cannot get Tail and if Tail comes we cannot get Head. Similarly, in the throw of a Dice the six phases numbered 1, 2, 3, 4, 5 and 6 are "Mutually Exclusive". There are no sample points in common in "Mutually Exclusive Events".

In case of Mutually Exclusive events, probability is calculated by addition theorem.

$$P(A \text{ or } B) = P(A) + P(B)$$
$$P(A \cup B) = P(A) + P(B)$$

Where, $P(A \cup B)$, is the probability of *A* union *B*.

(IV) **Independent Events :** Events are said to be "Independent Event" if the occurrence of one does not affect the outcome of the other. Two events are Independent when they have no influence on each other. The result of first toss of a coin does not affect the result of successive tosses at all.

(V) **Dependent Events :** If the occurrence of the one event affects happening of the other event, then they are said to be "Dependent Events". For example, the probability of drawing a queen from a pack of 52 cards is 4/52 or 1/13 if t happens that a Queen is drawn and is not replaced in the pack,. The probability of drawing again a Queen would be 3/51. Thus, the outcome of the first event has affected the outcome of the second event. Thus, they are Dependent Events. Probability of this type is also called as conditional probabilities. If *A* and *B* are dependent events then conditional probability of *B* (when *A* is given) : $P(B/A) = \dfrac{P(A, B)}{P(A)}$

Note : The question of Dependence or Independence of Events is relevant when experiments are consecutive and not simultaneous.

(VI) **Complementary Events :** To any event *A*, there is an event which is not *A*. This type of event is denoted by 'Not *A*' or A^C or $\overline{A}$ and called complementary of *A*. A^C contains all the outcomes of the experiments which are not in *A*. Thus, by the definition there are no smaple points common in *A* and A^C. So they are Mutually Exclusive.

For Example,

Let $S = (HH, HT, TH, TT)$, when 2 coins are fossed

here, if A = Similar faces *i.e.*, $A = \{HH, TT\}$

then A^C = Not Similar faces *i.e.*, $A^C = \{HT, TH\}$

here A & A^C are mutually exclusive events and No points are common.

(VII) **Exhaustive Events :** Two or more events are said to be "Exhaustive Events" if their totality makes the whole "Sample Space".

$S = \{1, 2, 3, 4, 5, 6\}$ be a Sample Space

For example, throwing of a dice furnishes six Exhaustive Events.

When a die is thrown

Let

here if A = Even Nos. (2, 4, 6) &

i.e. B = Odd Nos. (1, 3, 5)

then A & B are "Exhaustive Events", since their totality makes

"Whole Sample Space"

here $A \cup B = \{1, 2, 3, 4, 5, 6\} = S$ Sample Space

If the possible outcome of any exhaustive events are $A_1, A_2, A_3 ....A_n$ then the total of their probabilties will be 1 $P(A_1) + P(A_2) + P(A_3)..... + P(A_n) = 1$

(VIII) **Equally Likely Events :** The events are said to be '*Equally Likely*' or '*Equally Probable*' if none of them is expected to occur in preference to other. For example, in tossing of a coin all the outcomes of Head & Tail are Equally Likely, if the coin is not biased. Similarly, if it is throwing of an unbaised dice all the possible outcomes 1, 2, 3, 4, 5, 6 are Equally Likely.

(IX) **Overlapping Events :** Two events are said to be overlapping if the events have at least one outcome in common, hence they can happen at the same time.

The probability of ocurrance of some one over two overlapping events is the sum of the probabilities of the two individual events *minus* the probability of their common outcomes.

If two events A and B are overlapping partially, then the probability of A or B will be calculated by Addition Theorem.

$$P(A \text{ or } B) = P(A) + P(B) - P(A \text{ and } B)$$

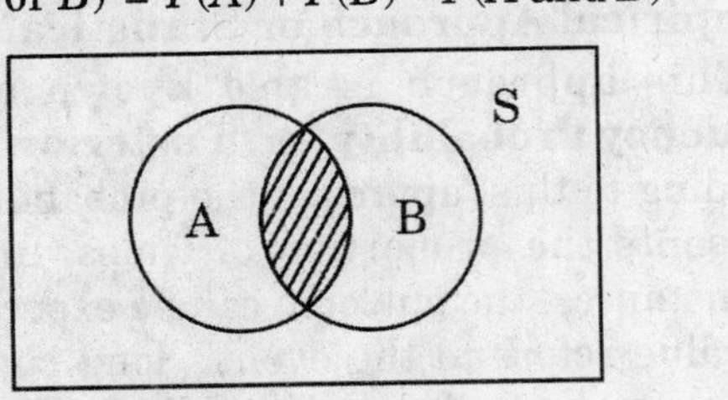

Fig. 1

Favourable Events : The number of outcomes of a Random Experiment which result in the happening of a particular event is called as *"Cases Favourable to the Event."* For example,

(i) In a toss of two coins, the number of cases favourable to the event can be said "Exactly One Head" which are 2, *viz., HT, TH*.

(ii) In drawing a card from a pack of cards the case favourable to getting a "Spade" is 13 and 'Getting of a Queen of Spade' is only one.

(7.4) MEANING AND DEFINITIONS OF PROBABILITY

In our day to day life we often use the word 'Chance' or 'Likely'. For example, it is likely to rain today. I have very small chance of winning lottery, Ramesh (may be) has chance of getting first division. Chance of winning the test series by India is 50-50. There are 50-50 chances of a student passing the examination. In all these sentences an idea of uncertainity is acknowledged. *Geothe* remarked that *"There is nothing more frightful than action in ignorance."*

In Statistics, the word 'Probability' is used in some different way. In Statistics, a probability is a numerical value that measures the uncertainity that the particular event will occur. A few definitions of probability are as follows :

(1) According to *Connor*, *"Probability is an attitude of mind towards uncertain events."*

(2) According to *Laplace*, *"Probability is the ratio of favourable events to the total number of equally likely events."*

If a randum experiment results in n mutually exclusive, equally likely and exhaustive outcomes out of which m are favourable to the occurrence of an event A, then the probability of the occurrence of A, usually denoted by $P(A)$ is given by

$$P(A) = \frac{m}{n} = \frac{\text{The number of favourable outcomes}}{\text{The total number of outcomes}}$$

Thus, probability is a concept which measures numerically the degree of certainty or uncertainty of the occurrence of an event.

(7.5) MEASUREMENT OF PROBABILITY OR DEFINITIONS OF PROBABILITY

There are four methods of measuring Probabilities. Often they are considered as Definitions of Probability. They are as follows :

Approaches or Definitions

↓

1. Classical or Mathematical or a Priori Approach
2. Empirical Approach or Statistical Approach
3. Subjective Approach
4. Modern Approach or Axiomatic

However, the following is the broad classification of the different schools of thought :

Probability

↓

- Objective
  - Classical
  - Empirical Approach
    - Modern Approach
- Subjective

The Objective Probability is based on certain laws of nature which are undisputed or on some experiments conducted for the purpose. This is not based on the impressions of individuals as is the case with subjective probability. These theories, therefore, are free from personal bias and ensure objectivity. The two approaches to objective probability are :

(1) Classical Approach, (2) Empirical Approach.

1. Classical or Mathematical or a Priori Approach

The classical approach is based on a *priori* laws of nature. It employs logic to derive probability measures to certain undisputed law of nature. Being based on abstract mathematical logic. It is also called as 'Abstract' or 'Mathematical'.

Definition : *If there are 'n' Exhaustive, Mutually Exclusive and Equally Likely outcomes of an event 'A' and 'm' cases of them are favourable to the happening of that event, then probability of the event 'A' is :*

$$P(A) = \frac{m}{n} \qquad \text{(J. Bernoulli)}$$

or $$P(A) = \frac{\text{Number of outcomes favourable to the occurrence of 'A'}}{\text{The total number of outcomes}}$$

It may be noted that the Probability, as defined above is only a "Ratio of two Numbers" in which the Numerator (m) is the *"Number of Favourable Cases"* and the Denominator (n) is the *Total Number* of Possible Outcomes satisfying certain conditions, Therefore, for the calculation of Probability the following steps should be followed :

Step 1 : Enumerate possible outcomes of the experiments, such that they satisfy three criteria of being (a) Mutually Exclusive, (b) Exhaustive, and (c) Equally Likely. Count the number (n) of such outcomes.

Step 2 : Check how many of these cases are favourable to the event for which the Probability is desired.

Let this number be 'm'

Step 3 : Devide 'm' by 'n' and the result gives the Probability of the Event (A).

Thus $$P(A) = \frac{m}{n}$$

or $$\text{Probability} = \frac{\text{Favourable Events}}{\text{Total Events}}$$

Note : If any of the three criteria, *viz.*, 'Mutually Exclusive', 'Exhaustive' and 'Equally Likely' are not satisfied, this is not practicable.

Remarks : Obviously the number of cases favourable to complementary event A, *i.e.*, non-happening of event A, are ($n - m$). That 'A' will not occur or happen is denoted by $q(A)$.

If there are 'm' possible outcomes favourable to 'A' and 'n' possible outcomes unfavourable to the occurrence of 'A', and on these pssible outcomes are equally likely and mutually exclusive then the probability that 'A' will occur (happen) by $P(A)$ is :

$$P(A) = \frac{m}{m+n}$$

Sum of p and q is equal to 1, therefore, we come to the conclusion that

$p + q = 1$, then $1 - p = q$, $1 - q = p$

Example :

The probability of getting a king in a draw from a pack of 52 cards.

$$p = \frac{4}{52} = \frac{1}{13} \text{ and not occurring a king.}$$

$$q = 1 - \frac{1}{13} = \frac{12}{13} \text{ or } \frac{52-4}{52} = \frac{48}{52} = \frac{12}{13}$$

Remarks : Probability that event A will not occur denoted by $P(A')$ is

$$P(A') = \frac{\text{Number of outcomes not favourable occurrence of 'A'}}{\text{Exhaustive number of outcomes}}$$

$$= \frac{n-m}{n} = 1 - \frac{m}{n} = 1 - P(A)$$

Limitations : This definition has the following limitations :

(i) The phrase 'Equally Likely' has been used in these definitions. It means that we are trying to define probability in terms of equal probability. How do you know whether the probability are euqal, before you meausre them.

(ii) This definition has only limited applications. For example, coin tossing, die throwing and similar game of chance.

(iii) Classical concepts fails if 'm' cannot be predetermined as the outcome in a large number of random trials.

2. Empirical Approach or Statistical Approach

This approach is also known as **"Relative Frequency Probability"** or **"Posteriori Probability"**. According to this, approach the probability of an event represents the proportion of times, under identical circumstances, the outcome can be expected to happen. The value refers to the event's long run frequency of occurrence. According to *Von Mises, "If the experiment be repeated a large number of times under essentially, identical conditions, the limiting value of the ratio of the number of times of events 'A' happens to the total number of trails of the experiments as the number of trails increases indefinitely, is called the probability of the occurrence of 'A'."*

$$P(A) = \lim_{n \to \infty} \left(\frac{m}{n}\right)$$

where, lim = Limitations

m = Number of times an event 'A' occurs

n = Number of times the experiment is performed

∞ = Infinite

Hence, according to *Croxton* and *Cowden*, *"Probability is the limit of the relative frequency of success in an infinite sequence of trials."*

For Example : Out of 10,000 products made by a machine, 400 products are of inferior quality can be probability of inferior products = 400/10,000 = 0.04

Similarly, there are 1,000 workers in a factory. The number of workers earning wages over ₹ 100 per day is 50.

Then, $P = \frac{50}{1,000} = 0.05$

Since in the relative frequency approach, the probability is obtained objectively by relative empirical observations, it is also known as statistical probability.

3. Subjective Approach

Subjective concept of probability measures the confidence that an individual has in the truth of a particular proposition. Hence for happening or not happening of an event is bound to vary with person to person. It is a calculative guess of say an experienced businessman and is based on his believe and experience. To forecast the demand, predicting price etc. is done on the basis of subjective probabilities.

In the subjective or personal interpretation of a probability, a probability is interpreted as a measure of degree of belief, or as the qualified judgement of a particular individual.

The probability is determined between 0 (impossible) and 1 (surety).

i.e., $\frac{\text{Number of outcomes favourable to the occurrence of 'A'}}{\text{The total number of possible outcomes}}$

The probability of not happening (occuring) 'A'

$$= q\,(A) = \frac{n}{m+n}$$

$$= \frac{\text{Number of outcomes not favourable to the occurrence of 'A'}}{\text{Total number of possible outcomes}}$$

On the basis of above two formulas we can say that

$$p + q = \frac{m}{(m+n)} + \frac{n}{(m+n)} = \frac{m+n}{m+n} = 1$$

where $p(A) = p$

and $q(A) = q$

For example, if we toss a coin, the probability of the Head coing up is : $p = ½$, because number of favourable event is one and the total number of possible outcomes is 2.

The probability of Head not coing up is :

$$q = \frac{1}{2}.$$

4. Modern Approach or Axiomatic Approach

In this approach no precise definition of probability is given. This modern concept to probability combines both the objective and subjective concepts of probability. Under this approach probability is express as a set function. The theory is based on certain axioms or postulates. In fact, modern theory of probability is based on the axiomatic approach introduced by the Russian mathematician, "A. N. Kolmogorov" in 1934. Before giving axiomatic definition of probability we shall explain certain concepts used therein.

Axiomatic Probability

Definition : Given a sample space of a random experiment, the probability of the occurrence of any event A is defined as a probability function $P(A)$ satisfying the following axioms :

Axioms 1 : The probability of an event exist is real and non-negative, *i.e.*,

$$0 \leq P\,(A) \leq 1$$

Axioms 2 : The probability of the entire sample space is 1, *i.e.*,

$$P(S) = 1,\ P(\phi) = 0$$

S = Certain Events, ϕ = Impossible Event

Axioms 3 : If $A_1\ A_2\ A_3$..... be a finite or infinite sequence of disjoint event of S, then

$$P\,(A_1 \cup A_2 \cup A_3 \cup .... \cup A_n)$$
$$= P\,(A_1) + P\,(A_2) + P\,(A_3) + ... P\,(A_n)$$

$P\,(A)$ = The sum of the probabilities of simple event, comprising the events A

$$= \frac{\text{Number of sample points in } A}{\text{Total no. of sample points in } S}$$

or $P\,(A) = \frac{n(A)}{n(S)} = \frac{n(A)}{N}$

Thus, if two events A and B are mutually exclusive, the probability (P) of happening events A and B.

$$P\,(A \cup B) = P(A) + P(B)$$

Where, $\cup$ = Union

Exercise 7(A)

1. What is the probability of getting a king or queen from a well shuffled pack of 52 cards ?

   $\left[\textbf{Ans. } \frac{2}{13}\right]$

2. What is the probability of drawing a king in a drawn from a pack of 52 cards ?

   $\left[\textbf{Ans. } \frac{4}{52} \text{ or } \frac{1}{13}\right]$

3. A single letter is selected at random from the word 'PROBABILITY'. What is the probability tha it is a vowel ?

   $\left[\textbf{Ans. } \frac{4}{11}\right]$

4. A dice is thrown. Find the probability of getting a digit less than 4.

$\left[\textbf{Ans.} \frac{1}{2}\right]$

5. A bag contains 6 white balls and 9 balck balls. What is the probability of drawing a black ball ?

$\left[\textbf{Ans.} \frac{3}{5}\right]$

6. A bag contains 10 white and 20 red balls. Find the probability of drawing a red ball from the bag.

$\left[\textbf{Ans.} \frac{2}{3} \text{ or } 0.667\right]$

7. From a pack of 52 cards one card is drawn. What is the probability that it would be (i) queen, (ii) a card of red colour and (iii) a king of diamond.

$\left[\textbf{Ans.} \text{ (i) } \frac{1}{13}, \text{ (ii) } \frac{1}{52}\right]$

8. Two cubical die where faces are marked with digits 1 to 6 are thrown simultaneously. Find the probability that the sum of the digits on the face that turn up is (i) 8, and (ii) 11.

$\left[\textbf{Ans.} \text{ (i) } \frac{5}{36}, \text{ (ii) } \frac{1}{18}\right]$

9. Find the chance of throwing 10 exactly in one throw of 3 dice.

$\left[\textbf{Ans.} \frac{9}{216} \text{ or } \frac{1}{24}\right]$

10. Find the chance of throwing more than 15 in one throw of 3 dice. *(JAC, 2020)*

$\left[\textbf{Ans.} \frac{10}{216} \text{ or } \frac{5}{108}\right]$

11. What is the chance that a non-leap year should have 53 Tuesdays ?

$\left[\textbf{Ans.} \frac{1}{7}\right]$

12. Find the probability of the occurrence of 5 in throwing a die.

$\left[\textbf{Ans.} \frac{1}{6}\right]$

13. If a coin is tossed twice, find the probability of getting one head. *(JAC, 2025)*

$\left[\textbf{Ans.} \frac{1}{2}\right]$

14. What is the chance of occurring 53 Sundays in a leap year ? *(JAC, 2025)*

$\left[\textbf{Ans.} \frac{2}{7}\right]$

(7.6) PROBABILITY THEOREMS

OR

BASIC RULES OF PROBABILITY

Probability Theorems or basic rules of probability can be divided into four parts. They are as follows :

Probability Theorems

or

Basic Rules of Probability

↓

(1) Addition Theorem
(For Simultaneous Trials)

(2) Multiplication Theorem
(For Consecutive Trials)

(3) Theorem of Conditional Probabilities
(If sub-events are not independent)

(4) Bayes' Theorem
(Rule for the Inverse Probability)

(1) Addition Theorem or Addition Law of Probability (For Simultaneous Trials)

Addition Theorem of probability applies in two cases :

(i) When events are Mutually Exclusive.

(ii) When events are not Mutually Exclusive.

Case I : When Events are Mutually Exclusive : Addition Theorem is stated as follows, "If two events are Mutually exclusive and the probability of the one event is $P(A)$, while that of the other is $P(B)$ then the probability of either one event or the other occurring is the sum $P(A) + P(B)$.

Now if A and B are mutually exclusive events, then

$$P(A \cup B) = P(A) + P(B)$$

In other words,

$$P(A \text{ or } B) = P(A) + P(B)$$

If there are more than two mutually exclusive events

$$P(A \cup B \cup \ldots \cup Z) = P(A) + P(B) + \ldots + P(Z)$$

Addition Law of Probability

1. If A and B are two mutually exclusive events.
   - The probability that either event A or event B will occur in a single trial is given by
     $P(A \text{ or } B) = P(A) + P(B)$
2. If the events are not mutually exclusive
   - $P(A \text{ or } B) = P(A) + P(B) - P(A \text{ and } B \text{ together})$
3. In case of overlapping, *i.e.*, if the events have at least one outcome in common.
   - $P(A \text{ or } B) = P(A) + P(B) - P(A \text{ and } B)$
4. $P(\text{Neither } A \text{ nor } B) = 1 - P(A) + P(B)$

***Illustration* 10(A)**

A bag contains 8 white, 4 black, 6 yellow and 6 red balls. What is the probability of getting a white or red ball at random in a single draw of one ? *(J.A.C. 2015, 20)*

Solution :

$$\text{Total balls} = 8 + 4 + 6 + 6 = 24$$

Probability of getting a white ball

$$= \frac{8}{24} = \frac{1}{3}$$

Probability of getting a red ball

$$= \frac{6}{24} = \frac{1}{4}$$

∴ Probability of getting a white or red ball

$$= \frac{1}{3} + \frac{1}{4} = \frac{4+3}{12}$$

$$= \frac{7}{12} \textbf{ Ans.}$$

***Illustration* 10(B)**

A bag contains 2 white, 5 black and 3 red balls. What is the probability of drawing a white or a black or a red ball in a single draw ? [*Mock Test Paper (JAC)*]

Solution :

Let, A — a White Ball

B — a Black Ball

C — a Red Ball

$$P(A \cup B \cup C) = P(A) + P(B) + P(C)$$

$$= \frac{2}{10} + \frac{5}{10} + \frac{3}{10} = \mathbf{1} \quad \textbf{Ans.}$$

***Illustration* 11(A)**

From a pack of 52 cards one card is drawn at random. What is the probability that it will be Queen of clubs or King of diamond ? (*JAC*, 2016)

Solution :

Drawing a Queen of clubs or King of diamonds are mutually exclusive events.

∵ Probability of drawing a Queen of clubs

$$= \frac{1}{52}$$

∵ Probability of drawing a King of diamonds

$$= \frac{1}{52}$$

Therefore, the probability of drawing a Queen of clubs or a King of diamonds is

$$= \frac{1}{52} + \frac{1}{52} = \frac{1+1}{52} = \frac{2}{52}$$

$$= \frac{\mathbf{1}}{\mathbf{26}} \quad \textbf{Ans.}$$

***Illustration* 11(B)**

What is the probability of getting a king or a queen from a well shuffled pack of 52 cards ?

[*Mock Test Paper (JAC)*]

Solution :

Let A = *a* king laid, B = *a* Queen Card.

Thus $P(A \cup B) = P(A) + P(B) - P(A \cap B)$

$$= \frac{4}{52} + \frac{4}{52} - 0 = \frac{\mathbf{8}}{\mathbf{52}} \quad \textbf{Ans.}$$

***Illustration* 12(A)**

In a single throw of two dice, what is the probability of getting a total of 8 ? (*JAC*, 2015, 19)

Solution :

Let the event of coming 8 as total on the faces of dice be '*A*'.

Event '*A*' can happen as follows :

(2, 6) (3, 5) (4, 4) (5, 3) (6, 2) = (5 Points)

∴ No. of favourable cases = 5

and total number of cases = 36

$$\therefore \quad \text{Required probability} = \frac{\mathbf{5}}{\mathbf{36}} \quad \textbf{Ans.}$$

***Illustration* 12(B)**

If a die is thrown, what is the probability of getting a 5 or a 6 ?

Solution :

Total number of possible outcomes when a dice is thrown = 1 × 6 = 6

The probability that one five or one six occurs are mutually exclusive events.

$$P(A \text{ or } B) = P(A) + P(B)$$

$$P(5 \text{ or } 6) = P(5) + P(6)$$

$$= \frac{1}{6} + \frac{1}{6} = \frac{2}{6}$$

$$= \frac{\mathbf{1}}{\mathbf{3}} \quad \textbf{Ans.}$$

***Illustration* 12(C)**

If a throw of two dice, find the chance of getting either a total of 7 or 11

Solution :

Total number of possible outcomes when two dice are thrown.

$$n(CS) = 6 \times 6 = 36$$

Number of result of getting the sum of 7

$$(A) = \{(1,6),(6,1),(2,5),(5,2)(3,4),(4:3)\}$$

Therefore, P (A) = 6

Number of result of getting the sum of 11

$$(B) = \{(5, 6), (6, 5)\}, P(B) = 2$$

$$P(A) = \frac{6}{36} \text{ and } PB = \frac{2}{36}$$

∵ Both the events are completely exclusive. Hence the probability of getting the sum of 7 or 11 is.

$$P(A) + P(B) = \frac{6}{36} + \frac{2}{36} = \frac{8}{36}$$

$$= \frac{\mathbf{2}}{\mathbf{9}} \quad \textbf{Ans.}$$

Corrolary of Addition Theorem

If P (A) and P (B) be the probability of two mutually exclusive events A and B then the probability of not happening the events of A and B (neither A nor B).

$$P(\text{neither A nor B}) = 1 - [P(A) + P(B)]$$

***Illustration* 13**

If a pair of dice is thrown, find the probability that the sum is neither 7 nor 11.

Solution :

Event A		
Dice		*Sum*
I	II	(I + II)
1	6	7
2	5	7
3	4	7
4	3	7
5	2	7
6	1	7

Event B		
Dice		Sum
I	II	(I + II)
6	5	11
5	6	11

Let A denote the event of getting a sum of '7' and 'B' that of 11.

The exhaustive outcomes in a throw of 2 dice are

$$6 \times 6 = 36.$$

6 outcomes being favourable to the event 'A'

$$\therefore \quad P(A) = \frac{6}{36} = \frac{1}{6}$$

2 outcomes being favourable to the event 'B'

$$\therefore \quad P(B) = \frac{2}{36} = \frac{1}{18}$$

The probability that the sum is neither 7 nor 11

$$= P(A \cap B)$$
$$= 1 - (P \cup B)$$
$$= 1 - \{P(A) + P(B)\}$$
$$= 1 - \left(\frac{1}{6} + \frac{1}{18}\right)$$

$$\therefore \quad \text{Required Prob.} = 1 - \frac{3+1}{18} = 1 - \frac{4}{18} = \frac{14}{18}$$

$$= \frac{\mathbf{7}}{\mathbf{9}} \qquad \textbf{Ans.}$$

Case II : When Events are not Mutually Exclusive : (Overlapping Events) If 'A' and 'B' are any two events and are not mutually exclusive, then

$$P(A \cup B) = P(A) + P(B) - P(A \cap B)$$

or

$$P(A \text{ or } B) = P(A) + P(B) - P(AB)$$

Thus, in the above formula the theorem of addition as explained in case I (that is, when events are mutually exclusive) is restricted by subtracting overlapping part of event 'A' and 'B'.

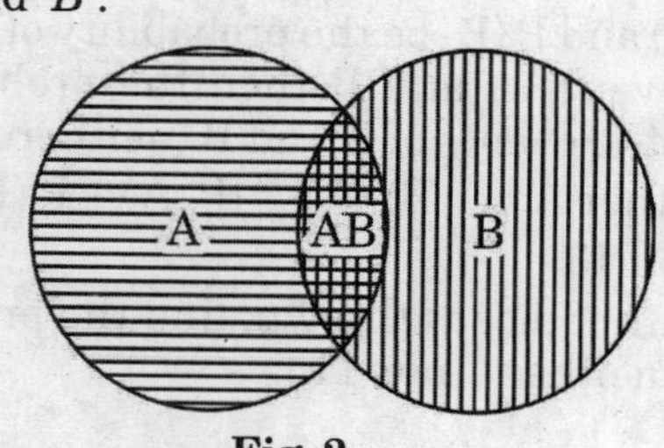

Fig. 2

***Illustration* 14(A)**

A bag contains 30 balls, numbered from 1 to 30, one is to be drawn at random. Find the probability that (i) in the first draw it is a multiple of 5 or 7, and (ii) in the second draw it is multiple of 7.

***Solution* :**

We have, total ways = 30 (n)

(i) Let A = Multiple of 5 = 5, 10, 15, 20, 25, 30 (6 points)

$\therefore$ Probability of getting, multiple of 5 = $\frac{6}{30}$ or $\frac{1}{5}$

and Let B = Multiple of 7 = 7, 14, 21, 28 (4 points)

$\therefore$ Prob. of getting, multiple of 7 = $\frac{4}{30}$ or $\frac{2}{15}$

Here, these events are mutually exclusive. (No point in common)

$\therefore$ Required Probability = $P(A) + P(B)$

$$= \frac{6}{30} + \frac{4}{30} = \frac{10}{30} = \frac{\mathbf{1}}{\mathbf{3}} \quad \textbf{Ans.}$$

(ii) Let A = Multiple of 3 = 3, 6, 9, 12, 15, 18, 21, 24, 27, 30 (10 points)

$\therefore$ Probability of getting of 3 multiples = $\frac{10}{30}$

& let B = Multiple of 7
= 7, 14, 21, 28 (4 points)

$\therefore$ Probability of getting multiple of 7 = $\frac{4}{30}$

Here, 21 is common multiple because it is a multiple of 3 as well as that of 7.

Hence, Probability of getting 3 or 7

$$P(A \text{ or } B) = P(A) + P(B) - P(AB)$$

$$\therefore \quad P(A \text{ or } B) = \frac{10}{30} + \frac{4}{30} - \frac{1}{30} = \frac{\mathbf{13}}{\mathbf{30}} \qquad \textbf{Ans.}$$

***Illustration* 14(B)**

If a dice is thrown, What is the probability of gelling a number less than 4 or an even number ?

***Solution* :**

Let less than 4 be A and even number be B.

The numbers less than 4 on a dice are : 1, 2, and 3 the even numbers on a dice are : 2, 4 and 6 since these two events have a common outcome 2, they are overlapping events.

$\therefore$ P (less than 4 or even)

= P(A) (less than 4) + P(B) (even) − P(AB) (less than 4 and even)

$$= \frac{3}{6} + \frac{3}{6} - \frac{1}{6} = \frac{\mathbf{5}}{\mathbf{6}} \qquad \textbf{Ans.}$$

Inclusion-Exclusion Formula in case of 3 events : Similarly, in case of three events where some events are not mutually exclusive, common multiple or common events will have to be separated.

$$P(A + B + C) = P(A) + P(B) + P(C) - P(AB) - P(AC) - P(BC) + P(ABC)$$

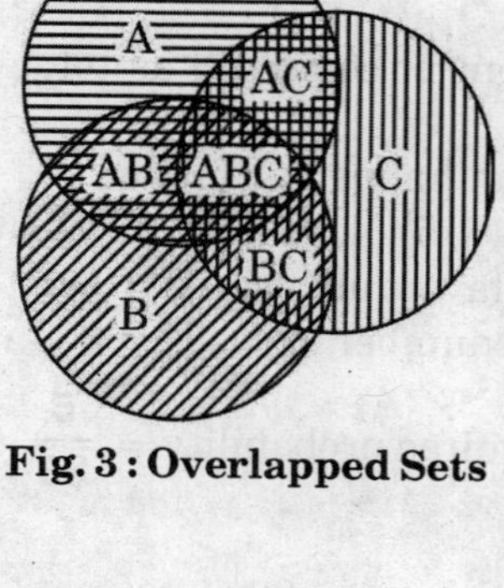

Fig. 3 : Overlapped Sets

***Illustration* 15**

The probability that a contractor will get a plumbing contract is 2/3 and the probability that he will get an electric contract is 5/9. If the probability of getting at least one contract is 4/5, what is the probability that he will get both ?

***Solution* :**

Let A = Plumbing contract and B = Electric contract

Thus, $P(A) = \frac{2}{3}, P(B) = \frac{5}{9}, P(A \text{ or } B) = \frac{4}{5}$

$$P(A \text{ or } B) = P(A) + P(B) - P(A \& B)$$

$$\frac{4}{5} = \frac{2}{3} + \frac{5}{9} - P(A \& B)$$

or $$P(A \& B) = \frac{2}{3} + \frac{5}{9} - \frac{4}{5}$$

$\therefore$ $$P(A \& B) = \frac{30+25-36}{45} = \mathbf{\frac{19}{45}} \quad \textbf{Ans.}$$

***Illustration* 16**

The probability that a contractor will get a plumbing contract is 2/3 and the probability that he will not get an electric contract is 5/9. If the probability of getting at least one contract is 4/5, what is the probability that he will get both ?

***Solution* :**

Let A and B denote the events that the contractor will get 'plumbing' and 'electric' contracts respectively. Thus, we are given :

$$P(A) = \frac{2}{3}, P(B^C) = \frac{5}{9}, P(A \text{ or } B) = \frac{4}{5}$$

$\therefore$ $$P(B) = 1 - P(B^C) = 1 - \frac{5}{9} = \frac{4}{9}$$

and $P(A \cup B)$ = Probability that contractor gets at least one contract = 4/5

or $P(A) + P(B) - P(A \& B) = 4/5$

$$\frac{2}{3} + \frac{4}{9} - P(A \& B) = \frac{4}{5}$$

or $$P(A \& B) \ \frac{8\ 0}{1\ 0\ 0} = \frac{30+20-36}{45}$$

$$= \frac{50-36}{45} = \mathbf{\frac{14}{45}} \quad \textbf{Ans.}$$

Hence, the probability that the contractor will get both the contracts is **14/45.**

***Illustration* 17(A)**

A Salesman is known to sell a product in 3 out of 5 attempts while an other Salesman is 2 out of 5 attempts. Find the probability that (i) No sale will be effective when then both try to sell the product, and (ii) Either of them will succeed in selling the product.

***Solution* :**

For the first salesman

$$P(A) = 3/5 \text{ and } P(\overline{A}) = 2/5$$

For the second salesman

$$P(B) = 2/5 \text{ and } P(\overline{B}) = 3/5$$

(i) Probability that both will not be able to sell

$$P(\overline{A} \cap \overline{B}) = \frac{2}{5} \times \frac{3}{5} = \frac{6}{25} = \mathbf{0.24} \quad \textbf{Ans.}$$

(ii) Probability that either A or B will succeed is

$\therefore$ $$P(A \text{ or } B) = P(A) + P(B) - P(AB)$$

$$= \frac{3}{5} + \frac{2}{5} - \left(\frac{2}{5} \times \frac{3}{5}\right) = 1 - \frac{6}{25}$$

$$= \frac{19}{25} = \mathbf{0.76}$$

Hence, probability that either of them will succeed in selling the product $= \mathbf{\frac{19}{25}} = \mathbf{0.76}$ **Ans.**

***Illustration* 17(B)**

In a business a man can make a profit of ₹ 3,000 with probability of 0.6 or to take a loss of ₹ 1,000 with probability 0.4. Determine his expectations. (*JAC*, 2017)

***Solution* :**

$$\text{Expectation} = 3{,}000 \times 0.6 - 1{,}000 \times 0.4$$
$$= 1{,}800 - 400 = 1{,}400$$

Exercise 7(B)

Based on Addition Theorem

1. From a pack of 52 cards, one card is drawn. What is the chance of drawing a king or ace ?

   $\left[\textbf{Ans. } \frac{2}{13}\right]$

2. A card is drawn from a pack of cards. What is the probability that it is either a king of hearts or queen of diamonds. (*JAC*, 2023)

   $\left[\textbf{Ans. } \frac{1}{26}\right]$

3. In a throw of two dice, find the chance of getting a total of either 2 or 8 or 12.

   $\left[\textbf{Ans. } \frac{7}{36}\right]$

4. What is the probability of getting an even number in rolling a fair dice ?

   $\left[\textbf{Ans. } \frac{1}{2}\right]$

5. Find out the probability of getting a total of either 7 or 11 in a single throw of two dice.

   $\left[\textbf{Ans. } \frac{2}{9}\right]$

6. A bag contains 16 white, 8 black, 12 yellow and 12 red balls. What is probability of drawing of a black or yellow ball in a single draw ?

   $\left[\textbf{Ans. } \frac{5}{12}\right]$

7. If two dice are thrown : (i) What is the probability throwing two sixes ? (ii) What is the probability of 9 ? (iii) What is the probability of not throwing a total of 9 ? (*JAC, 2023*)

[**Ans.** (i) $\frac{1}{36}$, (ii) $\frac{1}{9}$, (iii) $\frac{8}{9}$]

8. A bag contains 4 white, 9 black, 6 red and 3 green balls. Find the probability of getting either a white or a black or a green ball in a single draw ?

[**Ans.** $\frac{8}{11}$ or 0.727]

9. A bag contains 3 red, 5 black and 5 yellow balls. What is the probability of drawing either a red or yellow in a single draw ? (*JAC, 2024*)

[**Ans.** $\frac{8}{13}$]

10. In an experiment of tossing two dice, fnd the probability that the sum of numbers is greater than 9.

[**Ans.** $\frac{1}{6}$]

11. One purse contains 1 rupee and 4 half rupee coins, a second contains 2 rupee and 3 half-rupee coins and a third contains 3 rupee and 2 half-rupee coins. One purse is selected at random out of these and a coin is taken out from it. What is the probability that it is a rupee coin ?

[**Ans.** $\frac{2}{5}$]

[**Hint :** Use addition theorem.]

12. If the probability of the horse *A* winning the race is $\frac{1}{5}$ and the probability of the horse *B* winning the same race is $\frac{1}{6}$, what is the probability that one of the horses will win the race ?

[**Ans.** $\frac{11}{30}$] [**Formula :** $P(A + B) = P(A) + P(B)$]

When Events are not Mutually Exclusive

13. What is the chance of drawing of a spade or a king from a deck of cards ?

[**Ans.** $\frac{4}{13}$]

14. There are 100 tickets numbered from 1 to 100. They are well shuffled and one ticket is drawn at random. Find the probability that the number on the ticket drawn is square of an integer.

[**Ans.** $\frac{1}{10}$]

15. A bag contains 25 balls, numbered from 1 to 25, one is to be drawn. Find the probability that the number of the drawn ball will be a multiple of 5 or 7.

[**Ans.** $\frac{8}{25}$]

16. From 50 tickets consequently marked with the first 50 numeral, one is drawn at random. Find the probability of its being a multiple of 3 or 4.

[**Ans.** $\frac{24}{50}$ or $\frac{12}{25}$]

17. A person is known to hit the target 3 out of 4 shots, whereas another person is known to hit the target 2 out of 3 shots. Find the probability of the target being hit at all when they both try ?

[**Ans.** $\frac{11}{12}$]

18. The probability that a contractor will get a plumbing contract is $\frac{2}{3}$ and the probability that he will get an electric contract is $\frac{4}{9}$. If the probability of getting atleast one contract is $\frac{4}{5}$, what is probability that he will get both ?

[**Ans.** $\frac{14}{45}$]

(2) Multiplication Theorem or Multiplication Law of Probability

Multiplication Theorem is applied in two cases :
(i) When events are Independent,
(ii) When events are Not Independent.

To understand Multiplication Law of Probability, you should have a clear-cut concept of "Independent Events." Though, this term has been discussed earlier, for the convenience of students, we are going so explain this term here also.

Independent Events

- Two events are independent if the happening of one has no effect on the happening of another.

For Example,

1. On rolling a dice and tossing a coin together
   A : The event that number 6 turns up.
   B : The event that head turns up.
2. In shooting a target
   A : Event that the first trial is missed.
   B : Event that the second trial is missed

In both these cases events A and B are independent.

3. In drawing a card from a well shuffled pack
   A : Event that first card is drawn
   B : Event that second card is drawn without replacing the first.
   C : Event that second card is drawn after replacing the first.

In this case A and B are not independent but A and C are independent.

Multiplication Theorem

- If the events A and B are independent then :
  $P(\text{A and B}) = P(A) \times P(B)$
- Probability to happening at least one event out of two events :
  $P(\text{not A and B}) = 1 - P(\text{A and B together})$
- Dependent Events or Conditional Probability :
  $P(\text{A and B}) = P(A) \times P(B/A)$
  $P(\text{A and B}) = P(B) \times P(A/B)$

Case I : When Events are Independent : The probability that two or more independent events happen on any one occasion is the product of the chances of their happening simultaneously. In other words, "If two events are Mutually Independent and the probability of the one is p_1 while that of the other is p_2, the probability of two events occurring simultaneously is the product of p_1 and p_2."

(When the probability of happening event 'B' is not affected by the happening of the event 'A', then event 'B' is asid to be independent of A.)

$$P(A \text{ and } B) = P(A) \times P(B)$$

In case of more than two independent events,

$$P(A, B, C...n) = P(A) \times P(B) \times P(C) .... \times P(n)$$

Case II : When Events are Not Independent or When Events are Dependent : When probability of happening of an event is affected by the happening of another event then it is said that happening of one event is Dependent on the other. For instance if events 'A' and B are so related that the occurrence of 'B' is affected by the occurrence of 'A' then, 'A' and 'B' are called Dependent Events. The probability of event 'B' depending on the occurrence of the event 'A' is called conditional probability.

$$P(A \text{ and } B) = P(A) \times P(B/A)$$

or $$P(A \text{ and } B) = P(B) \times P(A/B)$$

Remarks : The Multiplication Theorem will hold good if the events belong to the same set.

For details and examples see 'Conditional Probability'.

Here $P(B/A)$ means Probability of 'B' given 'A'. Here probability of 'B' is based on the assumption that event 'A' has already happened. For instance, if two cards are withdrawn from the pack one by one and in the first card drawn is not placed in the pack (*i.e.*, without replacement), then it is Dependent Event.

***Illustration* 18 (Independent Events)**

What is the probability of getting all the tails in five throws of a coin ?

Solution :

The probability of getting Tail in the 1st throw $= \frac{1}{2}$

The probability of getting Tail in the 2nd throw $= \frac{1}{2}$

The probability of getting Tail in the 3rd throw $= \frac{1}{2}$

The probability of getting Tail in the 4th throw $= \frac{1}{2}$

The probability of getting Tail in the 5th throw $= \frac{1}{2}$

The probability of getting Tails in all the throws

$$= \frac{1}{2} \times \frac{1}{2} \times \frac{1}{2} \times \frac{1}{2} \times \frac{1}{2} = \frac{1}{32}$$ **Ans.**

***Illustration* 19**

A dice is thrown twice. What is the probability that it falls with number 6 upwards in the first throw and with an odd number upwards in the second throw ?

Solution :

Throwing of a dice first and second time is independent of each other.

Let A = No. 6 appears and

B = An odd no. appears

Thus the probability of getting 6 upwards in the first throw $P(A) = \frac{1}{6}$

Now, odd numbers of the dice : 1, 3, 5

Hence, the probability of getting odd number upwards

$$P(B) = \frac{3}{6}$$

Then,

$$\text{Required Prob} = P(A).P(B) = \frac{1}{6} \times \frac{3}{6}$$

$$= \frac{3}{36} = \mathbf{\frac{1}{12}}$$ **Ans.**

***Illustration* 20**

'A' speaks truth in 50% cases and 'B' in 80% cases. In what percentage of cases are they likely to contradict each other in stating the same fact ?

Solution :

The speaking of truth or false (*i.e.*, lie) of 'A' is independent of speaking of truth or false of 'B'.

The probability of speaking truth by 'A' $= \frac{50}{100}$

The probability of speaking false by 'A' $= 1 - \frac{50}{100}$

$$= \frac{50}{100}$$

Similarly, probability of speaking truth by 'B'

$$= \frac{80}{100}$$

Probability of speaking false by 'B' $= 1 - \frac{80}{100}$

$$= \frac{20}{100}$$

Now speaking truth by 'A' and false by 'B' or speaking false by 'A' and truth by 'B'

= To contradict each other.

Hence, Required probability of contradicting each other

$$= \left(\frac{50}{100} \times \frac{20}{100}\right) + \left(\frac{50}{100} \times \frac{80}{100}\right)$$

$$\therefore \quad \text{Reg'd Prob.} = \frac{10}{100} + \frac{40}{100} = \frac{50}{100}$$

= 50% **Ans.**

Illustration 21

A lot contains 10 items of which 3 are defective. Three items are choosen from the lot at random one after another without replacement. Find the probability that all the three are defective.

Solution :

Let A, B and C are three defective items which are drawn in I, II and III drawn respectively.

$\therefore$ Probability of being defective of three items are

$$P(A \cap B \cap C) = P(A) \times P(B) \times P(C)$$

$$\therefore \quad \text{Req'd Prob.} = \frac{3}{10} \times \frac{2}{9} \times \frac{1}{8} = \mathbf{\frac{1}{120}} \quad \textbf{Ans.}$$

Note : Since after draw, the item is not replaced, the total number of items (*i.e.*, n) will go on decreasing by 1.

***Illustration 22* (Dependent Events)**

In a bag there are 10 white and 15 black balls. If they are drawn at a time and the ball is placed after each draw, what is the probability of getting the first ball white, second black and the third white ?

Solution :

In this problem, the ball drawn is placed in the bag each time.

So every event is independent.

$$\text{Probability of drawing white ball first} = \frac{10}{10+15} = \frac{10}{15} = \frac{2}{5}$$

$$\text{Probability of drawing black ball next} = \frac{15}{10+15} = \frac{15}{25} = \frac{3}{5}$$

$$\text{Probability of white ball again} = \frac{10}{10+15} = \frac{10}{25} = \frac{2}{5}$$

$$\therefore \quad \text{Required Probability} = \frac{2}{5} \times \frac{3}{5} \times \frac{2}{5} = \mathbf{\frac{12}{125}} \quad \textbf{Ans.}$$

Illustration 23

In a bag there are 5 red and 3 white balls. Find the probability that the first ball is red, second white, third red and so on, if they are drawn in succession. (*JAC*, 2018)

Solution :

In this question, the ball is drawn in succession. It means it is not placed in the bag again. So the number of balls in the bag will go decreasing by 1 each time.

$\therefore$ Probability of 1st ball being Red (P)

$$= \frac{5}{5+3} = \frac{5}{8}$$

Probability of 2nd ball being White (P)

$$= \frac{3}{4+3} = \frac{3}{7}$$

Probability of 3rd ball being Red (P)

$$= \frac{4}{4+2} = \frac{4}{6}$$

Probability of 4th ball being White (P)

$$= \frac{2}{3+2} = \frac{2}{5}$$

Probability of 5th ball being Red (P)

$$= \frac{3}{3+1} = \frac{3}{4}$$

Probability of 6th ball being White (P)

$$= \frac{1}{2+1} = \frac{1}{3}$$

Probability of 7th ball being Red (P)

$$= \frac{2}{2}$$

Probability of 8th ball being Red (P)

$$= \frac{1}{1} \text{ (There is No. White ball, left)}$$

$\therefore$ Probability of drawing ball in succession

$$= \frac{5}{8} \times \frac{3}{7} \times \frac{4}{6} \times \frac{2}{5} \times \frac{3}{4} \times \frac{1}{3} \times \frac{2}{2} \times \frac{1}{2}$$

$$= \mathbf{\frac{1}{56}} \quad \textbf{Ans.}$$

Exercise 7(C)

1. A bag contains 5 black and 4 white balls. 3 balls are drawn one by one without putting them. Find the probability that the drawn 3 balls are of the same colour. (*JAC*, 2023)

   $\left[\textbf{Ans. } \frac{1}{6}\right]$

2. A bag contains 4 white, 5 red and 6 green balls. Three balls are drawn at random. What is the probability that a white, a red and a green ball are drawn ?

   $\left[\textbf{Ans. } \frac{24}{91}\right]$

3. One bag contains 5 red balls and 3 white balls. A second bag contains 4 red balls and 7 black balls. If one ball is drawn at random from each bag, what is the probability that both are of the same colour ?

   $\left[\textbf{Ans. } \frac{5}{22}\right]$

4. Three groups of children contain respectively :
   3 girls and 1 boy
   2 girls and 2 boys
   1 girl and 3 boys
   One child is selected at random from each group. Show that the chance that the three selected consist of 1 girl and 2 boys is 13/32.
   [**Ans.** 13/32]
   [**Hint :** P_1 = Girl from the first, boys from second, boy from the third.

$$= \frac{3}{4} \times \frac{1}{2} \times \frac{3}{4} = \frac{9}{32}$$

P_2 = Boy from the first, girl from the second, boy from the third.

$$= \frac{1}{4} \times \frac{1}{2} \times \frac{3}{4} = \frac{3}{32}$$

P_3 = Boy from the first, boy from the second and girl from the third.

$$= \frac{1}{4} \times \frac{1}{2} \times \frac{1}{4} = \frac{1}{32}$$

$$\text{Joint } P = \frac{9}{32} + \frac{3}{32} + \frac{1}{32} = \frac{13}{32}$$

5. Find the chance of drawing a king, a queen and a knave in that order from a pack of cards in three consecutive draws, the cards drawn are not being replaced.

[**Ans.** $\frac{8}{16,575}$]

6. Find the probability of drawing 2 white balls in succession from a bag containing 40 red and 60 white balls, the balls drawn not being replaced.

[**Ans.** $\frac{3540}{9900}$ or 0.3575]

7. A dice is cst three times. What is the probability :
(a) of getting there 6's in succession ?
(b) of not getting there 6's in succession ?
(c) that the same face appears three times ?

[**Ans.** (a) $\frac{1}{216}$, (b) $\frac{215}{216}$, (c) $\frac{6}{216}$ or $\frac{1}{36}$]

Corrolaries of Multiplication Theorem

(1) Probability of Happening atleast one Event : Sometimes several independent events are given and we have to find out probability of happening of atleast one event out of such events. In such a case first of all joint or compound probability of not happening of events will have to be found out and then this joint probability will be deducted from 1, the resultant figure will be required probability of happening of atleast one event.

Formula : P (Atleast one event)
= 1 – (Probability of not happening the events)

or P = 1 – Compound Probability of not happening of the events

or $P = \{(1-p_1)(1-p_2)(1-p_3) \dots (1-p_n)\}$

or, Probability of happening at least one event out of two events A and B :
= 1 – P (A not) × P (B not) or 1 – P (A and B together)
(See Illustration 24 and 25)

Probability of happening at least one event out of three events A, B, C :
= 1 – P (A not) × P (B not) × P (C not)
(See Illustration 26)

Illustration 24

A person is known to hit the target in 3 out of 4 shots, whereas another person is known to hit 2 out of 3 shots. Find the probability of the target being hit at all when they both try. (*JAC*, 2011)

Solution :

Let there be two persons 'A' and 'B'.
Probability of 'A', to hit the target $P(A)$

$$= \frac{3}{4}$$

Probability of 'A' not hitting the target $P(A^C)$

$$= 1 - P(A) = \frac{1-3}{4} = \frac{1}{4}$$

Probability of 'B', to hit the target $P(B)$

$$= \frac{2}{3}$$

Probability of 'B', not hitting the target

$$= P(B^C) = 1 - P(B) = \frac{1-2}{3} = \frac{1}{3}$$

∴ Probability of not hitting the target by (A^C and B^C)

$$= \frac{1}{4} \times \frac{1}{3} = \frac{1}{12}$$

Probability of the target being hit at all

$$= 1 - \frac{1}{12} = \mathbf{\frac{11}{12}}$$ **Ans.**

Illustration 25

It is 8 to 5 against a person who is now 40 years old living till he is 70 and 4 to 3 against a person now 50 living till he is 80. Find the probability that one of them would be alive 30 years hence ?

Solution :

Probability of a person that he would not be alive upto 30 years = 8/13

Probability of other person that he would not be alive upto 30 years = 4/7

Since both events are independent, therefore, probability of not living alive both of them upto 30 years $= \frac{8}{13} \times \frac{4}{7} = \frac{32}{91}$

∴ Probability of living alive atleast one of them upto the age of 30 years

$$= 1 - \frac{32}{91} = \mathbf{\frac{59}{91}}$$ **Ans.**

Illustration 26

A problem in Statistics is given to three students 'A', 'B' and 'C' whose chances of solving it are $\frac{1}{2}$, $\frac{1}{3}$ and $\frac{1}{4}$ respectively. What is the probability that the problem will be solved ?

Solution :

Probability of not solving the problem by 'A'

$$= 1 - \frac{1}{2} = \frac{1}{2}$$

Probability of not solving the problem by 'B'

$$= 1 - \frac{1}{3} = \frac{2}{3}$$

Probability of not solving the problem by 'C'

$$= 1 - \frac{1}{4} = \frac{3}{4}$$

Probability of not solving the problem by all of them

$$= \frac{1}{2} \times \frac{2}{3} \times \frac{3}{4} = \frac{1}{4}$$

Probability (P) that atleast one of them solves the problem $= 1 - \frac{1}{4} = \mathbf{\frac{3}{4}}$ **Ans.**

Alternatively :

Probability that problem will be solved

= P (Atleast one of them solves the problem)

= 1 – P (None of them solves the problem)

$$= 1 - \left(1-\frac{1}{2}\right) \times \left(1-\frac{1}{3}\right) \times \left(1-\frac{1}{4}\right)$$

$$= 1 - \frac{1}{2} \times \frac{2}{3} \times \frac{3}{4}$$

$$= 1 - \frac{1}{4} = \mathbf{\frac{3}{4}}$$ **Ans.**

(3) Conditional Probability or Theorem of Conditional Probability

If sub-events are not independent, and the nature of dependence is known, we have the Theorem of Conditional Probability. In other words, Conditional Probability is the probability of an event in the sub-population or the reduced sample space. This theorem is more or less corollary of the Multiplication Theorem.

The theorem of conditional probability is that the probability that both of the two dependent events can happen is the product of the probability of the first sub-event and the probability of the second after the first sub-event has happened.

Notation : P (A and B) = $P(A) \times P(B/A)$

or P (A and B) = $P(B) \times P(A/B)$

where, $P(B/A)$ = Conditional probability of 'B', when 'A' has already happened.

Similarly, $P(A/B)$ = Conditional probability of 'A', when 'B' has already happened.

In case of three events

$$P(ABC) = P(A) \times P(B/A) \times P(C/AB)$$

Example : If out of a pack of cards shuffled and drawing one card from it, a Queen turns out each time. Here, the probability of a Queen is 4/52 or 1/13. If Queen is not restored or placed in the pack, then chance of drawing one Queen from the pack in a second reshuffling is 3/51 or 1/17. Therefore, the probability of turning up of two Queens simultaneously $= \frac{4}{52} \times \frac{3}{51} = \frac{12}{2652}$.

The term conditional probability is often known as probability due to partial exhaustion of sample space.

***Illustration* 27 (Without Replacement)**

In a bag, there are 10 black and 10 white balls. Calculate the probability of drawing the black balls in succession if the ball drawn first is not replaced ?

Solution :

Let A = a black ball; B = a white ball

Here, probability of drawing black ball in first draw

$$\Rightarrow \quad P(A) = \frac{10}{10+10} = \frac{10}{20} = \mathbf{\frac{1}{2}}$$

After first draw, there remains 10 white and 9 balck balls (because the ball is not replaced)

Probability of drawing black ball in the second draw

$$\Rightarrow \quad P(B/A) = \frac{9}{10+9} = \mathbf{\frac{9}{19}}$$

Therefore, probability drawing of black ball in succession

$$P(A \,\&\, B) = P(A) \times P(B/A)$$

$$= \frac{1}{2} \times \frac{1}{19} = \mathbf{\frac{9}{38}}$$ **Ans.**

***Illustration* 28**

Four cards are drawn without replacement. What is the chance that all are from different suits ?

Solution :

In a pack of cards we have four suits, each suit having 13 cards. If a card is drawn from the pack it's chance of having from any suit = 52/52. After drawing one card only 51 cards are left in the pack and from three suits (*i.e.*, 39 cards) one card is to be drawn.

Drawing of second card of any other suit

= 39/51

Similarly, probability of drawing of the third card, being from another suit = 26/50

Similarly, probability of drawing of the fourth card, being from another suit = 13/49

Therefore, probability of four cards of different suits

$$= \frac{52}{52} \times \frac{39}{51} \times \frac{26}{50} \times \frac{13}{49}$$

$$= \frac{13 \times 13 \times 13}{17 \times 25 \times 49}$$

$$= \mathbf{\frac{2197}{20825}}$$ **Ans.**

***Illustration* 29**

Four cards are drawn in succession without replacement. What is the chance that all are Aces ?

Solution :

Total no. of cards in a pack = 52

Probability of Ace in the first draw $= \frac{4}{52}$

Probability of Ace in the second draw $= \frac{3}{51}$

Probability of Ace in the third draw $= \frac{2}{50}$

Probability of Ace in the fourth draw $= \frac{1}{49}$

Probability of Aces in four draws

$$= \frac{4}{52} \times \frac{3}{51} \times \frac{2}{50} \times \frac{1}{49}$$

$$= \frac{1}{13 \times 17 \times 25 \times 49}$$

$$= \frac{1}{270725}$$ **Ans.**

Exercise 7(D)

Probability of Happening at least one Event

1. A problem in statistics is given to four students. A, B, C and D whose chances of solving it are $\frac{1}{2}, \frac{1}{3}, \frac{1}{4}$ and $\frac{1}{4}$ respectively. What is the probability that the problem will be solved?

   [**Ans.** $\frac{13}{16}$]

2. Two dice are thrown once. What is the probability of getting at least '6'?

   [**Ans.** $\frac{11}{36}$]

3. One card is drawn at random from each of the two packs of cards. What is the probability that at least one will be queen of hearts?

   [**Ans.** $\frac{103}{2704}$]

4. A bag contains 5 white and 3 black balls. Two balls are drawn at random one after another without replacement. Find the probability that both the balls drawn are black.

   [**Ans.** $\frac{3}{28}$]

   [**Hint :** $P(AB) = P(A) + P(B/A)$]

5. Find the probability of drawing a king, a queen a knave in this from a pack of cards in three successive draws presuming that cards are not replaced?

   [**Ans.** $\frac{64}{132600}$]

6. In a bag there are 5 white and 8 black balls. 3-3 balls are drawn twice in such a way that (i) prior to drawing of the second time balls are replaced and (ii) balls are not replaced. Find the probability that in the first time 3 white balls will be drawn and the second time 3 red balls will be drawn.

   [**Ans.** (i) $\frac{140}{20{,}449}$, (ii) $\frac{7}{429}$]

7. Five cards are to be drawn in succession and without replacement from an ordinary pack of playing cards :

   (a) What is the probability that there will be no ace among five cards drawn ?

   (b) What is the probability that the first three cards are aces and the last two cards are kings ?

   (c) What is the probability that only the first three cards are aces ?

   (d) What is the probability that an ace will appear only on the fifth draw ?

   [**Ans.** (a) $\frac{205476480}{311875200}$ or $\frac{35673}{54145}$ (b) $\frac{288}{311875200}$ or $\frac{1}{1082900}$ (c) $\frac{54144}{311875200}$ or $\frac{846}{487305}$ (d) $\frac{18679680}{311875200}$ or $\frac{29687}{487305}$]

(4) Bayes' Theorem (Inverse Probability)

Bayes' Theorem is related with the rule for the Inverse Probability. Probability can be revised when new information relating to a Random Experiment is made available. The need for revising probability arises from a need to make better use of experimental information. "*Thomas Bayes*" (a British Mathematician) in 1763 propounded that probabilities be revised in accordance with the additional information.

It should be noted that where an event has occurred through one of the various mutually independent events or regions, the conditional probabilities shows that it has occurred due to particular region or event. This is called as "*Inverse*" or "Posteriori Probability".

If an event can only happen in conjunction with one of the '*n*' Mutually Exclusive & Exhaustive Events $p_1, p_2, p_3, \ldots, p_n$ and if the event actually happens then the probability that it was preceded by that particular event is given by :

$$= \frac{P_m p_m}{P_1 p_1 + P_2 p_2 + P_3 p_3 + \ldots}$$

Illustration 30

There are two bags, one containing 5 red and 7 white balls and the other containing 3 red and 12 white balls. One ball is drawn either from the first or from the second. Find the probability of drawing one Red ball.

Solution :

The one ball is drawn either from the first or the second bag.

Therefore, the probability of drawing one ball either from the first or second $= \frac{1}{2}$

$\therefore \quad P_1 = P_2 = \frac{1}{2}$ (equal prob.)

Total balls in the first bag

$= 5 + 7 = 12$ balls

Therefore, the probability of drawing a Red ball from the first bag

$$p_1 = \frac{5}{12}$$

Total no. of balls in the second bag

$= 3 + 12 = 15$

Therefore, the probability of drawing the Red ball from the second bag

$$p_2 = \frac{3}{15}$$

∴ Inverse probability of Red ball

$$= P_1 \times p_1 \times P_2 \times p_2$$

$$= \left(\frac{1}{2} \times \frac{5}{12}\right) + \left(\frac{1}{2} \times \frac{3}{15}\right)$$

$$= \frac{5}{24} + \frac{1}{10} = \frac{\mathbf{37}}{\mathbf{120}}$$ **Ans.**

***Illustration* 31**

There are 3 urns. First urn contains 5 red and 7 green balls. Second urn contains 5 red and 3 green balls and the third urn contains 8 red and 4 green balls. One red ball is drawn from an urn. Find the probability that it has been drawn from (i) First urn, (ii) third urn, (iii) second urn.

Solution :

Probability of drawing of one Red ball from the first urn :

$$p_1 = \frac{5}{12}$$

Probability of drawing one Red ball from the second urn :

$$p_2 = \frac{5}{8}$$

	Red	*Green*
Urn I	5	7
Urn II	5	3
Urn III	8	4

Probability of drawing one Red ball from the third urn :

$$p_3 = \frac{8}{12}$$

where $P_1 = P_2 = P_3 = 1/3$ (Prob. of selecting a bag)

(i) Inverse Probability of drawing one Red ball from first urn :

$$= \frac{P_1 p_1}{P_1 p_1 + P_2 p_2 + P_3 p_3}$$

$$= \frac{\frac{1}{3} \times \frac{5}{12}}{\left(\frac{1}{3} \times \frac{5}{12}\right) + \left(\frac{1}{3} \times \frac{5}{8}\right) + \left(\frac{1}{3} \times \frac{8}{12}\right)}$$

$$= \frac{5/36}{41/72} = \frac{\mathbf{10}}{\mathbf{41}}$$ **Ans.**

(ii) Inverse Probability of drawing one Red ball from the third urn :

$$= \frac{P_3 p_3}{P_1 p_1 + P_2 p_2 + P_3 p_3}$$

$$= \frac{\frac{1}{3} \times \frac{8}{12}}{\left(\frac{1}{3} \times \frac{5}{12}\right) + \left(\frac{1}{3} \times \frac{5}{8}\right) + \left(\frac{1}{3} \times \frac{8}{12}\right)}$$

$$= \frac{8/36}{41/72} = \frac{\mathbf{16}}{\mathbf{41}}$$ **Ans.**

(iii) Inverse Probability of drawing one Red ball from the second urn :

$$= \frac{P_2 p_2}{P_1 p_1 + P_2 p_2 + P_3 p_3}$$

$$= \frac{\frac{1}{3} \times \frac{5}{8}}{\left(\frac{1}{3} \times \frac{5}{12}\right) + \left(\frac{1}{3} \times \frac{5}{8}\right) + \left(\frac{1}{3} \times \frac{8}{12}\right)}$$

$$= \frac{5/24}{41/72} = \frac{\mathbf{15}}{\mathbf{41}}$$ **Ans.**

Exercise 7(E)

Inverse Probability

1. Suppose that any black ball has taken out from 3 bags; the first bag contains 3 balck and 7 white balls, second bag contains 5 black and 3 white balls and third bag contais 8 black and 4 white balls. Find the probability of drawing black ball out of first bag.

   $\left[\textbf{Ans. } \frac{36}{191}\right]$

2. There are three urns. In first urn there are 2 white and 3 black balls, second urn contains 1 white and 4 black balls, third urn contains 4 white and 1 black balls. One ball is drawn at random from an urn which is of white colour. Find the probability that this ball has come out from (i) first urn, (ii) third urn, (iii) second urn.

   $\left[\textbf{Ans. } \text{(i) } \frac{2}{7}, \text{ (ii) } \frac{4}{7}, \text{ (iii) } \frac{1}{7}\right]$

(7.7) APPLICATION OF PERMUTATION AND COMBINATION IN THE THEORY OF PROBABILITY

Rules of permutation and combination are often used in the theory of probability. In the chapter 5 of Business Mathematics rection we have studied permutations and combinations and fundamental rules of counting. We need not repeat them. To recaptulate **permutations** refer to different arrangements of object in a set where all elements are different and distinguishable. A **combination** is selection of object considered without regard to their arrangement. The number of combinations of objects all different is entirely different from the number of their permutations.

Counting assumes importance in the study of probability theory because as the chance of occurrence of an event has to be assessed by counting the outcomes favourable to the happening of the event from amongst all possible outcomes.

Fundamental Principle of Counting and formula of Permutation and Combinations

(1) If an event *'A'* occurs in exactly *'m'* ways and following it a second event can occur in exactly *'n'* ways then the events *'A'* and *'B'* can occur exactly in $m \times n$ ways.

If two events occur in any one way of $(m \times n)$ and a third event occurs in exactly *'o'* ways. Then three events will occur together in $(m \times n \times o)$ ways.

(2) Number of permutations of 'n' different things taking 'r' at a time $\Rightarrow {}^nP_r = \dfrac{n!}{(n-r)!}$ ...(1)

Where, n = number of all items

r = number of items taken together

(3) Number of ways of arranging things out of which 'p' are alike and one type, 'q' are alike and are of second type and 'r' are identical and are of third type and rest are all different $= {}^nP_r = \dfrac{n!}{(p!\ q!\ r!)}$

(4) Number of ways of selecting 'r' different things out of 'n' different things :

or

To find the number of combinations of 'n' different things taken r at a time :

$${}^nC_r = \frac{n!}{[(n-r)!\ r!]} \text{ or } \frac{\lfloor n}{\lfloor r \lfloor n-r} \quad ...(3)$$

Where ${}^nC_r$ = Number of combinations with 'r' things at a time

n = number of all items

Let us solve some problems on probability where the rules of permutation and combination are used.

***Illustration* 32**

There are four routes from Katihar to Patna. In how many different ways one person can go from Katihar to Patna through one route and come back through the other route ?

Solution

Routes for going from Katihar to Patna are : 4

But Routes for coming back from Patna to Katihar are : 3 (Because one cannot take the same route)

$\therefore$ No. of different ways for going & coming back are : $4 \times 3 = \mathbf{12}$ **Ans.**

***Illustration* 33**

If one room has 6 doors and four persons go into the room, then in how many different ways they can go inside through various doors ?

Solution

First person can go inside through any of the 6 doors.

Second person can go inside through any of the remaining $(6-1) = 5$ doors.

Third person can go inside through rest of the 4 doors.

Similarly fourth person can go inside through any of the remaining $4-1 = 3$ doors.

$\therefore$ Total no. of ways for going inside through various doors are $6 \times 5 \times 4 \times 3 = \mathbf{360}$

While solving the questions of probability, Permutation and Combination can be used, specially when we have to find the probability of a particular event to happen in a sample selected from the bulk.

Alternatively

$$n = 6, r = 4$$

$${}^nP_r = \frac{n!}{(n-r)!} = \frac{6!}{(6-4)!}$$

$$= \frac{6 \times 5 \times 4 \times 3 \times 2 \times 1}{2 \times 1}$$

$$= 6 \times 5 \times 4 \times 3 = \mathbf{360}$$ **Ans.**

***Illustration* 34**

4 strangers board a bus in which there are 6 empty seats. How many different ways can they be seated ?

Solution

$$n = 6, r = 4$$

$${}^6P_4 = \frac{6!}{(6-4)!} = \frac{6!}{2!}$$

$$= \frac{6 \times 5 \times 4 \times 3 \times 2 \times 1}{2 \times 1}$$

$$= 6 \times 5 \times 4 \times 3$$

= **360 ways** **Ans.**

***Illustration* 35**

In how many ways can be formed from the letters of the word COMMITTEE.

Solution

Here $n = 9$ and 3 letters M, T, E occur twice

Let p = M(2)

q = T(2)

r = E(2)

Thus, $${}^nP_r = \frac{n!}{p!q!r!} = \frac{9!}{2!2!2!}$$

$$= \frac{9 \times 8 \times 7 \times 6 \times 5 \times 4 \times 3 \times 2 \times 1}{2 \times 2 \times 2}$$

= **45,360** **Ans.**

***Illustration* 36**

In how many ways can the letters of the word BALLOON be arranged so that two L's do not come together ?

Solution

Here $n = 7$ and 2 letters L & O occur twice.

i.e. $p = 2, q = 2$

Now, Permutations

$$= \frac{7!}{2!2!}$$

$$= \frac{7 \times 6 \times 5 \times 4 \times 5 \times 3 \times 2 \times 1}{2 \times 2} = 1{,}260$$

Now, permutations with 2L together

$$= \frac{6!}{2!} = \frac{6 \times 5 \times 4 \times 3 \times 2 \times 1}{2} = 360$$

Now, No. of ways that two L's do not come together

$= 1{,}260 - 360 = \mathbf{900}$ **Ans.**

***Illustration* 37**

A bag contains 5 black, 3 white and 2 red balls. In how many ways can 3 balls be drawn ?

Solution

Total No. of balls $n = 10$

Possible ways to select 3 balls out of 10 balls are $^{10}C_3$

i.e. $\frac{10!}{3!7!} = \frac{10 \times 9 \times 8 \times 7!}{3 \times 2 \times 7!}$

$= \mathbf{120\ ways}$ **Ans.**

***Illustration* 38**

A person has 7 friends. In how many ways can be invite one or none of them of dinner ?

Solution

Total number to friends (n)

$= 7$

Possible ways to invite atleast one friend

$= 2^n - 1 = 2^7 - 1$

$= \mathbf{127\ ways}$ **Ans.**

***Illustration* 39**

A bag contains 8 green and 10 white balls. Two balls are drawn. What is the probability that one is green and other is white ?

Solution

Total no. of balls in the bag

$= 8 + 10 = 18$

Probability of getting one Green ball

$= {}^8C_1$

Probability of getting one White ball

$= {}^{10}C_1$

Probability of getting one Green and one White ball when two balls are drawn simultaneously

$= \frac{{}^8C_1 \times {}^{10}C_1}{{}^{18}C_2}$

$\therefore$ Required prob. $= \frac{8 \times 10 \times 2}{18 \times 17} = \mathbf{\frac{80}{153}}$ **Ans.**

***Illustration* 40**

A bag contains 8 white and 4 red balls. Five balls are drawn at random. What is the probability that 3 of them are white and red ?

Solution

Total no. of balls in the bag

$= 8 + 4 = 12$

Balls drawn $= 5$

No. of ways of drawing 5 balls out of 12 balls (P)

$= {}^{12}C_5$

No. of ways of drawing 3 White balls out of 8 balls

$(P) = {}^8C_2$

No. of ways of drawing 2 Red balls out of 4 balls (P)

$= {}^4C_2$

No. of favourable events

$= {}^8C_3 \times {}^4C_2$

$\therefore$ Required Probability (P)

$= \frac{{}^8C_3 \times {}^4C_2}{{}^{12}C_5}$

$= \frac{8 \times 7 \times 6}{3 \times 2 \times 1} \times \frac{4 \times 3}{2} \times \frac{5 \times 4 \times 3 \times 2 \times 1}{12 \times 11 \times 10 \times 9 \times 8}$

$= \mathbf{\frac{14}{33}}$ **or 0.424** **Ans.**

***Illustration* 41**

A bag contains 5 red and 8 green balls. Two draws of 3 balls each are made, the balls being replaced after the first draw. What is the chance that in the first draw the balls were all red and in the second all green ?

Solution

Total number of balls $= 5 + 8 = 13$

Number of ways of drawing 3 balls out of 13

$= {}^{13}C_3 = 286$ ways

Number of ways of drawing 3 balls out of 5 Red balls

$= {}^5C_3 = 10$ ways

$\therefore$ Probability of drawing 3 Red balls, $P(A)$

$= \frac{{}^5C_3}{{}^{13}C_3} = \frac{10}{286} = 0.034$

Number of ways of drawing 3 balls out of 8 Green balls

$= {}^8C_3 = 56$ ways

$\therefore$ Probability of drawing 3 Green balls, $P(B)$

$= \frac{{}^8C_3}{{}^{13}C_3} = \frac{56}{286} = 0.195$

$\therefore$ Probability of drawing 3 Red balls in first draw and 3 Green balls in 286 draw

$P(A \& B) \Rightarrow P(A) \times P(B)$

$= \frac{10 \times 56}{286 \times 286}$

$= \frac{{}^5C_3}{{}^{13}C_3} \times \frac{{}^8C_3}{{}^{13}C_3} = \frac{5}{143} \times \frac{28}{143}$

$= \mathbf{\frac{140}{20449}}$ **Ans.**

Explanation :

${}^5C_3 = \frac{5 \times 4 \times 3}{3 \times 2 \times 1} = 10,$

${}^{13}C_3 = \frac{13 \times 12 \times 11}{3 \times 2 \times 1} = 286,$

${}^8C_3 = \frac{8 \times 7 \times 6}{3 \times 2 \times 1} = 56$

$\therefore \frac{{}^5C_3}{{}^{13}C_1} = \frac{10}{286} = \frac{5}{143};$

$\frac{{}^8C_3}{{}^{13}C_1} = \frac{56}{286} = \frac{28}{143}$

***Illustration* 42**

There are 5 red and 8 black balls in a bag. Two successive draws of three balls each are made, the balls not being replaced after the first draw. What is the chance that in the first draw of the balls 3 are red and in the second 3 are black ?

Solution

Total Number of balls = 5 + 8 = 13

Number of ways of drawing 3 balls out of 13 = $^{13}C_3$

Number of drawing 3 Red balls out of 5 = $^5C_3$

∴ 1st Event, *i.e.*, probability of drawing 3 Red balls

$$= \frac{^5C_3}{^{13}C_3} = \frac{5}{143} \quad ...(1)$$

2nd event, *i.e.*, probability of drawing 3 black balls, since the balls are **not replaced** after the first draw, the bag will contain 5 – 3 = 2 red balls and 8 black balls.

Hence, probability of drawing 3 black balls out of 10 (2 + 8) = $^{10}C_3$

Probability of drawing 3 black balls out of 8 = $^8C_3$

Probability of drawing 3 back balls

$$= \frac{^8C_3}{^{10}C_3} = \frac{7}{15} \quad ...(2)$$

Probability of joint event, *i.e.*, probability of drawing 3 red balls in first attempt and 3 black balls in the second attempt

$$= \frac{^5C_3}{^{13}C_3} \times \frac{^8C_3}{^{10}C_3} = \frac{5}{143} \times \frac{7}{15}$$

$$= \mathbf{\frac{7}{429}} \text{ or } \mathbf{0.016}$$ **Ans.**

Illustration 43

From a pack of 52 playing cards, two are drawn at random. Find the probability that one is King and other is Queen.

Solution

Number of ways of drawing 2 cards out of 52 = $^{52}C_2$

Favourable ways of drawing a King and other a Queen = $^4C_1 \times {^4C_1}$

$$\therefore \text{ Required Probability} = \frac{^4C_1 \times {^4C_1}}{^{52}C_2} = \frac{4 \times 4}{\frac{52 \times 51}{2}}$$

$$= \frac{4 \times 4 \times 2}{52 \times 51}$$

$$= \mathbf{\frac{8}{663}} \text{ or } \mathbf{0.012}$$ **Ans.**

Illustration 44

From a pack of 52 cards, two cards are drawn at random. Find out the probability of drawing an Ace and a King.

Solution

Total number of ways of drawing two cards from a pack of 52 cards = $^{52}C_2$

∵ There are 4 Kings and 4 Aces in a pack of 52 cards. Also happening of an Ace or a King are Mutually Exclusive Events.

∴ No. of favourable cases = $^4C_1 \times {^4C_1}$

$$\therefore \text{ Required Probability } (P) = \frac{^4C_1 \times {^4C_1}}{^{52}C_2}$$

$$= \frac{4 \times 4 \times 2}{52 \times 51}$$

$$= \frac{8}{663}$$

= **0.012** **Ans.**

Illustration 45

In a factory, there are 6 skilled workers and 4 unskilled workers. What is the probability that (a) worker selected is skilled worker, (b) the two workers selected are skilled ?

Solution

(a) Favourable ways = $^6C_1 = 6$ (one skilled worker)

Total number of cases = $^{10}C_1 = 10 = (6 + 4)$

$$\therefore \text{ Required Probability} = \frac{6}{10}$$

(Prob. that worker selected is skilled workers) **Ans.**

(b)Number of ways of selecting 2 skilled workers

$$= {^6C_2} \; i.e., \binom{30}{2} \text{ ways}$$

= 15 ways

Total number of cases = $^{10}C_2$

$$\therefore \text{ Required Probability} = \frac{^6C_2}{^{10}C_2} = \frac{15}{45} = \mathbf{\frac{1}{3}}$$ **Ans.**

Illustration 46

A bag contains 5 white and 8 red balls. Two drawing of 3 balls are made such that (a) balls are replaced before the second trial, and (b) the balls are not replaced before the second trial. Find the probability that the first drawing will give 3 white and the second 3 red balls in each case.

Solution

(a) When the balls are replaced before the second trial :

Total no. of balls = 5 + 8 = 13

Probable Cases : Drawing of 3 White balls out of 13 = $^{13}C_3$

Favourable Ways : In first draw 3 White balls out of 5 White balls = $^5C_3$

∴ Probability of 3 White balls in first attempt

$$= \frac{^5C_3}{^{13}C_3} = \frac{5}{143}$$

In second draw 3 Red balls out of 8 Red balls = $^8C_3$

Probability of 3 Red balls in second draw

$$= \frac{^8C_3}{^{13}C_3} = \frac{28}{143}$$

Probability of happening of compound event (3 White balls in first draw and 3 Red balls in second draw)

$$= \frac{5}{143} \times \frac{28}{143} = \mathbf{\frac{140}{20449}}$$ **Ans.**

(b) When the balls are not replaced

Favourable ways : In first draw 3 white balls out of 5 White balls = $^5C_3$

Probability 3 White balls in first draw

$$= \frac{^5C_3}{^{13}C_3} = \frac{5}{143}$$

Since the balls are not replaced, the total no. of remaining balls

= 13 – 3 = 10 (2 white balls + 8 red balls)

∴ Probability of 3 Red balls in the second draw

$$= \frac{^8C_3}{^{10}C_3} = \frac{7}{15}$$

Probability of getting 3 White balls and 3 Red balls (without replcement)

$$= \frac{5}{143} \times \frac{7}{15} = \mathbf{\frac{7}{429}} \qquad \textbf{Ans.}$$

Illustration 47

A class consists of 10 boys and 5 girls. A committee of 3 students is formed. Find the number of events in the sample space when :

(i) It has 2 girls and 1 boy;
(ii) It has 2 boys and 1 girl;
(iii) All boys.

Solution

Total no. of students = 10 + 5 = 15 (3 has to be selected for a committee.)

Ways of forming the committee = $^{15}C_3$

Therefore, number of events in the sample space

$n(S) = {}^{15}C_3 = 455$

(i) If E_1 = 2 girls and 1 boy

then, $n(E_1) = {}^5C_2 \times {}^{10}C_1 = 10 \times 10 = \mathbf{100}$

(By Rule of Multiplication)

(ii) If E_2 = 2 boys and 1 girl

then, $n(E_2) = {}^5C_1 \times {}^{10}C_2 = 5 \times 45 = \mathbf{225}$

(iii) If E_3 = All boys

then, $n(E_3) = {}^{10}C_3 = \mathbf{120}$ **Ans.**

Exercise 7(F)

1. There are seven rooms in a hotel. In how many ways three persons can occupy different rooms ?
[Ans. 210]
2. In how many different ways the word SOFTWARE can be arranged taking all the letters of the word at a lime ?
[Ans. 40,320]
3. In how many ways can the letters of the word STATISTICS be arranged ?
[Ans. 50,400]
4. If a coins are tossed, find the chance that there should be two tails.
$\left[\textbf{Ans. } \frac{3}{8}\right]$
5. If 3 cards are drawn from a pack of 52 cards, what is the chance that all will be kings ? *(JAC, 2023)*
$\left[\textbf{Ans. } \frac{1}{5525} \text{ or } \frac{24}{132600}\right]$
$\left[\textbf{Hint}: P(E_2) = \frac{n(A)}{n(S)} = \frac{^4C_3}{^{52}C_3}\right]$
6. In a class there are 10 boys and 3 girls. 3 students are to be selected from the class. What is probability that 2 boys and 1 girl is selected ?
$\left[\textbf{Ans. } \frac{135}{286}\right]$
7. In a class there are 10 boys and 5 girls, 3 students are to be selected from the class. What is probability that 2 boys and 1 girl is selected ?
$\left[\textbf{Ans. } \frac{45}{91}\right]$
8. A bag contains 4 white, 5 red and 6 green balls. Three balls are drawn at random. What is the probability that a white a red and a green ball are drawn ?
$\left[\textbf{Ans. } \frac{24}{91}\right]$
$\left[\textbf{Hint}: \frac{^4C_1 \times {}^5C_1 \times {}^6C_1}{^{15}C_3}\right]$
9. A committee of 4 persons is to be appointed from 7 men and 3 women. What is probability that the committee contains : (i) exactly two women and (ii) atleast one women ?
$\left[\textbf{Ans. } \frac{3}{10}, \text{(ii) } \frac{5}{6}\right]$

(7.8) BERNOULLI'S TRIALS
OR
BERNOULLI'S THEOREM

This Theorem is associated with "James Bernoulli". A performance of Random Experiment with two possible outcomes is called a "Bernoulli Trials". Here, one trial is called as '*Success*' and another outcome as '*Failure*'. The probability of "Success" in a trial is denoted by 'p' and the probability of '*Failure*' is denoted by 'q', where $q + p = 1$.

If prob. of success in each trial is the same and Bernoulli's trials are repeated 'n' times, this compound experiment is known as independent repeated Bernoulli Trials.

Formula : $$P = \frac{\lfloor n}{\lfloor r \lfloor (n-r)} p^r q^{n-r}$$

$$= {}^nC_r p^r q^{n-r}$$

P = Probability of the happening of the event *i.e.*, success (Prob. of Success)

q = Probability of not happening of the event *i.e.*, failure (Prob. of Failure)

n = Total number of trials

r = No. of successes, $n - r$ = Number of failure trials

^nC_r = No. of combinations of 'r' things out of 'n'

Features : This theorem has the following features :

(i) The two outcomes 'Success' and 'Failure' are Mutually Exclusive. They are considered as two possible outcomes of a single trial.

(ii) Trials are independent and repeated.

(iii) The result of a trial is independent of the result of previous trials.

(iv) The notation for the probability of success in a trial is 'p' and that of failure is 'q' such that $p + q = 1$.

***Illustration* 48**

What is the probability of exactly four heads while tossing five coins ?

Solution

Number of trials $(n) = 5$

Frequency of Sucess (Head) = *i.e.*, $c = 4$

Failure trial or $n - 1 = 5 - 4 = 1$

$$p = 1/2, q = 1/2$$

Let X = No. of Heads

Now, to find

Now, $p_r = {}^nC_r . p^r . q^{n-r}$

Here ${}^5C_4 . \left(\frac{1}{2}\right)^4 . \left(\frac{1}{2}\right)^{5-4} = 5 \times \left(\frac{1}{2}\right)^5 = \frac{5}{32}$ **Ans.**

***Illustration* 49**

Eight coins are tossed together. Find out the probability of the following :

(a) At least 6 Heads, (b) No Head, (c) All Heads.

Solution

(a) Let X = No. of Heads

Now, to find $P(X \geq 6) = P(X = 6) + P(X = 7) + P(X = 8)$

$$n = 8; p = q = 1/2$$

here $P(X \geq 6) = {}^8C_6 \left(\frac{1}{2}\right)^6 \left(\frac{1}{2}\right)^{8-6} + {}^8C_7 \left(\frac{1}{2}\right)^7 \left(\frac{1}{2}\right)^{8-7}$

$$+ {}^8C_8 \left(\frac{1}{2}\right)^8 \left(\frac{1}{2}\right)^{8-8}$$

$$= \left(\frac{1}{2}\right)^8 \{{}^8C_6 + {}^8C_7 + {}^8C_8\}$$

$$= \left(\frac{1}{2}\right)^8 \{28 + 8 + 1\}$$

$$= \frac{37}{256}.$$ **Ans.**

(b) Let X = No. of Heads

Now, $P(X = 0) = {}^8C_0 \left(\frac{1}{2}\right)^0 \left(\frac{1}{2}\right)^{8-0}$

$$= \frac{1}{756}.$$ **Ans.**

(c) Let X = No. of Heads

Now, $P(X = 8) = {}^8C_8 \left(\frac{1}{2}\right)^8 \left(\frac{1}{2}\right)^{8-8}$

$$= \frac{1}{256}.$$ **Ans.**

***Illustration* 49(A)**

A coin is tossed three times. What is the probability of getting all the heads in 3 tossing ? (*JAC*, 2008, 12)

Solution

Total outcomes = 8

$P(3 \text{ Heads}) = \frac{1}{8}$ **Ans.**

Where Sample Space (S)

S = {$HHH, HHT, TTH, THT, HTH, TTT, THH, HTT$} (8 points)

and favourable point (HHH)

= 1 point only.

***Illustration* 50**

If one candidate out of ten fails on an average in an examination, what is the probability that 4 out of 5 will pass ?

Solution

Probability of student who fails

$$= \frac{1}{10}(q)$$

Probability of passing the exam.

$$= 1 - \frac{1}{10} = \frac{9}{10}(p)$$

Required prob. (that 4 out of 5 will pass)

$$\Rightarrow {}^5C_4 \left(\frac{9}{10}\right)^4 \left(\frac{1}{10}\right)^{5-4} = 5 \times \frac{9 \times 9 \times 9 \times 9}{10 \times 10 \times 10 \times 10} \times \frac{1}{10}$$

$$= \frac{32805}{100000} = \mathbf{0.32805}$$ **Ans.**

***Illustration* 51**

The chances of reaching safely at harbour is $\frac{1}{5}$. What will be the probability of reaching safely of 3 ships out of 5 ?

Solution

Probability of reaching the ship safely $(p) = \frac{1}{5}$

Thus, $q \Rightarrow 1 - p = 1 - 1/5 = 4/5; n = 5;$

Let X = No. of ships

Here $P(X = 3) = {}^5C_3 \left(\frac{1}{5}\right)^3 \left(\frac{4}{5}\right)^{5-3}$

$\therefore$ Required Prob. $= 10 \times \frac{1}{5 \times 5 \times 5} \times \frac{4 \times 4}{5 \times 5}$

$$= \frac{160}{3125}$$ **Ans.**

Exercise 7(G)

Bernoulli Theorem

1. Five coins whose faces are marked 2 or 3 are thrown. What is the chance of obtaining a total of 12 ?

   $\left[\textbf{Ans. } \frac{5}{16}\right]$

2. A coin is tossed thrice. What is the probability of getting : (i) all the heads, (ii) two heads in 3 tossing ?

   $\left[\textbf{Ans. } \text{(i) } \frac{1}{8}, \text{(ii) } \frac{3}{8}\right]$

3. Five marbles are drawn, with replacement from an urn that contains 4 white, 4 green and 12 black marbles. What is the probability of drawing exactly 3 marbles that are not white ?

   $\left[\textbf{Ans. } \frac{128}{625}\right]$

MISCELLANEOUS ILLUSTRATIONS

Illustration 52

A bag contains 5 white and 3 black balls and 4 balls are successively drawn out and not replaced. What is the chance that they are of different (alternative) colours ?

Solution

Four balls are drawn successively and not replaced.

Four balls of alternative colours can be drawn in the following ways :

(i) White, Black, White, Black, or

(ii) Black, White, Black, White

Since the ball drawn is not replaced, the number of balls will go on decreasing by one, each time.

Total number of balls = 5 + 3 = 8

Therefore,Probability of drawing White ball in first draw (p)

$$= \frac{5}{8}$$

Probability of drawing Black ball in second draw (p)

$$= \frac{3}{7}$$

Probability of drawing White ball in third draw (p)

$$= \frac{4}{6}$$

Probability of drawing Black ball in fourth draw (p)

$$= \frac{2}{5}$$

$$\text{Thus, } p\,(W, B, W, B) = \frac{5}{8}\times\frac{3}{7}\times\frac{4}{6}\times\frac{2}{5} \qquad ...(i)$$

Similarly, Probability of drawing a Black ball in the first draw (p),

$$= \frac{3}{8}$$

Probability of drawing a white ball in the second draw (p)

$$= \frac{5}{7}$$

Probability of drawing a Black ball in the thrid draw

$$(p) = \frac{2}{6}$$

Probability of drawing a white ball in the fourth draw

$$(p) = \frac{4}{5}$$

Thus,

$$p\,(B, W, B, W) = \frac{3}{8}\times\frac{5}{7}\times\frac{2}{6}\times\frac{4}{5} \qquad ...(ii)$$

$$= p\,(W, B, W, B) + p\,(B, W, B, W)$$

∴ Required Probability

$$= \left(\frac{5}{8}\times\frac{3}{7}\times\frac{4}{6}\times\frac{2}{5}\right)+\left(\frac{3}{8}\times\frac{5}{7}\times\frac{2}{6}\times\frac{4}{5}\right)$$

$$= \frac{1}{14}+\frac{1}{14}=\frac{2}{14}=\mathbf{\frac{1}{7}} \qquad \textbf{Ans.}$$

Illustration 53

In an urn there are 1 black and 3 white balls. In another urn there are 2 black and 1 white balls. A ball is drawn from the first and put into the second and then a ball is drawn from the second urn, show that the chance that is is white is $\left(\frac{5}{12}\right)$.

Solution

Here, there are two probabilities—(i) The replaced ball is balck, or (ii) it is of white colour.

(i) If the replaced ball is Black :

Probability of drawing a black ball from 1st urn (p)

$$= \frac{1}{3}$$

Now, in 2nd urn after putting one drawn black ball, total no. of black balls 2 + 1 = 3 and 1 white ball

∴ Probability of drawing 1 white ball from 2nd urn

$$(p) = \frac{1}{4}$$

Now, probability of drawing 1 black ball from 1st urn and probability of drawing 1 white ball from the 2nd urn $= \frac{1}{3}\times\frac{1}{4} = \frac{1}{12}$

(ii) **If the replaced ball is White :**

Probability of drawing 1 white ball from 1st urn (p)

$$= \frac{2}{3}$$

Now, drawn white ball is placed in the 2nd urn, so in 2nd urn now we have 2 white balls and 2 black balls.

∴ The probability of drawing 1 white ball from the 2nd urn

$$(p) = \frac{2}{4}$$

$$\therefore \text{ Joint Probability} = \frac{2}{3}\times\frac{2}{4} = \frac{4}{12}$$

Since, the event (i) and event (ii) are mutually exclusive the required probability

$$= \frac{1}{12} + \frac{4}{12}$$

$$= \frac{5}{12}$$ **Hence Proved**

***Illustration* 54**

A box contains 8 red, 3 white and 8 blue balls. If 3 balls are drawn at random, determine the probability that :

(i) all are red, (ii) all are white, (iii) 2 red and 1 white, (iv) at least 1 is white, (v) 1 of each colour is drawn, (vi) the balls are drawn in the order red, white and blue.

Solution

Total no. of balls = 8 + 3 + 9 = 20 balls

No. of ways of drawing 3 balls out of 20 balls

$= {}^{20}C_3 = 1140$

(i) When all are Red :

No. of ways of drawing 3 red balls

$$= {}^8C_3 = \frac{8 \times 7 \times 6}{3 \times 2} = 56$$

$$\therefore \quad \text{Probability} = \frac{{}^8C_3}{{}^{20}C_3} = \frac{56}{1140}$$

$= \mathbf{0.049}$ **Ans.**

(ii) When all are White balls :

No. of ways of drawing 3 white balls

$= {}^3C_3 = 1$

$$\therefore \quad \text{Probability} = \frac{{}^3C_3}{{}^{20}C_3} = \frac{1}{1140}$$ **Ans.**

(iii) When 2 Red and 1 White ball :

No. of ways of drawing 2 red and 1 white balls

$= {}^8C_2 \times {}^3C_1$

$$\therefore \quad \text{Probability} = \frac{{}^8C_2 \times {}^3C_1}{{}^{20}C_3} = \frac{28 \times 3}{1140}$$

$$= \frac{84}{1140} = \mathbf{0.073}$$ **Ans.**

(iv) When atleast 1 is White :

No. of ways of drawing 3 balls having no white ball $= {}^{17}C_3 = 680$

Probability of drawing atleast 1 is white ball

$$= 1 - \frac{{}^{17}C_3}{{}^{20}C_3}$$

$$= 1 - \frac{680}{1140}$$

$$= \frac{460}{1140} = \mathbf{0.40}$$ **Ans.**

(v) When 1 of each colour is drawn :

No. of ways of drawing 1 of each colour

$= {}^8C_1 \times {}^3C_1 \times {}^9C_1$

$$\therefore \quad \text{Probability} = \frac{{}^8C_1 \times {}^3C_1 \times {}^9C_1}{{}^{20}C_3}$$

$$= \frac{8 \times 3 \times 9}{1140} = \frac{216}{1140}$$

$= \mathbf{0.189}$ **Ans.**

(vi) When balls are drawn in the order Red, White and Blue :

No. of ways of drawing 3 balls

$= 20 \times 19 \times 18 = 6840$

Ways of drawing in order of Red, White & Blue

$= 8 \times 3 \times 9$

$$\therefore \quad \text{Probability} = \frac{8 \times 3 \times 9}{6840} = \frac{216}{6840} = \frac{27}{855}$$

$= \mathbf{0.03157}$ **Ans.**

***Illustration* 55**

In an examination 30% of the students have failed in Economics, 20% of the students have failed in History, 10% have failed both in Economics and History. One student is selected at random : (i) What is the probability that the student has failed in Economics if it is known that he has failed in History, (ii) What is the probability that the student has failed either in Economics or in History ?

Solution

Suppose E (Economics) and H (History) are events. It is also assumed that one student selected randomly fails in Economics and History.

Then $$P(E) = \frac{30}{100} = 0.3,$$

$$P(H) = \frac{20}{100} = 0.2$$

$$P(E \cap H) = \frac{10}{100} = 0.1$$

(i) Required probability that the randomly selected student has failed in Economics where it is given that he has failed in History :

$$P(E/H) = \frac{P(E \cap H)}{P(H)} = \frac{0.1}{0.2} = \frac{1}{2}$$

$= \mathbf{0.5}$ **Ans.**

(ii) Required probability that student selected randomly has failed in either Economics or History :

$$P(E \cup H) = P(E) + P(H) - P(E \cap H)$$

$= 0.3 + 0.2 - 0.1 = \mathbf{0.4}$ **Ans.**

***Illustration* 56**

'*A*' can solve 75% of the problems in Mathematics and '*B*' can solve 70%. What is the probability that either *A* or *B* can solve a problem choosen at random ?

Solution

Suppose

Let A = 'A' can solve the problem

Let B = 'B' can solve the problem

and $A \cap B$ = 'A' and 'B' both can solve the problem

$A \cap \overline{B}$ = 'A' can solve but 'B' does not

$\overline{A} \cap B$ = 'B' can solve but 'A' does not

$\overline{A} \cap \overline{B}$ = Neither 'A' and 'B' can solve the problem

$\overline{A \cup B}$ = Neither 'A' nor 'B' can solve the probelm

Here $P(A \cup B) = P(A) + P(B) - P(A) \times P(B)$

$$= \left(\frac{75}{100} + \frac{70}{100}\right) - \left(\frac{75}{100} \times \frac{70}{100}\right)$$

$$\therefore \text{ Required Prob.} = \left(\frac{3}{4} + \frac{7}{10}\right) - \left(\frac{3}{4} \times \frac{7}{10}\right)$$

$$= \frac{30 + 28 - 21}{40} = \mathbf{\frac{37}{40}}$$ **Ans.**

***Illustration* 57**

Out of 6 gentlemen and 4 ladies a committee of 5 is to be formed. In how many ways can this be done so as to include at least one lady in each committee ? (*JAC*, 2016)

Solution

There are 6 men and 4 women (ladies) *i.e.* There are 10 persons in all

$\therefore$ Total number of cases = $10C_5$

Now, there are cases where atleast one women (lady)

$$= {}^{10}C_5 - {}^{6}C_5 = 252 - 6$$

$$= 246$$ **Ans.**

Where, $${}^{10}C_5 = \frac{10!}{5!\,5!}$$

$$= \frac{10 \times 9 \times 8 \times 7 \times 6 \times \cancel{5!}}{\cancel{5!} \times 5 \times 4 \times 3 \times 2 \times 1}$$

$$= \frac{30240}{120} = 252$$

$${}^{6}C_5 = \frac{6!}{5!\,1!}$$

$$= \frac{6 \times \cancel{5!}}{\cancel{5!}} = 6$$ **Ans.**

***Illustration* 58**

In how many ways can the letters of the word 'DIRECTOR' be arranged so that the three vowels are never together ? (*JAC*, 2016)

Solution

Total letters in word DIRECTOR are 8 and 'R' letter occurs 2 times

$$\therefore \quad \text{Total ways} = \frac{8!}{2!}$$

Now, total no. of ways where 3 vowels of 8 do not come together are

$$= \frac{8!}{2!} - \frac{6! \times 3!}{2!}$$

$$= \frac{8 \times 7 \times 6 \times 5 \times 4 \times 3 \times \cancel{2!}}{\cancel{2!}} - \frac{6 \times 5 \times 4 \times 3 \times 2 \times 3 \times \cancel{2!}}{\cancel{2!}}$$

$$= 20160 - 720 = 19{,}440$$ **Ans.**

Exercise 7(H)

1. The producer of a pimple-remover medicated cream claims that there are 70% chances that his product will remove pimples of a person within a month. If 5 persons try the product, what is the probability that it will remove pimples of 3 persons within a month of its use ?
[**Ans.** 0.3087 or 31%]
2. Answer the following :
Given $P(A) = \frac{1}{4}, P(B) = \frac{1}{5}, P(A \cup B) = \frac{1}{3}$, find $P(A \cap B)$.
$\left[\textbf{Ans. } \frac{7}{60}\right]$
3. A committee of 4 persons is to be appointed from 6 men and 3 women. What is probability that the committee contains (i) exactly two women, and (ii) atleast one women ?
$\left[\textbf{Ans. (i) } \frac{3}{10}, \text{ (ii) } \frac{5}{6}\right]$
4. A box contains 100 bolts of which 10 are defective. Find the probability that a bolt choosen at random is not defective.
$\left[\textbf{Ans. } \frac{9}{10}\right]$
5. State what is probability of getting exactly 2 heads in 7 tosses of a fair coin.
$\left[\textbf{Ans. } P = {}^{7}C_2 \times \left(\frac{1}{2}\right)^7 = \frac{21}{128}\right]$
6. If a pair of dice is thrown, find the probability : (i) that the sum is neither 8 nor 10, (ii) that the sum is greater than 12.
[**Ans.** (i) 7/9, (ii) zero.]
7. A pair of dice is rolled. If the sum of the two dice is 9, find the probability that one of the dice showed 3.
$\left[\textbf{Ans. } \frac{1}{2}\right]$
8. A box contains 6 tickets. Two of the tickets carry a price of ₹ 5 each, the other four prices are of ₹ 1. If one ticket is drawn, what is the expected value of the price ?
[**Ans.** ₹ 2.33]
9. A candidate is selected for interviews for three posts. For the first there were 3 candidates, for the second 4 and for the third 2. What is the probability that the candidate is selected for atlest one post ?
[**Ans.** 3/4]

10. A person applies for a job in two firms, say X and Y. The probability of his being selected in firm X is 0.7 and being rejected in firm Y is 0.5. The probability of atleast one of his application being rejected is 0.6. What is the probability that he will be selected in one of the two firms ?
[**Ans.** 0.8]

11. A person is known to hit the target 3 out of 4 shots, whereas another person is known to hit the target 2 out of 3 shots. Find the probability that first person hits the target.
$\left[\textbf{Ans. } \frac{11}{12}\right]$

12. In a car factory machines A, B and C manufacture respectively 20%, 30% and 40% of the total. If their product 5%, 4% and 2% are defective. One car is drawn at random and is found defective. What is the probability that it was manufactured by machine B ?
$\left[\textbf{Ans. } \frac{2}{5}\right]$

13. The probability that a man will be alive in 25 years is 3/5 and the probability that his wife will be alive in 25 years is 2/3. Find the probability that :
(i) both will be alive, (ii) only wife will be alive, (iii) only man will be alive, (iv) atleast one of them will be alive.
$\left[\textbf{Ans. } \text{(i) } \frac{2}{5}, \text{(ii) } \frac{4}{15}, \text{(iii) } \frac{1}{5}, \text{(iv) } \frac{13}{15}\right]$

14. A university has to select an examiner from a list of 50 persons, 20 of them women and 30 men; 10 of them knowing Hindi and 40 not; 15 of them being teachers and the ramaining 35 not. What is the probability of the university selecting a Hindi knowing woman teacher ?
$\left[\textbf{Ans. } \frac{3}{125}\right]$

15. X can solve 80% of the problems while Y can solve 90% of the problems given in a Statistics book. A problem is selected at random. What is the probability that atleast one of them will solve the same ?
[**Ans.** 0.98]

16. 'A' can solve 90% of the problems of a book and 'B' can solve 70%. What is the probability that either of them can solve a problem choosen at random ? (*JAC*, 2008)
$\left[\textbf{Ans. } \frac{97}{100}\right]$

17. A committee of 5 is to be formed out of 6 men and 4 women. In how many ways can this be done when at least two women are included ? (*JAC*, 2025)
[**Ans.** 186 ways]

IMPORTANT FORMULAE

1. (i) $p = \dfrac{m}{m+n}$, (ii) $q = \dfrac{n}{m+n}$; $p + q = 1, q = 1 - p$.

$$p = \frac{\text{No. of favourable cases}}{\text{Total Number of cases}}$$

2. *Permutation*

(i) ${}^nP_r = \dfrac{n!}{(n-r)!}$; (ii) $\dfrac{n}{p!\,q!\,r!}$; (iii) $\dfrac{m+n+p+....}{m!\,n!\,p!}$

(iv) $\dfrac{R \times m}{R!\,m!\,m!\,m!}$ or $\dfrac{R \times m}{R\,!\,m\,!\,n\,!\,p\,!}$

3. *Combination*

$${}^nC_r = \frac{n\,!}{r\,!\,(n-r)!} \text{ or } {}^nC_r = \frac{{}^nP_r}{r!}$$

4. *Addition Theorem*

(i) In case of Mutually Exclusive events :
$P(A \text{ or } B) = P(A) + P(B)$

(ii) When events are not Mutually Exclusive :
$P(A \text{ or } B) = P(A) + P(B) - P(A \text{ and } B)$

5. *Multiplication Theorem*

(i) Independent Events
$P(A \text{ and } B) = p(A) \times P(B)$

(ii) Dependent Events or Conditional Probability
$P(A \text{ and } B) = P(A) \times P(B/A)$
$P(A \text{ and } B) = P(B) \times P(A/B)$

Probability of Happening Atleast One Event

$$1 - \{(1-p_1)(1-p_2)(1-p_3) \ldots (1-p_n)\}$$

6. *Bernoulli Trials :*

$$P = \frac{n\,!}{r\,!\,(n-r)!} p^r q^{n-r}$$
$$= {}^nC_r q^{n-r}$$

7. Bayes' Theorem (or Inverse Probability)

$$\frac{P_m p_m}{P_1 p_1 - P_2 p_2 + P_3 p_3}$$

THEORETICAL QUESTIONS

Long Answer Type Questions

1. Define probability.
2. Define probability and explain of Addition Theorem of Probability.
3. Define probability and explain the importance of this concept in Statistics.
4. What is probability ? Explain multiplication theorem of probability with example.
5. Explain the main theorems of probability giving examples.
6. Write short notes on :
(i) Independent Events, (ii) Dependent Events, (iii) Simple and Compound Events, (iv) Probability, (v) Events.
7. Explain the concepts of independent and mutually exclusive events in probability. State the theorems of total and compound probability.
8. State the addition theorem of probability for two events
(a) when they are mutually exclusive, and
(b) when they are not mutually exclusive.
9. Give the definition of probability of an event. For any two events A and B prove that
$$P(A \cup B) = P(A) + P(B) - P(AB)$$
10. State the addition and multiplication that of probability.

Short Answer Type Questions

1. Give the meaning of 'probability'.

2. State the importance of the concept of probability in statistics.
3. What do you understand by the term 'Probability' ? Explain.
4. Explain the addition theorem of probability.
5. Explain the multiplication theorem of probability.
6. What is inverse probability ?
7. What are the different types of events ? Explain.
8. Explain theorem of conditional probability.
9. What is Bernoulli theorem or Bernoulli Trials ?
10. What is conditional probability ?
11. Distinguish between :
    (i) Mutually Exclusive Events and Compound Events.
    (ii) Simple Events and Compound Events.
    (iii) Mutually Exclusive and Independent Events.

Very Short Answer Type Questions

1. Give mathematical definition of probability.
2. Give statistical definition of probability.
3. Explain the meaning of 'random experiment' in theory of probability.
4. What is sample space ?
5. Explain the meaning of 'events' in the theory of probability.
6. Explain simple and compound events.
7. Explain mutually exclusive events.
8. Explain the meaning of independent events.
9. What are the dependent events ?
10. Which definition will be applied to determine probability when events are not mutually exclusive ?
11. What is the probability of happening at least one event ? Explain.
12. Give the formula of Bernoulli theorem.

OBJECTIVE TYPE QUESTIONS

I. Multiple Choice Questions

1. If an event cannot take place, the probability will be : (*JAC*, 2016, 23)
   (a) + 1 (b) – 1
   (c) 0 (d) None of these
2. If the events *A* and *B* are mutually exclusive, then *AB* is :
   (a) A unit set (b) An infinite set
   (c) A Finite set (d) None of these
3. Those events which are included in sample space are call :
   (a) Sure events (b) Impossible events
   (c) Exhaustive events (d) None of these
4. The probability of drawing a red ball from a bag containing 4 red and 5 white balls is :
   (a) 4/5 (b) 3/5
   (c) 1/5 (d) 4/9
5. How many permutations can be made out of letters of the work TRIANGLE ?
   (a) 40,320 (b) 14,400
   (c) 5,040 (d) None of these
6. The probability of obtaining a total of 6 from two dice *A* and *B* in simultaneous throws is : (*JAC*, 2014)
   (a) 1/36 (b) 5/36
   (c) 1/6 (d) 5/6
7. The probability of 53 Sundays in randomly chosen leap year is :
   (a) 3/7 (b) 1/7
   (c) 2/3 (d) 2/7
8. The probability of obtaining a total of 9 in a single throw with two dice is : (*JAC*, 2016)
   (a) 1/12 (b) 1/18
   (c) 1/9 (d) None of these
9. The probability of getting at least two heads in a simultaneous throw of three coins if :
   (a) 1/4 (b) 1/2
   (c) 1/8 (d) 1/3
10. If (AB) = 20, (Ab) = 20, (aB) = 10, (a) = 50, then value of *N* will be :
    (a) 50 (b) 100
    (c) 75 (d) 200
11. In a single throw of two dice the probability of getting a total greater than 8 is :
    (a) 8/36 (b) 12/36
    (c) 5/8 (d) 4/16
12. The probability of drawing a black card or king from a pack of cards is :
    (a) 26/52 (b) 4/52
    (c) 7/13 (d) 2/13
13. The probability of drawing a lord of red colour in a single draw from a pack of cards is :
    (a) 4/52 (b) 2/52
    (c) 1/2 (d) 1/26
14. The probability of getting outcomes of more than 2 spats in a single throw of one six faced :
    (a) 1/3 (b) 2/3
    (c) 3/6 (d) 1/6
15. In a single throw of two dice, the probability of getting a total of atleast 10 is :
    (a) 3/36 (b) 1/10
    (c) 2/36 (d) 1/36
16. There are 150 fish of species *A* and 750 fish of species *B* in a pond. One fish is randomly picked up. What is the probability that it is of species *B* ?
    (a) 1/3 (b) 1/4
    (c) 1/2 (d) 3/4
17. The chance of drawing a red queen in a single draw from a pack of 52 cards is :
    (a) 1/52 (b) 1/26
    (c) 1/4 (d) 1/2
18. If two dice are thrown once then the probability of getting a total of 8 is : (*JAC*, 2020)
    (a) 1/12 (b) 3/8
    (c) 6/36 (d) 5/36
19. If $P(A/B) = P(A)$ then A and *B* are :
    (a) Mutually exclusive events
    (b) Dependent events
    (c) Independent events
    (d) Compound events

20. Two events 'A' and 'B' are not mutually exclusive and $P(A) = 1/4$, $P(B) = 2/5$, $P(A \cup B) = 1/2$, then $P(AB)$ is :
(a) 3/7 (b) 2/10
(c) 1/10 (d) None of these

21. Probability of getting a head in a single tossing of a coin is : *(JAC, 2015, 23, 25)*
(a) 1/6 (b) 2/6 (c) 1/2 (d) 1

22. A bag contains 5 blue and 4 black balls. Three balls are drawn at random. What is the probability that 2 are blue and 1 is black (without replacement) :
(a) 1/3 (b) 2/5
(c) 10/21 (d) 1/12

23. A packet contains 12 good pencils, 6 with minor defects and 2 major defects. A pencil is choosen at random. The probability that this pencil is not defective is :
(a) 1/2 (b) 4/5 (c) 3/10 (d) 3/5

24. Two balls to be drawn from a bag containing 5 red and 7 white balls. Find the chance that they will both be white :
(a) 7/12 (b) 5/7
(c) 7/22 (d) 10/22

25. Probability lies between 0 to 1.
(a) True (b) False

26. Probability involves the study of uncertain events.
(a) True (b) False

27. Probability theory had its origin in gambling games.
(a) True (b) False

28. A bag contains 3 black and 2 red balls. One ball is drawn randomly then what is the probability that it will be red :
(a) 3/5 (b) 2/5
(c) 1/5 (d) 2/3

29. If a card from a pack of 52 cards is drawn, what is the chance of drawing a face card or spade card ? *(JAC, 2024)*
(a) $\frac{11}{13}$ (b) $\frac{7}{26}$ (c) $\frac{11}{26}$ (d) $\frac{5}{3}$

30. What is the probability of getting the number 6 in a throw of a die ? *(JAC, 2024)*
(a) $\frac{6}{7}$ (b) $\frac{1}{3}$ (c) $\frac{1}{6}$ (d) $\frac{5}{7}$

31. If an event takes place certainly, the probability will : *(JAC, 2025)*
(a) + 1 (b) − 1 (c) 0 (d) $\frac{1}{2}$

32. What is the probability of getting numbers more than 3 in a throw of a die ? *(JAC, 2025)*
(a) $\frac{1}{3}$ (b) $\frac{1}{5}$ (c) $\frac{1}{2}$ (d) $\frac{1}{7}$

33. Probabilities lie between : *(JAC, 2026)*
(a) 0 to ∞ (b) − 1 to 1
(c) 0 to 1 (d) None of these

34. What is the probability of getting odd numbers if a die is rolled ? *(JAC, 2026)*
(a) $\frac{1}{2}$ (b) 2 (c) $\frac{1}{6}$ (d) $\frac{5}{2}$

35. What will be the probability of losing in a game if the winning probability is 0.3 ? *(JAC, 2026)*
(a) 0.5 (b) 0.6 (c) 0.7 (d) 0.8

[**Ans.** 1. (c), 2. (d), 3. (c), 4. (d), 5. (a), 6. (b), 7. (d), 8. (c), 9. (a), 10. (b), 11. (c), 12. (c), 13. (b), 14. (b), 15. (b), 16. (d), 17. (b), 18. (d), 19. (c), 20. (d), 21. (c), 22. (c), 23. (d), 24. (c), 25. (a), 26. (a), 27. (a), 28. (b), 29. (c), 30. (c), 31. (a), 32. (c), 33. (c), 34. (a), 35. (c).]

II. State whether the following statements are 'True' or 'False' :

1. Probability involves the study of uncertain events.
2. Probability lies between 0 to 1.
3. Probability involves the study of definite events.
4. Probability theory had its origin in gambling games.
5. If events are not mutually exclusive then $P(A \text{ or } B) = P(A) + P(B) - (P \text{ and } B)$.
6. If events A and B are undependent then $P(A \cap B) = P(A) + P(B)$.
7. If two events A and B are independent the probability that they will occur is given by $P(A) \times P(B)$.
8. The set of all possible outcomes of a random experiment is known as the sample space.
9. If the events are mutually exclusive then $P(A \text{ or } B) = P(A) + P(B)$.
10. $P(A \text{ and } B) = P(A) \times P(B)$ is based on the addition theorem of probability.

[**Ans.** 1. True, 2. True, 3. False, 4. True, 5. True, 6. False, 7. True, 8. True, 9. True, 10. False.]

III. Fill in the Blanks :

1. Probability lies between ...... to ....
2. Probability involves the study of .... events.
3. Probability theory had its origin in .... games.
4. To find the probability of mutually exclusive events .... theorem is used.
5. Two events are equally likely when one does not occur .... than the other.
6. $^5C_2$ = ...
7. The probability that the throw of two dies yields total of 5 is ....
8. $P(A \,\&\, B) = P(A) \times P(B)$ is based on .... theorem of probability.

[**Ans.** 1. 0 to 1, 2. Uncertain, 3. Gambling, 4. Addition, 5. More often, 6. 10, 7. 1/9, 8. Multiplication.]

8

INTERPOLATION AND EXTRAPOLATION

LEARNING OBJECTIVES

After studying this chapter, you will be able to know :

- **8.1 Introduction**
- **8.2 Meaning of Interpolation and Extrapolation**
  - **Assumptions of Interpolation and Extrapolation**
- **8.3 Necessity, Utility and Importance of Interpolation and Extrapolation**
- **8.4 Methods of Interpolation :**
  - **(I) Graphic Method** **(II) Algebraic Methods**
  - **8.4.1 Binomial Expansion Method**
  - **8.4.2 Newton's Method of Advancing Differences or Newton's Method of Finite Differences**
  - **8.4.3 Newton-Gauss Forward Method**
  - **8.4.4 Newton-Gauss Backward Method**
  - **8.4.5 Lagrange's Method**
  - **8.4.6 Sterling Formula**
  - **8.4.7 Parabolic Curve Method or Method of Fitting a Parabola**
  - **8.4.8 Newton's Divided Difference Method**
- **8.5 When and which Method should be used ?**
  - **Theoretical Questions : Long Ansswer Questions, Short Answer Questions, Very Short Answer Questions**
  - **Practical Problems**

ILLUSTRATIONS AND PRACTICAL PROBLEMS : AT A GLANCE

No. of Illustration		*No. of Problems*
1, 2	I. Graphic Method, II Algebraic Method	1, 2
3 to 9	Binomial Expansion Method/Missing Terms	3 to 12A
10(A) to 15	Newton's Method of Advancing Differences	13 to 17
16	Newton-Gauss Forward Method	18 to 20
17	Newton-Gauss Backward Method	21 to 23
18 to 22	Lagrange's Method	24 to 26
23	Sterling's Formula	27, 28
24, 25	Parabolic Curve	29, 30
26 to 28	Newton's Divided Difference Method	31 to 34
—	Miscellaneous Problems	35 to 38
28	**Total**	**38**

(8.1) INTRODUCTION

Interpolation is a statistical method of estimating the most likely figure of a dependent variable for a given independent variable (*i.e.*, subject). According to *"D.N. Elhance"*. *"Interpolation may be defined as the technique of obtaining the most likely estimates of certain quantity under certain assumptions."*

When the values are to be estimated for the future period, the methods of obtaining them is called *"Extrapolation"*. Thus, "Extrapolation" is made on the basis of past information.

Let us take an example to illustrate this fact.

Example 1 : We have been given population figure of India on the basis of Census Report for the years 1951, 1961, 1971, 1981, 1991 and 2001. On the basis of the data given for all these years we can estimate the population of India for 1965 or 1998. This part of estimate is called Interpolation, because Interpolation is the art of reading between the lines of a table.

Year	1951	1961	1965	1971	1981	1991	1998	2001
Population	...	...	?	....	....	..	?	...

(Given)

Let us take another example.

Example 2 : Annual income of a person is given below :

Year	2001	2003	2005	2007	2009
Income (in ₹)	10,000	12,000	15,000	20,000	30,000

If we have to know the income of that person for the year 2006 or 2008, it can be known by Interpolation. The process of estimating income in between two given years is called Interpolation.

Example 3 : If on the basis of population for the Census years 1951, 1961, 1971, 1981, 1991 and 2001 we want to estimate the population for the year 2007 or 2011, it will be called as Extrapolation because it lies outside given data.

Year :	1951	61	65	71	81	91	98	2001	2007	2011
Population (in Crores) :	Given	Given	?	Given	Given	88	?	100	×	×

Interpolation (65 to 98) Extrapolation (2007, 2011)

(8.2) MEANING OF INTERPOLATION AND EXTRAPOLATION

(1) **Meaning :** The main difference between Interpolation and Extrapolation is that Interpolation consists in a value which lies between two extremes points whereas extrapolation means reading a value that lies outside the two extremes points. For example, on the basis of Census figure for 1991 and 2001, we can estimate the population of 1995. It is Interpolation. If however, population for 2009 is to be estimated, it is Extrapolation.

(2) **Use :** Interpolation is used for calculating past missing data whereas Extrapolation is made for estimating for the future.

(3) **Correctness :** The result obtained from interpolation is more correct than that of extrapolation.

(4) **Method of Calculation :** For Inrterpolation Newton's Average Difference Method is considered to be more useful whereas for Extrapolation, Binomial Expansion Method or Lagrange's Method is considered to be more useful.

* Extrapolation some times (may be) helps in finding past records.

ASSUMPTIONS OF INTERPOLATION AND EXTRAPOLATION

(a) There is no **violent** or disturbing situation in the intervening period.

(b) There is **uniformity** in the changes of known figures. It means that there is **regularity in fluctuations** and the rise and fall is uniform.

(c) There is definite and **stable relationship** between both the variables.

(8.3) NECESSITY, UTILITY AND IMPORTANCE OF INTERPOLATION AND EXTRAPOLATION

The statistical technique of Interpolation and Extrapolation are of great practical use. The reasons are as under :

(i) It helps in the estimation of intermediate values.
(ii) It helps to estimate missing observations.
(iii) It may also be required in case when the data are insufficient due to gaps in coverage, or are inadequately collected.
(iv) It is also required to bring the uniformity in the data so that they may be fit for comparison.
(v) Interpolation is used for making forecast.
(vi) Interpolation helps in the determination of Median and Mode.

(8.4) METHODS OF INTERPOLATION

Methods of Interpolation can be divided into two categories :

(I) Graphic Method
(II) Algebraic Methods.

The algebraic methods may be divided into following categories :

(1) Binomial Expansion Method, (2) Newton's Method of Advancing Differences, (3) Newton-Gauss Forward Method, (4) Newton-Gauss Backward Method, (5) Lagrange's Method, (6) Sterling's Formula, (7) Parabolic Curve Method, (8) Newton's Divided Difference Method.

(I) GRAPHIC METHOD

This is the simplest method of Interpolation and Extrapolation.

Procedure :

(i) In this method the available data are plotted on a graph paper by taking independent variable on the horizontal scale, *i.e.,* x-axis and the dependent variable on the vertical scale *i.e.,* y-axis.

(ii) The various points are noted on the graph paper and are joined so as to form a curve.

(iii) From the point on the x-axis, for which the values of y is to be Interpolated, a line parallel to y-axis will be drawn. From the point where this line cuts the curve a line parallel to x-axis will be drawn.

(iv) The point where this line cuts y-axis, value of y will be readout. This is the Interpolated figure.

(v) If Extrapolation is required, the curve obtained on the graph paper is advanced in tune with the curve and the required result is obtained.

***Illustration* 1**

The following table gives the profit of a firm for the period from 2004 to 2009. The figure for 2008 is missing. Interpolate the same by graphic method :

Year	2004	2005	2006	2007	2008	2009
Profit (Crores)	1.2	1.5	1.3	1.2	?	1.6

***Solution* :**

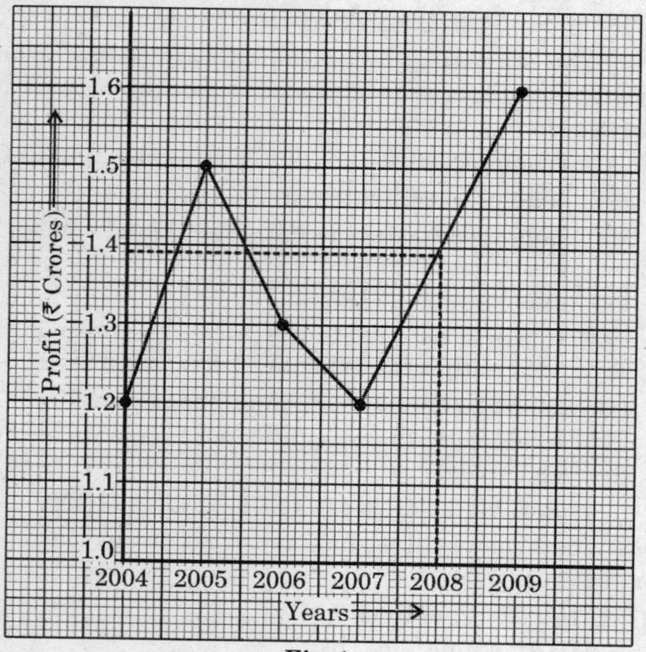

Fig. 1

The missing value is ₹ 1.39 crore. Thus estimated profit for the year 2008 may be ₹ 1.39 crore.

***Illustration* 2**

The following table gives the Population of India :

Year	1941	1951	1961	1971	1981
Population (in crore)	32	36	44	55	68.5

With the help of graph find the population for the year 1975 and 1981. (*JAC*, 2015)

***Solution* :**

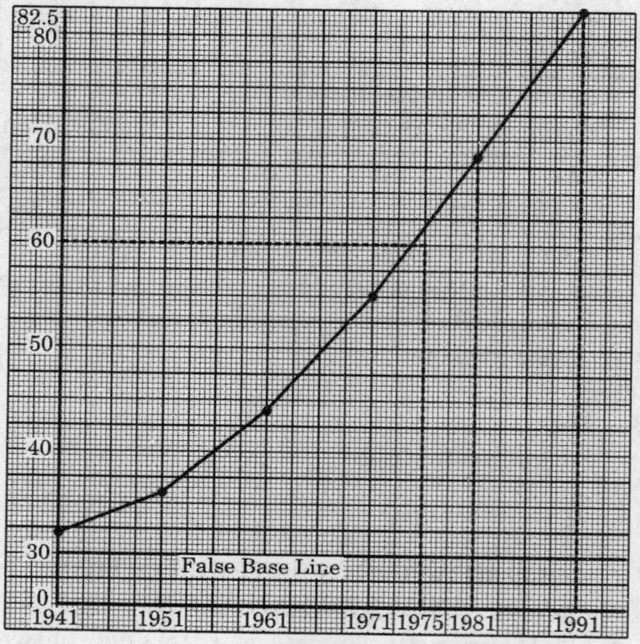

Fig. 2

To find estimated population for the year 1975 is an example of Interpolation since 1975 lies within the given sample data.

Now, To find estimated population for the years 1991 is an example of extrapolation since 1991 lies beyond the data.

$\therefore$ From the graph, population for the year 1975 = 60 crore and for 1991 = 82.5 crore.

(II) ALGEBRAIC METHODS

1. Binomial Expansion Method,
2. Newton's Method of Advancing Difference,
3. Newton-Gauss Forward Method,
4. Newton-Gauss Backward Method,
5. Lagrange's Method,
6. Sterling Formula,
7. Method of Fitting a Parabolic Curve,
8. Newton's Divided Difference Method.

8.4.1 Binomial Expansion Method

This method of Interpolation and Extrapolation is based on Binomial Theorem.

It is simple to understand and easy to calculate.

This method can be applied for Interpolation and Extrapolation both.

When to apply this method : This method is applicable under following conditions or situations :

(i) When the independent variable (x) advances by equal intervals, such as

5	10	15	20	25	: Difference 5
1969	1979	1989	1999	2009	: Difference 10

Note : Hence, when the independent variable (x) does not advance with equal distance or equal intervals, this method should not be applied to calculate Interpolation or Extrapolation.

(ii) The value of (x) of which the value of (y) is to be Interpolated is one of the class limits of x series. For example,

X :	50	60	70	80	90
Y :	10	12	?	16	20

Here the value of x advances with 10 units.

The value of y corresponding to $x = 70$ or 100 can be estimated according to this method but not corresponding to $x = 55$ or $x = 74$ or 75.

(iii) The tendency of y-variables should be either increasing or decreasing but it should not have sudden fluctuations.

Procedure : The method involves the following steps :

(i) The x-variable (including the value for which corresponding value of (y) is to be Interpolated or Extrapoled) are denoted by $x_0, x_1, x_2, x_3, x_3, \ldots\ldots$.

(ii) Similarly y-variable is denoted by $y_0, y_1, y_2, y_3 \ldots\ldots$.

(iii) According to the number of known values of (y), the *leading difference* is taken equal to zero (0). For example, if in a series, 4 values of y are known, then the fourth leading difference will be zero.

Symbolically,

$$\Delta_0^n \text{ or } (y-1)^n = 0$$

Where 'n' is equal to the number of known values of y.

(iv) According to the number of known values of y and taking the leading difference equal to zero, the formula $\Delta_0^n = 0$ or $(y-1)^n = 0$ will be expanded :

$$\Delta_0^n = (y-1)^n = 0$$

$$= y^n - ny_{n-1} + \frac{n(n-1)}{1\times 2} y_{n-2} - \frac{n(n-1)(n-2)}{1\times 2\times 3} y_{n-3} + \frac{n(n-1)(n-2)(n-3)}{1\times 2\times 3\times 4} y_{n-4} = 0$$

Hence, if we have 5 known values of y, then

$$\Delta_0^5 = (y-1)^5 = 0$$

$$= y^5 - 5y_{5-1} + \frac{5(5-1)}{1\times 2} y_{5-2} - \frac{5(5-1)(5-2)}{1\times 2\times 3} y_{5-3} + \frac{5(5-1)(5-2)(5-3)}{1\times 2\times 3\times 4} y_{5-4} - \frac{5(5-1)(5-2)(5-3)(5-4)}{1\times 2\times 3\times 4\times 5} y^{5-5} = 0$$

$$= y^5 - 5y^4 + 10y^3 - 10y^2 + 5y^1 = 0$$

While applying this formula power is used as subscript.

Simple Method of Deducing the Formula

(i) If we have 5 known values of y, then write y_5 first and then write by reducing 1, such as, $y_5, y_4, y_3, y_2, y_1, y_0$.

(ii) First (y) will be positive (+), next one negative (–), again positive, then again negative and so on. Thus, $+y_5, -y_4, +y_3, -y_2, +y_1, -y_0$

(iii) **Numerical Coefficient :** Numerical coefficient of various y's will be calculated as follows :

First numerical coefficient is 1 but this is not written. Coefficient of next y' s is ascertained by using this formula :

$$\frac{\text{Numerical coefficient of the previous (preceding) } y \times \text{Subscript of preceding } y}{\text{Rank in Sequence of the preceding (previous) } y}.$$

For example, if there are 5 known values of y, in the Binomial expansion of $(y-1)^5$, 1 will be the coefficient of y_5,

and Coefficient of $y_4 = \frac{1\times 5}{1} = 5$, that is, $5y_4$

Coefficinet of $y_3 = \frac{5\times 4}{2} = 10$, that is, $10y_3$

Coefficient of $y_2 = \frac{10\times 3}{3} = 10$, that is, $10y_2$

Coefficient of $y_1 = \frac{10 \times 2}{4} = 5$, that is, $5y_1$

and Coefficinet of $y_0 = \frac{5 \times 1}{5} = 1$, that is, y_0

i.e., $y_5 - 5y_4 + 10y_3 - 10y_2 + 5y_1 - y_0 = 0$

Some Binomial Expansion

No. of Known Values	*Formula*	*Binomial Expansion*
2	$(y-1)^2 = 0$	$y_2 - 2y_1 + y_0 = 0$ (*JAC*, 2023, 24)
3	$(y-1)^3 = 0$	$y_3 - 3y_2 + 3y_1 + y_0 = 0$
4	$(y-1)^4 = 0$	$y_4 - 4y_3 + 6y_2 - 4y_1 + y_0 = 0$
5	$(y-1)^5 = 0$	$y_5 - 5y_4 + 10y_3 - 10y_2 + 5y_1 - y_0 = 0$
6	$(y-1)^6 = 0$	$y_6 - 6y_5 + 15y_4 - 20y_3 + 15y_2 - 6y_1 + y_0 = 0$
7	$(y-1)^7 = 0$	$y_7 - 7y_6 + 21y_5 - 35y_4 + 35y_3 - 21y_2 + 7y_1 - y_0 = 0$
8	$(y-1)^8 = 0$	$y_8 - 8y_7 + 28y_6 - 56y_5 + 70y_4 - 56y_3 + 28y_2 - 8y_1 + y_0 = 0$

Numerical Coefficient used in Binomial Epansion can also be represented in the form of Pascal's Triangle.

Pascal's Coefficient Triangle

n	*Binomial Coefficients*	*Total*	2^n
1	1 + 1	2	2^1
2	1 + 2 + 1	4	2^2
3	1 + 3 + 3 + 1	8	2^3
4	1 + 4 + 6 + 4 + 1	16	2^4
5	1 + 5 + 10 + 10 + 5 + 1	32	2^5
6	1 + 6 + 15 + 20 + 15 + 6 + 1	64	2^6
7	1 + 7 + 21 + 35 + 35 + 21 + 7 + 1	128	2^7
8	1 + 8 + 28 + 56 + 70 + 56 + 28 + 8 + 1	256	2^8

Interpolation

Illustration 3

Using any Interpolation method find out the likely Index Number for 2013 from the following table :

Year	2011	2012	2013	2014	2015
Index No.	100	107	y_2	157	210

Solution :

Let the missing term be (y_2)

Year	2011	2012	2013	2014	2015
Index No. (y)	$100y_0$	$107y_1$	$y_2 = ?$	$157y_3$	$210y_4$

∴ The equation will be :

$$(y-1)^4 = 0$$

The equation will be expanded as follows :

$$y_4 - 4y_{4-1} + \frac{4(4-1)}{1 \times 2} y_{4-2} - \frac{4(4-1)(4-2)}{1 \times 2 \times 3} y_{4-3} + \frac{4(4-1)(4-2)(4-3)}{1 \times 2 \times 3 \times 4} y_{4-4} = 0$$

on solvingy $\quad {}_4 - 4y_3 + 6y_2 - 4y_1 + y_0 = 0$

By putting the values,

$$210 - (4 \times 157) + 6y_2 - (4 \times 107) + 100 = 0$$

or $\quad 210 - 628 + 6y_2 - 428 + 100 = 0$

or $\quad 6y_2 = -210 + 628 + 428 - 100$

or $\quad 6y_2 = 1056 - 310$

or $\quad 6y_2 = 746$

or $\quad y_2 = \frac{746}{6} = 124.33$

Thus, Index for year 2013 = **124** **Ans.**

***Illustration* 4(A)**

The age of mothers and the average number of children born per mother are given in the table below. Interpolate the average number of children per mother :

Age of Mothers (years)	*No. of Children*
15—19	0.7
20—24	2.1
25—29	3.5
30—34	?
35—39	5.7
40—44	5.8

***Solution* :**

Let x = Mothers, y = No. of children & let the missing term (y_3).

Note : No. of Children must be integer.

	y	
15—19	0.7	y_0
20—24	2.1	y_1
25—29	3.5	y_2
30—34	?	y_3
35—39	5.7	y_4
40—44	5.8	y_5

here, 5 values of y are known, therefore, we have

$$(y-1)^5 = 0$$

or $y_5 - 5y_4 + 10y_3 - 10y_2 + 5y_1 - y_0 = 0$

By substituting the known values, we get

$5.8 - (5 \times 5.7) + 10y_3 - (10 \times 3.5) + (5 \times 2.1) - 0.7 = 0$

or $5.8 - 28.5 + 10y_3 - 35 + 10.5 - 0.7 = 0$

or $10y_3 = -5.8 + 28.5 + 35 - 10.5 + 0.7$

or $10y_3 = 47.9$

or $y_3 = \frac{47.9}{10}$

= **4.97 or 4.8 children** **Ans.**

***Illustration* 4(B)**

Interpolate the missing value

x	50	55	60	65	70
y	80	95	?	108	115

***Solution*:** (*JAC* 2024)

By Bionomial Expenion Method

x	y	
50	80	y_0
55	95	y_1
60	?	y_2
65	108	y_3
70	115	y_4

$$(y-1)^4 = 0$$

$$y_4 - 4y_3 + 6y_2 - 4y_1 + y_0 = 0$$

$$115 - 4 \times 108 + 6y_2 - 4 \times 95 + 80 = 0$$

$$115 - 432 + 6y_2 - 380 + 80 = 0$$

$$115 + 80 - 432 - 380 + 6y_2 = 0$$

$$195 - 812 + 6y_2 = 0$$

$$6y_2 = 812 - 195$$

$$6y_2 = 617$$

$$y_2 = \frac{617}{6} = 102.83 \textbf{ Ans.}$$

Interpolating Two or More Missing Values (Binomial Expansion) :

If two or more values are missing in a series, they can be estimated or determined by Binomial Expansion Method easily. If two values are missing, we need to **Form two equations** and solve them simultaneously to find out the missing values.

Procedure : (i) The first equation is formed by taking Binomial Expansion of the leading differences equal to the number of known values equal to zero.

(ii) The above Binomial Expansion is written again and the **subscripts are raised by one** and in the end instead of y_0, we have y_1.

For example, if 5 values of y are known and 2 are unknown. In that case, the Binomial Expansion will be written as :

$y_5 - 5y_4 + 10y_3 - 10y_2 + 5y_1 = 0$ ...(i)

$y_6 - 5y_5 + 10y_4 - 10y_3 + 5y_2 - y_1 = 0$ ...(ii)

***Illustration* 5**

Estimate the production for the year 1989 and 1999 with the help of following data :

Year	*Production* (in lakh tons)
1984	180
1989	?
1994	250
1999	?
2004	320
2009	400

***Solution* :**

Let the production for the years 1989 & 1999 be y_1 and y_3 respectively.

Year	(x)	*Production* (y)	(In lakh ton)
1984	x_0	180	y_0
1989	x_1	?	y_1 (Unknown)
1994	x_2	250	y_2
1999	x_3	?	y_3 (Unknown)
2004	x_4	320	y_4
2009	x_5	400	y_5

The number of known values = 4, the values of y_1 and y_3 unknown

$\Delta_0^4 = y_4 - 4y_3 + 6y_2 - 4y_1 + y_0 = 0$ ...(i)

By adding 1,

$\Delta_1^4 = y_5 - 4y_4 + 6y_3 - 4y_2 + y_1 = 0$ ...(ii)

Substituting the known values,

$320 - 4y_3 + (6 \times 250) - 4y_1 + 180 = 0$ ...(i)

or $320 - 4y_3 + 1{,}500 - 4y_1 + 180 = 0$

or $-4y_3 - 4y_1 = -2{,}000$

or $4y_3 + 4y_1 = 2{,}000$ ...(iii)

Substituting the known values in equation (ii),

$400 - (4 \times 320) + 6y_3 - (4 \times 250) + y_1 = 0$ ...(ii)

or $400 - 1280 + 6y_3 - 1,000 + y_1 = 0$

or $6y_3 + y_1 = 2,280 - 400$

$= 1,880$ ...(iv)

By multiplying equation (iv) by 4, and subtracting equation (iii) from it

$24y_3 + 4y_1 = 7,520$

$4y_3 + 4y_1 = 2,000$

$20y_3 = 5,520$

$\therefore \quad y_3 = \frac{5,520}{20} = 276$

By substituting this value of y_3 in equation (iii),

$4 \times 276 + 4y_1 = 2,000$

or $1,104 + 4y_1 = 2,000$

or $4y_1 = 2,000 - 1,104 = 896$

$\therefore \quad y_1 = \frac{896}{4} = 224$

Production in 1989 = **224 lakh tons**

Production in 1989 = **276 lakh tons**

When there is Abnormal Fluctuation in the Values

Sometimes there is abnormal fluctuation (either increase or decrease) in the values. In that case, before finding out the estimated value of the unknown variable it is necessary to readjust the abnormal value taking into consideration uniform rate of increase or decrease, as the case may be. In other words, the abnormal values should first be re-estimated assuming it to be unknown.

Illustration 6

The population of a district for different year is given below. Estimate the population for 2004 :

Year	*Population* (in thousand)
1979	20
1984	22
1989	26
1994	85
1999	35
2004	?
2009	43

Solution :

In the above data there is a sudden increase in the population in the years 1994. First of all we should estimate population for 1994 assuming it to be unknown.

Year	*Population* (in thousand)
1979 x_0	20 y_0
1984 x_1	22 y_1
1989 x_2	26 y_2
1994 x_3	85 y_3
1999 x_4	35 y_4
2004 x_5	? y_5
2009 x_6	43 y_6

Known values of $y = 5$

$\Delta_0^5 = y_5 - 5y_4 + 10y_3 - 5y_2 + 5y_1 - y_0 = 0$ ...(i)

$\Delta_1^5 = y_6 - 5y_6 + 10y_4 - 10y_3 + 5y_2 - y_1 = 0$ ...(ii)

By putting the values,

$y_5 - (5 \times 35) + (10 \times y_3) - (10 \times 26) + (5 \times 22) - 22 = 0$

$\Rightarrow \quad y_5 - 175 + 10y_3 - 260 + 110 - 20 = 0$

$\Rightarrow \quad y_5 + 10y_3 - 455 + 110 = 0$

$\Rightarrow \quad y_5 + 10y_3 = +345$ ...(iii)

or $43 - 5y_5 + (10 \times 35) - 10y_3 + (5 \times 26) - 22 = 0$

$\Rightarrow \quad 43 - 5y_5 + 350 - 10y_3 + 130 - 22 = 0$

$\Rightarrow \quad -5y_5 - 10y_3 + 523 - 22 = 0$

$\Rightarrow \quad -5y_5 - 10y_3 = -501$ ...(iv)

By adding two equations,

$y_5 + 10y_3 = +345$

$-5y_5 - 10y_3 = -501$

$-4y_5 = -156$

$\therefore \quad y_5 = 39$

$\therefore$ Population in 2004 = 39 thousand

Now for estimating the values of y_3, substituting the value of y_5 in equation (iii),

$39 + 10y_3 = 345$

$\Rightarrow \quad 10y_3 = 345 - 39$

$\Rightarrow \quad 10y_3 = 306$

$\Rightarrow \quad y_3 = 30.6$

$\therefore$ Population in 1994 = **30.6 thou.**

Thus, estimated population for the year 2004 may be 39 thousand. **Ans.**

Illustration 7

Interpolate the population of 1971 and 1991 from the following data :

Year	1971	1981	1991	2001	2011
Population (in lakh)	?	2514	?	3168	3613

Solution :

Year		*Population* (in lakh)	
1971	x_0	?	y_0
1981	x_1	2514	y_1
1991	x_2	?	y_2
2001	x_3	3168	y_3
2011	x_4	3613	y_4

Known values of $y = 3$, unknown values = 2

Therefore, Δ_0^3 and Δ_1^3 will be expanded

$\Delta_0^3 = y_3 - 3y_2 + 3y_1 - y_0$ ...(i)

$\Delta_0^1 = y_4 - 3y_3 + 3y_2 - y_1$ ...(ii)

Substituting the known values, we get

$3,168 - 3y_2 + (3 \times 2,514) - y_0 = 0$ ...(i)

and $3,613 - (3 \times 3,168) + 3y_2 - 2,514 = 0$ ...(ii)

On solving both equations,

$-3y_2 - y_0 = -7,542 - 3,168$

$= -10,710$ ...(iii)

$\Rightarrow \quad 3y_2 = 8,405$ ...(iv)

Equation (iv), $3y_2 = 8,405$

$\Rightarrow \quad y_2 = \frac{8,405}{3}$

$= 2801.7$

(Estimated population for the year 1991)

On putting the value of y_2 in equation (iii),

$-3 \times \frac{8,405}{3} - y_0 = -10,710$

or $\quad -y_0 = -10710 + 8405 = -2305$

or $\quad y_0 = 2305$

(Estimated population for the year 1971)

Thus, Estimated Population of 1971

= 2305 lakh

Estimated Population of 1991

= 2801.7 lakh

Extrapolation (By Binomial Expansion Method)

Illustration 8

The following table gives the sales of a concern for the following years :

Year	*Sales of Cloth* (in lakh *yd*)
1989	125
1994	163
1999	204
2004	238
2009	282

Assuming the conditions to be the same estimate the sales for the year 2014.

Solution :

Year	*Sales of Cloth* (in lakh *yd*)
1989 x_0	125 y_0
1994 x_1	163 y_1
1999 x_2	204 y_2
2004 x_3	238 y_3
2004 x_4	282 y_4
2014 x_5	? y_5

Here $\Delta_0^5 = 0$, (Known values of $y = 5$)

$(y-1)^5 = y_5 - 5y_4 + 10y_3 - 10y_2 + 5y_1 - y_0 = 0$

Now, putting the values

$y_5 - (5 \times 282) + (10 \times 238) - (10 \times 204) + (5 \times 163)$

$-125 = 0$

$\Rightarrow y_5 - 1,410 + 2,380 - 2,040 + 815 - 125 = 0$

$\Rightarrow \quad y_5 = 3,575 - 3,195$

$\Rightarrow \quad y_5 = 380$

Thus, Estimated sales for year 2014

$y_5 =$ **380 lakh *yd*** **Ans.**

Illustration 9

The population of a district is given below for different years. Find the population for year 2010.

Year	*Production* (Million)
2005	7
2006	9
2007	36
2008	14
2009	16

Solution :

In the above data there is a sudden increase in population for the year 2007.

So first of all population for 2007 will be estimated assuming it to be unknown.

Year	*Production* (Million)
2005 x_0	7 y_0
2006 x_1	9 y_1
2007 x_2	36 y_2
2008 x_3	14 y_3
2007 x_4	16 y_4
2010 x_5	

Known values of $y = 4$

Substituting the values, we get

$(y-1)^4 = 16 - (4 \times 14) + 6y_2 - (4 \times 9) + 7$

$= 16 - 56 + 6y2 - 36 + 7$

$6y_2 = -16 + 56 + 36 - 7$

or $\quad 6y_2 = 92 - 23$

or $\quad 6y_2 = 69$

$\therefore \quad y_2 = \frac{69}{6} = 11.5$ million

Estimate for 2010

$(y-1)^5 = y_5 - 5y_4 + 10y_3 - 10y_2 + 5y_1 - y_0 = 0$

By putting the values in the above equation

$y_5 - (5 \times 16) + (10 \times 14) - (10 \times 11.5) + (5 \times 9) - 7 = 0$

$y_5 - 80 + 140 - 115 + 45 - 7 = 0$

$\Rightarrow \quad y_5 = +202 - 185$

$\Rightarrow \quad y_5 = 17$

$\Rightarrow \quad y_5 = 17$ million

Thus, Estimate Population for year 2010

= 17 million **Ans.**

8.4.2 Newton's Method of Advancing Differences or Newton's Method of Finite Differences

Newton's Method of Advancing Differences is also called as "Newton's Method of Finite Differences".

Applicability : This method is applicable where the independent variable x advances with equal intervals. In other words, when variation in x advances by equal increments, this method is used. We can interpolate and extrapolate any value by using this method. However, this method gives the best result when interpolation is to be made near the beginning of the values or series.

This method is called finite or Advancing Differences Method because after finding out differences in the values of 'y' the process is extended further till only one difference remains. The algebraic signs (+) and (–) are taken into account the differences are calculated.

Procedure : The following are the procedures for determining the unknown values by "Newton's Method of Advancing Differences :

Step :

(i) Independent variable (x) is denoted by $x_0, x_1, x_2, x_3, ..., x_n$.

(ii) Dependent variable (y) is denoted by $y_0, y_1, y_2, y_3, ..., y_n$.

(iii) The values of 'y' to be Interpolated is denoted by y_x.

(iv) Now the relevant finite differences are found out by preparing the table which is called as **"Table of Finite Differences"**.

(v) In table of finite differences apart from the column of independent variable (x) and dependent variable (y) there will be one less columns of finite difference than the number of known values of y (*i.e.*, dependent variable). For example, if the known values of y is 5 ($y_0, y_1, ... y_4$) then there will be four columns for finite differences. These columns will be turmed as 1st difference, 2nd difference, 3rd difference and 4th difference. These differences will be denoted by Δ^1, Δ^2, Δ^3 and Δ^4.

(iv) The differences of different column are calculated as follows :

In 1st column $y_1 - y_0 = \Delta_0^1$, $y_2 - y_1 = \Delta_1^1$, $y_3 - y_2 = \Delta_2^1$. In 2nd column with the help of the difference of 1st column $\Delta_1^1 - \Delta_0^1 = \Delta_2^1 - \Delta_1^1 = \Delta_1^2$ .... etc.

Similarly, differences of other columns are calculated.

The table given below shows the method of calculating advancing differences :

Table of Advancing (Finite) Differences

Independent Variable (x)	*Dependent Variable* (y)	*Advancing Differences* *1st Difference* Δ^1		*2nd Difference* Δ^2		*3rd Difference* Δ^3		*4th Difference* Δ^4	
x_0	y_0								
		$y_1 - y_0$	Δ_0^1						
x_1	y_1			$\Delta_1^1 - \Delta_0^1$	Δ_0^2				
		$y_2 - y_1$	Δ_1^1			$\Delta_1^2 - \Delta_0^2$	Δ_0^3		
x_2	y_2			$\Delta_2^1 - \Delta_1^1$	Δ_1^2			$\Delta_1^3 - \Delta_0^3$	Δ_0^4
		$y_3 - y_2$	Δ_2^1			$\Delta_2^2 - \Delta_1^2$	Δ_1^3		
x_3	y_3			$\Delta_3^1 - \Delta_2^1$	Δ_2^2				
		$y_4 - y_3$	Δ_3^1						
x_4	y_4								

Formula :

$$x = \frac{\text{Item of Interpolation} - \text{Item of Origin}}{\text{Difference in (two) Adjoining Values}}$$

$$y_x = y_0 + \Delta_0^1 + \frac{x(x-1)}{1 \times 2}$$

$$= \Delta_0^2 + \frac{x(x-1)(x-2)}{1 \times 2 \times 3}$$

$$= \Delta_0^3 + \frac{x(x-1)(x-2)(x-3)}{1 \times 2 \times 3 \times 4}$$

$$= \Delta_0^4 + ...$$

Where, y_x = The figure to be Interpolated

y_0 = The value of Independent variable at "origin".

Δ_0^1, Δ_0^2, Δ_0^3, Δ_0^4 .... are the 1st, 2nd, 3rd and 4th leading differences of the 0 order. The table of advancing differences clearly shows that there is relationship between various leading differences and the values of y. If the values of leading differences are known values of y can be found out. The relationship is of the following nature :

$$\Delta_0^1 = y_1 - y_0$$

$$\Delta_0^2 = \Delta_1^1 - \Delta_0^1$$
$$= y_2 - y_1 - (y_1 - y_0)$$
$$= y_2 - 2y_1 + y_0$$

$$\Delta_0^3 = \Delta_1^2 - \Delta_0^2$$
$$= \Delta_2^1 - \Delta_1^1 - (\Delta_1^1 - \Delta_0^1)$$
$$= \Delta_2^1 - \Delta_1^1 - \Delta_1^1 + \Delta_0^1$$
$$= (y_3 - y_2) - (y_2 - y_1) - (y_2 - y_1) + (y_1 - y_0)$$
$$= y_0 - y_2 - y_2 + y_1 - y_2 + y_1 + y_1 - y_0$$
$$= y_3 - 3y_2 + 3y_2 - y_0$$

From the above relation it is obvious that

$$y_0 = y_0$$
$$y_1 = y_0 + \Delta_0^1$$
$$y_2 = y_1 + \Delta_1^1$$

$= (y_0 + \Delta_0^1) + (\Delta_0^2 + \Delta_0^1)$

$= y_0 + 2\Delta_0^1 + \Delta_0^2$

$y_3 = y_2 + \Delta_2^1$

$= (y_0 + 2\Delta_0^1 + \Delta_0^2) + (\Delta_1^2 + \Delta_1^1)$

$= (y_0 + 2\Delta_0^1 + \Delta_0^2) + (\Delta_0^3 + \Delta_0^2) + \Delta_0^2 + (\Delta_0^2 + \Delta_0^1)$

$= y_0 + 3\Delta_0^1 + 3\Delta_0^2 + \Delta_0^3$

Numerical Coefficient for y_0, y_1, y_2 and y_3 :

1

1 + 1

1 + 2 + 1

1 + 3 + 3 + 1

These are called the items of Binomial Expansion which are $(1 + 1)^0$; $(1 + 1)^1$; $(1 + 1)^2$ and $(1 + 1)^3$: On generalisation, we get the formula :

$$y_x = y_0 + x\Delta_0^1 + \frac{x(x-1)}{1\times 2}\Delta_0^2 + \frac{x(x-1)(x-2)}{1\times 2\times 3}\Delta_0^3 + \ldots$$

Where,

$$x = \frac{\text{Year of Interpolation (–) year of Origin}}{\text{Difference between adjoining values}}$$

***Illustration* 10(A)**

The following are the annual premiums charged by an insurance company for a policy of ₹ 1,000. Estimate the premium payable at the age of 26 :

Age (in years)	20	25	30	35	40
Premium (₹)	23	26	30	35	42

***Solution* :**

Item to be Interpolated is 26.

Table of Finite Difference

Age (in years) (x)		*Premium* (y)		*Finite Difference* 1st Difference Δ^1		2nd Difference. Δ^2		3rd Difference. Δ^3		4th Difference. Δ^4	
20	x_0	23	y_0	+3	Δ_0^1						
25	x_1	26	y_1			+1	Δ_0^2				
				+4	Δ_1^1			0	Δ_0^3		
30	x_2	30	y_2			+1	Δ_1^2			1	Δ_0^4
				+5	Δ_2^1			+1	Δ_1^3		
35	x_3	35	y_3			+2	Δ_2^2				
				+7	Δ_3^1						
40	x_4	42	y_4								

Here,
$$x = \frac{26-20}{5} = 1.2$$

From this table we get $\Delta_0^1 = 3,\ \Delta_0^2 = 1,\ \Delta_0^3 = 0,\ \Delta_0^4 = 1$

Newton's Advancing Difference Formula,

$$y_x = y_0 + x\Delta_0^1 + \frac{x(x-1)}{1\times 2}\Delta_0^2 + \frac{x(x-1)(x-2)}{1\times 2\times 3}\Delta_0^3 + \frac{x(x-1)(x-2)(x-3)}{1\times 2\times 3\times 4} = \Delta_0^4$$

Substituting the known values :

$$y_x = 23 + (1.2\times 3) + \frac{1.2\,(1.2-1)}{1\times 2}\times(1) + \frac{1.2\,(1.2-1)(1.2-2)}{1\times 2\times 3}\times(0) + \frac{1.2\,(1.2-1)(1.2-2)(1.2-3)}{1\times 2\times 3\times 4}\times(1)$$

$y_x = 23 + 3.6 + 0.12 + 0 - 0.014 =$ ₹ 26.706.

Hence premium payable at the age of 26 years will be ₹ 26.70 (Approx.). **Ans.**

***Illustration* 10 (B)**

The following table shows the value of an immediate life annuity for ₹ 100 paid :

Age in Years	40	50	60	70
Annuity	6.2	7.2	9.1	12.0

Interpolate the annuity for the age 42.

Solution :

Age (in years) (x)		Annuity (y)		Advancing Difference Δ^1		Δ^2		Δ^3	
40	x_0	6.2	y_0						
				1.0	Δ_0^1				
50	x_1	7.2	y_1			0.9	Δ_0^2		
				1.9	Δ_1^1			0.1	Δ_0^3
60	x_2	9.1	y_2			1.0	Δ_1^2		
				2.9	Δ_2^1				
70	x_3	12.0	y_3						

$$x = \frac{\text{Value to be Interpolated} - \text{Value of Origin}}{\text{Difference between adjoining values}}$$

$$= \frac{42-40}{10} = 0.2$$

$$\therefore \quad y_x = y_0 + x\,\Delta_0^1 + \frac{x(x-1)}{1\times 2}\,\Delta_0^2 + \frac{x(x-1)(x-2)}{1\times 2\times 3}\,\Delta_0^3$$

$$= 6.2 + 0.2\times(1) + \frac{0.2(0.2-1)}{1\times 2}\times(0.9) + \frac{0.2(0.2-1)(0.2-2)}{1\times 2\times 3}\times(0.1)$$

$$= 6.2 + 0.2 - 0.072 + 0.0048 = \mathbf{6.3328}$$ **Ans.**

***Illustration* 11**

Calculate the likely minimum temperature for a maximum of 35° C by Newton's Method :

Max. Temperature	36	34	32	30	28
Min. Temperature	21	19	16	12	11

Solution :

On Arranging the Data in Ascending Order

Temp. (x)		Temp. (y)		Advancing Differences: 1st Diff. Δ^1		2nd Diff. Δ^2		3rd Diff. Δ^3		4th Diff. Δ^4	
28	x_0	11	y_0								
				+ 1	Δ_0^1						
30	x_1	12	y_1			+ 3	Δ_0^2				
				+ 4	Δ_1^1			− 4	Δ_0^3		
32	x_2	16	y_2			− 1	Δ_1^2			+ 4	Δ_0^4
				+ 3	Δ_2^1			0	Δ_1^3		
34	x_3	19	y_3			− 1	Δ_2^2				
				+ 2	Δ_3^1						
36	x_4	21	y_4								

$$x = \frac{\text{Value to be Interpolated} - \text{Value of Origin}}{\text{Difference between adjoining values}}$$

$$= \frac{35-28}{2} = \frac{7}{2} = 3.5$$

$$y_x = y_0 + x\,\Delta_0^1 + \frac{x(x-1)}{1\times 2}\,\Delta_0^2 + \frac{x(x-1)(x-2)}{1\times 2\times 3}\,\Delta_0^3 + \frac{x(x-1)(x-2)(x-3)}{1\times 2\times 3\times 4}\,\Delta_0^4$$

$$= 11 + (3.5 \times 1) + \frac{3.5(3.5-1)}{2} \times (3) + \frac{3.5(3.5-1)(3.5-2)}{6} \times (-4) + \frac{3.5(3.5-1)(3.5-2)(3.5-3)}{24} \times (4)$$

$$= 11 + 3.5 + 13.125 - 8.75 + 1.093$$

Estimated Temp. = **19.968 or 20° C (approx)** **Ans.**

Alternative Method

$$X = \frac{x_x - x_0}{x_1 - x_0} = \frac{35-36}{34-36} = \frac{-1}{-2} = 0.5$$

Difference Table

Temp.		Temp.		Advancing Differences							
				Δ_1		Δ_2		Δ_3		Δ_4	
36	x_0	21	y_0								
				– 2	Δ_0^1						
34	x_1	19	y_1			– 1	Δ_0^2				
				– 3	Δ_1^1			0	Δ_0^3		
32	x_2	16	y_2			– 1	Δ_1^2			+ 4	Δ_0^4
				– 4	Δ_2^1			4	Δ_1^3		
30	x_3	12	y_3			+ 3	Δ_2^2				
				– 1	Δ_3^1						
28	x_4	11	y_4								

$$y_x = 21 + (0.5 \times -2) + \frac{0.5(0.5-1)}{1 \times 2} \times (-1) + \frac{0.5(0.5-1)(0.5-2)}{1 \times 2 \times 3} \times (0) + \frac{0.5(0.5-1)(0.5-2)(0.5-3)}{1 \times 2 \times 3 \times 4} \times (4)$$

$$= 21 - 1 + 0.125 + 0 - 0.156 = 21.125 - 1.156 = 19.969$$

or y_x = **20°C (approx.)** **Ans.**

Intrapolation in Frequency Distribution

First change the frequency distribution into cummulative table, then Interpolate.

***Illustration* 12**

From the following table, find the number of students who obtained less than 45 marks and also find the percentage of students getting less than 45 marks :

Marks	30—40	40—50	50—60	60—70	70—80
No. of Students	31	42	51	35	31

Solution : **Newton's Advancing Difference Method**

Marks (*x*)		*No. of Students* (*y*)		*Finite Differences*							
				Δ_1		Δ_2		Δ_3		Δ_4	
Less than 40	x_0	31	y_0								
				42	Δ_0^1						
Less than 50	x_1	73	y_1			+ 9	Δ_0^2				
				51	Δ_1^1			– 25	Δ_0^3		
Less than 60	x_2	124	y_2			– 16	Δ_1^2			37	Δ_0^4
				35	Δ_2^1			+ 12	Δ_1^3		
Less than 70	x_3	159	y_3			– 4	Δ_2^2				
				31	Δ_3^1						
Less than 80	x_4	190	y_4								

Here, $x = \frac{45-40}{10} = \frac{5}{10} = 0.5$

$$y_x = y_0 + x\,\Delta_0^1 + \frac{x(x-1)}{1\times 2}\Delta_0^2 + \frac{x(x-1)(x-2)}{1\times 2\times 3}\Delta_0^3 + \frac{x(x-1)(x-2)(x-3)}{1\times 2\times 3\times 4}\Delta_0^4$$

$$= 31 + 0.5\times(42) + \frac{0.5(0.5-1)}{1\times 2}\times(9) + \frac{0.5(0.5-1)(0.5-2)}{1\times 2\times 3}\times(-25) + \frac{0.5(0.5-1)(0.5-2)(0.5-3)}{1\times 2\times 3\times 4}\times(37)$$

$$= 31 + 21 - 1.125 - 1.5625 - 1.4453$$

$52 - 4.1328 = 47.8672 \approx 48$ (Students)

Total Number of Students = 190

Number of Students getting less than 45 marks = 48

Percentage of students obtaining less than 45 marks = $\frac{48}{190}\times 100 =$ **25.26%**

***Illustration* 13**

From the following data of wages of 500 workers of factory, find the number of workers :

(a) Whose wage is more than 170b but not more than 200.

(b) Whose wage is less than 170 but not more than 200.

Wages not more than ₹ 100 = 150 workers
Wages not more than ₹ 150 = 180 workers
Wages not more than ₹ 200 = 240 workers
Wages not more than ₹ 250 = 400 workers
Wages not more than ₹ 300 = 500 workers

Solution :

Newton's Advancing Differences Table

Wages less than (₹)		*No. of Workers*		Δ_1		Δ_2		Δ_3		Δ_4	
100	x_0	150	y_0								
				30	Δ_0^1						
150	x_1	180	y_1			30	Δ_0^2				
				60	Δ_1^1			70	Δ_0^3		
200	x_2	240	y_2			100	Δ_1^2			– 230	Δ_0^4
				160	Δ_2^1			– 160	Δ_1^3		
250	x_3	400	y_3			– 60	Δ_2^2				
				100	Δ_3^1						
300	x_4	500	y_4								

Here, $x = \frac{x_n - x_0}{x_1 - x_0} = \frac{170-100}{50} = \frac{70}{50} = 1.4$

$$y_x = y_0 + x\,\Delta_0^1 + \frac{x(x-1)}{1\times 2}\Delta_0^2 + \frac{x(x-1)(x-2)}{1\times 2\times 3}\Delta_0^3 + \frac{x(x-1)(x-2)(x-3)}{1\times 2\times 3\times 4}\Delta_0^4$$

$$= 150 + 1.4\times(30) + \frac{1.4(1.4-1)}{1\times 2}(30) + \frac{1.4(1.4-1)(1.4-2)}{1\times 2\times 3}\times(70) + \frac{1.4(1.4-1)(1.4-2)(1.4-3)}{1\times 2\times 3\times 4}\times(-230)$$

$$= 150 + 42 + 8.4 - 3.92 - 5.152$$

$$= 191.328 \approx 191 \text{ (Workers)}$$

No. of workers having wages more than 170 but less than 200 = 240 – 191 = **49**

No. of workers having wages less than 170 but not less than 150 = 191 – 180 = **11** **Ans.**

Illustration 14

Using Newton's Method, Interpolate the no. of workers, earning ₹ 24 or more but less than ₹ 25.

Income (₹)	Less than 20	Less than 25	Less than 30	Less than 35	Less than 40
No. of Workers	296	599	804	918	966

Solution :

Newton's Advancing Difference Method

Income (in ₹) (x)		No. of Workers (y)		Finite Differences Δ_1		Δ_2		Δ_3		Δ_4	
Less than 20	x_0	296	y_0								
				303	Δ_0^1						
Less than 25	x_1	599	y_1			−98	Δ_0^2	7			
				205	Δ_1^1				Δ_0^3		
Less than 30	x_2	804	y_2			−91	Δ_1^2	25		18	Δ_0^4
Less than 35	x_3	918	y_3	114	Δ_2^1		Δ_2^2		Δ_1^3		
					Δ_3^1	−66					
Less than 40	x_4	966	y_4	48							

Here $x = \dfrac{x_x - x_0}{x_1 - x_0} = \dfrac{24-20}{25-20} = \dfrac{4}{5} = 0.8$

$$y_x = y_0 + x\,\Delta_0^1 + \frac{x(x-1)}{1\times 2}\Delta_0^2 + \frac{x(x-1)(x-2)}{1\times 2\times 3}\Delta_0^3 + \frac{x(x-1)(x-2)(x-3)}{1\times 2\times 3\times 4}\Delta_0^4$$

$$= 296 + (0.8\times 303) + \frac{0.8(0.8-1)}{1\times 2}(-98) + \frac{0.8(0.8-1)(0.8-2)}{1\times 2\times 3} + \frac{0.8(0.8-1)(0.8-2)(0.8-3)}{1\times 2\times 3\times 4}(18)$$

$$= 296 + 242.2 + 7.84 + 0.224 - 0.3168$$

$$= 545.94 \approx 546 \text{ (Workers)}$$

Hence, the number of workers earning less than ₹ 24 = 546

The number of workers earning less than ₹ 25 = 599

∴ The number of workers earning ₹ 24 or more but less than ₹ 25 = 599 − 546 = **53** **Ans.**

Illustration 15 (Extrapolation)

Extrapolate the population of a town for 2015 from the following table :

Year	1979	1989	1999	2009
Population (in thousand)	22	27	34	42

Solution :

Table of Finite Difference

Year		Population (in Thousands)		Advancing Differences					
1979	x_0	22	y_0						
				5	Δ_0^1				
1989	x_1	27	y_1			2	Δ_0^2		
				7	Δ_1^1			−1	Δ_0^3
1999	x_2	34	y_2			1	Δ_1^2		
				8	Δ_2^1				
2009	x_3	42	y_3						

$$x = \frac{\text{Item of Interpolation} - \text{Item of Origin}}{\text{Difference between two adjoining items}}$$

$$= \frac{2015 - 1979}{10} = \frac{36}{10} = 3.6$$

Using Newton's Formula, we have

$$y_x = y_0 + x\,\Delta_0^1 + \frac{x(x-1)}{1 \times 2}\,\Delta_0^2 + \frac{x(x-1)(x-2)}{1 \times 2 \times 3}\,\Delta_0^3$$

Substituting the values known

$$y_x = 22 + 3.6 \times (5) + \frac{3.6(3.6-1)}{1 \times 2} \times 2 + \frac{3.6(3.6-1)(3.6-2)}{1 \times 2 \times 3} \times (-1)$$

$$= 22 + 18 + 9.36 - 2.496 = 46.864$$

Thus,Estimated Population for 2015 = **46.864 thousand** **Ans.**

8.4.3 Newton-Gauss Forward Method

Newton-Gauss Forward Method or formula is applied in the following two cases :

(i) Where independent variable (x) advances by "Equal Intervals",

(ii) Where the figure to be Interpolated is in the middle of the series.

Formula :

$$y_x = y_0 + x\,\Delta_{y0}^1 + \frac{x(x-1)}{1 \times 2}\,\Delta_{y-1}^2 + \frac{x(x+1)(x-1)}{1 \times 2 \times 3} + \Delta_{y-1}^3 + \frac{x(x+1)(x-1)(x-2)}{1 \times 2 \times 3 \times 4}\,\Delta_{y-2}^4 + ...$$

Note : Where, $\underline{|2}$ or 2 = 2 × 1

$\underline{|3}$ or 3! = 3 × 2 × 1

Procedure : In this method of Interpolation, differences are found out, but the value preceding the values to be Interpolated is denoted by (x_0) and previous values are denoted by x_1, x_2, x_3, ...

Similarly, the corresponding values of 'y' are denoted, such as $\Delta_{y0}^1\ \Delta_{y-1}^2,\ \Delta_{y-1}^3,\ \Delta_{y-2}^4,$ .....

Where, $x = \frac{\text{Item to be Interpolated} - \text{Preceding Item}}{\text{Difference between Adjoining Items}}$

***Illustration* 16**

Estimate the value of 'y' if 'x' is 3.75 from the following table :

x	2.5	3.0	3.5	4.0	4.5	5.0
y	24.145	22.043	20.225	18.644	17.262	10.047

***Solution* :**

x	y		Difference Δ_1		Δ_2		Δ_3		Δ_4	
2.5	24.145	y_{-2}								
			– 2.102	Δ_{y-2}^1						
3.0	22.043	y_{-1}			+ 0.284	Δ_{y-2}^2				
			– 1.818	Δ_{y-1}^1			– 0.047	Δ_{y-2}^3		
3.5	20.225	y_0			+ 0.237	Δ_{y-1}^2			+ 0.009	Δ_{y-2}^4
			– 1.581	Δ_{y-0}^1			– 0.038	Δ_{y-1}^3		
4.0	18,644	y_1			+ 0.199	Δ_{y-0}^2			+ 0.006	Δ_{y-1}^4
			– 1.382	Δ_{y-1}^1			– 0.032	Δ_{y-0}^3		
4.5	17.262	y_2			+ 0.167	Δ_{y-1}^2				
			– 1.215	Δ_{y-2}^1						
5.0	16.047	y_3								

$$x = \frac{3.75 - 3.5}{4.0 - 3.5} = \frac{0.25}{0.5} = 0.5$$

Using Newton-Gauss Forward Method

$$y_x = y_0 + x\,\Delta^1_{y-0} + \frac{x(x-1)}{1\times 2}\Delta^2_{y-1} + \frac{(x+1)x(x-1)}{1\times 2\times 3}\Delta^3_{y-1} + \frac{(x+1)x(x-1)(x-2)}{1\times 2\times 3\times 4}\Delta^4_{y-2}$$

By putting the known values, we have

$$y_x = 20.225 + (0.5\times 1.581) + \left\{\frac{0.5(0.5-1)\times(0.237)}{2}\right\} + \left\{\frac{(0.5+1)\,0.5(0.5-1)\times(0.038)}{6}\right\}$$

$$+ \left\{\frac{(0.5+1)\,0.5(0.5-1)(0.5-2)(0.5-2)\times(0.009)}{24}\right\}$$

$$= 20.225 - 0.7905 - 0.029625 + 0.0023750 + 0.0002109 = 19.40746$$

Thus, the value of y when x is 3.75 = **19.40746**

8.4.4 Newton-Gauss Backward Method

Newton-Gauss Backward Method is used in the following cases :

(i) When the figure to be Interpolated falls at the end of the series, and

(ii) Variation in the x-variable is by equal intervals.

Formula : $$y_x = y_0 - x\,\Delta^1_{y-1} + \frac{x(x+1)}{1\times 2}\Delta^2_{y-1} - \frac{(x+1)\,x(x-1)}{1\times 2\times 3}\Delta^3_{y-2} + \frac{(x+1)\,x(x-1)(x-2)}{1\times 2\times 3\times 4}\Delta^4_{y-3}$$

Where, $$x = \frac{\text{Item succeeding the item to be Interpolated} - \text{Item to be Interpolated}}{\text{Difference between adjoining items}}$$

***Illustration* 17**

Estimate the value of y when $x = 23$ from the following data :

x	5	10	15	20	25	30
y	25	32	40	47	55	64

***Solution* :**

x	y		Δ^1		Δ^2		Δ^3		Δ^4	
5 $x-4$	25	$y-4$								
			7	Δ^1_{y-4}						
10 $x-3$	32	$y-3$			+1	Δ^2_{y-4}				
			8	Δ^1_{y-3}			−2	Δ^3_{y-4}		
15 $x-2$	40	$y-2$			−1	Δ^2_{y-3}			4	Δ^4_{y-4}
			7	Δ^1_{y-2}			+2	Δ^3_{y-3}		
20 $x-1$	47	$y-1$			+1	Δ^2_{y-2}			−2	Δ^4_{y-3}
			8	Δ^1_{y-1}			0	Δ^3_{y-2}		
25 $x-0$	55	$y-0$			+1	Δ^2_{y-1}				
			9	Δ^1_{y0}						
30 $x+1$	64	$y+1$								

$$x = \frac{25-23}{25-20} = \frac{2}{5} = 0.4$$

$$y_x = y_0 - x\,\Delta^1_{y-1} + \frac{x(x+1)}{1\times 2}\Delta^2_{y-1} - \frac{(x+1)x(x-1)}{1\times 2\times 3}\Delta^3_{y-2}$$

$$= 55 - (0.4\times 8) + \frac{0.4(0.4+1)}{2}\times 1 - \frac{(0.4+1)(0.4)(0.4-1)(0)}{6} = 55 - 3.2 + 0.28 - 0 = \mathbf{52.08}$$

8.4.5 Lagrange's Method

This method is associated with the name of a famous French mathematician, "Lagrange". In other words, *Lagrange's formula is applicable in case of unequal intervals or when the values of x are not equidistant.* Lagrange's Formula can be used both for Interpolation and Extrapolation.

This should be noted that Lagrange's formula should be used in such cases where Binomial Expansion Method or Newton's Method seems to be inapplicable or unsuitable.

Formula :

$$y_x = (y_0)\frac{(x-x_1)(x-x_2)(x-x_3)(x-x_4)\ldots.(x-x_n)}{(x_0-x_1)(x_0-x_2)(x_0-x_3)(x_0-x_4)\ldots(x_0-x_n)} + (y_1)\frac{(x-x_0)(x-x_2)(x-x_3)(x-x_4)\ldots.(x_0-x_n)}{(x_1-x_0)(x_1-x_2)(x_1-x_3)(x_1-x_4)\ldots(x_1-x_n)}$$

$$+ (y_2)\frac{(x-x_0)(x-x_1)(x-x_3)(x-x_4)\ldots.(x-x_n)}{(x_2-x_0)(x_2-x_1)(x_2-x_3)(x_2-x_4)\ldots(x_2-x_n)} + (y_3)\frac{(x-x_0)(x-x_1)(x-x_2)(x-x_4)\ldots.(x-x_n)}{(x_3-x_0)(x_3-x_1)(x_3-x_2)(x_3-x_4)\ldots(x_3-x_n)}$$

$$+ (y_4)\frac{(x-x_0)(x-x_1)(x-x_2)(x-x_3)(x-x_5)\ldots.(x-x_n)}{(x_4-x_0)(x_4-x_1)(x_4-x_3)(x_4-x_5)\ldots(x_4-x_n)}$$

Where, x = The figure for which Interpolation is to be done.

$y_0, y_1, y_2, y_3, \ldots.$ are known values of y corresponding to the known values of $x_0, x_1, x_2, x_3, \ldots.$

The formula is expanded both ways according to the given number of values.

***Illustration* 18**

In the following table 'h' is the height above sea-level and 'p' is the barometric pressure calculate 'p' when h = 5,280.

h	0	4,763	6,942	10,593
p	27	25	23	20

Solution :

Height above Sea-level $h = (x)$		*Barometric Pressure* $p\ (y)$	
0	x_0	27	y_0
4763	x_1	25	y_1
6942	x_2	23	y_2
10593	x_3	20	y_3

By using Lagrange's Formula :

$$y_x = \frac{(27)(5{,}280-4{,}763)(5{,}280-6{,}942)(5{,}280-10{,}593)}{(0-4{,}763)(0-6{,}942)(0-10{,}593)} + (25)\frac{(5{,}280-0)(5{,}280-6{,}942)(5{,}280-10{,}593)}{(4{,}763-0)(4{,}763-6{,}942)(4{,}763-10{,}593)}$$

$$+ (23)\frac{(5{,}280-0)(5{,}280-4{,}763)(5{,}280-10{,}593)}{(6{,}942-0)(6{,}942-4{,}763)(6{,}942-10{,}593)} + (20)\frac{(5{,}280-0)(5{,}280-4{,}763)(5{,}280-6{,}942)}{(10{,}593-0)(10{,}593-4{,}763)(10{,}593-6{,}942)}$$

or $$y_x = (27)\frac{(517)(-1{,}662)(-5{,}313)}{(-4{,}763)(-6{,}942)(-10{,}593)} + (25)\frac{(5{,}280)(-1{,}662)(-5{,}313)}{(4{,}763)(-2{,}179)(-5{,}830)} + (23)\frac{(5{,}280)(517)(-5{,}313)}{(6{,}942)(2{,}179)(-3{,}651)}$$

$$+ (20)\frac{(5{,}280)(517)(-1{,}662)}{(10{,}593)(5{,}830)(3{,}651)}$$

or $y_x = -0.353 + 19.23 + 6.43 - 0.402$

or $y_x = 24.815$

Thus, when 'h' is 5,280; p = **24.815**

***Illustration* 19**

Using Lagrange's Formula, estimate from the following data the number of workers getting income not exceeding ₹ 26 per day :

Income Not exceeding	15	25	30	35
No. of Workers	36	40	45	48

Solution :

Income (x)		No. of Workers (y)	
15	x_0	36	y_0
25	x_1	40	y_1
30	x_2	45	y_2
35	x_3	48	y_3

Given, $x = 26$

$$y_x = (y_0)\frac{(x-x_1)(x-x_2)(x-x_3)}{(x_0-x_1)(x_0-x_2)(x_0-x_3)} + (y_1)\frac{(x-x_0)(x-x_2)(x-x_3)}{(x_1-x_0)(x_1-x_2)(x_1-x_3)}$$
$$+ (y_2)\frac{(x-x_0)(x-x_1)(x-x_3)}{(x_2-x_0)(x_2-x_1)(x_2-x_3)} + (y_3)\frac{(x-x_0)(x-x_1)(x-x_2)}{(x_3-x_0)(x_3-x_1)(x_3-x_2)}$$

By substituting the known vlaues,

$$y_x = (36)\frac{(26-25)(26-30)(26-35)}{(15-25)(15-30)(15-35)} + (40)\frac{(26-15)(26-30)(26-35)}{(25-15)(25-30)(25-35)}$$
$$+ (45)\frac{(26-15)(26-25)(26-35)}{(30-15)(30-25)(30-35)} + (48)\frac{(26-15)(26-25)(26-30)}{(35-15)(35-25)(35-30)}$$
$$= (36)\frac{1\times-4\times-9}{-10\times-15\times-20} + (40)\frac{11\times-4\times-9}{10\times-5\times-10} + (45)\frac{11\times1\times-9}{15\times5\times-5} + (48)\frac{11\times1\times-4}{20\times10\times5}$$
$$= \frac{54}{-125} + \frac{792}{25} + \frac{-297}{-25} + \frac{-264}{125} = -\frac{54}{125} + \frac{792}{25} + \frac{297}{25} - \frac{264}{125}$$
$$= \frac{5,125}{125} = 41.016 = \textbf{41 workers}$$

Illustration 20

Find the value of log (656) using Lagrange's formual of Interpolation.

Given : log (654) = 2.8156 log (659) = 2.8189 log (658) = 2.8182 log (661) = 2.8202

Solution :

(x)		(y)	
log 654	x_0	2.8156	y_0
log 658	x_1	2.8182	y_1
log 659	x_2	2.8189	y_2
log 661	x_3	2.8202	y_3

Given, $x = 656$

$$y_x = (y_0)\frac{(x-x_1)(x-x_2)(x-x_3)}{(x_0-x_1)(x_0-x_2)(x_0-x_3)} + (y_1)\frac{(x-x_0)(x-x_2)(x-x_3)}{(x_1-x_0)(x_1-x_2)(x_1-x_3)}$$
$$+ (y_2)\frac{(x-x_0)(x-x_1)(x-x_3)}{(x_2-x_0)(x_2-x_1)(x_2-x_3)} + (y_3)\frac{(x+x_0)(x+x_1)(x+x_2)}{(x_3-x_0)(x_3-x_1)(x_3-x_2)}$$

By substituting the given values,

$$y_{656} = (2.8156)\frac{(656-658)(656-659)(656-661)}{(654-658)(654-659)(654-661)} + (2.8182)\frac{(656-654)(656-659)(656-661)}{(658-654)(658-659)(658-661)}$$
$$+ (2.8189)\frac{(656-654)(656-658)(656-661)}{(659-654)(659-658)(659-661)} + (2.8202)\frac{(656-654)(656-658)(656-659)}{(661-654)(661-658)(661-659)}$$
$$= (2.8156)\frac{(-2)(-3)(-5)}{(-4)(-5)(-7)} + (2.8182)\frac{(2)(-3)(-5)}{(4)(-1)(-3)} + (2.8189)\frac{(2)(-2)(-5)}{(5)(1)(-2)}$$
$$+ (2.8202)\frac{(2)(-2)(-3)}{(7)(3)(2)} = 0.6033 + 7.0455 - 5.6378 + 0.8057$$

$\therefore$ y_{656} = **2.8167** **Ans.**

***Illustration* 21**

Determine the percentage number of criminals under 35 years :

Age	0—25	25—30	30—40	40—50
Percentage of Number of Criminals	52.0	15.3	16.8	10.3

Solution :

Age (x)		*% of Criminals* (y)	
Under 25 years	x_0	52.0	y_0
Under 30 years	x_1	67.3	y_1
Under 40 years	x_2	84.1	y_2
Under 50 years	x_3	94.4	y_3

We have $x = 35$ (years)

By putting the known values in Lagrange's formula, we get

$$y_{35} = (52.0)\frac{(35-25)(35-40)(35-50)}{(25-30)(25-40)(25-50)} + (67.3)\frac{(35-30)(35-40)(35-50)}{(30-25)(30-40)(30-50)}$$

$$+ (84.1)\frac{(35-25)(35-30)(35-50)}{(40-25)(40-30)(40-50)} + (94.4)\frac{(35-25)(35-30)(35-40)}{(50-25)(50-30)(50-40)}$$

$$y_{35} = (52.0)\frac{(5)(-5)(-15)}{(-5)(-15)(-25)} + (67.3)\frac{(10)(-5)(-15)}{(5)(-10)(-20)} + (34.1)\frac{(10)(5)(-25)}{(15)(10)(-10)} + (94.4)\frac{(10)(5)(-5)}{(25)(20)(10)}$$

or $\quad y_{35} = -10.4 + 50.475 + 42.05 - 4.72$

or $\quad y_{35} = 92.525 - 15.12 = 77.405$

Percentage of criminals under 35 years = **77.4%** **Ans.**

***Illustration* 22 (Extrapolation)**

The population of a certain town is given below in the years mentioned. Estimate population for the year 2015.

Year	1979	1989	1999	2005	2009
Population (in thousand)	22	27	34	39	42

Solution :

Extrapolation by Lagrange's Formula

Year (x)		*Population* (in thousand) (y)	
1979	x_0	22	y_0
1989	x_1	27	y_1
1999	x_2	34	y_2
2005	x_3	39	y_3
2009	x_4	42	y_4

Population for 2015 is to be estimated.

Thus $x = 2015$

By using Lagrange's formula

$$y_x = (y_0)\frac{(x-x_1)(x-x_2)(x-x_3)(x-x_4)}{(x_0-x_1)(x_0-x_2)(x_0-x_3)(x-x_4)} + (y_1)\frac{(x-x_0)(x-x_2)(x-x_3)(x-x_4)}{(x_1-x_0)(x_1-x_2)(x_1-x_3)(x_1-x_4)}$$

$$+ (y_2)\frac{(x-x_0)(x-x_2)(x-x_3)(x-x_4)}{(x_2-x_0)(x_2-x_1)(x_2-x_3)(x_2-x_4)} + (y_3)\frac{(x-x_0)(x-x_1)(x-x_2)(x-x_4)}{(x_3-x_0)(x_3-x_1)(x_3-x_2)(x_3-x_4)}$$

$$+ (y_4)\frac{(x-x_0)(x-x_1)(x-x_2)(x-x_3)}{(x_4-x_0)(x_4-x_1)(x_4-x_2)(x_4-x_3)}$$

By substituting the known values, we have

$$y_{2015} = (22)\frac{(2015-1989)(2015-1999)(2015-2005)(2015-2009)}{(1979-1989)(1979-1999)(1979-2005)(1979-2009)}$$

$$+ (27)\frac{(2015-1979)(2015-1999)(2015-2005)(2015-2009)}{(1989-1979)(1989-1999)(1989-2005)(1989-2009)}$$

$$+ (34)\frac{(2015-1979)(2015-1989)(2015-2005)(2015-2009)}{(1999-1979)(1999-1989)(1999-2005)(1999-2009)}$$

$$+ (39)\frac{(2015-1979)(2015-1989)(2015-1999)(2015-2009)}{(2005-1979)(2005-1989)(2005-1999)(2005-2009)}$$

$$+ (42)\frac{(2015-1979)(2015-1989)(2015-1999)(2015-2005)}{(2009-1979)(2009-1989)(2009-1999)(2009-2005)}$$

or $$y_{2015} = (22)\frac{26\times16\times10\times6}{(-10)(-20)(-26)(-30)} + (27)\frac{36\times16\times10\times6}{10\times-10\times-16\times-20} + (34)\frac{36\times26\times10\times6}{20\times10\times-6\times-10}$$

$$+ (39)\frac{36\times26\times16\times6}{20\times16\times6\times-4} + (42)\frac{36\times26\times16\times10}{30\times20\times10\times4}$$

$$y_{2015} = 3.52 - 29.16 + 159.12 - 351 + 262.08 = 424.72 - 380.16 = 44.56$$

Estimated population for the years 2015 = **44.56** **Ans.**

8.4.6 Sterling Formula

Like the Newton-Gauss formula's, the sterling formula is to be applied when :

(i) The figure to be Interpolated is in the middle of the series.

(ii) When the variation in (x) series is, by equal increments.

Formula : $$y_x = y_0 + x\frac{\Delta^1_{y-1} + \Delta^1_{y0}}{2} + \frac{x^2}{2}\Delta^2_{y-1} + \frac{x(x^2-1)}{3\times2\times1}\cdot\frac{\Delta^3_{y-2} + \Delta^3_{y-1}}{2} + \frac{x^2(x^2-1^2)}{4\times3\times2\times1}\Delta^4_{y-2}$$

$$x = \frac{\text{Item of Interpolation} - \text{Item of origin}}{\text{Difference between two adjoining items}}$$

***Illustration* 23**

Using the Sterling formula, Interpolate the value of y when $x = 15$:

x	10	12	14	16	18	20
y	50	60	75	95	120	150

Solution

Interpolation by Sterling's Formula

x		y		*Differences* Δ^1	Δ^2	Δ^3
10	x_{-2}	50	y_{-2}			
				$10\,\Delta^1_{y-2}$		
					$5\,\Delta^2_{y-2}$	
12	x_{-1}	60	y_{-1}			
				$15\,\Delta^1_{y-1}$		$0\,\Delta^3_{y-2}$
14	x_0	75	y_0		$5\,\Delta^2_{y-1}$	
				$20\,\Delta^1_{y0}$		$0\,\Delta^3_{y-1}$
					$5\,\Delta^2_{y0}$	
16	x_{+1}	95	y_{+1}			
				$25\,\Delta^2_{y+1}$		$0\,\Delta^3_{y0}$
					$5\,\Delta^2_{y+1}$	
18	x_{+2}	120	y_{+2}			
				$30\,\Delta^2_{y+2}$		
20	x_{+3}	150	y_{+3}			

We have $x = \frac{15-14}{2} = \frac{1}{2} = 0.5$

Here, $y_{15} = y_0 + x\frac{\Delta^1_{y-1}+\Delta^1_{y0}}{2} + \frac{x^2}{2}\Delta^1_{y-2} + \frac{x(x^2-1^2)}{6} + \frac{\Delta^3_{y-2}+\Delta^3_{y-1}}{2}$

$= 75 + (0.5)\frac{15+20}{2} + \frac{(0.5)^2}{2} \times (5) + \frac{0.5(0.5^2-1^2)}{6} \times \frac{0+0}{2}$

$= 75 + 8.75 + 0.625 + 0 = \mathbf{84.375}$

8.4.7 Parabolic Curve Method or Method of Fitting a Parabola

Under this method Trend equation is found out and then the values are Interpolated.

Procedure :

(1) The independent variable is denoted by (x).
(2) Dependent variable is denoted by (y).
(3) Decide the power for which the parabolic curve will be used. It is (n – 1), where n = number of known quantities (x, y).
(4) Take the (x) for which (y) is to be Interpolated as origin.
(5) Obtain the deviations from the origin for different given values of (x).
(6) With the help of parabolic curve, values of constants are calculated. a, b, c etc. are constants which are to be found out and (y) is a function of (x).
(7) Substitute the different values of (x) and (y) in the parabolic curve equation. One of the equations formed $y_a = 0$
(8) Solve these equations for the value of a. This is the required value of y to be Interpolated.

Equation of the Parabolic Curve :

$$y = a + bx + cx^2 + dx^3 + ... + nx^n$$

The power to which this equation is to be raised depends upon the number of known pairs (x, y).

Parobolic Curve Equations

No of known Values (n)	*Degree of Parabolic Curve (n – 1)*	*Equations*
2	(2 – 1) = 1	$y = a + bx$
3	(3 – 1) = 2	$y = a + bx + cx^2$
4	(4 – 1) = 2	$y = a + bx + cx^2 + dx^3$
5	(5 – 1) = 2	$y = a + bx + bx^2 + dx^3 + ex^4$
⋮		
n	$(n-1) = n-1$	$y = a + bx + cx^2 + dx^3 + ex^4 + ... + nx^n$

Remarks :

1. The curve drawn according to this equation is the best, because it passes through all the points.

2. With the help of a parabolic curve both interpolation and extrapolation can be made.

3. This method should be used when the values of X be equidistant.

Drawbacks :

1. When the number of quantities (x, y) known is large, it is difficult to solve the simultaneous equations.

2. If figures to be Interpolated are more than one this becomes a lengthy process.

Illustration 24

From the following value, find out the value of y for $x = 6$:

x	3	6	7	9
y	168	?	120	72

Solution

In series (y) known values are three. Therefore, parabola of (3 – 1) = Equation of 2nd degree will be fitted. Hence, the equation will be :

$$y = a + bx + cx^2$$

Point of origin of (x) variable $x = 6$

x	y	$(x-6)$
3	168	– 3
6	? (y)	0
7	120	+ 1
9	72	+ 3

Substituting the known values, we get

$168 = a - 3b + 9c$ ...(i)

$y_0 = a$ ...(ii)

$120 = a + b + c$ ...(iii)

$72 = a + 3b + 9c$ ...(iv)

Now $y_0 = a$

∴ Add equation (i) and (iv),

$$168 = a - 3b + 9c$$
$$72 = a + 3b + 9c$$
$$240 = 2a + 18c \quad ...(v)$$

By multiplying equation (iii) by 3,

$$360 = 3a + 3b + 3c \quad ...(vi)$$

Now add equations (i) and (vi),

$$168 = a - 3b + 9c$$
$$360 = 3a + 3b + 3c$$
$$528 = 4a + 12c \quad ...(vii)$$

By multiplying equation (v) by 2,

$$480 = 4a + 36c \quad ...(viii)$$

Now subtract equation (viii) from equation (vii),

$$528 = 4a + 12c$$
$$480 = 4a + 36c$$
$$- \quad - \quad -$$
$$48 = -24c$$

$$\therefore \quad c = -\frac{48}{24} = -2$$

For calculating the value of a, the value of c will be substituted in equation,

$$528 = 4a + (12 \times -2)$$
$$\Rightarrow \quad 528 = 4a - 24$$
$$\Rightarrow \quad 4a = 528 + 24$$
$$\Rightarrow \quad 4a = 552$$
$$\Rightarrow \quad a = \frac{552}{4}$$
$$\therefore \quad \boxed{a = 138}$$

Since $a = y$, therefore $y = 138$ **Ans.**

Illustration 25

Find the cube value of 5 from the following data :

x	3	4	5	6	7
Cube Value	27	64	?	216	343

Solution :

Known values of y are four. Therefore, the parabola of (4 – 1) = Equation of 3rd order will be fitted Hence the equation is.

$$y = a + bx + cx^2 + dx^3$$

Point of origin $x = 5$

x	y	$x = x - 5$
3	27	– 2
4	64	– 1
5	? (y)	0
6	216	+ 1
7	243	+ 2

We have to find value of y.

By substituting the values, we get

$$24 = a - 2b + 4c - 8d \quad ...(i)$$
$$64 = a - b + c - d \quad ...(ii)$$
$$y_0 = a \quad ...(iii)$$
$$216 = a + b + c + d \quad ...(iv)$$
$$343 = a + 2b + 4c + 8d \quad ...(v)$$

Add (ii) and (iv) equations,

$$64 = a - b + c - d$$
$$216 = a + b + c + d \quad ...(vi)$$
$$280 = 2a + 2c$$

Add (i) and (v) equations,

$$27 = c - 2b + 4c - 8d$$
$$343 = c + 2b + 4c + 8d$$
$$370 = 2a + 8c \quad ...(vii)$$

Thus, we have two new equations (vi) and (vii).

In order to find out the value of a we will have to eliminate x. Hence equation (vi) is to be multiplied by 4.

$$1120 = 8a + 8c \quad ...(viii)$$

Now equation (vii) subtracted from (viii),

$$1120 = 8a + 8c$$
$$370 = 2a + 8c$$
$$- \quad - \quad -$$
$$750 = 6a$$
$$a = \frac{750}{6}$$
$$\therefore \quad a = 125$$
$$\therefore \quad y_0 = a \text{ or } y_0 = 125$$ **Ans.**

8.4.8 Newton's Divided Difference Method

This method of Interpolation is applicable where the independent variable (X) advances by unequal intervals. However, this method can be used even in such cases where X-variable is having equal intervals.

Cases of Applying this Method

(i) Where independent variable (*i.e.*, X-variable) or group of classes advances with unequal intervals. For example,

1980, 1990, 2005 or 0—5, 5—15, 15—30, 30—70, ...

(ii) In this method divided difference is calculated by dividing the difference of adjoining y's by the corresponding difference of x's.

(iii) The dependent variable (y-variable) should have a definite trend (either or increasing or decreasing), *i.e.*, shohuld not have sudden fluctuations.

Method of Calculation

Step 1. Express independent variable values as x_0, x_1, x_2, ... and dependent variable values as y_0, y_1, y_2 ...

Step 2. Find the divided difference. For finding out divided difference in each of the value of (y), deduct its previous value and divide it by the difference of corresponding values of (x),

For Example :

X	Y	*Divided Difference*
10 x_0	120 y_0	$\frac{265-120}{20-10} = \frac{145}{10} = 14.5 \; \Delta_0^1$
20 x_1	265 y_1	

Step 3. Denote each divided difference with notations like $\Delta_0^1\ \Delta_1^1\ \Delta_2^1$. Δ_0^1 will be the first leading difference. In the first column we will have *three* divided differences.

Step 4. In the second column *two* divided differences will be calculated with the help of *three* divided differences as obtained in the column 1 (*i.e.,* Δ^1). This difference will be denoted by $\Delta_0^2\ \Delta_1^2$. Δ_0^2 will be the *second* leading difference.

Step 5. In the third column we will have only one divided difference which will be called third leading difference Δ_0^3. These differences are found out upto the order, which is one less than the known values of (y). If four value of y are known, then *three* leading divided difference will we found out.

Step 6. Use the following formula to obtain the desired result :

Symbolically,

$$y_x = y_0 + (x - x_0)\ \Delta_0^1 + (x - x_0)(x - x_1)\ \Delta_0^2 + (x - x_0)(x - x_1)(x_1 - x_2)\ \Delta_0^3 + (x - x_0)(x - x_1)(x_1 - x_2)(x_1 - x_3)\ \Delta_0^4 + \ldots$$

Were, x = The given value of 'x' for which 'y' is to Interpolated or Extrapolated.

$\Delta_0^1, \Delta_0^2, \Delta_0^3, \ldots\ldots\ldots, \Delta_0^n$ are the first, second, third and nth leading divided differences.

Divided Difference Table

Independent Variable (x)	*Dependent Variable* (y)	Δ^1	Δ^2	Δ^3
x_0	y_0			
		$\frac{y_1 - y_0}{x_1 - x_0} = \Delta_0^1$		
x_1	y_1		$\frac{\Delta_1^1 - \Delta_0^1}{x_2 - x_0} = \Delta_0^2$	
		$\frac{y_2 - y_1}{x_2 - x_1} = \Delta_1^1$		$\frac{\Delta_1^2 - \Delta_0^2}{x_3 - x_0} = \Delta_0^3$
x_2	y_2		$\frac{\Delta_2^1 - \Delta_1^1}{x_3 - x_1} = \Delta_1^2$	
		$\frac{y_3 - y_2}{x_3 - x_2} = \Delta_2^1$		
x_3	y_3			

Illustration 26

Apply Newton's Divided Difference Method and estimate the number of plumbers getting ₹ 150 per day.

Income per day (₹)	100	180	200	250
No. of Plumbers	130	250	310	360

Solution :

Divided Difference Table

No. of Plumbers (x)		*Income* (₹) (y)		Δ^1	Δ^2	Δ^3
100	x_0	130	y_0			
				$\frac{250-130}{180-100} = \frac{120}{80} = 1.5\ (\Delta_0^1)$		
180	x_1	250	y_1		$\frac{3-1.5}{200-100} = \frac{1.5}{100} = 0.015\ (\Delta_0^2)$	
				$\frac{310-250}{200-180} = \frac{60}{20} = 3\ (\Delta_1^1)$		$\frac{-0.0280 - 0.015}{250 - 100} = -0.00029\ (\Delta_0^3)$
200	x_2	310	y_2		$\frac{1-3}{250-180} = \frac{-2}{70} = -0.0285\ (\Delta_1^2)$	
				$\frac{360-310}{250-200} = \frac{50}{50} = 1\ (\Delta_2^1)$		
250	x_3	360	y_3			

1.5 (Δ_0^1), 0.015 (Δ_0^2), – 0.00029 (Δ_0^3) are the leading differences.

Now x = ₹ 150

$$y_x = y_0 + (x - x_0)\ \Delta_0^1 + (x - x_0)(x - x_1)\ \Delta_0^2 + (x - x_0)(x - x_1)(x - x_2)\ \Delta_0^3$$

$$= 130 + (150 - 100) \times 1.5 + (150 - 100)(150 - 180) \times 0.015 + (150 - 100)(150 - 180)(150 - 200) \times (-0.00029)$$

$$= 130 + 75 - 22.5 - 21.75 = 160.75 = 161$$

∴ **161 Plumbers** **Ans.**

Illustration 27

The following table gives normal weight of babies during the last first six months of life :

Age (in months)	0	2	3	5	6
Weight (in lbs.)	5	7	8	10	12

Estimate the weight of a boby at the age of 4 months.

Solution :

Table of Divided Difference

Age (in months) (x)		*Weight* (in lb.) (y)		Δ^1	Δ^2	Δ^3	Δ^4
0	x_0	5	y_0				
				$\frac{7-5}{2-0} = 1\ (\Delta_0^1)$			
2	x_1	7	y_1		$\frac{1-1}{3-0} = 0\ (\Delta_0^2)$		
				$\frac{8-7}{3-2} = 1\ (\Delta_1^1)$		$\frac{0-0}{5-0} = 0\ (\Delta_0^3)$	$\frac{0.0825-0}{6-0}$
3	x_2	8	y_2		$\frac{1-1}{5-2} = 0\ (\Delta_1^2)$		
				$\frac{10-8}{5-3} = 1\ (\Delta_2^1)$		$\frac{0.33-0}{6-2} = 0.0825\ (\Delta_1^3)$	$= 0.01375\ (\Delta_0^4)$
5	x_3	10	y_3		$\frac{2-1}{6-3} = 0.33\ (\Delta_2^2)$		
				$\frac{12-10}{6-5} = 2\ (\Delta_3^1)$			
6	x_4	12	y_4				

Here, $x = 4$ and $1\,(\Delta_0^1)$, $0\,(\Delta_0^2)$, $0\,(\Delta_0^3)$, $0.01375\,(\Delta_0^4)$ are leading differences.

$$y_x = y_0 + (x - x_0)(\Delta_0^1) + (x - x_0)(x - x_1)\Delta_0^2 + (x - x_0)(x - x_1)(x - x_2)\Delta_0^3 + (x - x_0)(x - x_1)(x - x_2)(x - x_3)\Delta_0^4$$

Now substituing the values,

$$= 5 + (4 - 0) \times 1 + (4 - 0)(4 - 2)(0) + (4 - 0)(4 - 2)(4 - 3)(0) + (4 - 0)(4 - 2)(4 - 3)(4 - 5)(0.01375)$$

$$= 5 + 4 + 0 + 0 + (4 \times 2 \times 1 \times -1 \times 0.01375)$$

$$= 5 + 4 - 0.11$$

$$= 9 - 0.11$$

$$= 8.99$$

$$y_x = 8.9$$

∴ **8.9 lbs.** **Ans.**

Illustration 28

From the following data, estimate the probable number of workers earning between ₹ 30 and ₹ 40 per week :

Weekly Income	15—20	20—30	30—45	45—55	55—70
No. of Workers	73	97	110	180	140

Solution :

Table of Divided Differences

Weekly Income (x)		*No. of Workers* (y)		Δ^1	Δ^2	Δ^3	Δ^4
Below 20	x_0	73	y_0				
				$\frac{170-73}{30-20} = 9.7\ (\Delta_0^1)$			
Below 30	x_1	170	y_1		$\frac{7.3-9.7}{45-20} = -0.096\ (\Delta_0^2)$		
				$\frac{280-170}{45-30} = 7.3\ (\Delta_1^1)$		$\frac{0.428+0.096}{55-20} = 0.0149\ (\Delta_0^3)$	
Below 45	x_2	280	y_2		$\frac{18-7.3}{55-30} = 0.428\ (\Delta_1^2)$		$\frac{-0.0194-0.0149}{70-20} = 0.00068\ (\Delta_0^4)$
				$\frac{460-280}{55-45} = 18\ (\Delta_2^1)$		$\frac{(-0.348)-(0.428)}{70-30} = -0.0194\ (\Delta_1^3)$	
Below 55	x_3	460	y_3		$\frac{9.3-18}{70-45} = -0.348\ (\Delta_2^2)$		
				$\frac{600-460}{70-55} = 9.3\ (\Delta_3^1)$			
Below 70	x_4	600	y_4				

$9.7\ (\Delta_0^1), -0.096\ (\Delta_0^2), 0.0149\ (\Delta_0^3), 0.00068\ (\Delta_0^4)$ are the leading differences

Now, x = below 40

$\therefore \quad y_x = y_0 + (x-x_0)(\Delta_0^1) + (x-x_0)(x-x_1)\Delta_0^2 + (x-x_0)(x-x_1)(x-x_2)\Delta_0^3 + (x-x_0)(x-x_1)(x-x_2)(x-x_3)\Delta_0^4$

Subsituting the values

$$y_x = 73 + (40-20)(9.7) + (40-20)(-0.096) + (40-20)(40-30)(40-45)(0.0149)$$
$$+ (40-20)(40-30)(40-45)(40-55)(-0.00068)$$
$$= 73 + (20 \times 9.7) + (20 \times 10 \times -0.096) + (20 \times 10 \times 0.5 \times 0.0149) + (20 \times 10 \times -5 \times -15 \times 0.00068)$$
$$= 73 + 194 - 19.2 - 14.9 - 10.2 = 222.7$$
$$\approx \textbf{223 workers}$$

Ans.

(8.5) WHEN AND WHICH METHOD SHOULD BE USED ?

1. **In case of equal distance in the independent variable *x* or when independent variable advances by equal intervals :**
   (i) Binomial Expansion Method,
   (ii) Newton's Advancing Differences Method.
2. **In case of unequal intervals in the value of *x* :**
   (i) Lagrange's Method,
   (ii) Newton's Method of Divided Differences.
3. **When value to be interpolated lies in the middle of the series and variable of *x* advances by equal intervals :**
   (i) Newton-Gauss Forward Method,
   (ii) Sterling's Formula.

Note : Newton's formula is fairly easy but binomial expansion method is the easiest to apply.

THEORETICAL QUESTIONS

Long Answer Type Questions

1. What is meant by interpolation ? What are the assumptions on which methods of interpolation are based ?
2. What do you mean by interpolation and extrapolation ? Explain briefly their usefulness in statistical studies.
3. Discuss the utility of interpolation and extrapolation to businessman. What are the different methods known to you for interpolation ?
4. Explain clearly the difference between interpolation and extrapolation. Discuss briefly their neccessity and usefulness in statistical studies.
5. Discuss any two methods of interpolation you know of stating clearly the assumptions involved.
6. Distinguish between interpolation and extrapolation. Describe the different methods of interpolation.

7. What do you understand by the term interpolation and extrapolation ? Discuss briefly their neccessity and usefulness in statistical studies. Also, explain any method of interpolation.

Short Answer Type Questions

1. Explain the meaning of interpolation.
2. What is meant by extrapolation ?
3. Distinguish between interpolation and extrapolation.
4. What are the assumptions of interpolation ?
5. State the utility of interpolation and extrapolation.
6. Explain in brief parabolic curve method of interpolation.
7. What do you mean by Newton's method of finite or advancing differences ?
8. Describe graphical method of interpolation.
9. Describe binomial expansion method.

Very Short Answer Type Questions

1. State two assumptions of interpolation.
2. When Newton-Gauss Method is used for interpolation ? Give the formula.
3. When Newton's method for divided differences is used ? Give formula for calculating interpolation by this method.
4. Give the name of any two algebraical Methods of interpolation.
5. When Binomial Expansion method is used ? What are the conditions for using this method ?
6. What is the need of interpolation ? Give any two points.
7. Differentiate between interpolation and extrapolation. Give any two points.

PRACTICAL QUESTIONS

(I) Graphic Method

1. From the following data, estimate the profit for the year 2004 by using the graphic method : (Lakh ₹)

Year	1999	2001	2003	2005	2007	2009
Profit	8	10	15	18	20	25

2. Estimate graphically the annual sales of pencils in 2003 from the following records :

Year	1993	1997	2001	2004	2009
Sales (Lakh Dozen)	25	30	40	55	60

(II) Algebraic Methods

Binomial Expansion Method

3. The quantity of annual production of cement in ton is given in the following table. Find out the missing quantity by appropriate method in interpolation :

Year	1999	2001	2003	2005	2007	2009
Quantity (ton)	44	90	?	160	270	390

[**Ans.** 2003 = 104.6 tons]

4. From the following, interpolate the missing figure : (*JAC*, 2017)

x	20	25	30	35	40	45
y	55	60	?	72	75	80

[**Ans.** 67]

5. Estimate the missing value in the following table :

Year	2010	2011	2012	2013	2014	2015
Value	786	852	881	?	940	1052

[**Ans.** 898.4 or 898 (Approx.)]

6. Estimate the missing term in the following table :

x	1	2	3	4	5	6	7
y	2	4	8	?	32	64	128

[**Ans.** 16.1]

7. The profit of a business concern is shown in the following table :

Year	2010	2011	2012	2013	2015
Profit (lakh ₹)	587	592	595	599	608

Estimate the profit of 2014 by interpolation.

[**Ans.** 2014 = ₹ 604 lakh]

8. By Binomial method, interpolate the missing figure : (*JAC*, 2020)

Year	2010	2011	2012	2013	2014	2015
Profit (lakh ₹)	50	45	?	38	35	30

[**Ans.** 2012 = ₹ 41 lakh]

9. By applying Binomial method estimate export figures for the year 2005 and 2008 from the following data :

Year	2003	2004	2005	2006	2007	2008	2009
Exports Crore ₹	16	20	?	28	31	?	42

[**Ans.** 2005 = 24.37, 2008 = 35 (₹ in crore)]

10. Interpolate the missing values in the following table :

Year	1961	1971	1981	1991	2001	2011
Population (in lakh)	360	—	425	—	465	501

[**Ans.** 1991—443.05; 1971—400.70]

11. The following table give the age composition of post graduate students. Find the missing figure :

Age (years)	15—17	17—19	19—21	21—23	23—25	25—27
No. of Students	18	25	33	?	56	59

[**Ans.** 45]

12. The population of a district is give below for different year. Find the population for the year 2010 :

Year	2005	2006	2007	2008	2009
Population (in lakh)	7	9	36	14	16

[**Ans.** 17 Lakh]

12A. Interpolate the missing value : (*JAC*, 2025)

Year	2000	2001	2002	2003	2004	2005
Production	173	149	145	?	131	141

[**Ans.** 2003 = 139.2]

Newton's Advancing Difference Method

13. In the following table life expectancy for different age has been shown. Estimate life expectancy for the age 16 :

Age (in years)	10	15	20	25	30	35
Life Expectancy	35	33	29	27	22	20

[**Ans.** 32 years]

14. The number of admission in a school is as under. Find the number of admission in 2016 :

Year	1990	1995	2000	2005	2010	2015
Admission	66	114	150	195	240	275

[**Ans.** 281]

15. The following are the annual premiums charged by an insurance company. Estimate the premium payable at the age of 17 year :

Year	55	45	35	25	15
Premium Payable (₹)	18.3	16.1	14.3	12.6	11.1

[**Ans.** ₹ 11.4]

16. From the following table, find the number of students who obtained (i) less than 45 marks, (ii) less than 55 marks, and (iii) between 45.55 marks :

Marks	30 – 40	40 – 50	50 – 60	60 – 70	70 – 80
No. of Students	31	42	51	35	31

[**Ans.** (i) 48 approx, (ii) 72.36, (iii) 120]

17. Estimate the expectation of life at the age of 16 years using the following data :

Year	10	15	20	25	30	35
Premium Payable (₹)	35.4	32.3	29.2	26.0	23.2	20.4

[**Ans.** 32.19 years or 32.2 years]

Newton-Gauss Forward Method

18. From the following values, interpolate the value of y when $x = 15$ by Newton-Gauss method :

x-Variable	10	12	14	16	18	20
y-Variable	50	60	75	95	120	150

[**Ans.** $y = 84.37584$]

19. Estimate the expectation of life at the age of 35 :

Age (in years)	20	30	40	50
Expectation of Life (year)	36	32	24	16

[**Ans.** 28.25 years]

20. Given th values :

x	14	17	31	35
y	68.7	64.0	44	39.1

Calculate the value of y of corresponding to $x = 27$.

[**Ans.** 49.59 or 50]

Newton-Gauss Backward Method

21. Using Newton's Backward Formula, find the annual premium of the age of 33 from the following data :

Age (years)	24	28	32	36	40
Annual Premium (₹)	28.06	30.19	32.75	34.94	40.00

[**Ans.** 35.00375]

22. Interpolate the value of y at $x = 35$ by the Newton-Gauss Background Method :

x	10	20	30	40	50
y	45	48	54	65	80

[**Ans.** 60]

23. The population of town is given below. Estimate the population for the year 2005 :

Year	1971	1981	1991	2001	2011
Population ('000)	46	66	81	93	101

[**Ans.** 96,200]

Lagrange's Method

24. Calculate the missing value from the given table by Lagrange's Method :

x	5	8	9	11	12
y	121	?	73	25	16

[**Ans.** 100]

25. From the following data, interpolate the value of y when $x = 6$:

x	3	7	9	10
y	168	120	72	63

[**Ans.** 147]

26. Determine by Lagrange's formula, the percentage number of criminals under 35 years :

Age below	25	30	45
% of Criminals	60	70	100

[**Ans.** 80%]

Sterling's Formula

27. From the following data, interpolate the value of y, when $x = 15$:

x	10	12	14	16	18	20
y	50	60	75	95	170	150

[**Ans.** 84.375]

28. Using Sterling's formula, find the value of y, when $x = 15$:

x	4	6	8	10	12
y	80	86	96	104	114

[**Ans.** 100]

Parabolic Curve Method

29. The amount of sales of a firm Muzaffarpur is given below. Interpolate its sales in 2006-07 :

Year	2005-06	2006-07	2007-08	2008-09
Sales (in thousand ₹)	200	240	350	400

[**Ans.** 293.4 thousand]

30. The following table give the cube of the item. Find the cube of 2.5 :

Size of item	1	2	3	4
Cube value	1	8	27	64

[**Ans.** 15.375]

Newton's Divided Difference Method

31. The following table gives the normal weight of a baby during the first six months of life.
Estimate the weight of baby at the age of 4 months by Newton's Divided Difference Method :

Age (in months)	0	2	3	5	6
Weight (in lbs.)	4	6	7	9	11

[**Ans.** 7.92 or 8 lbs.]

32. From the following data by using Newton's Divided Difference Method find out the number of candidates who secured more than 20 marks but not more than 30 marks :

Marks	0—10	10—20	20—40	40—50
No. of Candidates	120	145	350	150

[**Ans.** 174 Candidates.]

33. Estimate the missing figure in the following table by applying Newton's Divided Difference Method :

x	20	22	25	30	35
y	73	93	198	?	1198

[**Ans.** 573]

34. Apply Newton's Divided Difference Method and find out the number of children getting 6 toffees :

Toffees (per child)	3	5	7	8	10
No. of Children	180	154	120	110	90

[**Ans.** 135]

Miscellaneous Problems

35. Find out y_2 from the following :

x	1	2	3	4	5
y	2.000	?	2.0646	2.0954	2.1253

[**Ans.** 2.0328]

36. Estimate the population of 2005 :

Year	1971	1981	1991	2001	2011
Production (000	46	66	81	93	101

[**Ans.** 96.8368 (in thousand]

37. From the following, interpolate the missing figure :

x	25	30	35	40	45	50
y	55	60	?	72	80	80

[**Ans.** 67]

38. Extrapolate the population of a town for 2007 from the following table :

Year	1971	1981	1991	2001
Population (in thousand)	22	27	34	42

[**Ans.** 46.864]

OBJECTIVE TYPE QUESTIONS

I. Multiple Choice Questions

1. At the interpolation of continuous series is not cumulated under :
(a) Binomial expansion method
(b) Newton's method
(c) Lagrange's method (d) All the above

2. Binomial expansion method is based on :
(a) Multiplication theorem (b) Additive theorem
(c) Binomial thorem (d) None of these

3. Value obtained by interpolation :
(a) Is equal to actual value
(b) Is less than actual value
(c) Is more than actual value
(d) Is the maximum possible estimate of actual value

4. When there is unequal difference in X series them appropriate method for interpolation is : (*JAC*, 2019)
(a) Binomial expansion method
(b) Lagrange's method
(c) Newton's method
(d) Sterling's formula

5. Which is the method that can be used in any type of question of interpolation ?
   (a) Newton's method
   (b) Binomial expansion method
   (c) Lagrange's method
   (d) None of these
6. Binomial exampansion method of interpolation is used when there are sudden rise and fall in y series.
   (a) True (b) False
7. Lagrange's formula will give the same result as is obtained by Binomial and Newton Formula.
   (a) True (b) False
8. Newton's formula is based on Binomial expansion.
   (a) True (b) False
9. The simplest method of interpolation is : (*JAC*, 2023)
   (a) Graphic method
   (b) Lagrange method
   (c) Newton's divided method
   (d) None of these
10. In interpolation $(y-1)^5 = 0$ or Δ_0^5 equals : (*JAC*, 2025)
   (a) $y_2 - 2y_1 + y_0 = 0$
   (b) $y_3 - 3y_2 + 3y_1 + y_0 = 0$
   (c) $y_4 - 4y_3 + 6y_2 - 4y_1 + y_0 = 0$
   (d) $y_5 - 5y_4 + 10y_3 - 10y_2 + 5y_1 - y_0 = 0$
11. Linear Interpolation is : (*JAC*, 2025)
   (a) Easy (b) Precise
   (c) Easy & precise (d) None of these
12.

x	25	30	35	40	45	50
y	55	60	?	72	75	80

It is related to (*JAC*, 2025)
   (a) Interpolation (b) Extrapolation
   (c) Both (a) and (b) (d) None of these

[**Ans.** 1. (a), 2. (c), 3. (d), 4. (b), 5. (c), 6. (b), 7. (a), 8. (a), 9. (a), 10. (d), 11. (c), 12. (a).]

II. State whether the following statements are 'True' or 'False' :

1. A technique of estimating a past figure is termed as extrapolation.
2. The simplest method of interpolation is graphic method.
3. Parabolic curve method is also known as method of simultaneous equations.
4. Binomial expansion is appropriate when independent variable advances by unequal intervals.
5. Lagrange's formula can be used in such a case when in independent variable (X) difference is equal or unequal.
6. Newton's advancing difference method is also called finite difference method.

[**Ans.** 1. False 2. True 3. True 4. False 5. True 6. True.]

I. Fill in the blanks

1. .... gives forecast for the future. (*JAC*, 2020, 24)
2. The simplest method of interpotation is .... method.
3. ....the method is also called simultaneous equation.
4. Binomial expansion method is appropriate when the indent variable X advances by ....
5. The technique of estimating any value between the range of values given is known as ....

[**Ans.** 1. Extrapolation, 2. Graphic, 3. Parabolic Curve, 4. Equal Intervals, 5. Interpolation.]

Notes

Appendix

Business Mathematics and Statistics

LOGARITHMS

	0	1	2	3	4	5	6	7	8	9	*Mean Differences*								
											1	2	3	4	5	6	7	8	9
10	0000	0043	0086	0128	0170	0212	0253	0294	0334	0374	4	8	12	17	21	25	29	33	37
11	0414	0453	0492	0531	0569	0607	0645	0682	0719	0755	4	8	11	15	19	23	26	30	34
12	0792	0828	0864	0899	0934	0969	1004	1038	1072	1106	3	7	10	14	17	21	24	28	31
13	1139	1173	1206	1239	1271	1303	1335	1367	1399	1430	3	6	10	13	16	19	23	26	29
14	1461	1492	1523	1553	1584	1614	1644	1673	1703	1732	3	6	9	12	15	18	21	24	27
15	1761	1790	1818	1847	1875	1903	1931	1959	1987	2014	3	6	8	11	14	17	20	22	25
16	2041	2068	2095	2122	2148	2175	2201	2227	2253	2279	3	5	8	11	13	16	18	21	24
17	2304	2330	2355	2380	2405	2430	2455	2480	2504	2529	3	5	8	10	12	15	17	20	22
18	2553	2577	2601	2625	2648	2672	2695	2718	2742	2765	2	5	7	9	12	14	16	19	21
19	2788	2810	2833	3856	2878	2900	2923	2945	2967	2989	2	4	6	8	11	13	15	17	19
20	3010	3032	3054	3075	3096	3118	3139	3160	3181	3201	2	4	6	8	11	13	15	17	19
21	3222	3243	3263	3284	3304	3324	3345	3365	3385	3404	2	4	6	8	10	12	14	16	18
22	3424	3444	3464	3483	3502	3522	3541	3560	3579	3598	2	4	6	8	10	12	14	15	17
23	3617	3636	3655	3674	3692	3711	3729	3747	3766	3784	2	4	6	7	9	11	13	15	17
24	3802	3820	3838	3856	3874	3892	3909	3927	3945	3962	2	4	5	7	9	11	12	14	16
25	3979	3997	4014	4031	4048	4065	4082	4099	4116	4133	2	3	5	7	9	10	12	14	15
26	4150	4166	4183	4200	4216	4232	4249	4265	4281	4298	2	3	5	7	8	10	11	13	15
27	4314	4330	4346	4362	4378	4393	4409	4425	4440	4456	2	3	5	6	8	9	11	13	14
28	4472	4487	4502	4518	4533	4548	4654	4579	4594	4609	2	3	5	6	8	9	11	12	14
29	4624	4639	4654	4669	4683	4698	4713	4728	4742	4757	1	3	4	6	7	9	10	12	13
30	4771	4786	4800	4814	4829	4843	4857	4871	4886	4900	1	3	4	6	7	9	10	11	13
31	4914	4928	4942	4955	4969	4983	4997	5011	5024	5038	1	3	4	6	7	8	10	11	12
32	5051	5065	5079	5092	5105	5119	5132	5145	5159	5172	1	3	4	5	7	8	9	11	12
33	5185	5198	5211	5224	5237	5250	5263	5276	5289	5302	1	3	4	5	6	8	9	10	12
34	5315	5328	5340	5353	5366	5378	5391	5403	5416	5428	1	3	4	5	6	8	9	10	11
35	5441	5453	5465	5478	5490	5502	5514	5527	5539	5551	1	2	4	5	6	7	9	10	11
36	5563	5575	5587	5599	5611	5623	5635	5647	5658	5670	1	2	4	5	6	7	8	10	11
37	5682	5694	5705	5717	5729	5740	5752	5763	5775	5786	1	2	3	5	6	7	8	9	10
38	5798	5809	5821	5832	5843	5855	5866	5877	5888	5899	1	2	3	5	6	7	8	9	10
39	5911	5922	5933	5944	5955	5966	5977	5988	5999	6010	1	2	3	4	5	7	8	9	10
40	6021	6031	6042	6053	6064	6075	6085	6096	6107	6117	1	2	3	4	5	6	8	9	10
41	6128	6138	6149	6160	6170	6180	6191	6201	6212	6222	1	2	3	4	5	6	7	8	9
42	6232	6243	6253	6263	6274	6284	6294	6304	6314	6325	1	2	3	4	5	6	7	8	9
43	6335	6345	6355	6365	6375	6385	6395	6405	6415	6425	1	2	3	4	5	6	7	8	9
44	6435	6444	6454	6464	6474	6484	6493	6503	6513	6522	1	2	3	4	5	6	7	8	9
45	6532	6542	6551	6561	6571	6580	6590	6599	6609	6618	1	2	3	4	5	6	7	8	9
46	6628	6637	6646	6656	6665	6675	6684	6693	6702	6712	1	2	3	4	5	6	7	7	8
47	6721	6730	6739	6749	6758	6767	6776	6785	6794	6803	1	2	3	4	5	5	6	7	8
48	6812	6821	6830	6839	6848	6857	6866	6875	6884	6893	1	2	3	4	4	5	6	7	8
49	6902	6911	6920	6928	6937	6946	6955	6964	6972	6981	1	2	3	4	4	5	6	7	8
50	6990	6998	7007	7016	7024	7033	7042	7050	7059	7067	1	2	3	3	4	5	6	7	8
51	7076	7084	7093	7101	7110	7118	7126	7135	7143	7152	1	2	3	3	4	5	6	7	8
52	7160	7168	7177	7185	7193	7202	7210	7218	7226	7235	1	2	2	3	4	5	6	7	7
53	7243	7251	7259	7267	7275	7284	7292	7300	7308	7316	1	2	2	3	4	5	6	6	7
54	7324	7332	7340	7348	7356	7364	7372	7380	7388	7396	1	2	2	3	4	5	6	6	7

	0	1	2	3	4	5	6	7	8	9	Mean Differences								
											1	2	3	4	5	6	7	8	9
55	7404	7412	7419	7427	7435	7443	7451	7459	7466	7474	1	2	2	3	4	5	5	6	7
56	7482	7490	7497	7505	7513	7520	7528	7536	7543	7551	1	2	2	3	4	5	5	6	7
57	7559	7566	7574	7582	7589	7597	7604	7612	7619	7627	1	2	2	3	4	5	5	6	7
58	7634	7642	7649	7657	7664	7672	7679	7686	7694	7701	1	2	2	3	4	4	5	6	7
59	7709	7716	7723	7731	7738	7745	7752	7760	7767	7774	1	1	2	3	4	4	5	6	7
60	7782	7789	7796	7803	7810	7818	7825	7832	7839	7846	1	1	2	3	4	4	5	6	6
61	7853	7860	7868	7875	7882	7889	7896	7903	7910	7917	1	1	2	3	4	4	5	6	6
62	7924	7931	7938	7945	7952	7959	7966	7973	7980	7987	1	1	2	3	3	4	5	6	6
63	7993	8000	8007	8014	8021	8028	8035	8041	8048	8055	1	1	2	3	3	4	5	5	6
64	8062	8069	8075	8082	8089	8096	8102	8109	8116	8122	1	1	2	3	3	4	5	5	6
65	8129	8136	8142	8149	8156	8162	8169	8176	8182	8189	1	1	2	3	3	4	5	5	6
66	8195	8202	8209	8215	8222	8228	8235	8241	8248	8254	1	1	2	3	3	4	5	5	6
67	8261	8267	8274	8280	8287	8293	8299	8306	8312	8319	1	1	2	3	3	4	5	5	6
68	8325	8331	8338	8344	8351	8357	8363	8370	8376	8382	1	1	2	3	3	4	4	5	6
69	8388	8395	8401	8407	8414	8420	8426	8432	8439	8445	1	1	2	2	3	4	4	5	6
70	8451	8457	8463	8470	8476	8482	8488	8494	8500	8506	1	1	2	2	3	4	4	5	6
71	8513	8519	8525	8531	8537	8543	8549	8555	8561	8567	1	1	2	2	3	4	4	5	5
72	8573	8579	8585	8591	8597	8603	8609	8615	8621	8627	1	1	2	2	3	4	4	5	5
73	8633	8639	8645	8651	8657	8663	8669	8675	8681	8686	1	1	2	2	3	4	4	5	5
74	8692	8698	8704	8710	8716	8722	8727	8733	8739	8745	1	1	2	2	3	4	4	5	5
75	8751	8756	8762	8768	8774	8779	8785	8791	8797	8802	1	1	2	2	3	3	4	5	5
76	8808	8814	8820	8825	8831	8837	8842	8848	8854	8859	1	1	2	2	3	3	4	5	5
77	8865	8871	8876	8882	8887	8893	8899	8904	8910	8915	1	1	2	2	3	3	4	4	5
78	8921	8927	8932	8938	8943	8949	8954	8960	8965	8971	1	1	2	2	3	3	4	4	5
79	8976	8982	8987	8993	8998	9004	9009	9015	9020	9025	1	1	2	2	3	3	4	4	5
80	9031	9036	9042	9047	9053	9058	9063	9069	9074	9079	1	1	2	2	3	3	4	4	5
81	9085	9090	9096	9101	9106	9112	9117	9122	9128	9133	1	1	2	2	3	3	4	4	5
82	9138	9143	9149	9154	9159	9165	9170	9175	9180	9186	1	1	2	2	3	3	4	4	5
83	9191	9196	9201	9206	9212	9217	9222	9227	9232	9238	1	1	2	2	3	3	4	4	5
84	9243	9248	9253	9258	9263	9269	9274	9279	9284	9289	1	1	2	2	3	3	4	4	5
85	9294	9299	9304	9309	9315	9320	9325	9330	9335	9340	1	1	2	2	3	3	4	4	5
86	9345	9350	9355	9360	9365	9370	9375	9380	9385	9390	1	1	2	2	3	3	4	4	5
87	9395	9400	9405	9410	9415	9420	9425	9430	9435	9440	0	1	1	2	2	3	3	4	4
88	9445	9450	9455	9460	9465	9469	9474	9479	9484	9489	0	1	1	2	2	3	3	4	4
89	9494	9499	9504	9509	9513	9518	9523	9528	9533	9538	0	1	1	2	2	3	3	4	4
90	9542	9547	9552	9557	9562	9566	9571	9576	9581	9586	0	1	1	2	2	3	3	4	4
91	9590	9595	9600	9605	9609	9614	9619	9624	9628	9633	0	1	1	2	2	3	3	4	4
92	9638	9463	9647	9652	9657	9661	9666	9671	9675	9680	0	1	1	2	2	3	3	4	4
93	9685	9689	9694	9699	9703	9708	9713	9717	9722	9727	0	1	1	2	2	3	3	4	4
94	9731	9736	9741	9745	9750	9754	9759	9763	9788	9773	0	1	1	2	2	3	3	4	4
95	9777	9782	9786	9791	9795	9800	9805	9809	9814	9818	0	1	1	2	2	3	3	4	4
96	9823	9827	9832	9836	9841	9845	9850	9854	9859	9863	0	1	1	2	2	3	3	4	4
97	9868	9872	9877	9881	9886	9890	9894	9899	9903	9908	0	1	1	2	2	3	3	4	4
98	9912	9917	9921	9926	9930	9934	9939	9943	9948	9952	0	1	1	2	2	3	3	4	4
99	9956	9961	9965	9969	9974	9978	9983	9987	9991	9996	0	1	1	2	2	3	3	3	4

ANTILOGARITHMS

	0	1	2	3	4	5	6	7	8	9	*Mean Differences*								
											1	2	3	4	5	6	7	8	9
.00	1000	1002	1005	1007	1009	1012	1014	1016	1019	1021	0	0	1	1	1	1	2	2	2
.01	1023	1026	1028	1030	1033	1035	1038	1040	1042	1045	0	0	1	1	1	1	2	2	2
.02	1047	1050	1052	1054	1057	1059	1062	1064	1067	1069	0	0	1	1	1	1	2	2	2
.03	1072	1074	1076	1079	1081	1084	1086	1089	1091	1094	0	0	1	1	1	1	2	2	2
.04	1096	1099	1102	1104	1107	1109	1112	1114	1117	1119	0	1	1	1	1	2	2	2	2
.05	1122	1125	1127	1130	1132	1135	1138	1140	1143	1146	0	1	1	1	1	2	2	2	2
.06	1148	1151	1153	1156	1159	1161	1164	1167	1169	1172	0	1	1	1	1	2	2	2	2
.07	1175	1178	1180	1183	1186	1189	1191	1194	1197	1199	0	1	1	1	1	2	2	2	2
.08	1202	1205	1208	1211	1213	1216	1219	1222	1225	1227	0	1	1	1	1	2	2	2	3
.09	1230	1233	1236	1239	1242	1245	1247	1250	1253	1256	0	1	1	1	1	2	2	2	3
.10	1259	1262	1265	1268	1271	1274	1276	1279	1282	1285	0	1	1	1	1	2	2	2	3
.11	1288	1291	1294	1297	1300	1303	1306	1309	1312	1315	0	1	1	1	2	2	2	2	3
.12	1318	1321	1324	1327	1330	1334	1337	1340	1343	1346	0	1	1	1	2	2	2	2	3
.13	1349	1352	1355	1358	1361	1365	1368	1371	1374	1377	0	1	1	1	2	2	2	3	3
.14	1380	1384	1387	1390	1393	1396	1400	1403	1406	1409	0	1	1	1	2	2	2	3	3
.15	1413	1416	1419	1422	1426	1429	1432	1435	1439	1442	0	1	1	1	2	2	2	3	3
.16	1445	1449	1452	1455	1459	1462	1466	1469	1472	1476	0	1	1	1	2	2	2	3	3
.17	1479	1483	1486	1489	1493	1496	1500	1503	1507	1510	0	1	1	1	2	2	2	3	3
.18	1514	1517	1521	1524	1528	1531	1535	1538	1542	1545	0	1	1	1	2	2	2	3	3
.19	1549	1552	1556	1560	1563	1567	1570	1574	1578	1581	0	1	1	1	2	2	3	3	3
.20	1585	1589	1592	1596	1600	1603	1607	1611	1614	1618	0	1	1	1	2	2	3	3	3
.21	1622	1626	1629	1633	1637	1641	1644	1648	1652	1656	0	1	1	2	2	2	3	3	3
.22	1660	1663	1667	1671	1675	1679	1683	1687	1690	1694	0	1	1	2	2	2	3	3	3
.23	1698	1702	1706	1710	1714	1718	1722	1726	1730	1734	0	1	1	2	2	2	3	3	4
.24	1738	1742	1746	1750	1754	1758	1762	1766	1770	1774	0	1	1	2	2	2	3	3	4
.25	1778	1782	1786	1791	1795	1799	1803	1807	1811	1816	0	1	1	2	2	2	3	3	4
.26	1820	1824	1828	1832	1837	1841	1845	1849	1854	1858	0	1	1	2	2	3	3	3	4
.27	1862	1866	1871	1875	1879	1884	1888	1892	1897	1901	0	1	1	2	2	3	3	3	4
.28	1905	1910	1914	1919	1923	1928	1932	1936	1941	1945	0	1	1	2	2	3	3	4	4
.29	1950	1954	1959	1963	1968	1972	1977	1982	1986	1991	0	1	1	2	2	3	3	4	4
.30	1995	2000	2004	2009	2014	2018	2023	2028	2032	2037	0	1	1	2	2	3	3	4	4
.31	2042	2046	2051	2056	2061	2065	2070	2075	2080	2084	0	1	1	2	2	3	3	4	4
.32	2089	2094	2099	2104	2109	2113	2118	2123	2128	2133	0	1	1	2	2	3	3	4	4
.33	2138	2143	2148	2153	2158	2163	2168	2173	2178	2183	0	1	1	2	2	3	3	4	4
.34	2188	2193	2198	2203	2208	2213	2218	2223	2228	2234	1	1	2	2	3	3	4	4	5
.35	2239	2244	2249	2254	2259	2265	2270	2275	2280	2286	1	1	2	2	3	3	4	4	5
.36	2291	2296	2301	2307	2312	2317	2323	2328	2333	2339	1	1	2	2	3	3	4	4	5
.37	2344	2350	2355	2360	2366	2371	2377	2382	2388	2393	1	1	2	2	3	3	4	4	5
.38	2399	2404	2410	2415	2421	2427	2432	2438	2443	2449	1	1	2	2	3	3	4	4	5
.39	2455	2460	2466	2472	2477	2483	2489	2495	2500	2506	1	1	2	2	3	3	4	5	5
.40	2512	2518	2523	2529	2535	2541	2547	2553	2559	2564	1	1	2	2	3	4	4	5	5
.41	2570	2576	2582	2588	2594	2600	2696	2612	2618	2624	1	1	2	2	3	4	4	5	5
.42	2630	2636	2642	2649	2655	2661	2667	2673	2679	2685	1	1	2	2	3	4	4	5	6
.43	2692	2698	2704	2710	2716	2723	2729	2735	2742	2748	1	1	2	3	3	4	4	5	6
.44	2754	2761	2767	2773	2780	2786	2793	2799	2805	2812	1	1	2	3	3	4	4	5	6
.45	2818	2825	2831	2838	2844	2851	2858	2864	2871	2877	1	1	2	3	3	4	5	5	6
.46	2884	2891	2897	2904	2911	2917	2924	2931	2938	2944	1	1	2	3	3	4	5	5	6
.47	2951	2958	2965	2972	2979	2985	2992	2999	3006	3013	1	1	2	3	3	4	5	5	6
.48	3020	3027	3034	3041	3048	3055	3062	3069	3076	3083	1	1	2	3	4	4	5	6	6
.49	3090	3097	3105	3112	3119	3126	3133	3141	3148	3155	1	1	2	3	4	4	5	6	6
.50	3162	3170	3177	3184	3192	3199	3206	3214	3221	3228	1	1	2	3	4	4	5	6	7

	0	1	2	3	4	5	6	7	8	9	Mean Differences								
											1	2	3	4	5	6	7	8	9
.51	3236	3243	3251	3258	3266	3273	3281	3289	3296	3304	1	2	2	3	4	5	5	6	7
.52	3311	3319	3327	3334	3342	3350	3357	3365	3373	3381	1	2	2	3	4	5	5	6	7
.53	3388	3396	3404	3412	3420	3428	3436	3443	3451	3459	1	2	2	3	4	5	6	6	7
.54	3467	3475	3483	3491	3499	3508	3516	3524	3532	3540	1	2	2	3	4	5	6	6	7
.55	3548	3556	3565	3573	3581	3589	3597	3606	3614	3622	1	2	2	3	4	5	6	7	7
.56	3631	3639	3648	3656	3664	3673	3681	3690	3698	3707	1	2	3	3	4	5	6	7	8
.57	3715	3724	3733	3741	3750	3758	3767	3776	3784	3793	1	2	3	3	4	5	6	7	8
.58	3802	3811	3819	3828	3837	3846	3855	3864	3873	3882	1	2	3	4	4	5	6	7	8
.59	3890	3899	3908	3917	3926	3936	3945	3954	3963	3972	1	2	3	4	5	5	6	7	8
.60	3981	3990	3999	4009	4018	4027	4036	4046	4055	4064	1	2	3	4	5	6	6	7	8
.61	4074	4083	4093	4102	4111	4121	4130	4140	4150	4159	1	2	3	4	5	6	7	8	9
.62	4169	4178	4188	4198	4207	4217	4227	4236	4256	4256	1	2	3	4	5	6	7	8	9
.63	4266	4276	4285	4295	4305	4315	4325	4335	4345	4355	1	2	3	4	5	6	7	8	9
.64	4365	4375	4385	4395	4406	4416	4426	4436	4446	4457	1	2	3	4	5	6	7	8	9
.65	4467	4477	4487	4498	4508	4519	4529	4539	4550	4560	1	2	3	4	5	6	7	8	9
.66	4571	4581	4592	4603	4613	4624	4634	4645	4656	4667	1	2	3	4	5	6	7	9	10
.67	4677	4688	4699	4710	4721	4732	4742	4753	4764	4775	1	2	3	4	5	7	8	9	10
.68	4786	4797	4808	4819	4831	4842	4853	4864	4875	4887	1	2	3	4	6	7	8	9	10
.69	4898	4909	4920	4932	4943	4955	4966	4977	4989	5000	1	2	3	5	6	7	8	9	10
.70	5012	5023	5035	5047	5058	5070	5082	5093	5105	5117	1	2	4	5	6	7	8	9	11
.71	5129	5140	5152	5164	5176	5188	5200	5212	5224	5236	1	2	4	5	6	7	8	10	11
.72	5248	5260	5272	5284	5297	5309	5321	5333	5346	5358	1	2	4	5	6	7	9	10	11
.73	5370	5383	5395	5408	5420	5433	5445	5458	5470	5483	1	3	4	5	6	8	9	10	11
.74	5495	5508	5521	5534	5546	5559	5572	5585	5598	5610	1	3	4	5	6	8	9	10	12
.75	5623	5636	5649	5662	5675	5689	5702	5715	5728	5741	1	3	4	5	7	8	9	10	12
.76	5754	5768	5781	5794	5808	5821	5834	5848	5861	5875	1	3	4	5	7	8	9	11	12
.77	5888	5902	5916	5929	5943	5957	5970	5984	5998	6012	1	3	4	5	7	8	10	11	12
.78	6026	6039	6053	6067	6081	6095	6109	6124	6138	6152	1	3	4	6	7	8	10	11	13
.79	6166	6180	6194	6209	6223	6237	6252	6266	6281	6295	1	3	4	6	7	9	10	11	13
.80	6310	6324	6339	6353	6368	6383	6497	6412	6427	6442	1	3	4	6	7	9	10	12	13
.81	6457	6471	6486	6501	6516	6531	6546	6561	6577	6592	2	3	5	6	8	9	11	12	14
.82	6607	6622	6637	6653	6668	6683	6699	6714	6730	6745	2	3	5	6	8	9	11	12	14
.83	6761	6776	6792	6808	6823	6839	6855	6871	6887	6902	2	3	5	6	8	9	11	13	14
.84	6918	6934	6950	6966	6982	6998	7015	7031	7047	7063	2	3	5	6	8	10	11	13	15
.85	7079	7096	7112	7129	7145	7161	7178	7194	7211	7228	2	3	5	7	8	10	12	13	15
.86	7244	7261	7278	7295	7311	7328	7345	7362	7379	7396	2	3	5	7	8	10	12	13	15
.87	7413	7430	7447	7464	7482	7499	7516	7534	7551	7568	2	3	5	7	9	10	12	14	16
.88	7586	7603	7621	7638	7656	7674	7691	7709	7727	7745	2	4	5	7	9	11	12	14	16
.89	7762	7780	7798	7816	7834	7852	7870	7889	7907	7925	2	4	5	7	9	11	13	14	16
.90	7943	7962	7980	7998	8017	8035	8054	8072	8091	8110	2	4	6	7	9	11	13	15	17
.91	8128	8147	8166	8185	8204	8222	8241	8260	8279	8299	2	4	6	8	9	11	13	15	17
.92	8318	8337	8356	8375	8395	8414	8433	8453	8472	8492	2	4	6	8	10	12	14	15	17
.93	8511	8531	8551	8570	8590	8610	8630	8650	8670	8690	2	4	6	8	10	12	14	16	18
.94	8710	8730	8750	8770	8790	8810	8831	8851	8872	8892	2	4	6	8	10	12	14	16	18
.95	8913	8933	8954	8974	8995	9016	9036	9057	9078	9099	2	4	6	8	10	12	15	17	19
.96	9120	9141	9162	9183	9204	9226	9247	9268	9290	9311	2	4	6	8	11	13	15	17	19
.97	9333	9354	9376	9397	9419	9441	9462	9484	9506	9528	2	4	7	8	11	13	15	17	20
.98	9550	9572	9594	9616	9638	9661	9683	9705	9727	9750	2	4	7	9	11	13	16	18	20
.99	9772	9795	9817	9840	9863	9886	9908	9931	9954	9977	2	5	7	9	11	14	16	18	20

LATEST MODEL PAPER

JHARKHAND ACADEMIC COUNCIL (JAC), RANCHI

BUSINESS MATHEMATICS–XII

Time : 3 *Hours*, 15 *Minutes*] [*Max. Marks* : 80

General Instructions :

1. This Qusestion Booklet has two parts — **Part -A** and **Part - B.**
2. **Part-A** is of MCQ type having **30** marks and **Part-B** is of Subjective type having **50** marks.
3. The candidate has to answer in the Answer Booklet which will be provided separately.
4. **Part-A** — There are **30** Multiple Choice Questions having four (4) options (a, b, c & d) The candidate has to write the correct option in the Answer Booklet. All questions are compulsory. Each question carries 1 mark. There is no negative marking for wrong answer.
5. **Part-B** — There are three sections : Section- A, B & C. This part is of Subjective Type having Very Short Answer, Short Answer & Long Answer Type questions total number of question is 22. **Section-A** Question Nos. **31-38** are Very Short Answer Type. Answer any **6** questions. Each question carries **2** marks. **Section-B** Question Nos. **39-46** are Short Answer Type. Answer any **6** questions. Each question carries **3** marks. **Section-C** Question Nos. **47-52** are Long Answer Type, Answer any **4** questions. Each question carries **5** marks.
6. Candidate has to hand over his/her Answer Booklet to the invigilator compulsorily before leaving the examination hall
7. Candidates can take away the Question Booklet after completion of the Examination.

Part-A
Multiple Choice Type Questions

Questions Nos. 1 to 30 are Multiple Choice Type. Each question has four option and write it in the Answer sheet. Each question carries 1 mark.

1. Which term will be 27 the sequence 5, 7, 9, 11, ... :
   (a) 13 (b) 12
   (c) 11 (d) 10
2. If in an A.P. third term is 18 and 7th term is 30, the 17 term is :
   (a) 60 (b) 12
   (c) 24 (d) 16
3. The sum of first five terms of the series 2, 8, 32... is :
   (a) 682 (b) 748
   (c) 996 (d) 1024
4. Four harmonic means are inserted between 1 and $\frac{1}{16}$. The first harmonic mean from the beginning is :
   (a) $\frac{1}{7}$ (b) $\frac{1}{4}$
   (c) $\frac{1}{13}$ (d) $\frac{1}{10}$
5. Which term of H.P. $1, \frac{1}{5}, \frac{1}{9}, \ldots$ is $\frac{1}{25}$?
   (a) 6 (b) 7 (c) 8 (d) 9
6. If ${}^nP_4 = 360$, then the value of n will be :
   (a) – 5 (b) – 6
   (c) 6 (d) None of these
7. 7! – 5! is equal to :
   (a) 5,040 (b) 4,920
   (c) 5,703 (d) 5,000
8. The number of ways to arrange the letter of the word BIPIN is :
   (a) 120 (b) 60
   (c) 130 (d) None of these
9. If $\begin{vmatrix} x & 8 \\ 3 & 3 \end{vmatrix} = 0$, then the value of x is :
   (a) 7 (b) 3
   (c) 8
   (d) None of these
10. The value of $\begin{vmatrix} 9 & 3 \\ 12 & 4 \end{vmatrix}$ is :
    (a) 0 (b) 4
    (c) 6 (d) 12

11. If $A = \begin{bmatrix} 3 & 1 \\ 7 & 6 \end{bmatrix}$, $B = \begin{bmatrix} 4 & 7 \\ 5 & 2 \end{bmatrix}$, then A + B = :

(a) $\begin{bmatrix} 12 & 7 \\ 35 & 12 \end{bmatrix}$ (b) $\begin{bmatrix} 7 & 8 \\ 12 & 8 \end{bmatrix}$

(c) $\begin{bmatrix} -1 & -6 \\ -2 & 4 \end{bmatrix}$ (d) $\begin{bmatrix} 3 & 7 \\ 5 & 6 \end{bmatrix}$

12. If $A = \begin{bmatrix} 2 & 5 \\ 7 & -8 \end{bmatrix}$ then A′ is :

(a) $\begin{bmatrix} 2 & -8 \\ 5 & 7 \end{bmatrix}$ (b) $\begin{bmatrix} 5 & 2 \\ -8 & 7 \end{bmatrix}$

(c) $\begin{bmatrix} 2 & 7 \\ 5 & -8 \end{bmatrix}$ (d) $\begin{bmatrix} 7 & -8 \\ 2 & 5 \end{bmatrix}$

13. The number of elements in the power set of 1, 2, 3, 4, 5 is :

(a) 16 (b) 32
(c) 64 (d) 80

14. If A = {a, b, c, d}, B = {b, d, e, f} then the vlaue of A ∩ B will be If universel set x = {1.2.3 ... 20} :

(a) {a, b, c, d, e, f} (b) {b, d}
(c) {d, e, f} (d) {c, d, e}

15. Out of 20 members in a family, 11 like to take tea and 14 like coffee. Assume that each one likes atleast one of the two drinks. Find how many like both coffee and tea ?

(a) 2 (b) 3
(c) 4 (d) 5

16. Null set is a .... of all sets :

(a) set (b) sub-set
(c) super set (d) single for set

17. If $y = \sqrt{x} + \frac{1}{\sqrt{x}}$, then $\frac{dy}{dx}$ at $x = 1$

(a) 1 (b) $\frac{1}{2}$

(c) $\frac{1}{\sqrt{2}}$ (d) 0

18. $\int x^6\, dx = ?$

(a) $7x^7 + C$ (b) $\frac{x^7}{7} + C$

(c) $6x^5 + C$ (d) $6x^7 + C$

19. The value of $6\int x^2.dx$ is :

(a) $2x^3 + c$ (b) $6x^2 + c$
(c) $5x^4 + c$ (d) $7x + c$

20. Mean of 5, 8, 11, 16, 15 is :

(a) 10 (b) 11
(c) 12 (d) 13

21. 80, 100, 90, 170, 60, 50, 40 is meadian :

(a) 80 (b) 170
(c) 90 (d) 60

22. ....divides the total number of observations in two equal parts :

(a) Median (b) Mode
(c) Mean (d) None of these

23. The arithmetic mean of 5, 10 and 15 is :

(a) 5 (b) 10
(c) 15 (d) 30

24. The G.M. of two numbers 4 and 16 shall be :

(a) 8 (b) 10
(c) 9 (d) 12

25. Average speed can be calculated by :

(a) $\overline{X}$ (b) G.M.
(c) H.M. (d) None of these

26. Geometric Mean of the series 3, 9, 27 is :

(a) 7 (b) 9
(c) 5 (d) 8

27. The most important factor causing seasonal variations are :

(a) Growth of population
(b) Change in fashion
(c) Weather and Social Customs
(d) Technological Improvement

28. Least square method is used for calculating trend.

(a) True (b) False

29. If two dice are thrown once then probability of getting a total of 8 is :

(a) 1/12 (b) 3/8
(c) 6/36 (d) 5/36

30. When there is unequal difference in X series then appropriate method for interplation is :

(a) Binomial expansion method
(b) Lagrange's method
(c) Newton's method
(d) Sterling's formula

[**Ans.** 1. (d), 2. (a), 3. (b), 4. (b), 5. (b), 6. (c), 7. (b), 8. (b), 9. (c), 10. (a), 11. (b), 12. (c), 13. (b), 14. (b), 15. (d), 16. (b), 17. (d), 18. (b), 19. (a), 20. (b), 21. (a), 22. (a), 23. (b), 24. (a), 25. (c), 26. (b), 27. (c), 28. (a), 29. (d), 30. (b)]]

Part-B
Subjective Type Questions

Section-A
Very short answer type questions

Answer any *six* questions.

31. Find : $1 + \frac{1}{2} + \frac{1}{4} + \frac{1}{8} + ...$ to ∞.
[Ans. : See Page No. 24 Part-(A) Example-5]

32. If ${}^9P_r = 3024$, find the value of r.
[Ans. : See Page No. 54 Part-(A) Example-6]

33. Find the value of $\begin{vmatrix} 9 & 3 \\ 12 & 4 \end{vmatrix}$.
[Ans. : See Page No. 79 Part-(A) Example-6A]

34. If $n(A) = 25$, $n(A \cup B) = 47$ and $n(A \cap B) = 9$ then fixed $n(B - A)$.
[Ans. : See Page No. 127 Part-(A) Example-1]

35. If the value of Mode and Mean is 8 and 68 respectively, find the value of Median.
[Ans. : See Page No. 59 Part-(B) Illustration-13A(i)]

36. If Arithmetic Mean of two items is 5 and G.M. is 4, find their H.M.
[Ans. : See Page No. 88 Part-(B) Illustration-17]

37. Find the probability of drawing a red card in a single draw from a well shuffled pack of ordinary playing cards.
[Ans. : See Page No. 130 Part-(B) Illustration-3]

38. Find the 10th term of the A. P. 3, 8, 13, 18, ...
[Ans. : See Page No. 5 Part-(A) Example-6(A)]

Section-B
Short answer type questions

Answer any six questions $3 \times 6 = 18$

39. Sum up the series :

$$\frac{3}{4} - \frac{5}{4^2} + \frac{3}{4^3} - \frac{5}{4^4} + \frac{3}{4^5} - \frac{5}{4^6} + ...\infty$$

[Ans. : See Page No. 25 Part-(A) Example-10]

40. In how many wags can a team of 11 be chosen from 15 cricketers if two of then can only be wicketkeepres ?
[Ans. : See Page No. 69 Part-(A) Example-23]

41. Solve the following equations by matrix method :

$$5x + 3y + z = 16$$
$$2x + y + 3z = 19$$
$$x + 2y + 4z = 25$$

[Ans. : See Page No. 102 Part-(A) Example-21]

42. If $t = \sqrt{x + \sqrt{x + \sqrt{x \infty}}}$ then prove that $\frac{dt}{dx} = \frac{1}{2t - 1}$
[Ans. : See Page No. 145 Part-(A) Example-11]

43. Calculate the Median from the following data :

Income (In ₹)	*No. of Workers*
150	15
160	40
180	30
190	20
200	10

[Ans. : See Page No. 31 Part-(B) Illustration-3]

44. Find out the value of the trend by three-yearly moving average :

Year	*Value*
1985	10
1986	15
1987	12
1988	18
1989	15
1990	22
1991	19
1992	24
1993	20
1994	26
1995	22
1996	30
1997	25

[Ans. : See Page No. 103 Part-(B) Illustration-5B]

45. The age of mothers and the average number of children born per mother are given in the below : Interpolate the average number of children per mother

Age of mothers (years)	*No. of Children*
15—19	0.7
20—24	2.1
25—29	3.5
30—34	?
35—39	5.7
40—44	5.8

[Ans. : See Page No. 163 Part-(B) Illustration-4A]

46. Find the value of n and r if ${}^nC_r = 56$ and ${}^nP_r = 336$.
[Ans. : See Page No. 65 Part-(A) Example 5(B)]

Section-C
Short answer type questions

Answer any four questions $5 \times 4 = 20$

47. If ${}^9P_r = 3024$, find the value of r.

[**Ans. :** See Page No. 54 Part-(A) Example-6]

48. In how many ways 12 different things can be equally distributed among 4 persons ? If they are divided in four groups instead to giving to 4 persons, what will be the number of ways ?

[**Ans. :** See Page No. 69 Part-(A) Example-20]

49. A college gives 30 medal Football (F), 15 in Basketball (B) and 20 in Cricket (C). These medals goes to 58 persons out of which 3 persons get 3 medals in 3 games. How many persons get 2 and only 2 medals ?

[**Ans. :** See Page No. 130 Part-(A) Example-3]

50. In a Carnival 10 ladies ate Lollipops as follows :

No. of . Ladies	1	2	3	4
No. of . Lollipops	3	4	5	8

Find the average number of Lollipops eaten by a lady.

[**Ans. :** See Page No. 8 Part-(B) Illustration-5]

51. In a bag there are 5 red and 3 white balls. Find the probability that the first ball is red, second white, third red and so on, if they are drawn in succession.

[**Ans. :** See Page No. 142 Part-(B) Illustration-23]

52. Using any Interpolation method find out the likely Index Number for 2013 from the following table :

Year	2011	2012	2013	2014	2015
Index No.	100	107	y_2	157	210

[**Ans. :** See Page No. 162 Part-(B) Example-3]

XC-BMT-(OPT.)- C

BMT
Commerce

Examination Paper, 2026

Jharkhand Academic Council, Ranchi

BUSINESS MATHEMATICS-XII

(OPTIONAL)

Time : 3 Hours 15 Minutes] [*Max. Marks* : 80

General Instructions :

1. This Question Booklet has *two* Parts—**Part-A** and **Part-B**.
2. **Part-A** is of MCQ Type having **30** marks and **Part-B** is of Subjective Type having **50** marks.
3. The candidate has to answer in the Answer Booklet which will be provided separately.
4. **Part-A** — There are **30** Multiple Choice Questions having four **(4)** options **[(a), (b), (c) and (d)]**. The candidate has to write the correct option in the Answer Booklet. **All** questions are compulsory. Each question carries **1** mark. There is no negative marking for wrong answer.
5. **Part-B** — There are *three* sections : **Section-A, B & C**. This part is of Subjective Type having Very Short Answer, Short Answer & Long Answer Type questions. Total number of questions is **22**.
   Section-A — Question Nos. **31 – 38** are Very Short Answer Type. Answer any **6** questions. Each question carries **2** marks.
   Section-B — Question Nos. **39 – 46** are Short Answer Type. Answer any **6** questions. Each question carries **3** marks.
   Section-C — Question Nos. **47 – 52** are Long Answer Type. Answer any **4** questions. Each question carries **5** marks.
6. Candidates has to hand over his/her Answer Booklet to the Invigilator compulsorily before leaving the examination hall.
7. Candidates can take away the Question Booklet after completion of the Examination.

Part-A

Multiple Choice Type Questions

Questions Nos. **1** to **30** are Multiple Choice Type. Each question has *four* options. Select the correct option and write it in the Answer Sheet. Each question carries 1 mark. **1 × 30 = 30**

1. How many terms are there in the A.P. 7, 13, 19, ..., 205 ?
   (a) 30 (b) 35 (c) 34 (d) 31
2. Geometric mean of 4 and 9 is :
   (a) 6 (b) 7 (c) 6.5 (d) 12
3. Harmonic mean of a and b is :
   (a) $\frac{2ab}{a+b}$ (b) $\sqrt{ab}$ (c) $\frac{a+b}{2}$ (d) $\frac{a+b}{2ab}$
4. The first term of a G.P. is 5 and the common ratio is – 2. What is the 6th term ?
   (a) – 100 (b) 100 (c) – 160 (d) 160
5. The value of the determinant having two rows identical is :
   (a) – 1 (b) 1 (c) 0 (d) None of these
6. 0 ! is equal to :
   (a) 1 (b) ∞ (c) 0 (d) 5
7. The nth term of a G.P. is :
   (a) $a + (n - 1)d$ (b) ar^{n-1} (c) ar (d) $\frac{a}{r}$
8. If 4, x and 9 are in G.P., x is equal to :
   (a) 4 (b) 6 (c) 9 (d) 36

9. If the ratio of the consecutive terms of a progression are same, then it is known as :
(a) Geometric progression (b) Common ratio
(c) Arithmetic progression (d) Common difference

10. Value of $^{60}C_{60}$ is :
(a) 1 (b) 0 (c) 60 (d) – 1

11. The value of the determinant $\begin{vmatrix} x^2 & x \\ 5x & 5 \end{vmatrix}$ is :
(a) 0 (b) 5 (c) 1 (d) 25

12. If $\begin{bmatrix} 2 & x \\ 5 & 0 \end{bmatrix} = \begin{bmatrix} 2 & 1 \\ 5 & 0 \end{bmatrix}$ then the value of x is :
(a) 2 (b) 5 (c) 1 (d) 0

13. Which is null set in the following ?
(a) 0 (b) {0} (c) {ϕ} (d) ϕ

14. If universal set $\Omega = \{1, 2, 3, 4, 5, 6, 7\}$ and $A = \{1, 3, 4, 5\}$:
(a) {1, 3, 5, 6, 7} (b) {2, 6, 7} (c) {1, 3, 4, 5} (d) {4, 6, 7}

15. The geometric mean of 3 and 75 is :
(a) 15 (b) 20 (c) 25 (d) 30

16. Null set is a .... of all sets.
(a) Subset (b) Power set
(c) Universal set (d) All of these

17. Which of the following is a measure of central tendency ?
(a) Arithmetic Mean (b) Median (c) Mode (d) All of these

18. Which of the following is difficult to compute in the measures of central tendency ?
(a) Mean (b) Median (c) Mode (d) Geometric Mean

19. Mode of 5, 6, 10, 6, 0, 12, 6, 13, 17, 6 is :
(a) 6 (b) 0 (c) 12 (d) 5

20. Probabilities lie between :
(a) 0 to ∞ (b) – 1 to 1 (c) 0 to 1 (d) None of these

21. The differential coefficient of $4x^4$ with respect to x will be :
(a) $16x^4$ (b) $16x^3$ (c) $9x^3$ (d) $15x^3$

22. If $y = x^5 + x^2$, then $\frac{dy}{dx}$ is :
(a) $5x + 2y$ (b) $6x^4 + 3x^3$ (c) $5x^4 + 2x$ (d) $5 + 2$

23. If the mode is 28 and mean is 25 then median is :
(a) 25 (b) 28 (c) 26 (d) 50

24. If $^nC_{18} = {}^nC_6$ then n is equal to :
(a) 20 (b) 12 (c) 24 (d) 6

25. If $A = \{a, b, c, d\}$, $B = \{b, d, e, f\}$ then the value of $A \cap B$ is :
(a) $\{a, b, c, d, e, f\}$ (b) $\{b, d\}$ (c) $\{a, e, f\}$ (d) $\{c, d, e\}$

26. Harmonic mean of 5 and 15 is :
(a) 7 (b) 7.2 (c) 7.5 (d) 7.8

27. The most important factor causing seasonal variations is :
(a) Growth of population (b) Change in fashion
(c) Weather and social customs (d) Technological improvement

28. What is the probability of getting odd numbers if a die is rolled ?
(a) $\frac{1}{2}$ (b) 2 (c) $\frac{1}{6}$ (d) $\frac{5}{2}$

29. What will be the probability of losing in a game if the winning probability is 0.3 ?
(a) 0.5 (b) 0.6 (c) 0.7 (d) 0.8

30. The simplest method of interpolation is :
(a) Extrapolation (b) Graphic
(c) Lagrange method (d) None of these

Part-B
Subjective Type Questions
Section-A
Very Short Answer Type Questions

Answer any *six* questions. **$2 \times 6 = 12$**

31. If the third term of an A.P. is 18 and seventh term is 30, find the 17th term.

32. The second term of a G.P. is 27 and 7th term is $\frac{1}{9}$. Find the first term and the common ratio.

33. Find the sum of five terms of the given harmonic series $\frac{1}{2}, \frac{1}{4}, \frac{1}{6}, \ldots$

34. In how many different ways can 20 different pearls be set on a necklace ?

35. Find the value of : $\begin{vmatrix} 2 & 2 & 3 \\ 3 & 4 & 5 \\ 6 & 7 & 9 \end{vmatrix}$

36. What is the time series ?

37. Calculate the mean of 14, 3, 0, 4, 5, 6.

38. What will be the geometric mean of 20, 50, 27 and 30 without using log table ?

Section-B
Short Answer Type Questions

Answer any *six* questions. **$3 \times 6 = 18$**

39. Find the Arithmetic Mean of the following data :

Size	0	1	2	3	4	5	6	7	8
Frequency	1	9	26	59	72	52	29	7	1

40. Find median from the following table :

Marks	10	20	30	40	50
No. of students	3	7	10	4	6

41. In moderately skewed distribution arithmetic mean is 32 and median is 36. Find out the mode.

42. Find out the value of the trend by three-yearly moving average :

Year	1995	1996	1997	1998	1999	2000	2001
Value	10	15	12	18	15	22	19

43. Using any interpolation method find out the likely index number for 2013 from the following table :

Year	2011	2012	2013	2014	2015
Index	100	107	$\frac{1}{2}$	157	210

44. The average income of 100 people is ₹ 20 and the average income of 150 people is ₹ 25. Find the average income of 50 people.

45. Explain the merits of Geometric Mean.

46. If $y = 5x^4 - 3x^3 + 1$, then find $\frac{dy}{dx}$.

Section-C
Long Answer Type Questions

Answer any *four* questions. **5 × 4 = 20**

47. Find mode from the following table :

Size	0-10	10-20	20-30	30-40	40-50	50-60
Frequency	40	30	18	12	10	5

48. A person was appointed at a salary of ₹ 700 per month. The condition of appointment was that he would receive ₹ 740 per month in the second year, ₹ 780 per month in the third year and so on the salary will increase. Find the total salary he would expect to have received by the end of 10 years.

49. Find the inverse of the following matrix $A = \begin{bmatrix} 0 & 1 & 2 \\ 1 & 2 & 3 \\ 3 & 1 & 1 \end{bmatrix}$.

50. In a school there are 20 teachers who teach Mathematics or Physics. Out of them 12 teach Mathematics and 4 Physics and Mathematics. State how many teachers teach Physics.)

51. Evaluate : $\begin{vmatrix} 1 & a & b+c \\ 1 & b & c+a \\ 1 & c & a+b \end{vmatrix}$.

52. Find the H.P. whose 7th term and 12th term are $\frac{1}{10}$ and $\frac{1}{25}$ respectively.

●●